Sandy Carpenters

Sociology

THIRD EDITION

**McGraw-Hill
Book Company**

*New York
St. Louis
San Francisco
Düsseldorf
Johannesburg
Kuala Lumpur
London
Mexico
Montreal
New Delhi
Panama
Rio de Janeiro
Singapore
Sydney
Toronto*

Paul B. Horton
Chester L. Hunt
Professors of Sociology
Western Michigan University

Sociology

Library of Congress Cataloging in Publication Data
Horton, Paul B.
  Sociology.
  Bibliography: p.
  1. Sociology.   I. Hunt, Chester L., joint
author.
HM51.H64 1972   301   79-38585
ISBN 0-07-030425-4

SOCIOLOGY

1 2 3 4 5 6 7 8 9 0 D O D O 7 9 8 7 6 5 4 3 2

This book was set in Clarendon Light by Black Dot, Inc., and
printed and bound by R. R. Donnelley & Sons Company. The
designer was Betty Binns; the drawings were done by Vantage
Art, Inc. The editors were John Hendry and David Dunham.
John F. Harte supervised production.

Contents

Preface

What should an introductory sociology textbook try to do? First and most important, we believe it should capture the interest of the student and demonstrate both the process and challenge of scientific observation and analysis of social behavior in a readable and interesting way.

Second, an introductory sociology textbook should seek to cultivate in the student the habit of scientific analysis of social data. Unless the student gains a sophisticated awareness of his own ethnocentrism and some ability to objectify his observations, his sociology course has failed in one of its major objectives.

Third, an introductory sociology textbook should present the basic concepts and descriptive materials of sociology clearly and intelligibly. These should be illustrated so vividly that they "come alive" and become part of the student's thinking vocabulary. Concepts should not be learned simply as definitions to be memorized, but as accurate, descriptive names for the ways people act and the things people build. Concepts are far more than a professional vocabulary to be used in advanced studies: They are even more important as tools for identifying and understanding a process or idea. Many sociology students will find that the introductory course is a terminal course as well, and the basic concepts should be tools for continuing social observation and analysis.

In this textbook we have tried to do these things. Whether we have succeeded is for the reader to judge. We have generally avoided esoteric sources in favor of others more easily available to most students. We have often used literary and popular sources for purposes of illustration. We have done this to emphasize the fact that sociology is the disciplined observation and analysis of everyday life and that the concepts and insights of sociology are applicable to all that goes on around the student.

We note that some recent textbooks contain very few footnotes or citations. It is true that footnotes and citations *do* clutter up a book. But we believe that students should constantly be reminded of the evidential basis for the conclusions of sociology. Therefore we have documented heavily in order to present sociology as a scientific and scholarly discipline, not as an exercise in popular journalism.

We have sought to minimize the overlap with other sociology courses. This textbook is not an encapsulated encyclopedia of the entire sociology curriculum. We have intentionally not emphasized "social problems" material in the belief that the introductory course should concentrate upon principles and concepts and should leave specialized topics and problem-oriented materials for later courses.

In this third edition, we have recognized the renewed interest in social and cultural evolution by reorganizing the two chapters on culture, one of which—"The Evolution of Culture"—is largely new. The "Social Institutions" chapter has been extensively re-written, with material on organizations and bureaucracy withdrawn and incorporated in a new chapter, "Formal Organizations." The "Social Power" chapter has a new section on coercion and disruption, and a new section on separatism and territorially based minorities in the "Race and Ethnic Relations" chapter gives attention to the American Indians and Mexican-Americans. In the "Social Movements" chapter, descriptions of Zionism, the commune, Women's Lib, and the New Left replace earlier illustrations of types of social movements. These changes, and numerous minor changes and updatings, make this third edition a major revision of our book.

Many instructors may find the *Instructor's Manual*, prepared by Ellen P. Robin, a useful aid. It provides a wide range of teaching suggestions and a liberal supply of objective and essay examination questions for each chapter.

The accompanying *Study Guide and Source Book* has been revised by Bruce J. Cohen for this third edition of *Sociology*. Many students find it helpful during study and review, a source of related materials, and a yardstick by which to measure their mastery of the text materials.

We owe a debt of appreciation to many people, and especially to the McGraw-Hill staff for their dedicated competence, to a number of our colleagues for their candid criticisms and helpful suggestions, to Ellen P. Robin and Bruce J. Cohen for their careful preparation of supplementary materials, and to Frederick J. Ashby for his imaginative line drawings.

Paul B. Horton
Chester L. Hunt

Sociology and society

For centuries man has pondered the societies he has developed. Some of our oldest documents, going back five thousand years or more, record men's efforts to analyze and understand their social order. In this search men have sought truth from many sources by using many methods, some highly successful, some less so. Some of the sources of truth are described in Chapter 1, "Science and the Search for Truth." This chapter shows that although each source of truth has its uses, only through scientific investigation can reliable knowledge about human society be discovered. Chapter 2, "Fields and Methods of Sociology," tells how scientific methods are used in sociological investigation. All phenomena can be studied scientifically, but the techniques of study must be fitted to the materials studied. Just how sociologists try to make this adaptation is described in Chapter 2.

In our time and for some centuries to come, for better or worse, the sciences, physical and social, will be to an increasing degree the accepted point of reference with respect to which the validity (Truth) of all knowledge is gauged. *(George A. Lundberg,* Can Science Save Us? *Longmans, Green & Co. Ltd., London, 1947, p. 36.)*

Sociology: The science of the origin and evolution of society, or of the forms, institutions, and functions of human groups. (Webster's New Collegiate Dictionary, *G. & C. Merriam Co., Publishers, Springfield, Mass., 1970.)*

Sociology: The intellectual discipline concerned with developing systematic, reliable knowledge about human social relationships in general and about the products of such relationships.... *(Thomas Ford Hoult,* Dictionary of Modern Sociology, *Littlefield, Adams & Co., Totowa, N.Y., 1969, p. 307.)*

The values, beliefs, and formal affiliations in the field of sociology bind it too closely to the governing structures and the powerful interests of our society.... In our attempts to share the prestige of "science" we [sociologists] have pursued the development of "scientific" methodology at the expense of meaningful content and have developed "scientific" theories at the expense of a knowledge of society. We have willfully turned from the problems of our time, and he who interests himself in a confrontation with reality is dismissed as a "mere journalist." *(Sociology Liberation Movement, handbill, 1968.)*

Sociology is the taking of what everyone knows and putting it into words that nobody can understand. *(Anonymous)*

Science and the search for truth

A pathologist after elaborate preparation places a slide under the microscope and adjusts the lens carefully. A Purari war party watch carefully as they place their canoe in the water, for unless it rocks, the raid will not be successful. A man steps from a new station wagon, cuts a forked twig, and carries it around holding it above the ground, while a well-drilling crew stands by, waiting to drill where the twig tells them water will be found. A woman in Peoria, anxious over her teen-age daughter, prays to God for guidance. A physician leafs through the pages of a parasitology textbook as he tried to identify the puzzling skin rash of his patient. A senator scans the latest public opinion poll as he wonders how to vote on the farm bill.

Each of these persons is seeking guidance. Their problems vary, and their sources of truth are different. Where shall man find truth? How can he know where he had found it? In the million years, more or less, of man's life on this earth, he has sought truth in many places. What are some of them?

SOME SOURCES OF TRUTH

Intuition

Galen, a famous Greek physician of the second century, prepared an elaborate chart of the human body, showing exactly where it might be pierced without fatal injury. How did he know the vulnerable spots? He just *knew* them. True, he had learned a good deal of human anatomy through his observations and those of his associates; but beyond this, he relied upon his intuition to tell him which zones were fatal. *Intuition is any flash of insight (true or mistaken) whose source the receiver cannot fully identify or explain.* Hitler relied heavily upon his intuition, much to the distress of his generals. His intuition told him that France would not fight for the Rhineland, that England would not fight for Czechoslovakia, that England and France would not fight for Poland, and that England and France would quit when he attacked Russia. He was right on the first two insights and wrong on the last two.

Intuition is responsible for many brilliant hypotheses, which can later be tested through other methods. Perhaps intuition's

greatest value is in the forming of hypotheses. As a source of knowledge, of conclusions, intuition is less satisfactory. True, sometimes intuition takes the form of a shrewd leap to a sound conclusion, based upon a mass of half-remembered experience and information. But how can such intuitive knowledge be tested and verified? Often it can't be. Anaximander propounded a theory of evolution in the sixth century B.C., but not until the nineteenth century A.D. were the facts available to indicate that his theory was essentially correct. Intuitive knowledge often can't be tested at the time it is offered. Sometimes it cannot be tested at all, or at least not until it is too late to make any difference, as Hitler eventually discovered.

Authority

Two thousand years ago, Galen knew more about human anatomy than any other mortal; as recently as 1800, physicians were still quoting him as an authority. Aristotle stated that a barrel of water could be added to a barrel of ashes without overflowing, and for two thousand years thereafter, a student who might suggest trying it out would be scolded for his impertinence. For many centuries, creative thought was stifled by Aristotelian authority, for since an authority is *right*, any conflicting ideas must be wrong. Authority does not discover new truths, but it can prevent new truth from being discovered or accepted.

Dangerous though authority may be, we cannot get along without it. Our accumulation of knowledge is too great for anyone to absorb, so we must rely upon specialists who have collected the reliable knowledge in a particular field. An authority is a necessary and useful source of knowledge—*in the field in which he is an authority.* Science recognizes no authorities on "things in general."

Authority is of several sorts. *Sacred au-*

thority rests upon the faith that a certain tradition or document—the Bible, the Koran, the Vedas—is of supernatural origin. Or it is a faith that a certain group or institution— the medicine men, the priests, the church— is constantly receiving supernatural guidance. *Secular* authority arises not from divine revelation but from human perception. It is of two kinds: *secular scientific* authority, which rests upon empirical investigation, and *secular humanistic* authority, which rests upon the belief that certain "great men" have had remarkable insight into human behavior and the nature of the universe. The search for truth by consulting the "great books" is an example of the appeal to secular humanistic authority.

The layman's problem is finding a qualified authority.

Some fields—counseling and psychological services, health and diet, for example— are cluttered with many self-styled "authorities" without professional training in these fields. The most reputable of authorities is likely to become a foolish incompetent when he strays beyond his specialty. The general who pontificates on crime prevention, the

business executive who endorses a food fad, the physician who gives prescriptions for labor-management problems—each of these may be making a fool of himself. He may also be making fools of his listeners.

The layman (and everyone is a layman in all fields except that of his specialty) has no choice; he *must* rely upon authority since he cannot become an expert on everything. It is presumptuous for the layman to disagree with the qualified authorities on a question of fact upon which the authorities have reached an agreement. The layman's problem is how to find and recognize a qualified authority on the matter which concerns him.

No scientific authority, however, has the final word on human knowledge. The scientist respects the qualified authority, but still questions his basic assumptions and verifies his conclusions. A man who is considered an expert in a given field deserves to have his views considered seriously, but the weight of authority does not close the door upon further investigation. Today's scientific authority becomes the springboard to tomorrow's research. Thus knowledge grows, relentlessly converting today's "final" pronouncements into tomorrow's midpoints and side streets along the road to expanding knowledge.

Tradition

Of all sources of truth, tradition is one of the most reassuring. Here is the accumulated wisdom of the ages, and he who disregards it may expect denunciation as a scoundrel or a fool. If a pattern has "worked" in the past, why not keep on using it?

Tradition, however, preserves both the accumulated wisdom and the accumulated bunkum of the ages. Tradition is society's attic, crammed with all sorts of useful customs and useless relics. A great deal of "practical experience" consists in repeating the mistakes of our ancestors. One task of social science is to sort out our folklore into the true and the merely ancient.

Common sense

For thousands of years people's common sense told them that the earth was flat, that big objects fell faster than small ones, that stone and iron were perfectly solid materials, and that a person's true character was betrayed by his facial features; yet today we know that none of these statements is true.

When we do not know where our ideas come from or what they are based on, we sometimes call them "common sense." If we call them common sense, we do not have to prove them, for then others will join us in the collective self-deception of assuming that they have already been proved. If one presses for proof, he is told that the idea has been proved by experience. The term "common sense" puts a respectable front on all sorts of notions for which there is no systematic body of evidence that can be cited.

Common sense and tradition are closely interwoven, with many common-sense propositions becoming part of a people's traditional lore. If a distinction is to be drawn, it may be that traditional truths are those which have long been believed, while common-sense truths are uncritically accepted conclusions (recent or ancient) which are currently believed by one's fellows.

What often passes for common sense consists of a group's accumulation of collective guesses, hunches, and haphazard trial-and-error learnings. Many common-sense propositions are sound, earthy, useful bits of knowledge. "A soft answer turneth away wrath," and "Birds of a feather flock together," are practical observations on social life. But many common-sense conclusions are based on ignorance, prejudice, and mistaken interpretation. When medieval Europeans noticed that feverish patients were free of lice while most healthy people were lousy, they made the common-sense conclusion that lice would cure fever and therefore sprinkled lice over feverish patients. Not until the fever subsided would the lice

Tradition and common sense say:	Scientific investigation finds that:
Men are intellectually superior to women.	Neither sex is superior in inherited intellectual capacities.
Colds are caused by chills and wet feet.	Colds are caused by viruses, although exposure may lower resistance.
One's character shows in his face.	There is no dependable association between facial features and personality characteristics.
A man who cheats at cards will cheat in business.	Honesty in one situation tells little about one's behavior in a different situation.
Spare the rod and spoil the child.	Serious delinquents usually have been punished more severely than most nondelinquents.
The genius or near-genius is generally delicate, impractical, unstable, and unsuccessful.	The genius and near-genius group is above average in health, emotional adjustment, and income.
Pornographic literature encourages sex crimes and perversions.	There is no evidence to link pornographic literature with disapproved sexual behavior.
The black race is especially talented in music but inferior in intellect.	Scientists find no convincing evidence of differences in innate racial capacities.

remain. Common sense, like tradition, preserves both folk wisdom and folk nonsense, and to sort them out one from the other is a task for science.

Science

Only within the last two or three hundred years has the scientific method become a common way of seeking answers about the natural world. Science has become a source of knowledge about man's *social* world even more recently; yet in the brief period since man began to rely upon the scientific method, he has learned more about his world than he learned in the preceding ten thousand years. The spectacular explosion of knowledge in the modern world parallels man's use of the scientific method. What makes the scientific method so productive? How does it differ from other methods of seeking truth?

CHARACTERISTICS OF SCIENTIFIC KNOWLEDGE

Verifiable evidence

Scientific knowledge is based on verifiable evidence. By evidence we mean concrete factual observations which other observers can see, weigh, measure, count, or check for accuracy. We may think the definition too obvious to mention; most of us have some awareness of the scientific method. Yet only a few centuries ago medieval scholars held long debates on how many teeth a horse had, without bothering to look into a horse's mouth to count them.

At this point we raise the troublesome methodological question, "What is a fact?" While the word looks deceptively simple, it is not easy to distinguish a fact from a widely shared illusion. Suppose we define a fact as a *descriptive statement upon which all qualified observers are in agreement*. By this definition, medieval ghosts were a fact, since all medieval observers agreed that ghosts were real. There is, therefore, no way to be *certain* that a fact is an accurate description and not a mistaken impression. Research would be easier if facts were dependable, unshakable certainties. Since they are not, the best we can do is to recognize that a fact is *a descriptive statement of reality which scientists, after careful examination and cross-checking, agree in believing to be accurate.*

Since science is based on factual verifiable evidence, science can deal only with questions about which such evidence can be found. Questions like, "Is there a God?" "What is the purpose and destiny of man?" or "What makes a thing beautiful?" are not scientific questions because they cannot be treated factually. Such questions may be terribly important, but the scientific method has no tools for handling them. Scientists can study human *beliefs* about God, or man's destiny, or beauty, or anything else, and they may study the *personal and social consequences* of such beliefs; but these are studies of human behavior, with no attempt to settle the truth or error of the beliefs themselves.

Science then does not have answers for everything, and many important questions are not scientific questions. The scientific method is our most reliable source of factual knowledge about human behavior and the natural universe, but science with its dependence upon verifiable factual evidence cannot answer questions about value, or aesthetics, or purpose and ultimate meaning, or supernatural phenomena. Answers to such questions must be sought in philosophy, metaphysics, or religion.

Each scientific conclusion represents the most reasonable interpretation of all the available evidence—but new evidence may appear tomorrow. Therefore *science has no absolute truths*. An absolute truth is one which will hold true for all times, places, or circumstances. All scientific truth is tentative, subject to revision in the light of new evidence. Some scientific conclusions (e.g., that the earth is a spheroid; or that innate drives are culturally conditioned) are based upon such a large and consistent body of evidence that scientists doubt that they will ever be overturned by new evidence. Yet the scientific method requires that *all* conclusions be open to reexamination whenever new evidence is found to challenge them.

This receptivity to new evidence is easy to state but not always easy to maintain. Scientists are also human beings, and despite their commitment to scientific detachment, they sometimes refuse to examine new evidence if it conflicts with established scientific traditions. Galileo's colleagues refused to look through his telescope and see the moons of Jupiter; Lavoisier insisted that stones (meteorites) could not fall from the air because there were none up there; all the scientists of the Paris Academy pronounced Edison's phonograph a humbug because they knew that the human voice could not be reproduced from a disk. Harvey's circulation of the blood, Pasteur's microbes, and Simmelweis's discovery that physicians spread childbed fever were all rejected for many years after their discovery. A more recent survey [Warner, 1938][1] found that many of the psychologists who rejected Rhine's findings on extrasensory perception had read none of his published research. To maintain an open-minded willingness to examine new evidence is so difficult a task that even scientists do not always succeed.

Ethical neutrality

Science is knowledge, and knowledge can be put to differing uses. Atomic fission can be used to power a city or to incinerate a nation.

[1]Bracketed references in the text are to sources described in full in the Bibliography at the end of the book.

Every use of scientific knowledge involves a choice between values. Our values define what is most important to us. Science tells us that overeating and cigarette smoking will shorten our life expectancy. But can science tell us which we should choose—a longer life or a more indulgent one? Science can answer questions of fact, but has no way to prove that one value is better than another.

Science, then, is ethically neutral. Science seeks knowledge, while society's values determine how this knowledge is to be used. Knowledge about bacteria can be used to preserve health or to wage germ warfare. Knowledge about group organization can be used to preserve a democracy or to establish a dictatorship.

Since science is ethically neutral, no field of inquiry is too sacred to explore. Scientific discoveries sometimes destroy revered myths, undermine established institutions, and challenge cherished values. Versalius laid the foundations of medical science by

Evidence consists of verifiable facts.

robbing graves to get corpses to dissect; the human body was too "sacred" to cut up. Kinsey's studies of human sexual behavior a few years ago and Masters and Johnson's more recent studies [1966; 1970] have aroused a chorus of protest from those who feel that human sexual behavior is "too intimate" for scientific inquiry. But science recognizes no "improper" questions. *Any* questions on which verifiable evidence can be secured is a proper question for science. Science acts on the belief that, if scientific knowledge undermines established beliefs, institutions, and practices, then these beliefs, institutions, and practices need to be revised.

Science may be ethically neutral, but *scientists* are not. Each scientist has his own value system which he cannot totally divorce from his work. Perhaps he should not. There is sharp debate among scientists as to whether their scientific disciplines should be committed to a neutral search for knowledge, or to the attainment of certain social goals. For example, should the physicist accept an assignment to develop a more deadly bomb, or should the sociologist show an oppressive, undemocratic government how to keep its people enslaved? These questions are discussed in the following chapter in a section on the roles of the sociologist.

OBSERVATION—THE BASIC TECHNIQUE OF SCIENTIFIC METHOD

The word "evidence" keeps popping up in discussions of scientific method. What is evidence and where is it found? Evidence consists of verifiable facts of all kinds and is found through scientific observation. But scientific observation is not the same as looking at things. Each of us has been looking at things all his life, but this activity does not make him a scientific observer, any more than a lifetime of swatting flies makes him an entomologist. Wherein does scien-

tific observation differ from just looking at things?

Accuracy

Scientific observation is *accurate*. The scientific observer is extremely careful to make certain that things are as he describes them. The statement, "My backyard is full of dead trees," is of uncertain accuracy unless the trees have been examined by an expert to be sure they are dead and not merely dormant. Or the statement, "Families are larger than they used to be," is of low accuracy. *What* size families, and *where*, are more numerous than they were *when*? If we say, "The proportion of American families with four or more children has grown substantially in the past decade," the statement is more accurate. Painstaking checking, rechecking, and cross-checking to produce carefully stated propositions are the price of scientific accuracy.

Precision

Scientific observation is *precise*. The statement, "My backyard is full of dead trees," is not precise, even though it may be accurate. What is meant by "full of" dead trees? If the sentence reads, "All the trees in my yard are dead," or "There are twenty dead trees in my yard," the statement gains in precision. While accuracy refers to the truth or correctness of a statement, *precision refers to degree or measurement*. If the above statement about family size is revised to read, "The proportion of American families with four or more children increased from 6.6 percent of all families in 1948 to 11.1 percent in 1965, then declined to 10.3 by 1969," the statement is more precise.

In a laboratory experiment the scientist weighs, measures, counts, or times each development with great care. A report which read, "I took some hot salt water, added a pinch of copper sulfate and a little nitric acid, let it cool for a while . . ." would be almost useless. How much water? How hot? How much salt, copper sulfate, and acid? Cooled for how long, and to what temperature? Unless quite precise, an observation is of limited value to science.

Since scientific writing seeks precision, science avoids colorful or extravagant language. While literature may aim to arouse the feelings of the reader, science aims to convey accurate information. Tennyson's lines, "Every moment dies a man; every moment one is born," is good literature. To be good science, it should be written, "In the entire world, according to 1960 figures, every 11⅛ seconds, on the average, dies a man, woman, or child; every 4⅞ seconds, on the average, an infant is born." Literary writing may be intentionally vague, imprecise, and fanciful, stimulating the reader to wonder what is meant (e.g., whether Hamlet was really insane). The dramatic sweep of the novelist and the provocative imagery of the poet have no place in scientific writing. Yet good scientific writing need not be dull, and should never plod through an insufferable mass of ill-arranged detail. Good scientific writing is clear, is easily understood by a qualified reader, and gets its suspense from a readable procession of significant facts and interpretations.

How much precision is needed? This depends upon what we are studying. In measuring atoms, a millionth of an inch may be too large an error, whereas at an agricultural experiment station, a variation of several feet may be unimportant. A social scientist might observe the behavior of a mob of "several hundred" persons without counting them, just as an entomologist can describe a "large" swarm of bees without counting them. Science, however, always seeks *as much precision as the particular problem requires.* If the conditions of observation make

this degree of precision impossible, the scientist must suspend judgment until more precise observations can be collected.

System

Scientific observation is *systematic.* A scientific investigation defines a problem, then draws up an organized plan for collecting facts about it. Suppose the question is, "How does the dropout rate of college students who marry while in college compare with the dropout rate of unmarried students?" One might try to answer the question by simply recalling the students he has known; but this sample would be small; it might not be typical; and one's memory is imperfect. Conclusions based on casual recollections are not very reliable. If our research plan calls for a systematic check on the college records of several thousand students, then our dropout rates for single and married students are based on dependable factual data. Unless these data have been collected as part of an organized systematic program of scientific observation, they are likely to be spotty and incomplete. Anecdotes, personal recollections, offhand opinions, and travelogue impressions may suggest an hypothesis which is worth testing; but no scientist would base a conclusion upon such data.

Records

Scientific observation is *recorded.* Man's memory is notoriously fallible. Data which are not recorded are not dependable. No laboratory scientist would attempt to memorize a detailed experiment. He writes it out completely, recording each operation and reaction, so that his procedures and findings can be accurately known and verified by other scientists.

In the field of human behavior, the need for recorded observation is less fully realized. Suppose a professor were to say, "A number of women students have majored in this field, and while some do excellent work, on the average they don't quite measure up to the men students in this field." What, exactly, is this professor saying? Unless he has actually recorded and computed average scores for both groups, he is in effect saying, "I have mentally recalled the grades of hundreds of my students, and have mentally added the scores and mentally computed averages for male and female students; and I have found the female average to be lower." Such a feat of memory would be impossible. All conclusions based on recalling a mass of unrecorded data are untrustworthy.

In fact, such conclusions based on informal recollection may be worse than useless, for they generally express the prejudices of the observer, masquerading as a scientific conclusion. Since memory is imperfect, we often "remember" things the way we prefer them to have been rather than as they actually were. Prejudice, wishful thinking, and habitual attitude all operate to twist our observations to fit our preferences. It is important, therefore, that evidence be recorded as quickly as possible; the longer we wait the more greatly our prejudices, preferences, and afterthoughts may have distorted it. The following accounts of a disaster as reported by one of the survivors show the progressive changes made by time:

Man's memories of themselves aren't accurate. One month after the sinking of the Litch I questioned the survivors for a second time. The stories had altered—in some cases radically. When the ship blew up it was honorable and acceptable to save one's own skin. Later, as we got closer to civilization and normal society, many men remembered something new, how they had struggled to save others at the risk of their own lives.

My notes on a signalman, made ten minutes after he was rescued, read, "After I jumped over, I swam as fast as I could, I swam upwind like you always told us. I had no life jacket and got scared. I saw someone floating with his head under water. It was Mr. —. His back was broken; I could tell by the funny way it angled just below the neck. I said to myself if he's dead there's no use in his wasting the life jacket. I took the jacket from him and held on to it. I don't know what happened to Mr. —'s body."

When I interviewed the same man a month later he told me this: "I swam from the ship as fast as I could. I swam upwind just like you always told us. I saw someone floating with his head under water. It was Mr. —. Although his back was broken and his head had been submerged, I figured maybe the doctor could do something for him. I pulled his head out of the water and tied the jacket tie under his chin so that his head'd stay in the air. I trod water for about an hour, just holding onto Mr. —'s life jacket for a rest occasionally. I saw a raft about five hundred yards away. I thought maybe the doctor or a hospital corpsman might be on it. I swam over to it. The doctor wasn't there. We paddled over where Mr. — had been, but there was no sign of him."

I met the signalman on the street in Washington a couple of months ago—five years after the Litch sank. His story had changed more. Now it was he, the signalman, who had the life jacket. When he saw that Mr. — had a broken back, the signalman removed his life jacket and gave it to the injured officer. "I knew he was dead, but figured maybe there was a chance in a thousand he might be saved. It was my duty to try to help him, so I gave him my jacket." (*From William J. Lederer*, All the Ships at Sea, *William Morrow & Company, Inc., New York, 1950, pp. 203–204. Reprinted by permission of William Sloane Associates.*)

Objectivity

Scientific observation is *objective*. This means that, insofar as is humanly possible, the observation is unaffected by the observer's own belief, preferences, wishes, or values. In other words, *objectivity* means the *ability to see and accept facts as they are, not as one might wish them to be*. It is fairly easy to be objective when observing something about which we have no preferences or values. It is fairly easy to study objectively the mating practices of the fruit fly, but less easy to view the mating practices of the human being with objective detachment. On any matter where our emotions, beliefs, habits, and values are involved, we are likely to see whatever agrees with our emotional needs and values. Few Americans, for example, could record a detailed description of the workings of the polygamous family system without including many words and phrases which would betray their disapproval. If a set of scientific observations is reported objectively, the reader will be unable to know whether the observer likes or dislikes what he has reported. Yet many experiments have shown that even our simplest observations are affected by our feelings and expectations. For example, in one investigation [Harvey, 1953] most observers judged a white disk imprinted with the name "Eisenhower" to be larger than disks of the same size with random names from the phone book; poor children generally estimated the size of coins to be larger than did children from prosperous homes; and a leaf-shaped piece of green cloth was judged to be greener than a donkey-shaped piece of the same cloth.

Many questions which should be clear-cut scientific questions arouse violent controversy because we find it hard to be objective or even to be sure *when we are* being objective. The question, "Does cigarette smoking promote lung cancer?" is not an impossibly difficult scientific question; yet each new study provokes bitter emotional reaction. The data are now quite conclusive, but this conclusion is displeasing to many people. The tobacco industry, which can draw a mountain of conclusion from a molehill of scientific evidence when preparing advertising claims, insists that we need more evidence before drawing conclusions on *this* question. Cigarette smokers with an appetite to defend are also practicing their newly discovered habit of withholding judgment until more data are available. Some ardent battlers against the cigarette "knew" the answer long before any studies were conducted. On

this question few are disinterested and few can be fully objective.

To be objective is perhaps the most taxing of all scientific obligations. It is not enough to be willing to see facts as they are. One must know what his biases are if he is to guard against them. A *bias* is simply *a tendency, usually unconscious, to see facts in a certain way because of one's habits, wishes, interests, and values.* Thus, in a racial incident one observer sees a white person insulting or abusing a black while another observer sees a black acting presumptuously and provocatively. One observer sees black people courageously asserting their democratic rights, while anothers sees them foolishly "asking for trouble."

Seldom are "the facts" so undebatable that bias does not distort them. *Selective perception is a tendency to see or hear only those facts which support our beliefs and overlook the others.* Many experiments have shown that most people who observe a social situation will see and hear only what they expect to see and hear. If what we expect to see isn't there, we see it anyway! This is dramatically shown in a famous experiment [Allport and Postman, 1947] in which observers were shown a picture of a roughly dressed white man holding an open razor and arguing violently with a well-dressed Negro who was shown in an apologetic, conciliatory posture; then the observers were asked to describe the scene. Some of them "saw" the razor in the Negro's hand, where they expected it to be. Others perceived it correctly, but in passing on a description of the scene (A described it to B, who described it to C, and so on), they soon had the razor in the black man's hand, where it "belonged." Even though they were not emotionally involved in the situation, had ample time to study it, and were making a conscious effort to be accurate in what they saw and reported or heard, the observers' unconscious biases still led many of them to "see" or "hear" a fact that wasn't there.

If the student is inclined to doubt that people often see and hear what they expect to see and hear, let him try a simple experiment. At a party, greet each arriving guest with a broad smile, a hearty handshake, and a murmured, "Pity to see you here this evening," and speed each departing guest with, "Glad you must leave so early!" Many will hear what they expect to hear, not what was actually spoken. This is why, if one is convinced that black people are lazy, Jews are pushy, businessmen are crooked, or cops are brutal, he will seldom "see" anything that conflicts with these expectations. Bias is like a sieve which allows to pass through it only what is supposed to pass through. Bias screens out our perceptions, generally admitting to our consciousness only those perceptions which agree with the biases.

Some common threats to objectivity, then, are vested interest, habit, and bias. Objectivity does not come easily to an observer, but it can be learned. One can become more objective as he becomes aware of his biases and makes allowance for them. Through rigorous training in scientific methodology, through studying many experiments and noting many examples of objective and nonobjective uses of data, an observer may eventually develop some ability to cut through many layers of self-deception and to perceive facts with a greater degree of scientific objectivity. The scientist also has another powerful ally—the criticism of his fellows. The scientist publishes his work so that it may be checked by other scientists who may not share his biases and who come to the problem with a different point of view. This process of publication and criticism means that shoddy work is soon exposed, and the scientist who lets his bias dictate his uses of data is pilloried by his fellows.

In writing his observations, the scientist uses objective language. For example, consider these statements:

The increasing American military commitment in Vietnam was accompanied by more frequent peace demonstrations and by increasing public debate over the wisdom of this policy.

Increasing American agression in Vietnam aroused a mounting chorus of public indignation at our arrogant and brutal denial of self-government to the Vietnamese people.

Our rising determination to prevent the Communist enslavement of Vietnam was harassed by the mounting frenzy of our own Communist sympathizers and peace-at-any-price appeasers.

The first of these statements is written in the neutral, descriptive language of the social scientist, while the other two are fiercely partisan. Polemical writing may be appropriate in debate, but not in science.

In recent years, polemical papers have been appearing at the annual meetings of academic societies such as the American Sociological Association, and in the new "underground" journals devoted to "radical" sociology. In these papers, objectivity, neutrality, and rigorous passion for accuracy are secondary to sweeping generalizations, strident accusations, and passionate commitment to social action. This does not mean that scientific method is changing. Instead, it reflects a debate, currently raging in all the sciences, over whether their authors' primary commitment is to scientific knowledge or to social action [Horton and Bouma, 1971].

Trained observation

Scientific observations are made by *trained* observers. A billion people watch the sun and the moon sweep across the sky, but more sophisticated observers possess certain knowledge which tells them that is not exactly what happens. The untrained observer does not know what to look for or how to interpret it. He does not know the pitfalls which lead to inaccurate observation, nor is he fully aware of the tricks his own limitations and biases may play on him. Startling reports of weird phenomena generally come from uneducated, unsophisticated persons, and are discounted by the experts. When some remarkable observations are reported, the scientist will want to know: (1) What is the observer's general level of education and sophistication? Is he a member of a superstition-ridden folk group, or of a well-informed and somewhat skeptical population? Ghosts, spells, magic, and other supernatural happenings are very real to some groups, but are an amusing absurdity to others. (2) What is his special knowledge or training in this particular field? Does he have the knowledge to discern whether this event has a perfectly natural explanation? Thus the biologist among the ship's passengers is less likely to see a sea monster than are the members of the crew, and the meteorologist sees fewer flying saucers than people with no special knowledge of atmospheric phenomena.

The Bridey Murphy case of some years ago shows the dangers of amateur investigation. A Colorado businessman who dabbled in hypnotism drew from a hypnotized housewife a fascinating account of her earlier life as Bridey Murphy in Ireland over a hundred years ago. This tale aroused great interest, became a best-selling book [Bernstein, 1956] which was syndicated in over forty newspapers, and stimulated a rash of books and articles on hypnotism, reincarnation, and occult topics. If this businessman had been a trained psychologist, he would have known that almost any hypnotized subject in a deep trance will babble freely about earlier incarnations (or future incarnations) if asked about them. A trained observer would have checked the childhood experiences and associations of this housewife to see whether she might be dredging up childhood recollections while in a trance. When the checking was done by less gullible observers, the Bridey Murphy affair promptly collapsed [Gardner, 1957, chap. 26]. Most sensational tales of weird phenomena would be discredited by naturalistic explanations if a scientifically trained observer were present.

Many events happen without any scientific observer on the sidelines. If each sea monster broke water before a panel of ichthyologists, each ghost materialized before the searching gaze of psychologists, and each revolution were staged before a team of visiting sociologists, our knowledge would be far more complete. But for many phenomena, the only reports we have are the casual impressions of untrained observers who happened to be there; these reports may be interesting and possibly useful, but must be interpreted most cautiously by scientists.

Controlled conditions

Scientific observation is conducted under *controlled conditions*. Laboratories are popular with scientists because they are handy places to control heat, light, pressure, time intervals, or whatever is important. We have a scientific experiment when we *control all important variables except one*, then see what happens when that one is varied. Unless all variables except one have been controlled, we cannot be sure which variable has produced the results. For example, if we wish to study the effects of phosphates on plant growth, all other factors—seed, soil, water, sunlight, temperature, humidity—must be the same for all the sample plots; then the varying amounts of phosphates on different test plots can be held responsible for different growth rates. This is the basic technique in all scientific experimentation— allow one variable to vary while holding all other variables constant. (There are some statistical procedures, such as *multiple correlation* and *multiple regression analysis*, which enable the research scholar to work with two or more variables simultaneously. But these procedures are of interest only to the advanced student.)

Failure to control all variables is a most

common error in scientific method and accounts for most false conclusions. For example, the promotion of antihistamines as a cold cure a few years ago was based on several experiments in which half the patients reporting with cold symptoms were given an antihistamine pill, while the other half were given a blank pill which contained no medicine. This latter half were the "control group," used as a base for measuring the effectiveness of the new pill upon the test group. The findings were encouraging, with many more of the test group reporting that their colds had gone away. These findings were enthusiastically and uncritically reported in popular magazines, and dozens of "cold-stopper" manufacturers climbed on the gold-filled band wagon.

These experiments were honestly conducted, but further research disclosed a serious error in method. Although the men reporting for treatment believed they were

Much that is important cannot be dragged into the laboratory.

all getting the same pill, the physician knew which pill each man received. Thus when the man made his before-and-after reports to the physician, the unconscious bias of the

physician apparently led him to shade the reports in the direction which would support the findings he hoped to get. When a national test of the Salk polio vaccine was arranged, the standard safeguards were used to guard against the unconscious bias of the persons conducting the experiment. Using the "double-blind" technique, identical appearing doses of vaccine and of blanks were numbered and recorded in a secret code book, so that neither the patients nor the physicians giving the injections and reporting each case had any way of knowing which way to shade their reports. This meant that we could *know* that the findings were due to the vaccine and not due to unconscious bias. Deliberate dishonesty is exceedingly rare among serious scientists, but unconscious bias is a constant hazard, requiring research controls which make it more difficult for bias to operate.

Since laboratories are such convenient places to control the conditions of observation, scientists use them whenever possible. But much that is important cannot be dragged into a laboratory. Volcanoes and earthquakes cannot be staged in a test tube, nor can we study the courtship process very realistically by herding some couples into a laboratory. Both physical and social scientists frequently must observe phenomena in their natural setting. Techniques may range from lowering a bathysphere to the ocean floor to giving a questionnarie to a group of army recruits. If we remember that the basic scientific procedure is the conducting of accurate observations, while laboratories, instruments, and IBM cards are merely *tools* of observation, this difference in technique will not confuse us.

When phenomena—riots, panics, disasters, flying-saucer sightings—must be observed in their natural setting where the conditions of observation are not under the scientist's control, the scientist can only evaluate the observation in the light of the surrounding conditions and circumstances. Was the observer an interested bystander or an emotionally involved participant? Was the observer calm, relaxed, and comfortable, or was he excited, terrified, exhausted, hunger-crazed, or otherwise incapable of accurate observation? What were the lighting conditions and other visual circumstances? It is not surprising that sailors, traditionally a highly superstitious group who often suffered prolonged isolation, danger, hunger, thirst, and exhaustion, should have peered through ocean spray or evening haze and seen enticing mermaids and terrifying monsters which other observers have been unable to verify.

The scientific critic will trust a reported observation only insofar as the conditions of observation have been controlled. On this basis, science is skeptical of the claims of spiritualism and mind reading. A spiritualist can conduct a very convincing seance in his own stage setting, but spirtualists are loath to attempt a seance where the room, furnishings, and lighting are controlled by the scientist. The professional mind reader is very convincing in a theater setting, but he is unwilling to attempt a reading under scientifically controlled conditions. Until spiritualists and mind readers will make demonstrations under conditions which preclude the possibility of deception, scientists will dismiss the one as a fraud and the other as entertainment.

In these several respects, then, scientific observation differs from looking at things. We spend our lives looking at things, and this activity brings us much information, many impressions, and numerous conclusions. But these conclusions are clouded by accident of coincidence, by selective memory, and by personal bias. Therefore, before accepting any generalization as true, the critical observer wants to know what it is based upon. Is this conclusion based upon a systematically collected body of scientific evidence, or is it an offhand reaction to haphazard observation?

The scientific method (some would prefer to say scientific methods) includes a great deal. The scientist must accumulate considerable background information on the problem. Then he formulates an *hypothesis.* This is a carefully considered theoretical statement which seeks to relate all the *known* facts to one another in a logical manner. The hypothesis is then tested by scientific research. For example, the hypothesis that cancer is a virus disease is based upon a great deal of observation; it relates known facts in a logical manner; and it is now being tested through many research projects. Eventually an hypothesis is confirmed, rejected, or revised, and in this manner a science grows.

There are several steps in scientific research. They are easy to list but not always easy to follow.

1. *Formulate the problem,* that is, find a problem of some apparent scientific importance and define it so that it can be studied scientifically. Suppose the question arises as to whether fraternity membership is a hindrance to academic success. Our hypothesis might be, "Fraternity members receive lower grades than comparable nonmembers."

2. *Plan the research design,* outlining just what is to be studied, what data will be sought, where and how they will be collected, processed, and analyzed. In the above example, we should need to decide how to select and match the samples of fraternity members and nonmembers, where to secure data on the grades, and what mechanical and statistical procedures to use in analyzing these data and in arriving at conclusions.

3. *Collect the data* in accordance with the research design. Often it will be necessary to change the design to meet some unforeseen difficulty.

4. *Analyze the data.* Classify, tabulate, and compare the data, making whatever tests and computations are necessary to help find the results.

5. *Draw conclusions.* Was the original

hypothesis confirmed or rejected? Or were the results inconclusive? What has this research added to our knowledge? What implications has it for sociological theory? What new questions and suggestions for further research have arisen from this investigation?

SOCIOLOGY AS A SCIENCE

Science may be defined in at least two ways: (1) A science is a body of organized, verified knowledge which has been secured through scientific investigation; (2) a science is a method of study whereby a body of organized verified knowledge is discovered. These are, of course, two ways of saying much the same thing.

If the first definition is accepted, then sociology is a science *to the extent that it develops a body of organized verified knowledge* which is based on scientific investigation. To the extent that sociology forsakes myth, folklore, and wishful thinking and bases it conclusions on scientific evidence, it is a science. If science is defined as a method of study, then sociology is a science *to the extent that it uses scientific methods of study.* All natural phenomena can be studied scientifically, if one is willing to use scientific methods. Any kind of behavior —whether of atoms, animals, or adolescents —is a proper field for scientific study.

During most of man's history, few of his actions were based on verified knowledge, for man through the ages has been guided mainly by folklore, habit, and guesswork. Until a few centuries ago, very few people accepted the idea that man should find out about the natural world by systematic observation of the natural world itself, rather than by consulting his oracles, his ancestors, or his intuition. This new idea created the modern world. A few decades ago, man began acting on the assumption that this same approach might also give useful knowledge about man's social life. Just how far he has replaced folklore with knowledge in this area will be explored in the chapters which follow.

THE DEVELOPMENT OF SOCIOLOGY

Sociology is the youngest of the social sciences. Auguste Comte in France coined the word "sociology" in his *Positive Philosophy,* published in 1838. He believed that a science of sociology should be based on systematic observation and classification, not on authority and speculation. This was a relatively new idea at that time. Herbert Spencer in England published his *Principles of Sociology* in 1876. He applied the theory of organic evolution to human society and developed a grand theory of "social evolution" which was widely accepted for several decades, then discarded for several decades, and is today regaining a partial acceptance in modified form. Lester F. Ward, an American, published his *Dynamic Sociology* in 1883, calling for social progress through intelligent social action which sociologists should guide. All these founders of sociology were basically social philosophers. They proclaimed that sociologists should collect, organize, and classify factual data, and derive sound social theories from these facts; but very often their method was to think out a grand system of theory and then seek facts to support it. So while they called for scientific investigation, they did relatively little of it themselves. Yet they took the necessary first steps, for the *idea* of a science of sociology had to precede the building of one.

A Frenchman, Emile Durkheim, gave the most notable early demonstration of scientific methodology in sociology. In his *Rules of Sociological Method,* published in 1895, he outlined the methodology which he pursued in his study of *Suicide,* published in 1897. Instead of *speculating* upon the causes of suicide, he first planned his research design and then collected a large mass of data on the characteristics of people who commit suicide, and then derived a theory of suicide from these data.

Courses in sociology appeared in many universities in the 1890s. The *American Journal of Sociology* began publication in 1895, and the American Sociological Society (now the American Sociological Association) was organized in 1905. Whereas most of the early European sociologists came from the fields of history, political economy, or philosophy, many of the early American sociologists had been social workers, ministers, or ministers' sons; and nearly all were from rural backgrounds. Urbanization and industrialization were creating grave social problems, and these early sociologists were groping for "scientific" solutions. They saw sociology as a scientific guide to social progress. The early volumes of the *American Journal of Sociology* contained relatively few articles devoted to scientific description or research, but carried many sermons filled with exhortation and advice. For example, a fairly typical article in 1903, "The Social Effects of the Eight Hour Day," contains no factual or experimental data, but is entirely devoted to a recital of all the social benefits which the writer assures us will follow from the shorter working day [McVay, 1903]. But by the 1930s, the several sociological journals were well filled with research articles and scientific descriptions. Sociology was becoming a body of scientific knowledge with its theories based upon scientific observation rather than upon armchair speculation or impressionistic observation.

SUMMARY

In his search for truth, man has relied upon: (1) *intuition*, ranging from brilliant imagination to naïve guesswork; (2) *authority*, which tells him what is true; (3) *tradition*, which finds truth in whatever has been long accepted as true; (4) *common sense*, a convenient catchall which includes casual observation plus any or all of the above sources; and (5) *science*, the newest method of seeking truth. Science differs from other sources of truth in that (1) since scientific truth is based on verifiable evidence, science studies only those questions on which verifiable evidence can be secured, making no attempt to answer many important questions of value, purpose, or ultimate meaning; furthermore science realizes that all scientific truth is tentative, subject to revision in the light of new evidence; and (2) science is ethically neutral, seeking to discover knowledge no matter what values or institutions it may undermine or reinforce.

The basic technique of scientific investigation is *observation*. Scientific observation differs from just looking at things in that scientific observation is: (1) *accurate*, seeking to describe what really exists; (2) as *precise* and exact as is necessary; (3) *systematic*, in an effort to find all the relevant data; (4) *recorded* in complete detail as quickly as possible; (5) *objective*, in being as free from distortion by vested interest, bias, or wishful thinking as is humanly possible; (6) *conducted by trained observers*, who know what to look for and how to recognize it; (7) *conducted under controlled conditions* which reduce the danger of fraud, self-deception, or mistaken interpretation. The several steps in a scientific research project are: (1) Formulate the problem; (2) plan the research design; (3) collect the data; (4) analyze the data; and (5) draw the conclusions.

Whether the study of man's social relationships is a science is often debated. Sociology is a very new science, recently emerged from the speculations of nineteenth-century social philosophers and social reformers. To the extent that man's social life is studied through scientific methods so that a body of verified knowledge is developed—to that extent these studies become social sciences.

Questions and projects

1. Does the rigorously trained scientist make use of any sources of truth other than scientific observation in his daily life? Which ones? How often?

2. Distinguish between the critical and uncritical uses of authority.

3. Will a scientist ever make use of sacred authority?

4. Discuss the proposition: "Modern man should discard all ideas which are not scientifically verified." Should he? Can he?

5. Can scientists prove that ghosts and spirits do not exist, or that fortune telling and mind reading do not work? Why are scientists so skeptical?

6. Suppose a foreman says, "I've supervised all kinds of workers, and the black workers just don't measure up to white standards." What would be necessary for this statement to be a scientifically justified conclusion?

7. Suppose you were a reporter for the campus paper, writing a news account of a violent confrontation between students and police. Should you try to write it with strict objectivity, or should you "slant" it, using polemical language and omitting certain facts while emphasizing others in order to support the side which you felt to be morally right?

8. Suppose you wished to get an accurate description of a riot which happened five years ago in a city of 100,000 people. Make an outline showing where you would look for data, and suggest the limitations or inadequacies of each type or source of data.

9. Read Sinclair Lewis's novel *Arrowsmith*. What are some of the difficulties Martin had to meet in becoming rigorously scientific?

10. Suppose you, a college student, were to take a summer job working as a laborer in a factory. Make a list of the biases which might distort your impressions of factory workers as you size them up. Subject these lists to class comparison and criticism.

11. Prepare three statements of some issue or event, one written as a neutral scientist, the second as a supporter, and the third as an opponent.

Suggested readings

*Beck, William S.: *Modern Science and the Nature of Life*, Harcourt Brace & World, Inc., New York, 1957, chap. 3, "The Nature of Science." A brief essay on the history and nature of the scientific method.

*Chase, Stuart, with Edmund De S. Brunner: *The Proper Study of Mankind*, Harper & Row, Publishers, Incorporated, New York, 1956. A highly readable treatise on the contribution of social science to the solution of human problems.

*Dunham, Barrows: *Man against Myth*, Little, Brown and Company, Boston, 1947. A critical examination of some of the major myths of the Western world.

*Evans, Bergen: *The Natural History of Nonsense*, Alfred A. Knopf, Inc., New York, 1946. An entertaining examination of many popular myths and superstitions, which are demolished with a rare blend of wit and learning.

*Gardner, Martin: *Fads and Fallacies in the Name of Science*, Dover Publications, Inc., New York, 1957. Earlier edition under the title, *In the Name of Science*, G. P. Putnam's Sons, New York, 1952. An interesting account of many unscientific and pseudoscientific theories and the cults which promote them.

*Inkles, Alex: *What is Sociology*, Prentice-Hall, Inc., Englewood Cliffs, N.J., 1965. A brief description of what sociology is and what sociologists do.

Kaufmann, Felix: *Methodology of the Social Sciences*, Oxford University Press, Fair Lawn, N.J., 1944, especially chaps. 10, 14, and 15. A penetrating discussion of major questions of scientific method in the social sciences; for the more advanced student.

*MacDougall, Curtis D.: *Hoaxes*, Dover Publications, Inc., New York, 1958. An entertaining survey of frauds in art, history, science, literature, politics, and journalism.

Vine, Margaret Wilson: *An Introduction to Sociological Theory*, David McKay Company, Inc., New York, 1969. Outlines the contributions of each of the pioneers of sociology.

* An asterisk beside a citation indicates that the work is available in a paperback edition.

Fields and methods of sociology

"Extensive empirical investigation, both by the commission [President's Commission on Obscenity and Pornography] and by others, provides no evidence that exposure to or use of explicit sexual materials play a significant role in the causation of social or individual harms such as crime, delinquency, sexual or nonsexual deviancy or severe emotional disturbances. Empirical investigation thus supports the opinion of a substantial majority of persons professionally engaged in the treatment of deviancy, delinquency, and antisocial behavior that exposure to sexually explicit materials has no harmful causal role in those areas." (*Excerpts from panel majority report, quoted in the* New York Times, *October 1, 1970, p. 20.*)

The senate voted overwhelmingly to denounce the recent report of the Presidential Commission on Obscenity and Pornography and to reject its major findings [by a] 60-to-5 roll call vote. . . . The resolution specifically rejected commission findings that there was no evidence to suggest that exposure to explicit sexual materials would cause criminal behavior in youths or adults or adversely affect moral attitudes towards sex or sexual behavior. (New York Times, *October 14, 1970, p. 30.*)

"I have evaluated the report and categorically reject its morally bankrupt conclusions and major recommendations. The commission contends that the proliferation of filthy books and plays has no lasting effect on a man's character. If that were true, it must also be true that great books, great paintings, and great plays have no ennobling effect on man's conduct. Centuries of civilization and ten minutes of common sense tell us otherwise. . . . American morality is not to be trifled with. The Commission on Pornography and Obscenity has performed a disservice and I totally reject its report." (*President Richard M. Nixon, quoted in the* New York Times, *October 25, 1970, p. 71.*)

The [Commission] Chairman, William Lockhart, Dean of the University of Minnesota law school, said in a radio interview today that he assumed Mr. Nixon had not read the report . . . Mr. Lockhart said the commission was directed by Congress to test scientifically certain assumptions about the effects of pornography, not to please the

President, and added, "My hope and expectation is that when the research papers are studied in a calm atmosphere uncomplicated by election appeals, the result will be a far more careful appraisal of public policy in this emotionally charged area." (New York Times, *October 26, 1970, p. 74.*)

A report published today on the effects of legalized pornography in Denmark said that a sharp drop in the number of sex crimes had accompanied the easing of the laws over the past three years.... The 200-page report was [first of a series of 10 research studies] prepared for the Federal Commission on Pornography and Obscenity, whose findings were denounced last week by the United States Senate and the Nixon Administration. (New York Times, *November 9, 1970, p. 4.*)

What will you say when you go home next weekend and your younger sister asks, "Sociology? Well, what *is* sociology?" If you reply, "Sociology is the scientific study of human social relationships with special emphasis upon groups and institutions," she may say, "Oh," and you will guess that she is as confused as you are. If you tell her, "Sociology is the scientific study of social problems, like race conflicts, crime, divorce, etc.," your definition will give her *some idea* of what sociology is about, and may be a pretty good description to give to someone who would be puzzled by a more technical definition. But your answer will not be entirely correct, for sociology is much more than the study of social problems. As a student of sociology, you need a better definition.

THE FIELD OF SOCIOLOGY

First of all, *forget whatever you have read about sociology in popular magazines and newspapers*, for most of it is absurd. When a magazine writer wishes to make some of his offhand guesswork sound more impressive,

he may preface it with the phrase, "Sociologists fear that . . . ," "Sociologists are alarmed by . . . ," or "Sociologists are wringing their hands over. . . ." This journalistic device helps a writer to speak authoritatively without knowing very much about the subject. Often a writer sets up his "straw man" by attributing to sociologists the viewpoints which he is about to demolish. For example, one magazine writer [Bliven, 1960] lists nine developments over which he states that "the sociologists, of course, are wringing their hands. . . ." Of these nine propositions, six would be flatly rejected by most sociologists, two are marginal, and only one bears much resemblance to what most sociologists believe. Such writing makes for colorful journalism, but it has the effect of caricaturing the sociologist as a frustrated do-gooder in a perpetual state of shock over the mess we are in.

Sociology is interested in the way groups interact with one another.

Careless use of the term "sociologist" is also confusing. Magazine and newspaper writers, social workers, labor leaders, government officials, or anyone else who is interested in social relations may be described as sociologists. This is incorrect. A sociologist is one who has earned advanced degrees or pursued other advanced studies in sociology (not in psychology, theology, social work, or some other field) and is engaged in teaching, research, or other professional work in the field of sociology.

No formal definition of sociology is very satisfactory. Short definitions do not really define; long, explicit definitions are usually cumbersome. Yet a definition of some sort is needed, and sociology is often defined as *the scientific study of man's social life*. Man behaves differently from other animals. Man has unique forms of group life, pursues customs, develops institutions, creates values. Sociology applies scientific methods to the study of these phenomena in the search for scientific knowledge. It may be helpful at this point to discuss some definitions in reverse—to state through comparison what sociology is not.

Sociology is science, not social philosophy. A science is a body of knowledge; a philosophy is a system of ideas and values. A social philosophy is a set of ideas about how men *ought* to behave and treat one another; a social science studies how they actually *do* behave, and the consequences of this behavior.

Sociology is social science, not socialism. Socialism is a social philosophy with a political program, whereas sociology is a search for scientific knowledge. Socialists sometimes find in sociological research some material they can use in their propaganda; so do Republicans and Democrats. Some sociologists are socialists; many more are Republicans or Democrats.

Sociology concentrates its study upon man's group life and the products of his group living. The sociologist is especially interested in the customs, traditions, and values which emerge from group living, and in the way group living is, in turn, affected by these customs, traditions, and values. Sociology is interested in the way groups interact with one another and in the processes and institutions which they develop. Sociology is subdivided into many specialized fields, of which a partial list includes:

Applied Sociology
Collective Behavior and Mass Communication
Community
Comparative Sociology
Crime and Delinquency
Cultural Sociology
Demography
Deviant Behavior
Formal and Complex Organizations
Human Ecology
Industrial Sociology
Law and Society
Leisure, Sports, Recreation, and the Arts
Marriage and the Family
Mathematical Sociology
Medical Sociology
Methodology and Statistics
Military Sociology
Political Sociology
Race and Ethnic Relations
Rural Sociology
Social Change
Social Control
Social Organization
Social Psychology
Sociological Theory
Sociology of Education
Sociology of Occupations and Professions
Sociology of Religion
Sociology of Small Groups
Sociology of Knowledge and Science
Stratification and Mobility
Urban Sociology

These topics are not the exclusive property of sociology, for other fields share our interest in them. For example, our interest in communication and public opinion is shared by psychology and political science; criminology is shared with psychology, political science, law and police science, and so on. No science can fence itself off from other sciences, least of all sociology. Our field is especially close to those of psychology and anthropology, and overlaps theirs so constantly that any firm boundaries would be arbitrary and unrealistic. The more we learn about man's behavior, the more we realize that no one field of knowledge can fully explain him.

THE METHODS OF SOCIOLOGICAL RESEARCH

The methods of sociological research are basically those outlined in the preceding chapter and used by all scientists. As Karl Pearson has remarked, "The unity of all science consists alone in its method, not in its material. The man who classifies facts of any kind whatever, who sees their mutual relation and describes their sequences, is applying the scientific method and is a man of science" [1900, p. 12].

While scientific methods are basically alike for all sciences, scientific *techniques* differ, for techniques are the particular ways in which scientific methods are applied to a particular problem. Each science must, therefore, develop a series of techniques which fits the body of material it studies. What are some of the techniques of sociological research?

Cross-sectional, longitudinal, and ex post facto studies

Every study has some sort of time setting. A study which limits its observations to a single point in time is called a *cross-sectional* study. For example, Freedman, Whelpton, and Campbell [1959] interviewed a national sample of 2,713 young married women to discover their childbearing frequency and expectations. If the study extends over time, describing a trend or making a before-and-after set of observations, it is called a *longitudinal* study. Thus Campbell and McCormack [1957] sought to find out whether military training develops authoritarian attitudes. They gave an authoritarianism scale (a questionnaire designed to measure

authoritarian attitudes) to Air Force cadets at the beginning of Air Force training, and repeated the test a year later. Contrary to expectation, the retest showed authoritarian attitudes lower than the original test. While a single study, on a rather small sample, is not conclusive, this study points up the danger of simply making assumptions about the personality effects of any kind of experience.

An *ex post facto* study seeks to trace a present situation back to some earlier factors which may have been involved. For example, Glick [1957, p. 112] compared divorcées with married persons as to their age at marriage, and found divorce among those married before the age of eighteen to be almost three times as common as among those marrying between the ages of twenty-two and twenty-four. A great deal of sociological research is of the ex post facto sort.

Planned experiments

All sciences use planned experiments. An experiment may be either a laboratory experiment or a field experiment. In the laboratory experiment, the materials or people are brought into the laboratory for study. In laboratory experiments with people, the people are recruited, assembled, and perhaps paid for engaging in the experiment. Dollard's famous frustration-aggression studies [1939] were conducted by assembling a number of students as experimental subjects, supposedly to study the effects of fatigue upon task performance; then these students were subjected to intense frustration through prolonged boredom, nonarrival of promised food and games, and other intentional annoyances, while their aggressive responses were catalogued.

The field experiment takes the research out among the people instead of bringing the people to the research laboratory. A massive field experiment, involving the vaccination of several million children, established the value of the Salk polio vaccine. A continuing series of field experiments are seeking to find effective ways of promoting the practice of birth control in underdeveloped countries and among disadvantaged groups in the United States [Berelson, 1966].

The concept of any experiment is quite simple: Hold all variables constant except one; cause it to vary and see what happens.

A *variable* is anything which differs from person to person, group to group, time to time, or place to place—age, education, income, and many others. As an example, suppose we want to know whether abolishing grades would increase learning or increase loafing. To test this by experiment, we would need a *control group* of classes which follow the usual teaching and grading procedures, and an *experimental group* of classes using whatever experimental procedure is being tested. To "hold all other variables constant," the control and experimental groups would need to be alike in caliber of student, subject studied, quality of teaching, students' work load, students' finances, and anything else likely to affect their performance. We would also need a reliable instrument to measure learning outcomes (after reaching agreement upon *what* learning outcomes were important). Then the results of the trial could be objectively determined. If the experimental group shows greater or lesser learning gains than the control group, and this difference is confirmed by repetitions of the experiment conducted by other scholars (replication studies), then significant conclusions can be drawn.

There are two common ways of setting up experimental and control groups. One is the *matched-pair* technique. For each person in the experimental group, another person like him in all important variables (such as age, religion, education, occupation, or anything important to this research) is found and placed in the control group. Another technique is the *random-assignment* technique, in which statistically random assignments of persons to experimental and control groups are made—such as assigning the first person to the experimental group, the next to the control group, and so on. Suppose we wish to measure the effectiveness of an experimental treatment program for delinquents in a reformatory. Using one technique, we should match each delinquent who received the experimental treatment (experimental group) with another delinquent, matched for other variables thought important, who received only the usual treatment (control group). Using the random-assignment technique, every second (or third, or tenth) delinquent would be assigned to the experimental group upon arrival at the reformatory, with the others becoming the control group. Wherever the researcher is permitted to make assignments in this way, the random-assignment technique is far easier and at least as accurate; but often, when the research situation precludes this technique, the matched-pair technique may be used.

Sometimes the research situation provides ready-made experimental and control groups. For example, during World War II there was some debate over whether it was more efficient to use Negro troops in segregated or in mixed units. A few experimental units were organized with black platoons within white infantry companies. Some time later a sample of servicemen were asked how they would feel about serving in such a mixed outfit. As shown in Figure 1, it was found that the servicemen who actually served in mixed companies offered the least objection, while those in divisions with no mixed companies were the most unfavorable. In other words, those who were nearest to the mixed companies liked them best. And, while most of those in mixed companies had objected strongly *before* their organization, they offered the least objection after having actual experience in a mixed company. This

Question:

"Some Army divisions have companies which include black platoons and white platoons. How would you feel about it if your outfit was set up something like that?"

Infantrymen in a company which has a black platoon (80)

Infantrymen in other companies in the same regiment (68)

Field Artillery, Antitank, and HQ units in the same division (112)

Cross section of other Field Force units which do not have black platoons in white companies (1,450)

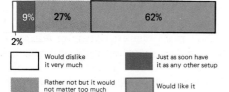

☐ Would dislike it very much	■ Just as soon have it as any other setup
▨ Rather not but it would not matter too much	▧ Would like it

FIGURE 1

Attitudes toward serving in a company containing Negro and white platoons among men who have done so and men who have not (Europe, June, 1945).

Source: Reproduced from Samuel A. Stouffer et al., *Studies in Social Psychology in World War II,* vol. 1, *The American Soldier: Adjustment during Army Life,* Princeton University Press, Princeton, N.J., 1949, p. 54.

experiment clearly showed that a great change in attitude took place as a result of enforced contacts.

These research findings formed the basis for the decision to end segregation in the armed services. For many years, the Army found that integration reduced racial conflict and permitted a more efficient use of troops [Nichols, 1954]. Currently, civilian racial friction has spread to the Army, but the basic principle is still valid that, other things being equal, contact promotes acceptance.

Planned experiments in sociology face certain difficulties. An experiment involving thousands of people may be prohibitively expensive. It may take many years to complete an experiment. Our values forbid us to use people for any experiments which may injure them. When people are unwilling to cooperate in an experiment, we cannot force them to do so (although we may occasionally trick them into unconscious cooperation). Furthermore, when people realize that they are experimental subjects, they begin to act differently, and the experiment may be spoiled. Almost any kind of experiment upon people *who know they are being studied* will give some interesting findings which may vanish soon after the experiment is ended. This is known as the Hawthorne effect, named after some experiments with temperature, humidity, rest periods, and other working conditions at the Hawthorne plant of Western Electric Company [Roethlisberger, 1949]. It was found that *any* change in the working conditions—more humidity, less humidity, longer rest periods, shorter rest periods—was followed by a temporary gain in work output. In medicine, this is known as the "placebo effect." In medical research, many subjects in the control group who are given placebos (pills containing no medicines of any kind) report that they feel much better. These show how the findings of many experiments may be due to the attention the subjects are getting, not to the factor which is being tested.

Planned experiments upon human subjects are most reliable when these subjects do not know the true object of the experiment. They may be given a rationale, a reasonable explanation of what the experimenter is doing, but this rationale may be a harmless but necessary deception which conceals the true purpose of the experiment. For example, an experiment to determine the effect of background music upon work output in a factory might be explained as a trial to see whether workers *liked* music. But as Kelman points out [1966] the use of deception in social research poses the ethical question of distinguishing between harmless deception and intellectual dishonesty, and may even produce errors in the outcome (subjects may detect the deception and begin second-guessing the researcher!).

Because of all these limitations, social sciences (excepting psychology) make limited use of planned experiments. We use them wherever practical, but depend more heavily on other techniques.

Observational studies

Observational studies are like planned experiments in all respects except one: In the planned experiments the scientist arranges for something to happen so that he can observe what follows, whereas in the observational study the scientist observes something which happens, or has already happened, by itself. Both rely upon systematic observation under controlled conditions in a search for verifiable sequences and relationships. Both are used in all the sciences, but the procedures for using them vary according to the material being studied. The types of studies which follow are not mutually exclusive, for a study may use several different techniques.

Impressionistic studies These are informal descriptive and analytic accounts, based on observations which are less fully controlled than in more formal studies. They definitely are *not* a rambling, incoherent recital of whatever one happens to recall having seen, but are an organized presentation of thoughtful, purposeful observations. Suppose a sociologist with a special interest in the family makes a tour of Russia. He is alert for information on the Russian family, asks questions about Russian family life of most of the people he meets, scans the papers and magazines for their pictures of family life. He returns home with some very definite impressions of Russian family life, but they are not based on a systematic, scientifically controlled investigation—on an orderly search of the published literature, on a scientifically constructed sample of informants, and so on. If he is a responsible scholar, he will call his judgments impressions, and will not state them as scientifically established conclusions.

No matter how elaborate, carefully planned, and systematically conducted a study may be, if the recorded data consist of the impressions of the observer, it is classed as an impressionistic study. Thus the Lynds [1929, 1937] spent many months in "Middletown" (Muncie, Indiana); they systematically searched the newspaper files, interviewed virtually everyone who held a position of authority or was locally said to be important, and participated in community life. They ended up with a large mass of impressions which were highly perceptive and probably accurate, but largely unverifiable except through long and costly research.

Impressionistic studies are highly useful in social science. They provide many hypotheses and research leads, and suggest many insights which might be overlooked by other methods. The best of the impressionistic studies hold an honored place in sociological literature.

Statistical comparative studies If information obtained from an experiment has already been written down somewhere it is sensible to look up the record. Much sociological research consists of looking up recorded statistical facts and comparing and interpreting them. For a simple example, consider the question, "Now that women have greater freedom to lead an interesting and independent life without marriage, are more women remaining single?" The answer is easily derived from census data, which show the proportion of single women dropping from 24.3 percent in 1890 to 19.2 percent in 1969. (These figures give the percentage of all American women fourteen years old or older, who had never been married, with correction for changes in the age distribution of the population.) Many such questions can be answered quickly by checking data in the annual *Statistical Abstract of the United States*, which summarizes statistics collected by many government and other agencies and should be found in any library. Other questions may require study of more specialized statistical sources, such as the many *Special Reports* issued by the Bureau of the Census.

Many research questions involve a comparison of several kinds of statistical data from several sources. For example, Lander [1954] wondered about the relation between juvenile delinquency and overcrowded, substandard housing. From court records he compiled delinquency rates for 155 census districts in Baltimore, and from census data he found the average number of persons per room and the percentage of officially substandard housing units for each census district. He found that delinquency rates closely followed rates of overcrowding and substandard housing, but that this association disappeared when he controlled the other variables, such as race, income, education, and occupation. However, he found one variable—home ownership—which remained highly associated even when all others were controlled. He concluded that home ownership was an index of family

stability, and that this connection helped to explain the lower delinquency rates in areas where home ownership prevailed.

Sometimes the research scholar must go out and collect the raw statistical data himself. For example, what factors have produced the fairly large nonstudent "fringe" which hangs around the edges of the major universities? In seeking an answer, Whittaker and Watts [1969] administered a standard psychological test to a sample of nonstudents and to a sample of students at Berkeley. They found the students and nonstudents to be from similar backgrounds, but found the nonstudents to be more interested in the arts than practical concerns, more impulsive, less self-disciplined, less integrated in personality, less distinctly masculine or feminine (more nearly "unisex") in personality, and more socioemotionally maladjusted.

Many people "have no use for statistics." Often they do not like statistics because they do not understand them. Statistics, like shotguns, are dangerous when handled by the ignorant, as is shown in Huff's entertaining little book, *How to Lie with Statistics* [1954]. Those who know the uses and abuses of statistics realize that statistics are nothing more or less than *organized, measured facts*. They are as trustworthy or untrustworthy as is the scientific method of the person who compiles them. To reject statistics is but a way of rejecting facts.

Sociologists make a great many comparative statistical studies. As almost any kind of research is likely to involve statistical organization and comparison of facts at some point or other, the sociologist must be something of a statistician, and the citizen who hopes to be intelligently aware of the world he lives in must have some understanding of statistical interpretation.

Questionnaire and interview studies Sometimes the facts we need are not recorded anywhere, and we can find them only by asking people. For example, what is the "ideal-size family" in the eyes of American young people? This question has some importance for population prediction, business planning, educational planning, and many other purposes. We can find the answer only by asking people what they think is the ideal size for a family. Questionnaire and interview studies are systematic ways of asking questions under scientific controls. A questionnaire is filled out by the informant himself; an interview schedule is filled out by a trained interviewer who asks the questions of the informant. Both methods have their pitfalls, which the trained sociologist should be able to avoid. While it is fairly easy to get purely factual information quite accurately (e.g., "Do you own or rent your home?" "Are you married?"), surveys of attitudes and opinions have greater margins of error. The informants may not understand the question; they may pick an answer even though they do not have any firm opinion on the matter; they may give an "acceptable" answer rather than the real one; or they may be swayed by the way the question is worded. A survey may also give false conclusions because the sample of persons surveyed is not a representative cross section of the population. Questionnaire and interview studies, like other research methods, must be used by trained scholars who are aware of their pitfalls.

Even though questionnaire and interview studies have a margin of error, they may still be useful, for they are more reliable than guesswork. For example, after victory over Germany in 1944, the Army had more men in uniform than were needed. *Which* men should be demobilized? This was an explosive question, with grave consequences for morale. The Army made a questionnaire study [Stouffer, 1949, chap. 11] in which several thousand servicemen were asked:

After the war when the Army starts releasing soldiers back to civilian life, which of these two groups of men do you think should be released first? (Check only one.)
——Men with dependents
or
——Men over 30 years of age

This question was repeated several times, each time presenting an answer choice between a different pairing of such criteria as overseas service, combat experience, length of time in service, age, and number of dependents. Responses showed that the largest number of servicemen would give first priority to men who have seen combat, next priority to married men with children, and so on. Using these responses, the Army developed a point system for determining eligibility for discharge. That this approach was highly practical was shown by the fact that the Army discharge policy proceeded with very little criticism or resentment, either from servicemen or from civilians.

Participant-observer studies No man will fully know what it feels like to be a mother, nor will any civilian completely understand army life. Some things can be fully understood only by experiencing them. The *participant observer* seeks insight by taking part himself in whatever he is studying. If he wishes to understand labor unions, he will join one, work in the shop, attend the union meetings, possibly become a minor union official or a union organizer. If he wishes to study a religious sect, he will join it and try to share in its worship. Through his own participation, together with the opportunity for very intimate observation, he may gain insights which no amount of *external* observation would provide.

At the height of the flying-saucer craze, an interesting cult arose in a Midwestern American city. A small group of believers received certain "revelations" that the earth would soon be destroyed, and that only a faithful few would be rescued by flying saucers and carried to a friendly planet. Several participant observers joined the group, concealing their scientific identities and taking part in the group's activities until it dissolved some months later [Festinger, 1956]. In another instance, a white novelist [Griffin, 1961] was commissioned by Ebony magazine to make a participant-observer study of Negro life. With his hair trimmed short and his skin darkened by a drug, he traveled about the South, where everyone identified him as a black. Although he was a native Southerner, he found that his view of Negro life from the inside brought many surprising revelations.

The participant observer seeks insight by taking part himself.

There are pitfalls in this technique. The participant observer may become so emotionally involved that he loses his objectivity. Or he may overgeneralize; that is, he may assume that what he finds in the group he studies is also true of all other groups. Since his data are largely impressionistic, his conclusions are not easily verified. Yet the participant observer is not just "looking at things," but is applying a sophisticated scientific methodology [Bruyn, 1966] which has given us many insights and suggested many hypotheses for further study.

Is it ethical to pretend to be a loyal member of a group in order to study it? Is such a deception justifiable? It is not easy to say when a deception ceases to be harmless. Perhaps the best answer is that a reputable scientist will be careful not to injure the people he is studying.

The *eyewitness account* is an amateur, small-scale participant-observer study. How do people act after a disaster, such as a tornado or an explosion? What happens at a religious revival, a riot, a picket-line disturbance? Rarely is there a visiting sociologist, pencil in hand, ready to record the event. Social scientists often seek eyewitness accounts from persons who were there. A detailed eyewitness account, collected as soon as possible after the event, is a useful source of information. Such accounts must be used with care, for the eyewitness is usually an untrained observer, and his own excitement or involvement may have impaired his accuracy and objectivity. Yet the eyewitness account is a priceless source of data for the social scientist.

Case studies The case study is a complete, detailed account of some phenomenon. It may be a life history of a person, or a complete account of a brief event. The case history of a group—a family, a clique, a union, a religious movement—may suggest some insights into group behavior. An accurate, detailed account of a riot, a panic, an orgy, a disaster, or any social event may have scientific value. An unhappy family, a happy family, a community, an organization—almost any phenomenon can be studied by the case-study technique.

Perhaps the greatest value of the case study is in the suggestion of hypotheses, which can then be tested by other methods. Most of our reliable knowledge about juvenile deliquency, for instance, has developed through the testing of hypotheses which were suggested by early case studies of delinquents [Thomas, 1923; Shaw, 1931]. Much of our present knowledge of personality disorganization stems from hypotheses suggested by a classic collection of case studies in Thomas and Znaniecki's *The Polish Peasant in Europe and America* [1923]. These hypotheses are not often *tested* by the case-study method, but by other methods.

A generalization cannot be based upon a single case, for a case can be found to "prove" almost anything. Generalizations must be based upon a large mass of carefully processed data, and the collection of a great many case studies is expensive. Also it is difficult to "add up" a number of case studies or compute averages or other statistical computations. Therefore we seldom use case studies when seeking to test a hypothesis. But after the hypothesis has been tested and we have arrived at some sound generalizations, a good case study may give a beautiful illustration of these generalizations. For example, there is conclusive evidence that juvenile delinquency is closely associated with unsatisfactory family life [Glueck and Glueck, 1959]. A case study showing how unsatisfactory family life has apparently encouraged delinquency in a particular family makes a vivid illustration of this generalization [Shaw, 1938].

SOME DIFFICULTIES IN SOCIOLOGICAL RESEARCH

Complexity of phenomena

Social phenomena are so complex, subtle, and elusive that the sociologist sometimes wonders where to begin. Yet a science is defined, not by the simplicity of its raw materials, but by the rigor of its methods. To some extent, the subtlety and elusiveness of phenomena are in proportion to our ignorance about them. The causes of a patient's fever, which may elude the layman, may be easily perceptible to the pathologist. As any science gains in maturity and knowledge, its con-

fusing complex phenomena become somewhat more orderly and systematic, and its data somewhat less puzzling and elusive.

It is unlikely, however, that any amount of knowledge will ever make our phenomena appear as orderly as those of the natural sciences. Boyle's law deals with only three variables—volume, temperature, and pressure of enclosed gases, all of which are easily controlled; criminal behavior deals with two or three dozen variables, none of which is very easily controlled. The truly great complexity of social phenomena poses a lasting challenge to the methodology of sociological research.

Constant change

Social phenomena are constantly changing. How can scientific truth be based upon data which are so slippery that today's truth is untrue tomorrow? This real difficulty is not peculiar to the social sciences, for many sciences must make allowance for changing phenomena. The geographer's landscape is constantly changing, although very slowly. The meteorologist must allow for shifting wind systems. The immunologist and the entomologist must concern themselves with changes in the tolerance or resistance of bacteria, viruses, and insects. The social sciences, however, study phenomena which are vastly more changeable than the phenomena of most other sciences.

But, as already stated, it is not the materials but the methods of study which identify a science. Since many of the phenomena of sociology are constantly changing, each sociological generalization must have a time-and-place qualification. Therefore, when we speak of "the family," we must show whether we are speaking of the family in all its forms and variations or whether we are speaking of, say, the contemporary, urban, American, middle-class family.

All sciences must qualify their generalizations by stating the conditions under which they hold true. The physicist must say, "Water boils at 100 degrees centigrade—providing it is chemically pure and at an atmospheric pressure of 14.7 pounds per square inch." And the sociologist may say, "Contact and association between members of prejudiced groups will reduce prejudices, *provided* these contacts are cooperative and equalitarian in nature."

The very great changeability and variability of the phenomena of sociology compel the sociologist to qualify his generalizations with especial care. The student will find many carefully qualified statements such as, "In the contemporary American middle-class family, education and the drive to 'get ahead' are major goals," or "among the small, nontypical samples studied to date, young American married couples living with in-laws are as happily married as those living by themselves." This incessant hedging may become tiresome to the student, who may be tempted to agree with the definition of sociology as "the science that is never sure of anything." Yet careful qualification is the price of accuracy, and the scientist never intentionally generalizes beyond the limitations of his data.

Unpredictability of behavior

Some critics maintain that, since all people are different, human behavior is unpredictable. People may even deliberately change their behavior in order to upset our predictions. A science can predict and sometimes control. Can sociology?

It is true that all persons are different in some respects. It is also true that all persons are alike in some respects. Sociology seeks to learn more about the ways in which people are different and the ways in which they are alike and act alike, so that their behavior can be understood and predicted.

In considering scientific prediction, the student must grasp two principles. First, *predictions hold true only under certain stated conditions.* The physicist can predict with great exactness the behavior of a specially manufactured ball rolling down a perfectly smooth plane in a vacuum chamber. If asked to predict the behavior of a driverless truck rolling downhill, his prediction must be less exact, since the conditions are not fully controlled.

The sociologist can rarely predict what any one person will do.

Accurate and exact prediction, in any science, is possible only when all variables can be controlled or mathematically calculated. The agronomist may predict, "About 20 percent of these seeds will fail to grow, if placed in good Indiana soil about May 15 and if temperature and rainfall conditions are similar to those of last year." Likewise, the sociologist may predict, "About 20 percent of the male teen-agers in this particular slum area will be officially recorded as delinquent this year, if social influences and law-enforcement practices in the area remain like those of last year." But if several of the variables cannot be controlled, then accurate prediction is impossible. For example, will we have a "white Christmas" next winter?

The meteorologist cannot predict, unless he knows what the wind systems and pressure areas are going to be next December. Or, what will the population of the United States be by the end of the century? The demographer cannot predict this without knowing what the birth rates, death rates, and rates of migration are going to be during the rest of the century; and these, in turn, hinge upon such variables as age at marriage, the popularity of large families, the level of prosperity, the progress of medical science, and several other variables.

The problem of prediction, then, is similar in all sciences. Our success in prediction is in proportion to our ability to predict or control all of the variables involved. As the following chapters will show, there are some topics upon which sociologists are able to make reasonably dependable predictions.

A second principle of scientific prediction derives from the fact that *most scientific prediction deals with collectivities, not individuals.* The agronomist predicts what proportion of seeds will grow, without telling which little seed will die. The chemist predicts the behavior of several billion hydrogen and oxygen atoms, without predicting the behavior of any single atom of hydrogen or oxygen. The sociologist can rarely predict what any one person will do, although he may be able to predict what most of the members of a group will do. In other words, the sociologist may predict the *probability* of an action, just as the life insurance actuary predicts the probability that an insured will die. Predictions may be useful even when we cannot predict the behavior of any particular individual. It is not necessary to know *which* persons will die of typhoid fever to know that polluted water is deadly. Nor need we stop predicting population movements just because we cannot name the persons who are going to move. Sociological prediction can be a useful basis for social policy if it can fortell what certain *groups or proportions* of people are going to do; it is

quite unnecessary to predict the behavior of each individual.

In the making of *socially significant* predictions, the social sciences already compare favorably with the natural sciences. The natural scientist can predict to the minute the next eclipse of the sun, but cannot predict the next flood or drought as accurately as the social scientist can predict the next recession. Natural science prediction is most accurate in artifical laboratory situations, and least accurate when directed to those matters upon which important social decisions hinge. On questions like, "How soon can we expect a major breakthrough in cancer research?" or "Which raw materials will be indispensable and which will have become inessential by the twenty-first century?" natural science is not very helpful. In the making of socially significant predictions, neither natural nor social scientists have attained any great accuracy, but the social scientists appear to be at least as successful as their critics.

PURE AND APPLIED SOCIOLOGY

A distinction between pure and applied science is drawn in every scientific field. *Pure science* is a search for knowledge, without primary concern for its practical use. *Applied science* is the search for ways of using scientific knowledge to solve practical problems. A biochemist who seeks to learn how a cell absorbs food or how a cell ages and grows old is working as a pure scientist. If he then tries to find some substance or procedure which will control the aging process, he is working as an applied scientist. A sociologist making a study of "the social structure of a slum neighborhood" is working as a pure scientist; if he then follows with a study of "how to prevent delinquency in a slum neighborhood," he is working as an applied scientist. Many people view sociology entirely as an applied science—trying to solve social problems. Properly viewed, it is both a pure and an applied science. For unless a science is constantly searching for more basic knowledge, its "practical applications of knowledge" are not likely to be very practical.

Practical applications of sociological knowledge are not widely appreciated. Some sociologists are employed by corporations, government bureaus, and social agencies, usually as research scholars, and sociologists are sometimes consulted by legislative committees who are planning new legislation. But the private citizen rarely bases his social decisions upon sociological knowledge. If a man wants to know how to fertilize artichokes, he generally collects some scientific data before deciding. But how are social-policy decisions made? Each year dozens of communities vote on whether to allow liquor to be sold by the glass in taverns and restaurants. Arguments about automobile accidents, crime drunkenness, and other evils are hurled around with abandon. But has any *comprehensive, carefully controlled* comparison of communities with and without liquor sale by the glass ever been conducted? Your authors know of none. For many years, citizens' groups have been crusading against pornography, although until 1970 there was virtually *no scientific evidence* upon whether pornography was a dangerous stimulant or a harmless outlet for salacious impulses. And, as noted earlier, when the first substantial body of research evidence was finally presented by the President's Commission on Obscenity and Pornography, the report was condemned and its recommendations rejected by President Nixon and by the Senate *before the entire series of reports was published.*

On many social questions, such as the causes and treatment of crime and delinquency, drug and alcohol addiction, sex offenses, the causes and consequences of racial discrimination, or the adjustment of the family to a changing society, there *is* considerable scientific knowledge, but this knowledge is rejected by many persons who prefer their prejudices. As a nation, we have only begun to apply scientific methods to our thinking about social issues.

Popular sociology

A great deal of sociological material gets into print through the agency of people who are not sociologists. The popular magazines are studded with articles on crime, family life, sex, education, suburbia, social class—practically every sociological topic imaginable. This is popular sociology—treatment of sociological topics, often by writers without much formal sociological training, and aimed at a popular audience. Popular sociology at its worst is seen in articles like the "sex-and-sin" exposés upon which certain men's magazines dwell so fondly. Such articles are generally descriptively inaccurate, with a total lack of the interpretative analysis which would fit the facts into a relevant social context. At the opposite pole are many magazine writers who do a fairly creditable job of popularizing sociological findings. Perhaps the best-known popular "sociologist" is Vance Packard, whose books on social class [*The Status Seekers*, 1959; *The Pyramid Climbers*, 1962] and other topics [*The Sexual Wilderness*, 1968] have been read by millions—and severely criticized by sociologists [Petersen, 1960; Goldner, 1963; Simon, 1969]. The writings of the sociological popularizers often contain inaccuracies and instances of misplaced emphasis, doubtful interpretation, oversimplification, and too-sweeping generalization. Yet it is likely that popular understanding of sociological topics has been greatly increased by such writers.

Why isn't popular sociology written by professional sociologists? For the same reason that popular medicine and popular science are usually written by journalists, rather than by physicians and scientists. Popular writing is a special skill which few scientists or professors have mastered. Furthermore, the scientist's passion for accuracy and for a careful qualification of his statements is a positive handicap in popular writing. His unwillingness to oversimplify, to overdramatize, or to indulge in grandly sweeping generalization all make his writing more accurate but less exciting. Sociologists write for the scholarly audience, while journalists popularize sociology, more or less accurately, for the public.

THE ROLES OF THE SOCIOLOGIST

What is the proper task of the sociologist? Should he merely observe human action with the calm, detached curiosity of the ecologist who counts the lemmings as they dive into the sea? Or should he plunge into social action to avert the dangers he foresees? Should the professor of sociology encourage students to develop a detached understanding of social phenomena, or should he inspire them to man the barricades for social reform? What is the proper role for the sociologist in a changing society?

The sociologist as research scientist

Like all scientists, sociologists are concerned with both collecting and using knowledge. They share in these tasks in various ways.

Conducting scientific research As a scientist, the sociologist's foremost task is to discover and organize knowledge about social life. A number of full-time research sociologists are employed by universities, government agencies, foundations, or cor-porations, and many sociologists divide their time between teaching and research. Many university sociologists are engaged in "funded" research, with all or part of their salaries and their research expenses paid from research grants made by government agencies, foundations, or corporations. These grants are made to sociologists who submit an acceptable proposal for research on a particular topic. Since little research can be conducted without research funds, this gives the funding agencies great power to influence the direction of sociological research.

Radical critics of sociology (including some sociologists) claim that, behind a facade of ethical neutrality and objectivity, sociologists have prostituted their research talents to the support of the interests of the funding agencies, and have thus supported militarism, racism, and other forms of oppression [Gouldner, 1962, 1970; Frederichs, 1970, pp. 82–85]. These and other criticisms of "establishment sociology" are repeated in the various handbills and newsletters of the Sociology Liberation Movement, a loosely organized network of critical graduate students with the support of some professors.

Whether sociological research has been widely corrupted in this manner may be debated [Horton and Bouma, 1971]. What is indisputable is that problems of bias and partisanship are present in all research, and that research findings are often helpful to the interests of some people and damaging to the interests of some other people [Becker, 1967]. Even the definition of a research problem may carry an implicit bias. For example, if we state a research problem as, "What characteristics of poor people contribute to their poverty?", we imply that the "blame" rests mainly on the poor people themselves; but if we define the problem as, "What social arrangements produce poverty?", then the blame is placed upon "society."

Throughout most of the history of sociology, sociologists were often accused of being radical subversives whose research and teaching were a threat to established institutions and vested interests. Many older sociologists today, still bearing the scars of the anti-Communist witch-hunts of the 1950s, are puzzled and hurt when students and younger sociologists accuse them of having been lackeys of capitalistic oppression all their lives! But the question of the responsibility of the scientist to his society is as old as science itself, and will not soon be settled.

Another task is to clear away the intellectual rubbish.

Correcting popular nonsense Another task of the sociologist as a scientist is to clear away the intellectual rubbish of misinformation and superstition which clutters so much of our social thinking. Sociologists have helped to bury a great deal of nonsense about heredity, race, class, sex differences, deviation, and nearly every other aspect of behavior. It is due partly to the findings of sociology that today we rarely hear an educated person argue that the white race is innately superior, that women are intellectually inferior to men, that behavior traits are inherited, that punishment

reforms criminals, or that rural people are less "immoral" than urbanities—ideas which nearly every educated person accepted a half century ago. By helping replace superstition and misinformation with accurate knowledge about human behavior, sociologists are perhaps performing their most important function.

Making sociological predictions Sociological prediction should be of interest to legislators and all others who are concerned with social policy, for every major policy decision makes certain assumptions about the present and future structure of society. When a legislator says, "We need new laws to curb campus disorders," he is predicting that the new laws he proposes *would* curb campus disorders without creating greater problems. The legislator who says, "Students and administrators themselves, under present laws, can best handle the problem," is making a different set of predictions. Every policy recommendation implies a set of assumptions and predictions. What sort of predictions do sociologists offer? Here are a few samples, offered without explanation or documentation at this point, as examples of the kind of predictions sociologists can make:

Urban sprawl will spread rapidly along the superhighways and will result in the eventual creation of regional planning and administrative authorities.

The trend toward the employment of mothers will continue until most women are working for a substantial portion of their married lives.

Birth rates will, sooner or later, fall to approach death rates, or death rates will rise to approach birth rates.

Farm organizations have passed the peak of their power; and are likely to decline in membership and in power.

There is no certainty that any one of these

predictions will be fulfilled, only a strong likelihood that most of them will come true. Such predictions help to clarify the kind of social setting in which we must function for the next generation or two.

The sociologist as policy consultant

Sociological prediction can also help to estimate the probable effects of a social policy. Every social policy decision *is* a prediction. A policy (e.g., federal grants for Head Start) is begun in the hope that it will produce a desired effect (e.g., narrow the educational gap between poor and more prosperous children). Policies have often failed because they embodied unsound assumptions and predictions. Sociologists can help to predict the effects of a policy, and thus contribute to the selection of policies which achieve the intended purposes. For example:

What effect would the removal or the addition of the death penalty have upon the murder rate? (Practically none.)

What effects do brotherhood propaganda and "education for brotherhood" efforts have on race prejudices? (Practically none.)

If welfare payments were witheld from illegitimate mothers, what effect would this have upon illegitimacy rates? (Little or none.)

What would be the effect of intensified law enforcement upon campus marijuana use? (Little or no reduction, with aggravation of other student-police problems.)

Would lower birthrates and a small-family norm increase marital happiness? (Yes; there is research evidence that smaller families are better in every way.)

Would publishing the names of juvenile delinquents help to reduce delinquency? (No; it would more likely increase it.)

Would the suppression of obscene literature help to reduce sex crimes and sex immorality? (Our limited evidence suggests that it would have no effect.)

These are a few of the many social-policy questions which sociologists could help to settle. So far our society has not generally accorded the sociologist a status as technical expert on social-policy matters. The image of the sociologist as a professional bleeding heart, so often reflected in the popular press, does not help the public to visualize the sociologist as a technical expert. Congressional committees, however, often consult sociologists and other social scientists when holding hearings on proposed legislation. In some areas, especially in criminology and race relations, the conclusions of sociologists (and other social scientists) have had considerable influence. It was, in considerable part, the findings of sociologists and psychologists which led the United States Supreme Court to rule that "segregated schools are inherently unequal" [*Brown v. Board of Education of Topeka*, 1954].

One of the greatest services any scholarly group can offer is to show the society what policies are most likely to work in achieving its objectives. This is a service which sociologists are qualified to perform.

The sociologist as technician

Today sociologists are increasingly finding employment with government departments, corporations, hospitals, large welfare agencies, and other large organizations. Aside from research, they are engaged in planning and conducting community action programs; advising on public relations, employee relations, problems of morale or of "intergroup relations" within the organization; working on human relations problems of many sorts. The "staff sociologist" is found in all kinds of large organizations [*Business Week,* 1959]. Often he has specialized in social psychology, industrial sociology, urban or rural sociology, or the sociology of complex organizations.

In such positions the sociologist is working as an applied scientist. His employer has engaged him to use his scientific knowledge in pursuing certain values—a harmonious and efficient working force, an attractive public image of the industry, or an effective community action program. This role raises a question of ethics. When a sociologist accepts employment as a technician, pursuing values chosen by his employer, has he compromised his scientific integrity? To take an extreme example, there is evidence [Monroe, 1962] that gambling operators engaged social scientists to find out why people do or do not gamble, so that the operators could learn how to attract more customers. (We do not know whether any sociologists were included.) Would this be a form of scientific prostitution?

The radical critics of "establishment sociology" charge that sociologists have "sold out" whenever they serve as technicians or research scholars in any kind of effort to maintain or improve the efficiency of the government, military, capitalistic, or welfare establishments. Thus, not only are sociologists (if any) working in war-related activities condemned, but even sociologists working in programs to improve the health of poor children in Mississippi, to increase agricultural output in Peru, or to teach birth control in Indian villages are accused of supporting "oppression." This is the classic view of the revolutionist—any attempt to make the present system work better, or to help people to find better lives within the system, is "oppressive" because it helps to perpetuate the system.

There is no simple answer to the question of what technician appointments it is proper for the sociologist to accept. Each sociologist's answer will be found partly in the prevailing views of the academic world at that moment and partly in his own conscience.

The sociologist as teacher

Teaching is the major career of most sociologists. In addition to the concerns and problems of teaching in any field, the problem of value neutrality versus value commitment is a particularly acute question for the sociologist. For example, in his course on "poverty," should he supervise an objective study of facts, theories, and policies—possibly sympathetic but as objective as possible? Or should he design the course to produce dedicated advocates of the action program he favors? Should he seek to convert his students to conservatism, liberal reformism, or revolutionary activism? For some decades, the ethics of university teaching have demanded that the teacher refrain from all conscious "indoctrination," but this question is now under spirited debate [Horton and Bouma, 1971].

The sociologist and social action

Scientists seek to discover knowledge. Should scientists also tell the society how this knowledge *should* be used? For example, the geneticists already know something about human heredity, and before very long it may be possible to control the genetic makeup of babies, and "order" babies according to a specifications list. Who should decide what sort of baby should go to whom? The scientists? The parents? The government?

The basic question is whether science—specifically sociology—should be value-free. For example, sociologists know some things about population growth, race relations, urban development, and many other matters involving questions of public policy. Should sociologists become public advocates of birth-control programs, racial integration, urban renewal, and many other programs which they may consider socially desirable?

Early sociologists gave an emphatic "yes" to this question. Without an adequate foundation of scientific knowledge, they rushed into support of all sorts of public policies they believed wise. Between 1920 and 1940, many sociologists shifted to the view that sociology should be a more nearly "pure" science, discovering knowledge, but not attempting to decree how it should be used. They sought to build sociology on the model of physics or chemistry, as a value-free science. As such, it should be committed to no values except those of free scientific inquiry. Sociologists generally avoided involvement in controversial issues and sought the status of "pure" social scientists.

More recently, this view has been challenged in both physical and social science. *The Bulletin of the Atomic Scientists* carries many articles by scientists urging their fellows to claim a larger role in making the decisions relative to the uses of nuclear science discoveries. Many sociologists today believe that sociologists should claim a major role in making decisions about public policy and should involve themselves in the major issues of our society [Lindesmith, 1960; Horowitz, 1964; Stein and Vidich, 1964; A. Lee, 1966; Becker, 1967]. They charge that sociologists have buried themselves in "safe" research topics, leaving the really important questions to nonsociologists—questions such as, "How can poverty be reduced?" "How can schools be integrated?" How can communities be organized for more civilized social living?" "Should the goals and values of American society be altered to promote human welfare?" They feel that sociologists not only should say what society *might* do about problems of race conflict, population growth, birth control, drug addiction, divorce, sex deviation,

medical care, etc.; they feel that sociologists have a duty to say what our society *should* do about such problems. Books like Shostak's *Sociology in Action* [1966] provide some concrete examples of how sociologists are involving themselves in social issues and constructive social action and show what they have learned from these experiences.

Sociology today, in common with all the other social sciences, has some members who insist that, both individually and as an academic discipline, sociologists should openly and publicly support the "radical reconstruction of society."[1] This question is receiving much attention in sociological literature [Douglas, 1970; entire Winter, 1970-1971, issue of *Sociological Focus*]. Whether sociology should be value-free is an unsettled question, but sociologists are agreed upon the following propositions:

(1) Sociologists should show the relationships between values. In short, sociologists may say, "If *this* is what you want, *here* is what you must do to get it." If stable, enduring marriages are more important than marriage happiness, then divorce should be made more difficult; if *happy* marriages represent the more important value, then fairly easy divorce should permit the unhappily married to separate and try again. If we wish to arrest urban blight and suburban sprawl, some private property rights will have to be sacrificed. If we wish to clean up polluted rivers, we must be prepared to spend a lot of tax moneys in doing so. Sociologists may clarify what value sacrifices must be made if we wish to attain certain other values.

(2) A sociologist *as an individual* may properly make value judgments, support causes, and join reform movements, like any other citizen. As a scientist, he may not know whether television violence is harmful to children, and therefore make no public

---

[1] See any issue of *Social Policy* or *The Insurgent Sociologist*.

recommendations; but as a parent he makes a decision according to his beliefs and values. As a scientist, he may not be able to say whether gambling should be forbidden or whether contraceptives should be distributed to unmarried coeds; but as a citizen he is free to express his opinions and support his own value judgments.

A citizen is perfectly justified in supporting causes.

Beyond this, there is no complete agreement among sociologists concerning what role they should assume. Most sociologists have some firm opinions on what policies society should follow and are in considerable agreement with one another upon many of these policies. Possibly the time will come when the social policies which seem best to most sociologists will also seem best to the rest of the society. As persons who cannot and would not divorce themselves from the society in which they live, most sociologists hope so.

THE STUDY OF SOCIOLOGY

Some students will learn little in a sociology course because they feel that they already know everything worth knowing about social life. Confident that more wisdom is found by opening a lid than a book, and having made the same encounters in a score of different bars and exchanged the same insights in a dozen different pads, they already know all about LIFE. Those who feel this way will learn very little, here or elsewhere. A lifetime of eating food does not make one a dietitian. Each student, true enough, has been having social experiences all his life, and from these he has learned many things, some true and some false. To separate truth from falsehood is one of the objectives of sociology. Only those students who are willing to learn—who are willing and able to subject their beliefs, assumptions, and practices to objective scientific scrutiny—will gain much from the study of any of the social sciences.

The use of concepts in sociology

Every field of study makes the student memorize many words to which that field attaches special meanings. This is not an idle ritual; it is done because precise concepts are necessary. First, *we need carefully expressed concepts to carry on a scientific discussion.* How would you explain machinery to a person who had no concept of "wheel"? How useful to a specialist would a patient's medical history be if his physician had recorded it in the language of the layman? The several dozen sociological concepts which will harass the student in this book are necessary for a clear discussion of social phenomena. Secondly, *the formulation of concepts leads to increased knowledge.* Some accurate descriptive knowledge must be organized before a concept can be framed. Then the analysis and criticism of this new concept point up the gaps and errors in present knowledge. The *use* of the concept often calls attention to the facts and relationships which may have been overlooked. Years ago, while studying migration, Park [1928] framed the concept of the *marginal man* who is on the fringes of two groups or two ways of life while fully belonging to neither. The use of this concept quickly led to the recognition that there were many kinds of marginal persons—the person of mixed racial ancestry, who belongs clearly to neither race; the foreman, who is not clearly either "management" or "labor"; the ambitious climber, no longer in the working class yet not securely a middle-class person; and many others. Sound concepts like that of the marginal man lead to increased knowledge.

Most of the concepts of sociology are expressed in words which also have a popular meaning, just as the term *order* has one meaning in zoology, another at the restaurant table, and still another at a law-and-order political rally. Every science appropriates some common words and makes them into scientific concepts by giving them a specific definition. Sociology is no exception.

Careers in sociology

If a subject interests a student, he may wonder what possibilities it holds for a career. A combination of courses which constitutes an undergraduate major or minor in sociology is not, in itself, preparation for a professional career as a sociologist. Undergraduate majors and minors are useful mainly as background preparation for other careers: (1) In *social work*, the better jobs demand a graduate degree in social work, and usually recommend a strong undergraduate major in sociology. (2) *The professions*—medicine, law, engineering—are increasingly urging more undergraduate social science upon their students, since some understanding of people and society is necessary for success in these professions [T. Turner, 1958; Boodish, 1957]. (3) *Secondary schools* present a growing demand for sociology teachers, with about one-fourth of the schools offering sociology as a separate course and another one-fourth including sociology in a composite course [S. Anderson et al., 1964; Wright, 1965]. (4) *Civil service positions* often include undergraduate sociology among the acceptable educational qualifications for a wide variety of positions in lower and middle brackets. (5) *Newly emerging careers* are to be found in many sorts of action programs —local human relations councils, fair employment practices commissions, economic opportunity programs, foreign aid programs, and many others. Such careers are too new and too rapidly expanding to have developed any rigidly standarized courses of professional preparation, but sociology majors are often sought for these positions.

An M.A. degree is usually sufficient to obtain a teaching position at a junior college or community college, but promotions and university appointments usually require a Ph.D., which is even more necessary for a distinguished career in sociology than it is in the other sciences. Among those scientists with enough "professional standing in the scientific community" to be listed in the 1970 National Register of Scientific and Technical Personnel, a doctor's degree was held by 76 percent of the sociologists, as compared with 66 percent of the psychologists, 42 percent of the economists, 41 percent of the physicists, 36 percent of the chemists; the sociologists were exceeded only by the anthropologists, 90 percent of whom held a doctorate. Of all sociologists, about 84 percent are employed by educational institutions, with the remainder scattered among many employers, mainly government agencies and private foundations. Teaching is the major activity of 58 percent of sociologists, with 22 percent engaged primarily in research, and 16 percent in management and administration, most often management and administration of research.

Until recently, the demand exceeded the supply of persons with doctorates in practically all fields. About 1970, cutbacks in government funding and in weapons and aerospace research cost many Ph.D.'s their jobs, especially in the physical sciences and engineering. Meanwhile, the rate of growth of college enrollments began to slow down, while graduate school output of Ph.D.'s was still rising. Consequently, the employment outlook for graduating Ph.D.'s for the decade of the 1970s ranges from rather poor in some fields (e.g., nuclear physics) to fairly good in others. In sociology the employment prospects are relatively good, according to the forecasts of the National Academy of Sciences [1969, p. 154].

For most students, sociology will not be a career but merely a part of their general liberal arts education. Whatever career they enter, including that of housewife, they will be members of a society, residents in a community, participants in many groups, and carriers of the culture to the next generation. The study of sociology may aid them to fill with greater insight these varied roles which are their destiny.

SUMMARY

Sociology attempts to study society scientifically. Each social science has its own focus, and sociology's is upon man's group life and the social products of this group life.

The methods of sociological research include studies which are *cross-sectional, longitudinal,* or *ex post facto.* They may be *planned experiments,* or they may be *observational studies* of several kinds—*impressionistic studies, statistical comparative studies, questionnaire* and *interview studies, participant-observer studies,* and *case studies.* Some difficulties in sociological research pose a challenge to our methodology —the complexity of social phenomena and the limitations of possible prediction when one is working with many variables.

Sociology, like all sciences, may be either *pure* or *applied. Pure sociology* searches for new knowledge, while *applied sociology* tries to apply sociological knowledge to practical problems. A good deal of more or less accurate sociology is popularized by professional journalists, who are sometimes incorrectly called sociologists.

The sociologist in his professional role as a social scientist tends to be a pure scientist who devotes himself to discovering and teaching truth; occasionally he makes sociological predictions. He may function as an applied scientist when employed as a technician or consultant, or when he fills his private role as citizen. Whether sociologists as scientists and teachers should select, recommend, and actively promote those policies which they believe society *should* follow is an unsettled question.

The study of sociology will be successful only if the student is willing to learn about matters which he may think he is already familiar with. He must learn some concepts which are needed for a precise scientific discussion. Granted a willingness to engage in serious preparation, he may even find a prospective career in sociology.

Questions and projects

1. How would you define sociology to an uneducated person with no understanding of the fields of knowledge? How would you define it to a well-educated person whose education had included no sociology?

2. What is a sociologist? How is the term often misused?

3. What is the difference between social science and social philosophy? Which do you think is more important?

4. Are sociologists interested in social reform?

5. Why are sociologists sometimes confused with socialists? What is the difference?

6. How do you "control" a variable? In studying the possible effects of student marriage on college achievement, what other variables would need to be controlled? How could they be controlled?

7. Why are planned experiments rather rare in sociology?

8. What precautions are needed in using eyewitness accounts as sources of scientific data?

9. How does the participant-observer technique differ from merely looking at things? Isn't everyone a participant observer?

10. What are the pros and cons of defining the so-

ciology teacher's role as including the active promotion among his students of the values, goals, and social policies he believes right?

11. When you are in an informal student "bull session," listen to each statement with these questions in mind: "How scientifically sound is this statement? Is it based upon scientific fact or upon guesswork, folklore, and wishful thinking? Could it be documented with adequate scientific support?" At the conclusion, try to estimate what proportion of the statements could be scientifically substantiated.

12. Write a brief, impressionistic account of some group or some community you have observed. Then list several of your generalizations about the group, and outline a research project for collecting the empirical data which would enable you to test the accuracy of these statements.

Suggested readings

Adams, Samuel Hopkins: "The Juke Myth," *Saturday Review*, Apr. 2, 1955, pp. 13ff.; reprinted in **Edgar A. Schuler et al. (eds.):** *Readings in Sociology*, 4th ed., Thomas Y. Crowell Company, New York, 1970, pp. 47–51. An amusing account of the method whereby the author of a famous study arrived at some highly dubious conclusions about heredity and crime.

Allport, Gordon W., J. S. Brunner, and E. M. Jandorf: "Personality under Social Catastrophe: Ninety Life-histories of the Nazi Revolution," *Character and Personality*, 10:1–22, 1941; reprinted in **Clyde Kluckhohn and Henry A. Murray (eds.):** *Personality in Nature, Society, and Culture*, Alfred A. Knopf, Inc., New York, 1949, pp. 347–366. Shows how a collection of life histories can be used in arriving at scientific generalizations.

*****Bates, Alan P.:** *The Sociological Enterprise*, Houghton Mifflin Company, Boston, 1967. A brief paperback telling what sociologists do and how they become sociologists. Chap. 5, "Training for Careers in Sociology," and Chap. 6, "Careers in Sociology" are especially recommended.

*****Douglas, Jack R. (ed.):** *The Relevance of Sociology*, Appleton Century Crofts, 1970. Significant

essays on the question of objectivity, value neutrality, and value commitment in sociology.

Form, William, and Sigmund Nosow, with Gregory P. Stone and Charles Westie: *Community in Disaster*, Harper & Row, Publishers, Incorporated, New York, 1958. A case study of community reaction to a severe tornado, showing how eyewitness accounts and other observational data can be used in sociological research.

*****Freeman, Howard E., and Clarence C. Sherwood:** *Social Research and Social Policy*, Prentice-Hall, Englewood Cliffs, N.J., 1970. A brief statement of how social research can be designed to contribute to humane social policy.

*****Labovitz, Sanford, and Robert Hagedorn:** *Introduction to Social Research*, McGraw-Hill Book Company, New York, 1971. A brief, readable explanation of research methodology, giving enough information to enable a student to interpret fairly sophisticated research.

Lantz, Herman R.: *People of Coal Town*, Columbia University Press, New York, 1958. A largely impressionistic case study of a community. Gives few statistics and no sweeping generalizations, but presents some hypotheses and interesting sociological description.

Lazarsfeld, Paul F., William H. Sewell, and Harold L. Wilensky: *The Uses of Sociology,* Basic Books Inc., Publishers, New York, 1967. A comprehensive review of the practical applications of sociology to a wide range of problems.

McCormick, Thomas C., and Roy G. Frances: *Methods of Research in the Behavioral Sciences,* Harper & Row, Publishers, Incorporated, New York, 1958. A brief handbook on planning and conducting a social research project.

*****Petersen, William (ed.):** *American Social Patterns,* Doubleday & Company, Inc., Garden City, N.Y., 1956. An Anchor paperback containing a good collection of sociological research examples.

Phillips, Bernard S.: *Social Research,* The Macmillan Company, New York, 1966. A standard text in social research methods.

*****Shostak, Arthur B. (ed.):** *Sociology in Action: Case Studies in Social Problems and Directed Social Change,* Dorsey Press, Homewood, Ill., 1966. Tells how sociologists may become involved in social action.

Statistical Abstract of the United States, published annually by the Bureau of the Census, and *The World Almanac and Book of Facts,* published annually by the Newspaper Enterprise Association. Two useful sources of statistical and factual information on practically any subject, available in any library. Every student should be familiar with them.

Culture and

personality

Part two shows how man creates an intricate type of adjustment to life called culture and how culture in turn shapes his behavior. Chapter 3, "The Structure of Culture," tells what culture is and how it becomes a part of man's life. Chapter 4, "The Evolution of Culture," deals with the processes through which culture grows and develops. Chapter 5, "Personality and Socialization," shows how individual personality is developed through the interaction of heredity, environment, culture, and both group and unique experience. In Chapter 6, "Role and Status," we see how most behavior is organized into a series of roles which men can fill easily only if they are properly prepared. Chapter 7, "Social Control and Social Deviation," shows how most people are led to act as they are expected to act, and attempts to explain the deviations of the minority.

The structure of culture

"You said the fellow you killed provoked you?"

"So it was."

"He insulted Asiak?" [an Eskimo wife]

"Terribly."

"Presumably he was killed as you tried to defend her from his advances?"

Ernenek [her husband] and Asiak looked at each other and burst out laughing.

"It wasn't so at all," Asiak said at last.

"Here's how it was," said Ernenek. "He kept snubbing all our offers although he was our guest. He scorned even the oldest meat we had."

"You see, Ernenek, many of us white men are not fond of old meat."

"But the worms were fresh!" said Asiak.

"It happens, Asiak, that we are used to foods of a quite different kind."

"So we noticed," Ernenek went on, "and that's why, hoping to offer him at last a thing he might relish, somebody proposed him Asiak to laugh [have sexual intercourse] with."

"Let a woman explain," Asiak broke in. "A woman washed her hair to make it smooth, rubbed tallow into it, greased her face with blubber, and scraped herself clean with a knife, to be polite."

"Yes," cried Ernenek, rising. "She had purposely groomed herself! And what did the white man do? He turned his back to her! That was too much! Should a man let his wife be so insulted? So somebody grabbed the scoundrel by his miserable little shoulders and beat him a few times against the wall—not in order to kill him, just wanting to crack his head a little. It was unfortunate it cracked a lot!"

"Ernenek has done the same to other men," Asiak put in helpfully, "But it was always the wall that went to pieces first."

The white man winced. "Our judges would show no understanding for such an explanation. Offering your wife to other men!"

"Why not? The men like it and Asiak says it's good for her. It makes her eyes sparkle and her cheeks glow."

"Don't you people borrow other men's wives?" Asiak inquired.

"Never mind that! It isn't fitting, that's all"

"Refusing isn't fitting for a man!" Ernenek said indigantly. "Anybody would much rather lend out his wife than something else. Lend out your sled and you'll get it back cracked, lend out

**your saw and some teeth will be missing, lend out
your dogs and they'll come home crawling, tired—
but no matter how often you lend out your wife
she'll always stay like new."** (*Hans Ruesch,* Top
of the World, *Harper & Row, Publishers, Incorporated, New York, 1950; Pocket Books, 1951, pp.
87–88.*)

As this incident shows, a particular social
situation gets its meaning from the culture
in which it appears. A situation has very different meanings in two different societies.
The members of each society are so completely immersed in their own body of beliefs
and customs that they generally fail to sense
that they are obeying *belief* and *custom*, and
fail to wonder why they believe and act as
they do. Only by imaginatively stepping outside his own body of belief and custom can a
man become aware of their actual nature.
From their life experiences, people develop a
set of rules and procedures for meeting their
needs. The set of rules and procedures, together with a supporting set of ideas and
values, is called a *culture*. This chapter and
the one which follows are devoted to the
explanation of this very important concept.

We commonly say that a person is cultured
if he can identify operatic arias, read a
French menu, and select the right fork. But
people who are bored by the classics, eat
peas with their knives, and speak in four-letter words also have culture. Like most
sociological concepts, "**culture**" is a word
with both a popular and a sociological
meaning.

The classic definition of culture, framed by
Sir Edward Tylor [1871, vol. 1, p. 1], reads,
"Culture . . . is that complex whole which
includes knowledge, belief, art, morals, law,
custom and any other capabilities and habits acquired by man as a member of society."
Stated more simply, *culture is everything
which is socially learned and shared by the
members of a society.* The individual receives culture as part of his social heritage,
and, in turn, he may reshape the culture and
introduce changes which then become a
part of the heritage of succeeding generations.

*Material culture consists of any
physical substance which has
been changed by man.*

This social heritage may be divided into
material and *nonmaterial culture.* Nonmaterial culture consists of the words people
use, the ideas, customs, and beliefs they
hold, and the habits they follow. Material
culture consists of man-made objects such
as tools, furniture, automobiles, buildings,
irrigation ditches, cultivated farms, roads,
bridges, and in fact, any physical substance
which has been changed and used by man.
Such man-made objects are called *artifacts.*
In the game of baseball, for instance, the
gloves, bats, uniforms, and grandstands are
a few elements of material culture. The nonmaterial culture would include the rules of
the game, the skills of the players, the concepts of strategy, and the traditional behavior of players and spectators. The material culture is always the outgrowth of the
nonmaterial culture and is meaningless
without it. If the *game* of baseball is forgotten, a bat becomes just a stick of wood.

The destruction of World War II, while the

most extensive in history, has left little lasting physical impression because men retained the knowledge and skills (nonmaterial culture) needed to rebuild their ruined cities. The Pyramids of Egypt, on the other hand, would not be rebuilt, for they are entirely divorced from the nonmaterial culture that led to their construction—a culture that would include both the methods of construction and the values that inspired the Pharaohs to want to build such monuments. Today the value system that motivated their behavior has disappeared, and the Pyramids are merely monuments to a dead culture, of interest only as a tourist attraction. People are likely to place a great value on impressive parts of the material culture, even though these may easily be replaced if the relevant nonmaterial culture is active, or may be completely useless if the nonmaterial culture which produced them has disappeared. Since *the heritage of ideas is the most important part of man's culture,* the major emphasis of this book will be on this nonmaterial culture.

Whereas a culture is a system of norms and values, a *society* is *a relatively independent, self-perpetuating human group who occupy a territory, share a culture, and have most of their associations within this group.* They may have some contacts with other societies, but if these become too numerous, the societal boundaries become blurred. For example, the American Indian tribes were undoubtedly societies before the coming of the Europeans, but today so many of their activities are with other groups that it is doubtful whether each tribe is still a society. As Lenski defines it, "A society exists to the degree that a territorially bounded population maintains ties of association and interdependence and enjoys autonomy" [Lenski, 1970, p. 9]. Thus societal boundaries may be more or less clearly defined according to how much social interaction is with people outside that society. Size is not a factor; some

isolated primitive societies today number only a few hundred, or even a few dozen people, and many societies have disappeared as the group completely died out.

The ties of association and interdependence which bind people together into a society are obviously a part of culture. Without societies, culture could not develop. Yet the boundaries of culture and society are not always identical. For example, Roman law is the foundation of the legal systems of both France and Germany, yet these are usually considered separate societies. Conversely, some aspects of a culture may fail to spread throughout the entire society. A single society may include two or more languages and several religious faiths. Cultures exist within societies; however, some aspects of the culture may not be shared by all members of the society, and some aspects of the culture may extend beyond the society's boundaries.

CULTURE AS A SYSTEM OF NORMS

Since culture tells us the way in which things should be done, we say that culture is *normative*, which is another way of saying that it provides standards of proper conduct. For shaking hands, we extend the right hand; our culture defines this as proper. For scratching our heads we may use either hand; our culture has no norm for head scratching. The term "norm" has two possible meanings. A *statistical norm* is a measure of what actually exists; a *cultural norm* is a concept of what is expected to exist. The famous Kinsey studies sought to find some statistical norms of sexual behavior in the United States. The effort infuriated many people who confused statistical with cultural norms. A cultural norm is a set of behavior *expectations*, a cultural image of how people are supposed to act. A culture is an elaborate system of such norms —of standardized, expected ways of feeling and acting—which the members of a society follow more or less perfectly. Except where otherwise indicated, it is the cultural norms to which the sociologist refers. These norms are of several kinds and several degrees of compulsion, as seen in the following classification.

Folkways

Social life everywhere is full of problems— how to wrest a living from nature, how to divide up the fruits of toil or good fortune, how to relate ourselves agreeably to one another, and many others. Man seems to have tried every possible way of dealing with such problems. Different societies have found a wide variety of workable patterns. A group may eat once, twice, or several times each day; they may eat while standing, seated in chairs, or squatting on the ground; they may eat together, or each may eat in privacy; they may eat with their fingers or use some kind of utensils; they may start with wine and end with fish, start with fish and end with wine, or they may reject both fish and wine as inedible. And so it goes for thousands of items of behavior. Each trait is a selection from a number of possibilities, all of which are more or less workable. Through trial and error, sheer accident, or some unknown influence, a group arrives at one of these possibilities, repeats it, and accepts it as the normal way of meeting a particular need. It is passed on to succeeding generations and becomes one of the ways of the folk—hence, a folkway. *Folkways are simply the customary, normal, habitual ways a group does things.* Shaking hands, eating with knives and forks, wearing neckties on some occasions and sport shirts on others, driving on the right-hand side of the street, and eating toast for breakfast are a few of our many American folkways.

New generations absorb the folkways, partly by deliberate teaching, but mainly by observing and taking part in the life about them. The child is surrounded by folkways. Since he constantly sees these ways of doing things, they become to him the only real ways. If he chances to hear of the customs of other groups, they appear as quaint oddities and not as practical, realistic ways of getting things done. Even the most primitive society will have a few thousand folkways; in modern, industrialized societies they become even more numerous and involved. Sorting out the proper folkway becomes so difficult that Emily Post was able to earn a sizeable fortune as an interpreter of our folkways, even though her fat volume does not catalog those followed by all Americans, but lists only some of the nonoccupational folkways of the urban upper class.

Folkways are simply the customary ways a group does things.

Mores

Some of the folkways are more important than others. If one uses the wrong fork for one's salad, there is momentary embarrassment but no great injury. But if, in our society, a woman chooses anyone but her husband to sire her child, many aspects of financial obligation, property inheritance rights, family relationships, and sentimental linkage become disrupted. We therefore recognize two classes of folkways: (1) those which should be followed as a matter of good manners and polite behavior and (2) those which *must* be followed because they are believed essential to group welfare. These ideas of right and wrong which attach to certain of the folkways are then called *mores*. By the mores we mean *those strong ideas of right and wrong which require certain acts and forbid others*. ("Mores" is the plural of the Latin word *mos*, but the singular form rarely appears in sociological literature.)

The members of a society normally share a sublime faith that violation of their mores will bring disaster upon them. Outsiders, however, often see that at least some of the group's mores are irrational. They may include food taboos which make cattle, hogs, or horses unfit to eat; modesty taboos which forbid exposure of the face, the ankle, the wrist, the breast, or whatever is considered "immodest"; language taboos which forbid misuse of certain sacred or obscene words; and many others. Such taboos seem very important to their believers but may be entirely unknown in other cultures and seem to have no necessary connection with group welfare. It is not necessary that the act forbidden by the mores should actually be injurious. If a society believes that the act is injurious, it is condemned by the mores. Mores are *beliefs* in the rightness or wrongness of acts.

Mores are not deliberately invented or thought up or worked out because someone decides they would be a good idea. They emerge gradually out of the customary practices of the people, largely without conscious choice or intention. Mores arise from a group decision that a particular act seems to be harmful and must be forbidden (or, conversely, that a particular act is so necessary that it must be required). Originally, then,

mores are a practical group judgment about group welfare. For example, suppose that through some coincidence several members of a tribe have nasty accidents after swimming in a certain pool. The tribe draws the logical conclusion that there is something dangerous about the pool. As soon as they firmly agree that people should stay away from the pool, the mores have defined this act as wrong. Persons who swim in the pool thereafter are likely to expect misfortune, and others who know of their act will wait to see how they are punished. Thus any misfortune will be interpreted as a punishment and will reinforce these mores. Before long, their origin is forgotten and people think of a dip in this pool as being wrong *in and of itself*, not just because it seems to have been followed by misfortune. In this way, mores, which originate as practical group judgments of the effects of actions, become transformed into absolutes—into things which are right because they are right, and wrong because they are wrong. In other words, *mores become self-validating and self-perpetuating*. They become sacred. To question them is indecent, and to violate them is intolerable. Every society punishes those who violate its mores.

Mores are taught to the young, not as a set of practical expedients but as a set of sacred absolutes. Wherever the mores are firmly established, obedience is automatic. When fully internalized by the individual, the mores control behavior by making it psychologically very difficult for him to commit the forbidden act. For example, we do not refrain from eating our children or our enemies because of an intellectual decision that cannibalism is impractical or wasteful, but because the idea of cannibalism is so repellent to us that the thought of eating human flesh never seriously occurs to us. Most of us would be unable to eat human flesh even if we tried to do so. Mores function by making their violation emotionally impossible. In a society with a clearly defined, firmly implanted set of mores, there is very little personal misconduct.

Some people claim that mores are just group opinions and are not the same as "real" right and wrong. They argue for absolute standards of morality, claiming that the nature of the universe makes certain actions definitely wrong and others definitely right, regardless of time, place, or circumstances. This is an important ethical issue but one which has had meaning for only philosophers and theologians. As far as the behavior of most people is concerned, "mores" is simply another word for "real" right and wrong. For, as Sumner [1906] has observed, the mores can make anything right and prevent condemnation of anything. Our mores define the killer as either a villain or a hero, according to the circumstances. Medieval mores made it right for the church to tolerate prostitution and even share in its income. Most of the Reformation churchmen, both Catholic and Protestant, who ordered the torture and burning of heretics were not cruel or evil, but were decent and often kindly men who did what the mores of the time and place required them to do. Mores of our recent past have approved child labor, slavery, and persecution of minorities, and have condemned pacifism, woman suffrage, and sex education. At all times and places, good people feel pure and righteous when following the mores, whatever they may be.

Institutions

Some clusters of folkways and mores are more important than others; for example, those concerned with forming families and raising children are more important than those concerned with playing football. Organized clusters of folkways and mores dealing with functions which the society considers to be highly important are embodied in the *social institutions* of the society. Institutions include behavior norms, values and ideals, and systems of social relationships. For a formal definition we suggest: *An institution is an organized system of social relationships which embodies certain common values and procedures and meets certain basic needs of the society.* In most complex societies there are five "basic" institutions which consist of family life, religion, government, education, and the organization of economic activities. Beyond these the concept tapers off into less significant clusters of behavior patterns like those surrounding baseball, hunting, or beekeeping, which are sometimes loosely called institutions, but probably should not be included because they are so much less important.

Institutions are among the most formal and compelling of the norms of a society. As already outlined, folkways emerge from the trial-and-error experience of the group; some of the folkways come to be viewed as essential to group welfare, and are therefore supported by the mores; when the folkways and mores surrounding an important activity become organized into a quite formal, binding system of belief and behavior, an institution has developed. For example, banking, corporate enterprise, investment markets, checking accounts, and collective bargaining are economic institutions which began with simple barter thousands of years ago and passed through many stages of development. An institution thus includes a set of behavior patterns which have become highly standardized, a set of supporting mores, attitudes, and values, and generally a body of traditions, rituals and ceremonies, symbols and vestments, and other paraphernalia. Social institutions will be treated in detail in later chapters, but are introduced here because the concept must be used throughout our discussion.

Laws

While some of the mores function simply as mores, there is a strong tendency for them to become incorporated into the laws of a society. Many people will obey the mores automatically or because they want to do the "right" thing. A few people, however, are tempted to violate the mores. These people may be forced to conform by the threat of legal punishment. Thus the law serves to reinforce the mores. Those who still will not conform are punished, imprisoned, or even executed.

Some observers believe that law can be effective only when it seeks to support mores which are already firmly accepted by most members of the society. National prohibition is offered as an example. The Eighteenth Amendment was ratified in 1918 to end all sale of intoxicating beverages in the United States. It clearly expressed the mores of many persons and groups. But for many others, the prohibition amendment was not a legal sanction of *their* moral beliefs, but an effort by the state to impose an unreasonable restriction. To these people the use of alcoholic beverages was a part of family social life and sometimes of religious celebration. The members of these groups reinforced one another's belief that prohibition was absurd and obedience unnecessary. The bootlegger who sold liquor illegally became not a criminal to be reported to the police, but a folk hero somewhat in the Robin Hood tradition. Under these circumstances, law enforcement was ineffective. The illegal consumption of alcohol was widespread, corruption was rampant in police departments, and the public in general became disgusted with the prohibition law. The Eighteenth Amendment was repealed in 1933, only fifteen years after it had been introduced. Other examples of laws unsupported by the mores include the Fugitive Slave Act, widely violated by persons who believed that escaped slaves should be helped to escape their owners; World War II price and rationing controls, widely violated by Americans who believed that they had an automatic right to buy anything they could pay for; and the current laws forbidding the sale, ownership, or use of marijuana. Such examples show how difficult it is to enforce successfully a law which is not supported by the mores of most of a nation's people.

Seldom, however, is any law in agreement with the mores of *all* groups of people in a society. Nor can we measure the precise degree of agreement needed between laws and the mores for the law to be effective. Perhaps a better way to state the relationship between law and mores is to say the law *is most effective when it is in harmony with changes which are affecting the mores.* Some examples of conflict between law and the mores will illustrate this idea. National prohibition was passed at a time when social changes tended to make the mores permissive rather than restrictive. The Fugitive Slave Act faced a mounting opposition to slavery which undercut any effort to support slavery by legislation. Increasingly strict divorce laws in the twentieth century (reduced number of grounds, waiting periods, interlocutory decrees) failed to stem a rising divorce rate. In other words, all three examples are of cases in which the trend of the mores was in the opposite direction from that indicated by the law.

This does not mean that law is always ineffective when it is in opposition to the mores of a part of the population. A case in point is the civil rights legislation since 1960, which has certainly increased the opportunity for minority groups to vote, to find a job appropriate for their capabilities, and to enjoy full access to public accommodations. The opposition to the law was bitter and formidable, but it came at a time when the trend toward equal treatment of the races was undermining the mores supporting segregation. Under these circumstances the law and the trend of the mores are working in harmony and tend to support each other. Similar civil rights legislation passed just after the Civil War in a different type of racial climate was completely ineffective.

In complex societies, law also becomes a means of regulating many kinds of behavior which are not clearly covered by the mores. Our culture changes rapidly, while mores change more slowly, and new situations must be handled in an orderly way. A vast array of laws and regulations—building codes, zoning ordinances, business law, traffic codes, and many others—has developed to regulate matters which are too detailed, specialized, technical, or changeable to be controlled successfully by mores. Some sociologists [Odum, 1947, pp. 227-229] have used the term *stateways* to include all this regulatory machinery of the state, and this is a useful label since the term *law* is used in many other contexts. Scientific laws, for instance, are statements of an "orderly and dependable sequence presumably of a causative character" [Fairchild, 1957, p. 171].

THE STRUCTURE OF CULTURE

A culture is not simply an accumulation of folkways and mores; it is an *organized system* of behavior. Let us see some of the ways in which it is organized.

Cultural traits and complexes

The smallest unit of culture is called a *trait*. This is a somewhat arbitrary definition since what is a single unit to one individual may appear as a combination of units to another. Hoebel's definition [1949, p. 499] is apt at this point: "A reputedly irreducible unit of learned behavior pattern or material product thereof." Traits of the material culture would include such things as the nail,

the screwdriver, the pencil, and the handkerchief. Nonmaterial culture traits would include such actions as shaking hands, tipping hats, the practice of driving on the right-hand side of the road, the kiss as a gesture of affection between the sexes, or the salute to the flag. Each culture includes thousands of traits, and some widespread traits are a part of many cultures.

Is the dance a trait? No; it is a collection of traits, including the dance steps, some formula for selecting the performers, and a musical or rhythmic accompaniment. Most important of all, the dance has a meaning—as a religious ceremonial, a magical rite, a courtship activity, a festive orgy, or something else. All these elements combine to form a *culture complex*, a cluster of related traits. Another cluster of objects, skills, and attitudes forms the football complex.[1] The saying of grace, the reading of the Bible, and evening prayers may form a family religious complex. Similarly, there is a dating complex which includes many activities and attitudes with which students may have some familiarity.

The complex is intermediate between the trait and the institution. An institution is a series of complexes centering upon an important activity. Thus the family includes the dating complex, the engagement-and-wedding complex, the honeymoon complex, the child-care complex, and several others. Some complexes are parts of institutions; others, revolving around less important activities—such as stamp collecting—are simply independent complexes.

Subcultures and countercultures

Every complex society includes some groups of people who share some complexes which are not shared by the rest of that society. Immigrant groups, for example, develop

---

[1] This term should not be confused with the term in psychology (e.g., inferiority complex) where the meaning is quite different.

a blend of the culture of their host nation and of the mother country. Economic groups, whether of high, low, or middle status, usually develop ways of behavior that mark the group off from the rest of society. The adolescent has special styles of behavior, thought, and dress, and a private vocabulary which adults can scarcely translate, so that one may speak of "teen-age culture." Institutions tend to produce behavior patterns not required outside of the institutional setting, and the expressions "culture of the school" or "culture of the factory" suggest special sets of behavior patterns. Such terms as "army life," "preacher's kid," and "ivory tower" evoke pictures of a cultural setting different from the conventional.

Clusters of patterns such as these, which are both *related to the general culture of the society and yet distinguishable from it, are called subcultures.* The subcultures in our society include occupational, religious, national, regional, social-class, age, and sex subcultures, and many others. Literature abounds in descriptions of subcultures, ranging from serious studies like Coleman's *The Adolescent Society* [1961] or Liebow's study of black men in *Talley's Corner* [1967] to Clausen's lighthearted description of carnival life in *I Love You Honey, but the Season's Over* [1961].

Subcultures are important because each complex society has, not a single, uniform culture, but a common core of traits and complexes plus an assortment of subcultures. The individual lives and functions mainly within certain of these subcultures. The immigrant may live within the immigrant subculture, and the army wife on a military post may have very little contact with civilian people or civilian values. The child passes through several age subcultures and behaves according to their values, often distressing his mother, who applies the values of a different age subculture.

Several sociologists feel that the term counterculture should be applied to designate those groups which not only differ from the prevailing patterns but sharply challenge them. The delinquent gang, for instance, is not a group with no standards or moral values; it has very definite standards and a very compelling set of moral values, but these are quite the opposite of conventional middle-class precepts. Youth trained in this culture are influenced *against* the dominant cultural norms; hence "countercultural." Similarly, the "hippie" conforms to a culture depicting work as undesirable, chastity as "square," flag-waving patriotism as passé, and the accumulation of material possessions as irrelevant. [Yablonsky, 1968; Roszak, 1969].

The individual lives and functions mainly within certain subcultures.

Most subcultures serve to reinforce the dominant cultural patterns by offering a variety of ways in which the individual may respond to the basic values of the larger society while still retaining allegiance to his particular subculture. The counterculture, on the other hand, serves to reinforce the individual's rejection of the patterned ways of the society. The delinquent may be accused of being disloyal to the conventional mores, but he comforts himself by resolute adherence to the mores of the gang. The gang mores sustain him in deviant behavior by proclaiming that everyone steals, that "squealing" is the worst possible sin, and that only dopes go to school, save money, or try to hold steady jobs.

Countercultures arise out of the needs of individuals to find group support for their failure to follow the dominant patterns [Yinger, 1965, p. 233]. The growth of such countercultures may be expected to reflect the quality of frustration within a society.

Age, sex, class, and occupational subcultures are probably inevitable in a complex culture, and economic specialization tends to increase them. Whether national, religious, and regional subcultures are desirable has been a subject of debate. Some Americans feel that such subcultures add a variety and richness to their national life; others argue that true Americanization requires total cultural conformity. The existence of such subcultures is strengthened by the diversity of national backgrounds but is weakened by the standardizing effects of television and other mass-communication media.

Cultural integration

The culture of the Plains Indians centered upon the buffalo. From its carcass they drew most of their material culture, as they used its flesh, hides, tendons, bones, sacs, membranes, and many other parts for one purpose or another. Their religion was mainly directed at ensuring the success of the buffalo hunt. Their status system measured success largely according to man's hunting skill. Their nomadic way of life was attuned to the buffalo migrations. In other words, the different parts of the culture all fitted together in an interrelated system of practices and values. When the white man killed off the buffalo, he did so in a deliberate and successful effort to demoralize the Indian by destroying the focal point of his culture.

Just as a pile of bricks is not a home, a list of traits is not a culture. A culture is an *integrated system* in which each trait fits into the rest of the culture. It is no accident that hunting peoples worship hunting gods, fishing peoples worship sea gods, and agricultural peoples worship sun and rain gods. The different parts of a culture must fit together if the culture is to function efficiently. Over a period of time, a people tends to reject or discard inharmonious elements, gaining from their elimination a reasonably integrated culture.

Linton [1936, pp. 189-195, 348-354] illustrates the concept of integration with a description of the Tanala of Madagascar. Their main crop was rice, grown on dry land by slash-and-burn agriculture. An extended family group of several adult males with their wives and children formed the basic social unit. This extended family formed a cooperative work force of the right size for clearing the land and growing rice. As land became exhausted, the village would move on to fresh lands. The family heads formed a tribal council, whose main task was to reassign land annually to different families according to their size and needs. This system of land tenure prevented any great differences in wealth or income, and the society was quite democratic and equalitarian. The authority of the family head was limited and rested upon his abilities in personal leadership more than upon inheritance. Religion was centered upon ancestor worship, the founders of a family receiving special veneration. Whenever a family became much larger than necessary for working efficiency, it was likely to divide, some members remaining at home, some members leaving under the leadership of a new founder, who was thus assured of great honor. When attacked by unfriendly neighboring tribes, the people simply fled into the jungle, for their flimsy, temporary villages could be easily rebuilt. Thus their family life, religion, tribal structure, defense measures, and economic procedures all fitted together into an efficient, mutually harmonious system.

Stated somewhat differently, the culture of the Tanala was highly integrated around the dry-rice complex.

All this changed when wet-rice growing spread to the Tanala from neighboring peoples. It was adopted first as an individual hobby rather than as a family activity. It took a lot of work to prepare the necessary dikes and ditches along the river. Furthermore, the season was continuous and unending, so that such land never reverted to tribal ownership for the annual reassignment. Thus, private ownership of land appeared, and differences in wealth developed. Disputes within each family arose over the division of work time between family work and private hobby, and over the sharing of the wet-rice crop. When the dry-rice land was exhausted and it was time to move the village, the wet-rice growers declined to abandon their laboriously prepared wet-rice plots. When white men arrived, they found a landed nobility of wet-rice aristocrats, living in permanent homes in well-fortified villages, and a landless proletariat of dry-rice growers, living in simple shelters and moving farther and farther away from the river, while the tie between the two branches of each family gradually weakened. In a few more generations, they would have become two entirely separate societies. The addition of an important new culture trait had disrupted the existing integration and was promoting a new integration within each of two separating societies.

Failure to appreciate the integration of culture leads to many failures in dealing with other cultures. When the American Indians were herded onto reservations and supplied with cattle by the government, the Indians hunted the cattle instead of tending and milking them as expected. The idea of tending and milking cows did not tie in with anything in their culture; to introduce a completely foreign complex was a far more complicated task than had been first imagined. Today, the industrialization of the un-developed areas of the world is delayed because "backward" patterns are tightly interwoven into the native culture. For example, the Bantu of South Africa are overgrazing their lands with oversized herds of scrawny, infected cattle. Reduction of herds and selective breeding are clearly indicated; but in the Bantu culture a man's wealth and status and his ability to purchase wives are measured by the number, not the quality, of his cattle. To introduce scientific livestock practices will require changes in customs and values which weave through the entire culture. Since a culture is integrated, we cannot change one part of it without producing some change in the whole.

ETHNOCENTRISM

Oliver Wendell Holmes once observed that "the axis of the earth sticks out visibly through the center of each and every town and city." Sumner called this outlook *ethnocentrism*, formally defined as "that view of things in which one's own group is the center of everything and all others are scaled and rated with reference to it" [Sumner, 1906, p. 13]. Stated less formally, ethnocentrism is the habit of every group of taking for granted the superiority of its culture. We assume, without thought or argument, that monogamy is better than polygamy, that young people should choose their own mates, and that it is best for the young married couple to live by themselves. Our society is "progressive," while the non-Western world is "backward"; our art is noble and beautiful, whereas that of other societies is grotesque and degraded; our religion is true; others are pagan superstitions. Ethnocentrism makes our culture into a yardstick with which to measure all other cultures, which are good or bad, high or low, right or queer in proportion as they resemble ours. It is expressed positively in such phrases as "chosen people," "progressive," "superior race," "true believers," and negatively by epithets like "foreign devils," "infidels," "heathen," "backward peoples," "barbarians," and "savages." Like the Bostonian who "didn't need to travel because he was already here," we are usually quick to recognize ethnocentrism in others and slow to see it in ourselves. Thus it was often remarked that Americans could not possibly believe Hitler's claim that the Germans were a nation of supermen, because they knew this could be true only of Americans!

All known societies are ethnocentric. The "backward" native peoples, to whom we feel so superior, have a similar feeling of superiority to us. Even while they are adopting our technology, they generally consider most of the rest of our culture quaint and absurd. Worsley describes the New Guinean's evaluation of white men:

> The Europeans were not regarded as all-powerful, but as rather pathetic, ignorant people who could be easily cheated or stolen from. Their ignorance of sorcery was lamentable. "These are not men; they are merely gods," said the natives, judging the whites to be beings whose lives were inferior to those of living men. Again, they spoke the indigenous tongues very badly; why should one bother trying to make out their uncouth speech? (*Peter Worsley,* The Trumpet Shall Sound, *MacGibbon & Kee, London, 1957, pp. 208–209.*)

Most, if not all, groups within a society are also ethnocentric. Caplow [1958, p. 105] studied 55 sets of six organizations each, including fraternities, churches, insurance companies, colleges, and many others. He found that members overestimated the prestige of their own organizations eight times as often as they underestimated it. Ethnocentrism is a universal human reaction, found in all known societies, in all groups, and in practically all individuals.

In an apparent exception to ethnocentrism, a few persons reject their group or some part of its culture. There are anti-Semitic Jews, blacks who reject and deny their black identity, aristocrats who lead revolutions, priests who abandon their faith, and so on. This rejection of one's group or its culture is a form of deviant behavior that will be discussed in Chapter 7.

No one can help being ethnocentric.

Although ethnocentrism is partly a matter of habit, it is also a product of both deliberate and unconscious cultivation. We are trained to be ethnocentric to such a degree that it is doubtful whether any one can avoid being ethnocentric. Our culture complex of nationalistic patriotism is perhaps the greatest source of deliberately cultivated ethnocentrism. From early childhood we learn about national heroes and the national mythology. Self-appointed patriotic organizations comb our textbooks and pounce upon any statements lacking in ethnocentric coloration. Anybody who is of doubtful commitment to nationalistic loyalties may be denounced as an undesirable citizen. Thus, the United States and the Philippines have had "un-American" and "un-Philippine" activities committees which investigated people who were suspected of deviating from true ethnocentric devotion to national principles.

College students should find ethnocentrism easy to understand, since they experience so much of it. They are subjected to a barrage of ethnocentric cultivation from before they arrive until the moment of graduation—when the alumni office takes over. College newspapers and annuals, pep rallies, trophy cases, and countless "bull sessions" all combine to convince the neophyte that Siwash U. has unique virtues denied to all lesser institutions. Rush week reaches a high point in ethnocentric indoctrination. An elaborate drama is staged to allow the pledge to perceive how only this particular fraternity has the social values, the illustrious membership, the burnished traditions, and the shimmering prestige which make joining it a privilege. Other fraternities are counterfeits, to whose members one condescends; the unaffiliated student one simply ignores. Without the successful cultivation of ethnocentrism, few fraternities could meet the payments on the mortgage, and every college "homecoming" would be a flop!

There are many other sources of ethnocentrism. Almost every race, social class, regional or sectional group, occupational group, recreational group, or group of any other kind encourages the ethnocentrism of its members.

Personality and ethnocentrism

All groups stimulate the growth of ethnocentrism, but not all members of the group are equally ethnocentric. There is some evidence that many people in American society develop a personality which is basically more ethnocentric than that of other people. How can we explain this? One answer is that some of us are strongly ethnocentric as a defense against our own inadequacies.

Many research studies have explored this hypothesis. One group of studies [O'Connor, 1952; Brown, 1953] finds that the ethno-

centric person is apt to have difficulty in following abstract reasoning and tends to be intolerant of ambiguity in a threatening situation. By the first criticism we mean that he had difficulty in placing specific events in the framework of a complicated chain of reasoning and therefore easily accepts simplified explanations that fit ethnocentric prejudices. "Intolerance of ambiguity" means that the ethnocentric person sees the experiences of life as polar opposites with no indeterminate shadings; that is, everything must be either "good" or "bad," with no confusing mixtures. This polarity is especially necessary when he feels that his status or his group's welfare is involved; his need for security demands that his enemies and friends must be clearly identified. He cannot attribute adversity either to his own limitations or to a complex chain of events, but must fix the blame on some specific personal or ideological devil. In this way he can simplify a baffling world and escape the need to deal realistically with his own shortcomings.

Two large-scale research projects and a number of smaller projects stimulated by their findings have given us information on the kinds of people most apt to hold strong ethnocentric views. One of them, *The Authoritarian Personality* [Adorno, 1950], sought to discover the personality types most apt to accept a fascist philosophy. Most of the data were gathered through interviews with people on the West Coast of the United States during and after World War II. The authors developed a scale designed to measure ethnocentrism. They found that the ethnocentric personality is not prejudiced just against one group but against many. The people they questioned who denigrated Negroes also expressed suspicion of other minorities in the society, and were distrustful of many "foreign" groups and influences.

Another major study, *Communism, Conformity, and Civil Liberties* [Stouffer, 1955], gives some characteristics of people who are apt to be ethnocentric. This study developed a "tolerance" scale to measure attitudes toward nonconformists. The scale would seem to include the same attitudes that were measured on the ethnocentrism scale, and when both tests were given to the same group, the correlation was in the expected direction. The result suggests that people classified as ethnocentric are also apt to be intolerant of nonconformists. From these and other studies of ethnocentrism, Altus and Tabejian [1953] arrive at some general characteristics of the kinds of Americans who are most likely to be highly ethnocentric. Five social categories among whom ethnocentrism has been found to be high are women, older people, the less educated, those who are less active in community affairs, and the religiously orthodox. The categories may be more ethnocentric because these groups are somewhat restricted in their interaction with other groups in our society. Seclusion of one kind or another is obviously characteristic of the aged, the less educated, and those who are inactive in community affairs. It is also true that many women are still confined to contacts with their families and those in the immediate neighborhood, although this situation is rapidly changing. The religiously orthodox develop an intense and unquestioning loyalty to a religious creed while living in a society which permits religious variation. Religious orthodoxy, with its sharp distinction between truth and error, would seem to appeal to the desire of the ethnocentric person for definite, unambiguous answers and a positive identification of good and bad people.

These studies have also found ethnocentrism to be higher among people with certain personality characteristics: the sexually inhibited, those with obsessions and compulsions, those with paranoid feelings (feelings of persecution), those with stunted egos (lack of self-confidence), and the poorly socialized (ruthlessly self-centered). While this is not the place for a detailed psycho-

analytic interpretation of ethnocentrism, it is clear that individual differences in ethnocentrism are related both to the group affiliations and to the personality structure of the individual.

We should remember that not everyone in each of these categories is highly ethnocentric; these are group averages. Also we often find that a particular form of ethnocentrism is a local tradition which one absorbs along with the rest of the culture, without necessarily becoming ethnocentric about other topics. Thus, Southern whites learned a set of ethnocentric reactions to blacks; but Prothro [1952] found no evidence that Southerners were more ethnocentric about other groups than comparable persons from other parts of the country. The intense ethnocentrism which some localities, such as Boston, cultivate in matters of local pride and history may not extend to other topics. In other words, it takes more than one ethnocentric reaction to identify a highly ethnocentric person.

Effects of ethnocentrism

Is ethnocentrism good or bad for people? First, we should have to decide how to define "good" and "bad," and even then we might find the question very unsettled. Ethnocentrism gets us into many of our muddles; yet it is doubtful whether groups can survive without it.

Promotion of group unity, loyality, and morale Ethnocentric groups seem to survive better than tolerant groups. Ethnocentrism justifies sacrifice and sanctifies martyrdom. The attitude, "I prefer my customs, although I recognize that, basically, they may be no better than yours," is not the sort of faith for which dedicated believers will march singing to their death.

Ethnocentrism reinforces nationalism and patriotism. Without ethnocentrism, a vigorous national consciousness is probably impossible. Nationalism is but another level of group loyalty. Periods of national tension and conflict are always accompanied by intensified ethnocentric propaganda. Perhaps such a campaign is a necessary emotional preparation for the expected sacrifices.

Protection against change If our culture is already the world's most perfect, then why tinker with alien innovations? From the Biblical Hebrews to nineteenth-century Japan, ethnocentrism has been used to discourage the acceptance of alien elements into the culture. Such efforts to prevent culture change are never entirely successful; change came to both the Hebrews and to the Japanese. Yet if people share a serene, unquestioning faith in the goodness of their culture—a conviction so completely accepted that no proof is necessary—then change is delayed.

Ethnocentrism also acts to discourage change.

Ethnocentrism also acts to discourage change in the internal arrangements of a culture. Privileged and wealthy groups are apt to feel that their society is "the best of all possible worlds," since a society which treats them so well must be good. Those who

can buy the symbols of success but have not yet been fully accepted socially—the "new rich"—are apt to hold an even stronger belief in the virtues of the aristocratic group they hope to join. In either case a defense of the group distracts attention from the weakness of the individual while preserving the class system against change.

While ethnocentrism provides rationalization for the privileged, it also brings compensation to those of low status. An example is seen in the attitude of Southern "poor whites" toward blacks. Myrdal [1944, pp. 597–599] found that the poor whites, low in income and social status, were the strongest exponents of the doctrine of white supremacy. As Sinclair Lewis writes, "Every man is king so long as he has someone to look down upon." Black Power advocates today who promote racial pride ("black is beautiful") are essentially pleading for a greater degree of ethnocentrism among blacks as a means of building self-esteem and group loyalty while providing emotional protection against white disrespect.

In discouraging culture change, ethnocentrism is undiscriminating. It discourages both the changes which would disrupt the culture and the changes which would help it attain its goals. Ethnocentrism led the Biblical Hebrews to reject both the pagan gods who would have disrupted their culture and the superior farming techniques of their neighbors which would have advanced their culture. Since no culture is completely static, every culture must make some changes if it is to survive. Ethnocentrism in India today helps to keep her from turning Communist, but India may not remain non-Communist unless she rapidly modernizes her technology and controls her population growth, and these changes are delayed by ethnocentrism. In an age of atom bombs and push-button warfare, when the nations must probably either get together or die together, ethnocentrism helps to keep them tied to concepts of national sovereignty. Under some circumstances, then, ethnocentrism promotes cultural stability and group survival; under other circumstances, ethnocentrism dooms the culture to collapse and the group to extinction.

CULTURAL RELATIVISM

We cannot possibly understand the actions of other groups if we analyze them in terms of *our* motives and values; we must interpret their behavior in the light of *their* motives, habits, and values if we are to understand them. Consider, for example, the administration of justice in the far North. The Canadian Mounties are occasionally called to go into the arctic region to apprehend Eskimos who have committed a murder. This action in terms of our culture is a crime, and the individual has violated the mores. In the culture of many Eskimo tribes, however, the killing may have been justified, since their mores demand that a man avenge an injury committed upon a kinsman. This type of revenge is not considered unruly or deviant but is the only kind of action which an honorable man could take. We would condemn the man who takes the law into his own hands and seeks revenge, while they would condemn the man who has so little courage and group loyalty as to allow his kinsman to go unavenged.

Few culture traits are so disturbing to most Americans as the primitive practice of head hunting—an apparently useless and bloodthirsty pastime. However, this trait nearly everywhere has a fairly complex meaning. The Marindese of New Guinea, a quite gentle and affectionate people, hunted heads in order to provide names for their children [Van der Kroef, 1952]. Since they firmly believed that the only way a child could get a name and a separate identity was to take it from a living person, they hunted

heads from neighboring tribes. A Marindese husband had a moral obligation to have one or two head names on hand, in case he was presented with a child. Thus head hunting, like any other important trait, was deeply integrated into a total cultural system within which it was moral and necessary.

The goodness or badness of a cultural trait depends upon its setting.

These illustrations show what we mean by cultural relativism—that *the function and meaning of a trait are relative to its cultural setting.* A trait is neither good nor bad in itself. It is good or bad only with reference to the culture in which it is to function. Fur clothing is good in the arctic, but not in the tropics. Premarital pregnancy is bad in our society, where the mores condemn it and where there are no comfortable arrangements for the care of illegitimate children; premarital pregnancy is good in a society such as that of the Bontocs of the Philippines, who consider a woman more marriageable when her fertility has been established, and who have a set of customs and values which make a secure place for the children. Adolescent girls in the United States are advised that they will improve their marital bargaining power by remaining chaste until marriage. Adolescent girls in New Guinea are given the opposite advice, and in each setting the advice is probably correct. The rugged individualism and peasant thrift of early America would produce great unemployment if they were widely practiced in our present mass-production economy. From such examples we see that *any cultural trait is socially "good" if it operates harmoniously within its cultural setting to attain the goals which the people are seeking.* This is a workable, nonethnocentric test of the goodness or badness of a culture trait.

The concept of cultural relativism does not mean that all customs are equally valuable nor does it imply that no customs are harmful. Some patterns of behavior may be injurious in any milieu, but even such patterns serve some purpose in the culture, and the society will suffer unless a substitute is provided.

Sociologists are sometimes accused of undermining morality with their concept of cultural relativism, and their claim that almost "everything's right somewhere." If right and wrong are merely social conventions, say our critics, one might as well do whatever he wishes. This is a total misunderstanding. It is approximately true that "everything's right somewhere"—but not everywhere. The central point in cultural relativism is that in a particular cultural setting, certain traits are right because they work well in that setting, while other traits are wrong because they would clash painfully with parts of that culture. This is but another way of saying that a culture is integrated, and that its various elements must harmonize passably if the culture is to function efficiently in serving human purposes. The person who invokes cultural relativism to excuse his own unconventional behavior is showing that he does not understand the concept, and perhaps that he has no concern for the welfare of his society.

REAL AND IDEAL CULTURE

In most societies some behavior patterns are generally condemned yet widely practiced. In some places these illicit behavior patterns have existed for centuries side by side with the norms which are supposed to outlaw them. Malinowski cites as an example of this type of behavior, the Trobriand islanders, a group whose incest taboos extend to third and fourth cousins.

If you were to inquire into the matter among the Trobrianders you would find that . . . the natives show horror at the idea of violating the rules of exogamy and that they believe that sores, disease and even death might follow clan incest. . . .

[But] from the point of view of the native libertine, *suvasova* (the breach of exogamy) is indeed a specially interesting and spicy form of erotic experience. Most of my informants would not only admit but actually did boast of having committed this offense or that of adultery (kaylasi); and I have many concrete, well-attested cases on record. (*Bronislaw Malinowski,* Crime and Custom in Savage Society, *Routledge & Kegan Paul, Ltd., London, 1926, pp. 79, 84.*)

Like all societies, the Trobrianders have some standardized ways of evading punishment. Malinowski [p. 81] observes, "Magic to undo the consequences of clan incest is perhaps the most definite instance of methodical evasion of law."

This case illustrates the difference between the real and ideal culture. The ideal culture includes the formally approved folkways and mores which people are supposed to follow (the cultural norms); the real culture consists of those which they actually practice (the statistical norms). For example, Warriner [1958] found that many residents of a town in Kansas, a legally "dry" state at the time of his research, drank in private while supporting the "temperance" morality in public. He concluded that the official morality served to prevent a disruptive public controversy, without interfering with their drinking behavior. There are many such divergences between the real and the ideal culture in our society. As a sample, Williams lists ten examples of "patterned evasion" of our formally approved norms:

1. Prohibition vs. the bootlegging and speak-easy industry, prior to repeal of the Eighteenth Amendment; organized gambling.
2. Impersonal, disinterested governmental services vs. political graft, "fixing," "status justice."
3. Family mores vs. prostitution.
4. Classroom honesty vs. accepted patterns of "cribbing."
5. Promotion by technical competence vs. nepotism, racial discrimination (as seen, for example, in the systematic evasion of civil service laws).
6. Universalistic legal justice vs. white-collar crime, the public defender system, bias in jury selection, racial discrimination.
7. Prescribed patterns of sexual behavior vs. the patterns revealed by studies of actual behavior.
8. Legal rules regarding divorce vs. actual court practice ("void" divorces, the "alimony racket").
9. Professional codes vs. such practices as fee splitting among doctors, violations of state and federal statutes and administrative regulations by retail pharmacists, ambulance chasing among lawyers.
10. Ethical concepts of truth vs. some advertising, financial transactions, etc. ("business is business"). (*Robin M. Williams, Jr.,* American Society, *Alfred A. Knopf, Inc., New York, 1970, pp. 421–422.*)

A clash between the real and ideal culture patterns is generally avoided by some kind of rationalization which allows people to "eat their cake and have it." For example, Lowie [1940, p. 379] describes some Burmese villages which are Buddhist, and whose inhabitants are therefore forbidden to kill any living thing, yet are dependent upon the murderous occupation of fishermen. They evade this contradiction by not literally killing the fish, which ". . . are merely put out on the bank to dry after their long soaking in the river, and if they are foolish and ill-judged enough to die while undergoing the process, it is their own fault."

No society is free of such inconsistencies, and complex societies like ours have many patterns which are formally condemned, enthusiastically practiced, and skillfully rationalized. We cherish monogamous marriage but tolerate quasi-legalized prostitution. The practices seem to be incompatible, but there is little conflict between them since our culture trains us both to applaud the virtuous woman and to tolerate the prostitute. Tax evasion is legally and morally wrong, but apparently it is practiced by most people who have a good opportunity. Business life demands rigid honesty, but alongside this uprightness may be found a pattern of bribery and special favors which is said to facilitate the making of business agreements. All are equal before the law in America—except blacks, immigrants, poor people, radicals, women, children, and the unemployed. Such contradictions could be extended into an impressive list for any modern society.

In the long-run viewpoint, the clash between real and ideal culture patterns may simply illustrate the fact that we have gone only part way in developing social control, and that eventually there may be a greater consistency between the actual behavior and the moral precepts of the culture. The extension of the voting privilege regardless of race or sex narrows the gap between precept and practice in our democratic mores. The abolition of child labor and the social security provisions for the aged and the handicapped are fulfilling the implications of the humanitarian mores in areas which have often been neglected. These and many other developments exemplify what Sumner [1906, p. 66] called a "strain toward consistency in the mores." In spite of frequent discrepancies, there is still a strong tendency for a society, sooner or later, to bring its various ideas and practices into harmony with one another.

On the other hand, in some circumstances it may be possible that the illicit patterns of behavior allow society to engage in conduct which seems essential to the welfare of the group but for which it has not been able to find a moral sanction. Thurman Arnold expressed this viewpoint in a book called *The Folklore of Capitalism* [1937]. He argued that the large-scale consolidation of industry was an essential part of modern technological development. This trend, however, is inconsistent with the American mores which sanction the value of small-scale competitive business. To meet the situation, he claims that the United States evolved unenforceable antitrust laws which expressed our moral condemnation of bigness in business, and at the same time permitted business to gain the advantages of continued consolidation. This procedure reminds us of the practice in some primitive societies in which courtship and marriage regulations are so complicated that most marriages occur through a type of elopement which is vigorously condemned by the mores. If the couple are unusually awkward, they may be caught and severely beaten, but ordinarily they are able to make good their escape. After a period of penance, they are welcomed back into the social group. Thus society is able to maintain the expression of sentiments sacred to the mores, along with the existence of a useful practice in violation of the mores, thereby promoting a type of adjustment which seems necessary to the smooth functioning of the society.

Real and ideal patterns are both definitely a part of the culture. The real patterns are not mentioned in formal statements or deliberately taught as part of the program of church and school, but they are transmitted by an informal communication network of gossip and advice which may be even more effective than the formal channels. For this reason it is sometimes suggested [Yinger, 1965, p. 75] that the terms *overt* and *covert* might indicate their nature. Ideal patterns are overt, that is, openly announced, while the real patterns are often covert, transmitted in an unofficial and perhaps clandestine fashion.

CULTURE AND HUMAN ADJUSTMENT

Is culture a help or a burden to mankind? Some of each. It helps him to solve some problems, gets in his way as he grapples with others, and itself creates still others.

Culture and biological adjustment

Man's culture contains many gadgets which help him in his unremitting battle with nature. Since man freezes and sunburns easily, he wears clothes and builds houses. Nature offers wild fruits, seeds, and berries; man domesticates them and increases their yield. His hands are poor shovels, but his bulldozers remake the surface of the earth. He cannot run fast, swim well, or fly at all; yet no living thing travels so fast as he. Man was created a fragile, delicate being, quickly prey to death through heat or cold, thirst or hunger. Through his culture, man can moisten the desert and dry the swampland, can survive arctic cold and tropic heat, and can even survive a trip through outer space.

While culture helps man to adjust to his environment, it also interferes with his biological adjustment in many ways. Every culture offers many examples of patterns harmful to man's physical well-being. The Hindu belief that man should not kill anything has filled India with stray dogs, scrawny cattle, and all manner of parasites, wasting food and spreading diseases. Man has improved his weapons until he can destroy the entire human race. He follows methods of agriculture and land use which destroy the soil and flood the land. He pollutes the air, fouls the streams, and poisons his foods. If he is rich enough he generally eats, smokes, and drinks more than is good for him. He eats polished rice or white bread which are stripped of vital food elements, while he may pass up beef, pork, horse meat, snake meat, snails, milk, or whatever valuable source of nourishment is under taboo in his society. If he were descended from cats instead of anthropoids, he would be better equipped for the night hours he likes to keep.

In nearly every culture men (and women) have twisted, stretched, squeezed, gouged, painted, trimmed, and scarred the human body in an effort to be beautiful. The clumsy platters inserted in the slit lips of the Ubangi, the foot binding as practiced upon upper-class female children in classical China, and the precarious high heels of our women are all efforts to improve upon nature by deforming and distorting the natural body contours—along with those interesting Western devices intended to squeeze, shift, uplift, and supplement various parts of the female anatomy. Our culture causes men to wrap themselves in useless garments in the summer while in winter women expose their legs to the icy blasts. Our culture encourages men to dangerous overexertion in sports, yet encourages them to miss healthful exercise by taking a car for a trip to the corner, and by hauling their children to school even when they would be better off walking. Automobile buyers have been more interested in a stylish appearance than in passenger safety, and only a minority of drivers fasten their seat belts. Our culture includes traits that lead communities to build new hospitals and other traits that cause them to oppose fluoridation programs to reduce tooth decay. American culture includes both the scientific milieu that developed an effective polio vaccine and the folkways and vested

interests that make it difficult to pursue an effective mass-immunization program for making efficient use of this vaccine. When the values of the culture are not in harmony with the needs of biological adjustment, the culture may cause man to work against his own physical welfare.

Is culture, then, good or bad for man? It may be either. Culturally sanctioned behavior may prolong life, or it may prevent man from using nature for his own physical welfare.

Culture and social adjustment

Just as culture may either promote or impair man's physical health, so it may either encourage or impede the harmonious operation of the society and the development of well-adjusted personalities. World birth rates have barely begun to fall in response to worldwide recognition that the large-family pattern has plunged the world deeply into a population crisis. In the Ottoman Empire the military and agricultural activities were highly valued, while commerce was disdained to such an extent that the Turks could not maintain their leadership in a world increasingly dominated by industrialism. In the Philippines the culture encourages an extremely high status for the legal profession with the result that other occupations are neglected while the country has thousands of lawyers without a practice.

The cultural guides to religious belief and family formation may also have mixed effects. The religious emphasis on the next world may cause the individual to ignore the need for making practical day-to-day adjustments in this world. Similarly a family-determined choice of marriage partners may lead to a rule of the elders which retards social change, while the belief in romantic choice of mates by individuals may lead them on a fruitless round of divorce and remarriage in search of ecstatic happiness probably unattainable by the human family.

The culture includes patterns of behavior, organized into a series of ascribed and achieved roles, and thus provides for getting the routine work of society accomplished. The culture may ascribe roles to people without providing adequate preparation for them, or may require a succession of roles which impose painful transitions upon individuals. It may build conflicting pressures into a role so that few individuals can possibly avoid mental conflict, or it may require difficult role choices of individuals or encourage role ambitions which doom most persons to failure. It may overelaborate these roles to a point of impracticality. It is said that Marie Antoinette was unable to get a glass of cold water; court etiquette required it to pass through so many hands that it was always tepid by the time it reached her. Rivers [1912] tells how on Torres Island in Melanesia, canoe building was surrounded with such an elaborate set of magical rites and taboos that only a small group of hereditary canoe builders dared to try to build one. Others were familiar with the manual skills for canoe building, but since they lacked the secret magic, it was unthinkable that they should build the craft. Therefore when the hereditary canoe-builder families died out, the Torres Islanders went without canoes despite their desperate need for them. If this deliberate frustration seems stupid to the reader, let him try to explain why in our society, any people should be hungry, ill-housed, or ragged while food rots in warehouses and men rot in unemployment! In our society our building codes, union rules, and other monopolistic practices in the construction industry make building unnecessarily complicated and costly. In every society the culture organizes the work of the society in ways that are sometimes cumbersome and impractical; yet, without a culturally organized system for getting things done, most of them would not get done at all.

SUMMARY

Culture consists of the socially learned behavior norms and values shared by a human group. *Material culture* is made up of the artifacts man constructs on the basis of cultural norms. *Nonmaterial culture* comprises the behavior patterns, values, and social relationships of a human group. *Folkways* are types of behavior which have the force of custom but do not necessarily have a moral connotation, while *mores* attach the ideas of right and wrong to some kinds of behavior. The mores may become sanctified by religion and strengthened by incorporation into law as part of the *stateways*. *Institutions* are organized systems of social relationships which embody common values and procedures and meet basic needs of the society.

A *trait* is the simplest unit of culture; related traits are grouped into *culture complexes*. A *subculture* is the behavior and value system of a group which is a part of the society, but which has certain unique cultural patterns. A *counterculture* is a subculture which is not merely different from, but sharply opposed to, the dominant values of the society.

A culture is an *integrated* system of behavior with its supporting ideas and values. In a highly integrated culture all elements fit harmoniously together. During periods of change, a culture is imperfectly integrated until a new integration is completed. The adoption of Western technology by underdeveloped countries will inevitably bring many other changes in their traditional culture.

All societies and all groups assume the superiority of their own culture; this reaction is called *ethnocentrism*. We are ethnocentric because of ignorance, habit, training, and as a defense against our own inadequacies. Ethnocentrism (1) promotes group unity, loyalty, and morale, and thereby reinforces nationalism and patriotism; (2) protects a culture from changes, including those needed to preserve the culture. Sociology does not either applaud or condemn ethnocentrism; rather, it seeks to understand it and its effects upon society.

Cultural relativism describes the fact that the function and meaning of a culture trait depend upon the culture in which it operates. Traits are judged "good" or "bad" according to whether they work efficiently within their own culture.

Every society has an *ideal culture*, including the patterns which are supposed to be practiced, and a *real culture*, including illicit behavior which is formally condemned but widely practiced. Clashes between the two are evaded by rationalization. In some cases, illicit patterns are ways of getting necessary tasks done and thus, even though the mores do not approve the illicit actions, may actually contribute to cultural stability.

Culture both aids and hinders human adjustment. It enables man to survive in an inhospitable physical environment, although in many respects it sustains habits which are physically injurious. We could not live without culture; sometimes it is not easy to live with it.

Questions and projects

1. Which would give the greater understanding of the culture of the Romans—studying the ruins, sculpture, and public works that have been excavated or studying the records of the nonmaterial culture preserved in literature, letters, and legal documents? Why?

2. How do you differentiate between society and culture?

3. What is meant by the statement that, when firmly established, the mores operate automatically? Does this happen in our society?

4. Why, when the government first gave cattle to the American Indians, did the Indians hunt and kill the cattle instead of herding and milking them?

5. Apply your knowledge of the integration of culture in evaluating the proposal that our society should return to the "simple life."

6. Is ethnocentrism the opposite of cultural relativism? Explain.

7. Is there any difference between ethnocentrism and patriotism? Are the most ethnocentric groups also the most patriotic?

8. In what ways does ethnocentrism aid in national survival in the modern world? In what ways does it jeopardize national survival?

9. What effects do you think an extended trip around the world is likely to have upon one's ethnocentrism?

10. Cheating in college is sometimes defended on the ground that it is necessary if a student is to reach the goal of graduation. Is this position defensible in terms of cultural relativism? Why or why not?

11. Are there any respects in which the real campus subculture differs from the ideal campus subculture?

12. In a perfectly integrated culture, would there be any divergence between the real and ideal culture patterns?

13. Apparently, culture can be both a help and a hindrance to man. How can this be?

14. Make a list of ten folkways on the college campus that are different from those in the rest of the community. Make a list of the folkways and mores of fraternity life.

15. Select an occupational group and describe the *special* behavior which is typical of that occupation.

16. Describe the traits, complexes, attitudes, and values making up a subculture with which you are familiar.

Suggested readings

Armez, Nancy L., and Clara E. Anthony: "Contemporary Negro Humor as Social Satire," *Phylon,* 29:339–436, Winter, 1968. The role of humorists in depicting the incongruity between real and ideal culture.

Coleman, James S.: "The Adolescent Subculture and Academic Achievement," *American Journal of Sociology,* 65:337–347, January, 1960. Relation of teen-age values to academic achievement.

Crist, Raymond: "The Latin-American Way of Life: Cultural Factors Making for Unity," *American Journal of Economics and Sociology,* 27:171–183, April, 1968. Role of the church, language, and family as unifying factors.

Hall, Edward T.: "Our Silent Language," *Americas,* 14:5–8, February, 1962; reprinted in *Science Digest,* 52:19–23, August, 1962. Description of nonverbal cues which indicate differences between North and South American cultural norms.

Linton, Ralph: *The Study of Man,* Appleton-Century-Crofts, Inc., New York, 1936. A classic analysis of the role of culture in human affairs. Chaps. 5, 6, 20, and 25 are especially recommended.

Lipset, Seymour Martin: "The Value Patterns of a Democracy: A Case Study in Comparative Analysis," *American Sociological Review,* 28:515–531, August, 1963. A comparison of value systems in Australia, Canada, Great Britain, and the United States.

*****Michener, James A.:** *Return to Paradise,* Random House, Inc., New York, 1950; Bantam Books, 1952, section entitled, "Povenaa's Daughter." A popular writer's hilarious tale of ethnocentric Americans' inability to comprehend the customs of Polynesian society.

Miner, Horace: "Body Ritual among the Nacirema," *American Anthropologist,* 58:503–507, June, 1956; The Bobbs-Merrill Company, Inc., Indianapolis, reprint S-185. An anthropologist describes the quaint customs and odd values of a well-known modern culture which the student may recognize.

*****Roszak, Theodore:** *The Making of a Counter Culture,* Doubleday & Company, Inc., Garden City, N.Y., 1969. Describes the growing resistance to a technological society and the efforts to find alternative cultural patterns.

Sale, J. Kirk, and Ben Appelbaum: "Report from Teeney-Boppersville," *New York Times Magazine,* May 28, 1967, pp. 25ff.; or "The Hippies: Philosophy of a Subculture," *Time,* July 7, 1967, pp. 18–22; or *****Lewis Yablonsky:** *The Hippie Trip,* Western Publishing Company, Inc., Racine, Wis., 1968. Popularized descriptions of a rapidly changing subculture.

Williams, Robin M., Jr.: *American Society,* Alfred A. Knopf, Inc., New York, 1970, chap. 10, "Institutional Variation and the Evasion of Normative Patterns." A perceptive discussion of the differences between our real and ideal cultures.

The cars of the migrant people crawled out of the side roads onto the great cross-country highway, and they took the migrant way to the West. In the daylight they scuttled like bugs to the westward; and as the dark caught them, they clustered like bugs near to shelter and to water. And because they were lonely and perplexed, because they had all come from a place of sadness and worry and defeat, and because they were all going to a new mysterious place, they huddled together; they talked together; they shared their lives, their food, and the things they hoped for in the new country. Thus it might be that one family camped near a spring, and another camped for the spring and for company, and a third because two families had pioneered the place and found it good. And when the sun went down, perhaps twenty families and twenty cars were there. . . .

Every night a world created, complete with furniture—friends made and enemies established; a world complete with braggarts and with cowards, with quiet men, with humble men, with kindly men. Every night relationships that make a world, established; and every morning the world torn down like a circus.

At first the families were timid in the building and tumbling worlds, but gradually the technique of building worlds became their technique. Then leaders emerged, then laws were made, then codes came into being. And as the worlds moved westward they were more complete and better furnished, for their builders were more experienced in building them.

The families learned what rights must be observed—the right of privacy in the tent; the right to keep the past black hidden in the heart; the right to talk and to listen; the right to refuse help or to accept, to offer help or to decline it; the right of son to court and daughter to be courted; the right of the hungry to be fed; the rights of the pregnant and the sick to transcend all other rights.

And the families learned, although no one told them, what rights are monstrous and must be destroyed: the right to intrude upon privacy, the right to be noisy while the camp slept, the right of seduction or rape, the right of adultery and theft and murder. These rights were crushed, because the little worlds could not exist for even a night with such rights alive.

And as the worlds moved westward, rules became laws, although no one told the families. It is

The evolution of culture

unlawful to foul near the camp; it is unlawful to eat good rich food near one who is hungry, unless he is asked to share.

And with the laws, the punishments—and there were only two—a quick and murderous fight or ostracism; and ostracism was the worst. For if one broke the laws his name and face went with him, and he had no place in any world, no matter where created.

In the worlds, social conduct became fixed and rigid, so that a man must say "Good morning" when asked for it, so that a man might have a willing girl if he stayed with her, if he fathered her children and protected them. But a man might not have one girl one night and another the next, for this would endanger the worlds.

The families moved westward, and the technique of building the worlds improved so that the people could be safe in their worlds; and the form was so fixed that a family acting in the rules knew it was safe in the rules. (*John Steinbeck*, The Grapes of Wrath, *The Viking Press, Inc., New York, 1939, pp. 264–266.*)

This excerpt from Steinbeck shows how new rules and patterns of behavior develop among people who are forced to grapple with a new set of problems and experiences. The emergence of a subculture embodying definite rules and patterns of behavior among an apparently unorganized horde of migrants illustrates the universal tendency of man to bring a culturally based order out of what would otherwise be social chaos. In this chapter we are concerned with the emergence of culture, and with the question of whether any definite evolutionary trends can be observed in its development. Since man is a part of the animal world, we start with a view of the differences between man and the other animals, and with an inquiry into the unique aspects of human culture.

THE DEVELOPMENT OF CULTURE

Subhuman societies

Many subhuman species have an orderly system of social life. Many bird species mate for a lifetime and (in contrast to humans) are absolutely loyal to their mates. Many species of insects, such as ants and bees, have an elaborate pattern of social life, complete with specialized occupations, lines of authority, and detailed distribution of duties and privileges. But the *subhuman social life is based upon instinct, not upon social learning.* Within a given species of ants, all anthills are very much alike, while human dwellings vary tremendously. For man is notably lacking in those inborn patterns of behavior which we call *instincts* in subhuman species. Instead man inherits a set of organic needs, urges, and hungers that we call *drives*, which he must satisfy in some way or other. In his trial-and-error efforts to satisfy his urges, man creates his culture, with its tremendous variations from society to society. Unable to rely upon instinct, man must build culture in order to survive.

As an animal, man is among the larger and more powerful of beasts. Fewer than a dozen other species will ordinarily attack an adult human unless wounded or provoked. Man's physical structure and processes are similar to those of other animals, and he shares many of their diseases. He has certain physical disadvantages. He is far from the strongest of animals; he lacks the physical agility of his cousins, the apes; his claws and teeth are puny weapons; and he has no hide, scales, or fur to protect him. He cannot hibernate or adjust organically to great temperature changes.

Man also has some advantages. He can digest a wider variety of foods than most other animals. His eyesight is fairly good at all distances from a few inches to many miles—a characteristic that many animals lack. Alone among the animals, he is well balanced on only two of his feet, freeing the other two for all sorts of mischief. He can oppose his thumb to each of his fingers and is capable of more delicate manipulations than any other animal. No chimpanzee, no matter how brilliant, could perform skillful surgery, for its hands lack dexterity.

Man's learning capacity

These advantages would mean little unless man had a greater learning capacity. This does not deny that other animals do think, reason, and learn, for their ability is shown by many tests. In some experiments a chimpanzee must figure out that he can get a banana, placed beyond reach, only by fitting together two sticks to make a longer one. In other experiments, where slugs must be put into a slot machine in order to get food, the chimpanzees quickly learn which size or color slugs are valuable, and sort out, hoard, hide, and steal them from one another in a quite human manner. Many such experiments with many species have clearly established that animals *do* learn, and apparently they learn *in the same way* that humans learn; they just do not learn as fast or as much. A famous experiment [Kellogg and Kellogg, 1933] in which a human infant and a chimpanzee infant were raised together and treated alike, showed that they behaved alike in many ways, but that before long the human greatly outdistanced the chimpanzee in learning.

Communication

Animals can learn; they can form interacting groups and have a social life; they can even communicate with one another at a very simple level. These facts lead a few scholars to conclude that some animals have a culture. Several experiments have shown that animal learning is affected by their social setting. For example, Kuo [1931] found that when kittens could watch the mother cat catching rats, 85 percent of them were catching rats themselves by the time they were four months old. Other kittens were raised with rats as companions; none of them killed the type of rats they grew up with and only 16 percent killed any kind of rats. This suggests that animals can learn

through example, and that it may be a form of social learning. But if cats have a "rat-killing culture," it is far removed from the hunting complex of the Plains Indians or the English gentry.

The idea of animal culture becomes rather farfetched if we try to imagine Leo the Lion acting in a manner governed by custom, tradition, or sacred ideal. As Myerson observes,

We cannot imagine him, for example, stopping in palpitating pursuit of a tawny female because some Leo the Saint, a hundred lion generations ago, reached the conclusion that burning desire might be satisfied only under very special circumstances. Nor can we visualize this same Leo aching for food yet withholding his mighty paw from a delicacy because that delicacy has been staked off for another lion or because old lions in a congress a hundred years before decreed private ownership in delicacies and forbade even ravenous hunger to satisfy itself except under strict rule and regulation.

We cannot imagine the young lion contemplating the life of some past Leo the Great and planning his entire career in emulation of the dead hero. . . . We cannot imagine him in agonies of self-condemnation because he has fallen short of an ideal which has been incorporated within him by the teaching and preaching of a thousand years and of countless lions. . . .

He does not foresee his own death, and knows nothing of his own birth. Sex means to him only the satisfaction that an individual of the opposite sex can bring him. It does not mean parenthood, domesticity, respectability, the fulfilling of an ideal, a responsibility, and the becoming part of a great racial sweep. (*Abraham Myerson,* Social Psychology, *Prentice-Hall, Inc., Englewood Cliffs, N.J., 1934, pp. 3–6. Adapted by permission.*)

It is fashionable to believe a great deal of nonsense about animal behavior. A faithful dog, gazing intently at his master, inspires all sorts of fanciful notions as to what he is thinking! Dogs are often credited with remarkable homing instincts; yet, for every dog who finds his way home across a continent, the lost-and-found ads list a hundred dogs who can not find their way home from the next block. Mama Bear is pictured as patiently "teaching" her cubs how to fish, yet we have no evidence that she is consciously trying to teach them anything. Perhaps she is just hungry! Only for man is there conclusive evidence of deliberate teaching and intentional communication of ideas.

This may be mankind's greatest advantage —*his ability to communicate his learnings to others.* The chimpanzee may learn how to get the banana, but he has no effective way of communicating his insight to others; each of his brothers must get the idea for himself, either through imitation or through his own imagination. Each chimpanzee stands, or rather crouches, on his own feet and must face the world without the advantage of simian learning. Man stands on the shoulders of his ancestors and brings to his problems a great heritage of accumulated wisdom.

Language and symbolic communications
Many animals can exchange feelings through growls, purrs, mating calls, and other sounds. Some animals give off odors or make bodily movements which convey meanings to one another. These sounds and motions are not *language,* for each is largely or entirely an inborn, instinctive response rather than an acquired, symbolic response. There is no evidence that a dog growls or barks because he wants to tell another dog something; perhaps he barks just because he feels like barking. As far as we know, no dog has yet developed a barking code (e.g., one short bark for "let's eat," two yips for "after you," etc.). A language is just such a code—*a set of sounds with a particular meaning attached to each sound.* A largely emotional or instinctive set of yips and yells is not a language, even though these sounds do serve to carry some accurate meanings to others of the species. A mother soon learns from her baby's cry whether he is hungry,

sick, or angry; but the baby is simply expressing his emotions, not using language. Only when an *artificial* meaning is attached to each sound, so that the sound becomes a symbol—only then do we have language. The idea of "chair" might be represented by any one of thousands of vocal sounds; when the members of a society agree in dependably recognizing one particular vocal sound as meaning "chair," then a *word* has been added to the language. We limit the term *language* to symbolic communication and exclude the exchange of meanings through instinctive cries and sounds as not being true language.

Some highly popular books and magazine articles have coined the term "body language" for the exchange of meanings through gestures and body postures [Fast, 1970]. There is no doubt that some meanings are exchanged in this way. The question has received a modest amount of scientific study [Hall, 1959, 1962], but the current popularizations are largely based upon intuition and guesswork, not upon scientific research. Furthermore, although "body language" may be a form of communication, it is not true *language,* since language is limited to communication through symbols.

Only man uses symbols; therefore, only man's communication reaches beyond the level of exchanging very simple feelings and intentions. With symbolic communication men can exchange detailed directions, share discoveries, organize elaborate activities. Without it, they would quickly revert to the caves and treetops.

Somewhat as speech separates man from the animals, the written language is a dividing line between primitive and civilized cultures. The man in the preliterate culture must memorize traditional lore, and the man with a fine memory is valued as a walking library. Old people are useful in a society which must rely on human memory to preserve its culture. But the human memory is not limitless. A culture dependent upon human memory and oral tradition must remain fairly simple. The use of writing allows an almost limitless expansion of the culture, since endless bits of lore can be stored away until needed. Techniques and processes of infinite complexity can be recorded in precise detail and endless variety. Even the illiterate person is affected by living in a literate culture, since his entire life is colored by the fact that others can draw upon the storehouse of the written word. The dictum of Pharaoh's court, "Thus it is written; thus it shall be done," is the basis of every civilized society.

Only man uses symbols.

Language is so intimately tied up with culture that every new addition to the group's cultural heritage involves additions to the language. In order to know a group one must learn to speak its language. Even special groups within a society, such as hoboes, soldiers, railroad men, or teen-agers have their own vocabularies. Each subculture has its vocabulary. College students are painfully aware that each new field of study forces them to learn many new words and to learn new meanings for many of the old ones.

Language is related to the rest of culture in other ways. Not only does culture produce language, but language helps or hinders

the spread of culture. It is difficult to think without language, for one's thoughts are likely to be vague until put into words. One can, perhaps, visualize objects or actions without using words, but ideas require language. Try visualizing ideas such as "goodness," "never," or "necessary" without using words! Sometimes an idea or concept is hard to translate because the language has no words with which to express it. The translation of papal encyclicals into classical Latin is complicated by the lack of Latin terms for modern words like "automation" and "atomic reactor." India's effort to limit the use of English and to employ the traditional Hindustani as the national language is facing similar difficulties. Either a whole new set of expressions must be hastily coined, or Hindustani must absorb words borrowed at a tremendous rate from other languages. Hence the zealous Indian attempt to support Hindustani was followed by a reluctant admission that English might have to be a language of university instruction for the indefinite future [Rao, 1956, pp. 1–12]. An adequate language is the indispensable means of communication through which culture is shared, transmitted and accumulated.

Language is so closely bound to culture that translators must have an understanding of the culture of both societies if they are to translate from one language to the other. The following anecdote is a case in point:

A story is making the rounds these days about some scientists who designed an English-to-Russian translating machine. To test the device they fed in the sentence, "The spirit is willing but the flesh is weak." Back came the translation: "The liquor is good but the food is lousy." *John G. Fuller, "Trade Winds,"* Saturday Review, 45:12, Feb. 17, 1962.

The accumulation of culture

A look at prehistory shows that man once lived very much like his animal cousins. Our early human ancestors lived in the open, wore no clothes, raised no crops, domesticated no animals, and used no fire. Archaeological reports indicate that hundreds of thousands of years passed before man learned to cook his food, plant crops, or build shelters. We who have come to expect a "new model" every year find it hard to visualize an era when man made no great change in his habits for perhaps a thousand generations and, like the animals, lived at the mercy of an unfriendly nature.

Man spent ages in making his early discoveries and inventions, but these became the *cultural base* for more rapid discovery and invention in the future. It took him several hundred thousand years to invent the

TABLE 1

If a million years* of human history were compressed into the lifetime of one seventy-year-old man

1,000,000 years of history	Compressed into one 70-year lifetime
1,000,000 years ago	*Pithecanthropus erectus is born.*
500,000 years ago	*He spends half his lifetime learning to make and use crude stone axes and knives.*
50,000 years ago	*And most of the next half in improving them.*
40,000 years ago	*Three years ago he began to use bone and horn tools.*
10,000 years ago	*Nine months ago the last ice age ended, and he left his cave dwellings.*
7,000 years ago	*Six or eight months ago he began to make pottery, weave cloth, grow crops, and domesticate animals.*
5,000 years ago	*About three months ago, he began to cast and use metals and built the Pyramids.*
3,000 years ago	*Ten weeks ago he invented the spoked wheel and began making glass.*
2,000 years ago	*Seven weeks ago, Christ was born.*
700 years ago	*Two weeks ago man finished the Crusades.*
185 years ago	*Five days ago he crossed the Delaware with Washington.*
60 years ago	*Yesterday he invented the airplane.*
25–30 years ago	*This morning he fought World War II.*
In the year 2,000 A.D.	*Tonight he will celebrate the arrival of the twenty-first century!*

* *Or several million years, according to some anthropologists.*

wheel; once invented, the wheel might then be used in thousands of other inventions. For this and other reasons, man's culture accumulated exceedingly slowly in pre-historic times, more rapidly in historic times, and with breakneck speed in modern times. Man's greatest problem today is how to adjust himself and his social arrangements to the speed with which his culture is changing. The accumulation of culture is treated in greater detail in Chapter 20.

Geographic factors in cultural development

Climate and geography are undoubtedly a factor in cultural development. Extremes of climate or topography are serious obstacles to many kinds of cultural development. Great civilizations do not flourish in the frozen Arctic, the torrid desert, the lofty mountain range or the tangled forest. Men can live in these areas and may develop ingenious means of coping with natural forces, but such areas have not produced great cities or highly developed civilizations. On the other hand, the earliest great civilizations known to the world developed in the lowlands of great river basins. When one speaks of ancient Egypt, Mesopotamia, or India, one is talking primarily of the river valleys of the Nile, Euphrates, Tigris, and Indus [Ogburn and Nimkoff, 1964, p. 71]. Only such areas met the requirements for an early civilization: (1) fertile land which could support a dense population, with part of the people free to engage in nonagricultural work, and (2) easy transportation to link together an extensive area.

Within the geographic extremes, however, it is hard to find any definite relationship. The best known attempt is probably that of Ellsworth Huntington, who developed the theory that civilization flourished best in the temperate zones [Huntington, 1924].

The temperate zones of climate do corre-

late fairly well at present with advanced civilization, but a shift in the time perspective gives a much different picture. The sunny lands of the Middle East were the homes of flourishing civilizations at a time when men in Europe were huddling in caves or tents. In temperate North America, the most advanced tribes were far behind the Mayas of Yucatan and Central America who built great cities and had developed a culture comparable to that of early Egypt. A look at history reveals that temperate zone areas now flourishing were at one time in a state of cultural stagnation, while splendid civilizations have flourished and then died in warmer climes. Any society is dependent on climate and natural resources; but there is no special type of geographic environment which guarantees human advance, and except for the extremes previously noted, there is no natural environment which dooms human effort to a limited plateau of achievement.

The possession of fertile farm lands or great mineral resources is an obvious advantage. Kuwait has one of the highest per capita incomes in the world, but was a land of poverty until the engineers of the Western world tapped its vast oil resources. Japan, with no mineral wealth and very little fertile farmland, has become a wealthy nation through effective social organization which has made it a workshop for the world. Truly, it seems that lack of natural resources is no insuperable handicap, while bountiful resources are no automatic guarantee of prosperity.

Ogburn and Nimkoff speak of cultural variation within the same physical setting:

. . . there are peoples living in essentially the same climate who have widely different cultures. In the southwestern part of the United States, the Hopi and the Navaho Indians have lived for centuries in the same locality but their cultures are quite different. The houses of the Hopi are built of adobe and may rise several stories like apartment houses. The Navaho live in a single room shaped much like the Eskimo domed snowhouse, but built of branches of trees. The Hopi are agriculturists and harvest crops. The Navaho are nomads and graze sheep. The religion and family life of the two groups are quite different. Since we find vastly different cultures under the same physiographic conditions, we must conclude that climate plays no precipitating or creative role in building the social heritage. *(William F. Ogburn and Meyer F. Nimkoff,* A Handbook of Sociology, *Routledge & Kegan Paul, Ltd., London, 1964, p. 77.)*

Many norms and institutions which originate in one climate are easily transportable into another climate. "High tea" has accompanied the British all over the world. Cultural tradition is often more important than physical environment in human behavior.

Modern man has been congratulating himself upon his ability to control his physical environment. Irrigation dams can make the desert bloom, air conditioning can cool the humid tropics, and through central heating, man can work in comfort in midwinter. He can even survive for brief periods in the airless cold of outer space or deep beneath the sea. But such dramatic achievements may be only temporary. Reservoirs silt up, irrigated lands salinate, and the combustible fuels which took millions of years to create may be gone in a few generations. Man's capacity to improve his environment has also made it possible for him to destroy it. Erosion carries away the soil, pollution destroys rivers, insecticides kill off both the beneficial and the harmful life forms, and noxious gases make air itself a doubtful commodity in our great cities. Man has made lakes where nature did not place them, but he has also polluted lakes until some are "dead" bodies of water unfit for either man or fish. And occasionally his most ambitious efforts to improve upon nature turn out to be a monumental blunder and an environmental disaster, as in the case of the Aswan High Dam in Egypt [Sterling, 1971].

It is dawning on man today that the natural environment consists of a series of interrelated ecological systems that he is currently disrupting at a rate which, if continued, will certainly impair the quality of life and probably threaten even man's survival. Many species have perished because of changes in their habitat, but man would be the first species to commit environmental suicide [De Bell, 1970; Klausner, 1971].

Man has congratulated himself on his ability to control his physical environment.

SOCIAL EVOLUTION

Evolution was one of the exciting ideas of the nineteenth century. While many scholars contributed to evolutionary theory, its most influential sponsor was the naturalist, Charles Darwin. After traveling the world and classifying tens of thousands of present life forms and fossil traces of earlier life forms, he developed, in his *Origin of Species* (1859), the theory that man had gradually evolved from lower orders of life as a result of progressive adaptation to the environment through the survival of biological forms best adapted to a competitive struggle. The early sociologists were intrigued by the question as to whether an evolutionary pattern could also be discerned in the development of man's culture and social life.

Auguste Comte in his *Positive Philosophy* (1851–1854) wrote of three stages through which he believed human thought inevitably moved: the theological, the metaphysical (or philosophical), and finally the positive (or scientific). Herbert Spencer, the sociological "giant" of the latter part of the nineteenth century, was enamored of "Social Darwinism". He saw social evolution as a set of stages through which all societies moved from the simple to the complex and from the homogeneous to the heterogeneous. Implicit in the thinking of both men was an optimism which saw the progress of society unfolding in a way that would gradually end misery and increase human happiness.

The course of two world wars, the appearance of economic depressions, and the rise of dictatorial governments did much to dampen this optimism and to make the idea of social evolution seem like a childish illusion. The cultural relativists denied that one could speak of a "higher" or "lower" type of culture and claimed that every culture was simply one of several possible ways of coping with the environment. The anthropologists denied that the direction of change is always from the simple to the more complex, and pointed out that many primitive tribes had a far more elaborate system of kinship classification than modern man. Even the ultimate triumph of the scientific approach to life over other approaches is doubtful; values remain central to theology, philosophy, and the humanities, and even appear to be creeping back into science. Culture historians such as Spengler and Toynbee deny the existence of any upward lineal progression of culture and claim that societies have moved in cycles in which democracy and dictatorship followed each other in sequence and in which advanced civilizations such as the Roman Empire rose, flowered, and were buried under successive waves of barbarians.

Ideas, however, are hard to kill. The notion of social evolution[1], which in the middle of

[1] In our discussion of social evolution we are heavily indebted to Richard P. Appelbaum, *Theories of Social Change,* Markham Publishing Co., Chicago, 1970.

the twentieth century seemed dead indeed, is very much alive today. One of the factors in its revival is a concern for the future of developing countries which have embarked on the path of industrialization. As developing countries become industrialized, they not only establish technological and economic structures similar to those of the western countries, but undergo related changes in religion, government, and the family as a part of this "modernization" [Moore, 1963, pp. 91–92; Levy, 1967, p. 190]. These developments would seem to indicate that social change is not simply a random process and that industrialization does bring other predictable social changes. For, as we recall, cultures are integrated.

If these nations, whose backgrounds are so different from those of the Western nations, are following a similar course of development, then perhaps there are some broad lines of movement which are part of a universal evolutionary pattern. We are hesitant to speak of these changes as "progress" in the sense of a happier or more just social system, but perhaps we can still speak of progress in terms of mastery over the environment. Thus Lenski suggests that progress be defined as "raising of the upper level of the capacity of human societies to mobilize energy and information in the adaptive process" [Lenski, 1970, p. 70]. Such a definition points out a possible direction to social and cultural change without raising such unanswerable questions as whether the laborer on the factory assembly line is happier than the craftsman in the medieval guild.

Are there common characteristics which all industrial societies share? Although the familial, religious, and governmental institutions of industrial societies may differ considerably, these differences are probably fewer than those of a century ago, while their industrial, commercial, and military institutions show great similarity. All steel mills, for example, must operate in much the same way, and cannot shut down for an afternoon siesta. Thus modern technology brings many common cultural characteristics to any people who embrace modern technology.

All industrial societies share certain common characteristics.

Are there any universal processes or directions of change throughout human societies? Parsons [1964, pp. 350–352] sees several, the first of which is the emergence of stratification (see Chapter 12) and the development of a political organization independent of kinship. In other words, the growth of technology means that someone has to be boss of every operation, and his authority does not rest upon his family connections but upon some other basis of assignment. The next two steps are seen as the appearance of a bureaucracy in which various degrees of authority are institutionalized and the emergence of money and markets which are mechanisms for mobilizing wealth and labor. His final pair of universal processes are more debatable: the acceptance of law which is equally binding on all members of the society and a democratic government which can support a consensus while still expressing an inevitable diversity.

Whether or not Parsons is right in all details is less important than the core of his argument, which is that social arrangements are not accidental or arbitrary but are moving in some definite directions. As societies adopt modern agricultural and industrial technology, they seem inevitably to experience accompanying changes which Smelser summarizes in this manner:

> In an emerging nation we may expect profound changes (1) in the *political* sphere as simple tribal or village authority systems give way to systems of suffrage, political parties, representation and civil service bureaucracies; (2) in the *educational* sphere as the society strives to reduce illiteracy and increase economically productive skills; (3) in the *religious* sphere, as secularized belief systems begin to replace traditionalistic religions; (4) in the *familial* sphere as extended kinship units lose their pervasiveness; (5) in the *stratificational* sphere, as geographical and social mobility tend to loosen fixed, ascriptive, hierarchical systems. (*Neil J. Smelser, "The Modernization of Social Relations," in Myron Weiner (ed.),* Modernization, *Basic Books, Inc., Publishers, New York, 1966, p. 111.*)

Biological and social evolution

Early social evolutionists assumed that man completed his biological evolution at some moment in the past, possibly 100,000 years ago, and then began his cultural evolution. We know today that culture has a far longer history—that he was using rude stone tools at least 500,000 years ago, while the age of such items of culture as language, customs, or kinship systems cannot even be estimated. It appears that cultural evolution began before our present level of biological evolution was reached. For instance, the early *hominids*, whose cultural development was extremely limited, had a cranial capacity in the range of 425 to 725 cubic centimeters, comparable to that of the larger apes today. While the beginnings of culture date back to this period, acceleration in cultural progress did not take place until the appearance of Neanderthal man about 150,000 years ago. Neanderthal man had a cranial capacity similar to that of modern man, averaging 1,500 cubic centimeters and ranging between 1,3000 and 1,600 cubic centimeters [Lenski, 1970, p. 152]. Thus both biological and cultural change moved together and presumably, are still evolving together.

Through selective breeding, man has already produced in nonhuman species "the most rapid evolutionary changes ever recorded" [Creed, 1969, p. 132]. Recent discoveries in genetics suggest the eventual possibility of producing evolutionary changes through direct modification of the genetic pattern, thus giving man great control over heredity, including his own. Man's growing ability to develop culture may be matched by his ability to control the hereditary potential with which he tackles the culture. In the prehistoric period, both man's biological capacity and his cultural storehouse were so limited that change was slow and difficult. In the modern era, the accumulation of culture and the prospect of controlling genetic quality set the stage for a period when man will have greater possibilities for controlling his world—for good or ill—than have ever before existed.

Conflict versus functionalist theories of evolutionary change

Although many scholars now accept the theory that all industrialized societies eventually develop cultures with certain similarities, controversy rages over the way in which these changes come about. One school of thought holds to the idea of balance, or equilibrium, and stresses the way that the various parts of society work together [Davis, 1949; Parsons, 1964]. The emphasis on equilibrium does not mean that society is unchanging, but it does imply that a harmonious relationship of different parts of society is the normal situation, and that disharmony or disequilibrium is a temporary phase of a readjustment process. The term *functionalism* is given to the approach which evaluates developments according to whether they promote equilibrium or disequilibrium—whether they stabilize or disorganize a social system. If a particular social change promotes equilibrium, it is seen as functional; if it has no particular effect upon equilibrium, it is nonfunctional; if it disturbs the social equilibrium, it is dysfunctional. Thus, political parties are functional in a democracy, while bombings, assassinations, and vote frauds are dysfunctional.

Conflict stimulates the search for new approaches.

It is not easy to foresee the long-term effects of any change. Developments which seem functional from one viewpoint may appear dysfunctional from another. Our interstate highway system, for example, is functional in that it simplifies travel, but dysfunctional in that it has chopped up cities, accelerated urban blight, and undermined the stability of the city. The important point, however, is not that any given change is, on balance, "good" (functional) or "bad" (dysfunctional); the major thesis is that social development comes through successive changes which promote harmonious cooperation among men.

An opposing point of view sees society as characterized by continuous conflict, in which any social change reflects the selfish interests of one party or another [Aron, 1954; Kerr, 1954; Coser, 1956; Dahrendorf, 1959, 1964]. While conflict is often regarded as wasteful and dysfunctional, it also has positive functions (see Chapter 14). Conflict forces the facing of issues and thus leads to their resolution. Conflict between groups promotes cohesion within each of the conflicting groups, stimulates the search for new approaches, and leads to new adaptations. Oftentimes, new ideas are best promoted by new groups, and the conflict which leads to their victory thus promotes social change. An appearance of social harmony is viewed as deceptive, since apparent peace is merely a period when opposing social forces are preparing for renewed battles to challenge the group which momentarily has been able to impose a system beneficial to itself. Karl Marx, over a century ago, taught that social evolution proceeded through continuous conflict between social classes over ownership of productive wealth [Marx and Engels, 1959, p. 18]. By contrast, Dahrendorf [1964, p. 107] feels that Marx overstressed the importance of property arrangements, and Dahrendorf finds the major source of conflict in the struggle for authority between rival groups.

While they argue about the source of conflict, the various conflict theorists agree that social evolution proceeds through the development and resolution of social conflict and, therefore, that the essential starting point for the analysis of social evolution is not cooperation but conflict. The differences between the functionalist and the conflict approaches are summarized in Table 2. Supporters of neither approach would claim that their set of assumptions holds true

TABLE 2

Assumptions of conflict and equilibrium approaches to social change

Equilibrium approach	Conflict approach
1. *Every society is a relatively persisting configuration of elements.*	1. *Every society is subject at every moment to social change: social change is ubiquitous.*
2. *Every society is a well-integrated configuration of elements.*	2. *Every society experiences at every moment social conflict: social conflict is ubiquitous.*
3. *Every element in a society contributes to its functioning.*	3. *Every element in a society contributes to its change.*
4. *Every society rests on the consensus of its members.*	4. *Every society rests on the constraint of some of its members by others.*

Source: Ralf Dahrendorf, "Towards a Theory of Social Conflict," in Amitai Etzioni and Eva Etzioni (eds.), Social Change, *Basic Books, Inc., Publishers, New York, 1964, p. 103.*

without exception, but that their assumptions are more consistently sound than those of their opponents.

It is not necessary to choose between the conflict and equilibrium theories, for while they place emphasis differently, both describe genuine social realities. It is certainly true that society is characterized by both cooperation and conflict (topics we will expand in Chapter 14, which deals with social processes). Society may be analyzed either from the standpoint of the strains which accompany a typically cooperative social system or from that of allegedly imposed cooperation arising from persistent conflict. Both viewpoints are relevant and useful in a full understanding of social reality.

SUMMARY

Man's accumulation of culture through the use of language is one of the main features which distinguishes him from the lower animals. Other animals may have physical strength and dexterity, but they lack the ability to communicate through language, the use of symbols which is essential if the learning of one generation is to be transmitted to the next.

Geographic factors require human adaptation, but they do not dictate the form which this cultural adaptation will take; they allow for a wide variety of cultural forms. Great cities have usually been the seedbeds of civilization, while cultural development has been more restricted in the isolated rural areas. The claim that the temperate climate favors high cultural attainment may seem to be true at the present day, but historical analysis indicates that tropical climates often gave rise to advanced civilizations while temperate areas were the homes of cavemen.

The idea of social or cultural evolution is regaining support. This is partly explained by the worldwide trend to industrialization, with the necessary changes which this imposes on all aspects of society. Social evolution does not exclude variation or mean that life is inevitably getting better. It does imply the certain universals are found in all industrializing societies. In prehistoric periods, cultural and biological evolution have moved together, with cultural evolution beginning before man's present level of biological evolution was attained. Cultural evolution seems to have accelerated after prehistoric man's braincase enlarged. Prospects for the control of the genes indicate that man soon may be in a position to exert some control over biological evolution in the human species. It is clear that cultural and biological change moved together in the past and may continue to do so.

The acceptance of an evolutionary viewpoint still leaves open the question as to how cultural development takes place. The functionalist explanation views society as an organism whose various parts are usually in a state of equilibrium; the conflict theorists view society as a perpetual struggle. According to the functionalist, evolution leads toward greater integration and cooperation; the conflict theorist holds that new forms of social life come about through the effort of antagonistic groups to gain or hold dominance.

Questions and projects

1. Distinguish between symbolic communication among humans and instinctive communication among animals.

2. Do animals have a culture? If your answer is yes, what limits are placed on such a culture?

3. Huntington argues that, since advanced civilization is found in the temperate zone, this type of climate must favor cultural development. What criticism can you make of this thesis?

4. Independent African countries have usually retained the language of the former colonial power for use in the schools. Do you feel that this practice is likely to continue?

5. Do geographic factors determine the nature of cultural development? Can geographic and biological factors be disregarded in making predictions about cultural development?

6. What factors led sociologists at one time to lose interest in the idea of social evolution?

7. Can one support the idea of social evolution while doubting that man is making ethical progress? Is it possible for man to continue his technical advance without progressing in the application of moral principles?

8. Does social evolution lead to uniformity? If not, what limits does it place on variation?

9. Would Karl Marx have been friendlier to a conflict theory or an equilibrium theory of society? Why?

10. Why is it difficult to classify particular developments as functional or dysfunctional?

11. It may soon become possible to control the genetic makeup of babies, "ordering" whatever combination of characteristics we desire. What conflicts would this create? Would this development be functional or dysfunctional?

12. Read the article "Genetics and Sociology: A Reconsideration" by Bruce Ecklund, *American Sociological Review*, 32:173-194, April, 1967. From the viewpoint of this article, what do you think of the prospects of drastically increasing educational achievement?

Suggested Readings

*Appelbaum, Richard P.: *Theories of Social Change*, Markham Publishing Co., Chicago, 1970. A concise and yet thorough summary of current sociological thought dealing with evolutionary theory.

Dahrendorf, Ralf: "Conflict Groups, Group Conflicts, and Social Change," in *Class and Class Conflict in Industrial Society*, Stanford University Press, Stanford, Calif., 1959, pp. 202-223. Reprinted in Peter Orleans and Sonya Orleans (eds.), *Social Structure and Social Process*, Allyn and Bacon, Inc., Boston, 1969, pp. 437-452. Examines conflict from the standpoint of its role both in promoting societal integration and in stimulating social change.

Darlington, C. D.: *The Evolution of Man and Society*, Simon & Schuster, Inc., New York, 1970. Presents the viewpoint that similar principles determine both biological and social evolution.

Eckland, Bruce K.: "Genetics and Sociology: A Reconsideration," *American Sociological Review*, 32:173-194, April, 1967. Argues that sociologists have failed to appreciate the importance of genetically transmitted potential and that heredity and culture interact in the evolution of human societies.

Feldman, Arnold S., and Christopher Hurn: "The Experience of Modernization," *Sociometry*, 29:378-395, December, 1966. Describes the cultural changes which take place when traditional societies modernize their procedures.

*Hall, Edward T.: *The Silent Language*, Fawcett Publications, Inc., Greenwich, Conn., 1959. A lively little book on the interaction of language and culture, listing many ways in which meaning is distorted because cultural norms cause the meaning of identical words to vary from one society to another.

*Helfrich, Harold W., Jr. (ed.): *The Environmental Crisis: Man's Struggle to Live with Himself*, New Haven, Yale University Press, 1970. A brief, readable, authoritative collection of essays on environmental problems and possibilities.

Klausner, Samuel Z.: *On Man in His Environment*, Jossey-Bass, Inc., Publishers, San Francisco, 1971. Outlines the kind of knowledge needed to "save" our environment, and how we might organize ourselves to develop and apply it.

Lenski, Gerhard: *Human Societies,* McGraw-Hill Book Company, New York, 1970. An introductory textbook with an evolutionary approach. Chap. 3, "Introduction to Evolutionary Theory," and Chap. 5, "Basic Evolutionary Trends," are a good introduction to this topic.

Lerner, I. Michael: *Heredity, Evolution, and Society,* University of California Press, Berkeley, 1968. A superbly illustrated treatment of the relationship of genetics to social decisions.

Lorenz, Konrad Z.: "Morals and Weapons," in *King Solomon's Ring,* Thomas Y. Crowell Company, New York, 1954, pp. 182–199; reprinted in **H. Laurence Ross (ed.),** *Perspectives on the Social Order,* McGraw-Hill Book Company, 1968, pp. 120–126. Contrasts the instinctive behavior of animals and the cultural behavior of man as a means of limiting in-group warfare.

Parsons, Talcott: "Evolutionary Universals in Society"; **Robert N. Bellah:** "Religious Evolution"; **S. N. Eisenstadt:** "Social Change, Differentiation, and Evolution." Three articles on social evolution, in *American Sociological Review,* June, 1954, Vol. 29. The articles by Parsons and Eisenstadt also appear in **Lewis A. Coser and Bernard Rosenberg (eds.),** *Sociological Theory: A Book of Readings,* The MacMillan Company, New York, 1969.

*Rostow, W. W.: *The Stages of Economic Growth,* Cambridge University Press, London, 1961. A well-known attempt to describe an evolutionary pattern of economic development.

Every man is in certain respects
> a. Like all other men
> b. Like some other men
> c. Like no other man (*Clyde Kluckhohn and Henry A. Murray (eds.),* Personality in Nature, Society and Culture, *Alfred A. Knopf, Inc., New York, 1949, p. 35.*)

Personality and socialization

There are some elements of a man's personality and socialization which he shares with all other men, some which he shares with some other men, and some which he shares with no other man. What these are and how they operate is the subject of this chapter.

THE MEANING OF PERSONALITY

Personality is one of those terms which is seldom defined in exactly the same way by any two authorities. All definitions of personality suggest that it represents a tendency for a person to act in a somewhat predictable manner. While some authorities are concerned with inborn predispositions which they credit to each person, others assume that behavior is largely a product of social experience. A quite satisfactory definition is offered by Yinger [1965, p. 141], who sees personality developing from the interaction of both elements: "Personality is the totality of behavior of an individual with a given tendency system interacting with a sequence of situations."

The phrase, "a given tendency system," suggests that the behavior of a person is fairly consistent. He acts much the same way day after day. When we remark, "Isn't that just like Ruth," we recognize that Ruth has a behavior "tendency system" that is quite characteristic of her. The phrase, "interacting with a sequence of situations," indicates that behavior is a joint product of a person's behavior tendencies and the behavior situations he encounters. To understand personality we need to know how behavior tendency systems develop through the interaction of the biological organism with various kinds of social and cultural experience.

FACTORS IN THE DEVELOPMENT OF PERSONALITY

The factors in personality development are: (1) biological inheritance, (2) physical environment, (3) culture, (4) group experience, and (5) unique experience.

Biological inheritance and personality

A brick house cannot be built of stone or bamboo; but from a pile of bricks, a great variety of houses can be built. Biological inheritance provides the raw materials of personality, and these raw materials can be shaped in a great many different ways.

Unlike many species, the human animal is sexually active throughout the entire year, and this characteristic guarantees the more or less constant association of the sexes. The human infant is born helpless and will survive only if given tender care for many years. Such biological facts provide a basis for man's group life. Some species are monogamous by instinct; man definitely is not. This is a biological fact which every society must deal with in some manner. Some of the similarities in man's personality and culture are due to his common heredity. As far as we know, every human group in the world inherits the same general set of biological needs and capacities. According to Montagu [1958, p. 85], these needs include oxygen, food, liquid, rest, activity, sleep, bowel and bladder elimination, escape from frightening situations, and the avoidance of pain. Our common heredity thus explains some of our similarities in personality, while individual differences in heredity explain some of the indi-

vidual differences in personality. But *group* differences in personality cannot be attributed to heredity unless there is convincing evidence that the groups differ in average inheritance.

The black Americans were taken from a number of tribes, mostly in West Africa. Promptly upon arrival, they began absorbing a culture and developing a personality quite different from that of their African kinsmen. Americans of many racial and national origins now share a common culture, and their differences in personality are not closely related to their different ethnic origins. We could cite dozens of examples of a rapid change in culture and personality without any change in heredity. All that we know of heredity suggests that the heredity of a group does not change rapidly enough to account for such changes in group behavior. What heredity does is to provide the set of needs, limitations, and capabilities with which other factors interact in shaping human personality.

In recent years, several semipopular books about biology and behavior have attracted a great deal of interest. They include Ardrey's *The Territorial Imperative* [1966], Lorenz's *On Aggression* [1966], Morris's *The Naked Ape* [1968], Tiger's *Men in Groups* [1969], and Tinbergen's *The Study of Instinct* [1969]. All of these authors (several zoologists, one anthropologist, and one playwright) claim that sociologists have underestimated the importance of biological factors in human personality and behavior. While none argues that specific human behavior traits are inborn, all hold that there are innate predispositions, common to all physically normal human beings, which influence personality and behavior more greatly than sociologists have believed. These writers draw heavily upon human parallels to animal behavior. They are provocative and stimulating, and offer interesting hypotheses, but most reviewers have considered their evidence inadequate for their conclusions. Yet these works remind us that questions about the biological factor in personality and behavior are far from settled.

Physical environment and personality

Some of our earliest manuscripts are attempts to explain human behavior in terms of climate and geography. Sorokin [1928, chap. 3] summarizes the theories of hundreds of writers, from Confucius, Aristotle, and Hippocrates down to the modern geographer Ellsworth Huntington, who have claimed that group differences in behavior are due mainly to differences in climate, topography, and resources. Such theories fit beautifully into an ethnocentric framework, for geography provides a respectable, apparently objective explanation of our national virtues and other peoples' vices.

As shown in Chapter 4, physical environment is a factor of some importance in cultural evolution. It is a factor of less importance in personality, for, whereas physical environment sets many limits upon cultural development, it imposes very few upon personality. Practically any kind of personality can be found in every kind of climate.

True, the physical environment has *some* influence upon personality. The Australian bushmen had a desperate struggle to stay alive, while it took the Samoans only a few minutes a day to gather more food than they could eat. Some regions, even today, can support only a very thinly scattered population, and density of population has some effects upon personality. But of the five factors discussed in this chapter, physical environment is the least important—far less important than culture, group experience, or unique experience.

Culture and personality

Some cultural experience is common to all mankind. Everywhere infants are nursed or fed by older persons, live in groups, learn to communicate through language, experience punishments and rewards of some kind, and have some other experiences common to the entire human species. It is also true that each society gives to virtually all its members certain experiences which many other societies do not offer. From the social experience common to virtually all members of a given society, there emerges a characteristic personality configuration which is typical of many members of that society. DuBois [1944, pp. 3–5] has called this the "modal personality" (taken from the statistical term, "mode," referring to that value which appears most frequently in a series). How the modal personality may vary between two different societies is seen in the following contrast.

Some cultural experiences are common to all mankind.

The anxious Dobuan [Fortune, 1932; Benedict, 1934, chap. 5] The Dobuan child in Melanesia might think twice about coming into this world, if he had any choice in the matter. He enters a family where the only member who is likely to care much about him is his uncle, his mother's brother, to whom he is heir. His father, who is interested in his own sister's children, usually resents him, for his father must wait until he is weaned before resuming sexual relations with his mother. Often he is also unwanted by his mother, and abortion is common. Little warmth or affection awaits the child in Dobu.

The Dobuan child soon learns that he lives in a world ruled by magic. Nothing happens from natural causes; all phenomena are controlled by witchcraft and sorcery. Illness, accident, and death are evidence that witchcraft has been used against one and call for vengeance from one's kinsmen. Nightmares are interpreted as witchcraft episodes in which the spirit of the sleeper has narrow escapes from hostile spirits. All legendary heroes and villains are still alive as active supernaturals, capable of aid or injury. Crops grow only if one's long hours of magical chants are successful in enticing the yams away from another's garden. Even sexual desire does not arise except in response to another's love magic, which guides one's steps to his partner, while one's own love magic accounts for his successes.

Ill will and treachery are virtues in Dobu, and fear dominates Dobuan life. Every Dobuan lives in constant fear of being poisoned. Food is watchfully guarded while in preparation, and there are few persons indeed with whom a Dobuan will eat. The Dobuan couple spend alternate years in the villages of wife and husband, so that one of them is always a distrusted and humiliated outsider who lives in daily expectation of poisoning or other misadventure. Because of numerous divorces and remarriages, each village shelters men from many different villages, so that none of them can trust either their village hosts or one another. In fact, no one can be fully trusted; men are nervous over their wives' possible witchcraft and fear their mothers-in-law.

To the Dobuans, all success must be secured at the expense of someone else, just as all misfortune is caused by others' malevolent magic. Effective magic is the key to success, and a man's success is measured by his accomplishments in theft and seduction.

Adultery is virtually universal, and the successful adulterer, like the successful thief, is much admired.

On the surface, social relations in Dobu are cordial and polite although dour and humorless. There is very little quarreling, for to give offense or to make an enemy is dangerous. But friends are also dangerous; a show of friendship may be a prelude to a poisoning or to the collection of materials (hair, fingernails) useful for sorcery.

What kind of personality develops in such a cultural setting? The Dobuan is hostile, suspicious, distrustful, jealous, secretive, and deceitful. These are rational reactions, for he lives in a world filled with evil, surrounded by enemies, witches, and sorcerers. Eventually they are certain to destroy him. Meanwhile he seeks to protect himself by his own magic, but never can he know any sense of comfortable security. A bad nightmare may keep him in bed for days. As measured by Western concepts of mental hygiene, all Dobuans are paranoid to a degree calling for psychotherapy. But simply to call them paranoid would be incorrect, for their fears are justified and not irrational; the dangers they face are genuine, not imaginary. A true paranoid personality *imagines* that other people are threatening him, but in Dobu, other people really *are* out to get him. Thus the culture shapes a personality pattern which is normal *and useful* for that culture.

The cooperative Zuñi [Benedict, 1934, chap. 4] The Zuñi of New Mexico are a placid people in an emotionally undisturbed world. The child is warmly welcomed, treated with tender fondness, and receives a great deal of loving attention. He is never disciplined or punished, yet becomes a well-behaved member of a society in which crime is rare and quarreling almost unknown.

Cooperation, moderation, and lack of individualism are carried into all Zuñi behavior. Personal possessions are unimportant and readily lent to others. The members of the matrilineal household work together as a group, and the crops are stored in a common storehouse. One works for the good of the group, not for personal glory. (Zuñi children do poorly on competitive examinations in the government schools, for it is impolite to answer any question whose answer may be unknown to one's classmates.)

The magical forces in the Zuñi world are never malevolent and often helpful. Since the supernaturals have the same tastes as living men, they need not be feared. Supernatural and magical aid is sought through many long ceremonials, yet the ceremonial dances are never frenzied or orgiastic. Violence or immoderation is distasteful, and even disagreements are settled without open bickering. For example, one wife who became weary of her husband's many amours decided to settle the matter. "So," she said, "I didn't wash his clothes. Then he knew that I knew that everybody knew, and he stopped going with that girl." Without a word the issue was settled [Benedict, 1934, p. 108]. Unlike most Indians, the Zuñi rejected alcohol because it tempts men to immoderate, undignified behavior. They do not use peyote or other drugs, or resort to self-torture or prolonged fasting in an effort to induce ecstasies, visions, or other unusual sensory phenomena. They desire only the normal sensory experience of moderate behavior. The individual Zuñi craves no power or leadership, and the necessary leadership roles must be thrust upon him. Responsibility and power are distributed; the group is the real functioning unit.

The Zuñi have no sense of sin. They have no picture of the universe as a conflict between good and evil, nor any concept of themselves as disgusting or unworthy. Sex is not a series of temptations but part of a happy life. Adultery is mildly disapproved, but is largely a private matter and a probable prelude to a change of husbands. Divorce is simple; the wife simply piles her husband's

things outside the pueblo, where he finds them, cries a little, and goes home to his mother. Since the family is matrilineal and matrilocal (descent follows the mother's family line, and family residence is with the mother's family), a divorce and the disappearance of the father does not seriously disrupt the life of the children. Yet divorce is not very common, and serious misconduct is very rare.

The normal personality among the Zuñi stands in stark contrast to that of the Dobuans. Where the Dobuan is suspicious and distrustful, the Zuñi is confident and trusting; where the Dobuan is apprehensive and insecure, the Zuñi is secure and serene. The typical Zuñi has a yielding disposition and is generous, polite, and cooperative. He is unthinkingly and habitually conformist, for to be noticeably different from his fellows is something neither he nor they can tolerate. Apparently this serves to control his behavior without the sense of sin and the guilt complexes found in many societies, including our own.

As the two foregoing sketches illustrate, personality differs strikingly from society to society. *Each society develops one or more basic personality types which fit the culture.* The Dobuans do not consciously or intentionally train their children to be hostile and suspicious; yet the atmosphere of constant treachery and fear has this result. Each culture, simply by being what it is, shapes personality to fit the culture. Let us consider some aspects of the culture which affect the process of personality development.

Norms of the culture From the moment of birth, the child is treated in ways which shape the personality. Each culture provides a set of general influences, which vary endlessly from society to society. As Linton writes,

In some [societies] infants are given the breast whenever they cry for it. In others they are fed on a regular schedule. In some they will be nursed by any woman who happens to be at hand, in others only by their mothers. In some the process of nursing is a leisurely one, accompanied by many caresses and a maximum of sensuous enjoyment for both mother and child. In others it is hurried and perfunctory, the mother regarding it as an interruption of her regular activities and urging the child to finish as rapidly as possible. Some groups wean infants at an early age; others continue nursing for years.

In the techniques of caring for infants there is an even greater cultural range. One society may make the baby the center of attention for the entire family, various adults constantly carrying it about, playing with it, and giving it anything it wants. Another society may regard infants as a nuisance and pay little attention to them outside the satisfaction of their physical needs. In some societies the child is in almost constant bodily contact with its mother during the first two years. Madagascar mothers keep their infants in the backs of their dresses, leaving them there even when working in the fields. In other societies this constant bodily contact is lacking, but the child is handled frequently. In still others it is rarely touched except at feeding time. In some societies the child is allowed to tumble about without interference. In others it spends its first eighteen months bound to a board, even its arms sometimes being wrapped. . . .

Turning to the more direct effects of culture patterns upon the developing individual, we have an almost infinite range of variations in the degree to which he is consciously trained, discipline or the lack of it and responsibilities imposed upon him. Society may take the child in hand almost from infancy and deliberately train him for his adult status, or it may permit him to run wild until the age of puberty. He may receive corporal punishment for even the smallest offense or never be punished at all. As a child he may have a claim upon the time and attention of all adults with whom he comes in contact or, conversely, all adults may have a claim upon his services. He may be put to work and treated as a responsible contributing member of the family group almost from the moment that he is able to walk and have it constantly impressed upon him that life is real and earnest. Thus in some Madagascar tribes children not only begin to work at an incredibly

early age but also enjoy full property rights. I frequently bargained with a child of six for some object which I needed for my collection; although its parents might advise, they would not interfere. On the other hand, the children in a Marquesan village do not work and accept no responsibility. They form a distinct and closely integrated social unit which has few dealings with adults. The boys and girls below the age of puberty are constantly together and often do not go home even to eat or sleep. They go off on all-day expeditions, for which no parental permission is required, catch fish and raid plantations for food, and spend the night in any house they happen to be near at sunset.

Examples of such cultural differences in the treatment of children could be multiplied indefinitely. The important point is that every culture exerts a series of general influences upon the individuals who grow up under it. These influences differ from one culture to another, but they provide a common denominator of experience for all persons belonging to a given society. (*Ralph Linton*, The Study of Man, *Appleton-Century-Crofts, Inc., New York, 1936. Copyright, 1936, and reprinted by permission of Appleton-Century-Crofts.*)

Some of the American literature on psychoanalysis and child development, drawing heavily upon the theories of Freud, has attached great importance to specific child-training practices. Breast feeding, gradual weaning, demand-feeding schedules, and easy and late induction to bowel and bladder training have often been recommended, with the opposite practices being blamed for all sorts of personality difficulties. These recommendations are generally unsupported by any carefully controlled comparative studies, although dramatic case histories may be cited in illustration. One serious effort [Sewell, 1952] to test these recommendations made a comparison of American children who had received differing child-training practices. This study found that no measurable adult personality differences were associated with any particular child-training practices. Studies of personality development in other cultures have likewise failed to substantiate Freudian theories of the results of specific child-training practices [Dai, 1957; Eggan, 1943]. Apparently, it is the total atmosphere, and not the specific practice, which is important in personality development. Whether a child is breast-fed or bottle-fed is unimportant; what *is* important is whether this feeding is a tender, affectionate moment in a warmly secure world, or a hurried, casual incident in an impersonal, unfeeling, unresponding environment.

Cultural personality types A society poses one or more personality types which children are urged to copy. Among most of the Plains Indians, the approved personality for the adult male was that of a vigorous, self-reliant, aggressive warrior. Under many circumstances, to take what he wanted from the weak was a virtue; any tendency to overlook insults or to compromise disagreements was a weakness. Since only these personality characteristics were admired and rewarded in males, they were the ones most boys developed.

The most widely approved personality in our culture is probably friendly and sociable, somewhat cooperative yet quite competitive and aggressively individualistic, progressive, yet practical and efficient. Many features of our social life conspire to develop these characteristics within us. We live in a society where sociability has a cash value. Cordiality is taught and cultivated as a necessity in almost any career. The child is trained to make all requests with a "Please," and receive all favors with a smiling "Thank you." Television commercials, clerks, and salesmen mount an unending barrage of smiling, friendly-sounding appeals. While much of this outward show of friendliness is phony, it nonetheless surrounds one with an atmosphere of sociability which probably leaves some residue. Our society forces people to develop an acute time conscious-

ness, since nearly everything is done on a time schedule. The American Indian's serene unconcern with time was exasperating to whites who had dealings with him, just as the white man's endless fretting and clock watching perplexed and bored the Indian.

Children are urged to copy,

Most of the world's people throughout past history could see little if any social change within their own lifetimes. They lived in an unchanging world, a world of customs supposedly unchanged over countless generations, of legends passed down from remote ancestors, and a world expected to extend endlessly into the future. Today we live in a culture permeated by change and expectations of change. Each child is surrounded by adults busily contrasting the present with their childhood reminiscences. Change is accepted, expected, and even discounted, as we base our future plans on the changes which we expect to have taken place by the time our plans mature. Cultural influences such as these help to develop the bustling, restless, energetic personality that is admired in our culture.

A close relationship between personality and culture should be expected, because in a sense, personality and culture are two aspects of the same thing. As Spiro [1951] has observed, "the development of personality and the acquisition of culture are not different processes, but are one and the same learning process. . . ." In a stable, well-integrated society, personality is an individual aspect of culture, while culture is a collective aspect of personality. This discussion could be prolonged indefinitely; but we have said enough to illustrate the point that every culture surrounds the individual with experiences that develop a normal personality, more or less perfectly reflected by most members of that society.

Subcultures and personality. This picture of a single approved personality type (for each sex and age level) in a society holds fairly true for the simple society with a well-integrated culture. But in a complex society with a number of subcultures, the picture changes. Are there personality differences between the Yankee and the Deep-Southerner? Does the sharecropper think and feel as does the urban professional? In a complex society, there may be as many "normal personality types" as there are subcultures.

The United States has many subcultures—racial, religious, ethnic, regional, social-class, perhaps even occupational. The boundary lines are indistinct, and some subcultures are more important than others. For example, the Catholic and Protestant subcultures probably affect less of a member's life than the Jewish subculture, and still less than the Amish subculture. Yet subcultures are real, and we have some justification for speaking of the "urban middle-class personality" or of the "typical salesman." Of course, we must not exaggerate; it is likely that personality similarities within our culture greatly outnumber personality differences between subcultures, and there are individual personality differences within each subculture. But the physician, the minister, the carnival worker, and the migrant fruit picker show some predictable

personality differences from one another. Therefore we cannot describe the normal American personality without first naming the subculture we have in mind.

Individual deviation from modal personality. In even the most conformist of societies, there is some individuality in personality. The modal personality merely represents a series of personality traits which are most common among the members of a group, even though comparatively few of them may have developed every one of the traits in the series. Wallace [1952a] used Rorschach tests on a sample of Tuscarora Indians, and concluded that only 37 percent of them showed all twenty-one of the modal personality traits which had been established as characteristic of the Tuscarora. Other similar studies [Kaplan, 1954; Wallace, 1952b] show that while a modal personality type characteristic of a society exists, it is not a uniform mold into which all members are perfectly cast. Likewise, in discussing the "typical" personality of nations, tribes, social classes, of occupational, regional, or other social groups, we must remember that the typical personality merely describes a series of personality traits, a *great many* of which are shared by *most* of the members of that group. Each society and each social group allows a certain amount of individual deviation from the modal personality. When this deviation extends beyond what the group or society considers "normal," then that person is considered to be a "deviant." Such deviation will be considered in some detail in Chapter 7.

SOCIALIZATION AND THE SELF

The infant enters this world as a biological organism preoccupied with his own physical comforts. He soon becomes a human being, with a set of attitudes and values, likes and dislikes, goals and purposes, patterns of response, and a deep, abiding concept of the sort of person he is. He gets these through a process we call *socialization*—the learning process which turns him from an animal into a person with a human personality. Put more formally, socialization is *the process whereby one internalizes the norms of his groups so that a distinct "self" emerges, unique to this individual.*

Group experience

As one's life begins there is no self, for the individual is simply an embryo sharing the life processes of the mother's body. Nor do birth and the severing of the umbilical cord produce any awareness of self. Even the distinction between the limits of the physical self and the rest of the world are a matter of gradual exploration as the infant discovers that the rattle or the bars on his crib belong to the external world, and are not a part of his body as are his toes and fingers.

The realization of a distinctive personality is an even more complicated process which continues throughout life. The child learns to differentiate between various other people by names—Daddy, Mummy, and Baby. At first, any man is a "daddy" and any woman a "mummy," but eventually he moves from names which distinguish a status to specific names which identify individuals, including himself. At about the age of two he begins to use "I," which is a sign of definite self-consciousness—that he is becoming aware of himself as a distinct human being [Cooley, 1908; Bain, 1936]. As time passes and social experiences accumulate, he forms an image of the kind of person he is—an image of self. One ingenious way of trying to get some impression of a person's self-image is the "Twenty Questions Test" [Kuhn and McPartland, 1954], in which the informant is asked to write twenty answers, exactly as they occur to him, to the question, "Who am I?" One's formation of his image of self is perhaps the most important single process in personality development.

Social isolates To some degree, personality is dependent upon physical-growth processes. But personality development is not simply an automatic unfolding of inborn potentials, as is shown by social isolates. Several times each year the newspapers report instances of neglected children who have been chained or locked away from the normal family group. They are always found to be retarded and generally antisocial or unsocial. Without group experience, human personality does not develop. The most dramatic reports are those of so-called feral children, separated from their families and supposedly raised by animals [Singh and Zingg, 1942; Krout, 1942, pp. 106–114]. Social scientists doubt that a child would live for long in the care of animals, and suspect that so-called feral children simply had been lost or abandoned by their parents and then discovered by others shortly thereafter [Ogburn, 1959].

An explanation of the reported "animal" behavior of feral children is offered by Bettelheim, who states that severe cases of infantile autism being treated at the Orthogenic School of the University of Chicago show symptoms like those of the feral children, although there was no claim that the Chicago children had ever been in a nonhuman environment.

During one year a single staff member had to have medical help more than a dozen times for bites she suffered from Anna, and the children regularly bare their teeth when annoyed or angry. Different, and again reminiscent of animals is their prowling around at night, in marked contrast to their quiet withdrawal to a corner during the day.... Then there is their great preference for raw food, particularly for raw vegetables.... Some of these children on seeing animals, respond as though they had found a dear, long-lost friend. One girl for example, became extremely excited on seeing a dog; she showed a strong desire to run toward it and cried or howled like an animal. . . . She fell on all fours, jumped like a dog with her head down and made biting gestures. Now had we believed in the feral origin of this girl—whose total life-history incidentally, is well known to us—we would probably have been convinced that, on seeing that wolflike creature, she was filled with memories of her happy times among wolves and was reverting to what she had learned from them. (*Bruno Bettelheim, "Feral Children and Autistic Children,"* American Journal of Sociology, *54: 458, March, 1959.*)

Bettelheim found that the autistic children in the Chicago clinic showed traits commonly attributed to "feral" children and concludes that the "feral" children were probably simply suffering from infantile autism—defined as "the inability to relate themselves in the ordinary way to people and situations from the beginning of life." He says that the autistic children known to the clinic had invariably been rejected by their parents and deprived of normal human love and concludes that this may be the real difficulty with the reported cases of feral children:

Study of the so-called feral children, and comparison of them with known and well-observed wild autistic children, suggests strongly that their behavior is due in large part, if not entirely, to extreme emotional isolation combined with experience which they interpreted as threatening them with utter destruction. It seems to be the result of some persons—usually their parents'—inhumanity and not the result, as was assumed, of animals'—particularly wolves'—inhumanity. To put it differently, feral children seem to be produced not when wolves behave like mothers but when mothers behave like nonhumans. The conclusion tentatively forced on us is that, while there are no feral children, there are some very rare examples of feral mothers, of human beings who became feral to one of their children. (*Bruno Bettelheim,* op. cit., *467.*)

It is highly doubtful, then, that allegedly feral children are examples of animal nurture. It does seem evident, however, that children who are emotionally rejected and deprived of normal loving care fail to develop the type of personality we usually consider human. This conclusion is consistent with the findings of a number of experiments in which animals were raised in isolation from their normal groups. Harlow [1961] raised monkeys in isolation, with only a heated terry cloth-covered wire framework as a substitute "mother," from which they received their bottle and to which they clung when frightened. As infants, they seemed satisfied with this substituted "mother," but as adults, they were almost entirely asocial. Many were apathetic and withdrawn; others were hostile and agressive. None showed the social group behavior of normal adult monkeys. Apparently the substitute mother met the infant's need for affection and security, but was unable to carry the monkey through any further stages of psychosocial development. Other animal experiments show similar failures of isolated animals to develop the behavior normal for their species [Krout, 1942, pp. 102–105]. Both animals and human beings need group experience if they are to develop normally.

Cooley and the looking-glass self Just how does a person arrive at a notion of the kind of person he is? He develops this concept of self through a gradual and complicated process which continues throughout life. The concept is an image that one builds only with the help of others. Suppose a girl is told by her parents and relatives how pretty she looks. If this is repeated often enough, consistently enough, and by enough different people, she eventually comes to feel and act like a beautiful person. But even a pretty girl will feel that she is an ugly duckling if, beginning early in life, her parents act disappointed and apologetic over her and treat her as unattractive. *A person's self-image need bear no relation to the objective facts.* A very ordinary child whose efforts are appreciated and rewarded will develop a feeling of acceptance and self-confidence, while a truly brilliant child whose efforts are frequently defined as failures will usually become obsessed with feelings of incompetence, and his abilities can be practically paralyzed. It is through the responses of others that one decides whether he is intelligent or stupid, attractive or homely, lovable or unlovable, righteous or sinful, worthy or worthless.

This "self" which is discovered through the reactions of others has been labeled the "looking-glass self" by Cooley [1902, pp. 102-103], who carefully analyzed this aspect of self-discovery. He may, perhaps, have been inspired by the words in Thackeray's *Vanity Fair:* "The world is a looking glass and gives back to every man the reflection of his own face. Frown on it and it will in turn look sourly upon you; laugh at it and with it, and it is a jolly, kind companion."

There are three steps in the process of building the looking-glass self: (1) our perception of how we look to others; (2) our perception of their judgment of how we look; (3) our feelings about these judgments. Suppose that whenever you enter a room and approach a small knot of people conversing together, the members promptly melt away with lame excuses. Would this experience, repeated many times, affect your feelings about yourself? Or if whenever you appear, a conversational group quickly forms around you, how does this attention affect your self-feelings? A wallflower is a person who learned early in life that he could not make conversation. How did he discover this?

Just as the picture in the mirror gives an image of the physical self, so the perception of the reactions of others gives an image of the social self. We "know," for instance, that we are talented in some respects and less talented in others. This knowledge came to us from the reactions of other persons. The little child whose first crude artistic efforts are sharply criticized soon concludes that he lacks artistic talent, while the child whose first efforts win praise from a considerate parent may build up a belief in his own ability in this field. As he matures, others will also give a reaction which may differ from that of his parents, for the social looking glass is one which is constantly before us.

Another difference between the functioning of the "looking glass" in early childhood and in later life is that the child may be deeply affected by the response of anyone with whom he comes in intimate contact, whereas the older individual is more discriminating in appraising the importance of the response he receives from various individuals. The baby-sitter's responses affect the child more than they affect the parent. Thus we say that as one matures he develops *reference groups* to whom he gives special attention [Rosen, 1955a]. A child may base his estimate of his musical talents on the opinions of parents regardless of their musical sophistication; an adult is more likely to give special attention to the opinions of musical experts and ignore the reactions of others. Not only do we become more selective in choosing the reference groups who comprise our social looking glass but we also are selective in the perception of the images which do influence us. We pay more attention to some reactions than to others; or we may misjudge the reactions of others. It may be that the ego-boosting remark which we take at face value is mere flattery; a scolding may have been caused by the boss's headache rather than by our own errors. Thus the looking-glass self which the individual perceives may easily differ from the image others have actually formed of his personality. Several research efforts have sought empirical evidence of the correlation between one's *perception* of responses of others and the *actual* judgments they have made of him. These studies find that there is often a significant variation between the individual's perception of how others picture him and the views they actually hold. Calvin and Holtzman [1953] found that individuals vary considerably in their ability to perceive accurately the judgments of others about them, and that the less well-adjusted person was less accurate in these perceptions. Another experiment by Miyamoto and Dornbusch [1956] found that a subject's self-conception is closer to his perception of a group's impression of him than to their actual reported impression of him, as is shown in Table 3.

In this study of ten groups totaling 195 subjects, the "perception of group response" is each subject's estimate of how the other members of the group rate him according to four characteristics—intelligence, self-confidence, physical attractiveness, and likeableness. The "actual group response" is the rating actually assigned to him by the others in the group. In most of these groups (of fraternity members and classmates who knew each other well) the subjects' self-conceptions were closer to their perceived response than to the actual response of the group to them. Clearly, it is our perception of the responses of others and not their

actual responses which shapes our self-image, and these perceptions are often inaccurate.

Mead and the generalized other The process of internalizing the attitudes of others has been aptly described by George Herbert Mead [1934, part 3, pp. 140–141] who developed the concept of "the generalized other." This "generalized other" is an individual's total impression of the judgments and expectations that other people have toward him. He then looks at himself as though he were another person and judges his actions and appearance according to these judgments of his "generalized other." This awareness of the "generalized other" is developed through the processes of "role taking" and "role playing." *Role taking* is an attempt to assume the behavior of a person in another behavior situation or role. (The concept of role will be more fully explained in Chapter 6.) In childrens' play, there is much role taking, as they "play house" ("You be the mama and I'll be the papa and you be the little baby"), play cops and rob-

TABLE 3

Self-conception as related to perceived and actual group response

Characteristic	Number of groups in which subjects' self-conceptions were closer to their perceptions of group response	Number of groups in which subjects' self-conceptions were closer to actual group response
Intelligence	8	2
Self-confidence	9	0(1 tie)
Physical attractiveness	10	0
Likeableness	7	3

Source: S. Frank Miyamoto and Sanford M. Dornbusch, "A Test of Interactionist Hypothesis of Self-Conception," American Journal of Sociology, 61:399–403, March, 1956. (The "1 tie" shown in the table means that in one of the ten test groups, the replies were so evenly divided that this group could not be placed in either column.)

bers, play with dolls, etc. *Role playing* is acting out the behavior of a role one actually holds (as when the boy and girl *become* papa and mama), whereas in role taking one only pretends to hold the role.

Our self-image is shaped by what we think others think of us.

Mead sees a three-stage process through which one learns to play adult roles. First, there is a preparatory stage (1–3 years) in which the child imitates adult behavior without any real understanding (as when the little girl cuddles her doll, then uses it as a club to strike her brother). Next comes the play stage (3–4 years) when children have some understanding of the behavior, but switch roles erratically. One moment the boy is a builder, piling blocks upon one another, and a moment later he knocks them apart; or at one moment he is a policeman and a moment later an astronaut. Finally comes the game stage (4–5 years and beyond) where role behavior becomes consistent and purposeful, with an ability to sense the role of the other players. To play baseball, each player must internalize his own role as well as the role of all the other players. Thus through child play, one develops an ability to see his own behavior in its relation to others, and to sense the reaction of the other persons involved.

It is through this awareness of others' roles, feelings, and values that the *generalized other* takes form in our minds. This generalized other is roughly equated with the standards or values of the community. By repeatedly "taking the role of the generalized other," one develops his concept of self—of the kind of person he is—as he repeatedly applies the judgments of this generalized other to his own actions. A failure to develop this capacity to adopt another's point of view (to take the role of another) seems to cripple personality development. Chandler [1970] tested a group of delinquent boys and found them to be several years retarded in their role-taking abilities. After several weeks of an "actor's workshop" in which each boy took all the roles in succession (aggressor, victim, arresting officer, judge), the boys gained several years in their role-taking skills. This supports Mead's theory that role taking is an essential learning process in socialization.

Other scholars have added the concept of the *significant other*. The significant other is the person whose approval we desire and whose direction we accept. As Woelfel and Haller [1971, p. 75] define the concept, "significant others are those persons who exercise major influence over the attitudes of individuals." These might be parents, admired teachers, certain playmates, and perhaps certain popular celebrities. The concept of the significant other and of the reference group have much in common, except that significant others are individuals, while reference groups are groups.

Two very popular terms which reflect one's sense of self are *identity* and *self-respect*. Identity is a sense of being a unique individual, distinct from all others, or of being part of a unique group, differing from other groups in ways which this group values. Thus the "search for identity" among black Americans today involves the effort to establish a "black" cultural heritage, distinct from those elements of "white" culture which blacks have absorbed. The problem in establishing a satisfactory sense of identity is that the individual or group needs to be distinguished by characteristics which carry prestige in the eyes of his generalized other. Often people are assigned an identity on a basis of race, nationality, religion, or occupation, and these characteristics of theirs may carry low prestige in the eyes of those who "count." Hence the person or group engages in a vigorous (but sometimes futile) struggle to find a more prestigious identity which is more highly respected by others and consequently by themselves [Merrill, 1957]. The feeling of self-respect is also socially determined. One's ability to respect himself is dependent on his perception of how he is rated by others, especially the others whom he considers important. The man whose interpretation of the generalized other leads him to perceive a favorable reaction to his own personality will develop a sense of self-respect. Otherwise he is likely to turn on himself, lack self-respect, and regard himself as unworthy and deficient.

Freud and the antisocial self Our treatment thus far implies a basic harmony between the self and society. In the words of Cooley:

A separate individual is an abstraction unknown to experience. . . . In other words "society" and "individuals" do not denote separate phenomena but are simply collective and distributive aspects of the same thing. . . . And just as there is no society or group that is not a collective view of persons, so there is no individual who may not be regarded as a particular view of social groups. He has no separate existence; through both the hereditary and the social factors in his life a man is bound into the whole of which he is a member, and to consider him apart from it is quite as artificial as to consider society apart from individuals. (*Charles Horton Cooley*, The Nature of Human Nature, *Charles Scribner's Sons, New York, 1902, pp. 1–3.*)

This concept of the socialized self was challenged by Freud, who saw no identity of self and society. Freud believed that the rational portion of human conduct was like the visible portion of an iceberg, with the larger part of human motivation resting in the unseen, unconscious forces which powerfully affect human conduct. He divided the self into three parts: the id, the superego, and the ego. The *id* is the pool of instinctive and unsocialized desires and impulses, selfish and antisocial; the *superego* is the complex of social ideals and values which one has internalized and which form his conscience; the *ego* is the conscious and rational part of the self which oversees the restraint of the id by the superego. Since society restricts the expression of aggression, sexual desire, and other impulses, the id is continually at war with the superego. The id is usually repressed, but at times it breaks through in open defiance of the superego, creating a burden of guilt that is difficult for the self to carry. At other times the forces of the id find expression in disguised forms which enable the ego to be unaware of the real underlying reasons for its actions, as when a parent relieves his aggressions by beating his child, believing that this is "for his own good." Thus Freud finds that the self and society are often opponents, and not merely different expressions of the same phenomena. He asserts,

If civilization imposes such great sacrifices not only on man's sexuality but upon his aggressivity we can understand better why it is hard for him to be happy in that civilization. . . .

We may expect gradually to carry through such alterations in our civilization as will better satisfy our needs and will escape our criticisms. But perhaps we may also familiarize ourselves with the idea that there are difficulties attaching to the nature of civilization which will not yield to any attempt at reform. . . .

In all that follows I adopt the standpoint, therefore, that the inclination to aggression is an original, self-subsisting instinctual disposition in man, and I return to my view that this constitutes the greatest impediment to civilization. (*Sigmund Freud*, Civilization and Its Discontents, Standard Edition of the Complete Psychological Works of Sigmund Freud, *vol. 21, The Hogarth Press, Ltd., London, 1962, pp. 115, 122. Quoted by permission.*)

Freud's theories have inspired bitter controversies, rival "schools," and numerous interpretations and revisions. His concepts represent ways of looking at personality rather than actual entities which can be verified through specific experiments. There is no simple empirical test which can be used to determine whether the superego, ego, and id are the best possible concepts to use in describing the component parts of the human personality. As our understanding of human nature grows, we may expect to develop additional forms of analysis which will relegate Freud's concepts to the status of pioneering ventures rather than ultimate truths. But the fact that theories are subject to revision and modification does not lessen the importance of their contribution. Most social scientists today agree that Freud was probably right in his claim that human motives are largely unconscious and beyond rational control, and do not always harmonize with the needs of an orderly society.

While Cooley and Mead describe the development of the self in somewhat different terms, their theories complement rather than oppose each other. Both contradict Freud in that they see self and society as two aspects of the same reality, while Freud sees self and society in eternal conflict. But all see the self as a social product, shaped and molded by the society.

Multiple groups and socialization In a complex society, one's group experience is not always consistent and harmonious. All complex societies have many groups with differing and sometimes opposing standards. The individual is presented with models of behavior which are rewarded at one time and condemned at another, or approved by some groups and criticized by others. Thus the boy learns that he should be tough and able to "stand up for his rights" and at the same time that he should be orderly, considerate, and respectful. Some people caution the girl that society demands modesty and maidenly reserve, while others show how a bold, provocative approach is rewarded. In a society where the individual participates in a number of groups, often with conflicting standards and values, he must work out some way of dealing with these opposing pressures. Failure to do so is likely to bring personal maladjustment and even mental illness. He may deal with this problem by compartmentalizing his life, developing a different "self" for each group in which he moves. Or he may select a favorite reference group to conform to and have his real life within, rejecting other groups, as in the case below:

"Thirteen arrests." The judge shook his head over my file. "Gang fightings, shootings, burglary, stealing a car . . . I don't know what to make of you. Your parents are hardworking, religious people in pretty good circumstances. Your IQ is extraordinarily high. Why do you do these things?

I shrugged. What a dumb question. Every boy I knew did these things. Maybe I just did more of them and better. ("*A Gang Leader's Redemption,*" Life, *Apr. 28, 1958, pp. 69ff.*)

This boy had adopted the standards of a delinquent peer group rather than those of his family. Research studies [Warner and Lunt, 1941, p. 351; Rosen, 1955b] have usually emphasized the power of the peer group to cultivate behavior patterns contrary to those of the family. Not all youth, however, are as firmly wedded to peer-group standards, and not all peer groups are as much in conflict with family or the society. Most youths find their principal extra-family group allegiance in athletic teams, church youth groups, neighborhood clubs, or youth cliques which are in harmony with the standards of adult society. Such groups frequently operate to support the parental standards (including what many would call snobbishness), as seen in this case:

Bill was a late adolescent who began to run around with a girl who not only lived on the other side of the railroad tracks, but who had most of the traits associated with that oft-used phrase. Bill's family was upper class, Bill was personally most attractive, and his mother knew the power of a peer group. Calling Bill to her, she explained with disarming friendliness that she had heard of his new girl and wanted to meet her. Wouldn't he bring her to the house, and to make it less formal, she would invite a few of his favorite friends. Upon securing Bill's wondering and semireluctant consent, the mother proceeded to promote, secretly, a gala event, to which she invited all of Bill's extended clique. Bill's relations with the new girl just barely survived until the end of the party. (*James H. S. Bossard,* The Sociology of Child Development, *Harper & Row, Publishers, Incorporated, 1948, p. 507.*)

Why do some youths select peer groups which generally support the socially approved adult values while others choose peer groups which are at war with adult society? The choice seems to be related to self-image. The habitual delinquent is usually one who sees himself as unloved, unworthy, unable, unaccepted, unappreciated; he joins with other such deprived youth in a delinquent peer group which reinforces and sanctions his resentful, aggressive behavior. The law-abiding youth sees himself as loved, worthy, able, accepted, appreciated; he joins with other such youth in a conforming peer group which reinforces socially approved behavior. Truly, seeing is behaving. How we see ourselves is how we behave.

Unique experience and personality

Why is it that children raised in the same family are so different from one another, even though they have had the same ex-

periences? The point is that they have *not* had the same experiences; they have had social experiences which are similar in some respects and different in others. Each child enters a different family unit. One is the firstborn; he is the only child until the arrival of the second, who has an older brother or sister to fight with, and so on. Parents change and do not treat all their children exactly alike. The children enter different peer groups, may have different teachers, and survive different incidents. Identical twins, in addition to having identical heredity, come very close to having the same experience. They enter a family together, often have the same peer groups, and are treated more nearly alike by other people; yet even twins do not share *all* incidents and experiences. *Each person's experience is unique in that nobody else perfectly duplicates it.* A detailed inventory of the daily experiences of the several children in the same family will reveal an impressive number of differences. So each child (excepting identical twins) has a unique biological inheritance, exactly duplicated by no one, and a unique set of life experiences, exactly duplicated by no one.

Furthermore, *experiences do not simply add up; they integrate.* Personality is not built by piling one incident upon another, like a brick wall. The meaning and impact of an experience depends upon the other experiences which have preceded it. When a popular girl is "stood up" by her date, this is not the same experience for her as it is for the wallflower. Psychoanalysis claims that certain incidents in one's experience are crucial because they color one's reaction to all later experience. "Psychological" movies often imply that psychoanalysis consists of probing into one's unconscious and dredging up *the* traumatic experience which caused all the trouble. This is a gross oversimplification. No woman has had her personality blighted *because* papa stomped on her dollie when she was five. But it is possible that such a traumatic episode might become the beginning of a series of mutual rejection experiences and thus color the meaning of a great many later experiences. This means that each person's experience is an infinitely complicated network of millions of incidents, each gaining its meaning and impact from all those which have preceded it. Small wonder that personality is complex!

Still another factor appears in the selection of roles to play within the family. Children imitate each other a great deal, but they also strive for separate identities. Younger children often reject those activities which their older siblings already do well and seek recognition through other activities. Parents may unwittingly aid this selection process. Mother may say, "Susie is mama's little helper, but I guess Annie is going to be a tomboy," whereupon Susie starts clearing the table while Annie turns a few handsprings. Sometimes a child in a well-behaved family selects the "bad boy" role, and scowls impressively while his parents describe their problem to the visitors. In large families a child may be hard pressed to find a role which has not already been annexed by an older sibling. Thus, in these and many other respects, each person's life experience is unique—unique in that nobody else has had exactly this set of experiences, and unique in that nobody else has the same background of experience upon which each new incident will impinge and from which it will draw its meaning.

Dynamics of the self

As already hinted, a person's self-image is a highly active factor in his behavior. There is a great deal of research showing how self-image affects task performance. For example, the famous study *Equality of Educational Opportunity* [Coleman, 1966, pp. 319–325] found that the most important variable associated with school learning was the child's self concept and sense of control over his environment—that is, the child's feeling that his efforts would make a difference. Effective teaching in school, plant, or army rests upon building the learner's confidence that he *can* do it! Conversely, the lack of a satisfactory self-image nearly always cripples learning or task performance, and often leads to antisocial or delinquent behavior [Schwartz and Tangri, 1965]. In fact, a great deal of behavior, ranging from mildly annoying habits like bragging and "knowing-it-all" to serious neuroses and delinquencies can be viewed as desperate efforts to repair an intolerable image of the self. Truly, the image of the self lies at the core of one's behavior system.

SUMMARY

Personality is one's total behavior tendency system. Our *heredity* gives us a set of needs and potentialities which other factors may channel and develop; our *physical environment* is relatively unimportant in personality development; our *culture* provides certain fairly uniform experiences for all members of our society; our *group experience* develops personality similarities within groups and differences between groups; the *unique experience* of each person shapes his individuality.

The normal personality differs dramatically from society to society, as is shown by the suspicious, treacherous, insecure Dobuan and the amiable, secure, cooperative Zuñi. Each society develops a normal personality, produced by the total experience of a person raised in the society. Such cultural influences include the norms of the culture, the ideal personality types presented as models, and many other kinds of experience. All these influences tend to develop a *modal personality* type for the society.

The more complex societies may have a number of subcultures, each developing its characteristic personality and reducing the overall uniformity of personality within the culture. Even in the simpler societies, there is no complete uniformity in personality; only a minority of the members share all the traits of the modal personality. In complex societies, the variation in personality is still greater.

Socialization requires group experience, and *social isolates* fail to develop a normal human personality. Socialization is heavily centered upon the development of the concept of *self*. Cooley saw a person forming his image of the self—the *looking-glass self*—in the "looking glass" of other peoples' reactions to him, and his feelings about those reactions. Mead emphasized *role taking* in child play as the learning process whereby one becomes aware of the feelings of others. Through applying the standards of this *generalized other* to his own actions, one develops an image of self. Freud saw the self as composed of unsocialized inborn impulses (the *id*) restrained by a socially acquired conscience (the *superego*) while the conscious or rational part of the self (the

ego) sought to keep a balance between id and superego. Cooley and Mead viewed the self and society as two aspects of the same thing, whereas Freud viewed the self as basically antisocial, with most personality difficulties arising from the clash between the impulses of the self and the restraints of society.

In a complex culture with many kinds of groups, one may have difficulty in developing a satisfactory self-image and an integrated system of behavior. One may resolve this problem by compartmentalizing his life and acting differently in each group, or by conforming to one group while, if possible, ignoring any others whose standards conflict with those of that one group. Failure to do either may bring confusion and maladjustment. While there are common elements in the experience of all men and even more in the experience of men within a particular society, each man is still unique. Thus each man is socialized in such a way that his personality is at the same time much like that of others in his society and yet unique.

Questions and projects

1. How do we know that personality is not simply the maturing and unfolding of inherited tendencies?

2. What might be some possible differences in social life and human personality if human infants were normally born (and nursed) in litters instead of one at a time?

3. It has been said that a person raised in one culture may learn to act like people in an adopted culture, but will never be able to think and feel like a person of his adopted culture. Do you agree?

4. Suppose the Dobuans were visited by a person who persistently acted in a straightforward, trusting, confident manner. Tell why you believe they would, or would not:
a. Admire him
b. Copy him

c. Fear him
d. Pity him

5. If culture develops similarities in personality within a society, how do we explain personality differences within a society? Are such personality differences greater within a simple or a complex society? Why?

6. How would you explain the fact that groups which have a major socializing influence upon one person may leave another person in the same vicinity unaffected?

7. Can you recall a specific "looking-glass" incident in your experience? Write it up, describing your actions, others' reactions, your perception of their reactions, and your feelings about that perception. How do you think this incident affected you?

8. How is the self a social product?

9. How do games contribute to the development of the self?

10. Do you feel that Freud and Cooley are in basic disagreement on the nature of the self? Explain.

11. How can children in the same family develop such strikingly different personality traits?

12. Explain how a number of types of annoying people—braggart, bully, gossip, Casanova—may be seeking to repair an unsatisfactory self-image.

13. For slavery to be profitable, it was necessary for slaves to *feel* inferior and *feel* fit only to be slaves. How were slaves in the United States made to feel inferior? Why has the self-image of black people in the United States been changing?

14. Write an account of a typical day in your life, listing all the standardizing cultural influences which you have experienced along with nearly every other American, and state how you suspect each has helped to shape your personality.

15. Prepare an analysis of the behavior of "Yank," the fireman in Eugene O'Neill's *The Hairy Ape*. Is his behavior consistent with what this chapter outlines about others and the concept of self?

Suggested readings

*Benedict, Ruth: *Patterns of Culture*, Houghton Mifflin Company, Boston, 1934; Penguin Books, Inc., Baltimore, 1946. Shows how each culture develops a behavior and personality which is normal and useful for that society.

Berreman, Gerald D.: "Aleut Group Alienation, Mobility and Acculturation," *American Anthropologist*, 66:231–250, April, 1964. A comparison of Aleuts who became alienated from Aleutian culture with those who remain loyal to the Aleut membership group, and comments upon the difficulties of retaining loyalty to an original ethnic group while becoming acculturated to a new one.

Bronfenbrenner, Urie: "The Changing American Child—A Speculative Analysis," *Merrill-Palmer Quarterly of Behavior and Development*, 7:73–84, April, 1961; reprinted in **Thomas E. Lasswell, et al.**, *Life in Society*, Scott Foresman and Company, Chicago, 1965. Appraises the effect of cold war competition in stimulating a shift from socialization for conformity to socialization for achievement.

*Danziger, K. (ed.): *Readings in Child Socialization*, Pergamon Press, New York, 1970. Eleven empirical studies and two theoretical papers on socialization, written for the advanced student.

Eysenck, Hans J.: *The Biological Basis of Personality*, Charles C Thomas, Publisher, Springfield, Ill., 1967. A comprehensive, authoritative sum-mation of the evidence on the biological factor in personality.

Garabedian, Peter G.: "Socialization in the Prison Community," *Social Problems*, 2:139–152, Fall, 1963. How "square Johns" learn to become "right guys" according to the definition of prison inmates.

*Goffman, Irwin W.: *Presentation of Self in Everyday Life*, Social Science Research Center, University of Edinburgh, 1956; Anchor paperback, Doubleday & Company, Inc., Garden City, N.Y., 1959. A detailed picture of how the self emerges through everyday experiences.

Havighurst, Robert J., and Allison Davis: "A Comparison of the Chicago and Harvard Studies of Social Class Differences in Child Rearing," *American Sociological Review*, 20:438–442, August, 1955. Two separate studies show that cultural influences on personality development differ from one social-class subculture to another, and also differ by region, religion, and ethnic group within the same social class.

Kuhn, Manford: "Self-attitudes by Age, Sex, and Professional Training," *Sociological Quarterly*, 1:39–55, January, 1960; Bobbs-Merrill Company, Inc., reprint S-156. Exploration of self-attitudes by members of different social categories through use of the Twenty Questions Test.

Leznoff, Maurice, and William A. Westley: "The Homosexual Community," *Social Problems*, 3:257–264, April, 1956. Describes efforts of homosexuals in a Canadian city to organize a "third-sex" community.

*__Mead, Margaret, and Martha Wolfenstein (eds.):__ *Childhood in Contemporary Cultures*, The University of Chicago Press, Chicago, 1955. A number of studies of patterns of child development in different cultures.

Merrill, Francis E.: "The Self and the Other: An Emerging Field of Social Problems," *Social Problems*, 4:200–207, January, 1957. An analysis of anxiety over others' image of the self in a society stressing achieved status.

Role and status

How am I to pursue any course single mindedly when some way along the line a person I respect is sure to say, "You are on the wrong track and are wasting your time." Uncle John telephones every Sunday morning. His first question is, "Did you go out last night?" He would think me a "grind" if I were to stay home Saturday night and finish a term paper. My father expects me to get an "A" in every subject and is disappointed with a "B". He says I have plenty of time for social life. Mother says, "That 'A' in Philosophy is very nice, dear, but please don't become so deep that no man is good enough for you." And, finally, Aunt Mary's line is careers for women. "Prepare yourself for some profession. This is the only way to insure independence and an interesting life. You have plenty of time to marry." *(Excerpt from a student report quoted in Mirra Komarovsky, "Cultural Contradictions and Sex Roles,"* American Journal of Sociology, *52:185–186, November, 1946.)*

Status is usually defined as the *rank or position of an individual in a group,* or of a group in relation to other groups. (In fact, some sociologists use the term *position* instead of *status.) Role* is the *behavior expected of one who holds a certain status.* Children occupy a status usually subordinate to adults' and are expected to show some degree of deference to adult authority. Soldiers occupy a status different from that of civilians, and their role calls for risks and duties which the general populace is not expected to bear. Women have a different status from men (and one which some women are determined to change). Each person may occupy a number of statuses and be expected to perform the roles appropriate to them. In a sense, "status" and "role" are two aspects of the same phenomenon. A status is a set of privileges and duties; a role is the acting out of this set of duties and privileges.

The norms of the culture are learned mainly through learning roles. While a few norms apply to all members of a society, most norms vary according to the statuses we fill, for what is correct for one status is wrong for another. Socialization, the process of learning enough of the folkways and mores to become a part of the community, is largely a process of learning role behavior.

SOCIALIZATION
THROUGH ROLE AND STATUS

Each person must learn to fill roles as child, student, parent, employee, organization member or officer, member of a particular racial and social class, citizen, resident of a community, and many others. Role learning involves at least two aspects: (1) We must learn to perform the duties and claim the privileges of the role, and (2) we must acquire the attitudes, feelings, and expectations appropriate to the role. Of these two aspects the latter is often the more important. Almost any young woman who can read can learn the mechanical skills of housekeeping fairly quickly; what she cannot learn quickly are the attitudes and expectations which can make housekeeping a satisfying and rewarding activity. One cannot fill a role successfully unless he has been socialized to accept that role as worthwhile, satisfying, and appropriate for him.

Imagine the mental state of a young German Jew, raised in a prosperous, cultivated home, who graduated from medical school just as the Nazi government closed the professions to Jews; at best, he could work only as a menial and live only as an outcast. Or consider the difficulties of a woman who has been socialized to view the role of housewife as the only really rewarding role for a woman, but who finds herself an unmarried career girl living alone and competing in a man's world.

Role training for most of the important roles begins early in childhood as one starts to form attitudes toward those roles and statuses. Most of the role training is painless and unconscious. Children "play house,"

play with the toys given them, watch and help mother and father, hear and read stories, listen to family talk and share in the countless incidents of family life. From all this experience, they gradually form a picture of how men and women act, and of how husbands and wives treat each other.

Social roles and personality

The little child who assumes the role of his father while playing house is aware that he must think and act in a different manner than when he is simply acting out his own role, that of child. At first he may have little understanding of the reasons which underlie his father's actions, but this understanding grows and his "pretend" roles will help prepare him for the time when he actually becomes a father. At a more mature level "pretend" role taking has been a helpful aid in assisting people to understand the reactions of others in a diagnostic and therapeutic technique known as the *psychodrama*, developed by Moreno [1940] and others. A husband, for example, may take the role of the wife while she assumes his role as they reenact in an unrehearsed dialogue some recent discussion or conflict. As each tries to play the part of the other, voicing the other's complaints and defenses, each may gain greater insight into the other's feelings and reactions.

The concept of role implies a set of expectations both of the one's own behavior and of the reciprocal behavior by other people in the situation. Whether a new role is taken on a pretend basis or as a genuine result of acquiring a new status, the person is forced to analyze the attitudes and behavior of himself and of those about him [Turner, 1956]. Obviously the self does not remain unchanged after this kind of experience. The married woman is in a different status from that of the single girl. Her role is different and in many ways she will seem a different person. Occupational roles also produce personality changes, so that without knowing a person's occupation we may say that he "acts like" a teacher, a farmer, a businessman, or a minister. Personality and role have a reciprocal relationship in that certain personal characteristics favor or hinder the playing of social roles, while social roles in turn tend to develop the personal characteristics required. The extrovert, for instance, is a personality type who may find it easy to adjust to the role of salesman while, conversely, the daily routine of the salesman helps to develop an extroverted type of personality. Thus there is a constant interaction between role and personality.

ASCRIBED AND ACHIEVED STATUS

Statuses are of two sorts: those *ascribed* to us by our society, irrespective of individual qualities or efforts, and those we *achieve* through our own efforts [Linton, 1936, chap. 8].

Ascribed status and role

If a society is to function efficiently, people must perform a vast number of daily chores willingly and competently. The simplest way to ensure the performance is to parcel most of the routine work of the society into a series of *ascribed* roles, and socialize people to accept and fill their ascribed roles. Since role training must therefore begin early in childhood, ascribed roles must be assigned according to some criterion which can be known in advance. Sex and age are universally used as a basis of role ascription; race, nationality, social class, and religion are also used in many societies.

Ascription by sex Although role training may be largely unconscious, it is no less real. As a noted American educator has re-

marked, "Adults ask little boys what they want to be when they grow up. They ask little girls where they got that pretty dress." No wonder that by adolescence, boys are becoming concerned about careers while girls are preoccupied with baiting the man trap! This is no accident, since a major part of the socialization process consists of learning the separate activities of men and women. The little girl plays with dolls, helps mother in the housework, and is rewarded for being a "little lady," while learning that "tomboy" activities, though possibly tolerated, are not really "ladylike." The boy finds out that dolls are for girls and babies and that no worse fate can befall him than to be a "sissy." Many years of differential training, if successful, will bring boys and girls to maturity with great differences in their responses, feelings, and preferences.

In mature life, sex differentiation continues, while the process of role definition becomes ever more complicated. The woman finds that she may have to become an economic provider as well as mother and housekeeper and that she must do this without robbing her husband of his masculine ego feelings. She must be an informed citizen, an intelligent conversationalist, and an active community worker, yet not neglect her primary duties in the kitchen and nursery. She must be a seductive siren, skillful, patient, and responsive, but she must also be a chaste creature, modest and demure, feeling the stir of passion only toward her husband! She must be a skillful—but not *too* skillful—sportswoman, yet remain a feminine clinging vine. She must be a household purchasing agent, a business manager, and a financial consultant when necessary; at all other times she must be completely ignorant of money matters. Her total role as wife and mother thus includes many different roles, some of them inconsistent with one another. It is little wonder women often find it difficult to play this complex and paradoxical role.

Nor is assuming the masculine role a simple task. The little boy must not be a sissy, but on the other hand he must become a gentleman, and the line between often seems thin and tenuous. In mature life he may find himself sharing in household tasks while his wife is on the night shift. If he wishes social approval in many groups today, he finds that even the rugged male must profess an interest in the arts and take part in social life.

Every society handles many tasks by making them part of a sex role. Yet most of the sex-linked functions can be performed equally well by either men or women, provided they are socialized to accept the tasks as proper for them. Thus in Pakistan, men are the household servants; in the Philippines, pharmacists are usually women, while men are preferred as secretaries; in the Marquesas, baby tending, cooking, and housekeeping are proper male tasks, while women spend much of their time primping; in many parts of the world the heavy agricultural labor is performed by women.

The definition of masculine and feminine roles is subject to infinite variation, yet every society has an approved pattern which the people are expected to follow. Individuals may be permitted to bypass some parts of the pattern at times, but they risk alienation from the society unless they can identify themselves with the role expected of their sex. A few individuals do fail to make this adjustment and become homosexuals or Lesbians, which means that they deviate from the roles expected of their own sex. While such individuals may attempt to develop a unique status for a "third sex," the task is difficult and they usually become marginal to the culture. Only a few societies have developed an accepted status for homosexuals, for example, the Plains Indians, who consider the homosexual to be one who has been stricken by the gods and who thereby merits special consideration. In the majority of cases the homosexual is normal

physically, and his condition is now viewed as a failure of socialization in relation to sex roles rather than as some type of biological deviation. Even in the cases of hermaphrodites, who are biologically intermediate between the sexes, their biological "closeness" to one sex or the other is less important than the social definition of them as "boy" or "girl" by their family and others [Jones and Scott, 1958, p. 49].

The influence of sex as a role determinant is under reappraisal at present, as seen in the popularity of long hair for men, unisex clothing styles which minimize sexual distinctiveness, the opening of sexually segregated schools such as Yale and Vassar to coeducation, and the insistence that men should share in household duties, while women are equally entitled to a career. Even dating behavior is said to be changing, with girls taking the aggressive role previously reserved for men (Winick, 1968, pp. 18–24).

Many of the considerations which presumably underlay our ascribed sex roles are themselves changing today. The assumption of vast innate sex differences in intellect and aptitude has been discredited. Greater dependability and availability of contraception and abortion has weakened the rationale for a "double standard" of sexual behavior. Declining family size means that women spend less time in child bearing and care. The shift from human to machine power means that greater masculine physical strength becomes less important. The Womens' Liberation Movement is demanding a wholesale overhaul of sex role ascription (see Chapter 21). No one doubts that men and women will continue to be different in recognizable ways, but current developments are narrowing the differences in their ascribed roles and opening more achieved roles to women.

Ascription by age Each society also ascribes different roles according to age. The adjustment of age status is a perennial task; almost as soon as a person adjusts to one age level, he enters another with different status and role. Just at the time when the youth is beginning to master the bewildering complexities of adolescence, he finds himself facing the responsibilities of adult life. And although the adult period is the longest single time span, retirement and old age often seem to come just when one has begun to reach a position where he can fully exploit his mature power. Each age period brings different opportunities and responsibilities, which is to say that each period affords a new status and requires the learning of new roles. At any age one may have trouble in adjusting to new status and role demands. The child who is "old before his time" is one who has reached for adult status before fully realizing the potential of his childhood roles; on the other hand, the immature adult represents an attempt to combine adult status with attitudes and behavior appropriate to childhood or adolescence.

In American society the socialization process is conspicuously inefficient in preparing for adolescence and for old age. In most primitive societies the adolescent period is not marked by any unusual stress. At any given age in most primitive societies, the individual has a clearly defined status and role; he, and everyone else, knows exactly what his duties and privileges are. Our society has no clearly defined age statuses, except for the relatively minor legal maturity at twenty-one, which, adding still greater confusion, is now rapidly changing to eighteen. The American youth and his parents have no standardized set of duties and privileges to guide them. Parents are uncertain about just how much "maturity" to concede to him, and they bicker with him endlessly about his choice of companions, the hours he keeps, his use of money, the use of the car, and whether he is old enough to marry. In most primitive societies the adolescent enters a period of training which ends in an elaborate cere-

mony, in which he may endure ordeals or submit to circumcision, tattooing, or scarification. Such ceremonies, called "rites of passage," establish his status and announce that the youth is now ready to assume adult responsibilities, and his successful role performance is almost guaranteed. Our closest equivalents are found in such events as confirmation or first Communion, getting a driver's license, holding a full-time job, graduating from high school or college, and getting married. Yet we lack any systematic preparation, or any general agreement upon the age, achievement, or type of ceremony which clearly establishes the transition into adult status.

The youth in most primitive societies (before white contacts disorganized them) had few painful choices to make. He had little freedom, but little anxiety. There were no competing religious groups, political parties, or social clubs. Since occupations were limited, the youth escaped conflicting advice on the type of career he should choose. Religion, government, social activities, educational training, and occupation—all these were traditional and clearly defined. By contrast the American youth learns that there are many different churches and that he may select from, or even reject them all; his political views, if any, often conflict with those of his parents; he must choose between continuing school and the instant pleasures of a car and spending money; in earning a living a young man must choose among thousands of occupations. With so many alternatives, it is small wonder that many youths vacillate wildly before settling down or that others make decisions contrary to their parents' hopes and dreams.

The transition to middle age is not a happy one in our society, especially for women. Our accent on youth and glamour dooms every woman to feel her desirability slipping away from her. The menopause is a relentless announcement that youth, glamour, and romance are over; instead, she can become "matronly." Plastic surgeons, cosmeticians, and beauticians make fortunes by catering to women's futile efforts to stave off the ravages of time. We suspect that many of the physical and emotional difficulties that sometimes accompany the menopause are due to this painful role transition. And for men, the middle years are rightfully called the "dangerous age," when they are notoriously prone to reckless romantic adventures.

Old age in many primitive or traditional societies is highly honored, perhaps because in such a society the ancient are closest to the source of hallowed tradition. Thus in pre-Communist China the grandmother was the reigning female in a multiple-family home, and the grandfather was a patriarch whose whim was close to law. In contemporary industrialized society old age is a nuisance. A rapidly changing society seldom looks to its aged for guidance, for people who were socialized two generations ago are likely to be behind the times. The compulsory retirement-at-age-sixty-five system is an expedient way of discarding the fossils. Three-generation households are scarce, and where they exist the aged are likely to be dutifully tolerated rather than revered as heads of the household. The role of the aged is a retirement in which their income is reduced, their responsibilities withdrawn, and their influence undermined; their main function in life is to divert themselves while waiting to die. The unhappy position of our aged illustrates the fact that a role transition is difficult when the characteristics which one develops in one role may become useless or even troublesome as he moves into the next role.

Among the Plains Indians, the warriors were trained from childhood to become aggressive, hostile, and uncompromising; then upon retirement from warrior to "old man" status, they were expected to be placid peacemakers. This called for an abrupt reversal in personality, and few of them could make the transition gracefully. An equally painful transition is demanded in our society. To be successful in the active adult role, one must develop independence and self-reliance, must learn to find satisfaction in useful work, and in being adviser and protector of the young. As an aged person, he must become dependent and submissive, able to respect himself with no useful work to do, and must learn to keep his advice to himself while being ignored or patronized by the young. Is it any wonder that many of our old people sicken and die soon after retirement, while many others become bored and fretful? The rapidly developing field of *geriatrics* indicates a serious concern with this topic, and the picture may change in the future. One such change is emphasis on the development of hobbies and activities that may be expanded on retirement, since they are not associated with either the family or the job. Another trend is the growth of specialized facilities which may provide pleasant living in a society segregated on an age basis. These include housing, either in rest homes or specially designed apartments; recreation centers, often given some name such as the Golden Years Club; or even the development of an entire village as a living place for retired people, such as Ryderwood, near Longview, Washington. These trends are already changing the status of elderly people, but at present their role involves difficult adjustments at a time of life when such adjustments are not easy to make.

Sex and age are only two of many examples of ascribed status. All such statuses involve roles which can be filled successfully only when one has been socialized to expect and appreciate the role.

We may today have developed a form of quasi-ascription through our trend towards *meritocracy*. A meritocracy is a social system in which status is assigned according to merit, and merit is most commonly measured by scores on standardized tests which control access to educational programs and occupational roles. Whether such tests are classified as means of role ascription or of role achievement depends upon the degree to which the scores are affected by conscious effort after one has passed the stage of early childhood. If one assumes that these scores are reasonably stable for an individual, then the result is a kind of caste system in which test scores, largely dependent upon heredity and early environment, may shape one's entire life. This means that a new type of ascribed status has developed, not directly dependent upon the status of one's ancestors, but perhaps equally rigid.

Achieved status and role

A social position which is secured through individual choice and competition is known as *achieved status*. Just as each person occupies a number of ascribed statuses, assigned without regard to individual ability or preference, so he occupies a number of achieved statuses which are secured through his ability, performance, and possibly good or ill fortune. The difference is aptly stated by Young and Mack:

"Princess" is an ascribed status; where there is a hereditary royalty a girl does not work her way up to being princess. She is *born* a princess, and whether she is pretty or ugly, tall or short, intelligent or stupid, a princess she remains. *Achieved statuses*, on the other hand, are not assigned at birth, but are left open to be filled by the persons who compete more successfully for them. Being male is an ascribed status. It is determined at birth; either you are male or you are not. Being a husband is an achieved status; it does not result automatically from one's being born a male but depends upon a male's own behavior in the future. Negro is an ascribed status. One cannot change his color to white. But policeman is an achieved status. One is not born a policeman; he becomes one through his own talent or choice or action. (*Kimball Young and Raymond W. Mack*, Sociology and Social Life, *American Book Company, New York, 1959, pp. 160-161.*)

Being a husband is an achieved status.

In traditional societies most statuses are ascribed, with one's occupation and general social standing determined at birth. Industrialized societies have a greater range of occupations, require a greater mobility of labor, and allow greater scope for the individual to change his status through his own efforts. The society stressing achieved status will gain in flexibility and its ability to place people in occupations best suited to their talents. The price it pays for these advantages is seen in the insecurity of those unable to "find themselves" and in the strain of constant adjustment to new roles. Achieved status requires the individual to make choices, not only of occupation but also of friends, organizations, schools, and place of residence. Further, it leads the individual into roles which were not foreseen or desired by his parents. In the traditional society, where statuses and roles are ascribed, the individual is trained from childhood and guided through life by rules of conduct which he has carefully learned in preparation for the roles he is destined to play. In a changing society where he is free to experiment, the individual meets situations far removed from the parental way of life and may have to feel his way awkwardly into unfamiliar roles.

Ascribed and achieved statuses are basically different; yet they interact with each other and may overlap. Thus it is easier for one with the ascribed status of male to reach the achieved status of President of the United States than it is for the one with the ascribed status of female. The achieved status of physician is open to both black and white, but in the United States whites reach it more easily than blacks. General social standing in the community (social-class status) is partly ascribed, reflecting the status of one's parents, and partly achieved through one's own accomplishments. At many points the boundaries between achieved and ascribed status are indistinct; yet the concepts are useful.

Psychic costs of achieved status

The ideal of the society which permits most statuses to be achieved is to place people according to their abilities. To some extent, this effort enables the highly talented to move upward, but it also destroys the alibi of the failures. In a society where most status is ascribed, the individual is not expected to improve his lot. He who receives low rewards and little prestige does not feel any guilt in occupying the lowly position in which society has placed him. He is taught that his role and status are right and proper. He can take pride in his accomplishments without any need to compare them with those of persons in other statuses. He is freed from the sense of insecurity, the nagging of ambition, or the sting of failure. Socialization is eased because he is not expected to change his status; he has only to learn and accept his social roles.

It is difficult to rationalize low status if hereditary barriers are removed and posi-

tions are open to all on the basis of ability. If positions are filled on competitive examinations and if adequate schooling is free to everybody, then the reason for low status must be incompetence, and this is not a comfortable explanation. The low-caste person in India could blame his status on the inexorable laws of the universe; the American university student who fails to graduate is hard put to find a similar justification. In self-defense the mediocre generally support the attempt to limit achievement by the imposition of seniority rules, group quotas, veterans' preference, and similar techniques.

Achieved status makes maximum provision for the attainment of roles on the basis of individual ability. It provides a high degree of choice and flexibility at the cost of psychic insecurity for the individual who has limited talents or has unequal opportunity to develop and employ them. The roles which accompany achieved statuses may be difficult to learn and mutually conflicting. In essence the achieved status probably represents both the most efficient use of the human potential and the greatest threat to the individual's peace of mind.

Status inconsistency

Each person holds a number of statuses at the same time, and some of them may be incompatible with the others. This conflict is called by several terms which are used more or less interchangeably by sociologists: *status inconsistency, status incongruity,* and *status discrepancy.* While some sociologists attempt to draw a distinction between these terms, any of them may be used to refer to *any kind of disparity between a person's several statuses.* One of his statuses may have more prestige than the others, as in the case of the poverty-stricken nobleman who sells real estate or opens a haberdashery. Or, the statuses may be socially defined as inappropriately linked; for example, when a person has an uncle who is younger than he is, or a nephew who is older, his age and kinship statuses are inconsistent. Any deviation from customary age relationships is regarded as status inconsistency. A teen-aged President is an impossibility under our Constitution, older people who marry part-ners young enough to be their children are criticized, and a ribald cynicism awaits the old man who proudly announces the birth of a child.

Another kind of status inconsistency is that in which a person is not accorded the status which he feels that he deserves. The new rich may fail to gain acceptance among aristocrats; the honorably discharged vet-eran, home from Vietnam, has been too young to buy a beer in many states; the Doc-tor of Chiropractic craves, but is denied, the status of Doctor of Medicine. Ethnic minori-ties and women often find that their ascribed status limits both their access to achieved sta-tuses and their rewards if they can surmount the obstacles. The prosperous Jew who can-not join the country club and the brilliant professional woman who is patronized by men are enduring the results of status in-consistency. One whose statuses are consist-ently low may be able to accept low status, but one who ranks high in some statuses and low in others is likely to feel that he is wronged when judged by his low rather than by his high-ranking statuses [Lenski, 1967, p. 298].

Several studies have been made of the be-havior of people with statuses which are generally perceived by others as inconsist-ent [Lenski, 1954; Mitchell, 1964; Treiman, 1966; Kelly and Chambliss, 1966; Broom and Jones, 1970], but there is no definite agreement upon the kind of behavioral re-sponse which can be expected. Perhaps this is because a person caught in the bind of status inconsistency may pursue either of two mutually contradictory courses of ac-tion. Since he is partially excluded from the desired status, he may identify with the

lower status group and take upon himself the attitudes and behavior of this group. He may thus be able to gain leadership in this group and then demand a degree of defer-ence from the rest of society. History tells of many who exacted a tribute as revolutionary leaders which they were denied as would-be members of the establishment. The colonial national in Asia and Africa who obtained a good job but was denied social recognition often became a nationalist leader of the in-dependence movement, just as the Womens' Liberation Movement today is almost en-tirely composed of educated women who re-ject the docile-housewife role as insulting.

A different reaction to status inconsist-ency is to deny any linkage to the undesired status, but to identify with the symbols of the desired status even more rigidly than those who have long enjoyed them without question. The new rich, whose humble an-cestry or ethnic origin inhibits his social acceptance, often indulges in ostentatious spending to prove his wealth, and may sup-port reactionary politics to prove his ideo-logical identity with the bastions of privilege —a process long noted among Texas oil millionaires. The immigrant who "made good" may change his name to hide ethnic identity and reduce his contacts with those of his own ancestry. One holding incon-sistent statuses may seek to reduce stress by identifying with either the lower or the higher aspects of his status characteristics, but one way or another, the situation affects his status definition and role behavior.

Role behavior

While a *role* is the behavior *expected* of one in a particular status, *role behavior* is the *actual* behavior of one who plays a role. Ac-tual role behavior may vary from expected behavior for a number of reasons: differ-ences of interpretation, personality char-acteristics which alter a role pattern, variations in degree of commitment to a given role, and possible conflict with other roles—all of which combine in such a way that no two individuals play a given role in exactly the same way. Not all soldiers are brave, not all priests are saintly, nor are all professors models of scholarly rectitude. There is enough diversity in role-behavior performance to give variety to human life, yet there is enough uniformity and predictability in role behavior to carry on the work of organizations even though the personnel is constantly changing.

While much role behavior is the unconscious playing of roles to which one has been socialized, some role behavior is a highly conscious, studied effort to project a desired image of the self. The concept of *dramatic role presentation* refers to a conscious effort to play a role in a manner which will create a desired impression among others. Conduct is regulated not only according to functional role requirements but also according to what the audience expects. Few of us will ever be movie stars, but everyone is an actor with a wide variety of audiences. The children in the home, the neighbors, the office force, fellow students in a school—all these, and many others, form audiences. As Goffman [1959, 1967] has noted, we put on a presentation of ourselves when the audience is present, acting out roles so that we give a dramatic picture of the self. The debutante making a grand entrance at a party, the policeman controlling traffic, the salesman making a pitch, the father lecturing his children, the tough guy on the playground —everyone at some time and place is essentially an actor putting on a presentation for the sake of the impression he makes on the audience. Sometimes the presentation becomes a group operation with everyone playing a supporting role as in the following example from a shipyard, where such impromptu "acting" began

"whenever word got around that the foreman was on the hull or in the shop or that a front office superintendent was coming by. Quarterman and leadermen would rush to their groups of workers and stir them to obvious activity. "Don't let him catch you sitting down", was the universal admonition, and where no work existed a pipe was busily bent and threaded or a bolt which was already in place was subjected to further and unnecessary tightening. This was the formal tribute invariably attending a visitation by the boss, and its conventions were as familiar to both sides as those surrounding a five-star general's inspection. To have neglected any detail of the false and empty show would have been interpreted as a mark of singular disrespect. (*Katherine Archibald*, Wartime Shipyard, *University of California Press, Berkeley, 1947, p. 159.*)

Role sets

The term *role set* is used to indicate that a status may have not just a single role, but a number of associated roles which function together [Merton, 1957, p. 369]. A wife, for example, relates not only to her husband but also to her children, to relatives, to neighbors, to her husband's business associates and probably to other parents in the Parent-Teacher Association or similar groups. Thus her role set involves a constellation of related roles, some of which may require drastically different types of adjustment. It is not uncommon for people to find that they fail to operate equally well in all aspects of their role set. The woman who is a charming social companion may be poor as a housewife, the teacher who enthralls a classroom may antagonize his fellow teachers, and the businessman who charms his customers may alienate his labor force.

ROLE STRAIN, ROLE CONFLICT, AND ROLE FAILURE

It would be ideal if each person could fill all roles in a role set with equal ease, but few people are able to do this. *Role strain* refers to *the difficulty people have in meeting their role obligations.* Role strain may arise through inadequate role preparation, role conflict, or role failure.

Inadequate role preparation

The little girl singing lullabies to her doll, the small boy building a model airplane, the maiden filling her hope chest, the apprentice copying the work techniques of the master craftsmen—all these are experiencing a *continuity of socialization* by learning skills and attitudes at one period of life which they can use at another. By continuity in socialization we simply mean that the experiences at each life stage are an effective preparation for the next stage. An example of how continuity in the socialization process provides a smooth transition into the adult role is seen in the child-training practices of the Cheyenne Indians, as described by Benedict.

The essential point of such child training is that the child is from infancy continously conditioned to responsible social participation while at the same time the tasks that are expected of it are adapted to its capacity. . . . At birth the little boy was presented with a toy bow and from the time he could run about servicable bows suited to his stature were specially made for him by the man of the family. Animals and birds were taught him in a graded series beginning with those most easily taken, and as he brought in his first of each species his family duly made a feast of it, accepting his contribution as gravely as the buffalo his father brought. When he finally killed a buffalo, it was only the final step of his childhood conditioning, not a new adult role with which his childhood experience has been at variance. (*Ruth Benedict, "Continuities and Discontinuities in Cultural Conditioning,"* Psychiatry, *1:161–167, May, 1938.*)

Such an easy transition from one status to the next is by no means universal. Our culture is characterized by built-in *discontinuities*, which make the socialization experience in one age period of little use in the next. In frontier America, boys and girls learned their adult roles by simply observing and taking part in whatever was going on around them—clearing land, planting crops, caring for babies, and so on. Today there is less opportunity for such continuity. Most adult male work is performed away from home, where boys and youths cannot watch and share it. Many households offer only a poor opportunity for a girl to learn the skills, attitudes, and emotional rewards of the housewife. Children and youths have few important tasks in most households, and much of the child's play activity is not closely related to adult tasks and responsibilities. Our maidens find that when they have internalized the roles of glamour girl and career woman as presented in magazines and movies, they are suddenly enveloped in maternity and housekeeping duties for which their previous experience has done little to prepare them. Then when they have become adapted to the housewife role, their children leave home, their housekeeping responsibilities diminish, and they must either face a late middle age of limited activity or transfer to roles much different from those they have known. When men reach the age of sixty-five they are apt to find that a life dominated by work has not prepared them for the leisure which comes with retirement.

Another imperfection in our socialization process is that the moral training of boys and girls introduces them mainly to the *formal* rules of social behavior rather than to the informal modifications of these rules which operate in the adult world. In other words, they are taught the ideal, not the real culture. The result is that young people become cynical as they find that the copybook maxims do not work out. The politician does not appear to be a public servant who negotiates a livable adjustment between bitter opponents, but a man who compromises on sacred principles; the businessman seems a greedy manipulator rather than an individual struggling to find his place in the market; the clergyman is apparently not one who mediates the ways of God to man, but a huckster who fails to live up to the ideals the church proclaims. Thus many young people graduate from a naive idealism directly into a naive cynicism without ever reaching an appreciation of the services of those who work out livable compromises with the unsolved problems of society.

Our culture is characterized by built-in discontinuities.

Some gap between the formal expressions of the mores and the actual adjustments of social life is probably found in all societies. The gap is probably far greater in a world so complex that the young have to find a considerable part of their socialization in separate educational institutions. Laboratory work, field experience, and "life-adjustment" education may narrow this gap, but there will probably always be some opposition between the precepts learned in church and school and the practices which hold sway in our competitive economic and social system.

Such discontinuities are also favored by rapid social change, since parents cannot possibly anticipate the type of world their children will face. While the emergence of new inventions is often recognized as a disrupting factor, the changing social climate is equally unpredictable. Thus the parent in Ceylon, who in the 1930s looked on Christianity as the religion of the enlightened and powerful, raised children who sometimes find this religious affiliation a social handicap now that Buddhism has become identified with resurgent nationalism in a newly independent country. Conversely, many an African, trained as a child to respect the traditions of the tribe and the authority of the chief, may grow up to live as an urban worker in a culture where chiefs are powerless and tribal traditions are irrelevant. The American farmer may carefully train his children in the attitudes and techniques appropriate to farming, although it is a predictable certainty that many of these children are headed for an urban life and work.

Such examples could be multiplied endlessly. They show how it is impossible to prepare young people for precisely the roles they will play as adults in a changing society. Since adult roles cannot be accurately predicted, socialization and education can be adequate only if they prepare the child to play any of a wide variety of roles. Memorization and rote learning in schools have been replaced, in theory, by efforts to develop abilities in "problem solving" and "adjustment," but how successfully may be debated. Yet the rapidity of change and the uncertainty of future role ascriptions makes flexibility and adaptability a necessary condition for survival.

Role personality and true personality

If role preparation were entirely adequate, each person would develop a personality which perfectly harmonized with his role demands. But imperfections in preparation, plus unpredictability of future role demands, make it certain that many people will develop a personailty which differs considerably from the *pattern of personality traits which the role requires—the role personality.*

For the ascribed roles and statuses, the divergence may be small enough so that little clash will occur between role personality and true personality. Thus most adult males can fill the male role simply by "being themselves."

For the achieved roles and statuses, which often are not selected until after one's adult personality has already been formed, considerable divergence between role and true personalities is fairly common. For instance, in the role of salesman a man needs to be friendly, extroverted, and perceptive of the reactions of others. Suppose his true personality is shy, withdrawn, contemplative, and insensitive to the reactions of others. Such a person is unlikely to become a salesman or to succeed as one. If he does succeed, he does it by masking his true personality with an outward show of friendliness and a deliberately cultivated attentiveness to the clues to other's reactions. This role playing is not easy to accomplish successfully and may entail a good deal of emotional strain. If the role playing is done successfully over a long period of time, however, the true personality may gradually be modified to come closer to the role personality. Mrs. Eleanor Roosevelt was a rather shy young woman and a hesitant and reluctant public speaker. In her role as wife to a politically ambitious but physically handicapped husband, she forced herself into vigorous political activity and became an eloquent speaker. Apparently she found the role a rewarding one, for long after her husband's death she accepted a diplomatic appointment, remained a tireless world traveler and public speaker, and became perhaps the most remarkable woman of her age. On the other hand, the wives of several men prominent in public life have rejected the role of politician's wife and divorced their husbands.

It is likely that a good deal of success and failure in achieved roles is explained by the degree to which the true personality coincides with the required role personality.

Personnel management today is much concerned with this coincidence and uses job analyses, psychological tests, depth interviews, and other devices in an effort to fit people into jobs where there will be little clash between true and role personalities.

Role conflicts

There are at least two kinds of role conflicts: conflicts between roles and conflicts within a single role. Often two or more roles (either independent roles or parts of a role set) may impose conflicting obligations upon a person. The employed wife finds that the demands of her job may conflict with home duties; the married student must reconcile student role demands with duties as husband or wife; the police officer must sometimes choose between violating his duty and arresting a friend. Or, within a single role, there may be a structured (built-in) conflict. The military chaplain, preaching a gospel of love, must sustain men in their readiness to kill, a role conflict which many chaplains find disturbing [Burchard, 1963; Zahn, 1969]. In many occupational roles, ranging from repairman to physician, there is a built-in "conflict of interest" in that the obligation to be honest with the customer or patient may conflict with the desire to make money, so that a number of needless repairs to car or body may be made. Very few roles are completely free from structured role conflicts.

There are several common processes which reduce role strain and protect the self from guilt. These include *rationalization, compartmentalization,* and *adjudication.* The first two are not conscious, intentional protective devices; if they were, they would not "work." Only when people are not aware of them will these processes function successfully.

Rationalization is a defense process whereby one redefines a painful situation in terms which are socially and personally acceptable. The classic illustration is the girl who becomes convinced that she is lucky she didn't marry that heel who jilted her. Rationalization conceals the reality of role conflict, preventing awareness that any conflict exists. Thus our belief in democracy and our denial of equality to women and to black people caused few anxieties as long as we believed that women and blacks were on the intellectual level of children. "All men are created equal," but slaves were not *men*, they were *property*. The Catholic doctrine (which Luther and Calvin also followed) of "just" and "unjust" wars makes it possible for Christians (on both sides) to commit mass murder with a clear conscience. Through rationalization, the situation is defined in such a way that there is no role conflict and therefore no role strain.

Compartmentalization reduces role strain by fencing one's roles off into separate parts of one's life and responding to only one set of role demands at a time. It has been noted that many cruel Nazi concentration camp guards and executioners were kindly, affectionate husbands and fathers. Their work and family roles were entirely separated. The businessman who conspires to violate the antitrust laws in the afternoon and speaks eloquently at a citizen's law-and-order meeting in the evening is not necessarily a hypocrite; he is merely switching roles. Within each role are found the pressures and justifications which make the expected role behavior seem necessary and good. Uniforms, judicial robes, surgical gowns and professional titles are aids in insulating roles from one another. Many people cannot "relax" (that is, cannot step fully outside a role) until they are "out of uniform."

If one is successfully socialized, he develops a wardrobe of role personalities, and slips into one or another as the situation demands. At home he is tender and indulgent; while working at the office he is brisk and formal. This process of switching role personalities creates the possibility of emo-

tional strain whenever the attitudes called for in one role clash sharply with those needed in the other. Many a businessman, faced with the necessity of laying off employees, finds it painful to ignore their human needs and treat them impersonally as "cost factors in production." The dishonesties, deceptions, and exploitations that are a part of many occupational roles are inconsistent with the usual moral and religious training. If the individual is not fully successful in fencing his behavior off into compartments, these cultural contradictions become mental conflicts within the individual. Some psychiatrists hold that such culture conflicts, and the mental conflicts they produce, are major causes of personality disorder.

He develops a wardrobe of role personalities.

Cultural conflicts and inconsistencies are probably found in every culture. In well-integrated cultures, these inconsistencies are so well rationalized, compartmentalized, and fenced off from one another that the individual does not sense them at all. Thus many primitives who treated one another with great tenderness were ruthlessly cruel to outsiders; their humanitarian mores applied only to tribal fellows, while outsiders were considered and treated like any other animals of the forest. By contrast, our belief in a universal God of all mankind makes it harder for us to bomb our enemies with a clear conscience (but we generally manage to, somehow). *Cultural contradictions are upsetting only when they subject the individual to conflicting pressures in a situation that demands a single action.* For example, should the maiden respond to her lover's tender persuasions, or remember what her mother told her? Should the employee, official, or soldier, when given an order which he feels to be dishonest or immoral, follow his conscience or protect his career and his family? When torn between the insistent demands of her aging, senile parents and the needs of her husband and children, what should a wife do? For many role conflicts, there is no satisfactory compromise. When role strain becomes unendurable, neurotic or psychotic behavior may follow.

Adjudication differs from the protective devices just discussed in being conscious and intentional. It is a formal procedure for turning over to a third party a difficult decision on a possible role conflict, thereby relieving the individual of responsibility or guilt. Much of the work of professional associations and the codes of ethics which they develop is devoted to the solution of role conflicts. The American Bar Association often hands down statements which serve as precedents in deciding the duties of the attorney to the court, to his clients, and to himself. The American Medical Association identifies as "unethical" that role behavior which constitutes a breach of trust either toward the client or toward other physicians. Cynics may argue that such professional associations usually operate to defend the interests of the profession. In many codes of ethics, the clauses protecting the competing members from one another greatly outnumber the statements protecting the clients or customers. Yet members of professions have been barred from the profession for viola-

ting the expected role behavior, and the need to justify action before one's peers does place some limitations upon behavior. In any event, a decision on proper role behavior by the professional association or labor union means that the individual is relieved of the duty of making his own decision in difficult cases.

Role failure

In a stable, well-integrated society with a high proportion of ascribed roles, most people fill these roles successfully. Most of the roles in any society can be filled by almost any member, if he has been adequately prepared for them. But in a rapidly changing and less well-integrated society like ours, where we cannot predict all adult roles in advance and where discontinuities limit role preparation, a good deal of role failure is inevitable. Some persons even fail in their ascribed roles of male and female, as in the case of the homosexual, or of the woman with the complex of hostile, resentful, and aggressive attitudes toward men which is called the *masculine-protest* pattern, or of the man who never outgrows his dependence upon mother. Even more persons fail in some of their achieved roles. Some of them fail to achieve the role they court—the boy (or girl) fails to become a physician or executive, or the girl fails to get a husband and become a wife and mother. Others achieve a role but fail to fill it successfully. Many husbands and wives fail as marital partners, and face either the often shattering experience of divorce or a lifetime of mutual frustration. Many parents fail to socialize their children successfully. Only a few in any occupation or profession can be spectacularly successful, because for each manager there must be many subordinates. Those who crave the highest levels of excellence in a particular role are usually frustrated. Role failures of many kinds and degrees keep swelling the ranks of unhappy, frustrated people.

SUMMARY

Socialization takes place largely through the learning of social roles. *Social status* is a position in society with consequent privileges and duties; a *role* is the behavior expected of those who occupy a particular status. *Role behavior* is affected by *dramatic role presentation*, in which the individual plays the role with a consciousness that spectators are evaluating his performance.

Roles and statuses are of two sorts: those which are *ascribed* to individuals according to sex, age, race, or other innate characteristics, and those which are *achieved* through personal choice or effort. A *meritocracy* in which people are given opportunities and jobs according to tested capacity brings a degree of ascription into statuses and roles which are supposedly open to achievement. In traditional societies, most statuses are ascribed, while in the industrial societies, more statuses are open to achievement.

Even in a single status, people are confronted with a related cluster of roles in what is known as a *role set*, and sometimes these various parts of the role set are difficult to integrate. We also play a number of roles which are relatively independent of each other but which often have a potential of mutual conflict.

Role conflict is minimized by a variety of techniques. These include *rationalization* which enables one to deny that conflict exists, *compartmentalization* which enables one to focus on one role at a time, and *adjudication* which provides a third party to render a decision on actual or potential role conflict. Apart from role conflict, there are several other hazards in role performance. One may fail in role behavior with consequent injury to the self.

The *role personality* may call for traits which are not a part of one's true personality. In such cases one may reject the role; or he may counterfeit the required role personality; eventually he may somewhat modify his true personality in the direction of the role personality. Organizing society's work by ascribing statuses ensures that most roles will be filled adequately, with a maximum of emotional security but some waste of unusual abilities. Opening many statuses to achievement probably makes more efficient use of talent, at the price of many failures and greater emotional insecurity.

Questions and projects

1. Are *role* and *status* two separate concepts or two aspects of the same phenomenon? Explain.

2. What is the function of children's play in socialization? How does play aid in role preparation?

3. Why is it a comparatively easy task to assume one's age roles in most primitive societies? Why do we not have a clearly defined set of age roles?

4. How does our culture make old age a difficult period? Is it a difficult period in all cultures? Ana-lyze our old-age problem in terms of discontinuities. In terms of conflicting roles.

5. Describe the shift from the status and role of a high school student to that of college student in terms of cultural continuities and discontinuities in socialization. From civilian to soldier.

6. In role preparation for most adult roles, which is more important: the attitudes and values which make that role acceptable, or the knowledge and skills necessary to fill the role? Illustrate for the

homemaker, schoolteacher, army officer, research scientist, and old-age roles.

7. Is there any conflict between your roles as college student and as son or daughter? If you are a married student, a third (and possibly a fourth) role is added. What possible role conflicts are added?

8. What social costs accompany an emphasis upon achieved status? Ascribed status?

9. In what respects is your present role as college student preparing you for later roles? In what respects is your present role experience irrelevant or even dysfunctional?

10. Are there any respects in which you are already assuming role personalities which differ from your true personality? Are you aware of any stresses which this acting a part produces?

11. What are the pros and cons of a meritocracy, as compared with alternative methods of status ascription or achievement?

12. Describe in some detail a role and status with which you are familiar and which involves a good deal of conflicting pressure within the role. How do persons in that role usually resolve these conflicts?

13. Describe some situation you know about in which a person has been under pressure to fill two or more conflicting roles. How did he resolve the conflict? Would you say his resolution was successful or unsuccessful?

Suggested readings

Epstein, Joseph: "The Struggle for Sexual Identity," *Harpers*, September, 1970, pp. 37–51. Portrays the homosexual as one who has failed in his ascribed role and therefore is subject to grave social maladjustment.

Goffman, Irwin: *Where the Action Is*, Doubleday & Company, Inc., Garden City, N.Y., 1967. A skillful analysis of role behavior.

Gowman, Alan G.: "Blindness and the Role of the Companion," *Social Problems*, 4:68–75, July, 1956. The process through which the companion develops a role relationship satisfactory to the blind person and the changes which occur in the definition of the situation.

Gullahorn, John T.: "Measuring Role Conflict," *American Journal of Sociology*, 61:299–303, January, 1956. An attempt to measure role conflicts of labor union leaders.

Komarovsky, Mirra: "Cultural Contradictions and Sex Roles," *American Journal of Sociology,* 52:184–189, November, 1946; The Bobbs-Merrill Company, Inc., reprint S-150. A classic discussion of the role conflicts of the college-educated woman.

McCord, Joan, and William McCord: "Effects of Parental Role Models on Criminality," *Journal of Social Issues*, 15:66–75, 1958. A study of social worker reports upon the parents of delinquents, showing that some popular ideas are unsound.

Steinmann, Anne: "Lack of Communication between Men and Women," *Marriage and Family Living*, 20:350–352, November, 1958. A role-centered analysis of communication difficulties between the sexes.

Wardwell, William, and Arthur L. Wood: "Extra-professional Role of the Lawyer," *American Journal of Sociology*, 61:304–307, January, 1956. A discussion of the community service responsibilities involved in the role of lawyer.

Winick, Charles: "Depolarization of Sex," *Annals of the American Academy of Political and Social Science*, 376:18–24, March, 1968. Describes the decreasing distance between masculine and feminine roles.

Social control and social deviation

The Hawaiians had long obeyed some of the *Kanawai* [laws]. They had always honored fathers and mothers, and their days had been long upon the land. They had utterly abolished idols before the Longnecks [whites] came.

Theft they had dealt with in a way that had served well enough, though it could scarcely have been pleasing to Jehovah. In the old days if a man took something from one below him in the social scale, it was not stealing; for that which was taken had in reality belonged by virtue of rank to the taker. And if a commoner made off with the calabash or the weapon of a superior, the injured man could go to the thief's house and take back his possession, along with anything else he saw that he wanted.

But when the *hoales* [white traders] came with their bean pots and silver spoons, their monkey wrenches and linen towels, their sawed lumber and their keen-edged axes, this method no longer served. Complaints from foreigners rang unceasingly in the governor's ears. White men did not want to go poking into native huts to find their lost articles. They wanted Boki to haul up the thief and arrange for restitution and punishment.

Gradually the enlightened chiefs saw what they must do. Some of them put their men in irons for proven theft or set them free only to work and pay for what they had stolen. The boy prince Kauikeaouli, when his beloved *kahu* was found accessory to a theft, consented quickly to the man's dismissal. "My *kahu* must go," he declared, "or by and by the foreigners will think that I myself am guilty."

The *haoles* applauded such measures. Here was a Commandment they liked to see enforced.

Then there was the Commandment forbidding murder in a few short words. Once, if a native killed in sudden anger, it was proper for the victim's relatives to avenge the deed, unless the murderer took shelter in a place of refuge. If the guilty man were of equal rank with the victim's avenger, there might be an appeal to the king or the governor or to the chief of the district. The aggrieved one and the accused would then sit cross-legged in the judge's yard and each would eloquently argue his case till the magistrate made his decision.

But these customs failed when Honolulu swarmed with hot-headed sailors, and brown and white alike drank rum and got *huhu* [very angry]. Again, as with theft, the traders wanted stern laws, strictly enforced, so that the riffraff of all nations would think twice before bashing their fellows on the head. They told the chiefs to build a lofty engine of death which would string up a murderer by the neck and leave him hanging limp from a rope's end—a potent reminder to the living to restrain themselves. (*Reprinted by permission of Dodd, Mead & Company from* Grapes of Canaan *by Albertine Loomis, pp. 227–229. Copyright 1951 by Albertine Loomis.*)

The disintegration of the traditional system of law and order when the European traders brought changes and new problems to Hawaii could be duplicated in many other lands. Changes in a society demand changes in its ways of maintaining social order. When the Hawaiian chiefs were shifting from their traditional customs to the jails and gallows suggested by the traders, they were seeking to adjust the techniques of social control to the needs of changing times —a problem which is a continuous concern of every modern society.

The study of *social control*—the means through which people are led to fill their roles as expected—begins with the study of the social order within which people interact. Consider, for example, the orderly arrangements which underlie the bustling confusion of a great city. Tens of thousands of people take their places and perform their tasks with no apparent direction. Thousands of vehicles butt their way through clogged canyons, missing by inches, but seldom actually colliding. Thousands of kinds of merchandise arrive at the proper places in the proper amounts at the proper times. Ten thousand people whom an individual never sees will labor on this day so that meals will be ready for him when needed, drinking fountains will flow, drains will carry off the wastes, bulbs will blink and glow, traffic will part to let him pass, and various conveniences will meet his other needs. A hundred people may serve him

within an hour, perhaps without a word from him to any of them.

This is what is meant by *social order*—a system of people, relationships, and customs operating smoothly to accomplish the work of a society. Unless people know what they may expect from one another, not much will get done. No society, even the simplest, can function successfully unless the behavior of most people can be reliably predicted most of the time. Unless we can depend upon police officers to protect us, workers to go to work on schedule, and motorists to stay on the right side of the road most of the time, there can be no social order. The orderliness of a society rests upon a network of roles according to which each person accepts certain duties toward others and claims certain rights from others. An orderly society can operate only as long as most people reliably fulfill most of their duties toward others and are able successfully to claim most of their rights from others.

How is this network of reciprocal rights and duties kept in force? Sociologists use the term "social control" to describe *all the means and processes whereby a group or a society secures its members' conformity to its expectations.*

SOCIAL CONTROL AND SOCIAL ORDER

How does a group or a society cause its members to behave in the expected manner? In a number of ways, whose relative importance is difficult to measure.

Social control through socialization

Fromm [1944] has remarked that if a society is to function efficiently, "its members must acquire the kind of character which makes them *want* to act in the way they *have* to act as members of society. . . . They have to *desire* to do what objectively is necessary for them to do."

People are controlled mainly by being socialized so that they fill their roles in the expected way through habit and preference. How do we compel women to accept the endless drudgery of household and child care? Mainly by socializing them so that they *want* husbands and children, and feel cheated without them. How is man, unlike the male of most other species, persuaded to exchange his freedom for a sense of social responsibility toward the offspring he sires? Mainly by cultivating within him a set of cherished sentiments and yearnings which this troublesome little creature promises to fulfill. As we stated in an earlier chapter, the crucial part of one's role preparation is his development of the attitudes and wishes which make the role attractive. Most role failures come, not because one is unable to perform the role's tasks, but because he is trapped in a role he does not really want or enjoy.

Socialization shapes our customs, our wishes, and our habits. Habit and custom are great time savers. They relieve us of the need for countless decisions. If we had to decide whether and how to perform each act —when to arise, whether and how to wash, shave, dress, and so on—few students would get to class at all! The members of a society are schooled in the same customs and tend to develop much the same set of habits. Thus habit and custom are great standardizers of behavior within a group. If all members of a society share similar socialization experiences, they will voluntarily and unthinkingly act in very much the same ways. They will conform to social expectations without any conscious awareness that they are "conforming," or any serious thought of doing otherwise. The American college male's attempt to date a cute coed arises from motives less academic than a wish to "conform to the courtship pattern"; yet such conformity is the result.

Social control through social pressure

In a novel by Sinclair Lewis, George F. Babbitt, a small-town realtor, somehow strays into "radical" notions about government and politics. Soon his business declines, his friends begin to avoid him, and he grows uncomfortably aware that he is becoming an outsider. Lewis describes with rare perception how Babbitt's associates apply a variety of subtle pressures until, with a sigh of relief, Babbitt scurries back into a comfortable conformity [Lewis, 1922, chaps. 32, 33]. In all human societies, and even in many nonhuman species, this tendency to conform to group pressure and example is evident. Nineteenth-century explorer David Thompson was impressed by the reckless, headlong flight of wild horses, and when his dull, placid packhorse escaped to join the wild horses, it amazed him to see how quickly it assumed their wild temperament "with nostrils distended, mane flying, and tail straight out" [Ryden, 1971, p. 106].

LaPiere [1954] sees social control as primarily a process growing out of the individual's need for status within his primary groups. He claims that these groups are most influential when they are small and intimate, when the individual expects to remain in the group for a long time, and when he has frequent contacts with them. All authorities agree that our need for acceptance within intimate groups is a most powerful lever for the use of group pressure toward group norms.

The individual experiences this group pressure as a continuous and largely unconscious process. Its operation is illustrated by the life of one of the author's acquaintances. He spent most of his working life as a small farmer in central Michigan; like most of his neighbors, he thought conservatively, voted Republican, and scolded labor unions. During World War II he moved to Detroit and worked in a war plant, joined a union, became a union officer, and voted Democratic. After the war, he retired to a small central Michigan village where he again thought conservatively, voted Republican, and scolded labor unions. He explained these about-faces by claiming that the parties and the unions had changed. He did not realize that it was *he* who had changed. Like most of us, he soon came to share the views of his group associates. This tendency to conform to group attitudes is so compelling that the Catholic church in France found it necessary to abandon its worker-priest program. This was an effort to stem the drift of French workers toward communism by sending out priests who would take ordinary jobs and work beside the workers, meanwhile leading them back to the church. After a ten-year trial, when it became evident that the workers were converting the priests to the Marxian view of the class struggle, the program was curtailed [Brady, 1954].

Our need for acceptance within intimate groups.

Social psychologists [Sherif, 1935; Bovard, 1951] have made a number of experiments which show how a person tends to bring his expressions in line with those of the group. The method in such experiments usually consists of asking the members for individual estimates, attitudes, or observations on a topic, then informing them of the group norm, and finally asking for a new expression from each member. Many of the informants modify their second expression in the direction of the group norm. In a series of ingenious experiments, Asch [1951], Tuddenham [1961], and others have shown that many people will even alter an observation which they *know* to be correct rather than oppose the group. Each subject in these experiments was surrounded by a group which, by secret prearrangement, made factual observations that the subject *knew* to be wrong; yet one-third of these subjects accepted the wrong observation when opposed by a unanimous group opinion to the contrary. Schachter [1951] has also shown experimentally how the member who sharply deviates from group norms in opinion is rejected by the group.

We often notice that a new member of a group is more carefully conformist and more fiercely loyal than the old members. Religious converts and naturalized citizens often show a zeal which puts lifelong members to shame. An experiment by Dittes and Kelley [1956] helps to explain this. They found that among members who equally value their membership in a group, those who feel *least accepted* are the most rigidly conformist to the group's norms. Meticulous conformity is a tool for gaining acceptance and status within a group, while rejection is the price of nonconformity.

It is probable that no other structure even approaches the tremendous controlling power of the group over the individual. Any parent who has tried to counter a teen-ager's argument, "*All* the kids are wearing them!" is fully aware of the controlling power of the group.

Informal primary-group controls Groups are of two kinds, primary and secondary; these concepts will be analyzed in detail in a later chapter. For our present discussion, it is sufficient to note that primary groups are small, intimate, informal groups, like the family, clique, or play group, while secondary groups are impersonal, formal, and utilitarian, like a labor union, trade association, church congregation, or student body.

Within primary groups, control is informal, spontaneous, and unplanned. The members of the group react to the actions of each member. When a member irritates or annoys the others, they may show their disapproval through ridicule, laughter, criticism, or even ostracism. When a member's behavior is acceptable, a secure and comfortable "belonging" is his usual reward. Many novelists have used the subplot in which a character violates the norms of his group in some way, is disciplined by group disapproval which he cannot endure, and must earn his way back into group acceptance through penitence and renewed conformity (like Sinclair Lewis's Babbitt).

In most primitive societies, where virtually all groups were primary groups, there was very little serious misconduct. Each person was born into certain kinship groups—for example, a family, a clan, and a tribe. He could not move on to another tribe or clan, for a man divorced from his kinship ties had no social existence—that is, no one was obligated to regard and treat him as a fellow human being. If a man were to survive, he *had* to get along with the groups in which he found himself. Since there was little privacy and no escape, the penalty of serious nonconformity was an intolerable existence. For example, the polar Eskimo institutionalized ridicule and laughter as a social control. The person who violated cultural norms was mercilessly ridiculed. Birket-Smith writes of the Chugach Eskimo:

Once a habitual thief entered a house, and an old woman sitting there began to sing:

Analurshe
Analurshe
Makes me ashamed

He was looking at me
While I was eating
Analurshe
Analurshe

He immediately left the house, but the children used to sing the song whenever they saw him. Thus he acquired the nickname Analurshe, i.e., Old Excrements, and after that he stopped stealing. (*Kaj Birket-Smith*, The Eskimos, *Methuen & Co., Ltd., London, 1959, p. 151.*)

Lowie describes the use of scorn and ridicule by a number of American Indian peoples:

When a Fox Indian boy in Illinois was taught not to steal and never to abuse his wife, his elder did not hold up to him any tangible punishment here or hereafter nor any abstract rule of morality. The clinching argument was, "The people will say many things about you, although you may not know it."

Gossiping sometimes took special forms of ridicule. An Alaskan youth thus reports his experience: "If you do not marry within your village, they joke about you—they joke so much that it makes it disagreeable." The Crow sang songs in mockery of a miser, a bully, or a man who should take back a divorced wife—the acme of disgrace. Certain kinsmen had the privilege of publicly criticizing a man for breaches of etiquette and ethics, and there was nothing he would fear more than to be thus pilloried. This system was developed by the Blackfoot along slightly different lines. "For mild persistent misconduct, a method of formal discipline is sometimes practiced. When the offender has failed to take hints and suggestions, the head men may take formal notice and decide to resort to discipline. Some evening when all are in their tipis, a head man will call out to a neighbor asking if he has observed the conduct of Mr. A. This starts a general conversation between the many tipis, in which all the grotesque and hideous features of Mr. A.'s acts are held up to general ridicule, amid shrieks of laughter, the grilling continuing until far into the night. The mortification of the victim is extreme and usually drives him into a temporary exile or, as formerly, upon the warpath to do desperate deeds."

A primitive man sacrifices half his property lest he be dubbed a miser; he yields his favorite wife if jealousy is against the code; he risks life itself, if that is the way to gain the honor of a public eulogy. **That is why savages of the same tribe are not forever cutting one another's throats or ravishing available women, even if they lack written constitutions, jails, a police force, and revealed religion.** (*Robert H. Lowie,* Are We Civilized? *Harcourt, Brace & World, Inc., New York, 1929. Copyright 1929, by Harcourt Brace & World, Inc., renewed © 1957, by Robert H. Lowie, and reprinted with the publisher's permission.*)

In many authenticated instances where primitives have violated important norms, they have committed suicide because they could not endure the penalty of group disapproval [Malinowski, 1926, pp. 94–99]. In such a group setting, the penalty for serious nonconformity is so unendurable as to make serious nonconformity quite rare. Likewise in complex cultures, wherever persons are trapped in primary group settings which they cannot easily escape, as in a prison cell or a military unit, this great controlling power of the primary group comes into operation.

In many societies, the group is held responsible for the acts of any of its members. For example, if a Tlingit Indian of the American Northwest murdered a member of another clan, his own clan had to provide for execution a person equal in social status to the murdered victim, while the actual murderer was punished by living with the knowledge that he had caused the execution of a clansman. In our military units, one dirty rifle or messy locker may deprive an entire company of their weekend passes. Such forms of collective punishment may seem unjust, *but they work!* A soldier whose indolence has once caused his company to lose their weekend passes is unlikely to repeat his error—or to be permitted to forget it!

A great deal of "leadership" and "authority" rest upon the skillful manipulation of the group as a control device. The successful schoolteacher, for example, often uses the class to maintain discipline; she manipulates the situation so that the child who misbehaves will look ridiculous before the class. But if she allows a situation to develop wherein the misbehaving child appears as a hero or a martyr to the class, her control is lost.

Normal people everywhere need and seek the approval of others, especially of the primary group associates upon whom they depend for intimate human response. English workers sometimes punish a fellow worker who has violated group norms by "sending him to Coventry." This means that no other worker will speak to him, answer him, or look at him, but acts as though he weren't there at all. Such a punishment is generally unendurable. The victim soon either does his penance or quits his job. Thousands of novels, dramas, and operas have elaborated this theme. Most people will give almost anything, even their lives if necessary, to retain this approval and the comforting feeling of belonging to the group that is most important to them. It is the overwhelming need for group approval and response that makes the primary group the most powerful controlling agency known to man.

Secondary-group controls As we shift from primary- to secondary-group situations, we also shift from informal to more formal social controls. Secondary groups are generally larger, more impersonal, and specialized in purpose. We do not use them to meet our need for intimate human response, but to help us to get certain jobs done. If a secondary group does not meet our needs, we can generally withdraw with no great anguish, for our emotional lives are not deeply involved. To maintain our status in the secondary group is desirable but not a desperate emotional necessity as it is in the primary group. True, it is possible in our society for people to change their primary groups—leave their families, divorce their mates, find new friends—but the process is generally painful. The secondary group is a less compelling control agency than the primary group.

The secondary group is still an effective control. Some of the informal controls still operate in the secondary group. No normal person wants to appear ridiculous at the union meeting, the church worship service, or the chamber of commerce banquet. Such informal controls as ridicule, laughter, gossip, and ostracism operate in secondary-group settings, but generally with a reduced impact. Meanwhile, other more formal controls are characteristic of secondary groups —parliamentary rules of order, official regulations and standardized procedures, propaganda, public relations and "human engineering," promotions and titles, rewards and prizes, formal penalties and punishments, and still others.

The more formal controls of the secondary group are most effective when reinforced by a primary group. A prize or decoration is more sweet when an admiring family and an applauding clique of close friends can watch the presentation ceremony. Within the large, impersonal secondary group may be many very closely integrated primary groups, such as squads within an army or work crews within a corporation. These primary groups can either reinforce or undermine the formal secondary-group controls and greatly affect the performance of the secondary group. Much of the human-engineering approach in industry is an effort to use these primary groups to reinforce the controls and the objectives of the corporations [Gross, 1953].

Special language as a social control An argot, a special vocabulary restricted to a particular subculture, serves important functions of social control. An argot promotes communication within the group, since each unique expression is freighted with meaning which only the group members can comprehend. Conversely the argot shields the group from outside influence which might introduce discordant ideas. Learning the argot thus not only strengthens the tie between the individual and the group; it also cuts down communication with the world outside. No individuals are entirely cut off from contacts outside the subculture, but as Bernstein [1966] observes, the argot serves to maximize the social barriers between the group and the rest of society.

Tuning in on the Scene

(Every subculture has its argot. This is one of dozens of possible examples.)

ALIVE—able to feel; with feeling, not necessarily happy; opposite of feeling depressed or alienated.
BEAUTIFUL—great, marvelous, a term of approval and admiration similar to groovy and outasight; an aesthetic word used for making an approving moral judgment on integrity, character, wisdom, reliability.
BURNED—cheated in a drug sale.
CO-OPTION, CO-OPTED—1. selling out. 2. the process by which the dominant culture absorbs the trappings of its undercultures without becoming changed itself.
DOWNER—tranquilizer or barbiturate.
FOOTBALLS—combination of dextroamphetamine and amphetamine.
FREAK OUT or FLIP OUT—1. orginally, to lose control after using drugs. 2. now, any aberrant behavior, from having a nervous breakdown to acting bizarrely.
FREE—1. acting spontaneously. 2. without restraints, inhibitions, or responsibilities. 3. acting without regard for tradition.
STRAIGHTEN ONE'S HEAD—to see the truth, to become aware.
LIBERATE—1. to steal. 2. to occupy by sit-in. 3. to break a cultural pattern. "LSD can liberate people."
LID—about 1 oz. of marijuana.
PEARLY GATES—certain morning glory seeds.
PLASTIC—phoney, fake.
POLITICO—term of derision toward activists, used by those to whom political action seems futile.
RAP—v. originally the compulsive talking under drugs; now, simply talk. n. a conversation, an aimless conversation.

SPACED OUT—having lost the sense of reality while under drugs.
UPPERS—stimulants; amphetamines.
WIPED OUT—whacked out, spaced out; under the influence of drugs.
"Treatises on slang should be printed in loose-leaf form—and, perhaps, in disappearing ink." **Theodore M. Bernstein** (*Abstracted from Ethel Grodzins Romm*, The Open Conspiracy: What America's Angry Young Generation Is Saying, *Stackpole Books, Harrisburg, Pa., 1970, pp. 240–246.*)

Language is a way of describing reality, and changes in language may change peoples' perceptions of reality. A redefinition which ascribes new meanings to familiar words may promote a redefinition of attitudes and relationships. For example, the recent use of the term "welfare rights" has had some success in changing the image of "welfare" from a charity (which the poor gratefully accept in whatever amount offered) to a "right" (for which the recipients may legitimately negotiate, bargain, and battle). The more violent of the New Left radicals have sought to deflect criticism of their window-smashing, bombing, and other disruptions by redefining the term "oppression" to include all of the established institutions of our society, and by describing as "violence" all the institution-sustaining procedures—rules, regulations, law enforcement, etc. Thus the violence of "trashing" and other disruptions is legitimated by being compared with "Establishment violence." Sometimes, words do redefine situations.

Control through force Many primitive societies succeeded in controlling the behavior of individuals through the mores, reinforced by the informal controls of the primary group, so that no formal laws or punishments were necessary. But with larger populations and more complex cultures, formal governments, laws, and punishments are developed. Wherever it becomes possible for the individual to become lost in the crowd, informal controls are inadequate and formal controls are necessary. For example, in a clan of one or two dozen adult kinsfolk, informal food sharing is practical; each person can take what he needs and contribute whatever he can catch, while informal group pressures can be trusted to prevent laziness and control greed. But in a village of hundreds of persons, it would be impossible to keep tabs on each person informally; individual laziness and greed would make a system of informal food sharing unworkable. Some *system* of assigning work and distributing rewards becomes necessary. Thus, with larger populations and cultural complexity comes a shift to impersonal secondary-group controls—laws, regulations, councils, and formalized procedures.

When the individual does not wish to follow these regulations, the group tries to compel him to do so. In such large groups he is too anonymous for informal group pressures to be brought to an effective focus upon him. Furthermore, in larger groups with complex cultures, some subcultures that conflict with the culture of the majority are likely to develop. The individual who rejects the conventional regulations of the society may find emotional support from other persons who think and act as he does. A few of the many current examples might include the Amish community, the hippie commune, the homosexual subculture, and perhaps the student-and-nonstudent communities adjacent to major universities. Although the member may fondly imagine that he is "free," he is still subject to group pressures, but these group pressures come from a nonconforming group which insulates him from the informal group pressures of conventional society. So conventional society sometimes uses force upon him—in the form of laws and formal punishments—to compel from him a required minimum of conformity. This force is not always successful, but is used in every complex society.

Ironically, some of the world figures most widely admired by American nonconformists (Castro, Che Guevara, Mao Tse-Tung) are noted for the severity of their punishment of nonconformists in their own countries!

Punishment of deviation

The punishments which all societies visit upon deviants range from nonacceptance and ridicule to every imaginable form of torture, mutilation, imprisonment, and death. Often the punishment has more the flavor of vindictive revenge than of intended control. The deviants sometimes accept punishment with stoical calm, as did the early Christians, and sometimes they protest bitterly over their persecution and oppression, as do today's hippies and radical leftists. The "persecution" theme is a useful promotional tactic which organizers have used for centuries. But although often exaggerated and sometimes provoked, the persecution of deviants is very real in every society.

At the very least, hostile glares and unkind remarks await the group who deviate from cultural norms (or the member of a deviant group who deviates from *their* group norms), but this is hardly "persecution." A denial of civil rights or an unequal enforcement of laws, however, might justifiably be termed "persecution." For example, Hamersma [1970] test-mailed stamped letters addressed to the Young Lords in Chicago, a group of Latin revolutionaries, and found that the letters were frequently delayed, opened, or never delivered. Huessenstamm [1971] found that when a selected group of students added Black Panther decals to their cars and attempted to continue driving in their usual manner, their traffic tickets multiplied astronomically! These are two recent experiments which document the perfectly obvious fact that

deviants suffer some forms and degrees of punishment in all societies. The severity of punishment varies with the tolerance level of the society or group in question, and the degree to which a particular deviation seems to threaten cherished values of other people. On balance, American society is probably more tolerant of deviation than most—possibly than any—of the world's other major societies.

The punishment of deviants is very real in every society.

Situational determinants of behavior

When a layman sees some behavior he does not like, he often attributes it to evil human nature, wicked impulse, weak character, or some other *individual* cause. What separates the sociologist from the layman here is the sociologist's habit of looking for *social* factors in the causation of behavior. True, when one individual or a few people change in character or behavior, the explanations may be purely individual. But when any *large number* of people change their character or behavior in the same way, we look for the probable cause in some change in the social and cultural influences upon behavior.

To a far greater degree than most people recognize, one's behavior in a particular situation is a result of the needs, pressures, and temptations of that situation. There is ample evidence that many people who would not cheat a blind newspaper man will cheat the national supermarket if they get a chance to do so; war veterans who did not rob their neighbors back home "liberated" many articles from the enemy population; people do things as part of a mob which they would never do as individuals. War atrocities are committed by all armies, including American armies [Taylor, 1970]. Whether a surrendering enemy is shot or taken prisoner depends more upon the circumstances at the moment of surrender than upon the character of the capturing troops [Draper, 1945]. Kinsey's data show that most civilian husbands are faithful to their wives, at least most of the time; but it appears that most overseas military personnel, when long separated from their wives, seized almost any attractive opportunity for infidelity. Labor union officials believe in labor unions —except for their own employees! So when the staff employees of the large unions seek to organize and bargain collectively with their bosses, these union official–bosses seem to react just like any other employers, even crossing picket lines when their office workers go on strike.[1] Boys from satisfactory homes in stable neighborhoods rarely become delinquent, but most boys from unsatisfactory homes in a slum neighborhood will become seriously delinquent [Glueck and Glueck, 1959; Reckless et al., 1957]. Argyris [1967] reports, "Not long ago, as a sociological experiment, two Detroit ministers went to work on an assembly line and soon found themselves cheating on quality, lying to their foremen and swearing at the machines." Their new work situation carried pressures and frustrations to which they responded like any other workers. Illustrations of how the total behavior situation

affects the behavior outcome could be multiplied almost without end. Many more are found in Chapter 16, "Collective Behavior."

True, the personality characteristics one brings to a situation are a factor in his behavior; occasionally they are the determining factor. A few people are honest in *all* situations; a few husbands will be faithful despite *any* temptation. But more often than our folklore admits, a situation develops a characteristic kind of behavior among most of the participants. This is why confrontations with police carry an unavoidable risk of "excessive use of force" by police. After hours, or sometimes days, of subjection to name-calling, insult, obscenity, and of pelting with bottles, rocks, and sometimes excreta, the police or guardsmen may "overreact" as they did at Chicago in 1965, at South Carolina State in 1968 [Nelson and Bass, 1970], or at Kent State and Jackson State in 1970 [President's Commission on Campus Unrest, 1970; Michener, 1971]. The only reliable way to prevent such fatal shootings is to arm police with only nonlethal riot weapons when in such confrontations. A major part of social control consists of trying to manipulate the kinds of situations which people enter, for we know that most of them will respond with the kind of behavior which a particular situation encourages.

This is not a complete catalog of the means of social control. There are many others which are described by Lumley [1925] and Landis [1956]—symbols, traditions, myths, legends, threats, intimidations, tortures, and still others—but they would be only an elaboration of the preceding outline.

SOCIAL DEVIATION

No society succeeds in getting all its people to behave as expected all the time. The term *deviation* is given to *any failure to conform to customary norms*. Deviation

---

[1] See "Pickets Cry 'Scab' at UAW Leaders," *Business Week*, March 20, 1971, p. 31.

takes many forms. The juvenile delinquent, the hermit, the ascetic, the hippie, the sinner and the saint, the artist starving in his garret and the miser gloating over his wealth—all have deviated from the conventional social norms.

In a simple society with a single set of norms, deviation is easy to define. In a complex society with many different competing norms, the problem grows more complicated. In a neighborhood where most of the boys are delinquent, and many of the adults repeatedly violate the law, who is the deviant—the delinquent or the nondelinquent? Obviously, deviation needs more detailed definition.

Basic types of deviation

Cultural and psychological deviation One may deviate from the norm in his social behavior, in his personality organization, or sometimes in both of these. Sociology is primarily interested in the *cultural deviant*, who deviates in his behavior from the norms of his culture. Psychologists are primarily interested in the *psychological deviant*, who deviates from the norm in his personality organization—the psychotic, the neurotic, the paranoid personality, and others. These two categories often converge. Deviant behavior may spring from personality abnormality, and many studies of deviant behavior report evidence of such an association. Radical political behavior is often interpreted as an outlet for emotional hostilities [Ernst and Loth, 1952; Almond, 1954; Hendin, 1971]. The prostitute is often explained as a product of an emotionally deprived childhood, in which she had little opportunity to integrate a secure personality [Greenwald, 1959]; and other sex deviations, along with alcoholism, drug addiction, and compulsive gambling, are often attributed to personality disorder of some sort.

Personality disorder, however, is far from the sole cause of deviant behavior. Although Hendin reports evidence that student revolutionaries come from a particular kind of unsatisfactory home life, he observes that "psychological forces alone [cannot] explain why students become revolutionaries at a particular time and place in history" [1971, p. 30]. And, while some psychologically abnormal people have a compelling urge to be bad, other psychologically abnormal people have an equally compelling urge to be good. These disturbed people become overconformists. The insecure, compulsive neurotic who *must* do his work perfectly, cannot stand disagreements, obeys all the mores, and finds comfort in meticulously following all the rules and regulations is fulfilling a neurotic need to conform. This shows that cultural and psychological deviation are related, but not in any simple cause-and-effect relationship. The puzzling question of why personality abnormality sometimes leads to deviant behavior and sometimes to conforming behavior is a problem which continues to interest both psychologists and sociologists.

Individual and group deviation A boy in a "good" neighborhood of stable families and conventional people may reject the norms which surround him and become a delinquent. In this case, the individual deviates from the norms of his subculture. He is thus an *individual deviant*. In a complex society, however, there may be a number of *deviant subcultures*, whose norms are condemned by the conventional morality of the society. Thus in the deteriorated areas of the city, Cohen [1955] and W. Miller [1958] find a delinquent subculture in which many of the youths participate. For many of them the life of the street gang is the only life that seems real and important. In such neighborhoods, delinquent behavior is as "normal" as law-abiding behavior. When boys from these neighborhoods become delinquent, they are not individually deviant from their subculture; it is their subculture (the group, not the boy) that is deviant from the conventional norms of the society. The delinquent episodes are not revolts against the area subculture but are "status-seeking mechanisms within the group" [Short and Strodtbeck, 1965. p. viii].

These delinquent boys are not individually deviant in the beginning; they are conforming normally to the norms of a deviant subculture. This subculture directs them into patterns which eventually result in many of them becoming individually deviant. As they graduate from the adolescent gang into adult society, their gang experience has placed them at war with conventional society, so that they often become and remain individual deviants.

Deviant groups tend to develop subcultures.

We therefore have two ideal types of deviants: (1) individual deviants, who reject the norms which surround them and deviate from their subculture; and (2) group deviants, wherein the individual is a conforming member of a deviant group. In practice, deviant persons are not sharply divided into two

such distinct groups. The "ideal type" always is a clearcut expression of an idea, while most real persons fall somewhere between the sharply contrasting images presented by the "ideal types." This is the reason for constructing the ideal types; they clearly express an idea. Meanwhile, we remember that very few people perfectly fit into an ideal type, but are intermediate; for example, few people are either "dominant" or "submissive"; most people show some of each characteristic.

In the case of deviant persons, many deviants are not perfect examples of either individual or group deviation, but show elements of both. Rarely is an individual deviant *completely* surrounded by conventional groups and influences. If he were, it is unlikely that he would ever deviate at all! But even the most carefully sheltered child hears about crimes and immorality, comes across literature his parents would censor, and observes other children violating the norms his parents revere. In other words, even a highly conventional subculture does not completely isolate the person from deviant patterns which he can observe and follow.

Furthermore, deviant persons tend to join with other similar persons into deviant groups. The "bad boys" in the schoolroom tend to form a clique, reinforcing one another's boisterous behavior. Individual hotrodders, hippies, drug addicts, or homosexuals tend to drift together into groups of deviants. These groups reinforce and sanction the deviation, give the member emotional protection against conformist critics, and possibly help to cultivate new deviants. These groups of deviants tend to develop a private language and a set of rigidly stereotyped behavior norms of their own. In short, they tend to develop subcultures. Thus it becomes hard to say whether the hippie of the 1960s was a deviant nonconformist or a rigidly conforming member of a deviant subculture. In practice, then, the distinction between the individual and the group deviant becomes blurred; yet the theoretical distinction is an important one, as our later discussion will elaborate.

Primary and secondary deviation The concepts of primary and secondary deviation, proposed by Lemert [1951, pp. 75–76], help to show how people may become confirmed deviants. *Primary deviation* is the deviant behavior of a person who is conformist in the rest of his life organization. His deviant behavior is so trivial, or so generally tolerated, or so successfully concealed that he is not publicly identified as deviant, nor does he consider himself a deviant, but views himself as a "decent fellow" who has a little secret or eccentricity. Lemert writes that "the deviations remain primary . . . as long as they are rationalized or otherwise dealt with as functions of a socially acceptable role" [1951, p. 75]. *Secondary deviation* is that which follows one's public identification as a deviant. Sometimes the discovery of a single deviant act (of rape, incest, homosexuality, burglary, drug use), or even a false accusation, may be enough to "label" one as a deviant (rapist, "dope fiend," etc.). This *labeling process* [Lemert, 1951, pp. 77; Becker, 1963, chap. 1] is highly important, for it is often the "point of no return" in the development of a deviant life organization. While engaging in no more than primary deviation, one still maintains a conventional set of statuses and roles, and is subjected mainly to the normal series of conformity-reinforcing group pressures and associations. But being labeled as "deviant" tends to be followed by isolation from these conformity-reinforcing influences. A person so labeled may be dismissed from his job or disbarred from his profession, ostracized by conventional people, and possibly imprisoned and forever branded as "criminal." He is almost forced into association with fellow deviants by his exclusion from conventional

society. As one becomes dependent upon his deviant associations and begins to use his deviation as a defense against the conventional society which has branded him, his deviation becomes the central focus of his life reorganization.

There is also a self-isolating factor in much secondary deviation. As one continues to repeat a deviant act, he may become increasingly bored and uncomfortable among conventional people, and may voluntarily begin to confine his associations to other deviants. Thus one moves from primary to secondary deviation.

It is likely that much of the disorganization and demoralization which often accompany deviation is due to the effects of secondary deviation. For example, it has been widely noted that LSD users are likely to become unmotivated, passive "dropouts." Many members of the hippie subculture report that LSD was the turning point in their change of philosophy and life style [Freedman, 1968]. But these are subjective impressions, and cannot be accepted as conclusive. A ten-year follow-up study of 247 subjects who received multiple doses of LSD under medical supervision found "little evidence that measurable, lasting personality, belief, value, attitude, or behavior changes were produced in the sample as a whole [and that LSD] becomes less attractive with continued use and, in the long-term, is almost always self-limiting" [McGothlin and Arnold, 1971, p. 35]. This suggests that any lasting demotivation and demoralization accompanying LSD usage may be due mainly to the conditions and associations surrounding its use, plus the possible self-selection of unstable persons who became LSD users. In this and many other instances, it is difficult to separate the effects of primary and secondary deviation.

Simmons [1970, pp. 122–124] has pointed out how a great many people experiment with deviation at some moments during their lives. Most of them eventually return to conformity. Labeling, isolation, and secondary deviation all impede this return to conformity and thus help to confirm people in a pattern of deviant life organization.

Culturally approved deviation

Deviant behavior is culturally evaluated. Some deviation is condemned; some is applauded. The wandering holy man of one society is the worthless bum of another; the rugged hero of the raw frontier is the uncouth boor of an urban community. In our society, the genius, the hero, the leader, and the celebrity are among our culturally approved deviants.

Causes of individual distinction There has been much speculation about what contributes to individual greatness. A large number of studies have compared leaders with followers, both among children and in adult groups; and some studies [Gibb, 1954] have also surveyed the "great men" of history to see what distinguished them from ordinary people. Most of the studies find that leaders (but not necessarily scholars or creative artists) tend to be taller than average. Several studies find that attractive appearance and dress are associated with leadership. Several find that leaders are considerably, *but not too greatly*, above average in intelligence; those who are greatly above average apparently seek learning or creative work instead of political or organizational leadership. Several studies find associations between leadership and self-confidence, sociability, will, dominance, or other traits. But these many studies do not agree in finding any consistent pattern of traits for great men or leaders.

Efforts to find *the* causes of greatness are probably doomed by the fact that there are many kinds of "greatness," and each may call for different personal qualities. The saint, the war hero, the revolutionist, the artist, the scientist, and the tycoon are far from uniform in their attributes or their paths to greatness. A look at some possible "causes" of greatness will reveal the difficulty of assigning any general causes of individual achievement. ·

1. Intelligence. Intelligence is more useful in some roles than in others. The intellectual mediocrity is unlikely to gain fame as a scientist or mathematician, but extraordinary intelligence is less necessary to the actor, the athlete, or the religious or political leader; in these roles, certain other qualities of talent, physique, character, or personality are especially important. Great intelligence may even be a handicap in some roles, as it may isolate the gifted person from ordinary people, or bar him from the comfortable oversimplifications which allow less perceptive men to act with confidence. Fools rush in—and sometimes succeed—where wiser men fear to tread because the wise are able to foresee the hazards and possible consequences of such rash action. All in all, the factor of intelligence in personal greatness is probably exaggerated in popular thought—possibly because it seems so unkind to suggest that behind the great man's sterling character, magnetic personality, and benign smile, there sometimes lurks a mediocre brain.

2. Special aptitudes. As implied above, the greatness of the athlete, the musician, the actor, the ballerina, the artist, and certain others rests more heavily upon special aptitudes than upon superior general intelligence. Some intelligence is necessary if one is to use his aptitudes effectively; yet many famous men have also been famous for their naïveté and poor judgment outside their field of special talent. The difference between the great artist and the rest of us seems to be found in a greater special aptitude, not in greater intelligence.

3. Motivation. We speculate much upon the topic of motivation, but actually we know relatively little. Motivation is clearly a factor in success, but just why a person becomes highly motivated is not easy to determine. Group pressure is probably a factor. For example, the drive for success and upward mobility in the United States appears to be stronger among Jews than gentiles and among middle-class than lower-class persons. Family tradition is probably a factor, but tradition is difficult to measure, since it cannot be separated from the other aids and opportunities which a distinguished family gives to its children.

Social scientists suspect that intense motivation is often *compensatory*. This is to say, one may be highly motivated as an unconscious response to some frustration or deprivation. Hitler and Napoleon may have drawn their motivation from their lonely, rejected childhoods, Richard III from his deformity, and Theodore Roosevelt from his childhood delicacy. We suspect that such wishes as the desire to win the affectionate approval of an unresponsive or demanding parent, the wish to humble a resented relative, or to prove one's worth to a skeptical hometown may form the core of many a successful person's motivation. Feelings of insecurity, inferiority, resentment, or hostility may thus find outlet through intense efforts at personal achievement. This possibility is difficult to prove, disprove, or measure, but it holds an important place in our thinking about motivation.

4. Personality traits. The effort to identify the personality traits which make for greatness has produced much speculation and many studies. But such studies are doomed to be contradictory and inconclusive because different roles require different personality traits. Physical courage is essential to a soldier but unnecessary to an artist; sociability and conviviality, useful to the businessman or politician, may be a positive interference in the career of the writer, artist, or scientist.

Popular thinking is confused by a number of popular stereotypes about individual distinction—the mad scientist, the temperamental musician, the Bohemian artist, and so on. Some of these stereotypes may not be entirely untrue, for the "self-fulfilling prophecy" may help them to become true. A "self-fulfilling prophecy" is one in which the prophecy starts a series of events that make it come true [Merton, 1957a, chap. 11]. (For example, if I point at a girl in the class and say, "You are going to blush! Watch her blush, everybody!" she nearly always blushes brightly.) If great musicians are expected to be highly temperamental, and their outbursts of rudeness and immaturity are excused as "artistic temperament," such outbursts may be encouraged. If the great actor or artist is expected to pursue his amours with a zest which others dare not imitate, we should not be surprised when he does so. However, very little empirical evidence either confirms or disproves these popular stereotypes, and the serious student will not rely upon them.

The stereotype of the mad genius, however, has been thoroughly exploded. The belief that extraordinarily gifted people are nearly always unstable, erratic, physically delicate, and precariously poised on a thin dividing line between genius and insanity is nonsense. We hear of child prodigies who mature into an ineffectual obscurity, and we may not realize that most child prodigies become distinguished adults—Mozart, Francis Bacon, John Stuart Mill, Albert Einstein, and Norbert Wiener, for example. The stereotype of the sexually irresponsible artist is fed by the Casanova types like Wagner and Liszt, although they were outnumbered by good family men like Bach and Mendelssohn. Several studies of great men of history have concluded that the majority of them were quite conventional in their personal and family relationships [Dempsey, 1958]. For many years, Terman [1959] followed the careers of a sample of 1,000 exceptionally gifted children (as measured by intelligence quotient, an admittedly imperfect measure, but the only practical one available). He found that, both as children and as adults, the gifted group is well above average in physical development, emotional stability, and nearly every other "desirable" attribute, and that their adult achievement is greatly above average. He furthermore found that, up to IQs of about 170, the more highly gifted among his sample average higher in most of these other respects. The mad genius makes good melodrama but poor social science.

Personality characteristics are doubtless extremely important factors in achievements, often the most important factors. A man's childhood experiences, his parental relationships, and his relations with wife and relatives all have profound effects upon his work. But we dare not generalize. One man's achievement is encouraged by an adoring wife and an admiring clan of relatives; another's is a refuge from a shrewish wife and a revenge upon disbelieving relatives. Bach was immersed in music by a large affectionate family of musicians; Mozart's interest in music was applauded by an exploitative father; Handel fought his way into music over the bitter protest of a tyrannical father. Many different kinds of social situations and personality attributes may enter into great achievement, and it is hazardous to generalize about them.

5. *Cultural evaluation.* The values of the culture determine whether a particular deviant is praised or pilloried. This is another example of cultural relativism. Some cultures, such as the Zuñi or Hopi, encourage very little deviation of any kind whatever; persons of remarkable individual achievement are rare in such a culture. Other cultures, such as the Haida or Kwakiutl, or the contemporary American culture, encourage individual distinction of certain approved sorts. In such cultures, persons of great achievement are fairly numerous, highly honored, and widely emulated. A culture may thus encourage or dis-

courage great personal achievement, direct it into one channel or another. or even block it completely. What would Einstein have accomplished in a society which had no need to count beyond ten? Beethoven among the American Indians might have added a new drum beat, but he would never have written the Ninth Symphony.

Some people will insist that a genius in any society would still find some way to express his talents through great achievements. Since we cannot reincarnate Einstein for a second try among the Hottentots, such statements cannot be either proved or disproved. But we suspect that when a primitive genius came up with a new idea, it was accepted and used only if it fitted in with the needs and values of his society; otherwise it was generally suppressed, ignored, or ridiculed, and thereby lost and forgotten. Thus the genius in any society is able to make only the kinds of contributions which are welcomed by at least some groups in his society.

6. *Luck.* Good fortune cannot make a genius of a dullard, but fortune can give or withhold a favorable opportunity to display one's abilities. Would Eisenhower have become President if there had been no World War II? Would he have been picked as Allied Commander if he had been a few years younger or a few years older? Great achievement requires not only that one have certain talents, but that he have them at just the right place at the right time. History is filled with gifted generals and statesmen, like Smuts, Masaryk, and Sequoia, who are buried in the footnotes because they led one of the minor nations. The factor of luck can easily be exaggerated by the cynic, but the serious student of individual achievement does not overlook it.

To summarize. A number of factors in extraordinary personal achievement are difficult to isolate and measure. Since different kinds of achievement differ so greatly in their requirements, there probably are no general "qualities of greatness." Popular thinking about greatness is confused by many romantic stereotypes, and fails to give proper weight to the social and cultural factors in individual achievement.

Culturally disapproved deviation

Most societies permit and reward deviation in the form of extraordinary achievements in activities already approved by the values of the culture. But most societies are unhappy about individual failure to attain the norms in approved activities, while deviation from the mores is even more severely disapproved.

Deviation through physical inability to conform Those with physical or mental defect may be incapable of normal achievements or normal social behavior. The term *mental defect* refers to limited learning capacity, through either inheritance or brain damage. The diagnosis and treatment of physical or mental defect lie largely outside the field of sociology. But sociologists are interested in beliefs about mental defect, and social policies concerning defectives. The popular belief that all mental defectives multiply like hamsters is incorrect. Birth rates are high only among the "high-grade morons" or borderline defectives; among the more seriously defective, the greater the defect, the lower tends to be the birth rate and the survival rate. Most of the inherited severe mental defect appears among children of normal parents who carry recessive gene defects, so that only a small fraction of severe mental defect could be prevented by sterilizing all mental defectives. Since all true mental defect and most physical defect is incurable at present, social policy is mainly concerned with preparing defectives to be as socially useful as their abilities permit.

Mental illness is a disorganization of behavior rather than a lack of learning capacity. In mental illness, a person who may be within the normal range of learning capacity is unable to perceive and respond to realities in an orderly and rational manner. His reality perceptions may be so distorted that he imagines that people are persecuting him or that he hears strange voices and commands, or he becomes disoriented and forgets where he is and what he is doing. His self-perceptions may become distorted, so that he becomes obsessed with his own worthlessness, sinfulness, or incompetence, or perhaps develops delusions of grandeur and power. His reactions to reality may become confused and erratic, or he may withdraw from reality into an inner world of fantasy.

The classification, diagnosis, and treatment of mental illness lie in the fields of psychology, psychiatry, and medicine. Sociologists are mainly interested in the social and cultural factors involved in producing mental illness, and in our social attitudes and policies toward it.

The causes of mental illness appear to be both physical and social, but in unknown proportions. All students of mental illness agree that heredity is a factor, but the exact degree and operation of the hereditary factor has not been established [Jost and Sontag, 1944; Kallman, 1946; Coleman, 1964, pp. 117–129]. The fact that mental illness often runs in a family is not very helpful, since the members of a family generally share both a similar heredity and a similar social experience. Yet each individual is biologically and biochemically unique. Williams [1956] has shown that individuals vary considerably, even in the size and location of internal organs, the chemical composition of body fluids, the number of branch arteries, the branching of trunk nerves, and many other respects. It is known that severe malnutrition can induce personality disorders [Keys, 1952; Wilder, 1952]. Kretschmer [1925] and Sheldon and Stevens [1942] have shown how at least some types of mental illness seem to show some association with constitutional body type, but constitutional factors and their exact roles remain to be established. The entire question of the hereditary, constitutional, or organic causation of mental illness is not yet settled.

There is widespread agreement among scientists that most mental illness is precipitated, or "triggered," by mental conflicts, especially the conflicts provoked by guilts, frustrations, and anxieties. Yet some people survive intense and prolonged stress without becoming disorganized, while others succumb quickly. Obviously, people differ in their ability to endure mental conflicts. It is not known whether this difference is partly physical; some people may be biologically better able to endure mental conflict without becoming disorganized. Certain physical changes or disorders may make a healthy person become susceptible to mental illness. There is widespread agreement among scientists, however, that the socialization process is extremely important. It may develop a secure and confident personality, well able to meet the stresses and conflicts of social life, or it may develop an insecure and complex-ridden personality, unable to survive even mild stress without disorganization.

Sociologists are especially interested in the ways a culture may create mental conflicts for individuals. The culture may impose difficult role transitions, such as our transition from youth into adulthood or from active adulthood into retirement. It may require difficult choices, so arranged that neither alternative is fully comfortable; an example is the American wife who is under pressure to get a job so that the family can live better, and also under pressure to stay home and take care of the family. Massive advertising campaigns guarantee that people's wants will constantly outrun their means; this fostering of desires may be economically useful, but it is emotionally costly. Our culture teaches many contradictory values: Be generous, but hang on to your money; be modest and unassuming, but be sure to get ahead; don't take advantage of others' hardship, but remember that business is business; be thrifty and saving, but keep spending lest you touch off a recession; be virtuous, but don't be inhibited; love your enemies, but extend no sympathies lest you be disloyal. Any complex, changing culture includes many such culture conflicts, and these become mental conflicts for individuals. To some students of mental illness, such conflicts within the culture are largely responsible for the mental conflicts which precipitate much of our mental illness [Horney, 1937].

Some cultural conflicts can encourage mental conflicts.

The simple well-integrated societies, then, should provoke fewer mental conflicts and have less mental illness than we have. There is some evidence that this is true [Carothers, 1947], but it is difficult to be certain. Many difficulties arise when an observer from our society tries to diagnose and measure mental illness in a different cultural setting. Sometimes later studies of a group have concluded that the earlier studies underestimated the amount of mental illness in that group [Kaplan and Plaut, 1956]. Furthermore, if increasing cultural complexity produces mental illness, then our rates should have increased during the past century. Whether they have is uncertain; one study [Goldhamer and Marshall, 1953] concludes that there was no noticeable increase between 1840 and 1940. Yet it is significant that "no field worker has reported a high rate of schizophrenia [our most common form of mental illness] in a stable primitive society which is isolated from white influences. Wherever schizophrenia is recorded, the society is in the process of change" [Miller and Swanson, 1960, p. 42; also Demerath, 1942]. Until more is definitely known, we may only conclude that it *seems likely* that the mental conflicts produced by the culture are a major factor in mental illness.

Social attitudes toward mental illness show a fascinating variety. Some primitive societies assumed that the mentally ill were supernaturally favored and gave them special privileges and recognition. Medieval Europeans blamed mental illness upon demon possession and therefore tortured and abused the victim to chase the demons from his miserable body. (There are no reliable data measuring the success of this heroic treatment!) Even today, many people cannot accept mental illness as an *illness* without connotations of humiliation or disgrace. This attitude is revealed in their preference for the euphemism "nervous breakdown," and by their unwillingness to admit that an illness is mental or to visit patients at a mental hospital, or to accept members back into the family when they are ready for release [Rock, 1968, pp. 217–218]. Such attitudes have the effect of prolonging mental illness, since they lead people to delay treatment, and make recovery more difficult even after treatment is sought. As long as such prescientific attitudes persist, they will remain among the "causes" of mental illness.

Physical-type theories of deviation The idea that certain body types are predisposed

to certain kinds of behavior is almost as old as human history. A number of modern scholars, including Lombroso [1912], Kretschmer [1925], Hooton [1939], Von Hentig [1947], and Sheldon [1949] have made studies claiming to find that certain body types are more prone to deviant behavior than others. The most recent and elaborate theory is that of Sheldon, who identifies three basic body types: endomorph (round, soft, fat); mesomorph (muscular, athletic); and ectomorph (thin, bony). For each type, Sheldon describes an elaborate series of personality traits and behavior tendencies. For example, he finds that delinquents and alcoholics are generally mesomorphs. He attributes neurosis largely to one's effort to be different from what his body type predisposes him to be.

Physical-type theories appear occasionally as "scientific" articles in popular magazines and Sunday papers. They have become quite popular, possibly because they seem to offer a simple, scientific way of classifying people and predicting or explaining their behavior. Social scientists, however, are quite skeptical of the body-type theories [Clinard, 1968, pp. 173–174]. Although these theories are supported by impressive empirical evidence, critics have noted serious errors in method which cast doubts upon their findings. For example, the process of classifying subjects into the several body types included no adequate methodological safeguards against unconscious bias; consequently, a borderline subject may have been placed in whatever body-type class he "belonged" in order to support the theory. The subject groups used in most of these studies were composed of institutionalized delinquents, who are not properly representative of all types of delinquents. Furthermore, the control groups of "normal" people were collected so unsystematically that it is doubtful whether they were a representative cross section of people. More carefully controlled research is continuing, and associations between body type and behavior continue to be claimed [Cortez and Gatti, 1970], but no reliable associations have yet been generally accepted by social scientists.

Psychoanalytic theories of deviant behavior Psychoanalysis is firmly rooted in Freud's concepts of the id, ego, and superego, as described in Chapter 5. Deviant behavior is attributed to conflicts between the id and the ego, or between the id and the superego. Crime, for example, takes place when the superego, the civilized self-control of the individual, is unable to restrain the savage, primitive, destructive impulses of the id [Zilboorg, 1943; Abrahamsen, 1944].

Do the id, ego, and superego represent major aspects of the human personality, or are they merely words that psychoanalysts quote to one another? Do death wishes, castration complexes, and Oedipal stages actually exist in the normal personality, or does the psychoanalyst unconsciously plant the expected symptoms in the patient's mind and dig them up in subsequent interviews? We do not definitely know. Psychoanalytic theory is almost totally unsubstantiated by empirical research, while a number of such efforts have been inconclusive or nonconfirmatory. In Chapter 5 we cited Sewell's findings [1952] which cast doubt on psychoanalytic theory about specific child-training practices. Barnes [1952] sought to test the Freudian theory of the successive oral, anal, and phallic levels of psychosexual development and concluded that "the Freudian theory of levels of psychosexual development has not been supported as a whole." In all, comparatively few empirical attempts to test psychoanalytic theory have been made. It would, in fact, be quite difficult to design research that would either establish or disprove the usefulness of such concepts as the id or the ego. But until such research is completed, psychoanalytic theory remains debatable, even though it is

widely used in the treatment of behavior disorders. Its clinical success is sometimes cited as proof of psychoanalytic theory; that is, since some of the patients improve under psychoanalytic treatment, the theory must be sound. But such claims for successful treatment are not accompanied by a comparison of these patients with a control group of untreated patients, many of whom improve without treatment. Consequently, we cannot know whether the patients improved because of the treatment or because of other factors.

If, without using psychoanalytic terminology, we merely state that culture often frustrates biological drives, little argument is possible. While the id may be debatable, there is no doubt about the existence of biological drives such as hunger and sex, or of the organic reactions associated with fear and anger. Clearly, too, culture often frustrates these drives and impulses. Our culture, for example, makes no socially approved provision for the sexual drives of those who are unmarried, widowed, or separated. If one gratifies such impulses in defiance of cultural taboos, he is engaging in deviant behavior. If, however, he disposes of the impulse by *repressing* it into his unconscious (to return to psychoanalytic theory), it does not go away, but remains as part of his unconscious motivation and may still give rise to deviant behavior of some kind. Thus the sex-starved spinster may repress her sex drives into her unconscious, where they remain active, perhaps impelling her to extreme prissiness, to religious fanaticism, to health anxieties, or to some other emotional "cover-ups." Stated in this less tortuous manner, psychoanalytic theory, while still unproved, becomes a highly plausible explanation for much deviant behavior.

Socialization failures and deviation Every member of a society is frustrated by the clash of his biological drives with the taboos of his culture. But not everyone becomes a deviant. Why, when most persons conform to the norms of the culture, do some become deviant? There is no convincing evidence that most of these deviants differ significantly from the conformists in their inherited or constitutional behavior impulses. Therefore, *social scientists assume that they are deviant because the socialization process has failed in some way to integrate the cultural norms into the individual's personality.* Where the socialization process is successful, the individual adopts the norms which surround him, and the approved goals and values of the culture become his own emotional needs, while the taboos of his culture become a part of his conscience. He *internalizes* the norms of his culture so that he automatically and mechanically acts in the expected manner most of the time. His lapses are rare, and both he and others recognize that they are lapses from his normal behavior.

Behavioral scientists are agreed that moral values and behavior norms are learned mainly in the family. Where the child is socialized in a happy, affectionate, conventional family, he usually develops a secure, well-adjusted personality, behaves conventionally in most respects, marries successfully, and provides a happy, affectionate, conventional home for his children, who then repeat the cycle. Where family life is unsatisfactory, the children often develop personality difficulties and behavior deviations. The Gluecks [1959], after many years of carefully controlled comparisons of delinquent and nondelinquent youth, predict that juvenile delinquency is at least a 90 percent probability when the "five highly decisive" factors in family life are unfavorable: father's discipline (harsh, erratic, unsympathetic); mother's supervision (indifferent, unconcerned); father's affection (lacking); mother's affection (cold, indifferent, hostile); cohesiveness of the family (unintegrated, empty of companionship).

Where all five of these factors are favorable, they find virtually no serious delinquency.

The exact manner in which one's family life molds personality into conforming or deviant channels shows an endless variety. Some families make no conscious effort to transmit the cultural norms to their children, while others try but fail, as is shown in this personal history taken from the authors' files.

As far back as I can remember anything, I can recall those scenes which always ended with my mother's tearful lament, "Why can't you be more like your brother?" while I kept to myself the thought, "Be like that big sissy? Not on your life." He was older and was expected to look after me, which I resented. So anything he counseled against, I promptly did. I think it was emotionally necessary for me not to be or do anything he was or did. He was studious; I avoided school books like they were disease germs. He was neat, orderly, punctual, and methodical; I shunned these weaknesses. He did exactly what our parents and teachers asked; I did nothing they asked. He was a "good boy," and they showed their pride in him on every occasion; they were never proud of me. He and my father were close confidants and companions; my only companions were other "bad boys" from whom my parents made strenuous—and unsuccessful—efforts to separate me. When I finally stood, dry-eyed, beside my father's casket while my brother sniffled, my only thought was, "Why don't you die too, you stupid square!"

We cannot be certain just why this boy rejected parental values and standards while his brother was accepting them. One might guess that his parents showed some favoritism and perhaps a lack of sympathetic interest, and made a clumsy use of the older brother as model. Yet a similar family atmosphere had an opposite effect upon another child, as is shown in this case, also taken from the authors' files.

All my life I have been competing with my older brother. From the first I felt that he was better, smarter, and more handsome than I. He was the one whom my parents loved the more, criticized more gently, praised more highly, and proudly showed off before the relatives and guests. I recall that at such moments, I harbored no feelings of resentment, but only feelings of wistful longing that I might also deserve such appreciation. I became very dutiful and obedient, and my intense efforts to do what they wished were sometimes rewarded.

Today, as a middle-aged adult, I feel a good deal of resentment toward them. I suppose that my dedicated efforts to earn their affection are responsible both for my success, which greatly surpasses my brother's, and for my anxieties and tensions, which are considerable. Although both parents have been dead for years, my persistent emotional need to seek approval through perfect performance is both my virtue and my curse. I often wonder what I would be today, had I received the warm acceptance my brother always enjoyed.

These two cases illustrate the fact that *there is no social situation which has uniformly predictable effects upon all persons in that situation.* All attempts to link predictably a particular behavior outcome with a particular type of family experience are doomed to failure. The most we can say is that certain kinds of family experience *usually* produce well-adjusted, conforming people, while family life which is deficient in certain characteristics is more likely to produce poorly adjusted personalities and behavior deviation. The specific deficiencies may be of many sorts—parental neglect or abuse, lack of sympathy and affection, harsh or erratic discipline, lack of family cohesiveness, excessive parental demands and unrealistic standards, or any of a number of other defects which keep the home from being a pleasant, comfortable place. Inadequate parents may fail in at least two general ways:

(1) They may fail to provide a satisfactory model of normal behavior for their children to copy. If the parents are themselves deviant persons, their children have little opportunity to learn the conventional behavior norms. There is a good deal of speculation upon the possibility that much alcoholism, drug addiction, sex deviation, marital inadequacy, and other behavior difficulty may stem from a boy's inability to identify with his weak, ineffectual father, so that the son was never able to form a satisfactory masculine self-image. Feminine difficulties are often attributed in like manner to a girl's unsatisfactory mother-model. This theory is plausible and widely accepted, although as yet largely unsubstantiated.

(2) Parents may strive to present a satisfactory model and to instill the cultural norms in their children, but they may still fail as parents if they are too demanding, too critical, too strict, too erratic, or too unloving. At any rate, a child sometimes develops a strong emotional need to resist parental goals and standards and to shock parents and others by unconventional behavior. A study of American ex-Communists by Ernst and Loth [1952] found that most of them were resentful, somewhat unhappy children of conventional, domineering parents, and had joined the Communist party briefly during young adulthood as a means of emancipation from and revenge upon their parents. Psychiatrists are convinced that some alcoholics are resentful persons who, probably unconsciously, are revenging themselves upon their families by destroying themselves [Podalsky, 1960; Fox, 1956]. L. Young [1954] studied 1,350 unmarried mothers, and concluded that most of them *wanted* an illegitimate child as a form of revenge, usually upon their mothers. An endless variety of behavior difficulties are often traced to some disturbance in the parent-child relationship. Such conclusions are difficult to prove or disprove, but are widely held by behavioral scientists.

Cultural conflicts and deviation In a well-integrated culture with a single set of behavior codes and moral values, socialization is smooth and untroubled. Parents express the cultural norms in their words and actions, and these are reinforced by the rest of the society. But in a heterogeneous, changing society there is no single set of norms; instead many sets of norms and values compete with one another. Many parents find that their efforts to train their children are undermined by other groups and influences. Parents who wish their teen-age children to remain chaste and sober must struggle, not only against the rash, exploratory self-confidence of youth, but also against a variety of commercial panderings and group encouragements which tempt youth to seek "sophistication" and indulgence. Our formal mores demand chastity until marriage, but young people are subjected to a ceaseless barrage of commercial sex stimulation, are exposed to a pseudoscientific literature which encourages and justifies indulgence, and are largely removed from any effective adult chaperonage. Is it surprising that most unmarried young people dally on the borders of unchastity while at least half of them step across it [Reiss, 1967]?

The extreme heterogeneity of American society produces many conflicting norms and values. A variety of immigrant groups have brought differing cultural traditions which are difficult to fuse into a common set of norms. Even the different branches of the Christian faith cannot agree on several questions of morality. Some Protestant groups condemn all alcoholic beverages, dancing, and all kinds of gambling as sinful, while certain other Protestant groups, together with the Catholics, claim that under certain conditions these activities are harmless. The Catholic Church condemns divorce and contraception, while most Protestant bodies will permit them. All American churches teach that one should be generous, sympathetic, and self-sacrificing, but our economic system rewards those who are ruthless, selfish, and grasping. This list of culture conflicts could be extended indefinitely. Many among today's youth angrily charge the society with "hypocrisy" and at-

tribute such cultural contradictions to the insincerity and duplicity of their elders. They fail to recognize that such inconsistencies and culture conflicts are found in virtually all societies, and especially in all heterogeneous, changing societies. But wherever they exist, culture conflicts encourage deviant behavior by undermining and weakening the common set of norms and values upon which social order depends. A fairly high rate of deviation is part of the price we pay for a complex, rapidly changing society.

Anomie and deviation From such a variety of conflicting norms arises a condition which Durkheim [1897] called *anomie*, a condition of "normlessness." He did not mean that modern societies have no norms; instead they have many sets of norms, with none of them clearly binding upon everybody, so that individuals become "normless." Later sociologists extended the term to include the state of mind in which the person has no firm sense of belonging to anything dependable or stabilizing. As Parsons writes, anomie is

. . . the state where large numbers of individuals are in a serious degree lacking in the kind of integration with stable institutions which is essential to their own personal stability and the smooth functioning of the social system. . . . The typical reaction of the individual is . . . insecurity. (*Talcott Parsons*, Essays in Sociological Theory, *The Free Press, New York, 1954, pp. 125, 126.*)

This approach implies that anomie arises from the confusion and conflict of modern society. People move about too rapidly to be bound to the norms of any particular group and, as a result, have no stable perspective from which to make decisions. In this sense anomie is the result of freedom of choice without the balance assumed to come from stable relationships to church, state, family, or community.

Merton [1938] suggests that anomie

comes not from freedom of choice but from the inability of many individuals to follow norms which they are perfectly willing to accept. He sees the major cause of this difficulty as a disharmony between cultural goals and the institutionalized means for reaching them. He notes that while our society encourages *all* its members to aspire to wealth and social position, our approved modes of attaining these goals are so restrictive that only a few have any realistic prospect of reaching them. True, an exceptional poor boy reaches wealth and fame, and these rare exceptions help to preserve the myth of equal opportunity. But a poor boy with a family background of ignorance and apathy and without valuable "connections" has to struggle for success even if he is highly talented. If he has only average abilities, he has still less chance of ever reaching the goals which our culture holds before him, unless he violates the rules for seeking them. So Merton concludes:

It is only when a system of cultural values extols, virtually above all else, certain common success-goals for the population at large while the social structure rigorously restricts or completely closes access to approved modes of reaching these goals for a considerable part of the same population, that deviant behavior ensues on a large scale. . . .

The moral mandate to achieve success thus exerts pressure to succeed, by fair means if possible and by foul means if necessary. (*Robert K. Merton, "Social Structure and Anomie," in his* Social Theory and Social Structure, *The Free Press, New York, 1957, chap. 3, pp. 146, 169.*)

The approved path to success in our society lies in education and occupational advancement. To many people, however, education is a frustrating, boring experience which they escape as soon as possible; occupational advancement eludes them, and the idea of saving and investing is not even seriously considered. Since these people still feel entitled to affluence, they proceed to look for other means than those society approves. These deviant routes to legitimate ends may include gambling, swindling, participation in the rackets, or resort to violent crime. When the condition of anomie becomes so widespread that deviancy becomes the rule rather than the exception, then social control may be considered to have completely broken down.

This substitution of illegitimate for legitimate means is only one of several possible reactions to the disparity between universalized goals and restricted methods of obtaining them. A full range of possible responses is given in Merton's typology [1957, pp. 140–57] illustrated in Table 4. (1) *Conformity* is an acceptance of both the conventional goals and the conventional, institutionalized means of seeking them. (2) *Innovation* is an attempt to attain the conventional goals through unconventional means (including illicit or criminal means). (3) *Ritualism* preserves the institutionalized means, which have become ends in themselves, as the goals are largely ignored or forgotten. The rituals, ceremonies, and routines are followed, but the original meanings or functions have become lost. (4) *Retreatism* abandons both the conventional goals and the institutionalized means for attaining them, as illustrated by most of the advanced alcoholics, drug addicts, hippies, skid-row bums, hermits, and other "dropouts." (5) *Rebellion* involves a retreat from the conventional goals and means, with an attempt to institutionalize a new system of goals and means. The revolutionists of today's New Left are generally uninterested in promoting a new set of institutionalized goals and means in place of the present one. Unlike Marxian Communists, who always offered a fairly detailed blue print of the new society, our New Left revolutionists are largely preoccupied with disrupting the present system [See A. Hoffman, 1968, 1971]. It is debatable whether they should be classed as revolutionists or simply as aggressive retreatists in Merton's typology.

TABLE 4

A typology of modes of individual adaptation

Modes of Adaptation	Culture Goals	Institutionalized Means
I. *Conformity*	+	+
II. *Innovation*	+	−
III. *Ritualism*	−	+
IV. *Retreatism*	−	−
V. *Rebellion*	±	±

Note: In the table above, (+) signifies "acceptance," (−) signifies "rejection," and (±) signifies "rejection of prevailing values and substitution of new values."
Source: Robert K. Merton, Social Theory and Social Structure, *The Free Press, New York, 1957, p. 140.*

Whereas Merton sees deviation growing from one's inability to achieve culturally inspired goals, Riesman [1950] sees deviation growing from the shift to *other-direction* in modern society. In traditional societies, according to Riesman, people are *tradition-directed;* that is, they are guided by a coherent set of traditions which they follow with little deviation. Some centuries ago, Western society became *inner-directed*, with people guided by a conscience which had internalized the rather authoritarian indoctrination of family and other groups in a stable community. Today man is increasingly *other-directed*, for the lack of a coherent tradition or a stable community is leaving him with no clear guide to conduct except the judgments of other people. But since modern societies have many groupings, with differing norms, other-direction provides no dependable guide to conduct. Consequently the behavior of the individual often lacks consistency and conforms to no dependable norm. Since it is impossible, in our complex and changing society, to reestablish stable communities, Riesman looks to the development of "autonomous" persons who can order their lives responsibly without being rooted in stable communities or being puppets of their peer groups. Whether this autonomy is possible remains an unanswered question.

McClosky and Schaar [1965] suggest that anomic normlessness may be simply one aspect of a negative and distrustful outlook on life and society. They present evidence that anomie appears, not only among Merton's frustrated failures, but also among the highly successful. They find that persons who score high on anomic scales also show high scores for hostility, anxiety, pessimism, authoritarianism, political cynicism, and other symptoms of alienation.

All authorities agree that anomie is not the only explanation for deviant behavior, but that anomie is an important factor. Just *how* important it is and exactly *how* anomie produces deviant behavior are still unsettled questions.

Significance of deviant behavior

Deviation is relative, not absolute People are not completely conformist or completely deviant. A completely deviant person would have a hard time staying alive. Even the more spectacular deviants, such as criminals or sex deviants, are generally fairly conventional in dress, food habits, recreation, and many other activities. And nearly all "normal" people are occasionally deviant. Kinsey [1948, p. 392, 576] has shown how over half our adults could be imprisoned for using techniques of lovemaking which were (and still are) forbidden by the laws of most states. A number of studies have shown that most people have committed a number of major crimes for which they could receive penitentiary sentences if all laws were fully enforced [Porterfield, 1946; Wallerstein and Wyle, 1947]. It is clear that nearly everyone in our society is deviant to some degree; but some are more frequently and broadly deviant than others, and some conceal their deviant actions more fully than others. To some extent, the recognized deviant is one who does openly what others do secretly.

Deviation from real or ideal culture? Since the real and ideal cultures often diverge, as mentioned in Chapter 3, conformity to one may be deviation from the other. For example, the ideal culture includes the cultural norm of obedience to all laws, yet practically no one obeys all laws.

Where important values are involved in the divergence between what people say (ideal culture) and what they do (real culture), this becomes an important distinction. In each discussion of deviation where this distinction is important, the normative base —real or ideal culture—should be either implied or expressly stated. For example, in any discussion of premarital chastity or of certain sex "crimes" which are widely practiced by married couples, the normative base should be specified.

Norms of evasion Whenever the mores forbid something that many people strongly wish to do, *norms of evasion* are likely to appear. These are the patterns through which people indulge their wishes without openly challenging the mores. For example, Roebuck and Spray [1967] show how the cocktail lounge functions to facilitate discreet sexual affairs between high-status married men and unattached young women.

The fact that a particular norm is often violated does not necessarily create a norm of evasion. It is only when there is a *pattern* of violation which is *recognized and sanctioned by one's group* that we have a norm of evasion. Patronizing a bootlegger became a norm of evasion when it became a standard, group-approved way of getting the forbidden alcoholic beverages. In becoming group-sanctioned, the evasion loses its moral censure. Among many groups, success in "fixing" traffic tickets or in seducing women will earn one the admiration of his fellows. Norms of evasion thus are a semi-institutionalized form of deviant behavior.

Deviation and social change Deviation is both a threat and a protection to social stability. On the one hand, a society can function efficiently only if there is order and predictability in social life. We must *know*, within reasonable limits, what behavior to expect from others, what they expect of us, and what kind of society our children should be socialized to live in. Deviant behavior threatens this order and predictability. If too many people fail to behave as expected, the culture becomes disorganized and social order collapses. Economic activity may be disrupted, and actual shortages may appear. The mores lose their compelling power, and the society's core of common values shrinks. Individuals feel insecure and confused in a society whose norms have become undependable. Only when most of the people conform to well-established norms most of the time can a society function efficiently.

On the other hand, *deviant behavior is one way of adapting a culture to social change.* No society today can possibly remain static for long. Even the most isolated of the world's societies faces sweeping social changes within the next generation. The population explosion, technological change, and the passing of tribal or folk cultures will require the more primitive peoples to learn new norms, while changing technology continues to demand adaptations from the more advanced peoples. But new norms are seldom produced by deliberative assemblies of people who solemnly pronounce the old norms outworn and call for new ones. While the grave deliberations of congresses, religious councils, and professional associations may accelerate or retard the development of new norms, their pronouncements more often serve to legitimate new norms which are well on the way to general acceptance. New norms emerge from the daily behavior of individuals, responding in similar ways to the impact of new social circumstances. The deviant behavior of a few individuals may be the beginnings of a new norm. As more and more people join in the deviant form of behavior, a new norm will eventually be established, and the behavior will cease to be "deviant."

The deviant behavior of one generation may become the norm of the next.

The emergence of new norms is neatly illustrated in the decline of the patriarchal family. In an agrarian society where all the family worked together under the father's watchful eye, it was easy to maintain male dominance. But changing technology moved the father's job to the shop or office, where he could no longer keep his eye on things; changing technology also began drawing the wife into jobs where she worked apart from her husband and earned her own paycheck. The husband was no longer in a strategic position to assert his male authority, and, bit by bit, it slipped from him. In the nineteenth century, the relatively independent, equalitarian woman with a mind of her own and a habit of firmly voicing it was a deviant; today she is commonplace, and the Women's Liberation Movement demands additional changes of sex status. Thus the deviant behavior of one generation may become the norm of the next.

Deviant behavior thus often represents tomorrow's adaptations in their beginnings. Without any deviant behavior, it would be difficult to adapt a culture to changing needs and circumstances. A changing society therefore needs deviant behavior as the incubator of the new norms it must develop if it is to operate efficiently. The question of *how much* deviation and *what kinds* of deviation a society should tolerate is a perpetual puzzle. It is easy now for most people to agree that the eighteenth-century republicans and the nineteenth-century suffragists were socially useful deviants, while the utopians were harmless and the anarchists were socially destructive. But which of today's deviants will prove tomorrow to have been today's trail blazers—the nudists, hippies, pacifists, marijuana users, commune members, free-lovers, one-worlders, or whom? It is difficult to say.

Not all forms of deviation will fit the above analysis. The behavior of the criminal, the sex deviant, or the alcoholic rarely contributes to the forging of a useful new social norm. At any particular moment, deviant behavior takes many forms, only a very few of which are destined to become tomorrow's norms. Much deviation is entirely destructive in its personal and social consequences. But *some* deviation is socially useful, as is indicated above. To separate the socially harmful from the socially useful deviations requires an ability to predict the social norms that tomorrow's society will require. Although sociologists cannot forecast future norms with any certainty of accuracy, they may forecast them somewhat more accurately than others who are not professionals in the study of culture and social change.

SUMMARY

A society must have *social order* if it is to function smoothly. A society maintains *social control* over its members in three principal ways. First, it socializes them so that they will want to behave as they should. Second, society imposes *group pressure* upon the individual so that he must conform or be punished by his group. This group pressure may be expressed through the informal controls of the primary group—approval and disapproval, praise, scorn, ostracism, etc.; or it may operate through the more formal controls of secondary groups—rules and regulations, standardized procedures, propaganda, rewards, titles, and penalties. Finally, control through *force* is used where other controls fail. But in many social situations, behavior is more greatly controlled by the needs and pressures of the situation—the *situational determinants of behavior*—than by the character one brings to the situation.

Social deviation arises whenever a person fails to conform to the usual norms of the society. Deviation may be individual, in that a person deviates from the normal behavior of his group; or it may be group deviation, in which the entire group deviates from social norms, so that the individual is a conforming member of a deviant group or subculture. In practice these two types tend to merge, since deviants tend to seek out other deviants and form deviant groups. *Primary deviation* is the deviant behavior of persons who hold conventional statuses and fill conventional roles in most of their behavior, while *secondary deviation* develops when people are publicly labeled as deviant, are to some degree isolated from conventional roles and associations, and use deviation as an "adjustment" to their social isolation. Deviants are also divided into *cultural deviants* and *psychological deviants*. Cultural deviants simply deviate from the expected behavior norms. Psychological deviants are deviant from the norm in their personality integration; in their social behavior they may be either deviant or conformist.

Some forms of deviation are approved—the leader, hero, genius, and saint are often (although not always) honored and revered. Efforts to determine which factors account for outstanding individual achievement are not very conclusive, but it appears that social circumstances and personality factors other than pure intelligence play a larger role in "greatness" than is generally known.

Many forms of deviation are disapproved by the culture. Deviation through physical *inability* to conform—often caused by physical or mental defect or illness—is usually viewed with sympathy. The role of social and cultural influences in producing mental illness cannot be exactly measured, but there is widespread agreement that our culture provokes mental conflicts which contribute to mental illness. Where there is no clear physical incapacity to conform, the causes of deviation are debatable.

Physical-type theories of deviation are popular but unproved. Psychoanalytic theories are popular and plausible, but also unproved. Most of the disapproved individual deviation probably stems, at least partly if not entirely, from failures in socialization, so that the norms and values of the culture are imperfectly integrated into the personality of the individual. The family plays the key role in socialization and is the main channel through which the child absorbs the society's norms and values. Unsatisfactory family life is, therefore, the principal factor in disapproved individual deviation. The family, however, is a part of the culture, and unsatisfactory family life is often a reflection of conflicts within the culture. Such conflicts surround cultural norms with uncertainty, and by thus imposing pressures upon individuals, help to produce a state of normlessness called *anomie*. The disharmony between our cultural goals and our means for attaining them encourage anomie and deviation.

Deviation is relative, not absolute, in that most people are deviant to some degree.

Wherever a particular pattern of deviation becomes widely followed and excused, it is called a *norm of evasion*. Whenever some aspect of a culture becomes unbearably confining, norms of evasion are likely to appear. In time, these may become the new norms. Thus deviation, while an enemy of social stability, is also a means of introducing the changed norms which become necessary if a changing society is to remain reasonably integrated and efficient.

Questions and projects

1. How does social order depend upon predictability of behavior?

2. Some ancient societies required many human sacrifices. Why did the victims consent to die quietly instead of revolting?

3. Evaluate this statement: "Only weaklings follow the herd. A person with true strength of character will do what he knows is right without being swayed by the group."

4. In the factory a "rate buster" is a worker on piecework who produces and earns so much that management may revise the piece rate downward. How do the other workers treat him? Is he anything like a "course spoiler" in college, who works so hard in a course that the professor begins to expect more from the other students?

5. What do you think of the Tlingit practice of holding the entire group morally responsible for the acts of each member? Does the practice make for effective social control? How widely could we follow it? Is it consistent with our ethos? Does our society have the kind of group structure in which such a practice is workable?

6. Under what circumstances will practically all students cheat? When will very few students cheat? How does this contrast in attitude illustrate "situational determinants of behavior"?

7. In a hippie commune, where each member is "free," what group controls might operate?

8. Why do "backward" or primitive societies have less crime and fewer violations of the mores than "progressive" societies like ours?

9. Distinguish between individual and group deviants. How do these two ideal types tend to merge in practice?

10. What do you think of the suggestion to publish the names of all juvenile delinquents?

11. How would you interpret the high crime rate of black people in terms of Merton's theory of cultural goals and institutionalized means?

12. Discuss these propositions: (1) "Norms of evasion are a threat to social stability." (2) "Norms of evasion are a protection to the stability of a society."

13. Read one of the disaster studies such as William Form, et al., *Community in Disaster*, Harper & Row, Publishers, Incorporated, New York, 1958, Harry E. Moore, *Tornados over Texas*, University of Texas Press, Austin, 1958, or Allen H. Barton, *Communities in Disaster*, Doubleday & Company, Inc., Garden City, N.Y., 1969. Show how social order breaks down and then is restored.

14. Compare and explain the differing success of two families in their effort to insulate their children from the influences of a slum neighborhood, as described in Betty Smith, *A Tree Grows in Brooklyn*, Harper & Row, Publishers, Incorporated, New York, 1943, and James T. Farrell, *A World I Never Made*, Vanguard Press, Inc., New York, 1936.

15. Read Michael E. Brown, "The Condemnation

and Persecution of Hippies," *Trans-action*, September, 1969, pp. 33–46. Do you think hippies are truly being persecuted, or do you think Brown exaggerates?

Suggested readings

*Becker, Howard S.: *Outsiders: Studies in the Sociology of Deviance*, The Free Press, New York, 1963, 1966. A concise description of how people become deviant, applied particularly to marijuana users and dance musicians.

Bernstein, Basil: "Elaborated and Restricted Codes: An Outline," *Sociological Inquiry*, 36:254–261, Spring, 1966. Analysis of the role of language in facilitating communication within the group and simultaneously isolating it from outside contacts.

Brown, Paula: "Changes in Ojibwa Social Control," *American Anthropologist*, 54:57–70, January, 1954. Tells how loss of traditional controls and lack of effective replacements leaves the Ojibwa with an unsolved problem of social control.

Clinard, Marshall: *Sociology of Deviant Behavior*, Holt, Rinehart and Winston, Inc., New York, 1968. A comprehensive textbook on deviation.

*Dinitz, Simon, Russel B. Dynes, and Alfred C. Clark (eds.): *Deviance: Studies in the Process of Stigmatization and Societal Reaction*, Oxford University Press, Fair Lawn, N.J., 1969. A comprehensive reader with essays and research studies on many kinds of deviance.

*Horney, Karen: *The Neurotic Personality of Our Time*, W. W. Norton & Company, Inc., New York, 1937. A classic description of how a competitive, stressful society encourages mental disorders.

Klapp, Orrin E.: "The Folk Hero," *Journal of American Folklore*, 62:17–25, January, 1949; and "Hero Worship in America," *American Sociological Review*, 14:53–62, February, 1949. A study of those who deviate through superfulfillment of cultural norms, and a study also of their admirers. Also,

Heroes, Villains, and Fools: The Changing American Character, Prentice-Hall, Inc., Englewood Cliffs, N.J., 1962. A study of deviant social types and of the society which poses them as models.

Lemert, Edwin M.: *Social Pathology*, McGraw-Hill Book Company, New York, 1951, chaps. 1–3. A perceptive outline of social deviation.

*McCaghy, Charles H., James K. Skipper, Jr., and Mark Lifton: *In Their Own Behalf: Voices from the Margin*, Appleton Century Crofts, 1968. A wide variety of deviants tell their own story.

Means, Richard L.: *The Ethical Imperative: The Crisis in American Values*, Doubleday & Co., Inc., New York, 1969. Argues that social control in a society rushing toward ecological disaster demands a new value system which sees both man and nature as intrinsically valuable.

Merton, Robert K.: *Social Theory and Social Structure*, rev. ed., The Free Press, New York, 1957, chaps. 3 and 4, "Social Structure and Anomie," and "Continuities in the Theory of Social Structure and Anomie." A classic statement upon anomie and deviation in modern society; chap. 11, "The Self-fulfilling Prophecy," is a description of the self-fulfilling prophecy as a basic process in society.

Sagarin, Edward: *Odd Man In: Societies of Deviants in America*, Quadrangle Books, Inc., Chicago, 1970. A readable description of a number of organizations which deviants have formed in the United States.

*Simmons, J. L.: *Deviants*, Glendessary Press, Berkeley, Cal., 1969. A brief, simply written paperback describing sympathetically the process of becoming deviant and the life of deviants.

PART THREE

Social organization

This section describes how society is organized. People are not independent units, like grains of sand on the beach. The members of a society are organized into many kinds of groups, organizations, and relationships. Chapter 8, "Social Groups," describes the kinds of groups which appear in any society—ours in particular. Chapter 9, "Social Institutions," describes how the norms of the culture and the relationships of a society are organized into working systems in order to meet people's needs. Chapter 10, "The Family," is a detailed description of one of these social institutions—probably the most important. Chapter 11, "Formal Organizations," describes the associational structures through which a complex society operates. Chapter 12, "Social Class," describes an extremely important set of status relationships among individuals, and shows how these relationships affect their entire lives. Chapter 13, "Social Mobility," shows how people change their class status.

Take each of us alone, a man apart from the Cheyenne people who remember the same things and wish for the same things. Take each one of us that way, and you have nothing but a man who cannot respect himself because he is a failure in the white man's way. A man who does not respect himself cannot make a good future. There is no strength in his spirit. Now take all of us together as Cheyenne people. Then our names are not the names of failures. They are the names of great and generous hunters who fed the people, fighters who died for freedom just as white men's heroes died, holy men who filled us with the power of God. Take us together that way and there is a drink for every man in the cup of self-respect, and we will have the strength of spirit to decide what to do and to do it. We will do good things as a tribe that is growing and changing that we cannot do as individual men cut off from their forefathers. (*From a statement by the Northern Cheyenne, quoted by Oliver la Farge in* Indian Affairs, *News letter of the Association for American Indian Affairs, Inc., no. 37, New York, June, 1960.*)

Social groups

The Cheyenne are not the only people who find that individual strength and character come from association with the group. All people, regardless of race or culture, find personality fulfillment through group life. The infant becomes "human" as he takes his place in the family; the autistic children mentioned in Chapter 5 are extreme examples of the personality distortion associated with a lack of normal family interaction. As the child moves beyond the family circle, he enters into still other group relationships which will continuously remold his personality until death ends the process.

While "group" is one of the most important concepts in sociology, there is no complete agreement upon a single definition. Such confusion is not because sociologists can't make up their minds! Confusions persist because most concepts (in sociology) are not invented and then put into use; instead, most sociological terms are words which have long been in general use and which sociologists come to use with a particular meaning.

Some terms continue to be used with more than one meaning, because to invent an entirely new set of several words to cover the several meanings would be even more confusing.

Consequently, there are several meanings of "group" in the sociological literature. In one usage, the term denotes *any physical collection of people* (e.g., "a group of people were waiting . . ."). In this usage, a group need share nothing beyond physical proximity. Many sociologists would call such a collection of people an *aggregation* or a *collectivity*.

A second meaning is that of *a number of people who share some common characteristic*. Thus, males, college graduates, physicians, old people, millionaires, commuters, and cigarette smokers would each be a group. *Category* would be a more satisfactory term, but sociologists often use "group" where "category" would be more precise, but perhaps would read more clumsily.

Another usage defines a group as *a number of people who share some organized patterns of recurrent interaction*. This would exclude all casual, momentary meetings of people whose interaction has no pattern of organization or repetition, such as the spectators at a traffic accident. This definition would include the family, the friendship clique, organizations like a club or church organization—any kind of collective contact between people who repeatedly interact according to some pattern of customary procedures and relationships.

Another quite common usage (which your authors prefer) is *any number of persons who share a consciousness of membership and of interaction*. By this definition, two persons waiting for a bus would not be a group, but would become a group if they started a conversation, a fight, or any other interaction. A number of people walking down a street would be an *aggregation* or a *collectivity*, not a group, unless something—a street orator, an accident, a suicide—caught their atten-

tion and held their interest, thus converting them into an *audience*, which is one kind of group (see p. 391). A busload of passengers would not ordinarily be a group because they have no consciousness of interaction with each other but simply happen to be in the same place at the same time. It is possible that interaction may develop in the course of the trip and groups may form. When children begin to play together, or boy meets girl, or businessmen discover a common interest in the stock market or the baseball game, groups begin to develop—transient and amorphous though they be. On occasion the entire aggregate may become a group, as in this instance related by Bierstedt.

Subway passengers in New York, for example, are notoriously indifferent to one another. But only the slightest stimulus is needed to transform [them] . . . into a social group. The writer was in a fairly crowded car one evening in the spring when a very young, very tipsy Scandinavian sailor happened to stroll in from the adjoining car. He began to sing aloud in his native language, a gay pleasant song, and the passengers, aroused from their reveries and their newspapers, responded warmly to his effort and began to exchange smiles with one another. With unexpected and indeed, unusual solicitude for subway passengers, several of the men in the car asked the sailor where he wanted to go and made sure that he did not ride past his destination. After he left, the remaining passengers, augmented now by others who were strangers to the episode, returned to their reveries and their newspapers. The spell was broken. What for a few transitory moments had been a social group became once again . . . people with no more in common than their accidental togetherness at the same time and place, enough to give them a consciousness of kind but not enough, without this extra stimulus, to induce them to enter into social relations with one another. (*Robert Bierstedt*, The Social Order, *McGraw-Hill Book Company, New York, 1957, p. 257.*)

The essence of the social group is not physical closeness but a consciousness of joint interaction. The passengers in the subway car were close together, but until the entry of the sailor gave them a common interest, they were not engaged in joint interaction. Other kinds of stimulus incidents may change an aggregation into a group. For example, a rate increase for passenger fares or a threat to discontinue commuter service may change an unstructured aggregation of passengers into an effective, self-conscious group, developing the usual group patterns as they seek to safeguard a privilege which they might lose. This consciousness of interaction depends on many factors and may be present even when there is no personal interaction between individuals. Thus we are members of a national group and think of ourselves as nationals even though we are acquainted with only a tiny fraction of those who make up our nation. Nevertheless, we interact through political campaigns, the payment of taxes, the use of government services, the response to symbols such as the flag and the national anthem, and perhaps most of all through our consciousness that as citizens of one nation we are bound together in a way that distinguishes us from the citizens of other nations. Thus the term "group" covers a wide variety of kinds of human association.

THE GROUP AND THE INDIVIDUAL

Our individualistic ethos tempts us to assume that the individual is in full command of his behavior and blinds us to the degree to which individual behavior is controlled by group experience. This assumption is revealed by the popular reaction to the announcement that some American soldiers held prisoner by the Chinese in the Korean War had collaborated with the enemy. There was a popular disposition to blame individual weaknesses and character defects, but a more scientific inquiry found that the cap-

tured soldiers had been demoralized by a systematic attack upon their group loyalties.

To explain this process we must describe the types of conduct in question. First, all evidence shows that the American soldiers were patriotic men who fought bravely and surrendered only in hopeless situations. There were no wholesale conversions to communism, for when prisoners were given their choice at the end of hostilities, only 21 Americans chose to remain with the Chinese forces as against over 20,000 Chinese prisoners who chose to go to Formosa rather than return to mainland China.

Critics of the conduct of the captive Americans point out that there were no organized escape attempts from prison camps and charge that approximately one in three of the Americans collaborated to some extent with the enemy. A death rate of 38 percent in the prison camps is also attributed, in part, to the American prisoners' lack of concern for the welfare of their comrades [*U.S. News and World Report*, 1955]. On the other hand, it is also true that conditions of physical terrain and distance from friendly territory made prison camp escape more difficult than in previous wars, that many Americans did resist the demands of their captors, that never before had American prisoners been placed under such intensive pressure to collaborate, and that the prisoner death rate in previous wars was comparable to that in the Korean conflict [Biderman, 1963]. In summary, it appears that the captured Americans stood up about as well as could be expected, but the Chinese and North Koreans were still able to use some of them in ways embarrassing to the United States.

Physical hardship, poor food, limited medical attention, and inadequate shelter played a part in weakening the resistance of the American prisoners, but these conditions were not considered sufficiently severe to account for their behavior. Torture and, more frequently, the threat of torture did take place on occasion but affected only a minority of the prisoners. The major means of demoralization used by the Chinese was something more powerful than physical force—*the systematic attack upon group ties*, described by Biderman [1960] and Schein [1960]. Just as "dying is easy for anyone left alone in a concentration camp,"[1] death came easily to prisoners of war who were isolated from their fellows.

The Chinese used such techniques as solitary confinement, isolation of small groups of prisoners, and frequent shifting of personnel to hamper the formation or survival of cohesive groups. More important, they also sought to divide the prisoners in their attitude to each other and to cut off the prisoners from any feeling of effective links with the homeland. Casual information gathered in interviews was used to convince them that all other Americans were informers and that they might as well give in too. If a prisoner resisted what he thought were improper demands from the Chinese, the whole unit was denied food or a chance to sleep until the objector had been forced to come round by his own buddies. The following description of mail censorship gives an idea of some of the procedures used:

Another method of isolating these people from each other was through their selection of mail. . . . This effectively separates people one from another by shearing away what ordinarily serves as a common basis for unified effort and unified activity. When two soldiers get together and compare their letters from home about their kids and about their family and about their house, this has a unifying effect. This binds men closer together. But when your letters are restricted to letters very often which announce some major or minor domestic crisis, when your letter turns out to be a notice from a collection company, or what a soldier calls a "Dear John" letter, this isn't the kind of thing you get together with your buddy and talk about. Consequently, men were deprived of

[1]An anonymous concentration-camp survivor, quoted in *Life*, Aug. 18, 1958. p. 90.

this common emotional basis for sticking together.

They also used this control of the mail to make men feel that what the Communist says about capitalism and what it does to its members was demonstrably true, in this respect: It said that our system of free enterprise leads to selfishness, grasping, caring only for what is in it for you, little regard for another individual, especially if he is not there. They said, "Your people at home have forgotten about you. They don't really care about you." What little mail you got was likely to bear this out. Of course this helped make men feel that they were alone and abandoned and isolated.

It was interesting that they routinely did not allow a photograph to come through. A man might get an intact letter in which it said "Here is a picture of me and the kids." No picture. This was almost invariably true, because they didn't want this kind of reminder. They didn't want to give him supports of an emotional kind. It is a diabolical kind of censorship and it is bound over a period of time to be extremely effective.

They cut these people apart, making them isolated and thus obviously much more helpless. (*Testimony before the permanent Subcommittee on Investigations; testimony of Major William E. Mayer, Medical Corps, United States Army, before the Committee on Government Operations, U.S. Senate, 84th Cong., 2d Sess. Cited in Eugene L. Hartley and Gerhart D. Wiebe,* Casebook in Social Processes, *Thomas Y. Crowell Company, New York, 1960, pp. 76–77. Our general treatment of this topic is based on testimony by Major Mayer and Major Marion R. Parnell.*)

Normally the GI is a gregarious soul, looking for amusement in the company of his buddies and anxious to maintain his home ties. Observers reported that over half of the first group of liberated American prisoners passed up an offer for a free long-distance phone call to the States and that, when given leave in Tokyo, they went to town alone. These are clues to the success with which they had been isolated—from their buddies, from their families, from everyone! How this separateness contrasts with the kind of group experience that makes a soldier effective may be seen in a dispatch by a World War II correspondent:

The ties that grow up between men who live savagely and die relentlessly together are of great strength. There is a sense of fidelity to each other among little corps of men who have endured so long and whose hope in the end can be but so small.

One afternoon while I was with the company, S. Sgt. Buck Eversole's turn came to go back to rest camp for five days. The company was due to attack that night.

Buck went to his company commander, and said, "Lieutenant, I don't think I better go. I'll stay if you need me."

The lieutenant said, "Of course I need you, Buck, I always need you. But it's your turn and I want you to go. In fact, you're ordered to go." . . .

I walked with him toward the truck in the dusk. He kept his eyes on the ground, and I think he would have cried if he knew how, and he said to me very quietly:

"This is the first battle I've missed that this battalion has been in, and I sure do hope that they have good luck."

And then he said:

"I feel like a deserter."

He climbed in and the truck dissolved into the blackness. I went back and lay down on the ground among my other friends, waiting for the night orders to march. I lay there in the darkness thinking —terribly touched by the great simple devotion of this soldier who was a cowboy— and thinking of the millions far away at home who must remain forever unaware of the powerful fraternalism in the ghastly brotherhood of war. (*Ernie Pyle*, Brave Men, *Holt, Rinehart and Winston, Inc., New York, 1944, pp. 197, 198.*)

The remarkable tenacity with which the German army survived years of unbroken defeats in World War II is testimony to the importance of group unity to fighting effectiveness. During the war the Allies nursed the hope that "psychological warfare" could undermine the German soldier's faith in his cause and his loyalty to his government and thus impair his fighting morale. Postwar studies [Shils and Janowitz, 1948] have shown that this approach was not very effective. It was rooted in the unsound theory that the soldier is sustained mainly by loyalty to his country and faith in the rightness of its cause, whereas postwar investigations found that he is sustained mainly by his unity with, and loyalty to, the small military units to which he is attached. As long as the soldier's immediate group— the primary group which we shall analyze within a few pages—remained integrated, he continued to resist. Even those who were critical of their "cause" remained effective soldiers because of their group loyalties. Among the comparatively few German deserters, their failure to have become fully absorbed into the primary-group life of the army was far more important than any political or ideological doubts. Long after their cause was clearly lost, most German units of all sizes continued to resist until their supplies were exhausted or they were physically overwhelmed.

Such is the sustaining power of a unified group. When bound to his fellow soldiers by shared experience and group loyalties, the soldier was able to face death itself in heroic fashion, but when he was cut off from the support of his group his fighting effectiveness quickly ebbed. Individual qualities certainly played a part, but beyond them was the vital question of whether the soldier was an isolated individual or a member of a group drawing strength from the consciousness of his relationship to others. Pasley [1955] has shown how, of the twenty-one American soldiers who defected to the enemy after being taken prisoner in Korea, eighteen had no close family ties and had never taken part in school activities or sports during their school life. This shows that these were men who had never really "belonged" and were therefore easily open to treason.

Is it only in warfare that the individual develops a sacrificial loyalty and a leonine courage? By no means. We cite research on military groups because they have been more intensively studied than most other kinds of groups, and from this study we have learned something about groups of all kinds. We see how the group is a vital social reality, with profound effect upon the behavior of individuals in all social situations. Cut a man off from all group ties, and in many cases he will soon sicken and die; unite him in group loyalty and his endurance and sacrifice are almost beyond belief.

SOME MAJOR GROUP CLASSIFICATIONS

In-groups and out-groups

There are some groups to which I belong—my family, my church, my clique, my profession, my race, my sex, my nation—any group which I precede with the pronoun, "my." These are *in-groups*, because I feel I belong to them. There are other groups to which I do not belong—other families, cliques, occupations, races, nationalities, religions, the other sex—these are *out-groups*, for I am outside of them.

The least advanced primitive societies live in small, isolated bands which are usually clans of kinsmen. It was kinship which determined the nature of the in-group and the out-group, and when two strangers met, the first thing they had to do was establish relationship. If kinship could be established, then they were friends—both members of the in-group. If no relationship could be established, then in many societies they were enemies and acted accordingly.

Modern society is based upon many ties besides those of kinship, but the establishment and definition of in-groups is equally important to us. People placed in a new social situation will usually make cautious conversational feints to find out whether or not they "belong." When we find ourselves

among people who are of our own social class, our religion, our political views, and who are interested in the same types of sports or music, then we may have some assurance that we are in an in-group. Members of the in-group are likely to share certain sentiments, laugh at the same jokes, and define with some unanimity the activities and goals of life. Members of the out-group may share many of the same cultural traits, but they lack certain essentials which are considered necessary to break into this particular social group.

In-groups and out-groups.

In modern society, we find that individuals belong to so many groups that a number of their in-group and out-group relationships may overlap. A member of a senior class will consider that a freshman belongs to an out-group; yet the same senior and freshman may both be members of an athletic team in which they have an in-group relationship to each other. Similarly, men who have an in-group relationship based on membership in the same church may discover that this association does not extend to economic relationships; and women who work together in the PTA may find that they are no longer in the same in-group when making plans for a party at the country club.

The fact that in-group and out-group classifications cut across many lines does not minimize their intensity; the subtlety of some distinctions makes exclusion even more painful. One may crave membership in a group which excludes him. Thus the "new rich" who have all the surface qualifications for admittance to "society" may still find themselves excluded from the social register. The teen-ager who hopes desperately for acceptance may find that no clique welcomes him; the housewife may be left out of the coffee klatsch; and the man on a work gang may find himself the butt of ridicule rather than one of a group of comfortable companions. Exclusion from the in-group can be a brutal process. Most primitive societies treated outsiders as part of the animal kingdom; many had no separate words for "enemy" and "stranger," showing that they made no distinction. Not too different was the attitude of the Nazis, who excluded the Jews from the human race. Rudolf Hoess, who commanded the Auschwitz concentration camp in which 700,000 Jews were put to death, characterized this slaughter as "the removal of racial-biological foreign bodies."[2]

It is impossible to understand the repeated brutalities of history without understanding in-groups and out-groups. This distinction makes it psychologically possible for even decent and humane men to commit cruel acts. Trevor-Roper writes:

Seventeenth-century Englishmen were generally tolerant and humane. Even in their civil war and revolution, they constantly remembered that their enemies were like themselves; they fought them with mildness and courtesy. Oliver Cromwell himself was ahead of his age in tolerance. But when Cromwell invaded Ireland, he assumed a new character. To him and his followers, the Irish

were quite different. A generation of ideological propaganda against creatures safely invisible in another island made it possible for Englishmen to regard the Irish as "sub-human," and for Cromwell (who was surprisingly tolerant of Roman Catholics in England) to write from Drogheda that his "knocking on the head" of obstinate Irishmen was "a righteous judgment of God" on "these barbarous wretches." (H. R. Trevor-Roper, New York Times Magazine, Sept. 17, 1961, p. 108.)

Three hundred years have brought remarkably little change in man's inhumanity to man, as the following contemporary account reveals:

War teaches the cheapness of life—not surprisingly, the specific lesson of the war in Vietnam is the cheapness of Vietnam life. They were "gooks" or "slants" or "slopes" and the sounds they made conveyed no sense. "A lot of these [American] people wouldn't think of killing a man," Bernhardt said of Company C. "I mean, a white man—a human, so to speak. You cannot say that a person over there who would shoot a Vietnamese for nothing would shoot a Caucasian for nothing, would shoot an American or an English-speaking person. Even if it was allowed. Even if you wouldn't go to jail or the chair or something." (Joseph Lelyveld, "The Story of a Soldier Who Refused to Fire at Songmy," New York Times Magazine, Dec. 14, 1969, p. 101. © 1969 by the New York Times Company. Reprinted by permission.)

People who commit cruel, inhuman acts upon out-groups are very often kindly, decent people who are compassionate towards fellow in-group members. But when an out-group has been dehumanized—no humane responses are expected. In Vietnam, the dehumanization of the Vietnamese out-group was encouraged by the nature of a war with no definite battle lines or boundaries, and where there was no sure way to distinguish enemy from civilian, so that every civilian is eyed as a possible enemy [Hammer, 1970].

In-groups and out-groups are important, then, because they affect behavior. From fellow members of an in-group, we expect rec-

[2]See Rudolf Hoess, *Commandant of Auschwitz*, tr by Constantine Fitzgibbon, The World Publishing Company, Cleveland, 1960, in which Hoess tells with nostalgic pride how efficiently he organized this operation; reviewed in *Time*, Mar. 28, 1960, p. 110.

ognition, loyalty, and helpfulness. From out-groups, our expectation varies with the kind of out-group. From some out-groups we expect hostility; from others, a more or less friendly competition; from still others, in-difference. From the sex out-group we may expect neither hostility nor indifference; yet in our behavior a difference undeniably remains. The twelve-year-old boy who shuns girls grows up to become a romantic lover and spends most of his life in matrimony. Yet when men and women meet on social occasions they tend to split into one-sex groups, for each sex is bored by many of the conversational interests of the other.

Social distance We are not equally in-volved in all our in-groups. One might, for example, be a passionate Democrat and a rather indifferent Rotarian. Nor do we feel equally distant from all our out-groups. A loyal Democrat will feel far closer to the Republicans than to the Communists. Bo-gardus [1958, 1959] and others [Westie, 1959] have developed the concept *social distance* to measure the *degree of closeness or acceptance we feel* toward other groups. While most often used with reference to racial groups, social distance refers to close-ness among groups of all kinds.

Social distance is measured either by direct observation of the relationships which people have with other groups, or more often by questionnaires in which people are asked the relationships in which they would ac-cept or reject members of certain other groups. In these questionnaires, a number of groups may be listed and the informants asked to check whether they would accept a member of each group as a neighbor, as a fellow worker, as a marriage partner, and so on through a series of relationships. Table 5

TABLE 5

Social distance on the campus: Percentage of students in 40 American colleges who would accept or reject personal contacts with other group members

Other groups	Work beside on job	Live on same block	Have as intimate friend	Date or allow child to date	Marry	Bar from social club	Bar from block
Italians	92%	84%	84%	76%	65%	4%	4%
Negroes	89	58	63	24	29	24	26
Jews	93	84	85	60	37	12	6
Japanese	90	74	72	46	24	11	8
Catholics	95	83	92	73	56	3	1
Filipinos	89	73	69	42	24	12	11
Protestants	95	96	92	83	74	1	1
Mexicans	88	66	68	45	31	15	14
Greeks	93	82	80	64	50	6	4
Irish	95	88	87	77	64	3	2
Polish	93	83	83	72	61	4	3

Source: Albert I. Gordon, Intermarriage, *Beacon Press, Boston, 1964, pp. 389–399.*

shows a study of social-distance reactions of a sample of college students to eleven different groups.

The social-distance questionnaires may not accurately measure what people actually would do if a member of another group sought to become a friend or neighbor. The social-distance scale is only an attempt to measure one's feeling of unwillingness to associate equally with a group. What a person will actually do in a situation also depends upon the circumstances of the situation (situational determinants of behavior), which will be illustrated at some length in the chapter on race and ethnic relations.

Reference groups There are groups which are important to us as models even though we ourselves may not be a part of the group. The opinions of "high society" may be important to the social climber who has not yet made the social register. At times the in-group and the reference group may be the same, as when the teen-ager gives more weight to the opinions of the gang than to those of his teachers. Sometimes an out-group is a reference group: American Indians wore war paint to impress their enemies, and little boys (of all ages!) show off to impress girls. A reference group is any group to which we *refer* when making judgments —any group whose value judgments become our value judgments. You will recall that we mentioned the concept of reference group when speaking of the "looking-glass" self, indicating that the young child is interested in the reactions of everyone with whom he is in contact, while the more mature person selects particular groups whose approval— or whose disapproval—he especially desires.

Stereotypes Out-groups are generally perceived in terms of stereotypes. A *stereotype* is *a group-shared image of another group or category of people.* Stereotypes can be positive (the kindly, dedicated family doctor), negative, (the unprincipled, opportunistic politician), or mixed (the dedicated, fussy, sexless old-maid school teacher). Stereotypes are applied indiscriminately to all members of the stereotyped group, without allowance for individual differences. Stereotypes are never entirely untrue, for they must bear *some* resemblance to the characteristics of the persons stereotyped or they would not be recognized. But stereotypes are always distorted, in that they exaggerate and universalize *some* of the characteristics of *some* of the members of the stereotyped group.

Just how stereotypes begin is not known. Once the stereotype has become a part of the culture, it is maintained by *selective perception* (noting only the confirming incidents or cases and failing to note or remember the exceptions), *selective interpretation* (interpreting observations in terms of the stereotype: e.g., Jews are "pushy" while gentiles are "ambitious"), *selective identification* ("they look like school teachers . . ."), and *selective exception* ("he really doesn't act at all Jewish"). All of these processes involve a reminder of the stereotype, so that even the exceptions and the incorrect identifications serve to feed and sustain the stereotype.

Stereotypes are nonetheless constantly changing. The dowdy old-maid school teacher is so rare today that this particular stereotype is virtually dead. A stereotype dies when confirming illustrations can no longer be found. Unflattering racial and ethnic stereotypes have become unfashionable in the mass media today (and, besides, the offended groups today are prepared to make effective protest against unflattering or inaccurate stereotypes). Racial and ethnic humor has almost entirely disappeared from the stage and screen, while the villain today rarely has any recognizable racial, ethnic, national, religious, or occupational identity.

The stereotyping process is continual. Any long-haired, bearded, blue-denimed youth today is likely to be treated as a hippie, even though relatively few of these youths share the hippie subculture. But the stereotyping process runs both ways, as the following letter from *Playboy* magazine reveals:

I am one who was born too late for the hippie movement. I sympathize with its goals and philosophy, but I've dressed and looked like a straight person all my life and it would be phony for me to change my appearance at this point. One night, a friend and I, wearing jackets and ties and relatively short hair visited a popular hippie coffeehouse in Los Angeles. We'd no sooner sat down than we hear someone loudly say, "There are two narcs in the room." The remarks, for our benefit, got more and more threatening, till we decided, for the sake of peace and love, to leave our expresso unfinished and departed. (*John Hawkins, in* Playboy, *December, 1970, p. 18.*)

Stereotypes are maintained by selective perception.

Another recently developed stereotype, widely held among certain younger people (some of whom talk much of "peace," "love," and "humanity") is the "pig" stereotype of the police officer—possibly the most cruel stereotype ever to appear in our society.

Stereotypes are important because people treat members of other groups in terms of the stereotyped views they hold of that

group. They interact, at least initially, with the stereotype rather than with the true person. This results in many individual injustices, since only some of the persons in a group fully fit the stereotype. Most important, however, is the tendency for interaction in terms of stereotypes to encourage people to become more like the stereotype. In this sense, the stereotype is a "self-fulfilling prophesy" (see page 136). In Chapter 5, we learned how people tend to become whatever other people seem to think they are (the "looking-glass self"). Thus the stereotype tends to mold group behavior in the direction of the stereotype. It is highly likely, for example, that the "pig" stereotype of the police officer serves to increase police brutality rather than to inspire a sympathetic sensitivity among the police.

Primary and secondary groups

Primary groups are those in which we come to know other people intimately as individual personalities. We do this through social contacts that are *intimate*, *personal*, and *total* in that they involve many parts of the person's life experience. In the primary group, such as family, clique, or set of close friends, the social relationships tend to be informal and relaxed. The members are interested in one another as persons. They confide hopes and fears, share experiences, gossip agreeably, and fill the need for intimate human companionship. In the *secondary group* the social contacts are *impersonal*, *segmental*, and *utilitarian*. One is not concerned with the other person as a person, but as a functionary who is filling a role. His personal qualities are not important; his performance—only that part, or segment, of his total personality involved in playing a role—is important. The secondary group might be a labor union or a trade association, a country club, or a PTA, or it might be two persons bargaining briefly over a store counter. In any case the group exists to serve a specific, limited purpose involving only a segment of the personalities of the members.

The terms "primary" and "secondary" thus describe a type of relationship rather than the relative importance of the group. The primary group may serve objective functions such as the provision of food and clothing, but it is judged by the quality of its human relationships rather than by its efficiency in meeting material needs. The secondary group may function in pleasant surroundings, but its principal purpose is to fulfill a specific function. One does not consider a home "good" just because the house is clean. Primary groups are not judged so much by their "efficiency" in performing some task as by the emotional satisfactions they bring to their members. Thus the quartet of ladies who meet for bridge Tuesday afternoons may play a pretty indifferent bridge game but share a lot of pleasant, gossipy conversation. Tournament and duplicate bridge are another matter. Here, virtual or total strangers meet and play to win. A "good partner" is a skillful player who wastes no time on distracting small talk. The major goal is a winning score (and master points chalked up), not sociability. A good lunch-table clique is one that has fun; a good labor union is one that succeeds in protecting its members' interests. Primary groups are judged by the satisfying human response they supply; secondary groups are judged by their ability to perform a task or achieve a goal. Although secondary groups sometimes also provide pleasant human relationships, sociability is ordinarily not their goal. In brief, *primary groups are relationship-oriented*, whereas *secondary groups are goal-oriented*.

Primary and secondary groups are important because feelings and behavior are different. It is in the primary group that personality is formed. In the primary group one find intimacy, sympathy, and a comfortable sharing of many interests and activities. In the secondary group one finds an effective mechanism for achieving certain purposes, but often at the price of suppressing one's true feelings. For example, the saleslady must be cheerful and polite, even when she has a splitting headache and the customer is a boor. The concepts are useful because they describe important differences in behavior.

Gemeinschaft and Gesellschaft

Somewhat similar to the concepts of primary and secondary groups are the concepts of *Gemeinschaft* and *Gesellschaft*, developed by the German sociologist Ferdinand Tönnies [1887, tr. 1957]. These two terms translate roughly as "community" and "society." The gemeinschaft is a social system in which most relationships are personal or traditional, and often both. A good example is the feudal manor, a small community held together by a combination of personal relationships and status obligations. Although great inequality existed, the lord of the manor was personally known to his subjects, while their duties to him were balanced by his obligation for their welfare. When money was used, economic transactions were governed by the concepts of a just price; more often the people involved simply carried out a network of customary obligations to one another. Written documents were scarce, formal contracts unknown, bargaining rare, and behavior of all types operated in traditional patterns that were known and accepted by all the community. Men had little hope of surpassing their fathers and equally little fear of falling behind the parental status. Except for occasional feast days, life was monotonous; but loneliness was rare in a community of lifelong neighbors.

In gesellschaft, the society of tradition is replaced with the society of contract. In this society neither personal attachment nor traditional rights and duties are important. The relationships between men are determined by bargaining and defined in written agreements. Relatives are separated as people move about and live among strangers. Commonly accepted codes of behavior have less force than rational—or "cold-blooded"—calculation of profit and loss. The gesellschaft flourishes in the modern metropolitan city. Some of the contrasting characteristics of gesellschaft and gemeinschaft relationships are summarized in this table:

Gemeinschaft relationships	Gesellschaft relationships
Personal	Impersonal
Informal	Formal, contractual
Traditional	Utilitarian
Sentimental	Realistic, "hard-boiled"
General	Specialized

MODERN TREND TOWARD SECONDARY-GROUP ASSOCIATION

Our sentiments and emotional ties are centered in primary groups, but an accelerating trend toward a gesellschaft society based on secondary groups has been irresistible in the modern era. The small principalities of feudal Europe have given way to national states, and the intimate association of master and workmen in the guild workshop has yielded to the giant corporation employing thousands of men. Population has moved from the country to the city, and lifetime residence in familiar surroundings has become a rarity as approximately one American family in five moves each year.

An industrialized urban society attacks the primary group in at least two ways. First, it increases the relative proportion of secondary-group contacts, as one activity after another is withdrawn from the primary group and assumed as a secondary-group function. Second, the primary-group associations which remain are at the mercy of secondary-group developments. Changes in industry may move the wage earner about, disrupting his local associations. Industrial changes also influence the roles played in the family. A prolonged depression, the result of a maladjustment of secondary relationships, may deprive the father of his earning power and substitute the wife and the relief administrator as symbols of authority. Changes in office and factory work lead to the employment of women, so that the mother has the same kind of career as the father, and both share in the domestic tasks of the home. Changes in the international political scene may take the husband or son out of the family locale and move him to the other side of the world. The worker's family must adjust itself to whatever working hours the corporation finds most profitable. Negotiations between the international union and the corporation may result in work changes which break up informal primary groups formed on the job. The "little red schoolhouse" where a small group of children and a teacher formed an intimate primary group lasting for years is succeeded by the consolidated school, drawing hundreds of children from a large area and shifting them about from class to class and teacher to teacher. Scores of similar examples show how primary groupings have become transient and changing units, swept along by the heedlessly changing trends of a gesellschaft society.

Such a trend is not universally welcomed. Critics maintain that it produces shallow and rootless personalities which lack the calm certainty and deep friendship that supposedly characterized personal relationships in the gemeinschaft setting. A visiting Filipino educator expressed this view in his reaction to America's largest city:

In New York, people seem so busy and so deeply concerned with their own affairs that they no longer know how to smile. Some of them wear masks like "guys and dolls" who conceal their inner world from the busy chatter outside. They walk hurriedly—tack! tack! tack!—on the side-walks, like robots, unfeeling and unconcerned. (*Vidal A. Tan, "Visit to America,"* Sunday Times Magazine, *Manila, Dec. 28, 1952.*)

Durkheim [1897], in his study of suicide, came to the conclusion that not only high rates of suicide but many other behavior difficulties are explained by the lack of traditional and personal ties in a secondary society, where the individual is engulfed by anomie. Many students of society have followed his lead in regarding the secondary trends of the modern world as an evil force, destructive of the relationships that assured man of membership in a warm and secure society where his tendencies toward crime or despair were curbed by his obligations to a stable and intimate social community.

Contributions of the gesellschaft

While the gesellschaft has brought problems to man, it has also brought benefits. The most obvious is the efficiency of large-scale impersonal organizations in which sentiment is subordinated to the need to get the job done in the most practical way. The tremendous advances in material comfort and in life expectancy in the modern world would be impossible without the rise of goal-directed secondary organizations, in which the paternal squire has been replaced by the efficiency expert and the production manager.

Nor has the rise of the gesellschaft and the accompanying division of labor had only materialistic advantages. These changes have opened channels of opportunity and specializations of function which, while they fragment society, also open a greater chance to develop individual talents. The contrast between the thousands of occupations in the metropolis and the handful of pursuits in the rural village shows how a society dominated by secondary groups opens the way for specialized careers. This process has gone so far today that not only

is the talented individual able to rise from an obscure background but society actively seeks out those whose abilities may be developed along professional, artistic, scientific, or managerial lines.

The secondary group also has a tendency toward the imposition of patterns of conformity on its members. In this way it offers a counterbalance to the prejudices or vested interests of the immediate locality. Since its boundaries extend beyond the primary group, it forces a consideration of events from a larger perspective. This difference in attitudes may be seen in the tendency of religious organizations, operating on a national or international scale, to espouse viewpoints which may be unpopular in local congregations. The reaction of the Southern Baptist Churches to the school-integration issue is a case in point. With a membership of white Southerners, most congregations have been strongly segregationist in their beliefs and practices. Prominent members, including some pastors, have been active in the efforts to keep racial separation in the schools. Nevertheless, when meeting as a national body somewhat removed from the pressures of local groups, the convention of the Southern Baptist Churches voted in 1954 to *endorse* the Supreme Court decision [Fey, 1954]. A similar type of reaction to the segregation issue occurred among Roman Catholics in Louisiana. Here the violently segregationist stand of local Catholics contrasted sharply with support for integration by the church as a whole as voiced by the Archbishop [*America*, 1957].

Lest these be viewed as isolated incidents peculiar to an especially violent racial controversy, we should add that this disparity between national and local views is common in many church groups on many questions. For example, a study [Glock and Ringer, 1956] of the Protestant Episcopal Church showed a wide divergence between statements of the national body and views of members of local congregations on eight out of nine issues. Such a divergence between national and local sentiment is sometimes attributed either to hypocrisy at the local level or to a misrepresentation of the "real" views of the organization at the national level. A more penetrating analysis would emphasize the fact that while the local group and the national organization interact, the national body has concerns which may override local feelings.

This tendency for the national organization to be more universal in its judgments and the local units to be more particularistic—that is, influenced by local concerns and personal attitudes—is not confined to churches and may be observed in the deliberations of business, labor, and political organizations. The emphasis on goals rather than on personal relationships and the need to accommodate a large number of individuals and localities tend toward an outlook which reaches beyond the primary group. Such an outlook is, however, not necessarily more liberal or humanitarian. Communist Russia and Nazi Germany are extreme examples of situations in which the goals of secondary organizations demanded action which violated the local code of human decency. The expulsion of the more well-to-do peasants in Russia from their farms and the large-scale use of concentration camps in Germany were motivated by goals beyond the usual concern of a local community, but they diminished rather than increased the area of human fellowship. Secondary groups may restrain local greed and shatter the bonds of provincialism, or they may let loose a ruthless force which transgresses the traditional mores in pursuit of organizational goals.

Persistence of primary groups

The secondary group has overshadowed but not destroyed the primary group. In fact, the two major primary groups, the clique and the family, appear to be stronger than ever.

The clique is a small group of intimates with intense in-group feelings based on common sentiments and interests. It may develop in almost any situation, and nearly every secondary group shelters a large number of cliques which add a highly personal note to an otherwise impersonal organization. As for the family, more people get married today, and get married earlier, than in any other period on which we have reliable data. Furthermore, today's family is steadily becoming less directed toward mundane goals and more concerned with human relationships. Yesterday's family was primarily a work crew, sometimes a brutally repressive one; today's family is primarily a companionship group, and a perfect example of primary-group persistence.

Primary groups persist in a secondary-group-dominated world because the human need for intimate, sympathetic association is a continuous need. Man cannot function well unless he belongs to a small group of people who really care what happens to him. Wherever people are ripped from family and friends and thrust into large, impersonal, anonymous groups, as in a college dormitory or an army camp, they feel such great need for primary groups that they promptly re-form them.

Primary groups in a secondary setting

If we classified groups according to the extent to which they show primary- or secondary-group traits, the result would be a listing of secondary groups such as the army, the corporation, and the national state, and a list of primary groups such as the family, the clique, and the gang. Proceeding in this fashion, we should then contrast the impersonal goal-directed nature of the large organization with the personal, relationship-oriented focus of smaller intimate groups. Such a separation is often assumed when we attempt to analyze the efficiency of large organizations. If we are interested in the productivity of industrial labor, we might study the goals, techniques, and rewards of the factory and then look at the character and training of the individuals who make up the labor force.

The fallacy of this approach is that it overlooks the extent to which every large organization is a network of small primary groups. A person is not simply a unit in an organization chart designed by top management; he is also a member of a smaller informal group with its own structure and its own system of statuses and roles defining the behavior of its members. In the factory the workman finds his place in a group of his fellows with its own leadership, from which the foreman is usually excluded, since his very position bars him from this in-group relationship. Since the workman needs the approval and support of his clique more than he needs the approval of his supervisors, he responds to the demands of management only as these demands are consistent with his primary-group relationships.

The influence of the primary group is one reason why incentive pay plans giving the worker a bonus for greater output have frequently been ineffective. The logic of such plans is that many workers who fail to exert their maximum efforts will work harder if paid in proportion to the work they do. The major defect in such plans is that their effective operation destroys the unity of primary groups. Rather than a number of equals cooperating together, the work gang would become a number of competing individuals each striving to outdo his fellows. Aside from the strain of continuous competition, this situation threatens the workers' social relationships. As a defense, factory cliques develop a norm of a "fair day's work." The man who attempts to ignore this norm is the butt of ridicule, ostracism, and possible violence. Management may employ time and motion study experts to decide a "reasonable" output, but new norms cannot be effec-

tive unless they are also accepted by the group [Roethlisberger and Dickson, 1939, chaps. 22, 23; Moore, 1947, chap. 15].

While the primary group in the secondary setting can be an obstacle, it can also be a positive aid in the accomplishment of organizational objectives. Gross [1953] has examined the way in which informal cliques that cut across formal work assignments may lead to cooperation and smoother functioning of the organization. He finds that the clique may even reinforce the idea of organization loyalty, as one private secretary reveals:

A private secretary is the top of the heap. You need something else beside the ability to type and take shorthand. You've got to feel that you are working for the company and not just for yourself. Now Mildred and Emma [other private secretaries], we see eye to eye on that. Louise—she's a good little stenographer, but she'll never be a secretary. She doesn't fit into our crowd. When we go out for coffee she usually tags along. Then she'll complain about her boss. She can't accept the idea that you don't work for a boss, you work for the company. (*Edward Gross, "Some Functional Consequences of Primary Controls in Formal Work Organizations,"* American Sociological Review, *18:372, August, 1953.*)

At times the primary groups may even violate the rules of the larger secondary organization in order to get things done. If the formal rules are not always workable in all situations, primary worker groups simply trim some corners—that is, break a few rules —in order to get the work out [Roy, 1955].

Perhaps the most dramatic of all illustrations of the influence of the group is found in studies of the extent to which American combat soldiers actually fired their guns in combat. Since the soldiers have been trained to shoot and may die if they fail to shoot, one would take their reaction for granted. Actually many men found that at the crucial moment they were unable to fire. In fact, studies in World War II [Marshall, 1947; Davidson, 1952] indicated that only 12 to

25 percent of combat soldiers in a position to fire were able to pull the trigger. Apparently the soldiers had been so strongly conditioned against taking human life that even when self-defense and the call of duty demanded that they kill the enemy, they were unable to overcome the effect of the mores of the civilian culture. Research on combat behavior found that patriotism, hatred of the enemy, military training, and fear of punishment are not very effective in making a man perform well in combat. The main variable that determines how well a man will fight is his degree of integration with his unit. Men who will not shoot to save themselves will shoot to save their comrades. Highly integrated units fought bravely. Poorly integrated units, although identical in individual abilities and training, fought poorly, with a high proportion of nonshooters, deserters, and mental breakdowns. The authors of the research study, *The American Soldier*, conclude that the primary group "served two principal functions in combat motivation: it set and emphasized group standards of behavior and it supported and sustained the individual in stresses he would otherwise not have been able to withstand" [Shils, 1950].

Training methods and combat techniques now are designed to create the closest possible unity of member and group. For example, two men are assigned to a foxhole instead of the men being scattered as much as possible. Instead of keeping silence in combat, men are now encouraged to yell and scream while attacking, as this binds them into a group. Officers are told to spend their time crawling from foxhole to foxhole to keep the group unified. In such ways, the primary group may be used to achieve secondary-group objectives.

Just as we cannot realistically consider the individual apart from society, so we cannot understand secondary and primary groups completely except in relation to each other. In modern society the functions and influence of primary groups have been weakened by a growth of impersonal, goal-directed secondary groups which are assuming an increasingly dominant role. Each of these secondary groups, however, creates a new network of primary groups that provide intimacy and personal response in an otherwise impersonal situation. While these and other primary groups are often destroyed or modified by the impact of secondary groups, the primary groups in turn exert a major influence on the secondary groups. Primary groups may resist the goal-directed efforts of secondary organizations, or they may help to integrate disparate parts of the organization, and provide an emotional security which reinforces the individual's ability to play the roles demanded by his status in the secondary group.

GROUP DYNAMICS

For a long time sociologists were busy trying to convince a skeptical world that the group was real and not simply a collection of individuals. Only recently have sociologists turned their attention to the specific factors which affect the functioning of groups. *Group dynamics* is *the study of the relationships of group members to one another.* Obviously many possible patterns may occur. A group may be dominated by one or two individuals, or it may involve the participation of all its members; leadership may be democratic or authoritarian, transitory or enduring; the group may stimulate productivity or hold it down; its atmosphere may be relaxed and friendly or tense and charged with hostility; it may forge new approaches to problems or stick to old routines. These and many other patterns have often been observed. The question arises, "What factors produce one or another type of group life and how can these factors be controlled?"

The academic interest of sociologists in expanding the frontiers of knowledge in this area has been stimulated by demands from organizations who want help in solving their problems. Social agencies such as the Boy Scouts and the YMCA and YWCA wish to use leaders more effectively and secure more intensive participation from their members. Governmental bodies hope to make their employees more efficient and more responsive to the needs of the people. The armed forces are constantly revising their policies in the search for the type of organization which will lead to the most effective use of military manpower. Industrial corporations seek knowledge which will help them plan their work groups in a way to minimize friction and to secure the maximum efficiency in their operations. Reformers and revolutionists want to know how to organize and unify the groups whose potential they wish to mobilize.

These practical needs, joined by the intellectual curiosity of scholars, have led to a field of research usually labeled either "group dynamics" or "small-group research." Such research painstakingly records the interaction which actually occurs in group activities, oftentimes using such devices as a conference room in which one-way visibility enables observers to see the interaction and record conversations without being noticed by the participants. The problems to be solved are difficult because groups are affected both by the specific way in which they are organized and also by the general cultural background of their members. In spite of the complexities of the task, however, this type of research is gradually enlarging our understanding of how groups function [Strodtbeck and Hare, 1954; Bales, 1959; Cartwright and Zander, 1960; Mann, Gibbard, and Hartman, 1967; T. Mills, 1967; Roby, 1968; Luft, 1970].

Communication patterns

One of the important problems in any group is communication among its members. Communication is not merely a matter of the language spoken and the types of printed or audiovisual material used to get across messages, even though these are important. Communication is also a matter of the structure of the group and the physical and social proximity of its members. Any group must devise some way for its members to share their information. There are many possible ways of arranging the flow of communication, and possibly not all these patterns have the same effect on the work of the group and the relationship among its members.

The influence of different patterns of communication in a problem-solving group has been listed by Bavelas [1953]. He arranged groups of five men in different communication patterns which may be described as the circle, the chain, the Y, and the wheel. In the circle everyone had an equal chance to communicate with everyone else; in the other patterns the man at the center has maximum communication and the others were restricted. Morale and leadership turned out to be closely related to centrality of position. Member satisfaction with the situation was greatest in the circle, where no one man emerged as a leader. In the wheel, where the man in the center became the leader, production was greater but group satisfaction less. As an offset to its lower production, the circle was found to adapt more quickly to new tasks than the other patterns.

Effective communication promotes the individual's satisfaction with the group and enables him to express himself freely and to receive the impressions of others. A centralizing of communication focuses the attention of group members on specific topics and promotes a concentration of effort. The implications for the organization of school classrooms and industrial work plans depend on whether the major emphasis is on routine productivity or on developing flexibility and achieving satisfaction in the group situation. Research on the lecture versus the discussion method of college instruction, for instance, reports that students memorize as much even in very large groups with the lecture method (analogous to the wheel pattern) but that they have greater stimulus to do their own thinking in the discussion method (analogous to the circle pattern) [Bloom, 1954, pp. 37–38]. These are a few examples of how small-group research can help in solving practical problems.

Therapeutic and encounter groups

Alcoholics Anonymous organizes the emotional support of the group in the effort to help an alcoholic control his drinking urges. The Synanon Houses use similar group-therapy techniques for drug addicts; Weight Watchers helps people to lose weight; even cigarette smokers are trying the therapeutic group approach. There are also a number of groups organized to help the members live with a difficult affliction—relatives of alcoholics or drug addicts, relatives of mental patients, released mental-hospital patients, homosexuals, dwarfs, blind people, the recently handicapped, and others [Sagarin, 1970]. This tendency for people who share an affliction to band together for understanding and mutual support in either overcoming or accepting it is a quite recent development.

Another relatively new form of group experience is the *encounter group*, broadly defined to include "all sensitivity, meditative, body, consciousness-expanding, and other current encounter experiences which take place in more than dyadic [two-person] groups" [Burton, 1969, p. 8n]. The objective of an encounter group may be educational, directed mainly at increased emotional and attitudinal learnings; or it may be therapeu-

tic, seeking to help members understand themselves and interact more comfortably with others. But while the therapeutic groups mentioned above will unite in one group a number of persons sharing the same affliction, a single encounter group may include people with all sorts of problems.

The encounter-group movement is quite new, its theory poorly developed, and its definitions and vocabulary are not established. The term "encounter group" thus covers a wide variety of kinds of group experience. The widely used term "T-group" an abbreviation for "training group," covers the entire range of manipulated group experience for the purpose of learning outcomes [Egan, 1970, p. 10]. The *sensitivity training* group is an educational encounter group which attempts to structure the communication with a group to maximize exchanges of meanings and attitudinal changes. It originated among educators seeking ways to stimulate learning [Golembiewski and Blumberg, 1970]. It later developed to include an effort to increase mutual understanding between hostile groups, such as management and labor, police and youth, blacks and whites, through a blunt, honest verbal confrontation in which each voiced attitudes and "gripes" at the "gut level" and presumably gained insights in the process [Bouma, 1969, pp. 149–153]. Such confrontations may increase sympathetic mutual understanding if skillfully conducted; otherwise they can easily confirm prejudices and intensify hostilities.

There is a rapidly spreading commercialized encounter-group movement whose objective is primarily the improvement of personal adjustment. An estimated six million customers are attending encounter-group sessions organized by over a hundred centers in the United States [Maliver, 1971, p. 39], patterned after the original provided by the Esalen Institute in California [Schutz, 1967]. Under more-or-less trained leaders, a number of people, usually strangers, will assemble, strip themselves of names, titles, social and professional statuses, all ordinary amenities and civilities, and sometimes clothing, so that they can cast aside all sham, pretense, and defense, and interact with complete "honesty." A series of exercises and "games" may be played to heighten contact and response. Touching, holding, caressing, and embracing is encouraged or demanded, but this is not expected to be erotic or to lead to sexual intercourse. Uninhibited verbal and physical interchange is encouraged, with occasional episodes of screaming or fighting. Such encounter sessions may be brief, but often are "marathon" sessions lasting twenty-four hours, a weekend, or even longer [Bach, 1966; Shepard and Lee, 1970]. These experiences are expected to increase insights into one's self, to relieve one of anxieties and "hang-ups," and to aid one in relating to others.

There is a rapidly spreading commercialized encounter-group movement.

There are too few evaluation studies to permit any firm conclusions about the effects of encounter-group experience. Schutz claims that 80 percent of his clients at Esalen "reported tangible benefits" [Burton, 1969, p. 23], but this is not a very careful evaluation study. Many participants feel exhilarated

and "free" after a session, but this feeling seldom endures, and some participants seem to become addicted to encounter-group sessions, which apparently fill their need for social contact or intimate group experience. In the only carefully controlled psychiatric study of encounter-group casualties published to date, covering 170 subjects in 18 different encounter groups, Yalom and Lieberman [1971] report that nearly ten percent became seriously disturbed, psychotic, or suicidal. Most group leaders have no professional training other than some experience at encounter centers. Persons with professional training in the behavioral sciences are not preferred as group leaders because they are said to be "too intellectual and remote." Most psychiatrists and other behavioral scientists are highly critical of any form of group therapy conducted by untrained and unsupervised laymen. When a patient's psychological defenses are stripped away and his psyche laid bare, with his guilts, anxieties, and repressed impulses exposed (as they are in psychiatric treatment), the therapist must know how to handle what he has "dug up" if the patient is to be helped rather than shattered. Orthodox behavioral scientists are highly critical, but it has not been established whether non-professionally conducted encounter groups are a useful therapy [Burton, 1969; Egan, 1970] or a highly profitable racket [Rakstis, 1970; Maliver, 1971].

SUMMARY

Both strength and weakness are largely the result of the manner in which a person is integrated into a network of groups. A fundamental distinction is that between *out-groups* and *in-groups*—a distinction which has been measured by the use of the concept of *social distance*. *Reference groups* are those which we accept as models and as guides for our judgments and actions. *Stereotypes* are distorted impressions of the characteristics of out-groups which have become widely accepted in a society. Emotional conditioning is largely the result of *primary-group* contacts, but our society is increasingly affected by the growth of *secondary-group* relationships. While many groups may be easily characterized as either primary or secondary, the two types of influence interact, each influencing the other.

Since the industrial revolution, the trend has been from the traditional *gemeinschaft* toward the *gesellschaft*. This has meant a loss of intimacy and security, which has been countered to some extent by the growth of new primary groups within a secondary-group setting.

Group dynamics studies interaction within groups, both to gain understanding and to solve organizational problems. Communication patterns within groups have been extensively studied. *Therapeutic groups* of many kinds bring group support and possibly understanding to troubled people. *Encounter groups* are an unproven and possibly dangerous form of group therapy.

Questions and projects

1. Why do sociologists have so many different definitions for the term *group*?

2. Comment on this statement: "A group is made up of individuals; and the characteristics of a group are the sum of the characteristics of its members."

3. Is courage an individual character trait or a response to group influences?

4. What differences are found in the in-group-out-group distinction in primitive and modern societies?

5. Why are primary and secondary groups important? In-groups and out-groups?

6. To what extent would you expect social distance to be related to geographical distance?

7. College is often an introduction to the complexities of secondary-group relationships. Is this experience worthwhile for a young woman whose major interests are centered in the primary-group relationships of family life?

8. Does the conduct of American prisoners of war in Korea show that a greater knowledge of communism is what our soldiers need? What does this experience reveal about the needs of combat troops?

9. How could decent, clean-cut American young men be guilty of war atrocities in Vietnam?

10. The early Christians were sometimes crowded into large prison cells and later marched into the Colosseum to be crucified or fed to the lions before thousands of spectators. They could have saved themselves by denying their faith, but few did so. Why?

11. How does a stereotype become a "self-fulfilling prophecy"?

12. In a recent experiment, conventionally groomed college students passing out peace literature in an airport were politely treated, while hippie-type students, behaving identically, were often abused, insulted, or jostled. Explain this in sociological terminology.

13. What do you think is the real reason the leaders of encounter groups so often are persons without professional training in the behavioral sciences?

Suggested readings

Bales, Robert F.: "How People Interact in Conferences," *Scientific American*, 192:31–35, March, 1955. A popular description of social interaction in the conference.

Bogardus, Emory S.: "Racial Distance Changes in the United States during the Past Thirty Years," *Sociology and Social Research*, 43:127–135, November, 1958. Shows how the acceptance and rejection of different racial or national groups changed during this period.

*****Egan, Gerard**: *Encounter: Group Processes for Interpersonal Growth*, Wadsworth Publishing Company, Belmont, Calif., 1970. A balanced general description of the encounter group movement.

Golembiewski, Robert, and Arthur Blumberg (eds.): *Sensitivity Training and the Laboratory Approach*, F. E. Peacock Publishers, Inc., 1970. A textbook on sensitivity training.

Gross, Edward: "Some Functional Consequences of Primary Groups in Formal Work Organizations," *American Journal of Sociology*, 18:368–373, August, 1953; The Bobbs-Merrill Company, Inc., Indianapolis, reprint S-106. A description of some ways in which primary groups may support the aims of secondary groups.

Janowitz, Morris: *Sociology and The Military Establishment*, Russell Sage Foundation, New York, 1962, 1965, chap. 4, "Primary Groups and Military Effectiveness," reprinted in **Alvin W. Gouldner and Helen P. Gouldner**, *Modern Sociology*, Harcourt, Brace & World, Inc., New York, 1962, pp. 70–82. An analysis of the role of primary-group relationships in various types of military situations.

Maliver, Bruce L.: "Encounter Groupers Up Against the Wall," *New York Times Magazine*, January 3, 1971, pp. 4ff. A popular description and critical appraisal of encounter groups.

*****Olmstead, Michael S.**: *The Small Group*, Random House, Inc., New York, 1959. A brief and highly readable description of small-group research.

Schein, Edward H.: "Interpersonal Communication, Group Solidarity and Social Influence," *Sociometry*, 23:148–161, June, 1960. Describes how group disintegration was used as a technique of psychological warfare against American prisoners in Chinese camps.

Shils, Edward A., and Morris Janowitz: "Cohesion and Disintegration in the Wehrmacht in World War II," *Public Opinion Quarterly*, 12:280–315, Summer, 1948; The Bobbs-Merrill Company, Inc., reprint S-263. Tells how morale and resistance continued in the German army as long as primary-group structures remained intact.

Warriner, Charles K.: "Groups Are Real: A Reaffirmation," *American Sociological Review*, 21:549–554, October, 1956; reprinted in **Milton Barron**, *Contemporary Sociology*, Dodd, Mead & Company, Inc., New York, 1964, pp. 120–127. Shows how the nature of the group is not completely represented by the individuals who compose its membership.

Social institutions

Duels of honour were private encounters about real or imagined slights or insults. The practice, considerably facilitated by the fashion of wearing a sword as part of everyday dress, seems to have spread over the rest of Europe from Italy from the end of the 15th century. Italy in any case was the great center of professional swordsmanship, and as the duel of honour became prevalent the nobility of Europe flocked to Milan to learn the secret strokes that fencing-masters had to teach. Men would fight on the slightest pretext and often, at first, without witnesses, but as this secrecy came to be abused (e.g., by ambushes) it soon became usual for duelists to be accompanied by friends or seconds. Later these seconds would also fight, to prove themselves worthy of their friends. . . .

In a rather different category is the *Mensur*, the student duel still a feature of German university life. Most German universities have long-established *Verbindungen* (fighting corps) with strict rules, distinctive uniforms and great prestige. . . . The *Schläger*, a heavy basket-hilted sabre is used, and the method of swordplay is quite different from that of normal fencing. In the Mensur the combatants take up a position on guard upright and quite close to each other with the sabre held above the head and the forearm in front of the face; it is a point of honour to remain immobile from the top of the head to the rear foot during a bout. The forearm is padded, the eyes protected by steel glasses and the neck is also protected. Cuts are delivered exclusively at the head, inflicting severe wounds. Defense is limited to blocking the strokes with the forearm and the hilt, and the duel continues by timed rounds until loss of blood compels one of the duelists to retire. In this way students can obtain the scars on head and cheek which are prized as marks of courage. (Encyclopaedia Britannica, *Encyclopaedia Britannica, Inc., Chicago, 1966, vol. 7, pp. 735–737. Reprinted by permission.* © 1966 *by* Encyclopaedia Britannica.)

Dueling was an institutionalized way for gentlemen of the sixteenth to eighteenth centuries to settle certain differences. A cluster of procedures (norms) had developed which transformed spontaneous brawls into highly formalized combats, with specialized roles (principals, seconds, attendants) and a supporting ideology which was generally accepted in the society. Alexander Hamilton had only two choices when challenged by Aaron Burr: accept the challenge, or retire from public life in craven disgrace. But dueling was already losing public approval in the United States and elsewhere. Only a few decades later, Abraham Lincoln was able to laugh off a dueling challenge by announcing an absurd choice of weapons—reportedly a peck of small potatoes at 20 paces!

Sociologists have not been entirely consistent in their use of the term *institution*. Some have applied the term to any large-scale organization, like the American Legion or the YMCA, using the term *association* for smaller organized groups like the local photography club. This makes the distinction between institution and association purely one of size and obscures the basic difference in nature between institution and association. The more common practice is to call any organized group of any size an association and to define an institution as "an organized way of doing something" [Bierstedt, 1963, p. 341]. Kingsley Davis [1949, p. 71] defines the institution as "a set of interwoven folkways, mores, and laws built around one or more functions." Hertzler [1961, p. 77] calls them "great clusters of established, accepted, and implemented ways of behaving socially." Clearly, the association is an organized *group of people* while an institution is an organized *system of behavior*.

All these definitions of institutions imply both a set of behavior norms and a system of social relationships through which these norms are practiced. Let us suggest a formal definition which clearly includes both ideas: *An institution is an organized system of social relationships which embodies certain common values and procedures and meets certain basic needs of the society.* In this definition, "common values" refers to shared ideas and goals; the "common procedures" are the standardized behavior patterns the group follows; the "system of relationships" is the network of roles and statuses through

which this behavior is carried out. Thus the family includes a set of common values (about love, children, family life), a set of common procedures (dating, child care, family routines), and a network of roles and statuses (husband, wife, baby, teen-aged child, fiancé), which form the system of social relationships through which family life is carried out. Five important basic institutions in complex societies are the familial, religious, governmental, economic, and educational institutions. Today, the values and procedures of science are so important and so highly standardized that some would add the "scientific institutions" to the list. The activities involved in social work or medical care have become so definitely patterned that we might speak of either of these systems of behavior as institutions. In referring to the Middle Ages one could speak of chivalry and knighthood as aspects of the institution of feudalism.

An institution embodies certain common values and procedures.

While they are separate concepts, institutions and associations are not entirely separate from each other. An institution is a set of relationships and a system of behavior, and these require *people*. Although the institution itself consists of relationships and norms, it is people who fill these relation-ships and practice these norms. And people organize themselves into groups, forming associations. Thus each institution has many satellite associations which carry out institutional behavior. By *institutional behavior* we mean the carrying of institutional norms and values into practice. Institutional behavior is carried out, in large part, through these satellite associations. The church has its organized local congregations, Sunday schools, clubs, and groups of many kinds, carrying out the work of the church; the school has its PTA, alumni association, athletic association; the state has its political organizations, voters' leagues, taxpayers' associations, and organized pressure groups. Institutions and associations are very much interrelated; yet the concepts are distinct and should not be confused. *The* church is a social institution; the First Methodist Church on Main Street is an association. *The* corporation is a social institution; the First National Bank and the Ford Motor Company are associations.

THE DEVELOPMENT OF INSTITUTIONS

The process of institutionalization

Institutions emerge as the largely un-planned products of social living. People grope for practical ways of meeting their needs; they find some workable patterns which harden through repetition into standardized customs. As time passes, these patterns acquire a body of supporting folklore which justifies and sanctions them. The custom of "dating" developed as a means of mate selection. Banks gradually developed as the need for storing, transferring, borrowing, and lending money gave rise to a series of practices for accomplishing these purposes. From time to time, men might gather to codify and give legal endorsement to these practices as they continued to develop and

change. In such manner, institutions arise.

Institutionalization consists of the establishment of definite norms which assign status positions and role functions in connection with such behavior. A norm is a group expectation of behavior. Institutionalization involves the replacement of spontaneous or experimental behavior with behavior which is expected, patterned, regular, and predictable. Thus the preinstitutional phase of a religious movement brings forth spontaneous ecstatic and often confused behavior as the followers of the new leader respond to his dynamic appeal. Every day is an adventure, and every religious meeting is an unpredictable sequence of emotional events in which no man is able to predict what he will do. As the institutionalized church emerges, the participants acquire definite roles, and their activities begin to follow a routine pattern. Some people are simply worshipers; others assume specialized roles such as choir member, clergyman, teacher, usher, secretary, janitor, and so on. Novelty and excitement fade as procedures come to be governed by definite norms, and the behavior of each participant becomes standardized and predictable.

A tavern brawl is noninstitutionalized behavior; a professional boxing match is institutionalized. A set of social relationships has become institutionalized when (1) a regular system of statuses and roles has been developed, and (2) this system of status and role expectations has been generally accepted in the society. Dating in American society meets both of these qualifications. A rather clearly defined set of courtship roles has emerged, in which the duties and privileges of each party are defined (he asks, she accepts, he pays, etc.), and safeguarded with some limitations or restraints (e.g., no all-night dates) intended to prevent complications; thus dating became part of our marriage and family institutions.

When we say that dating has become institutionalized, we mean that it is generally accepted by the society as a necessary and proper activity whereby young people mature emotionally and eventually find agreeable partners. Many societies have also institutionalized premarital sexual intercourse, making it a normal and expected part of the activities leading to marriage. Although premarital intercourse is fairly common in American society, it has not been institutionalized; that is, it is not a part of a standardized, approved, and culturally safeguarded pattern of behavior.

Even carefully organized patterns of behavior differ in the extent to which they receive social acceptance. In American society the corporation has full institutional status. The cooperative, on the other hand, would be classified as an *emergent* institution, not yet completely accepted as a proper and necessary part of society. The first six grades of the elementary school are accepted as necessary in all American localities, whereas the provision of "head start" or kindergarten facilities and junior colleges is a matter of controversy. Although the need for some basic social institutions is recognized in all societies, their forms vary. Time will see some subsidiary forms becoming accepted institutions and others passing from the scene.

Individual roles in institutional behavior

Not all roles are institutionalized. The "bad boy" and "mother's little helper" roles in the family are noninstitutionalized roles, while son and daughter are institutionalized roles. An institutionalized role is a set of behavior expectations that leaves little room for personal eccentricity. All judges act a good deal alike when on the bench, however much they differ at other times. Every Methodist minister and every Catholic priest finds that his duties and privileges are quite precisely defined by his institutional role; to deviate from his expected role in any way is hazardous. Even presidents and kings, apparently so powerful, are in fact most highly circum-

scribed in their freedom of action. If they fail to operate within the role expectations of the institution, they generally lose their influence.

An interesting example of the persistence of institutional roles is seen in the transition of the English coal mines from private to public ownership [Koening, 1948]. Under private ownership the miners were supervised by the "boss," an agent of the private capitalists who owned the mines. Acting in this role, the boss sought to get the greatest production at the least possible cost. When the government took over the mines, some of the miners thought the new ownership meant the end of annoying rules and regulations. The boss, however, was still with them. Although now an agent of the state, he still had the job of making the nationalized mines produce the greatest possible amount of coal at the lowest possible cost. Ownership and sometimes personnel had changed, but the system of roles which had grown up in response to institutional needs remained pretty much the same.

This lack of change in the role of the supervisor in the coal mines under nationalization is not an isolated example; similar experiences occur in other institutional settings. Occasionally a man contrasts the smooth and efficient way in which his secretary anticipates his needs in the office situation with the rather demanding attitude of his wife at home. Sometimes a discontented husband divorces the wife and marries the secretary, only to find that when the secretary assumes the role of wife, she begins to act like a wife! Many an employee who is promoted to a supervisory role tries to retain his old rapport with his former crew; this rarely succeeds, for the new role inevitably alters his relationship to the old buddies whom he now bosses.

It is true that individual personality differences do affect institutional behavior to some degree. One foreman is grouchy and another is cheerful; one professor is stimulating and another is dull. But the range of individual variation is limited and is greatly overshadowed by role requirements. The conflicts that arise within an institution are sometimes due to clashes of personality but more often to the clash of institutional roles. The foreman and the inspector clash because the foreman must keep production going while the inspector keeps finding defects that must be corrected. The salesman is frustrated when the credit manager refuses to extend more credit to a slow-paying customer. The university professor's wish to stimulate intellectual controversy on the campus may clash with the dean's or president's wish to avoid off-campus criticism. Many such clashes are inherent in the interrelation of roles within an institution. With some modification, Gertrude Stein's famous statement, "A rose is a rose is a rose," may be applied to institutional roles. A wife is always a wife; a husband is always a husband; and a supervisor is always a supervisor. The difference made by individual personalities in institutional roles is comparable to the difference between a mediocre and a highly talented actor in a dramatic production. The highly talented actor realizes more fully the potentialities of the part he is playing, but at the same time his expression must be channeled within the limitations of the role. Organizations function most smoothly when they can attract competent personnel, and sometimes they are handicapped by personnel unequal to the roles assigned them. Regardless of differences in personnel, however, the persistence of role requirements will require some degree of uniformity in the conduct of those who carry out a particular institutional role.

INSTITUTIONAL TRAITS

While each institution has its peculiarities, each institution is also like all others in some respects. If institutions are to function,

ways must be found to assign responsibility to different functionaries, formulate standards of behavior, maintain the loyalty of participants, and develop methods of dealing with other institutions. Since these are common problems, it is not surprising that similar techniques may develop in institutions with very different goals.

Cultural symbols

All institutions acquire symbols which serve as a shorthand reminder of the institution. The citizen is reminded of his allegiance to the state by the flag, to the church by a crucifix, crescent, or star of David, to the family by a wedding ring, to the alma mater by the school colors or animal totem (mascot), and to the business concern by brand names and trademarks. Music also has symbolic meanings. National anthems, school songs, religious hymns, and the singing "commercials" all use the art of melody to strengthen institutional ties. Buildings may become institutional symbols, so that it is hard to think of home without a house, religion without a church edifice, education without a school building, or government without the government house or king's palace.

Codes of behavior

The people involved in the activities of institutions must be prepared to carry out their appropriate roles. These roles are often expressed in formal codes, such as the oath of allegiance to the country, the marriage vows, the medical profession's oath of Hippocrates, and the codes of ethics of several other groups. As we saw in Chapter 7, these institutionally defined roles are an important part of social control.

A formal code of behavior, however impressive, is no guarantee of proper role performance. Husbands and wives may prove unfaithful to marital vows; citizens who fervently repeat the oath of allegiance may commit treason; and church members who have sworn fidelity to their religion may lapse into indifference. If the affirmation of a verbal or written code is the climax to a long process of attitude formation and role preparation, it may be observed; if not, and if there are no swift and sure punishments for violation, the code may be quietly ignored.

A formal code is only a part of the total behavior that makes up an institutional role. Much of the behavior in any role—parent, soldier, priest, professor, politician—consists of an elaborate body of informal traditions, expectations, and routines which one absorbs only through long observation and experience with the role. Children who have never lived in a harmonious family setting are likely to have difficulty in ever filling the roles of parent and husband or wife. They have had no good chance to observe these roles in successful operation or to absorb the attitudes needed for successful role performance. Like roles of all kinds, institutional roles can be filled most successfully by those who have fully learned the proper role attitudes and behavior.

Ideologies

An ideology may be loosely defined as a *system of ideas which sanction a set of norms.* The norms define how people are expected to act; the ideology explains *why* they should act that way, and why they sometimes fail to act as they should. The ideology of an institution includes both the central beliefs of the institution and an elaboration of these beliefs which will explain the rest of the world in terms acceptable to the participants in the institution. Whereas the repetition of an oath formally binds the individual to follow institutional norms, the ideology gives him a rational justification for the application of institutional norms to the problems of life.

For instance, juvenile delinquency is a problem in all complex societies. All institutions tend to develop an explanation for this problem consistent with their basic norms. Juvenile delinquency may be interpreted by the socialist as the result of capitalist exploitation, by the conservative businessman as the result of coddling by a paternalistic government, by the churchman as caused by the neglect of religious teaching and practice, by the educator as the result of an inadequate school system, and by the family-oriented persons as a symptom of the breakdown of the home.

The usefulness of an ideology is measured, not by its literal correctness, but by its ability to inspire the loyalty and cooperation of an institution's personnel. Any shortcoming in society is blamed upon competing institutions or upon the inadequate devotion of the institution's own followers. Institutional leaders claim credit for practically all favorable developments and define all problems as simply a challenge to greater efforts along present lines. Criticisms of institutional ideology are defined as heretical or subversive attacks which must be repelled. False doctrine (any belief that attacks the ideology) breaks down the attitudes supporting institutional role performance and so strikes at the heart of institutional functioning.

INSTITUTIONAL FUNCTIONS

Society is so complex and its forces so interrelated that it is impossible to foresee all consequences of a particular action. Institutions have *manifest* functions which are easy to recognize as part of the professed objectives of the institution, and *latent* functions which are unintended and may be unrecognized, or, if recognized, regarded as byproducts [Merton, 1957*b*, pp. 19–84]. Men with important institutional roles often fail to realize the latent effects of the activities they promote. Henry Ford, the founder of the company that bears his name, is a case in point. He cordially detested labor unions, big cities, mass credit, and installment buying; yet through his promotion of the assembly line and mass production he probably did more than any other one man to stimulate these very developments. The latent functions of an institution may support the professed objectives, or be irrelevant, or even lead to consequences quite damaging to the norms of the institution.

Manifest functions of institutions

Every institution has two types of manifest functions: (1) the pursuit of its objectives in a world which is often indifferent or hostile to these objectives and (2) the preservation of its own internal cohesion so that it may survive. The family, for instance, is concerned both with raising its children and with maintaining harmony and loyalty among its members so that it does not dissolve in the divorce courts. The national state must serve its citizens and protect its boundaries and, at the same time, escape the peril of revolution or conquest. The church which seeks to convert outsiders and increase its influence must also hold the loyalty of its members and enhance their feeling of satisfaction with the institution. When an institution fails in either of these manifest functions, it either suffers disorganization and change, or its necessary functions are absorbed into some other institution.

THE INTERRELATIONS OF INSTITUTIONS

No institution operates in a vacuum. The preceding sections of this chapter show that one cannot understand a social institution unless one studies its relationships with the rest of the culture. Religion, government, business, education, and the family all exist in a constant state of mutual interaction. Business conditions affect the number of people who feel able to marry; the marriage and birth rates affect the demand for goods. Education creates attitudes which influence the acceptance or rejection of religious dogma; religion, in turn, may either exalt scholarship because it reveals the truths of God or denounce scientific inquiry because it threatens the faith. Businessmen, educators, clergymen, and the functionaries of all other institutions seek to influence the acts of government, since governmental action may make the difference between success and failure in their institutional enterprises.

The interrelationship of institutions explains why institutions are seldom able to control their members' behavior in a manner fully consistent with institutional ideals. Schools may offer a standard curriculum to all children, but the reaction of students depends on many factors outside the control of educators. Children from a home which offers stimulating conversation and challenging reading materials are more apt to acquire intellectual interests than are children in homes where comic books and confession magazines are the reading fare and where television replaces conversation. Churches profess high ethical ideals, but their members often feel obligated to compromise these ideals in their adjustment to business, politics, or the process of securing a mate. Patriotism glorifies self-sacrifice and a devotion to the welfare of the state that conflict with many individual wishes and obligations.

The need to harmonize the roles which different institutions seek to impose on the same individuals has often led to a deliberate effort to arrange institutional alliances. Our nineteenth-century alliance between business and government made it possible for business to pursue maximum profits with government assistance instead of governmental restraint. A state church ensures that church and state will support, rather than oppose or undermine, each other. Education has such a profound influence on the rest of the society that other institutions attempt to capture it by controlling the schools. Business and labor associations attempt to influence the schools by propaganda in the guise of free "educational" materials; politicians investigate them to be sure they conform to the current standards of nationalism; and some churches operate schools of their own in an effort to guarantee that education will support religious indoctrination.

The family affects participation in other institutions and in turn is the object of concern by other parts of the social order. The state regulates the process of marriage and divorce and at the same time sets minimum standards for the care of children. The schools provide "family-life" courses and seek family cooperation through the formation of parent-teacher associations. Churches set ideals for family life and strive to keep the observance of family ceremonies in the religious setting. Business advertises its products as essential to proper family life.

Many work roles pose a conflict between career loyalty and family loyalty on the part of their functionaries. Business concerns try to secure "corporation wives" who will cheerfully adjust their family concerns to harmonize with the demands the corporation makes on its executives. The army discourages marriages for privates and tries, by providing living quarters, to enable the upper-rank officers to adjust their family life to the needs of military service. The most thorough effort to control family influence is seen in the Roman Catholic Church, which strives to free its priesthood entirely from family entanglements through the requirement of celibacy.

All institutions face the necessity of continuous adaptation to a changing society.

Changes in one institution compel changes in other institutions. Since family patterns change, the state sets up a system of social security. As workers drift from farm to factory, the church must revise its language, its procedures, and possibly its doctrines in order to remain "relevant" to the needs of an urbanized, industrialized society. No institution can avoid affecting other institutions or being affected by them, as is illustrated in this chapter.

All institutions must adapt to a changing society.

Institutional autonomy

The fact that institutions are interdependent does not mean that the defenders of any institution willingly surrender ideological or structural control. Rather, the goal is to preserve their freedom to act within a specific institution while at the same time seeking to influence, if not to dominate the leaders in other institutions. In all the basic institutions, patterns of behavior have developed which are intended to maintain some degree of independence and to prevent dominance by men associated with other institutions.

Unlike some other societies, past and present, American society has not encouraged the complete domination of any institution by another. It has fostered the separation of church and state, a rejection of widespread government ownership of industry, the preservation of private business enterprise, and a somewhat uncertain tradition of academic freedom for educational institutions. These methods of assuring institutional autonomy are not completely accepted, and leaders of each institution make a continued effort to increase its influence upon other social institutions. While distinctive attitudes and goals do develop in institutions, their members carry into one institutional arrangement the attitudes formed in another, and the social order is the stage for a continual interplay, adjustment, and competition among different institutional groups.

DUAL FUNCTION OF THE INTELLECTUALS

In all complex societies, social institutions are the objects of constant comment by the intellectuals, while the bureaucrats supervise institutional behavior. An intellectual is one who, regardless of education or occupation, devotes himself seriously to the analysis of ideas. The importance of ideology in sustaining loyalty to institutional norms leads all institutions to develop mixed attitudes of appreciation and fear toward those men who are able to manipulate ideas. Intellectuals are needed to perform the vital service of explaining social developments in terms harmonious with institutional norms. Communist intellectuals, for instance, have the task of showing how all recent history really fulfills the predictions of Marx and Lenin, although this task requires a spectacular distortion of the facts. China's 1966 campaign to destroy the influence of the intellectuals reflected Mao Tse-Tung's fear that the intellectuals were wavering in their support of the revolutionary regime [Bloodworth, 1966]. The intellectual cannot be fully trusted, because the training that

equips the intellectual to defend the ideology may also enable him to analyze its deficiencies. He may even develop a rival ideology more satisfying to the demands of the time. It is the intellectuals who promote revolutions and lead the attack upon entrenched institutions. Conversely, it is the intellectuals who are called upon to defend institutions under attack.

No institution can avoid the constant need to justify its basic beliefs and practices. Any institution needs intellectuals who are able to interpret the social situation in terms harmonious with the institutional ideology. The difficulties of the intellectual come from the fact that his devotion to the institution may be subordinated to his concern for the truth. Conflict is minimized when the two types of interest converge, as was illustrated by Adam Smith's argument that the pursuit of private gain by businessmen served the public good. But modern economists and environmental ecologists have come under criticism when their research led them to the conclusion that, under modern conditions, the public good may require some limits upon the quest for private gain [Helfrich, 1970].

Sometimes the intellectual is alternately praised and condemned during his lifetime, as were Plato, Galileo, Luther, Trotsky, and many others. In his youth, Milovan Djilas interpreted communism as the main hope for achieving social justice. His writings were widely quoted, and he became Vice-President of Yugoslavia. On more mature reflection he wrote a book describing communism as a new form of human exploitation [1957]; its publication resulted in his being imprisoned by the same authorities who had praised his previous works.

Recently, the basic features of American liberal democracy have come under heavy attack from intellectual critics, of whom Herbert Marcuse [1969] may be the most influential, while being vigorously defended by other intellectuals such as Sidney Hook [1969]. Intellectuals are often difficult for the institutional supporters to work with, since the intellectual who is a defender of the faith today may become a critic tomorrow. Nevertheless, no institution in the modern world escapes the constant appraisal of intellectual critics, and no features of the institution can long survive without some degree of intellectual support.

It is easy to see why Communist countries are constantly vacillating between freedom and greater restraints upon their intellectuals. The intellectual who is best able to defend established institutions is a man acknowledged to be devoted to the truth as he sees it regardless of institutional commitments. Such a man is both helpful and dangerous to the welfare of his institution—helpful because his support gains respect for established institutions, dangerous because his search for truth may lead him to conclusions which provide ammunition for institutional critics while weakening the convictions of its supporters. This dual role creates a problem of discipline for the society and a problem of conflicting loyalties for the intellectual.

INSTITUTIONAL STRUCTURES

Because the family is so basic to all social life, Chapter 10 is devoted to it. Space does not permit an equal treatment of each of the other basic institutions, but the following brief sketches of religious, educational, economic, and governmental institutions may provide a clearer idea of institutional structure and function.

RELIGIOUS INSTITUTIONS

Practices and organizations considered religious vary so much that it is difficult to find a really adequate definition. Frequently the suggestion is made that religion concerns man's effort to relate himself to supernatural forces. Such a definition, however, eliminates the humanists who try to organize a set of moral ideals without reference to a deity, as well as Buddhists, who certainly do not believe in God in the way in which the nature of God is understood in many religions. Perhaps, as a more inclusive definition, we might suggest that *religious institutions are the organized patterns of belief and behavior specifically devoted to a relationship between people and what they believe to be the ultimate reality.* This definition includes orthodox religious faiths, in which God is the ultimate reality, as well as organized humanists who see humanity as the ultimate reality. The totalitarian social philosophies, such as communism and fascism—which find the ultimate reality in the absolute truths, goals, and values they proclaim—have sometimes been described as rival religions, seeking to replace the traditional religions. It is probably best not to describe them as religions, however, since their primary focus is upon governmental-economic activities. As we noted previously, all institutions have some common elements, and the similarity of the competing claims of the totalitarian ideologies and orthodox religions is one reason why they have trouble in coexisting.

Functions of religious institutions cluster about three types of concerns: a pattern of beliefs called *doctrines,* which concern the nature of the relationship of man to the ultimate reality in the universe; *rituals* which symbolize these doctrines and keep man aware of their significance; and a series of *behavior norms* consistent with the doctrines. The work of explaining and defending the doctrines, carrying out the rituals, and reinforcing the desired behavior norms leads to a complex pattern of worship, teaching, evangelism, exhortation, and philanthropic works requiring a considerable investment of money and personnel.

TABLE 6

Traits of major American social institutions

Family	Religion	Government	Business	Education
ATTITUDES AND BEHAVIOR PATTERNS				
Affection	*Reverence*	*Loyalty*	*Efficiency*	*Love of*
Loyalty	*Loyalty*	*Obedience*	*Thrift*	*knowledge*
Responsibility	*Worship*	*Subordination*	*Shrewdness*	*Class attendance*
Respect	*Generosity*	*Cooperation*	*Profit making*	*Studying*
				"Cramming"
SYMBOLIC CULTURE TRAITS				
Marriage	*Cross*	*Flag*	*Trademark*	*School colors*
ring	*Ikon*	*Seal*	*Patent sign*	*Mascot*
Wedding veil	*Shrine*	*Mascot*	*Slogan*	*School song*
Coat of arms	*Hymn*	*Anthem*	*Singing*	*Seal*
"Our Song"			*commercial*	
UTILITARIAN CULTURE TRAITS				
House	*Church building*	*Public buildings*	*Shop, factory*	*Classrooms*
Apartment	*Church*	*Public works*	*Store, office*	*Library*
Furnishings	*equipment*	*Office*	*Office*	*Stadium*
Car	*Literature*	*equipment*	*equipment*	*Books*
	Liturgical	*Blanks and*	*Blanks and*	
	supplies	*forms*	*forms*	
CODE OF ORAL OR WRITTEN SPECIFICATIONS				
Marriage	*Creed*	*Charter*	*Contracts*	*Accreditation*
license	*Church law*	*Constitution*	*Licenses*	*Rules*
Will	*Sacred books*	*Treaties*	*Franchises*	*Curricula*
Geneology	*Taboos*	*Laws*	*Articles of*	*Graduation*
Marriage law			*incorporation*	*requirements*
IDEOLOGIES				
Romantic love	*Thomism*	*Nationalism*	*Laissez faire*	*Academic*
"Togetherness"	*Liberalism*	*States rights*	*Managerial*	*freedom*
Familism	*Fundamentalism*	*Democracy*	*responsibility*	*Progressive*
Individualism	*Neo-orthodoxy*	*Republicanism*	*Free enterprise*	*education*
			Rights of labor	*Three "r"s*
				Classicism

Source: Adapted from F. Stuart Chapin, Contemporary American Institutions, *Harper & Row, Publishers, Incorporated, New York, 1935, p. 16.*

Latent functions of religious institutions

Few Americans will object to the manifest functions of religious institutions—the worship of God and instruction in religious ideology and moral behavior. Some of the latent functions of the churches, however, bring consequences which often surprise even the faithful, while they may stimulate either approval or opposition from those who do not consider themselves very religious.

Christian missions in colonial areas have often served to stimulate nationalistic feeling. This was not the intention of the missionaries who, though not mainly concerned with government, usually considered Western rule essential to the progress of an underdeveloped area. Rather than a direct goal, the stimulus of nationalistic feeling was a latent result of the training received in mission schools and the need to treat potential converts with some measure of equality. The manifest function was simply to produce Christians, but the latent function has often been to train nationalist leaders who became bitter enemies of colonial rule.

The Christian emphasis on monogamous marriage has some latent consequences quite the opposite of the desires of churchmen. Protestant countries tend to emphasize the sexual exclusiveness of marriage and, partly in consequence, have a high divorce rate. Catholic countries generally prohibit or restrict divorce and, partly in consequence, have a greater number of more or less permanent extramarital relationships. Many among the lower classes react to the prohibition of divorce by setting up households without legal marriage and shifting mates when they wish. Most of the middle- and upper-class people are properly married, but a discontented husband may establish a relationship with a mistress which the wife is powerless to prevent, since divorce is either completely outlawed or religiously taboo. Thus both the Protestant and the Catholic approach to ideal family life have latent consequences which modify the monogamous character of the family.

One of the most often cited latent effects of religion is the relation between the "Protestant ethic" and the "spirit of capitalism." Protestant leaders of the Reformation had no desire to erect the spiritual foundations for a capitalistic society and often denounced capitalistic trends in their day. Yet the industrial revolution and the growth of large-scale business concerns was much more rapid in predominantly Protestant than in largely Catholic areas, and in mixed areas Protestants were much the more active in business development. This circumstance helps explain the economic depression in France which followed the revocation of religious tolerance and the expulsion of the Huguenots. The phrase "as rich as a Huguenot" became a popular stereotype, and the explusion of the Protestants slowed down French industry while accelerating business development in the countries where they settled as refugees.

The Protestant ethic made religious virtues of individualism, frugal living, thrift, and the glorification of work—practices which obviously favored the accumulation of wealth. These practices are usually attributed to the Protestant emphasis on individual responsibility rather than churchly sacraments, to the interpretation of worldly success as a sign that one was predestined for salvation, and to the reaction against the symbols of wealth which had been accumulated by the traditional church. None of these Protestant practices originated in a deliberate desire to encourage commerce, and perhaps for that reason, their effect was all the more potent. The classic presentation of this theory is found in Max Weber, *The Protestant Ethic and the Spirit of Capitalism.* While most social scientists accept Weber's theory as a plausible hypothesis, some disagree [see, for instance, Fanfani, 1955].

Catholics today are increasingly accepting the values of a business society, whereas the power of the Protestant ethic has been weakened by the installment buying and the general emphasis on leisure, recreation, and luxury in an affluent society. A few decades ago it was fashionable among Protestant leaders to glorify business activity, but in more recent years capitalism has come under heavy criticism, and modern Protestants are uncertain whether their identification with business development is a virtue to be proclaimed or a mistaken emphasis to be corrected.

Some research indicates that, regardless of the situation in the early days of the Industrial Revolution, religious affiliation bears little relation to economic ideology in twentieth-century America [Greeley, 1964; G. Bouma, 1970]. On the other hand, a Detroit survey found that the Protestant ethic was still viable. This survey indicated a greater commitment to work, thrift, and individualism among Protestants than among Catholics and also a more rapid social mobility [Lenski, 1961]. A replication of the study at a later date confirmed the findings on work attitudes but did not support the other Protestant-Catholic differences in the earlier survey [Lenski, 1971; Schuman, 1971]. Therefore whether the Protestant ethic still describes genuine Protestant-Catholic differences in the United States is uncertain; any such differences that may exist are apparently diminishing.

Another latent function of religious institutions in some societies is the promotion of sociability. In their worship and educational activities, as well as in the celebration of special occasions, churches draw people together. They provide companionship and "wholesome" recreation, along with courtship opportunities and training in leadership. Religious holidays in the United States are comparatively prosaic (with the possible exception of New Orleans' Mardi Gras), but in many societies they involve the whole community in elaborate pageantry. Among primitive societies it is common for religious holidays to be the occasion for orgies, when the customary restrictions on heavy drinking and sexual license are temporarily lifted. It often seems that one of the major functions of religious institutions is to draw people out of their isolation and to break the daily routine with distinctive celebrations.

Interrelation of religion and other social institutions

Religious organizations face a pressure to support other institutions. The national state often wishes to equate the good churchman with the good citizen. The forces of the existing order wish the churches to bless the status quo in the name of peace and responsibility. The forces of revolution wish the churches to endorse drastic change in line with religiously expressed ideas of equality and social justice. The functionaries of every institutional system crave the blessings, but not the ethical judgments, of the church; that is, they wish the church to endorse, but not to criticize or evaluate, their institutional practices.

Religious organizations have developed various means of coping with these threats to their independence and freedom of action. One method is that of the state church, sometimes designated the *ecclesia*. This may be found in a society where the great majority of the people are members of the same church. Under these circumstances a type of modus vivendi is worked out under which the church accepts the main features of the institutional life of the country and in turn is protected and oftentimes financially supported by the state. Somewhat attenuated versions of the state church are found in the Lutheran Church in Scandinavian countries and the Church of England in Great Britain. Tibet, before the Chinese Communist invasion, was a country in which state and church were so thoroughly intermingled that it was hard to tell them apart. Currently, Islam in Saudi Arabia and Roman Catholicism in Spain are vigorous examples of the state church practice. The state church not only accepts the main features of the society, but oftentimes accepts some measure of government control. The Spanish government, for instance, was given the right to approve or reject bishops nominated by the Vatican.

The *sect* and the *cult* are at the opposite pole from the ecclesia. The cult is a comparatively small religious organization which stresses the ecstatic experience of its members, is usually uninterested in most types of personal morality, and is relatively unconcerned about the ethics of governmental or economic activities. It is thus seldom directly concerned with interests affecting other institutions and asks only to be let alone. Cults have a special appeal for older rural migrants to urban centers. California is considered to be the most flourishing ground for such groups in the United States.

The sect is also comparatively small, but unlike the cult, its religious interest takes in a wide range of personal and social morality. Of all the religious groups, the sect is the most insistent that its members actually live according to its doctrines. Its mores may be greatly different from those of the general society. It may be pacifist in a warlike nation, collectivist in an individual economy, agrarian in an urban culture, and austere in an affluent society. The sect is so small that deviations are easily detected, and deviants may be expelled. The sect's variation from the ideals and practices of the general culture is tolerated (sometimes) only because it comprises so small a minority that it is not thought to be a threat. A nation which would not tolerate pacifist attitudes if they were widespread can ignore a few Quakers or Mennonites without seriously affecting its military power. The sect usually makes no serious attempt to sway the total society and asks only that the society tolerate its peculiar practices and beliefs.

Intermediate between the ecclesia and the sect or cult is the *denomination*. This is a religious organization which has a large membership but less than a majority of the nation's inhabitants. Since membership does not cover a majority of the country's citizens, the denomination does not feel the same pressure for support of state objectives that is found in the ecclesia, and it may hold viewpoints not generally accepted in the country. Thus in the United States, the Methodists have espoused a policy toward liquor and gambling which did not meet majority approval, and the Catholics have been in a similar position in regard to birth control. On the other hand, a large and widely dispersed membership is difficult to discipline, and the members of a denomination find themselves in agreement with the majority position on most questions considered vital by the national state. Occasionally a nation will subsidize different religious denominations on the ground that their activities work for the general good, but usually they are supported by the voluntary contributions of their members.

In summary, the ecclesia seeks to dominate secular life through an alliance with the state but finds that it must surrender some of its own autonomy in the process. The denomination may be at odds with secular society on some issues but is unable either to secure control of the state or to enforce a rigid pattern of conduct on its members. It seeks to secure both acceptance of its internal autonomy and a greater degree of influence in the total society. The sect withdraws from the rest of society in an effort to keep the faith pure and remove its members from pressures to conform to the larger society. The cult finds its major role in emotionally expressive activities, and its ethical demands are largely irrelevant to other social institutions.

Classification of a religious group as cult, sect, denomination, or ecclesia does not imply any value judgment concerning its validity or prestige. Rather the classification is an indication of a difference in type of emphasis and in pattern of relationship to the general society. There are, however, no churches which are "pure" types, and the classification is a continuum with degrees of difference rather than a dichotomy with absolute contrasts. Since no single church claims a majority of Americans, it is probably correct to say that the United States does not have an ecclesia and that all the larger groups are denominations.

EDUCATIONAL INSTITUTIONS

In early and primitive societies, no schools were necessary. Children learned what they needed to know by watching and taking part in whatever was going on. Education, along with everything else, was handled by the family or the clan. Schools became necessary when cultural complexity created a need for specialized knowledge and skill which could not easily be acquired by the watch-help method.

The complexity of modern life has not diminished the importance of the teaching functions of the family, but it has added the need for many types of instruction which require specialized educational agencies. In the early days of American life even elementary education in the "three Rs" was far from universal. Today, graduation from high school is regarded as a desirable minimum preparation, while higher education grows steadily more common. Nor is education ended in youth, since changes in science and technology may require retraining at any stage in one's working life. Education beyond literacy was, at one time, necessary only in the professions such as the ministry, law, and medicine, and as a sort of ornamental gloss for the rich. Today, advanced education is regarded as a necessity for a large portion of the population.

Manifest functions
of educational institutions

Whether it is basic general education or training in specific skills, the primary manifest function of education in American society is to prepare people for occupational roles. Practically all occupational roles require basic literacy, while many also demand some type of specialized training. The cybernetics revolution with computer controlled machines is rapidly cutting the demand for unskilled labor, while the market for professionals, semiprofessionals, and technicians is rapidly expanding.

The list of other manifest functions of education is quite extensive: preserving the culture by passing it on from one generation to the next; encouraging democratic participation by teaching verbal skills and developing the person's ability to think rationally and independently; enriching life by enabling the student to expand his intellectual and aesthetic horizons; improving personal adjustment through personal counseling and such courses as applied psychology, sex education, family living, drug abuse; improving the health of the nation's youth by providing physical exercise and courses in hygiene; producing patriotic citizens through lessons illustrating the country's glory; and finally, "building character." Some of these manifest functions may not actually be fulfilled, but they are nonetheless *intended* functions of the educational system. In fact, the manifest functions of the school have multiplied to such an extent that we often seem to assume that education can solve all the problems of society.

Latent functions
of educational institutions

Educational institutions also have latent functions, which include keeping youth off the labor market, weakening the control of parents, promoting the Americanization of immigrants, and altering the class system.

To a great extent, the complaints about the schools are a reaction to these latent functions. Keeping youth off the labor market may be attractive to labor unions, but it appears in a different light to farmers who need seasonal workers or to those remaining industrialists who rely on cheap and unskilled labor. Parents want their children to achieve higher status through education but are distressed when their children learn about ideas that conflict with parental norms; immigrant parents who wish children to cling to the practices and customs of a foreign culture have mixed feelings about the Americanization of the school. Altering the class system by enabling youth from low-income families to get the education needed for higher-status positions likewise meets with a mixed response. Some laud this as a step toward a better society; others fear the increase of competition or fear a shortage of workers who will be content with low-status jobs. The American school system is now engaged in probably the most bitter controversy in its history—over whether its latent functions should include the promotion of racial integration.

Educational autonomy

Educators are a relatively conservative group, somewhat more likely than the average person to be loyal citizens, to accept the prevailing economic institutions, and to be faithful churchmen and conventional family members. Nevertheless, educators have a rationale of their own and are restive when leaders of other institutions attempt to exert control over the schools. The rationale of the educator is that schools exist to disseminate the truth as it is discovered by each academic discipline. Usually this search for truth does not have revolutionary implications, but it frequently issues forth in a form some-

what different from that preferred by the representatives of other institutions. Further, the very process of intellectual inquiry is upsetting to those who have made an absolute commitment to institutional goals and accompanying ideologies. Hence the schools are often under suspicion of undermining the faith of citizens and are closely watched by representatives of other institutions.

The ideology used to safeguard the autonomy of educational institutions is *academic freedom*. This means that schools are to be run by their own authorities rather than being directly subservient to other institutions, and that professors are free to conduct research, publish, and teach their findings without fear of reprisal if the results of research should prove unpopular. From the point of view of educators, academic freedom is the passport to their search for truth wherever it may lead. From the viewpoint of society, this means of assuring educational autonomy may at times prove embarrassing to other institutions whose leaders feel that they have not received the proper support from the school. Its merits lie in the assurance that both students and the general public will receive what actually is the truth as the professor understands it, rather than some position to which the professor is forced to subscribe because of pressure.

In recent years, academic freedom has come under fire from militant students who want the university to be an agency of social reconstruction. Such students have firm ideas about the type of social change they wish to see, and they view the university, not as a place of intellectual inquiry, but as an arena in which their forces may be mobilized. In their view, the good professor is one whose teaching is *relevant;* that is, his teaching materials and ideas are designed so as to cultivate support for the radical students' social-policy objectives. Any reluctance to attack the established institutions makes the professor a sure target for the militant students, in much the same way that Nazi students ran liberal professors off the campus in the days of Adolph Hitler in Germany. Since academic tenure supports academic freedom by making it difficult to discharge unpopular professors, tenure thus is also under attack by militant students who, like the archreactionaries on the political right, tend to work for a university in which teaching supports their own ideologies. In spite of these attacks from both the left and the right, most educators continue to support academic freedom and tenure as the only means by which the educational institution can secure the degree of autonomy it requires for effective operation.

GOVERNMENTAL AND ECONOMIC INSTITUTIONS

While it would be possible to look at governmental and economic institutions separately, they are so closely intertwined that it seems most efficient to look at them together. Government does have other concerns besides economic activity, but fostering or carrying on the production of goods and services is such an important function of modern governments that governmental and economic policy are always closely related regardless of whether the prevailing ideology is socialist or capitalist.

Development of governmental-economic institutions

When man gained a subsistence by gathering nuts and herbs, there was little need for either trade or government. The extended family provided all the coordination needed at this stage of activity. Trade developed when a need was felt for an orderly and dependable way of obtaining resources controlled by another group. Economic institu-

tions emerged as man organized a division of labor and recognized private claims to property. The domestication of animals, the establishment of settled agriculture with claims to land, and the eventual development of industries all led to the development of economic and governmental systems of various degrees of complexity. In recent years, the specialization of labor has reached a point where over 30,000 different occupational titles are listed in the government publication, *Alphabetical Index of Occupations in the United States*, and an economic system has developed in which virtually no one subsists by his own efforts alone. The functions of government have grown so greatly that approximately 30 percent of the national income is expended by the several levels of government in the United States.

Even modern business makes use of tradition, ritual, and sentiment.

Governmental-economic institutions are more than standardized ways of doing things. As with all institutions, they also include supporting ideas, sentiments, traditions, and values. Canoe building among the Polynesians, the walrus hunt among the Eskimos, rice planting in the wet rice culture of Southeast Asia—all these involve ascribed roles, traditions, and elaborate rituals. These rituals bring the blessing of the gods on the undertaking and also solidify the cooperation of humans. Government is supported by a panoply of flag waving, martial music, impressive buildings, and the stirring sentiment of patriotism. Even modern business makes use of tradition, ritual, and sentiment. The singing commercial, stories of the charismatic business leaders, gifts to charity and public services, the recognition banquet for retiring employees—all these combine to make the business system take on the appearance of a warm-blooded collection of human beings rather than simply a cold economic machine.

Structures of governmental-economic institutions

In Chapter 4 we noted that the evolution of a money economy and of social stratification have been suggested as two of the inevitable developments in social evolution. This is another way of saying that modern economies require a medium of exchange more flexible than barter, so a monetary and credit system has developed. A modern economy also requires the coordination of the labor of many specialized functionaries and the enforcement of the rules whereby they operate.

Three different types of governmental-economic systems have emerged, each of which handles the problem of economic coordination differently.

Mixed economy This type of system may take either a capitalist or a socialist label, but these labels make little difference in the way the institutions function. Whether the society in point is the allegedly capitalist one of the United States or the allegedly socialist one of Sweden, the relation between government and the economy is similar in kind and differs somewhat in degree. In either case, a large part of the society's eco-

nomic activity is carried on by businessmen whose activities are dictated largely by what seems to be the best way to make profits. In each country, however, some enterprises are operated by the government, somewhat fewer in the United States than in Sweden. Similarly, government control of the supply of both credit and money does much to influence economic activity in each country, while variations in government expenditures also affect the level of business. Finally, both countries operate as welfare states in which the guarantee of a minimum level of subsistence is a governmental responsibility (less perfectly fulfilled in the United States than in Sweden). Government in each country is controlled by representatives elected by popular majorities.

Communist societies The term "democratic" is used in communist societies to describe a system in which people have no effective means of control but in which a one-party dictatorship claims to rule in their behalf. Agriculture is often organized in collective farms which usually draw bitter opposition from the farmers, with agricultural output lagging in communist countries. Overall coordination of the economy, including the level of prices and wages and the kind of goods produced, is determined by central planning agencies. In recent years, communist countries in Europe have reverted partially to a capitalist model where each industry makes more of its own business decisions and is expected to make a "profit" in its operations. These profits are retained by the government to be used as the government thinks best. Yugoslavia is the communist country which allows the individual enterprise the greatest degree of independence in operation. While there are variations between countries, some type of communist system operates in the Soviet Union, the satellite Eastern European countries, North Vietnam, China, Cuba, and (since late 1970) in Chile. Communism in the

Soviet Union did produce a high degree of economic development, but whether economic advance there was more or less rapid than it might have been under a capitalist system is still under dispute. Communism typically gains power in poor, underdeveloped countries with an archaic social system and constitutes the form of their effort to modernize themselves [Ebenstein, 1970].

Fascist societies A fascist society is ruled by a one-party dictatorship organized by a charismatic leader. The people have practically no voice in governmental affairs and find their satisfaction in the glorious strength of the nation. Military power and conquest were major features of Hitler's Germany and Mussolini's Italy, but Franco's Spain and Peron's Argentina functioned without military expansionism. Private ownership of business is tolerated, but the businessman is given limited freedom and is subject to detailed state direction. Welfare benefits are provided by the state and are as high as the stage of industrial development and the needs of the military will allow. All private interests are subordinated to the state. Labor unions become agencies for imposing state policy upon workers, while churches are either forced to support the regime or find their activities severely restricted. Fascism develops in countries with a relatively advanced economy and some democratic experience. Such countries may "turn fascist" when they have been unable to reconcile their social tensions or to solve their social problems democratically [Ebenstein, 1970].

All three of these governmental-economic systems are oriented to increased productivity. The mixed economies provide more scope to individual initiative, while communism and fascism limit individual freedom sharply and depend upon centralized government agencies for planning economic goals and activities. Insofar as they are industrialized, there tends to be a restriction of extreme wealth and a raising of the standards of the lower income level. Yet in all three types of societies, inequalities in income persist. In the communist society, inequalities in income stem from differences in bureaucratic position, while in the fascist society and in the mixed economies, property ownership and inheritance lead to great differences in income. Most of the developing countries have not yet settled neatly into any of these patterns, and the trend in these countries seems to be toward a one-party or military dictatorship in government with a mixture of governmental enterprise and private business in the economy.

Latent functions of governmental-economic institutions

The manifest functions of all three systems —communist, fascist, and mixed economy— are to maintain order, achieve consensus, and maximize economic production. No society is completely successful in any of these functions. The totalitarian communist or fascist societies seem most successful in maintaining order, at least temporarily, while the mixed economies have the best record in reaching a consensus which still allows expression of minority opinion, and they have also achieved the greatest success in economic production.

An analysis of the three types of societies indicates a high degree of similarity in their latent functions. One latent function of all modern governmental-economic institutions is the destruction of traditional culture. Customary forms of land tenure, religious belief, family organization, residential location, and many other established patterns of social life undergo change as industrialism develops. Social mobility is encouraged, one consequence of which is increased anomie and alienation.

Another latent function is the acceleration of ecological deterioration. Unless expensive and complicated precautions are taken, every increase in production leads to an increase in environmental destruction. Sometimes capitalists are blamed for this on the grounds that they are unwilling to let concern for ecological balance interfere with profits. However, the Soviet Union, without any capitalists except the state, has the same problem. Basically, the difficulty is that any system is reluctant to pay the costs of preventing pollution. A major reduction in pollution would probably require increases in production costs and in taxes, with a consequent drop in the standard of living, and will certainly require a halt in the world's population explosion. Neither communists nor capitalists will find it easy to carry pollution-reduction policies into effect.

INTERRELATIONSHIP OF GOVERNMENTAL AND ECONOMIC INSTITUTIONS

The relationship of business and government has been a bitter controversy. An important aspect of the eighteenth-century liberal movement was the effort to free business from the restrictions of merchantilist governments. In more recent years, charges have often been made that government is simply the servant of the big capitalists. In the communist countries, the boundaries between business and government have been blurred in very much the same way that the distinction between state and church is obscured in a theocratic state. In the mixed economies, the aim is to maintain a cooperative relationship in which both government and business operate to strengthen each other. Business finds that maintenance of private ownership gives the greatest protection to its autonomy. Governmental autonomy is preserved by breaking up powerful monopolies and by maintaining free elections, in which the majority can check the efforts of the wealthy to dominate the government. The balance is never perfect, but fluctuates between the twin extremes of a government which is simply a facade for control by business interests and one in which private owners are denied the power of independent decision.

The leaders of business, government, and religion in the United States have all been involved in attempts to subordinate one institution to the other. Educational leaders have attempted to maintain academic freedom as a guarantee of autonomy and at times have made efforts, usually unsuccessful, to control other institutions. Some degree of freedom of action has been preserved for leaders in all these institutions, but governments everywhere have been steadily gaining powers and functions. A major question of all times is how to give the governmental officials sufficient power to operate effectively and still preserve some degree of independence for other institutions.

SUMMARY

Social institutions are organized systems of social relationships which embody certain common values and procedures and meet certain basic needs of the society. Institutions develop gradually from the social life of a people. When certain activities have become the standardized, routinized, expected, and approved means of accomplishing important goals, this behavior has been *institutionalized*. An *institutionalized* role is one which has been standardized, approved, and expected, and is normally filled in a quite predictable manner, regardless of the person filling it. Each institution includes a cluster of *institutional traits* (codes of behavior, attitudes, values, symbols, rituals, ideologies), *manifest functions* (those functions which it is intended or believed to perform), and *latent functions* (those results which are unintended and unplanned).

Institutional leaders normally seek for each institution some degree of *institutional autonomy,* or independence from other institutions. Struggles over institutional autonomy have led to such church-state arrangements as the *sect, denomination,* and *ecclesia,* and to the development of the concept of *academic freedom* in educational institutions. Institutions are *interrelated,* so that changes in one institution affect the others in a continuous cause-and-effect relationship.

The analysis of particular institutions illustrates these characteristics of institutions. The latent functions of religious institutions may subvert their formal norms, as in rules resulting in family living outside of formal marriage. Latent functions of educational institutions, such as the promotion of social mobility or racial integration, may involve the schools in severe conflict, while latent functions of the governmental-economic institutions may lead to ecological destruction. In modern times, governmental institutions have overshadowed the others. In communist countries the government officials have direct control of the economy; in fascist countries they dominate it indirectly; and in the mixed economies the governmental and business leaders share societal control. The leaders in each institution seek both to preserve their institutional autonomy and to extend their influence over other institutions.

Questions and projects

1. What are five basic social institutions found in all complex societies? How does an institution differ from an association?

2. What is meant by the process of institutionalization? Is art an institution? Recreation? The United Nations? Marriage? Birth control? Science?

3. Do you think the increased rate of divorce in the family institution is related to changes in our economic institutions? If so, how?

4. Is it possible that a church could be an ecclesia in one country and a denomination in another? Can you think of an example?

5. What is the meaning of the statement that Weber's interpretation of the Protestant ethic refutes the Marxian emphasis on the primacy of economic factors in the interrelationship of institutions?

6. Are there any reasons why a person who is anxious to promote radical social change should defend the academic freedom of faculty who oppose radical social change?

7. Has the community college been institutionalized in terms of the role behavior expected of students, faculty, and administrators? How about the "free universities" that have appeared on or near the campus?

8. What is the difference between manifest and latent institutional functions? Can you think of any latent functions of educational institutions today? Of religious institutions?

9. The Socialist Worker's Party in the United States, a small group with no hope of winning an election, is bitterly critical of other parties who have missed the true path of Marxian socialism and is very proud of its own steadfast devotion to basic principles. What type of religious group does it resemble? What kind of motivation keeps parties of this type alive?

10. Make a comparison of the Communist Party and the Christian Church(es) as institutional structures. (William Ebenstein, *Today's Isms,* Prentice-Hall, Inc., Englewood Cliffs, N.J., 1970, chap. 1, is a good source on the Communist Party.) For each, identify its sacred writing, saints and martyrs, absolute truths, symbols, codes of behavior, manifest and latent functions, claims upon members, and recent examples of disorganization and reorganization.

11. From the Suggested Readings compare the articles by Sidney Hook with the one listed for Herbert Marcuse; or compare Berger with Neuhaus in *Movement and Revolution*. In each case, one defends present institutions while the other calls for revolution. Which do you think makes the more convincing case? Why?

Suggested readings

Abrecht, Milton C.: "Art as a Social Institution," *American Sociological Review*, 33:383–390, June, 1968. Presents art as a social institution, but one which does not follow exactly the type of format usually characterizing other institutions.

Bennett, William S., Jr., and R. Frank Falk: *New Careers and Urban Schools*, Holt, Rinehart and Winston, Inc., New York, 1970. Describes the institutionalization of the role of teacher aide.

*****Berger, Peter L., and Richard J. Neuhaus**: *Movement and Revolution*, Doubleday & Company, Inc., Garden City, N.J., 1970. Berger argues the case for the viability of the present structure of American society, while Neuhaus urges the need for revolution.

Douglass, H. Paul, and Edmund De S. Brunner: *The Protestant Church as a Social Institution*, Harper & Row, Publishers, Incorporated, New York, 1935, pp. 3–19; Reprinted in **Schneider, Louis,** *Religion, Culture, and Society,* John Wiley & Sons, Inc., New York, 1964, pp. 9–12. A vivid picture of both the advantages and the difficulties of research on this topic.

*****Goslin, David A.**: *The School in Contemporary Society,* Scott, Foresman and Company, Glenview, Ill., 1965; *****Smelser, Neil J.,** *The Sociology of Economic Life*, Prentice-Hall, Inc., Englewood Cliffs, N.J., 1963; *****Yinger, J. Milton,** *Sociology Looks at Religion,* The Macmillan Company, New York, 1961. Brief sociological description of these basic institutions.

Hertzler, J. O.: *American Social Institutions,* Allyn and Bacon, Inc., Boston, 1961. A comprehensive textbook on social institutions.

Hook, Sidney: "Real Crisis on the Campus," *Readers Digest*, August, 1969, pp. 41–45; "War against the Democratic Process," *Atlantic,* Apr., 1969, pp. 45–49. Two brief articles defending American liberal democratic institutions.

Hoult, Thomas Ford: *The Sociology of Religion,* Holt, Rinehart and Winston, Inc., New York, 1958, especially chap. 4, "The Institutionalization and Differentiation of Religion." Discusses principally the relationship of religion to other social institutions.

Hunt, Chester L.: "Moslem and Christian in the Philippines," *Pacific Affairs,* 28:331–350, Dec., 1955. Interaction among religious, economic, and political institutions in the southern Philippines.

Johnson, Benton: "Theology and the Positions of Pastors on Public Issues," *American Sociological Review,* 32:433–442, June, 1967. An illustration of consistency between religious ideology and stands taken on current issues. An example of one role of ideology in the religious institution.

Lewy, Guenter: "The Future of Islamic Religion," *Trans-action,* March, 1968, pp. 52–55. Suggests that Islam, although often bypassed by secular leaders, may adapt to a different but still vital role.

Marcuse, Herbert: "Student Protest Is Nonviolent Next to the Society Itself," *New York Times Magazine,* May 4, 1969, p. 137. A short statement of Marcuse's indictment of American society.

Merton, Robert K.: "Manifest and Latent Functions: Toward the Codification of Functional Analysis in Sociology," *Social Theory and Social Structure,* The Free Press, New York, 1957, pp. 19–84; reprinted in **Merton, Robert K.,** *On Theoretical Sociology,* The Macmillan Company, New York, 1967, pp. 73–138. A discussion of latent and manifest functions of institutions.

It happened one morning when Johnny [an American ex-GI] came to work and found Maggi, Kim Sing, Povenaaa, and three other men rolling dice. Teuru [Johnny's native girl] stood nearby, watching the game with interest, advising Maggi, "You better try harder! You need three more sixes!"

"What's the game?" Johnny asked.

"Dice," Teuru said.

"I can see that. What's it about?"

Teuru blushed and looked away, so Johnny asked Povenaaa. "Don't bother me now," the excited man cried. Suddenly there were shouts of triumph and Maggi swore the Chinaman had cheated, but Kim Sing grinned happily and picked up the dice.

"The damned Chinaman gets the baby," Povenaaa spat.

"Gets what?" Johnny asked.

"The baby."

"Whose baby?"

"Teuru's."

"I didn't know Teuru had a baby."

"She doesn't . . . yet."

"You mean . . . my baby?" Johnny fell back with his mouth gaping. Then he yelled. "Hey! What's this about my baby?"

"He won it," Maggi said disconsolately.

Grabbing Teuru the American cried, "What are they talking about?"

"When it's born," Teuru said. "All the people in Raiatea would like to have it. So we rolled dice."

"But it's your own baby!" he stormed.

"Sure," she said. "But I can't keep it. I'm not married."

"Your own flesh and blood!"

"What's he mean?" Teuru asked Maggi.

Johnny Roe looked beseechingly at the fat woman and asked, "Would you give away your own baby? Would you give away Major?"

The crowd in the vanilla shed burst into laughter and Johnny demanded to know the joke. "It's Major!" Povenaaa roared, punching Johnny in the ribs. "Major's not her baby. She's Hedy's."

"You mean that Hedy. . . ."

"Of course," Maggi explained. "Hedy had to go to Tahiti for a good time before settling down. So she gave me Major."

Johnny Roe had heard enough. He stormed off and bought two bottles of gin, and when Teuru found him he had returned to his Montparnasse days except that now he blubbered, "Our baby! You raffled off our baby with a pair of dice!"

The family

He kept this up for a whole day and Teuru became afraid that it was the start of another epic binge, so she broke the gin bottles and said, "All girls give away their first babies. How else could they get married?"

Johnny sat upright, suddenly sobered. "What do you mean, married?"

"What man in Raiatea would want a girl who couldn't have babies?"

"You mean . . . the men don't care?"

"Very much! Since people find I'm to have a baby, several men who never noticed me before have asked when you were going away."

"What happens then?" Johnny asked suspiciously.

"Then I get married."

Johnny fell back on his pillow and moaned, "It's indecent. By God, it's indecent." (*James A. Michener*, Return to Paradise, *Random House, Inc., New York, 1951, pp. 115–117.*)

Family patterns show a fascinating variation from society to society, and persons from one society who become involved in the family patterns of a different society generally react in a predictably ethnocentric manner. Why, if the family is so important, has mankind been unable to find and agree upon some ideal pattern of family life which best serves human needs?

In the most primitive societies, the family is the only institution. Among the polar Eskimos, there were no other institutions—no chiefs or formal laws, no priests or medicine men, no specialized occupations. Within the family all the business of living was fulfilled. In other words, they had no physical or social needs that called for an institutional structure other than that provided by their family.

As a culture grows more complex, its institutional structures become more elaborate. The family is an adequate structure for handling the economic production and consumption of primitive hunters and farmers. But what happens when they develop trade with neighboring or distant tribes? Before long the group includes traders, shippers, and other specialists whose work is no long-er a part of the family life of the society. Later, specialized craftsmen begin to produce trade goods, giving rise to further occupational differentiation. Economic institutions exist whenever economic functions are performed in routine ways by specialists, operating outside their family roles and functions.

In the most primitive societies, order is maintained with no formal laws, police, or courts. The only authority known in many simple societies is family authority; that is, certain family members have certain authority over others. With increasing tribal size and growing cultural complexity, more formal political organization is needed. Family heads are joined into tribal councils, tribes combine into confederations, and bureaucracies begin to develop. Warfare, in both primitive and modern societies, is a powerful stimulus to political organization, for only through political organization can an aroused rabble be mobilized for an effective military effort. In like manner, religious and educational institutions develop as professional functionaries, following standardized procedures, withdraw from the family certain activities too complicated for the family to handle well.

The family, then, is the basic social institution, from which the others have grown as increasing cultural complexity made them necessary. A study of the family will tell us something about the family and about institutions in general.

STRUCTURE OF THE FAMILY

Like all institutions, the family is a system of accepted norms and procedures for getting some important jobs done. The family is defined as a *kinship grouping which provides for the rearing of children and for certain other human needs.* If a society is to survive, people must find some workable

FIGURE 2

*Conjugal and
consanguine
family types.*

Conjugal family

The basic family unit consists of husband and wife and their
children, with a fringe of relatives.

Consanguine family (matrilineal)

The basic family unit consists of a group of sisters and
brothers, and the sisters' children, with a fringe of spouses.
(In the less common patrilineal form, it is the children of
the brothers who complete the family.)

and dependable ways of pairing off, conceiving and raising children, caring for the ill and aged, and carrying out certain other functions. These family functions vary less than the family forms through which people seek to meet them. In fact, if one were to list every possible way of organizing family life, a search of anthropological literature would probably reveal that each form of organization was the accepted pattern in at least one society. With only a few exceptions, where family patterns are concerned, everything is right some place.

Composition of the family group

When we speak of the family, we think of a husband and wife, their children, and occasionally an extra relative. This is called the *conjugal family*, since its core is the married couple; or it is sometimes called the "nuclear family." The *consanguine family* is founded, not upon the conjugal relationship of two people, but upon the blood relationship of a large number of kinspersons. The consanguine family is an extended clan of blood relatives together with their mates and children. Sometimes it is called the "joint" or "extended" family. There are certain technical differences between the joint and the extended family [see Queen et al., 1961, p. 69], but they need not concern us here. While Americans use the consanguine family pattern for family reunions and other ceremonial purposes, our important family functions proceed on a conjugal-family basis. Our folklore warns against in-laws and urges the couple to set up a household of their own. Our laws require a husband to maintain his wife in a home apart from other relatives if she insists, and she sometimes does. Our laws require parents to support their own children, but impose only slight obligation to care for their parents, and no obligation to care for brothers and sisters, cousins, uncles and aunts, nephews and nieces, or other relatives.

The consanguine family has a very different atmosphere. Whereas the conjugal family has a married couple at its core, surrounded by a fringe of blood relatives, the consanguine family has a group of brothers and sisters at its core, surrounded by a fringe of husbands and wives. In most instances of the consanguine family, a married man (or woman) remains primarily attached to his parental family, and remains a semioutsider in his wife's (or husband's) family. This has important consequences. One's principal responsibilities are toward the family into which one was born, not the family into which one has married. Thus a woman may depend not upon her husband but upon her brothers for protection and help in raising her children. Her husband does not escape, however, for he is saddled with his sister's children. [For descriptions of the consanguine family, see Linton, 1936, chap. 10; Murdock, 1949, chap. 3.]

In such a family, affection and responsibility are widely diffused among a fairly large group of people. Children are the joint responsibility of the entire family, and a child develops a relationship with his aunts very like that with his mother. He is surrounded by many adults, any of whom may momentarily act as parents toward him. The family tends to turn out personalities with less individuality than ours, since each child has more nearly the same socialization experience. Such a family protects the individual against misfortune. If a child's mother dies or is neglectful, good substitutes are at hand. The consanguine family offers little opportunity for individuality and little danger of loneliness or neglect.

Obviously the consanguine family is not practical everywhere. Where both the family of birth and the family of marriage are in the same village, it is easy to be with one's mate while fulfilling obligations to one's parental family. If they are in different villages, a strain is imposed. In a highly mobile, individualized, specialized society like ours, the consanguine family would be unworkable.

But for the Tanala of Madagascar, whose farm work required a cooperative team of a half dozen or more adult males, the consanguine family was ideal [Linton, 1936, chap. 12].

Where family patterns are concerned, almost everything is right someplace.

Forms of marriage

The path to marriage is lined with a variety of impediments, requirements, preliminaries, and ceremonials which would be downright discouraging—were not the objective so compelling. Rare is the society which simply allows a couple quietly to pair off and start playing house. While this happens with some frequency in contemporary American society, this is not the approved and expected (and therefore not the institutionalized) arrangement. Marriage is too important for such casual arrangements. Marriage is *the approved social pattern whereby two or more persons establish a family.* It involves not only the conceiving and rearing of children (who are sometimes conceived as an institutionalized preliminary to marriage), but also a host of other obligations and privileges affecting a good many people. Every society has, therefore, developed a pattern for guiding these marriages.

In this matter of guidance our ethnocentrism is likely to be evident. To us it is monstrous that parents should arrange and compel the marriage of two persons who may never even have met! How do they know whether they will love each other? Why are not their wishes consulted? Our reaction illustrates the usual error of ethnocentrism —assuming that people of another culture will think and feel as we should think and feel if transplanted into their situation. It overlooks the fact that most people wish and feel only what their culture trains them to wish and feel. We think of marriage as a romantic adventure with a person we have come to love. The girl in classical China, about to enter an arranged marriage with a stranger, eagerly anticipated her marriage as a desirable status and a comfortable companionship with a man she would come to love, because he had been wisely chosen by her parents. Each society viewed the other with an ethnocentric pity; we pitied their young people for their lack of freedom; they pitied our young people for their lack of parental assistance. In neither case did the young people themselves feel any need for pity. Today, of course, the Chinese family has changed rapidly and painfully in the Peoples' Republic [Levy, 1949, Chandrasekhar, 1959; Yang, 1959; Huang, 1961; Leslie, 1967, pp. 114–120].

Endogamy and exogamy Every society limits choice in marriage by requiring that one choose a mate outside his own group. This is called *exogamy.* In our society the prohibition applies only to close blood relatives; one may not marry his sister, first cousin, and certain other close relatives. Many societies extend the circle of prohibited kin to forbid marriage within the clan, the village, or sometimes even the tribe.

Most societies also require that mates be chosen within some specified group. This is called *endogamy.* Clan, village, and tribal endogamy are quite common among primitive societies. In our society, racial endog-

amy was required by law in many states until the U.S. Supreme Court held all such laws unconstitutional in 1967, while custom and social pressure strongly discourage racial intermarriage throughout our society. With varying degrees of pressure, we also encourage religious endogamy and class endogamy in our country.

Every society practices both exogamy and endogamy, as it specifies the limits of group closeness (exogamy) and the limits of group distance (endogamy) within which mates must be found. Sometimes between these two limits there is little room for hunting! The Aranda of Central Australia have a complicated marital pattern known to anthropologists as an "eight-class system with exogamy and indirect patrilineal descent." To skip the detailed explanations, this means that a man can marry only a woman from a particular group within the proper subsection of the opposite half of his tribe [Murdock, 1936, pp. 27–30]. In a number of societies, a formula such as this makes an actual choice unnecessary, for only one girl may be in the permissible category for a boy to marry. If there is none at all, then the couple who are supposed to become his parents-in-law normally adopt a marriageable girl from another family with a surplus. After all, an institution is a structure for meeting human needs, and it usually does so in one fashion or another.

Marital choice The process of arranging a marriage shows a fascinating range of possibilities. As shown above, some societies follow a formula whereby the children of certain socially designated kinsmen marry each other, so that the individual choices may be unnecessary. Where actual choices are necessary, they may be made in many ways. The couples can do their own choosing, sometimes with parental guidance or parental veto. The parents can arrange the marriage, with or without considering the couple's wishes. A wife may be purchased, or perhaps a complicated series of gifts are exchanged between families. Wife capture is not unknown. Each of these patterns is the standard way of arranging marriages in some of the world's societies. All of them work—within the society in which they exist—and are supported by the surrounding values and practices of the culture. Wife capture worked very well for the Tasmanians, who practiced village exogamy and were not greatly concerned over the differences between one woman and all the others. For our society, it would be less practical. This illustrates the concept of cultural relativity—a pattern which works well in one cultural setting might work badly in another. As Peters shows [1971], parental engagement of three-year-old girls to teenaged boys works out very well for the Shirishna of Brazil, while any attempt to impose the Western concepts of marriage would undermine Shirishna stability and invite chaos.

Monogamy and polygamy To all properly ethnocentric Americans, there is only one decent and civilized form of marriage —*monogamy*—one man to one woman (at a time). Yet a majority of the world's societies have practiced *polygamy*, allowing a plurality of mates. There are three theoretical forms of polygamy. One is *group marriage*, in which several men and several women are all in a marriage relationship with one another. While this is an intriguing theoretical possibility, there is no authentic instance of a society in which group marriage has been fully institutionalized, with the possible exception, at one time, of the Marquesans. A very rare form is *polyandry*, where several husbands share a single wife. The Todas of Southern India provide one of our few examples. Here, as in most other cases, polyandry was fraternal, meaning that when a woman married a man, she automatically became wife to all of his brothers, and they all lived together with little jealousy or discord. Toda polyandry becomes understandable when one learns that it accompanied female infanticide and a shortage of women [Murdock, 1936, pp. 120–121; Queen et al., 1961, chap. 2]. Only where some situation has created a shortage of women is polyandry likely to be found [Unni, 1958]. But the scattered handful of societies which practice polyandry serve to show how a practice which seems to us to be contrary to human nature can still be the accepted and preferred pattern for people who are socialized to expect it. The usual form of polygamy is *polygyny*—a plurality of wives, not usually sisters and generally acquired at different times during one's life.

Mention of polygyny will arouse a predictably ethnocentric response from almost any American. He conjures up images of female degradation and helpless enslavement and rises to impressive heights of moral indignation at such heathen brutishness (or possibly of harem delights as pictured in Hollywood's mass-produced daydreams). The facts are otherwise. It would be difficult to show that women have generally had a more satisfactory status in monogamous than in polygamous societies. Even in polygynous societies, most of the marriages are monogamous. It is generally only the more successful and powerful men who can afford or attract more than one wife. In many polygynous societies, the second wife fills the status function of the second Cadillac in our society. Far from feeling resentful, the first wife often urges her husband to take more wives, over whom she generally reigns as queen bee. Polygyny in operation takes many forms in different societies, all of them far removed from the imagination of the normal ethnocentric American.

Divorce What is to be done when a married couple can't stand each other? Although most societies make some provision for divorce, some make it very difficult or perhaps give the privilege of divorce only to the men. Some make divorce very simple. A-mong the Hopi, divorce is rather rare but very uncomplicated. The husband merely packs up and leaves, or in his absence his wife tells him to get lost by pitching his things outside the door.

The social and family structure of many societies makes divorce a fairly painless and harmless operation. In many societies where there is no great emphasis upon romantic love and no intense individual love attachments, divorce entails no great heartbreak. Where the consanguine family surrounds the child with a protective clan of kin, and designates the mother's brother as the responsible male in a child's life, the loss of a child's father is hardly noticed. The meaning of divorce depends upon how it relates to other aspects of the institution of the family. In our society, with its strong accent upon individual love attachments within an independent conjugal family unit, a divorce is likely to mean the collapse of the emotional world for both child and adult.

Other variations in family structure We could extend the list of "odd" family patterns indefinitely. Some societies, like ours, encourage an informal camaraderie between brother and sister; among others, such as the Nama Hottentots, brother and sister are expected to treat each other with great formality and respect, may not address each other directly, or even be alone together. Such *avoidances* are found in many societies. Mother-in-law avoidance is very common; the Crow husband may not look at or speak to his mother-in-law, or even use a word which appears in her name. In many societies, avoidance taboos demand extreme decorum toward certain relatives, while *privileged relationships* permit special familiarities with certain other relatives. Thus the Crow, who must act with great decorum toward his sister, mother-in-law, son-in-law, and his wife's brother's wife, is socially expected to show great familiarity toward his

sister-in-law, joke with her, and engage in various immodesties. Among the Nama Hottentots, brother-sister incest is the worst of all offenses, but cross-cousins[1] enjoy a "joking relationship" which includes loose talk, horseplay, and sexual intimacy. All this is merely to say that the family includes a varying number of people whose relationship to one another is defined differently in different societies.

Is there any sense in all this, or is the family an irrational jumble of odd notions and historical accidents? Two things we should remember. First, many different patterns will "work," as long as all members of the society accept them. Wife purchase, wife capture, or wives-for-the-asking—any one of these patterns works out acceptably, provided the people view it as the proper way to stake out a mate. Thousands of societies have been in existence at some time or other. It is not surprising that most of the possible ways of organizing human relationships have been tried out sometime, somewhere. Many of them have survived, showing that man is a highly adaptable animal, capable of being trained to find his satisfactions in a remarkable variety of ways.

Second, we invoke the concept of cultural relativity and repeat that how a custom works depends upon how it relates to the rest of its cultural setting. Where wife purchase exists, the transaction is not merely a way of arranging marriages but a central feature of the entire economic and social system. The consanguine family exists in certain societies because it is an efficient *economic* unit in such societies, and not just because it is nice to have the family together [Sahlins, 1957; Nimkoff and Middleton, 1960]. As we stated in the preceding chapter, institutions are interrelated.

---

[1]*Cross-cousins* are the children of a brother and sister with their respective mates; where the related parents are of the same sex, as in the case of two brothers or two sisters, the cousins are called parallel cousins.

FUNCTIONS OF THE FAMILY

The family in any society is an institutional structure which develops through a society's efforts to get certain tasks done. What are the tasks commonly performed through the family?

The sexual regulation function

The family is the principal institution through which societies organize and regulate the satisfaction of sexual desires. Most societies provide some alternative sexual outlets. With varying degrees of indulgence, each society also tolerates some sex behavior in violation of its norms. In other words, there is in all societies some deviation of the real culture from the ideal culture in sexual behavior. But all societies expect that most sexual intercourse will occur between persons whom their institutional norms define as legitimately accessible to each other. These norms sometimes allow for considerable sexual variety; yet no society is entirely promiscuous. In every society there are mores which forbid certain persons access to one another. What may look to us like promiscuity is more likely to be a complicated system of sexual permissions and taboos which we do not fully understand.

A clear majority of the world's societies allow young persons to experiment with sexual intercourse before marrying [Murdock, 1949, 1950]. Many societies think the idea of virgin marriage is absurd. Yet in such societies, this premarital sex experience is viewed as a preparation for marriage, not as a recreational pastime. Sometimes its principal purpose is to determine fertility; a girl who conceives shows her readiness for marriage. Most of these societies have not merely *allowed* premarital sexual behavior; they have *institutionalized* it. They have defined it as a proper and useful activity

and have developed a supporting set of institutional arrangements which make it safe and harmless. Since there is full social approval, there is no fear, shame, or disgrace. The family structure and living arrangements in such societies are generally of a sort where one more baby is no special inconvenience or burden. Premarital sex experience can be a useful and harmless preparation for marriage in a society which has institutionalized it. Ours has not, as many young people learn to their dismay.

Some societies provide for the sexual needs of virtually all adults; others do not. Many primitive societies provide for the unmarried through some form of sexual hospitality or occasional license. An unmarried or widowed brother may be permitted occasional access to his brother's wife. A widow may automatically become wife to her deceased husband's brother (the *levirate*); and, less commonly, the widowed husband becomes husband to his deceased wife's sister (the *sororate*). Celibacy is exceedingly rare in primitive societies. Contemporary Western societies are less solicitous. No approved sexual outlet is provided for the widowed or the unmarried adult. Just how easily Western societies *could* make such provision, without severe disruption of other institutions and values, is a matter of debate. Yet the war-decimated populations of countries like Germany and the Soviet Union have several millions of women who are condemned to a life without husband, legitimate children, or a legitimate sex and love experience. In this respect, contemporary Western society is, perhaps, less well organized than many primitive societies.

The reproductive function

Every society depends primarily upon the family for the business of producing children. Other arrangements are theoretically possible, and many societies arrange to accept children produced outside a marriage relationship. But no society has established a set of norms for providing children except as part of a family.

The socialization function

All societies depend primarily upon the family for the socialization of children into adults who can function successfully in that society. Thinkers from Plato to Huxley [1932, 1958] have speculated about other arrangements, and dozens of experiments in communal child rearing have been attempted and abandoned. After the Russian Revolution, the Soviet Union experimented with raising children in institutions, hoping to free their mothers for labor and to rear the children more "scientifically." But Russia never practiced this idea very widely, soon gave it up, and then did everything possible to strengthen the family [Alt and Alt, 1959]. In the Soviet Union today, school and family cooperate closely to socialize children for conformity, obedience, and altruism [Bronfenbrenner, 1970]. In modern Israel, children in the kibbutz (cooperative farm) are raised in communal cottages and cared for by nursery workers while the other women work elsewhere in the kibbutz. Parents are normally with their children for a couple hours a day and all day on Saturday. This communal rearing seems to work very successfully in the kibbutz [Bettelheim, 1964, 1969; Leon, 1970], although some critics disagree [Spiro, 1958]. Yet only a few of the Israeli children ever lived in the kibbutz, and the proportion is declining as the founders pass away and the youth find the kibbutz dull. To paraphrase an American ballad, "How you gonna keep 'em on the kibbutz, after they've seen Tel Aviv?" In Israel as elsewhere, the family survives as the standard institution for looking after children. The family is the child's first primary group, and this is where his personality development begins. By the time he is old enough to enter primary groupings outside the family, the basic foundations of his personality are already firmly laid.

One of the many ways in which the family socializes the child is through providing models for the child to copy. He learns to be a man, a husband, and a father mainly through having lived in a family headed by a man, a husband, and a father. Some socialization difficulties are encountered where such a model is missing and the child must rely upon the second-hand models he sees in other families or among other relatives [Biller, 1960; Santrock, 1970; Hartnagel, 1970]. There is no fully satisfactory substitute for a mother and a father, although they need not be the biological parents.

Sometimes, although both parents are present, they are not satisfactory models. If the father is an ineffectual, timid, hesitant incompetent in a society which expects men to be bold, confident, and successful, the son is torn between his need to identify with a father as a model and his growing awareness that he should not grow up to be like his father. A girl's mother may be aggressive and masculine, with a resentful hostility toward men; she may be exploitatively feminine, selfishly using femininity to manipulate men; she may be timid, overdependent, and insecure, lacking any confidence in her ability to function as a wife and mother. A girl with such a mother has no opportunity to imitate the attitudes and skills needed for a successful adult role in our society. Psychiatrists trace many personality difficulties to one's lack of suitable parental models. For example, a most dramatic form of role-model failure is that revealed in the "battered child" syndrome. A common cause of death among small children is being beaten to death by their parents. Research has found that the parents who beat their children are generally timid, ineffectual people who were battered children in their own childhood, whose own parents were inadequate role models, and who developed no confidence in themselves or in their ability to be adequate parents. In their inability to control their children, their bafflement and frustration often gives way to blazing, violent rage. In this way, the battered child syndrome is passed on from generation to generation [Helfer and Kempe, 1968].

The function of models in socialization can be seen in the role-taking play of children. Children often "play house," passing out roles among one another ("You be the mama, and you be the papa, and I'll be the little girl, and you be the baby!"). They proceed to act out these roles as they perceive them, and they perceive them largely as they have seen them being played in their own families. Many a parent, overhearing such play, has been chagrined to learn how his child perceives his behavior! All this, however, is more than just "play." Through such role taking, the child's perception of adult roles is refined and corrected ("You stop that and act like a papa is supposed to act, or we won't play!"). Such play probably contributes insights into the feelings of others. When in play a child "misbehaves" and is "punished" by the "papa," each of them probably gains some insight into the feelings of the real father who punishes a child. Both are also recognizing the boundaries of conduct when they define an act as misbehavior. Role-taking play is thus a way of socializing children to accept and fill both their present and their future family roles.

Socialization in the multiproblem family
A multiproblem family is one with a depressing assortment of problems and inadequacies. It is usually proverty-stricken and conflict-ridden, is often fatherless, and is beset by other problems such as unemployment and irregular work habits, alcoholism, drug addiction, illegitimacy, dependency, delinquency, and physical and mental illness. Such families fail to fulfill *any* of the family functions adequately, and thus socialize their children to continue the pattern of inadequacy and dependency. Malnutrition permanently blights their physical and intellectual growth, and contributes to their school failure [Birch and Gussow, 1970]. Every slum, rural or urban, and white or black, throngs with the "drifters"—children of disorganized lower-class families—who are deprived of love and affection, alienated from society, purposeless, and hopeless [Pavenstedt, 1967].

The affectional function

Whatever else he needs, man needs intimate human response. Psychiatric opinion holds that probably the greatest single cause of emotional difficulties, behavior problems, and even of physical illness, is *lack of love*, that is, lack of a warm, affectional relationship with a small circle of intimate associates [Fromm, 1956; Schindler, 1954, chap. 10; Hayanagi, 1968]. A mountain of data shows that the serious delinquent is typically a child whom nobody cares very much about. Infants who get good physical care but are not cuddled, fondled, and loved are likely to develop a condition medically known as *marasmus* (from a Greek word meaning "wasting away"). They lose weight, fret and whimper listlessly, and sometimes even die [Ribble, 1943, chap. 1]. Several studies have shown how children in the sterilized but impersonal atmosphere of hospital or foundling home will suffer in emotional development and often show startlingly high rates of illness and death [Spitz, 1945]. Lack of affection actually damages an infant's ability to survive.

The evidence is overwhelming that our need for companionship and intimate, affectionate human response is vitally important to us. Indeed, this is probably our strongest social need—far more necessary than, for example, sex. Many celibates are leading happy, healthy, and useful lives, but a person who has never been loved is seldom happy, healthy, or useful.

Most societies rely almost entirely upon the family for affectionate response. The companionship need is filled partly by the family and partly by other groupings. Many primitive societies had organizations and clubs somewhat like modern lodges and fraternities, filling much the same functions. Yet even these were often organized on a kinship basis and were, therefore, another aspect of the family.

The status function

In entering a family one inherits a string of statuses. One is ascribed several statuses within the family—age, sex, birth order, and others. The family also serves as a basis for ascribing several social statuses—as, for example, a white, urban, middle-class Catholic. In any society with a class system, the class status of a child's family largely determines the opportunities and rewards open to him, and the expectations through which others may inspire or discourage him. Class status can be changed through some combination of luck and personal efforts, as is described in Chapter 13, "Social Mobility." But each child *starts out* with the class status of his family, and this initial placement probably has greater effect upon achievement and reward than any other single factor. The assignment to a class may seem unfair; yet it is inevitable. The family cannot avoid preparing the child for a class status similar to its own, for the very process of living and growing up in such a family is preparation for its class status. The child normally absorbs from his family a set of interests, values, and life habits which make it easy for him to continue in the class status of his family and difficult for him to achieve a different class status.

The protective function

In all societies the family offers some degree of physical, economic, and psychological protection to its members. In many societies any attack upon a person is an attack upon his entire family, with all members bound to defend him or to revenge the injury. In many societies guilt and shame are equally shared by all family members. In most primitive societies the family is an extended food-sharing unit which starves or fattens together; as long as a man's relatives have food, he has no fear of hunger. And in many primitive societies, as in ours, very few persons outside one's family really care what happens to him.

The economic function

As stated earlier, the family is the basic economic unit in most primitive societies. Its members work together as a team and share jointly in their produce. In some societies the clan is the basic unit for working and sharing, but more often the family performs the function. This situation, however, is now changing, as will be seen in the following section.

THE CHANGING AMERICAN FAMILY

The family is a prime example of the interrelatedness of institutions, for the changes in the family mirror the changes in the other institutions with which it dovetails. For example, in most hunting societies the men are clearly dominant over women, who make inferior hunters because of their limited strength and incessant child bearing. But as the economic base shifts from the hunt to the garden, women's role in the family grows somewhat more influential, for women can and do perform most of the hoe agriculture. As the plow replaces the hoe, male dominance again tends to grow, for plowing generally calls for the greater strength of the male. Thus there is some relation between one's power within the family and the importance of his (or her) economic contribution. Other examples of interrelatedness will follow.

Changing family structure

The size of the American family has decreased It is no secret that the twelve-child families of the last century are rare today. The birthrate in the Western world began falling about a century ago. It reached a low during the great Depression of the 1930s, when in the United States it fell to 16.6 births per thousand in 1933, rose to 26.6 in 1947, and fell to 17.7 by 1969. Today's "smaller family," however, does not mean that all families are proportionally smaller. As Figure 3 shows, small and medium-sized families are about as common as they were a half century ago, but very large families are increasingly rare. As birth control becomes increasingly available to the poor and uneducated, this trend away from the very large family will probably continue.

Why has overall family size declined in the Western world? Contraceptive devices have provided the means but not the motive. Contraceptives are not the cause of smaller families any more than ropes are the cause of suicides. The motives for desiring smaller families carry us into many other aspects of the culture. The shift from an illiterate agricultural society to a literate, specialized, industrialized society has changed children from an economic asset into an expensive burden. Shifts in patterns of recreation, in aspirations for education and social mobility, and changing concepts of individual rights have all united to curb indiscriminate child bearing. At present, the

FIGURE 3
Family size in the United States since 1920.

Source: *Vital Statistics of the United States,* 1964, vol. 1, *Natality,* U.S. Department of Health, Education, and Welfare, pp. 1–11; *Statistical Abstract of the United States,* 1970, p. 50.

traditional idea that raising a large family is a noble service to society is rapidly being replaced by the idea that bearing many children is an act of irresponsible self-indulgence. There is also a growing recognition, which is fully supported by research evidence [Michel and Feyrabend, 1969], that excessive fertility is damaging to marital happiness. Thus changing technology, changing economics, and changing values are all involved in the change in family size.

The status of divorce has changed Divorce is the object of much agonized dismay by Americans who cannot accept divorce as an integral part of the modern American family system. A society can secure a very low divorce rate in at least five ways. First, it can deemphasize love. In many societies marriage is a working partnership, but not a romantic adventure as well. If less is expected of marriage, more will be "successful." Second, it can separate love from marriage. Romantic love appeared in Western societies several centuries ago, but only recently has it become the standard basis for marriage. A number of societies have a series of men's clubs for companionship, and allow men a wide freedom to prowl in search of sex adventure. Here again, less is demanded of the marriage. Third, the society can socialize its members to be so much alike in personality and expectation that practically all marriages will work out successfully. The stable, well-integrated society generally succeeds in accomplishing this leveling; our society does not. Fourth, familism may be so encompassing that divorce is intolerable. In other words, so many of one's necessities, privileges, and satisfactions may be connected to the marital and family ties that to sever the marital tie is to cancel nearly all the claims and privileges which make life tolerable. This was approximately true in early America, where divorce was legally simple but not very practical. Finally, divorce can be legally forbidden, or made

so difficult that most unhappily married couples are unable or unwilling to seek divorce as a solution. Our society has actually done none of these things. It socializes people so that they differ more and more greatly in personality and expectation, gives them values which lead them to expect a great deal of marriage and to demand a high level of love satisfaction in marriage, and provides no approved outlet for their frustrated marital needs when they fail. All this makes a fairly high rate of marital failure and divorce an inescapable part of our modern family structure. The American divorce rate increased gradually to its present peak of about one divorce for every three marriages. From being a rare example of moral disgrace, divorce has become a fairly common, more-or-less respectable way of dealing with an intolerable marriage.

Where children are involved, a divorce creates a broken home. But while divorce has been creating more broken homes, falling death rates have reduced the number of homes broken by the death of parents. When both causes of broken homes are combined, we find that we now have proportionately fewer broken homes than formerly [Landis, 1970, p. 6]. The proportion of children who reach adulthood under the care of their own parents is higher today than in the "good old days" when families were supposed to be stable. This suggests that the popular practice of blaming rising delinquency and other problems on broken homes is not supported by the facts.

The division of labor and authority has changed The traditional American family was highly patriarchal. A century ago, a married woman's property, earnings, and even her body were legally beyond her control and at her husband's disposal. Today both law and custom have changed. Even among groups whose family is often said to be patriarchal, such as Catholics, immigrants, or farmers, recent investigation shows that "the patriarchal family is dead" [Blood and Wolfe, 1960, p. 29]. In their investigation of 909 Detroit-area marriages, Blood and Wolfe found that power or domination of decision making was about equally divided between white husbands and wives [p. 35]. Black middle-class families resemble white middle-class families, but among black lower-class families, there is considerable research evidence that the wife is the more dominant, possibly because our economy offers more steady jobs to black women than to black men [Kephart, 1966, p. 209; Moynihan, 1965b; Aldous, 1969; Blood and Wolfe, 1969]. There are, however, a few research studies which contest the "black matriarchy" thesis [Hyman and Reed, 1969; Mack, 1971], thus calling into question a widely held conclusion among sociologists.

They differ more and more greatly in personality and expectation.

The "quiet revolution" in women's employment Perhaps the greatest change of all has been the increase in "working wives." Women workers today make up over one-third of our labor force. One-half of all women between eighteen and sixty-four years of age are in the labor force at any single moment, and four-fifths (81 percent) of these are married and living with their husbands. Nine out of ten married women work for some part of their married lives. Of all women workers, two-fifths (41 percent) have children under eighteen, and one-eighth (13 percent) have children under six years old. About one-third of all mothers with children under eighteen are employed, and about 4 million preschool children have working mothers. [All above data from Women's Bureau, 1970.] From these figures, the "normal" life pattern of the American woman emerges. Typically, she begins working before marriage, works until her children arrive, takes off a few years, then returns sometime after her children get into school [Smutz, 1959, p. 60]. Obviously, it has become normal for the American wife to work for a major part of her lifetime.

Historically, a woman who worked was living evidence that she had no husband able and willing to support her. A survey of 140 married women workers in 1908 found that only six husbands held jobs above the grade of unskilled laborer [Bureau of Labor Statistics, 1916, pp. 163–164]. The working wife, once a lower-class phenomenon, is increasingly common among the prosperous middle classes. There is no reason to believe that this trend will be reversed. The "American standard of living" now assumes two incomes. Of all families with annual incomes between $9,000 and $15,000, nearly half (48 percent) include a working wife [Women's Bureau, 1967, p. 4]. As the "normal" standard of living increasingly becomes insupportable on a single income, the pressure upon the nonworking wife to get a job is difficult to resist. The majority of the readers of this textbook will be either working wives or the husbands of working wives for a major portion of their married lives. Are working wives happier than housewives? Evidence on this question is mixed, but it is clear that the wife is happier if she works from choice rather than from necessity [Orden and Bradburn, 1969].

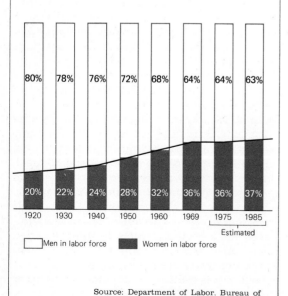

FIGURE 4

Women in the labor force (United States, 1920–1985).

80%	78%	76%	72%	68%	64%	64%	63%
20%	22%	24%	28%	32%	36%	36%	37%
1920	1930	1940	1950	1960	1969	1975	1985

Estimated

☐ Men in labor force   ■ Women in labor force

Source: Department of Labor. Bureau of Labor Statistics.

This quiet revolution has transformed the household division of labor. The work time of housewives has *not* been reduced by labor-saving devices; today's housewives work as many hours as those of a half-century ago [Hall and Schroeder, 1970]. The time once spent in hand-washing clothes and home-canning is now spent in putting in order a daily avalanche of toys, books, magazines, and hobby gear, chauffeuring children, attending PTA, and doing other tasks which grandmother did not do. Obviously, when the wife works, *something has to give.* Some of the housekeeping niceties may be sacrificed, and some tasks may be commercialized (sending out the laundry, buying prepared foods), but the major shift is a re-division of household labor among husbands and children. A French study finds that married women workers actually work, at job plus housework, only six to eight hours a week more than nonworking wives with several children [Stoetzel, 1956]. Blood and Wolfe's study shows that husbands of working wives must expect to help out more at home. Many of the male readers of this text will (if they have not already done so) eventually learn whether their masculinity will dissolve in dishwater!

Changing family functions

Structure and function are two aspects of the same thing. Changes in one are both cause and effect of changes in the other. What changes in function accompany the changes in family structure?

The sexual-regulation function probably shows no great change Nonmarital sexual behavior is fairly common, but according to Kinsey, at least 90 percent of all American sexual intercourse is marital [1948, p. 588]. There is a popular notion that virginity is rapidly fading among American youth, but the evidence indicates that there has been little if any increase in the proportion of persons having premarital sexual intercourse since the Kinsey study in 1948 [Ehrmann, 1959; Reiss, 1960, 1967; R. Bell, 1966; Robinson, 1968; Christensen and Gregg, 1970]. These and other studies show fairly constant proportions of about half of the brides and three-fourths of the bridegrooms having had some premarital intercourse, most often with future mate. One might also wonder whether premarital intercourse is evidence of the *failure* of family regulation of sex. Or are we developing premarital relations with an intended mate as a form of family regulation of sex? In other words, are we actually beginning to institutionalize premarital sex relations? Some scholars suspect so [Ehrmann, 1959; Reiss, 1960, 1967; R. Bell, 1966]. They point to the increasing acceptance of the "permissiveness with affection" pattern, in which serious emotional attachment rather than marriage is the primary test of propriety in sexual intimacy. The "situation ethics" concept is part of the "new morality" which would judge behavior, not according to moral absolutes, but according to whether the behavior is harmful or fulfilling for the particular persons in their particular situation [Kirkendall, 1961; Fletcher, 1966]. There is also the possibility that sexual intercourse, formerly institutionalized in American society only as a part of marriage, may become institutionalized as an independent, autonomous activity—as a legitimate form of play [Sprey, 1969]. It is significant that the currently popular sex books—runaway best sellers—[Masters and Johnson, 1966, 1970; Reuben, 1968; J, 1970] all abandon the old "married love" approach for the "sex-is-fun" approach. All indications would suggest that nonmarital sexual intercourse is becoming more nearly legitimated in our society. Meanwhile, improved antibiotics, contraceptives, and the spreading legalization of abortion are weakening some of the supports of the traditional moral code. Whether the "new

morality" is an enlightened adaptation to new conditions or a dangerous rationalization for self-indulgence and exploitation is an important question [Schur, 1964, pp. 63-118]. The cultural norm (virgin marriage) and the statistical norm (considerable premarital intercourse) are in glaring divergence. Young people, parents, friends, and relatives have generally conspired to maintain the illusion of virgin marriage, complete with pure white gown and veil, whereas perhaps half our brides should be wearing polka dots. The present trend toward greater candor about premarital sex relationships suggests that the cultural norm may be starting to move closer to the statistical norm, and the real and ideal cultures brought into closer correspondence.

The reproduction function is little changed True, birth rates are much lower than a century ago, but if one considers only the size of the *surviving* family, then the family reproductive function is not so greatly changed. A century ago, half the children died in infancy or childhood; today over 96 percent reach adulthood. Today's average American family of three surviving children (3.2, to be exact) is not far from what it has been through most of recent Western history. At present, the birth rate in the United States (when adjusted for age distribution) is falling, and probably will fall still farther. A recent Gallup Poll [February, 1971] shows that the percentage of Americans who consider four or more children to be the ideal-sized family has fallen from 40 percent in 1967 to only 23 percent in 1971. A further decline in family size, aside from its ecological implications, may be expected to increase family harmony. There is solid research evidence that the smaller families are less stressful, more comfortable, and "most satisfactory to spouses, parents, and children" [Nye, 1970, p. 225], and are happier and better adjusted [Hurley and Palonen, 1967]. Even when other variables are controlled (such as income, education, etc.), children in smaller families are more healthy, creative, and intelligent [E. Lieberman, 1970]. These are good reasons to be relieved that the trend is toward smaller families.

The socialization function claims increased attention The family remains the principal socializing agency, although the school and the peer group unquestionably fill important socializing functions. Other social agencies are occasionally called in for guidance. The major change has been in our *attention* to the socialization function. An earlier generation knew little about "personality development"; today nearly every literate parent knows about Dr. Spock [1945, 1957]. We know something today of the role of emotional development in school progress, career success, physical well-being, and practically all other aspects of the good life. Our great-grandparents worried about smallpox and cholera; we worry about sibling jealousies and peer-group adjustment.

How has the quiet revolution affected the socialization function? Does the child suffer when mother takes a job? There have been several dozen studies of this question [reviewed by Stoltz, 1960; Herzog, 1960; Nye and Hoffman, 1963]. The earlier studies failed to control for such variables as social class or family composition. As a result, the working-mother sample had a higher proportion of poor, uneducated slum dwellers, widows, and divorcées than the nonworking-mother sample. Such poorly controlled studies seemed to show that children suffered when mother worked. Later studies compared children of working mothers with children of *otherwise comparable* nonworking mothers. Although not entirely conclusive, these studies do not show any general tendency for children to suffer when the mother is employed. The Gluecks [1959] compared 500 delinquents with 500 nondelinquents, carefully matched for social class, age, ethnic-racial derivation, and in-

telligence. They found no difference between the delinquency rates of the children of nonworking and those of regularly employed mothers, while children of irregularly employed mothers had a higher delinquency rate. They attributed this higher delinquency rate to the fact that the irregularly employed mother more often had an unstable husband with poor work habits; they suspected that the mother herself was more often unstable and, consequently, was a poor mother whether working or not.

Whereas the Gluecks studied working-class mothers, Nye [1958] studied middle-class mothers and found greater delinquency among the children of working mothers. On the other hand, several studies [Nye, 1952, 1969; Douvan, 1963] find that part-time employment of the mother seems to be beneficial to the adolescent child. One study concludes that maternal employment is beneficial to sons but not to daughters [Farley, 1968]. Although the evidence is somewhat mixed, it is clear that *whether* the mother works is not very important, while the *kind* of mother she is and the kind of home she and the father provide are the important variables [Hoffman, 1963].

The affectional and companionship functions have gained Among Blood and Wolfe's 909 families, "Companionship has emerged as the most valued aspect of marriage today" [p. 172]. Here we have two apparently contradictory developments. We have become *more* dependent upon the conjugal family for affection and companionship while we have become *less* dependent upon the extended family, the clan of relatives. We are so mobile and so individualized in our interests that we sometimes find that we have nothing in common with our cousins, uncles, and aunts except our ancestors. The extended family is less effective in offering companionship, and this lack increases our dependence upon the immediate family. Furthermore, the primary community, the small group of neighbors who knew one another well and had much in common, has disappeared from the lives of most Americans. Urbanization and specialization have destroyed it. In an increasingly heedless, impersonal, and ruthless world, the immediate family becomes the bulwark of emotional support. A man may be insulted by his boss, patronized by his colleagues, and ignored by his neighbors, but at home he can be King Solomon to his wife and Hercules to his children! Herein lies one of the greatest functions and strengths of the family.

Herein also lies one of the greatest weaknesses of the modern American family. When the family fails to provide affection and companionship—the key functions of the modern American family—little is left to hold it together. Most of the other functions can be performed for the individual outside the family relationship. We can even question whether the married man is better off, economically or sexually, than the bachelor. Yet most people marry, perhaps because sex without enduring affection is not enough. Nonetheless, when we place so much responsibility upon the conjugal family group for providing the basic emotional support for the individual, many families will fail.

The status-definition function continues Many families continue to prepare children to retain the class status of the family; a considerable fraction seek to prepare their children for social mobility. They do this mainly by trying to give children the kind of ambitions, attitudes, and habits which prompt them to struggle for a higher status. At best, the effort is only partly successful. No family can fully succeed in socializing children in a way of life not practiced by the family.

The protective functions have declined The traditional family in Western society performed most of the functions of organized social work today—nursed the sick, gave haven to the handicapped and shelter to the aged. Today, we have a medical technology which only specialists and hospitals can handle. Today's urban household is an impractical place in which to care for many kinds of handicapped people. Family care of the aged was a practical arrangement when the aging couple stayed on the farm, joined by a married child and mate. The parents could retire gradually, shifting to less strenuous tasks, but remaining useful and appreciated. This pattern is available today to only a tiny minority, and many elderly couples feel—and are—useless and unappreciated in the homes of their children. Our rapid rate of social change and social mobility also means that many tensions may develop when three generations live under one roof. So for a variety of reasons—most of which have nothing to do with selfishness or personal irresponsibility—many of the protective functions of the traditional family have been shifted to other institutions.

The economic functions have changed most greatly A century ago the American family was a unit of economic production, united by shared work on the farm. Today only one-nineteenth of our families are farmers, and even the farm family is not the self-sufficient unit of the past. Except on the farm, the family is no longer the basic unit of economic production; this has shifted to the shop, the factory, the office. The family is no longer united by shared work, for its members work separately. Instead, the family is a unit of economic *consumption*, united by companionship, affection, and recreation.

THE FUTURE OF THE FAMILY

The American family has largely completed the transition "from institution to companionship"—from a family wherein the role of each person was rigidly fixed by tradition and enforced by law, custom, and social pressure to a family wherein the roles and tasks are arranged according to the wishes of the members [Burgess and Locke, 1953]. It is united not by work and external pressures but by shared interests and affections. It shows a far greater variety, since no uniform set of marriage roles and duties are impressed upon all without regard for individual preferences and aptitudes. Such a family has a far greater potential for personality development and individual fulfillment than the traditional pattern. This potential, though not always realized, influences the form our family is taking.

The modern American family has its critics, one of whom boldly entitles his strictures *The Death of the Family* [Cooper, 1970]. There are at least three developments which reveal the stresses in the modern American family.

The companionship family has a regard for individual preferences and aptitudes.

The generation gap

There has always been something of a "generation gap" between parents and maturing children. Today it sometimes appears to be such an unbridgeable chasm that Margaret Mead proposes that it can only be spanned when parents consent to sit at the feet of their children and learn the facts of life

[Mead, 1970]. But there is considerable evidence that the generation gap is in large part a myth [Holzman, Luria, and Sherman, 1968; Davis, 1969; Kandel and Lesser, 1969; Braungart, 1970; Brunswick, 1970; Himelhock, 1970; Walsh, 1970]. All these studies show that youths and their own parents are in far closer agreement than is often assumed. Walsh [1970] studied attitudes towards sexual permissiveness among several hundred college students and their own parents. He found that students perceived their parents' views quite inaccurately and overestimated their divergence in attitudes. He found a real generation gap of 14 percent disagreement with parents' attitudes, but the gap as imagined by the students was 48 percent. While there is a relatively small generation gap, there is a far larger "education gap." College youth diverge from non-college youth far more widely in their attitudes than either group diverges from their own parents [Seligman, 1969; Brunswick, 1970]. Furthermore, since only about one-third of today's college students have college-educated parents, any student-parent attitude comparison is more greatly a measure of education gap than of generation gap. Some degree of generation gap is inevitable in a rapidly changing society, but our modest generation gap today seems unlikely to threaten the family as an institution.

The commune

One alternative life style which appears to be currently spreading is the commune. Many communes are little more than a temporary living arrangement of college students or other young people trying to live cheaply, but many others are viewed by their members as an enduring alternative to the family. The commune is not exactly new, for American history is dotted with dozens of communal experiments of many sorts [Burton, 1939; Halloway, 1951; Bestor, 1950;

1970]. Only a few lasted as long as a generation, and all are gone today. The present commune movement is more widespread and varied than the earlier American experiments, and it is debatable whether any predictions can be ventured. Numbering possibly as many as several thousand, communes are of many kinds—political, religious, vegetarian, hippie, artistic, and others. Organization may be authoritarian or democratic, but in either case is generally informal. Resources and duties are shared, with much talk of love and, in most communes, easy access to drugs and sex, although orgiastic promiscuity is rare. Many communards work hard, especially at subsistence farming, with work informally organized and surrounded with a festive atmosphere. Work for cash income is sporadic, voluntary, and unorgainzed, and the main source of cash income in most communes is welfare [Berger, 1971]. Many communes are highly unstable, with "members" drifting in and out rapidly and the group soon dissolving, while some are more enduring. Little sociological observation has been reported and the published descriptions of commune life are mainly journalistic [Davidson, 1970; Hedgepeth, 1970; *Time*, Dec. 28, 1970, pp. 34–39; Houriet, 1971; Diamond, 1971].

One sociologist who has made systematic observations of commune life believes that the commune may be more than a fad. He believes that the isolated nuclear family is psychologically inadequate and that the commune is a contemporary effort to regain the security and emotional health of the consanguine family [Benjamin Zablocki, quoted by UPI, Feb. 19, 1971]. But very few communes have shown much stability. Hedgepeth [1970] has noted that communes which are not unified by a strong sense of purpose soon split up. Furthermore, there is an inherent contradiction in the commune. Most communes attempt to unite "free" individuals, guided only by "love," but soci-

ologists know of no instance where group life has endured on this "free" basis. In all enduring communes, such as the Hutterites or the kibbutz, the individual is tightly bound by group norms. It is doubtful whether any commune of "free" individuals can long endure.

Women's Liberation and changing sex roles

The feminist movement of the nineteenth century sputtered out several decades too soon, according to the Women's Liberation Movement (analyzed as a social movement in Chapter 21). There is no doubt that women's career accomplishments are far less then men's, as shown in Table 7. As compared with an employed woman, a man is 9 times as likely to earn over $10,000 a year, and 20 times as likely to earn over $15,000 [Women's Bureau, 1970, p. 19]. And in recent decades, women have been losing, rather than gaining, in occupational status and income [Knudson, 1969]. Even on the campus, women run a poor second, as shown in Table 8. How much of this achievement difference is due to discrimination, and how much is due to women's lesser motivation for career advancement? This is impossible to determine. Women are socialized to view their sex roles primarily as those of wives and mothers, and only secondarily in terms of a career. Women's Liberationists view this situation as cruel and unjust, and insist that both sexes should be socialized to expect equal rights and duties as respecting career, child care, and household responsibilities. When the young couple has children, why should it automatically be the wife who interrupts her career to baby-tend? Twenty-four-hour day-care centers, part-time jobs for both parents, and full equality in all kinds of educational and occupational opportunity are among Women's Liberation demands. But even this would be insuffi-

"Pay gap" between men and women gets wider			Unemployment rate: higher for women than men		
Median earnings per year, full-time workers	Women	Men	Rate of unemployment, average for year	Women	Men
1957	$3,008	$4,713	1960	5.9%	5.4%
1958	3,102	4,927	1961	7.2	6.4
1959	3,193	5,209	1962	6.2	5.2
1960	3,293	5,417	1963	6.5	5.2
1961	3,351	5,644	1964	6.2	4.6
1962	3,446	5,794	1965	5.5	4.0
1963	3,561	5,978	1966	4.9	3.2
1964	3,690	6,195	1967	5.2	3.1
1965	3,823	6,375	1968	4.8	2.9
1967	3,973	6,848	1969	4.7	2.8
1968	4,150	7,182			
1969*	4,457	7,664			

cient, because many other subtle forms of discriminiation are under attack—the language use of masculine gender to refer to all of peoplekind; the soft, yielding image of "femininity"; the "playmate" image of women as sexual toys; the double standard of declining sexual desirability with advancing age [I. Bell, 1970]—these are only some of the features of our society which Women's Liberation would like to change [Roszak and Roszak, 1970; also, *Trans-action*, special issue, "The American Woman," Nov.-Dec., 1970].

Anthropologists report that in all known societies, child care has been primarily a female responsibility. Women's other work has been of the kinds which fit in with her child-care responsibilities—work which is close to the home, is relatively monotonous, does not demand close concentration, is not dangerous, and can be carried on despite frequent interruptions [Brown, 1970]. In demanding a completely *equal* responsibility of both sexes for child care and household duties, with fully *equal* freedom of choice for work of all kinds, Women's Liberation is proposing a revolutionary departure from the experience of all known societies throughout history. While this proposal will not immediately be achieved, current trends are in its direction. The eventual consequences upon the society will be substantial, but not exactly predictable, since we have no experience upon which to base a prediction.

The ultimate goal of some Liberationists is a "unisex" role wherein all sex role dif-

TABLE 7

*The "second sex" is second
in more ways than one*

Women earn less than men in all kinds of jobs			Most women workers are in lower-paying jobs		
Median annual earnings, full-time workers			People employed as:	% of all women workers	% of all male workers
Occupation	Women	Men			
Scientists	$10,000	$13,200	Proprietors, managers	4%	14%
Professional, technical	6,691	10.151	Professional, technical	15	14
Proprietors, managers	5,635	10,340	Craftsmen	1	20
Clerical workers	4,789	7,351	Factory workers	15	20
Sales workers	3,461	8,549	Clerks, sales workers	42	13
Craftsmen	4,625	7,978	Service workers	16	7
Factory workers	3,991	6,738	Household workers	6	Less than 1%
Service workers	3,332	6,058			

*Latest data available is for 1969.
Sources: U.S. Department of Commerce, U.S. Department of Labor, and U.S. Department of Labor, National Science Foundation data for 1968. Reprinted by permission from Marijean Suelzle, "Women in Labor," Trans-action, November–December, 1970, p. 53. Copyright December, 1970, by Trans-Action, Inc., New Brunswick, New Jersey.*

ferences are cut to the irreducible biological minimum. The present trend is unmistakably unisex, with the sexes becoming more similar in personality [Montagu, 1969]. Men are losing many of their traditional "masculine" characteristics [Sexton, 1969]. Unisex clothing and hair styles are only the most obvious indication that sex differences of many kinds are quite rapidly diminishing [Winick, 1968, 1969]. In a small but suggestive research project, Heisel [1970] asked her students to identify each of 20 behavior characteristics as either "masculine," "feminine," or "equal." The percentage of replies designating an attribute as "equal" (rather than either "masculine" or "feminine") rose from 43 percent in 1965 to 63 percent in 1970. Other research shows that

children of working mothers perceive fewer sex role differences than children of nonworking mothers [Vogel, 1970], and the proportion of children now being raised by working mothers is higher than ever before. One psychiatrist remarks that "no behavior is demarkated as masculine or feminine any more" [Lief, 1970].

Sex roles are undeniably changing, and in directions which are compatible with the democratic, companionship family in an industrialized, mobile society. These sex role changes will *change* family life, but they will not destroy it. It is interesting to note that in the kibbutz, after more than a generation of successful communal living, the recent trend has been toward increasing the functional significance of the family at

TABLE 8

Women in campus leadership roles

Administrators	Public colls	Private colls	Over 10,000	Under 1,000	Coed colls	Women's colls
Presidents	3%	8%	0%	13%	5%	47%
Vice-presidents	0	4	0	8	2	17
Directors of development	1	3	0	3	2	6
Business managers	1	9	2	4	5	32
College physicians	9	7	10	5	7	13
Financial aid directors	9	23	12	32	15	67
Placement directors	14	30	10	33	21	73
Counseling directors	9	20	5	32	13	67
Deans of students	9	18	5	26	12	83
Head librarians	22	37	8	62	29	61
Academic deans	8	14	17	15	10	62
Associate or assistant academic deans	11	16	12	20	12	44
Counselors	19	22	16	26	17	51

Students	Public colls	Private colls	Over 10,000	Under 1,000	Coed colls
Student body presidents	4%	12%	2%	18%	5%
Class presidents	8	13	5	22	6
Student union board chairmen	13	15	11	16	12
Debate team captains	13	10	3	8	8
Judicial board chairmen	13	17	6	18	12
Activities committee chairmen	30	31	22	38	27
Freshman orientation chairmen	26	29	28	32	24
Newspaper editors	24	31	18	46	25
Yearbook editors	46	54	48	52	49
Literary magazine editors	23	41	16	63	30

Source: Reprinted from The Chronicle of Higher Education, *Nov. 30, 1970, p. 5.*

Note: These tables show the percentages of institutions where women have held various administrative (above) and student positions (below) for at least two out of the last three years. The private and under-1,000 categories do not include women's colleges.

the expense of the communal life of the kibbutz [Shepher, 1969]. Although many nonsociologists are predicting drastic changes in family structure, such as commune living, group marriage, triangular marriage, or individualized marriage contracts [see *The Futurist*, April, 1970], such changes are unlikely to become the norm. More authoritative predictions come from a noted sociologist [Bernard, 1970], and a home economist [East, 1970], who predict further changes in present directions—a further decline in the emphasis upon reproduction and household roles for women, a greater degree of male-female interaction as equals, and a continuation of the trend towards companionship, joy, and sexual fulfillment. This is the most probable future for the family—continuing change in present directions.

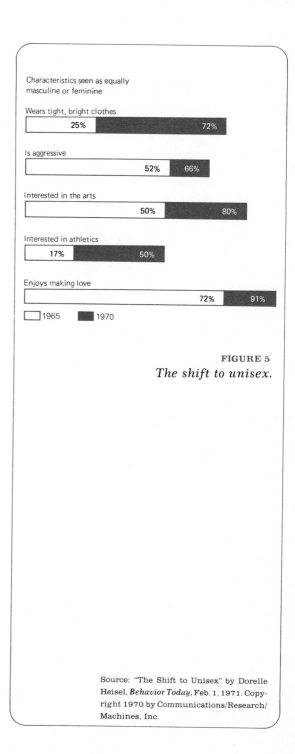

Characteristics seen as equally masculine or feminine

Wears tight, bright clothes
25% | 72%

Is aggressive
52% | 66%

Interested in the arts
50% | 80%

Interested in athletics
17% | 50%

Enjoys making love
72% | 91%

☐ 1965 ■ 1970

FIGURE 5
The shift to unisex.

The present trend is unmistakably unisex.

SUMMARY

The family is the basic social institution. It varies greatly in form. The Western family is normally *conjugal*, composed of man, wife, and children. But in many societies the family unit is *consanguine*, a much larger group

Source: "The Shift to Unisex" by Dorelle Heisel, *Behavior Today*, Feb. 1, 1971. Copyright 1970 by Communications/Research/Machines, Inc.

of blood relatives with a fringe of spouses. All societies practice *endogamy*, requiring selection of mates within some specified groups, as well as *exogamy*, requiring that one go outside certain of his groups for selection. Although most marriages are *monogamous*, many societies permit *polygamy*, generally *polygyny*, wherein it is the husband who has more than one mate at a time. Most societies provide for divorce, with wide variance in grounds and procedures. The fascinating variety of family forms shows how man's basic needs can be satisfactorily met under a great variety of institutional arrangements. In all societies the family performs certain functions—regulates sex relations, provides for reproduction, socializes children, offers affection and companionship, defines status, protects its members, and serves as a working and sharing team.

The present American family is in the midst of sweeping changes. It is perhaps a little smaller than a century ago. Divorce has become common and almost respectable. Male authority has declined, and the division of labor has changed since it has now become normal for the wife to hold a job during a considerable part of her married life. This development has aroused many alarms over the welfare of children, but the evidence suggests that these alarms are largely unjustified.

The sex-regulatory, reproductive, and status-definition functions of the family have probably been the least affected by recent social changes. In economic function, the production activities of the family have been largely absorbed by separate economic institutions, leaving the family mainly a unit of economic consumption. The protective functions have been largely shifted to other institutions. The socialization and affectional functions of the family have gained greatly in relative importance, both because of changes in other institutions and because of our increased knowledge about man's personal and social needs. Probably these trends will continue, and tomorrow's family in America will be more equalitarian, probably still smaller than today, and oriented toward companionship and family recreation. Some people suspect that the generation gap, the commune, or the demands of Women's Liberation may destroy the family. But the generation gap is in substantial part a myth. The commune is notably unstable, and while the demands of Women's Liberation would greatly change the family, it is not certain that they would weaken it. They might even strengthen it.

Questions and projects

1. Why is the family found in all societies? Would it be possible, with modern technology, to dispense with the family?

2. Why do American parents today play only a limited role in guiding the courtship choices of their children? Would it be desirable for them to play a larger role in determining marriage choices?

3. In a society such as the Trobriand, where a man has no special duties or particular affection for his own children, how can he possibly take a truly "fatherly" concern for his sister's children?

4. We use the term "uncle" for the brothers of our father or mother. Among the Todas the term "father" includes not only one's father but all his uncles. What is the importance of such variations in terminology? Some societies have no word for "illegitimate." What does the omission mean?

5. How do recent and current family changes illustrate the interrelationship of institutions?

6. Test-tube fertilization and incubator gestation of human beings may soon become feasible. Do you think women will ever prefer this to natural childbirth?

7. What do you consider the pros and cons of the current trend toward unisex roles?

8. In what ways does some research exaggerate the generation gap?

9. Is the commune likely to replace the family as the customary living arrangement? Why or why not?

10. Defend each of these positions: (1) "Divorce is a necessary and useful institution for a society like ours." (2) "Divorce is cause and evidence of family breakdown, and should be avoided."

11. Discuss these two propositions: (1) "The proper socialization of the child requires the intimate, continuous, affectionate supervision that only a full-time mother can give." (2) "An uninterrupted mother-child contact encourages an excessive dependence; the child develops most healthfully when cared for by several warmly responsive adults."

12. Discuss these two propositions: (1) "The American family is badly disorganized by the sweeping social changes of the past century." (2) "The American family is reorganizing itself to meet changing human needs in a changing society."

13. Prepare a statement of the reasons why you believe you will, or will not: (1) be a working wife, if you are female, or (2) have a working wife, if you are male. Then identify each reason as to whether it is a value judgment—a statement of what you like or dislike—or whether it is a statement of social forces and trends which may affect your decision.

14. Read John P. Marquand's *H. M. Pulham, Esq.*, Little, Brown and Company, Boston, 1941. How does the Pulham family prepare Harry for his sex role and class status, and generally socialize him to act in the expected manner?

15. Read Hans Ruesch, *Top of the World,* Harper & Row, Publishers, Incorporated, New York, 1950; Pocket Books, 1951, a novel about Eskimo life. Evaluate the Eskimo family as an institutional structure for meeting the needs of people in a particular environment.

Suggested readings

*Blood, Robert O., Jr., and Donald M. Wolfe: *Husbands and Wives*, The Free Press, New York, 1960. A research study of 909 marriages in the Detroit area, which presents evidence contradicting many widely held notions about the American family.

Doten, Dana: *The Art of Bundling*, Holt, Rinehart and Winston, Inc., New York, 1938. An entertaining account of the rise and fall of a quaint American custom, showing how it related to the other institutions of the period.

Folsom, Joseph K.: *The Family*, John Wiley & Sons, Inc., New York, 1934, 1943, chap. 1, "The Family Pattern." An interesting parallel-column comparison of the American and Trobriand family patterns.

Hess, Robert W., and Gerald Handel: *Family Worlds*, The University of Chicago Press, Chicago, 1959. A study of five differing but "typical" American families, showing how each has worked out an acceptable adaptation to the gratifications and stresses of family life.

*Komarovsky, Mirra: *Blue Collar Marriage*, Random House, Inc., New York, 1962; 1964. An interesting research study of working-class marriage, showing many contrasts with middle-class marriage.

*Lemasters, E. E.: *Parents in Modern America*, Dorsey Press, Homewood, Ill., 1970. A sociological analysis of the parental role.

*Linton, Ralph: *The Study of Man*, Appleton-Century-Crofts, New York, 1936, chap. 10, "The Family," chap. 11, "Marriage," and chap. 12, "Social Units Determined by Blood." An anthropologist's description of various forms of marriage and family life.

*Murdock, George P.: *Social Structure*, The Macmillan Company, New York, 1949. An anthropological study of the family and kinship systems of 250 societies.

*Queen, Stuart A., Robert W. Habenstein, and John B. Adams: *The Family in Various Cultures*, J. B. Lippincott Company, Philadelphia, 1952,

1961, 1967. Readable descriptions of the family in a dozen cultures, primitive and civilized, ancient and modern.

Reiss, Ira L.: *The Social Context of Sexual Permissiveness,* Holt, Rinehart, and Winston, Inc., New York, 1967. A recent study of premarital sex behavior.

*Roszak, Betty, and Theodore Roszak (eds.): *Masculine—Feminine: Readings in Sexual Mythol-* *ogy and the Liberation of Women,* Harper & Row, Publishers, Incorporated, Colophon Books, 1970. One of the best of many recent collections of readings on the Women's Liberation Movement.

Young, Kimball: *Isn't One Wife Enough? The Story of Mormon Polygamy,* Holt, Rinehart and Winston, Inc., New York, 1954. A readable analysis, by a Mormon and distinguished sociologist, of the only serious attempt to establish polygamy in America.

Formal organizations

My analysis of hundreds of cases of occupational competence led me on to formulate *The Peter Principle:*

IN A HIERARCHY EVERY EMPLOYEE TENDS TO RISE TO HIS LEVEL OF INCOMPETENCE

A New Science!

Having formulated the Principle, I discovered that I had inadvertently founded a new science, hierarchiology, the study of hierarchies.

The term "hierarchy" was originally used to describe the system of church government by priests graded into ranks. The contemporary meaning includes any organization whose members or employees are arranged in order of rank, grade, or class.

Hierarchiology, although a relatively recent discipline, appears to have great applicability to the fields of public and private administration.

This Means You!

My principle is the key to an understanding of all hierarchal systems, and therefore to an understanding of the whole structure of civilization. A few eccentrics try to avoid getting involved with hierarchies, but everyone in business, industry, trade-unionism, politics, government, the armed forces, religion, and education is so involved. All of them are controlled by the Peter Principle.

Many of them, to be sure, may win a promotion or two, moving from one level of competence to a higher level of competence. But competence in that new position qualifies them for still another promotion. For each individual, for *you,* for *me,* the final promotion is from a level of competence to a level of incompetence.

So, given enough time—and assuming the existence of enough ranks in hierarchy—each employee rises to, and remains at, his level of incompetence. Peter's Corollary states: *In time, every post tends to be occupied by an employee who is incompetent to carry out his duties.*

Who Turns the Wheels?

You will rarely find, of course, a system in which *every* employee has reached his level of incompetence. In most instances, something is being done to further the ostensible purposes for which the hierarchy exists.

Work is accomplished by those employees who have not yet reached their level of incompetence. (Laurence F. Peter and Raymond Hull, The Peter Principle, *William Morrow & Company, Inc., New York, 1969, pp. 25–27. Copyright © 1969, by William Morrow Co., Inc.)*

In this popular essay, Professor Peter has written, with tongue in cheek, on the tendency for incompetence to emerge in bureaucracies. Bureaucratic behavior, however, is only one of the many aspects of formal organization which interest sociologists. What are formal organizations and what is their importance?

Formal organizations are related to social organization as the parts are related to the whole. Social organization is that network of relationships between individuals and groups which binds them into a society. Formal organizations are only one aspect of social organization. They are distinguished from small, informal organizations such as friendship groups or work teams, and from social institutions such as religion or the family.

The friendship clique is an informal organization generally arising casually and operating according to no set rules to pursue some vaguely defined companionship goals. The formal organization is created deliberately and operates according to definite rules to pursue one or more specific goals. Blau and Scott offer a definition of a formal organization as "any social unit which has been deliberately organized for the explicit purpose of reaching a specific goal" [Blau and Scott, 1962, p. 5].

Informal organizations are *organized* groups, for all human groups have structure. But informal organizations have no *formal* organizational structure. They have leaders and followers, procedures and taboos, but there are no written rules, titles, or elective offices. Often the informal organizations are primary groups, while formal organizations are secondary groups. Like all secondary groups, formal organizations are segmental, utilitarian, and goal-oriented; but they may have primary groups or friendship cliques among their members. Formal organizations appear when a group becomes too large to organize its affairs informally.

Formal organizations differ from social institutions in that formal organizations are *associations of people* while institutions are *systems of norms and values*. Very often, however, formal organizations are ways of organizing the activities connected with an institution. Thus religion operates through a long list of church organizations, clubs, and societies; education has the PTA, the American Federation of Teachers, the accrediting agencies, and many others. Formal organizations are the associational structures through which much institutional behavior operates.

While the formal organization has membership requirements and rules which differentiate it from the rest of society, it nonetheless interacts with the rest of the society [Katz and Kahn, 1966, pp. 14–29]. The formal organization's activities stimulate a response in the society which, in turn, is fed back to the formal organization and modifies its operations. The automobile manufacturers, for example, have profoundly affected American life; yet public pressure has forced some very unwelcome changes upon the automobile industry. Unpopular models like the Edsel have been dropped, smaller cars have been marketed in response to consumer demand, and costly changes are reluctantly being made to increase safety and reduce pollution. The Roman Catholic Church has been a powerful influence in Western civilization, but current trends in scientific thought and social organization are profoundly changing the Roman Catholic Church. Although the formal organization is a separate entity, it is heavily involved in interaction with the rest of the society.

One prominent sociologist, Talcott Parsons, classifies the types of formal organizations under four headings: (1) economic production, (2) political power, (3) societal integration, and (4) pattern maintenance [Parsons, 1960, pp. 45–46]. Economic-production organizations carry on activities which add value to products or provide services (corporations, cooperatives). Political-power organizations are those which influence the allocation and operation of political power (political parties, organized pressure groups). Integrative organizations seek to maintain the order and unity of society through the resolution of conflicts (bar associations, arbitration panels, ethics committees). Pattern-maintenance organizations are those which offer channels of cultural transmission—that is, which pass on cultural patterns from generation to generation—such as schools and churches.

Parsons' list is incomplete for he omits what is possibly the most rapidly growing type of formal organization—that devoted to play—for example, the American Contract Bridge Association, the Antique Automobile Club of America, and thousands of local and regional organizations such as archers, bird watchers, and snowmobilists. Even organizations devoted to play still need some formal structure. Regardless of organizational focus, the coordination of their activities makes some degree of formal organization necessary for all large organizations.

VOLUNTARY ASSOCIATIONS

Voluntary associations are formal organizations in which all or most of the members are spare-time volunteers, sometimes with a small core of paid full-time professionals to handle the routines. There are many local voluntary organizations—church organizations, PTA, recreational clubs, neighborhood associations and others—which have volunteer officers, a minimum constitution (if anyone can find it), and bylaws or procedures which are highly "flexible" and sometimes forgotten or ignored. In such organizations, the informal aspects greatly overshadow the "formal organization" aspects, as the association operates vaguely and loosely according to Robert's *Rules of Order*. Where membership is fairly small, with a general consensus upon simple

goals, such informal operation is highly efficient. It completes desired tasks with a minimum of bureaucratic fuss. Where membership is large or geographically scattered and when goals or policies are controversial, a more formal and rigid organization develops. A large association with a scattered membership, such as the National Rifle Association or Rotary International, must have a bureaucracy with a paid professional staff that conducts routines and an elected board of directors that determines policies. In practice, however, the function of the board of directors is generally to approve the policies which the professional staff has developed and "sold" to the board. While the membership theoretically controls the organization, the actual control is by a small clique of officers and professionals in fulfillment of Michel's "iron law of oligarchy," which is discussed later in this chapter.

Functions of voluntary associations

An outlet for individual interests The major appeal of the voluntary association lies in its ability to provide a means of satisfying the proclivities of a number of citizens even though their interest is not shared by the total society. A few men who like to play golf can band together and provide a country club even though the city council may be cool to the use of tax money for adult playgrounds. A few individuals may band together to found a planned parenthood association to take action in a controversial field where it is politically unwise for the government to act. Rose [1954, p. 58] maintains that a variety of voluntary associations provide a type of "cultural pluralism," in which varied interests may be supported within the same society. Whatever the purpose, the voluntary association has the supreme merit of enabling a minority of the people to take some action toward realizing their aims without being held back by a hostile or indifferent majority.

A testing ground for social programs The voluntary association can develop a program and so demonstrate its value that it is ultimately taken over by the church or the state. The Sunday school began as an individual project by Robert Raikes, then was promoted through the London Sunday School Society, and is now an organic part of most Protestant churches. Planned parenthood programs, once too controversial for tax support, are today supported, in part, by federal grants. Most of the welfare functions of the modern state were born in voluntary associations which saw a social need, pioneered a program, and educated the public to the point where government was expected to assume the responsibility.

A channel of purposive social action The voluntary association enables the private citizen to share in the making of major social decisions. Many observers feel that this is a vital part of the democratic process. One sociologist observed:

More specifically, the hypothesis is that the voluntary associations have three important functions in supporting political democracy in the United States: (1) They *distribute power over social life* among a very large proportion of the citizenry, instead of allowing it to be concentrated in the elected representatives alone, so that the United States has a little of the character of the ancient Greek democratic city-state, as well as of the modern European centralized republic. (2) The voluntary associations *provide a sense of satisfaction with modern democratic processes* because they help the ordinary citizen to see how the processes function in limited circumstances, of direct interest to himself, rather than as they grind away in a distant, impersonal, and incomprehensible fashion. (3) The voluntary associations provide a social *mechanism for continually instituting social changes*, so that the United States is a society in flux, constantly seeking (not always successfully, but seeking nevertheless) to solve long-standing problems and to satisfy new needs of groups of citizens as these needs arise. (*Arnold Rose*, Theory and Method in the Social Sciences,

The University of Minnesota Press, Minneapolis, 1954, p. 52.)

Voluntary associations are important in all industrialized countries, and to a lesser extent are found in other areas as well, but in no other major country are they as numerous and influential as in the United States. Many European countries in the past have been suspicious of voluntary associations, feeling that they might represent a conspiracy against the state or the church. Even today the increase in voluntary associations in Europe has been mostly along the lines of cooperatives, church-sponsored societies, political parties, and labor unions. The notion that active participation in strictly voluntary single-purpose groups is both an obligation and an opportunity of the citizen is still primarily an American idea, not widely shared by the rest of the world [Cohen, 1960].[1] Even in the United States, however, only a minority of people are active in voluntary associations, with 46 percent of our adult population reporting no associational memberships and only 6 percent reporting four or more memberships in 1967 [Hyman and Wright, 1971]. Yet this minority that is active in voluntary associations has been showing a "small but noteworthy increase" in recent years [Hyman and Wright, 1971, p. 205], indicating the importance of voluntary associations in American life.

[1]Kenneth Little ("The Role of Voluntary Associations in West African Urbanization," *American Anthropologist*, 59:579–596, August, 1957) states that the West African cities may be an exception, with many associations, often based on tribal or kinship lines, involving many people and functioning to provide sociability and mutual aid as well as social control. More typical of the developing areas is the situation reported by Floyd Dotson ("A Note on Participation in Voluntary Associations in a Mexican City," *American Sociological Review*, 18:380–386, August, 1953) in a study of Guadalajara, the second largest city of Mexico, where he found voluntary organization was rudimentary and participation far less widespread than in American cities of comparable size. Similarly, Delbert C. Miller (*International Community Power Structure: Comparative Studies of Four World Cities*, Indiana University Press, Bloomington, 1970) in a study of community power in Seattle, Bristol, Lima, and Cordoba found that voluntary associations were most influential in Seattle.

ORGANIZATIONAL STRUCTURES

Almost by definition, organizations have structure. The *normative structure* is the cluster of norms—of expectations, rules, and procedures—written or unwritten, formal or informal. The *personnel structure* is the network of persons, roles, and statuses through which the activities of the organization are carried out. Both the normative and the personnel structures can be either closely or loosely organized.

Some organizations are *closely structured*, that is, authority is highly centralized and procedures are highly standardized with little autonomy for either local groups or individuals. Other *loosely structured* organizations have less centralization and allow more freedom of action. In the closely structured organization, roles are rigidly defined, even to the prescription of specific rules for most situations; in the loosely structured organization, the roles are less defined and may be adjusted by the individual or local group as the occasion warrants. Governmental and military organizations are normally closely structured organizations, with a precisely defined role and status for each rank, rigid obedience to orders, and detailed organization patterns. Business corporations may be classified in either category, according to their pattern of organization. The corporation which controls all activities by detailed direction from a central office would be in the closely structured category. The loosely structured approach is followed by many concerns which give their branch managers freedom to set their own policies as long as they show a good profit.

Associations with a similar ideology may differ in structure. The Catholic Church is closely structured, with a strong central authority, elaborate organization, and detailed rules and procedures. The Baptist Church is very loosely structured. Congregations are highly autonomous; they select and dismiss their own ministers, run their own affairs, and are very loosely tied together into a denominational organization. Likewise the Communists and Socialists both base their ideology on the writings of Karl Marx. Yet the Communist party is a closely structured organization, whereas the Socialist parties operate in a loosely structured system which somewhat resembles the congregationally organized Protestant churches.

Which is more effective—the closely structured or the loosely structured organization? This depends upon the size of the organization and the nature of its activities. A large army must be fairly closely structured; a smaller military unit can be quite loosely structured. Under some circumstances, loosely structured guerilla units are the more effective, as in the defeat of the carefully organized troops of General Braddock by a less orderly collection of French and Indians. Churches and political parties apparently can be effective with varying degrees of close or loose structuring. Any intrinsic superiority of one over the other is difficult to prove. The loosely structured organization is apt to pride itself on freedom, tolerance, and individual responsibility while being criticized for inconsistency, laxness, and ideological deviations. The closely structured unit prides itself on the purity and consistency of its ideology and the close integration of its component parts, while it is criticized as dogmatic, intolerant, and heedless of local problems far removed from the central office.

Formal and informal structures

In the armed forces a table-of-organization chart shows the exact rank and duties of every category of personnel. The recruit soon learns that he must "go through channels," that is, take up his business with the appropriate officer, without going over his head to any of this officer's superiors. In a short time, however, the perceptive soldier will learn that the organization chart does not really tell how the army operates. He will find that sometimes a sergeant or secretary has more to do with decision making than the commanding officer. As he continues in an army career he will, if successful, learn that there is a "shadow" table of organization, different for every unit and not printed in any headquarters, which he must learn in order to get things done. This shadow table is a list of the men who have "influence." Sometimes they are the men named in the official organization chart, sometimes not; but the individual who can discern the real pattern of power will find adjustment easy in the armed forces, whereas the man who relies on the official table of organization will experience bewildering delays and frustrations.

The individual who can discern the real pattern of power will find adjustment easy.

A crucial distinction must obviously be made between *authority* and *influence*. Authority is an official right to make and enforce decisions; influence is the ability to affect the actions of others apart from any authority to do so. Authority stems from

rank; influence rests largely upon personal attributes. Authority is based upon the status one holds; influence is based upon the esteem one receives. A professor has authority to make assignments and assign grades; he may have much or little influence upon his students, depending upon how they feel about him. An admired institutional officer will have both authority and influence; an unpopular officer has authority but little influence; a competent, popular subordinate may have much influence even though he has little authority.

This informal structure grows partly from the personality differences among individuals and partly from the fact that no system of roles is completely successful in meeting all the needs of the organization. In order to get things done, one may prefer to go outside regular channels and use the informal structure of the organization. This procedure is sometimes risky and must be handled skillfully if it is not to backfire; yet it is very common. Without informal structures and procedures, many things would not get done quickly or efficiently.

The real operation of an organization cannot be understood without understanding its informal structure. In an organization we may find the "operator" who can pull strings and get things done outside the usual channels; there is the old-timer whose support is valuable because he knows all the routines and because he knows "where all the bodies are buried"—that is, he knows of past errors and incidents which can be used as gentle blackmail; there are the friends and relatives of the higher officials who presumedly have influence upon them; there is the "fair-haired boy" who appears to have been selected for promotion; there is the subordinate who is so widely admired and respected that the officials find it wise to consult him; there is even the pariah who is so disliked that his support is to be avoided. The interplay of such personalities has great effect upon the decisions made by those in authority and upon the way these decisions are interpreted and carried out in practice. The interactions of authority and influence in the upper levels of government is perceptively described in the novel *Advise and Consent* [Drury, 1959] and in the several novels of C. P. Snow.

THE TENDENCY TOWARD OLIGARCHY

Prior to the nineteenth century most groups were organized under an authoritarian leadership in the belief that a few wise and experienced men, preferably of noble birth, could give more able direction than a mass of ordinary people. The nineteenth century saw the rise of numerous associations devoted to a different principle: democratic control through the decisions of the rank-and-file membership. Even these avowedly democratic associations, however, found that control tended to drift into the hands of a few leaders. This tendency was usually explained either as the action of power-hungry officials who had deliberately distorted the democratic goals of the group, or as a proof that ordinary men had not yet acquired enough education and experience to run an organization democratically.

About sixty years ago a European social scientist, Robert Michels, studied this persistence of authoritarian tendencies in an organization which considered itself the enemy of all dictatorial power, the German Social Democratic party. He concluded that the dominance of a small number of leaders was not due either to the immaturity of the membership or the lust for power of the leaders; rather it was the result of patterns which were inevitable in any organization. In his words: "It is organization which gives birth to the dominion of the elected over the electors, of the mandatories over the mandators, of the delegates over the delegators. Who says organization says oligarch"

[Michels, 1949, p. 41]. He called this the "iron law of oligarchy."

Oligarchy tends to develop in all formal organizations, of whatever type or size. Even rather small organizations, such as a local PTA or church "couples club," tend to be run by a rather small clique. Oligarchy flows directly from the pattern of participation of the ordinary member of the group. He usually attends meetings irregularly if at all; he is poorly informed about the problems of the organization; and he lacks the means of uniting with his fellow members to exercise real control. Under these circumstances a few able men who are willing to give time and attention to the task can easily assume control. They do not "seize" it; control is dumped in their laps by the members who do not want to bother themselves.

In large formal organizations, the necessary bureaucratization of the organization creates an ideal opportunity for oligarchy to develop. No large organization can possibly operate without a bureaucracy. The bureaucrats are highly knowledgeable about the organization; they have the prestige of their titles and write letters on organizational stationery; they hold the records and membership lists; they handle (and occasionally mishandle) the funds. Unless it is spectacularly inept, a bureaucratic oligarchy can quite easily perpetuate itself in office. A successful membership revolt is likely only when there is a division among the oligarchs, with rival factions bidding for membership support. A successful revolt installs new oligarchs who generally operate much like the ones they replace.

An exception to oligarchical rule The "iron law of oligarchy" simply expresses the tendency for all groups to fall under an oligarchical form of control. Is this necessarily true of all organizations, or is it simply the easiest of several patterns which an organization may follow? An illuminating example is found in a study [Lipset et al., 1956] of the internal control of the International Typographical Union. This union attracted attention because, unlike other unions and unlike most voluntary associations of any kind, the ordinary members were active in union affairs, and union officers found themselves constantly under the scrutiny of an effective opposition. Certain unusual features of the International Typographical Union seem to be related to its democratic structure, which includes: (1) a two-party system; (2) strong local units, large enough to influence the international union yet small enough for personal influence to operate within the local; (3) a network of social clubs which reinforce primary-group relations among printers and indirectly stimulate an interest in and acquaintance with union affairs; (4) union officers with salaries at about the same level as the earnings of working printers.

These features appear to meet certain problems that prevent many organizations from operating in a democratic manner. The two-party system means that the member who is unhappy with the union leadership has a channel at hand through which to express his grievances and to press for a change. Every civics student hears that the two-party system is essential to democratic government, but in private associations it is usually condemned as "factional," with the result that there is usually no effective means of organizing opposition to the office-holders who are in power.

The presence of strong local units with some authority of their own means that the individual can meet some situations through action in his local union and can use the local to influence action of the international union. The network of social clubs brings men together in a union atmosphere and increases the frequency with which they are reminded of organization matters. Finally, the union officers and members have about the same income, live on about the same plane, and retain the ease of communication which usually prevails among equals. The ability of officers to return to the trade without lowering their standard of living also reduces the urgency of retaining a union office.

The International Typographical Union, at the time described, was one example of an organization which had avoided the tendency toward oligarchy. Organization research is discovering a variety of other factors which may modify the oligarchical tendency. Thus a report on a Canadian farmers' organization indicates that a *lack* of internal political parties or "factions" and a variety of services which attracted those of different viewpoints was responsible for democratic participation [Craig and Gross, 1970, pp. 19–33].

Another variant from the ITU pattern was reported in a study in a store clerks' union [Rogow, 1968, pp. 132–145]. This study found that a high voting turnout of members induced by quasi-compulsory regulations actually favored control by a centralized leadership. These two examples indicate that while the ITU case is an example of escape from the "iron law of oligarchy," there are several possible patterns which may vary both from the typical oligarchical situation and from the ITU model.

Oligarchy usually arises from the indifference of most of the membership, allowing authority to drift into the hands of those who are willing to devote their time to the organization. But occasionally oligarchy is attained by deliberate manipulation of the membership by successful oligarchs. The United Mine Workers Union is an oligarchy which has successfully resisted efforts at membership control. The national officers did this by granting votes to pensioners who no longer pay dues but are dependent upon national officers for pensions, by placing nineteen out of twenty-three local unions under national office control and replacing locally elected officers with nationally appointed local officers, by use of organizational funds to support the political power of national officers, and (according to opponents within the union) by fraud [O'Hanlon, 1971, pp. 78-83]. A determined, crafty, and unscrupulous oligarchy is difficult for the membership to displace.

NATURE OF BUREAUCRACY

Role of the bureaucrat

When man first tackled projects which demanded an organizing of human activity beyond what family and clan organization could provide, bureaucrats first appeared. Some feel that perhaps the ancient irrigation and flood-control projects first gave rise to the need for a disciplined and organized division of labor [Wittfogel, 1957]. Bureaucrats are never very popular. Most men regard themselves, rightly or wrongly, as productive workers and look with suspicion upon the bureaucrat who "does no real work" but just organizes and records the work of others.

Bureaucracy is defined [Coser and Rosenberg, 1969, p. 445] as "that type of hierarchical organization which is designed rationally to coordinate the work of many individuals in pursuit of large scale administrative tasks." A bureaucracy, therefore, is a pyramid of personnel who conduct rationally the work of a large organization. Thompson [1961, pp. 13-17], drawing mainly on the work of Max Weber, presents the main characteristics of bureaucracy as (1) *specialization*, to assign each task to an expert; (2) *merit appointment and job tenure*, to ensure competent personnel; (3) *formalistic impersonality*, to see that a set of formal procedures is carried out impartially; and (4) a *chain of command*, to define each person's authority and responsibility.

Bureaucracy inevitably develops in all large organizations—government departments, churches, universities, voluntary associations, and private business concerns. Suppose, for example, a business concern has an office force of three persons. They can divide the work casually and informally, and each can get from the supply closet whatever office supplies he needs. Suppose the office force grows to 3,000. Now an orderly division of work and authority is necessary to get the work done; a set of formal policies is needed to keep the supplies in order, along with a system of inventory control and requisitions to keep supplies in stock and to prevent pilferage. Bureaucracy thus has at least three roots: the needs for efficiency, for uniformity, and for prevention of corruption.

In addition to these factors, the very complexity of modern organizations may lead to an increase in bureaucratic personnel. Research findings indicate that the greater the expertness involved, the higher the ratio of supervisors to other employees [Meyer, 1968, pp. 950-951]. This increase does not represent a surveilance of routine operations, but the need for increased communications to bring about the coordination of technical knowledge. Expert personnel may be motivated to carry out their duties without the constant supervision of a "boss," but the coordination of their work with that of the other experts is an involved and complicated process requiring constant communication through bureaucratic personnel concerned with the functioning of the organization as a whole.

Civil service as a bureaucratic model

While bureaucrats conducted routine government operations in ancient Egypt, Rome, and China, the great modern expansion of the civil service is due both to the expansion of government functions and to a new concept of the nature of the state. The state

is no longer the property of either an hereditary ruler or a successful politician but becomes the servant of the people. As such
it performs many functions which it did not
assume in an earlier era. If governmental
employees are not just loyal henchmen
claiming their just rewards, then a system
must be devised to obtain people who will
assume their responsibilities in an impartial and capable manner. To gain this type
of employee, civil service rules carefully
define qualifications, duties, authority, and
compensation. The civil service employee
ordinarily makes decisions, not to please
the political ruler or to gratify his own prejudices, but according to definite rules. His
income is not based on either his ability to
gather taxes or the generosity of the ruler;
he receives a salary according to his rank in
the governmental organization. His tenure
is usually for life, and he may be promoted
on the basis of seniority or proved competence; he can be dismissed only for wrong-
doing or lack of efficiency.

The civil service system is designed to secure uniformity of administration by employees who have a special competence for
the particular task to which they are assigned. The fact that it is still subject to
criticism, even though it has largely succeeded in reaching the objectives for which
it was established, reveals some of the problems of bureaucratic operation [Merton et
al. (eds.), 1952, pp. 397–424]. The criticisms
of civil service may be summarized as: (1)
creation of an invidious status, (2) rigidity
of performance, (3) division of responsibility and excessive clerical routine, (4)
bifurcation of focus [Selznick, 1943; Merton, 1949, pp. 151–160]. To some extent
these tendencies may be alleviated by
changes in the structure, but they appear in
all bureaucracies and are probably impossible to eliminate.

An *invidious status* is one which automatically tends to create ill will, resentment,
or animosity. It arises from the fact that al-

though the bureaucratic employee is supposed to be the servant of the public, he is
often in a position where he makes decisions that vitally affect the welfare of the
citizen. The clerk who informs a jobless man
that he is ineligible for unemployment benefits or tells a homeowner that his tax assessment has been raised is probably acting according to regulations, but he is in the
position of handing down a distasteful decision to the citizen who is nominally one
of his employers. It is easy for the bureaucrat to defend himself by citing the regulations and his duties as a public official,
but this Olympian detachment may simply
infuriate the citizen who already believes
himself the victim of an unfair decision.

Rigidity of performance characterizes the
actions of personnel who must follow a set
of rules. When conditions unforeseen by the
rules arise, the bureaucrat may be unable to
act constructively because the regulations
permit no exceptions. A striking example of
the difficulty of bureaucratic action in situations without a clear precedent is seen in
the case of Bernt Balchen, Admiral Byrd's
pilot on his historic South Pole flight:

According to a ruling of the department of labor, Bernt Balchen . . . cannot receive his citizenship papers. Balchen, a native of Norway, declared his intention in 1927. It is held that he has
failed to meet the condition of five years' continuous residence in the United States. The Byrd
Antarctic voyage took him out of the country, although he was on a ship carrying the American
flag, was an invaluable member of the Antarctic
expedition, and in a region to which there is an
American claim because of the exploration and
occupation of it by Americans, this region being
Little America.

The bureau of naturalization explains that it
cannot proceed on the assumption Little America
is American soil. That would be trespassing on
international questions where it has no sanction.
So far as the bureau is concerned, Balchen was out
of the country and technically has not complied
with the law of naturalization. (*Chicago Tribune*,
June 24, 1931).

A more amusing example of the bureaucrat's habit of blindly following the rules occurred when the cold wave of 1962 brought freezing temperatures to many Southern cities which had not had a freeze in decades. In at least one city the street department proceeded with its regular street-sprinkling schedule. The water promptly froze, bringing traffic to a standstill. After all, nobody *told* them not to water the streets that day.

It is often alleged that bureaucrats develop a habit of blindly following regulations, with an emotional incapacity to see any further than the rule book. Much bitter satire has been directed at the myopic bureaucrat with nose in the rule book and guided by all the initiative and imagination of an oyster! While many entertaining confirmations of bureaucratic rigidity can be collected, there is evidence that rigidity of performance is a characteristic of the bureaucratic system, not of the bureaucrats themselves. A careful comparison of bureaucrats with other personnel in nonbureaucratic positions concludes that "there is a small but consistent tendency for men who work in bureaucratic positions to be more intellectually flexible, more open to new experience, and more self-directed in their values than are men who work in nonbureaucratic organizations" [Kohn, 1971, p. 461]. Thus, rigidity of performance is not so much a product of blindly habituated bureaucrats as it is a product of the necessary rules of procedure by which any large organization must operate.

The disadvantages of rigidity are recognized by governmental administrators, and they try to reduce rigidity by giving more discretion to subordinate officials as well as by leaving some positions free to be filled by appointees selected without regard to the usual civil service regulations. But the granting of a great deal of discretionary authority to officials increases favoritism and corruption, and this in turn leads to a new set of regulations. Rigidity remains a

problem, and the bureaucrat usually has difficulty in coping with a situation not clearly defined by regulations.

Division of responsibility is another irritating aspect of bureaucracy. In order to be sure that a uniform policy is followed and all individuals are treated equally, it may be necessary to build up an elaborate file and to consult several officials at different levels of the hierarchy. The citizen often feels that he is getting the "runaround" as he tries to find some official whom he can pin down to a decision. If this difficulty is minimized by decentralization to give subordinate officials more power, then the bureau faces the danger of criticism because of favoritism and inconsistent decisions.

Bifurcation of allegiance is perhaps the most deep-rooted of the objections to any bureaucracy, civil service or otherwise. Bifurcation means a splitting off in two divergent paths. In the bureaucracy, this may take the form of a split between service to the clientele and adherence to the norms and procedures characteristic of the bureaucratic structure. Supposedly the bureaucracy exists to serve its clientele, and procedures are developed with service in mind. Actually the procedures sometimes become an end in themselves. For example, the prison and the mental hospital have the goal of rehabilitating inmates or patients. But in each institution an employee culture develops, oriented toward controlling the inmates or patients in the easiest way, which sabotages the formal goals of the prison or hospital [Dunham and Weinberg, 1960]. Every bureaucracy offers similar examples of means becoming ends. An office may go through the motions without ever actually solving a problem. A bureaucrat may handle a citizen's complaint by filing a report, or by referring him to Mr. X. The official who follows this path may feel that he has done all that could be expected according to the rules; but the public is dissatisfied because its needs have not been met. Efforts to punish an official are usually fruitless when he can prove that he has followed the letter of the regulations. Again, a greater amount of freedom for the official, though it would enable him to meet problems more realistically, would destroy uniformity in treatment and invite corruption.

A number of these dysfunctional tendencies in bureaucracy are summed up in the concept of *bureaupathology*, a word apparently coined by Thompson [1961, chap. 8]. All large impersonal organizations produce a great many tensions among their personnel. Anxieties and frustrations over promotions, criticisms, failures, lack of recognition, unwelcome demands of others, and conflicting pressures of many sorts all combine to produce great stress in the individual. He often responds in ways which reduce his tension but sabotage the goals of the organization. The insecure employee plays it safe by concentrating on report filing and record keeping. Buck passing and responsibility ducking are ways of keeping one's record "clean." Bureaupathic behavior is oriented to personal needs rather than to institutional goals. Since it arises from the anxiety and insecurity created by all large organizations, it is a problem in organizational theory, not in psychopathology.

Reactions to bureaucracy

The tendency for bureaucracies to accumulate rules and procedures is well known. In fact, many bureaucracies become so entangled in red tape that their daily work can be accomplished only by violating or evading some of the rules. Employees can stage a limited form of strike—a "work slowdown"—by simply abandoning their shortcuts and following the rule book. In this way the employees of the British Post Office slowed the mails to a crawl during a dispute in 1962 [*Time*, Jan. 19, 1962, p. 35].

The difficulties of bureaucratic organiza-

tion lead to attempts both to improve it and to revolt against it. The formal study of administration with a careful analysis of bureaucratic forms and functions is an attempt to make the bureaucracy an efficient instrument for meeting organizational needs. Training programs for businessmen, educators, public officials, and clergymen all stress courses in "administration" (a more popular term for bureaucratic procedures). Since bureaucracy is both a necessary and an annoying feature of all modern societies, efforts to improve bureaucracy are continuous and only partly successful.

Bureaucracies tend to accumulate rules and procedures.

Revolts against bureaucracy take many forms. In government they may be seen in the persistence of "machine politics." The political machine is sometimes regarded as an effort to outflank the bureaucracy, since the citizen who is frustrated by the bureaucracy may have his needs cared for by a political boss who gives preferential treatment in return for votes. The boss may be less honest than the bureaucrat but more skillful in primary-group relations. While he ignores red tape and violates rules, he gets things done.

Discontent with bureaucratic rule appears

among the members or clients of all kinds of formal organizations. The elaborate ecclesiastical structure of the major denominations is often threatened by irregular clergy or by less formal churches which provide religious solace to those who distrust the formalized organization. The elaborately organized business may be undercut by a smaller competitor which can more swiftly pursue profitable opportunities. Schools find themselves confronted with taxpayers' revolts which are due in part to a feeling of helplessness of the average citizen in dealing with educational administration. Labor-union leaders often find their control is jeopardized by wildcat strikes in which the rank and file take action that the official union leaders would rather suppress. Student discontent with the bureaucratic characteristics of the university is claimed to be a significant factor in contemporary campus protests [Otten, 1970].

Both the need for bureaucratic structures and the resentment which they arouse seem inherent in the nature of modern large-scale organizations. A growing understanding of the techniques of administration may enable institutions to function in ways that will lessen public resentment against bureaucratic red tape, but some degree of dissatisfaction will probably always remain. If future trends follow those of the past, we may expect to see rank-and-file revolts against bureaucratic rule followed by the rise of new bureaucracies differing in personnel but following essentially the same procedures as the old ones.

FREEDOM VERSUS COMPLIANCE

Possibly the crucial problem of formal organization is to secure compliance with basic policies without stifling individual freedom. If the organization becomes a vast bureaucratic machine with a few men at the top giving orders while the others are mere robots following standardized routines, the results are fatal both to organizational success and to individual development. The world, is not so simple that a handbook of rules can anticipate every situation, and any organization in which initiative is stifled will soon be so out of touch with the real world that its function will be impaired. Similarly, men are more than clerks or machines, and an organization will suffer if its personnel are deprived of any real voice in the decision-making processes. The formal organization seeks a high degree of compliance with at least the spirit of its announced goals; but if this conformity is purchased at the cost of stifled initiative and blunted thought, the cost to the organization is great.

Communications problems

In Chapter 8, we noted that the form of the communication chain makes a difference in the type of response. Morale is higher and communication more frequent in the circle with no designated leader, and lowest in the wheel where the man at the hub acts as director. This is also true of hierarchical versus egalitarian patterns. A system in which superiors give orders to subordinates is more likely to secure a uniformity of response, but also tends to dampen initiative and to repress feedback which might reveal problems. This is the reason why organizations often find a great deal of communication flowing from the top down and very little from the bottom up. A free flow of ideas which will stimulate suggestions, expose errors, and relieve anxiety through shared responsibility will also make it difficult to agree on one master plan or uniform solution. What is gained in stimulation to increased creativity must be balanced against possible loss in coordination of activity.

Patterns of communication which stimulate the flow of ideas are a stimulus to creativity, but other attitudes which encourage the acceptance of innovations are also important [Strother, 1969, pp. 7–16]. For instance, there is always a very real risk that an innovation may be impractical. Thus an organization which fosters creativity must also be willing to accept risk and uncertainty. Further, most innovations are disruptive and expensive in the short run while the "bugs are being worked out." A creative organization requires a long-term perspective in which short-term costs are considered less important than future gains.

Professional versus bureaucratic competence

All formal organizations need the expertise provided by professionals. [2]Economists, sociologists, biologists, and a host of others are employed by governments, business, labor unions, political parties, and even churches, as well as by many other organizations. As organizations become larger, more centralized, and more bureaucratic, the "professionalization" of personnel tends to increase [Montagu, 1968, pp. 138–145]. The professional differs from the other bureaucratic officials in his frame of reference. The bureaucrat looks to the rules and the policies of the organization to provide a justification for his decisions, while the professional is guided by the norms of his profession and by the opinions of professional colleagues who may be entirely outside the particular organization which employs him.

Consider the case of an economist hired by a labor union. His services are valuable to the union because it needs him to prove that union demands will not harm either the employer or the national economy. Because a layman is unable to marshal the statistics and logical arguments needed for this process, a professional economist is employed. If his professional judgment and the union's bargaining needs are in harmony, there is no problem; but if they clash, then his professional integrity and his desire for approval from his professional colleagues come into conflict with his desire for approval from the union leaders who employ him. Without their approval, he is soon unemployed. Without approval from his colleagues in the profession, he lacks the prestige and expertise which make him valuable. This is another example of the role conflict discussed in Chapter 6.

The professional may need less bureaucratic supervision than other personnel because he is presumably guided by a set of professional ethics which motivate him to perform conscientiously. But the professional's tendency to downgrade bureaucratic status and rank and to seek approval from the profession outside the organization inevitably presents a problem in administrative coordination. Many occupations are striving for professional status today: realtors, morticians, accountants, social workers, and even business managers, to name only a few.[3] In many cases, both these newer "professionals" and such traditional professionals as lawyers, physicians, and clergymen are salaried employees working for large organizations, It is no simple task to keep a balance between the freedom of the professional to follow the norms of his profession and the demands for loyalty to the organization which employs him.

University professors have a similar problem of whether their first commitment is to

[2]In this section we are indebted to Peter M. Blau and W. Richard Scott, *Formal Organizations*, Chandler Publishing Company, San Francisco, 1962, pp. 242–250, and to Victor A. Thompson, *Bureaucracy and Innovation*, University of Alabama Press, Tuscaloosa, 1969, pp. 69–70, 104–106.

[3]For a stimulating analysis of the efforts of a wide variety of occupations, ranging from librarians to funeral directors, to seek the status of a profession, see Harold L. Wilensky ("The Professionalization of Everyone?") *American Journal of Sociology*, 70:137–158, September, 1964.

their university or to their discipline. Those who seek national recognition among their fellow physicists, historians, or sociologists are called the "cosmopolitans," and those who look mainly to their own university for recognition are called the "locals" by one observer [Gouldner, 1957, p. 282]. The "local" has greater dedication to his particular college or university but somewhat less concern with academic colleagues outside his school, while the "cosmopolitan" is intensely concerned with the affairs of the international academic society, but may feel little loyalty to the college in which he is employed. Both types of professors are needed, but their goals and values are so different that the effort to coordinate their activities often leads to difficult conflicts.

Other kinds of professionals employed by the university may also experience role conflicts. Does the university psychiatrist owe his loyalty to his patient, observing the strict confidentiality of the physician-patient role model? Or is his loyalty to the administrators to whom he should reveal anything about the student that the administrators wish to know [Szasz, 1967]? Should the college physician or the college president make the decision whether the health service should dispense contraceptives to unmarried students? Such questions are not fully answered by existing codes of ethics of the professions.

Some authorities feel that the increasing professionalization of society is making the hierarchical bureaucratic forms of organization obsolete. Instead of an organization developed from the top with fairly rigid policies based upon rank or seniority, they envision a number of temporary task forces representing different professional skills; these task forces would be organized and reorganized for the needs of specific problems. The executives and managers in such a setup would not be decision makers, but would be liaison people who had learned enough technical jargon to be able to com-

municate between groups and thus achieve coordination [Toffler, 1970, pp. 128–129]. To date, no large-scale organization has been able to operate without a bureaucratic structure, but the very fact that alternatives are being considered points to the seriousness of the problem and the need to devise better methods for combining professional expertise with bureaucratic coordination.

Centralized control versus local initiative

The ideal pattern of a formal organization is one which has a group of experts at the top to decide general policies, and local functionaries to adapt them to specific situations. Actually, the organization has difficulty avoiding the twin dangers of (1) subversion of the central directives by local employees, or (2) their mechanical implementation in a way which fails to take varying conditions into account. A strict hierarchical supervision is likely to leave subordinate employees with so little freedom that innovation is stifled, while a more relaxed policy may mean that there is little resemblance between policies determined in the central office and practices in the field.

Some business concerns have sought to avoid this dilemma by the "horizontal" plan of organization which gives branch managers almost complete autonomy as long as they produce the desired results. Service agencies have found that reports enable the supervisor to react to lower-level communication rather than simply carry out orders from above. Sometimes a completely impersonal mechanism such as an assembly line determines operations so completely that there is little room for supervisory decision.

However, we do not mean to imply that top-level direction is always restrictive and the local representative always advances human freedom. In our discussion of secondary groups in Chapter 8, we noted that the top-level decision making (as represented by central headquarters) is often more universalistic in character and more removed from local prejudice than is the naive grass-roots reaction. The kings of Spain, for instance, usually planned humane policies toward the South American Indians, but the policies were frustrated by the king's inability to control the actions of distant personnel in his colonial administration. High-level policy changes are often frustrated by grass-roots personnel because they conflict with what the field personnel have been trained and rewarded for doing. Such difficulties are revealed by the following item:

> Agriculture Secretary Hardin has announced a dramatic new policy on pesticides. Henceforth USDA [United States Department of Agriculture] "will encourage those means of pest control which provide the least potential hazard to man, his animals, wildlife, and other components of the natural environment." But will such a policy statement redefine reality for Entomologist Durkin, County Agent Woodburn, and their colleagues across the land? It is not a difficult question to answer.
>
> The Agriculture Establishment has been committed to the use of hard pesticides at all levels of government, but especially at the local level. Commitments may be slowly changing in Washington but out in mid-America, where the 6,170 county agents and the 4,281 Extension specialists perform their "education" duties, little has changed.
>
> They are committed by 20 years experience—their life's work, really—to a certain point of view. Secretary Hardin can restate policy all he wants to from Washington, and President Nixon can reorganize anything he likes. At the local level nothing's going to change because the same people are going to be doing the job, and they're not equipped to do it any other way than the way they're doing it now. (Peter Montagu and Katherine Montagu, "The Great Caterpillar War and the Ecopolitics of Pesticides," Audubon, *January, 1971, p. 58.*)

The problems of balancing freedom and order, efficiency and justice, uniformity and flexibility, stability and receptivity to change—these problems are inherent in the nature of all large-scale organizations. Policies that are repressive or freedom-expanding may originate at either level. To maintain some tolerable balance is an enduring task of bureaucracy.

CYCLES OF ORGANIZATIONAL CHANGE

The birth or death of organizations is a frequent event. Voluntary associations are created and disappear with baffling speed. New business concerns are constantly being formed, and many of them quickly go into bankruptcy. Nation-states come and go; over thirty have been formed in Africa in the last twenty years, and in other parts of the world, nations such as Serbia and Montenegro have been absorbed into larger political units. Most churches survive for a long time, but many have merged in recent years. Some, such as the Shakers, lose their adherents and disappear, while the growth of such groups as the Mormons, Christian Scientists, and Jehovah's Witnesses testifies to the possibility of developing new religious organizations.

Not only do organizations experience birth and death, but they have a life cycle with fairly definite phases. It would be misleading to compare groups to people; yet they do have phases which may be roughly compared to youth, maturity, and old age. These various periods differ in many respects, as suggested by Dawson and Gettys [1948, pp. 705–709] and by Hertzler [1961, pp. 155–157]. While in some respects these are similar to the life cycle of social movements (see Chapter 21), there are significant differences. The typical life cycle of an organization has four stages: *formation, growth, formalism,* and *decay* or *revitalization.*

When people realize that they cannot accomplish their purposes through individual or informal efforts, the *formation* of an organization begins. Local snowmobilists form an organization to stage events and to fight off restrictive legislation; the business-man incorporates his enterprise; the legislature sets up a regulatory body such as the Pure Food and Drug Administration; ecumenically minded churchmen organize a World Council of Churches; the school board establishes a remedial reading clinic; all these and many others are examples of the formation phase.

The *growth* phase involves the elaboration and expansion of role structures within the organization. As problems and opportunities appear, new positions are added and the duties of their occupants are specified. In many large organizations the "vice-presidents-for-this" and the "vice-presidents-for-that" multiply as new organizational roles and titles are invented to meet expanding organizational needs. Each new role and procedure is an attempt to attain the manifest goals of the organization.

Formalism sets in when people start justifying organizational practices in terms of tradition rather than function. Statements such as "this is the way it is (has been) done," "we should follow the rules," or "we must maintain standards" are recited whenever change threatens. Formalism is sometimes described as a greater concern for forms, rituals, and appearances than for functions or results, but this description misses the point. *Formalism develops from the assumption that if the established forms are carried out, the desired results will follow.* Formalism has much in common with the popular image of bureaucracy, and includes the practices listed in the preceding discussion of bureaupathology. Since formalism leads to the waste of energy in ways that are irrelevant to organizational goals, many of the advantages of organized activity are lost, and decay or dissolution threatens the organization.

The final phase of *decay* occurs when the traditional routines become increasingly ineffective in functional terms—the busi-

ness concern loses money, schools hear charges that students fail to learn even though they attend classes, worshippers complain that church services are boring, governmental agencies are regarded as "tax eaters" rather than as servants of the public. How long an organization can continue sleepwalking depends mainly on the rate of social change. In a period of limited social change, organizations may survive indefinitely even though they are decadent. In periods of rapid social change, sharp competition makes the path from formalism to decay to death a short one.

It is possible, however, that the trend to formalism and decay can be reversed. *Revitalization* refers to the process by which an organization abandons the practices of the formalistic phase and begins again the consistent alignment of roles and organizational goals which marked the growth period. This process gives the organization a new lease on life, hence the term "revitalization."

People tend to develop a loyalty to existing practices, while revitalization requires a willingness to break with the past. Consequently, revitalization is aided by new leaders who lack vested interests and by new policies which provide a justification for breaking old routines. All types of organizations are aware of the dangers of formalism and decay. Business concerns, in particular, have developed certain strategies which facilitate revitalization. One of these strategies is the use of management consulting firms which promote the changes that the regular executives are either unable or unwilling to introduce. Another practice which has at least latent potentials for revitalization is the merger and reorganization. The merger brings new resources of personnel and facilities, prunes out "dead wood," or unnecessary personnel (often shattering peoples' lives), and forces a reorganization which presumably restores the organization to efficient operation.

Not all organizations pass through all these stages. Many organizations never survive the formation stage, and some pass quickly from growth to decay. Like all cyclical theories, this one poses the most typical sequence of stages through which organizations pass.

SUMMARY

Formal organizations are relatively enduring, deliberately organized groups operating according to a set of rules in pursuit of certain goals. These goals may encompass economic production, the pursuit of power, the integration of social organization through the resolution of conflict, the maintenance of patterns through the transmission of culture, and the enjoyment of various forms of play. *Voluntary associations*, which are especially numerous in the United States, provide people with an outlet for individual interests, a testing ground for action programs, and a channel for purposive social action.

Formal organizations may be either *closely or loosely structured*. The *informal structure* of a formal organization is an important aspect of organizational structure and may operate either to complement or to frustrate the formal chain of command. A *tendency toward oligarchy*, the rule of an organization by a small governing group, is a universal tendency; but an occasional organization remains truly democratic.

Bureaucracy is an administrative personnel which is specialized, appointed on merit, impersonal, and directed by a chain of command. While much criticized and ridiculed, bureaucracy is necessary and inevitable in all large organizations, arising from the need for efficiency, uniformity, and prevention of corruption. *Bureaupathology* is a name given to the defects of bureaucracy, including invidious status distinctions, rigidity, excessive red tape, and bifurcation of focus. Reactions to bureaupathology include efforts to improve bureaucracy through analysis and training and to bypass it by "string-pulling." The dilemma of *freedom versus compliance* is a major problem for all large organizations, which need both the initiative and high morale of personnel who have some freedom of action and yet must obtain personnel compliance with organizational policy.

Cycles of organizational change carry many organizations through a typical life cycle of *formation, growth, formalism,* and either *decay* or *revitalization*.

Questions and projects

1. Emerson made the statement, "An institution is the lengthened shadow of one man." As the terms are defined in this book, was he talking about institutions or formal organizations? Defend your answer.

2. What is meant by the life cycle of organizations? In what stage of this life cycle is the Catholic Church at the present time? The Protestant churches?

3. "Turn the rascals out" is a frequent battle cry in politics. Comment on the effectiveness of this procedure as a means of changing role behavior of officials and bureaucrats. As a means of changing political institutions.

4. Is it correct to say that modern labor unions are a latent effect of changes in business enterprise brought about by the industrial revolution?

5. Religious organizations are often charged with having abandoned the faith as originally conceived. How does this charge, if true, relate to the idea of the life cycle of organizations?

6. Why does dissatisfaction arise with bureaucratic developments? What is the major obstacle in eliminating bureaucratic features which cause resentment?

7. Can you cite any examples of bureaupathic behavior in any bureaucracy with which you are familiar? By college students? By professors?

8. What is the meaning of the "iron law of oligarchy"? Does it operate in campus politics? Do you think that the formation of opposition parties in campus politics increases participation?

9. Read and compare Lawrence F. Peter and Raymond Hull's *The Peter Principle* with C. Northcote Parkinson's *Parkinson's Law and Other Studies in Administration*. Are there any means by which the problems treated in these books can be ameliorated?

10. Read and compare two fictional or biographical presentations of organizational roles in James Gould Cozzens, *Guard of Honor* (army officer); A. J. Cronin, *The Keys to the Kingdom* (Catholic priest); Pearl S. Buck, *Fighting Angel: Portrait of a Soul* (missionary); Sara Lucille Jenkins, *Lost Lamp* (Protestant minister); Theodore Morrison, *Stones of the House* (college president); James Hilton, *Good-bye, Mr. Chips* (old schoolmaster); Cameron Hawley, *Executive Suite* (business executive); Fortune (editors of), *The Executive Life* (business executive).

Suggested readings

*__Blau, Peter M.__: *Bureaucracy in Modern Society*, Random House, Inc., New York, 1956. A simple and readable introduction to the nature and problems of bureaucracy.

Coser, Lewis A., and Bernard Rosenberg (eds.): *Sociological Theory: A Book of Readings*, The Mac-Millan Company, New York, 1969. Chapter 11, "bureaucracy," contains significant excerpts from Weber, Michels, Selznick, Merton, Gouldner, and Eisenstadt.

*__Etzioni, Amitai:__ *A Comparative Analysis of Complex Organizations*, The Free Press of Glencoe, Inc., New York, 1961. A comparative study of the circumstances and techniques under which formal organizations secure compliance from their personnel.

Grusky, Oscar, and George A. Miller (eds.): *The Sociology of Organization: Basic Studies*, The Free Press, New York, 1970. A comprehensive reader on formal organizations.

*__Lipset, Seymour M., Martin A. Trow, and James S. Coleman:__ *Union Democracy*, The Free Press of Glencoe, Ill., Chicago, 1956. A detailed description of how one organization evaded the "iron law of oligarchy."

*__Peter, Lawrence F., and Raymond Hull:__ *The Peter Principle*, William Morrow & Company, Inc., New York, 1969. A humorous yet serious discussion of the manner in which reaching the level of incompetency becomes an organization trait.

Rose, Jerry D.: "The Attribution of Responsibility for Organizational Failure," *Sociology and Social Research*, 53: 323–332, April, 1969. A study of how the careers of baseball managers are damaged by having managed losing teams, while baseball pitchers playing with losing teams apparently experience no harmful results to their careers.

*__Rosengren, William R., and Mark Lefton:__ *Organizations and Clients*, Charles E. Merrill Books, Inc., Columbus, Ohio, 1970. An analysis of organizations from the viewpoint of the clients they serve.

Thompson, Victor A.: *Modern Organization*, Alfred A. Knopf, Inc., New York, 1961, chap. 8, "Bureaupathology." An incisive analysis of some dysfunctional aspects of bureaucracy.

Tiger, Lionel: "Bureaucracy and Charisma in Ghana," *Journal of Asian and African Studies*, 1: 13–26. January, 1966. A study of a struggle between a charismatic president and a well-entrenched civil service.

Wilson, Thomas P.: "Patterns of Management and Adaption to Organizational Roles: A Study of Prison Inmates," *American Journal of Sociology*, 74: 146–157, September, 1968. A study finding that prisoners who participate in decision making have better relations with peers and superiors than those who simply take orders.

CAPTAIN: (. . . walks upstage, then turns to ROB-ERTS) I think you're a pretty smart boy. I may not talk very good, Mister, but I know how to take care of smart boys. Let me tell you something. Let me tell you a little secret. I hate your guts, you college son-of-a-bitch! You think you're better than I am! You think you're better because you've had everything handed to you. Let me tell you some-thing, Mister—I've worked since I was ten years old, and all my life I've known you superior bas-tards. I knew you people when I was a kid in Boston and I worked in eating-places and you ordered me around . . . "Oh bus-boy! My friend here seems to have thrown up on the table. Clean it up, please!" I started going to sea as a steward and I worked for you then . . . "Steward, take my magazine out to the deck chair!" . . . "Steward, I don't like your looks. Please keep out of my way as much as possible!" Well, I took that crap! I took that for years from pimple-faced bastards who weren't good enough to wipe my nose! And now I don't have to take it any more! There's a war on, by God, and I'm the Captain and you can wipe my nose! The worst thing I can do to you is to keep you on this ship! And that's where you're going to stay! Now get out of here. (*Thomas Heggen and Joshua Logan,* Mister Roberts, *Random House, Inc., New York, 1948, pp. 87–88*).

In these lines from the play *Mister Rob-erts,* the Captain explodes with resentment against those whose class origin is higher than his. Popular literature abounds with dramatic illustrations of class attitudes, class prejudices, and class-typed behavior. What is social class, and how does it affect behavior?

Aristotle observed two millenia ago that populations tended to be divided into three groups: the very rich, the very poor, and those in between. For Karl Marx the princi-pal social classes were the wage workers (the proletariat) and the capitalists (the bourgeoisie), with a middle group (the petty bourgeoisie) which was on the way out. Adam Smith divided society into those who lived on the rent of land, the wages of labor, and the profits of trade. Thorstein Veblen divided society into the workers who strug-

Social class

gle for subsistence and a leisure class which has become so wealthy that its main concern is a "conspicuous consumption" which proves how far this group has risen above the common herd. Franklin D. Roosevelt in 1937 gave a vivid description of lower-class life when he said in his inaugural address, January 20, 1937, "I see one third of the nation ill-housed, ill-clad, and ill-nourished." All these descriptions of social class imply that money separates people into different groupings.

ARE THERE SOCIAL CLASSES?

Although the concept of social class has long been used by sociologists, some sociologists today feel that it is not a useful concept [Faris, 1954; Nisbet, 1959; Lasswell, 1965]. They state that there are no definite boundaries or dividing lines for social classes, that persons placed in one class according to one measure belong in another class according to another, and that, consequently, the members of a "class" differ from one another too greatly for the concept of class to be valid.

The following pages will show why, despite the above objections, your authors believe that social class *is* a valid and useful concept.

WHAT IS SOCIAL CLASS?

Is social class purely a matter of money? If so, the rich gangster would out-rank the minister, nurse, or professor. While money is a factor, social class is not directly measured by one's bank account. A social class is defined as a *stratum of people of similar position in the social status continuum.* The social position of the janitor is not the same as that of the college president; a student

will not greet them in exactly the same manner. We are deferential toward those whose social position we believe to be above ours; we are condescending to those whom we consider socially below us. These processes of snubbing and kowtowing, of trying to claw one's way in or of shouldering out the person who doesn't "belong"—these provide the inexhaustible material for hundreds of novels, plays, movies, and television scripts every year.

The members of a social class view one another as social equals, while holding themselves to be socially superior to some other groups and socially inferior to still others. In placing a person in the proper social class, one asks such questions as: "To whose dinner party will he be asked as a social equal?" or "For whose daughter will his son be an 'acceptable' escort?" The members of a particular social class often have about the same amount of money; but what is much more important is that they have much the same attitudes, values, and way of life.

How many classes are there? This question is hard to answer. Classes are not sharply defined status groupings like the different ranks in an army. Social status varies along a continuum, a gradual slope from top to bottom, rather than a series of steps. As "youth," "middle age," and "old age," are points along an age continuum, social classes may be viewed as points along a status continuum. Consequently, the number of social classes is not fixed, nor do any definite boundaries and sharp status intervals separate them. Instead, persons are found at all status levels from top to bottom, just as persons are found at all weights and heights, with no abrupt gaps in the series.

Such a series can be broken up into any convenient number of "classes." Earlier students of social class broke up the status continuum into three classes—upper, middle, and lower. Later students found this division unsatisfactory for many communities, because it placed persons in the same class even when they were much too far apart to treat one another as equals. Later students have often used a sixfold classification by breaking each of these three classes into an upper and lower section. The top, or *upper-upper class*, is composed of the wealthy old families, who have long been socially prominent, and who have had money long enough for people to have forgotten when and how they got it. The *lower-uppers* may have as much money but have not had it as long, and their family has not long been socially prominent. The *upper-middle* class includes most of the successful business and professional men, generally of "good" family background and comfortable income. The *lower-middle* class takes in the clerks, other white-collar workers and semiprofessionals, and possibly some of the foreman and top craftsmen. The *upper-lower* class consists mainly of the steadily employed workers, and is often described as the "working class" by those who feel uncomfortable about applying the term, "lower," to responsible workmen [Miller and Riessman, 1961]. The *lower-lower* class includes the irregularly employed, the unemployable, migrant laborers, and those living more or less permanently on public assistance.

This sixfold classification, used by Warner and associates [1941, 1942] in studying an old New England town, is probably fairly typical of the large and medium-size cities in the more settled parts of the country. In the rapidly growing Western regions, "old family" may be less important. In smaller towns, the class system is less complex. In studying a small city in the Midwest, Hollingshead [1949] used a fivefold classification in which the two upper classes were combined into one. In a small rural community, West [1945] found no agreement among the residents upon the number of classes, although the status range probably would correspond to the bottom half of the six-class system of an urban society. Lynch [1959], studying the class system of an impoverished agricultural community in the Philippines, found only two classes—the self-sustaining and the destitute.

The number of social classes, therefore, varies from place to place; possibly it also varies with the observer's appraisal of the number of social strata whose members have the same general status. When we speak of, for example, the middle class, we do not refer to a group of people who are clearly set off from others by a definite status interval; we refer to a group of people who cluster around a midpoint in a status scale and who view and treat one another as social equals. The fact that the terms have no distinct boundaries does not keep the terms from being useful concepts and research tools. Social class is a significant social reality, not just a theoretical construct, for people *do* classify others as equals, superiors, and inferiors. Whenever people define certain other people as social equals and treat them differently from those who are not so defined, their behavior creates social classes.

GENESIS OF SOCIAL CLASSES

All complex societies have some system of stratification which unequally ranks people. The extent and kind of inequality varies tremendously, but there are always some accepted standards by which men distinguish their peers from their inferiors. This is true in Communist countries which deplore class divisions and in capitalist countries which may justify them; it is true in both democracies and autocracies and in agricultural as well as industrial societies. The only possible exception is in the most primitive food-gathering societies where people live by collecting such foods as fruits, nuts, roots, and berries. Here there is little possibility of any division of labor and hence little possibility of rank which may lead to group differentiation.

As soon as the society develops enough complexity to require coordination, the basis is formed for the development of social classes. Some men will be in charge of the work of other men, and their authority will inevitably be reflected in privileges which they try to pass on to their descendants. Warner describes the process in the following terms:

For example, among primitive peoples simple fishing expeditions may be organized so that the men who fish and handle each boat are under the direction of one leader. The efforts of each boat are directed by the leader and, in turn, each boat is integrated into the total enterprise by the leader's taking orders from his superior. The same situation prevails in a modern factory. Small plants with a small working force and simple problems possess a limited hierarchy, perhaps no more than an owner who bosses all the workers. But a large industrial enterprise with complex activities and problems, like General Motors, needs an elaborate hierarchy of supervision. . . . The same holds true for political, religious, educational, and other social institutions; the more complex the group and the more diverse the functions and activities, the more elaborate the status system is likely to be. (W. Lloyd Warner, with Marchia Meeker and Kenneth Eells, Social Class in America, Harper & Row Publishers, Inc., New York, 1960, pp. 8–9.)

Although social class includes many features besides occupation, it is fundamentally based on the division of labor. A complex society requires many workers with varying degrees of skills and many coordinators with varying realms of authority. Prestige and power attach to the higher-ranked occupations and in turn enable the men in these occupations to confer advantages on their descendants. Thus a group of people arise whose hereditary privileges are greater than are those of people who have descended from less highly regarded ranks.

An agricultural society with only two or three categories of responsibility may have a completely rigid system of stratification in which the gulf between nobles and commoners is never bridged. An industrial society is apt to have a far greater variety of occupations with greater ease of movement from one level to another, but distinct levels still remain. Social class, then, grows out of the system of division of labor, and the ease of movement from one level to another depends upon the complexity and flexibility of the occupational structure of the society. Class mobility within a society is a highly complicated topic and is considered in some detail in the following chapter.

People do classify others as equals, superiors, and inferiors.

Social classes as subcultures

It is, after all, this division into working class and business class that constitutes the outstanding cleavage in Middletown. The mere fact of being born upon one or the other side of the watershed roughly formed by these two groups is the most significant single cultural factor tending to influence what one does all day long throughout one's life; whom one marries; when one gets up in the morning; whether one belongs to the Holy Roller or Presbyterian church; or drives a Ford or a Buick; whether or not one's daughter makes the desirable high school Violet Club; or one's wife meets with the Sew We Do Club or with the Art

Each social class is a system of behavior, a set of values, and a way of life. While some overlapping and some exceptions occur, it remains true that the average middle-class child has a socialization vastly different from that of the average lower-class child. Let us take just one aspect of socialization—those experiences which shape ambition, education, and work habits—and see how they differ between two social-class worlds.

The typical upper-middle-class child lives in a class subculture where he is surrounded by educated, cultivated persons who speak the English language correctly most of the time, enjoy classical music, buy and read books, travel, and entertain graciously. He is surrounded by people who are ambitious, who go to work even when they don't feel like it, and who struggle to make their mark in the world. He is acquainted with the successes of ancestors, relatives, and friends, and it is normal for him simply to assume that, like them, he is going to amount to something in the world.

When he goes to school, scrubbed and expectant, he finds a teacher whose dress, speech, manner, and conduct norms are much like those he already knows. He is met by a series of familiar objects—picture books, chalkboard, and others—and introduced into a series of activities which are already familiar. The teacher finds him an appealing and responsive child, while he finds school a comfortable and exciting place. When the teacher says, "Study hard so you can do well and become a success some day," her exhortation makes sense to him. His parents echo these words; meanwhile he sees people like him—older brothers, relatives, family acquaintances—who actually *are* completing educations and moving on into promising careers. For him, to grow up means to complete an advanced education and get himself launched into a career.

The lower-lower-class child lives in a class subculture where scarcely anybody has a steady job for very long. To be laid off and go on relief is a normal experience, carrying no sense of shame or failure. He lives in a world where one can spend his weekends in drinking, gambling, and sexual exploration and miss work on Monday without sacrificing the respect of his friends or neighbors. In his world, meals are haphazard and irregular; many people sleep three or four to a bed; and a well-modulated speaking voice would be lost amid the neighborbood clatter.

He goes to school, often unwashed and unfed, and meets a woman unlike anyone in his social world. Her speech and manner are unfamiliar, and when he acts in ways that are acceptable and useful in his social world, she punishes him. The classroom materials and activities are unfamiliar. The teacher, who usually comes from a sheltered middle-class world, is likely to decide that he is a sullen, unresponsive child, while he soon concludes that school is an unhappy prison. He learns little. The school soon abandons any serious effort to teach him, defines him as a "discipline problem," and concentrates upon keeping him quiet so that the other children can learn. When the teacher says, "Study hard so you can do well and become a success some day," her words make no sense to him. They receive no reinforcement from his parents, who are apt to be hostile and uncooperative toward the school. More important, he sees almost nobody *like* him, nobody in his world, who actually *is* using school as a stepping-stone to a career. In his world, the flashy cars and flashy women are possessed by those who picked a lucky number, or got into the rackets, or found an "angle." Thus the school fails to motivate him. For him, "growing up" means to drop out of school, get a car, and escape from the supervision of teachers and parents. His horizon of ambition seldom extends beyond the next weekend. His work habits are casual and irregular. Soon he marries and provides for his children a life which duplicates the experiences of his own socialization. Thus the class system operates to prepare most children for a class status similar to that of their parents.

Such differences in class behavior are found in virtually every activity of life—food habits, personal care, discipline and child care, reading tastes, conversational interests, vocabulary and diction, religious behavior, sleeping arrangements, sex life. Even the procedures followed in making love, according to Kinsey [1948, pp. 355–357], show important class differences. This is what we mean in speaking of class subcultures—that a great many of the normal life experiences of people in one class differ from those of people in another class. It is true that there are no sharply defined boundaries. From top to bottom, one kind of behavior shades gradually off into another; for example, vocabulary gradually becomes less genteel and diction less precise as we descend the class continuum. But if we pick several points along this continuum for comparison, then the class differences are easy to see.

The culture of poverty

In the last decade it has been increasingly fashionable to refer to a culture of poverty [Lewis, 1959, 1966a, 1966b]. What this implies is that the poor form a subculture in which, as a result of their common experiences, they have developed certain attitudes and behavior patterns which have been transmitted from parent to child. These include the matricentric family, the casual resort to physical agression, a disdain of

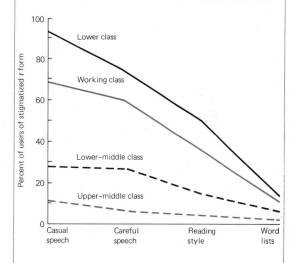

FIGURE 6

Class stratification of pronunciation.

The pronunciation of *th* as in *thing, through, three,* in New York City. Shown in percentages of stigmatized form *t* versus prestige form *th,* by social class and context.

(Slightly modified from William Labov, "Stages in the Acquisition of Standard English," in Roger W. Shur, ed., *Social Dialects and Language Learning,* National Council of Teachers of English, Champaign, Illinois, 1965, p. 83.)

thrift, and an apathetic attitude toward social mobility. The concept has been criticized [Roach and Gursslin, 1967; Glazer, 1971] on the grounds that it does not apply to such groups of the poor as the aged and the ill and that it may not apply equally to all ethnic groups. Further, the behavior patterns may not be so much norms or ideals as simply a pragmatic adjustment to what appear to be unalterable circumstances.

Whether all poverty-striken groups perfectly fit the Lewis "culture of poverty" pattern can be debated, but there is no question that distinct behavior patterns characterize those who are poor. To a highly significant degree, social classes are different cultural worlds.

Determinants of social class

What places one in a particular social class? Is it birth, money, occupation, or what? The answer to each question is "Yes," for all these attributes are involved.

Wealth and income Money is necessary for upper-class position; yet one's class position is not directly proportional to his income. An airline pilot has less status than a college professor at half the income; a clergyman may out rank a prizefighter at fifty times his income.

To understand the place of money in class determination, we must remember that a *social class is basically a way of life.* It takes a good deal of money to live as upper-class people live. Yet no amount of money will gain *immediate* upper-class status. The "new-rich" have the money, but they lack the way of life of the upper-class person. They can buy the house, cars, and clothes, and hire a decorator to select the proper furnishings, books, and paintings. It takes a little longer to learn the formal manners of the upper class, but some careful observation, plus intensive study of Emily Post or Amy Vanderbilt, will probably suffice. But to

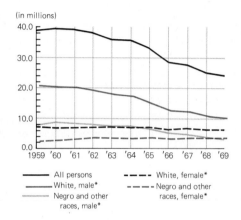

FIGURE 7
*Poverty in the United States:
Persons below the poverty level
by sex and race of head:
1959 to 1969.*

(in millions)

— All persons   – – – White, female*
— White, male*   – – – Negro and other
···· Negro and other   races, female*
       races, male*

*For persons in families, sex of head; for unrelated individuals, sex of the individual.
Source: Bureau of the Census, *Current Population Reports*, series p-60, no. 68, Dec. 31, 1969; no. 71, July 16, 1970.

acquire the attitudes and feelings and habitual responses of the upper-class person takes far longer. Unless one is born and socialized in an upper-class subculture, he is almost certain to make occasional slips which betray his plebeian origin. Novels and plays abound with social climbers who never quite "make it" because they occasionally use the wrong word or reflect the wrong attitude and thereby betray their humble origin. Most of the "new rich" are no more than marginal members of the upper classes during their lifetimes.

Their children, however, have a better chance, and for their grandchildren, a secure upper-class status is practically assured. Money, *over a period of time*, usually gains upper-class status. People who get money begin to live like upper-class people. By the time their grandchildren mature, they are becoming "old family," while the grandchildren have fully absorbed upper-class behavior. Thus the two requisites of upper-class status are fulfilled.

Money has other subtle overtones. Inherited money confers greater status than earned money, for inherited wealth shows family background. Income from investments also suggests family background. Income from genteel professions is better than wages; money from speculating on stocks is better than money from gambling on horses. The nature and source of one's income carry suggestions as to one's family background and probable way of life.

Money one used to have is almost as good as money one has now. The "real" aristocracy of the South, for example, no longer has great wealth, partly because its class values prevented it from engaging in the grubby scrabbling which eventually created the oil millionaires and the industrial magnates. Yet the impoverished aristocrat can still retain upper-class status as long as he has enough money to eke out an upper-class pattern of living, even though it is somewhat frayed around the edges.

Money, then, is an important determinant of social class, partly because of the way of life it permits or enforces, and partly because of what it suggests about one's family background and way of life.

Occupation Occupation is another determinant of class status. As soon as man developed specialized kinds of work, he also got the idea that some kinds of work were more honorable than others. In a primitive society, the spear maker, the canoe builder, and the medicine man each holds a definite social status because of his work. Classical China honored the scholar and despised the warrior; Nazi Germany reversed the formula. Table 9 gives a prestige ranking of some occupations in the United States, according to one national-opinion survey.

Just why one occupation *should* carry greater prestige than another is a question which has long fascinated social theorists. The high-prestige occupations generally receive the higher incomes; yet there are many exceptions. A popular night-club singer may earn as much in a week as a Supreme Court justice earns in a year. The relatively low-paid clergymen, diplomats, and college professors rank far above the higher-paid airline pilots and building contractors, and have about equal ranking with the far wealthier physicians and lawyers. The high-ranking occupations generally require advanced education, but again the correlation is far from perfect. The importance of the work is an unsatisfactory test, for how can we say that the work of the farm hand or policeman is less valuable to society than the lawyer or corporation director? In fact, it has been suggested that the low-ranking garbage collector may be the most essential of all workers in an urban civilization!

Obviously, the prestige ranking of occupations cannot be easily explained on a purely rational basis; yet it can hardly be an accident that all contemporary complex cultures have developed much the same hier-

TABLE 9

Distributions of prestige ratings,
United States, 1963

Occupation	Rank	Occupation	Rank
U.S. Supreme Court justice	1	Building contractor	31.5
Physician	2	Artist who paints pictures that are exhibited	
Nuclear physicist	3.5	in galleries.	34.5
Scientist	3.5	Musician in a symphony orchestra	34.5
Government scientist	5.5	Author of novels	34.5
State governor	5.5	Economist	34.5
Cabinet member in the federal government	8	Official of an international labor union	37
College professor	8	Railroad engineer	39
U.S. representative in Congress	8	Electrician	39
Chemist	11	County agricultural agent	39
Lawyer	11	Owner-operator of a printing shop	41.5
Diplomat in the U.S. foreign service	11	Trained machinist	41.5
Dentist	14	Farm owner and operator	44
Architect	14	Undertaker	44
County judge	14	Welfare worker for a city government	44
Psychologist	17.5	Newspaper columnist	46
Minister	17.5	Policeman	47
Member of the board of directors of a large		Reporter on a daily newspaper	48
corporation	17.5	Radio announcer	49.5
Mayor of a large city	17.5	Bookkeeper	49.5
Priest	21.5	Tenant farmer—one who owns livestock and	
Head of a department in a state government	21.5	machinery and manages the farm	51.5
Civil engineer	21.5	Insurance agent	51.5
Airline pilot	21.5	Carpenter	53
Banker	24.5	Manager of a small store in a city	54.5
Biologist	24.5	A local official of a labor union	54.5
Sociologist	26	Mail carrier	57
Instructor in public schools	27.5	Railroad conductor	57
Captain in the regular army	27.5	Traveling salesman for a wholesale concern	57
Accountant for a large business	29.5	Plumber	59
Public school teacher	29.5	Automobile repairman	60
Owner of a factory that employs about		Playground director	62.5
100 people	31.5		

Occupation	Rank	Occupation	Rank
Barber	62.5	Railroad section hand	77.5
Machine operator in a factory	62.5	Night watchman	77.5
Owner-operator of a lunch stand	62.5	Coal miner	77.5
Corporal in the regular army	65.5	Restaurant waiter	80.5
Garage mechanic	65.5	Taxi driver	80.5
Truck driver	67	Farmhand	83
Fisherman who owns his own boat	68	Janitor	83
Clerk in a store	68	Bartender	83
Milk route man	70	Clothes presser in a laundry	85
Streetcar motorman	70	Soda-fountain clerk	86
Lumberjack	72.5	Sharecropper—one who owns no livestock or	
Restaurant cook	72.5	equipment and does not manage farm	87
Singer in a nightclub	74	Garbage collector	88
Filling-station attendant	75	Street sweeper	89
Dockworker	77.5	Shoe shiner	90

Source: Robert W. Hodge et al., "Occupational Prestige in the United States, 1925–63," American Journal of Sociology, 70:290–292, November, 1964.

archy of occupational status. A survey of data from many countries by Inkeles [1960] finds that a particular occupation has about the same status rating in all urbanized, industrialized societies. Apparently the industrial system fosters certain attitudes, perceptions, and status relationships wherever it develops. And in all societies, industrial or preindustrial, we see that persons tend to be assigned a class status according to their occupation, and that people will find those occupations open to them which are appropriate to their present class status.

Occupation is an exceedingly important aspect of social class because so many other facets of life are connected with occupation. If we know a man's occupation, we can make some fairly accurate guesses about the amount and kind of education he has had, the standard of living he can afford, the kind of people he associates with, the hours he keeps, and the daily routines of his family life. We can even make some guesses about his reading tastes and recreational interests, his standards of moral conduct, and his religious affiliations. In other words, each occupation is part of a way of life that differs considerably from that which accompanies certain other occupations. It is one's total way of life that ultimately determines to which class one belongs. Occupation is one of the best clues to one's way of life, and therefore to one's social-class membership.

The underdeveloped countries have a class structure which reflects a society that has limited use for professional, white-collar, or highly skilled workers and hence has a small middle class and a very large lower class. This pattern is changing as these countries become industrialized. Mexico, for instance, is a nation which is making rapid strides in this direction, and Table 10 shows the changes in social-class distribution. The *popular* category (Mexican term for lower class) comprised only 40 percent of the population in 1960 as compared with 90 percent in 1890.

Education Social class and education interact in at least two ways. First, to get a higher education one needs money plus motivation. Lack of money is less of a barrier than it used to be, now that scholarships and student loans are so widely available; yet relatively few students complete college without some financial aid from their families. Even if it is no more than free room, board, and laundry for all or part of the year, this is a considerable help. Upper-class youths already have money for the finest schools; they also have family tradition and social encouragement. For the upper-class or upper-middle-class high school youth, the question is, "What college are you going to?"; lower-middle-class and perhaps upper-lower-class youths ask one another, "What will you do after graduation?"; lower-lower class youths are more likely to ask, "How soon can I quit school?" Second, one's amount and kind of education affects the class rank he will secure. Education is one of the main levers of the ambitious. Higher education not only brings occupational skills; it also brings changes in tastes, interests, goals, etiquette, speech—in one's total way of life.

Although a distinguished family background is a necessity for secure upper-class status, education may substitute for family background at the intermediate class levels. The middle classes are so large and move around so much that it is impossible to know the family background of each individual. Newcomers to a locality are likely to be accepted into whichever of the middle or lower classes their behavior fits them. Education, occupation, and expended income are three

TABLE 10

*Changing class structure in Mexico,
1895–1960 (percentages, varying bases)*

Classes and subclasses	1895	1940	1950	1956	1960
Upper					
Leisure	0.4	0.4	0.5	1.0	1.5
Semileisure	1.1	2.5	1.5	4.0	5.0
Subtotal	1.5	2.9	2.0	5.0	6.5
Middle					
Stable	6.1	6.1	8.0	15.0	17.0
Marginal	1.7	6.5	17.0	15.0	16.5
Subtotal	7.8	12.6	25.0	30.0	33.5
Transitional	00.0	6.5	20.0	20.0	20.0
Popular					
(lower class)	90.7	78.0	53.0	45.0	40.0

Source: Adapted from Howard F. Cline, Mexico, *Oxford University Press, Fair Lawn, N.J., 1963, table 30, p. 124.*

fairly visible clues, and with these are associated most of the other behavior characteristics which make one "belong."

Social scientists make great use of these three criteria—education, occupation, and income—in dividing people into social-class levels for research purposes. As we have already explained, these are fairly reliable clues to the total way of life distinguishing social classes. Furthermore, these criteria are fairly easy to objectify. It would, for example, be difficult to use "crude or cultivated speech" as a test of class rank in a research study, because speech, though easy to notice, is hard to measure.[1] Finally, the data on education, occupation, and income are available from the census reports, broken down by "census tracts," or areas of a few blocks each. Suppose a sociologist wishes to compare death rates, or polio rates, or average family size, or practically anything, as it varies among social classes. Using census data on occupation, education, and average income of the different census tracts within the community, he could easily locate an upper-class tract, a middle-class tract, and a lower-class tract for comparison. While social class involves more than these three criteria, they are adequate to identify social classes for most research purposes.[2]

Self-identification and class consciousness Most sociologists consider social class a reality even if people are not fully aware of it. American democratic beliefs emphasize equality and tend to inhibit a frank recognition of class lines. People will deny that there are social classes in their community, yet state this denial in terms

which reveal that classes really do exist. Lantz cites one of many such statements by the residents of a small town:

You see, this no-class idea makes it a good place to live. The Company houses are called "Silk Stocking Row" but I would feel as good with the mining superintendent's wife as I would with anybody else. You see, this is a melting pot. Our people, you see, all came from foreign countries. Why, my grandparents came from England. You see, I belong to the DAR. I can trace my family tree all the way back through the Revolutionary War into England. I take a great deal of pride in this. Why, I can trace my ancestry back to a captain who was a friend of Washington's in the Revolutionary War. (*Herman R. Lantz,* People of Coal Town, *Columbia University Press, New York, 1958, p. 216.*)

The belief that the American people lack "class consciousness" was supported by early surveys [Cantril, 1943; Gallup and Rae, 1940; *Fortune*, February, 1940], which found from 79 to 88 percent of the people claiming to be "middle-class"; yet Warner's [1941, p. 88] careful analysis of the actual class distribution of the population of "Yankee City" (Newburyport, Massachusetts) placed only 38 percent in the two middle classes, and other studies agree in findings that only a minority of people belong in the middle class. More recent surveys suggest that people may be resisting the word more than the reality. When informants are permitted to select the term "working class" rather than "lower class," they classify themselves in a way which more closely resembles the class division made by the social scientists [Centers, 1949; Manis and Meltzer, 1954, 1963; Hodge and Treiman, 1968].

Is one's class membership, then, determined by his feeling that he belongs in a particular class, or by the facts of his occupation, education, and income? Largely by the latter, for they determine his overall way of life. Yet his *feeling* of class identification is of some importance, for he tends to copy the behavior norms of the class with

---

[1]For a discussion of speech as an indication of social class, see William Labov, "The Effect of Social Mobility on Linguistic Behavior," *Sociological Inquiry*, 36:186–203, Spring, 1966.

[2]See Joseph A. Kahl and James A. Davis, "A Comparison of Indexes of Socioeconomic Status," *American Sociological Review*, 20:317–325, June, 1955, for a defense of the view that occupation is the best overall measure of class position. For a claim that a composite "index of status characteristics" is a better measure, see John L. Haer, "Predictive Utility of Five Indices of Social Stratification," *American Sociological Review*, 22:541–546, October, 1957.

which he identifies himself. Eulan [1956] found that those informants who placed themselves in a class in which they did not objectively belong, shared the political attitudes of the class they claimed rather than those of the class in which they belonged. Self-identification with a social class has some effect upon behavior, whether one actually is a member of that class or not.

Size of each social class

A number of studies show considerable agreement in placing something over half the population in the two lower classes (upper-lower and lower-lower, using Warner's six-class typology). Warner's 1941 study, and two national self-identification surveys in 1945 and 1946 [Centers, 1949] agree in placing about 57 percent of the pop-

ulation in the two lower classes. Davis [1952, pp. 22–23] concluded that each of the two lower classes provided about one-third of the elementary school children. Table 11 presents some more recent data on several groups, most of whom are probably lower-lower class. Most of these indices of lower-class status show a considerable drop in recent years, and it is probably true that the United States is becoming more nearly a middle-class society. We do not have recent estimates of the proportion in various classes, but it seems reasonable to assume that the two lower classes now represent less than half the population.

Class distribution, then, is changing in the United States. The middle class and possibly the upper classes are growing; the lower classes are shrinking. Changing technology is destroying lower-class jobs and creating middle-class jobs. In 1900, "unskilled laborers" constituted 13 percent of

TABLE 11

How large is our lower class? Proportion of United States population in selected educational, occupational, and income categories

Type of individual or group	Year	Approximate % of population	Year	Approximate % of population
Adults (18 or over) in labor force who did not complete high school	1947	67.0	1968	47.4
Adults in civilian labor force in "semiskilled" and unskilled positions	1960	43.6	1965	41.7
Adults with 4 grades of education or less	1947	11.0	1968	6.0
Family units with income under $3,000 (1967 dollars)	1947	27.4	1967	12.5
Household units reporting female head	1960	18.0	1968	20.0
Adult illiterates	1947	2.7	1960	2.4

Source: Statistical Abstract of United States, 1969, Monthly Labor Review, *93, July, 1970, p. 100.* Manpower Report to the President, *U.S. Department of Labor, March, 1969, p. 226.*

TABLE 12
Annual incomes of blue- and white-collar workers

	Sales workers	Clerical	Craftsmen & foremen	Operatives
Male	$7,367	$7,034	$7,705	$6,209
Female	2,248	4,002	4,145	3,506

Source: Statistical Abstract of the United States, *1970, p. 326.*

the labor force; by 1950 they had fallen to 8 percent, and are expected to fall to 4 percent by 1975; meanwhile the "professionals" in the labor force have risen from 4 percent in 1900 to 8 percent in 1950, and are expected to reach 14 percent by 1975 [National Education Association, 1959]. Almost every kind of middle-class job is expanding as the changes in economic life continually demand more technical and professional personnel. Furthermore, as technology changes the content of jobs, their status also changes. Historically, most factory jobs were dirty, filled by men who were comparatively unskilled and low paid. Today a growing fraction of factory jobs are clean, calling for highly trained and well-paid workers. Such workers seem likely to move into the middle class.

Measurement of classes is complicated by the fact that there are several criteria of membership in a given class and many families do not show *all* the characteristics of any one class level. For example, the "ideal type" lower-lower-class family would live in an urban slum or rural shack; one or more adult members would drink quite heavily, and the male family head would not be consistently in the household; the family would have little education or interest in education; and its low income would be derived partly from intermittent unskilled labor and partly from welfare sources. Probably comparatively few lower-lower-class families meet all of these conditions. While class differences are real, the boundaries

and membership of each class cannot be clearly fixed.

Blue-collar and white-collar class status

Frequently the decisive dividing line between the middle class and the lower class has been whether the occupation was manual or nonmanual. In recent years, there has been so much of a convergence of manual and nonmanual income levels that some authorities doubt that this is still a measure of social class. Two English sociologists [Goldthorpe and Lockwood, 1963, p. 133] have coined the word "embourgeoisment" to indicate that the working class is gradually taking on a middle-class (bourgeoisie) type of outlook. This viewpoint is supported by figures like those in Table 12 which show that average incomes of craftsmen and foremen are higher than those of clerical workers and sales workers.

There is also some evidence that perhaps the reverse process is occuring and that white-collar workers are becoming proletarianized or assuming working-class identification. Hamilton [1966] found that 52 percent of a sample of American clerks identified themselves as working class. He found this especially true of those who had come from blue-collar families who, since they found no advantages in income, retained their working-class self-identification. Whether one looks at the embourgeoisment of the blue-collar worker or the proletarianization of the white-collar worker, it is becoming clear that the old distinction between manual and nonmanual work is losing at least part of its meaning. Lenski [1966, p. 362] does point out, however, that clerks still have better mobility prospects than manual workers for moving into managerial, professional, or entrepreneurial posts. Since men guide themselves at least partly by their expectations, this difference in mobility prospects may be enough of a distinction to prevent a complete merging of blue-collar and white-collar social attitudes.

A convergence of manual and nonmanual income levels.

THE SIGNIFICANCE OF SOCIAL CLASSES

Determining life opportunities

From before one is born until he is dead, opportunities and rewards are affected by class position. Poor nutrition for the mother may affect the health and vigor of the fetus before birth, while total living conditions thereafter continue the advantages or handicaps of class position. One study of the relation between education (taken as a rough index of social class) and mortality reveals this in grim detail [Kitagawa and Hauser, 1967]: men between twenty-five and sixty-four with less than five years of education had a mortality index 49 percent higher than that of men with some college. For some women the difference was even greater, being 98 percent higher for those with less than five years of education than for college alumni. One would conclude from these figures that the chances of longevity are definitely greater in the higher social classes.

In mental health, the class differential is equally striking. Over two dozen studies have been made, all showing that the lower class has several times as much mental illness as the higher classes [Hollingshead and Redlich, 1953, 1958; Miller and Mishler, 1959; Rushing, 1969]. The "treatment" received by the lower-class mentally ill is sometimes only custodial, which simply removes the patient from society, rather than the complete medical and psychotherapeutic treatment which might effect a cure. In no other major form of health care is the disparity between the classes as great as in the treatment of mental illness [Hollingshead and Redlich, 1953; Robinson et al., 1954; Srole et al., 1962; Myers and Bean, 1968].

The school attended by the lower-class child has usually been one of the drab and dingy schools of the community built a half century or more ago. His teachers may be either dedicated mentors hopefully utilizing the latest educational methods or weary drudges who have long since given up in what seems a hopeless battle against ignorance and apathy. In any case, the effectiveness of the school is largely determined by the attitudes of the students which, in turn, reflect the spirit of the neighborhood. The neighborhood is likely to be an area of drab, crowded housing, of irregular family life, of persons whose goals are short-term just as their grasp on jobs, health, and housing is short-term.

When the lower-class youth comes to seek a job, he lacks the education, the work habits, and the poise or bearing to command a job with a promising future. The lower-class occupations, such as farm laborer or unskilled laborer, carry low wages, irregular employment, and few welfare or "fringe" benefits. Often they involve high accident danger or health hazard; yet this class can afford only the poorest living conditions and the least medical care. In wartime the lower-class youth is less likely to be deferred as a college student or an essential worker; when drafted he is less likely to become a commissioned officer or earn a specialist's rating. There is one place where his chances are better; he has a better chance of being killed, as is seen in Table 13. No comparable data are available for the Vietnam War, but since in 1969, college men composed only 10 percent of the total drafted [Alsop, 1970], it probably remains true that the higher one's social class the less the chances of his becoming a war casualty.

Coloring personality development

Since social classes are subcultures, the personality development of the child is affected in many ways [Davis and Havighurst, 1946; Sears et al., 1957; Havighurst and Davis, 1955; Coleman and Neugarten, 1971]. As has been already suggested, his goals, interests, and habits are affected by the kind of social world he lives in. The lower-class family is less stable, more often broken by death or separation. It is larger in size, yet occupies smaller living quarters. At almost every point of contact between child and parent, there are class differences in socialization experience. Middle-class child training encourages individual achievement and the urge to "succeed," encourages competition and rivalry while discouraging direct aggression, uses parental love systematically as a control device, avoids severe physical punishment, imposes numerous restrictions, and produces a good many

TABLE 13

Korean war-casualty rate per 10,000 occupied dwelling units; by median income of census tract, Detroit, Michigan

Median income, dollars	Casualty rate per 10,000 occupied DU's
Under 2,500	14.6
2,500–2,999	10.8
3,000–3,499	9.1
3,500–3,999	8.6
4,000–4,499	7.5
4,500–4,999	6.6
5,000–5,499	5.8
5,500 and over	4.6

Source: Albert J. Mayer and Thomas Ford Hoult, "Social Stratification and Combat Survival," Social Forces, 34: 155–159, December, 1955. Copyright © 1955, The University of North Carolina Press, Chapel Hill, N.C.

anxieties and guilt feelings. Lower-class child training more rapidly pushes the child into adult roles, places less stress on individual achievement, accepts the idea that the child will probably retain the social status of its father, seldom uses parental love as a systematic reward, uses physical punishments readily, imposes fewer restrictions upon organic functions and pleasures, accepts direct aggression and encourages agressive self-defense, places little stress on language facility, literacy, or school advancement, and probably produces fewer guilts and anxieties. Middle-class socialization is strongly oriented toward upward social mobility through risk taking; lower-class socialization in a risk-filled world is strongly oriented towards reducing risks by attaining economic security and stability [Miller and Riessman, 1961].

As compared with lower-class personality, adult middle-class personality tends to be more ambitious, more competitive but less aggressive physically, more rigidly conformist to conventional mores, outwardly more poised and self-assured, but possibly beset by greater inner guilts and self-doubts. Such differences are not predictably true for all members of either class, for there are many exceptions and much overlapping. But such differences are frequent enough to be socially significant [Barber, 1957, chap. 12].

Assigning social responsibilities and privileges

A lot of unpleasant work must be done in any society, and someone must be persuaded to do it. Occasionally special rewards may be used—honor for the warrior, or wealth and fame for the prizefighter, for example.

But each complex society relies mainly upon the class system to compel someone to do the drudgery. A combination of cultural background, educational limitation, and job discrimination all work together to make the lower-class person unable to compete for the better jobs; as a result, only the poorer jobs are left. The result, though it may be entirely unintentional, is no less real. Social class gets the grubby work of the world done by excluding part of the people from the nicer jobs.

The lower class also functions as a storehouse for surplus unskilled labor. Our economy requires a good deal of seasonal or irregular labor, especially in farm labor and construction projects. Those who are not continuously needed are "stored" in the low-

Two patterns of child rearing: Those conducive to educational achievement and those characteristic of low-income families

Conducive to achievement	Low income
1. *Child given freedom within consistent limits to explore and experiment.*	1. *Limited freedom for exploration (partly imposed by crowded and dangerous aspects of environment).*
2. *Wide range of parent-guided experiences, offering visual, auditory, kinesthetic, and tactile stimulation.*	2. *Constricted lives led by parents: fear and distrust of the unknown.*
3. *Goal commitment and belief in long-range success potential.*	3. *Fatalistic, apathetic attitudes.*
4. *Gradual training for and value placed on independence.*	4. *Tendency for abrupt transition to independence: parents tend to "lose control" of children at early age.*
5. *Educational-occupational success of parents; models as continuing "learners" themselves.*	5. *Tendency to educational-occupational failure; reliance on personal versus skill attributes of vocational success.*
6. *Reliance on objective evidence.*	6. *Magical, rigid thinking.*
7. *Much verbal communication.*	7. *Little verbal communication.*

Source: Adapted from Catherine S. Chilman, "Child Rearing and Family Relationship Patterns of the Very Poor," Welfare in Review, *3:10, January, 1965.*

er class, where the class subculture makes it possible to survive periods of unemployment and go on relief without guilt or sense of failure. The lethargy, lack of ambition, and willingness to accept squalor which middle-class people criticize so self-righteously are, in fact, the *necessary and useful* life adjustments of the lower class. Such attributes are necessary to the mental health and sanity of our "stand-by" unskilled labor supply.

The lower-class culture makes a positive contribution to the society. Men who seem to lack ambition and responsibility have shouldered jobs which were rough, monotonous, temporary in duration, often far from settled communities, yet essential to the economic life of the nation. The lower-class women, often frowned upon by higher-status women because of their irregular family life, have learned to adjust to the unreliable habits of fathers and husbands whose lives have been shaped by irregular and uncertain employment. These women have reared children in manless households and, at the same time, cleaned the homes and offices used by other classes. Lower-class life produces people able and willing to work and live under conditions which those raised in other class levels would find intolerable.

Other social classes also provide their members with distinctive subcultures that prepare them for specialized functions in society. Looking at the upper class, one sees a group which is removed from the fear of being unable to make a fairly adequate income. Their position in society does not have to be earned by unusual achievement, although they may feel a need to validate their status through some form of public service. At its best this class produces men like Franklin D. Roosevelt, the Rockefellers, and the Kennedys, who have been able to devote a major portion of their lives to public service without having to worry about personal fortune. The fact that all these men

accept government programs commonly identified with lower-class interests indicates both an emancipation from economic concern and an acceptance by the masses of the leadership of an elite whose wealth and background are strikingly different from those of the common man.

There is a lot of unpleasant work.

A most vulnerable aspect of upper-class claims to social usefulness is the existence of a group who become "jet-set" types and devote their time and money to expensive dissipation in an endless search for novelty to stimulate jaded senses dulled by little responsibility and much indulgence. Persons of this type may be a minority of the upper class, but they are very conspicuous in an era of mass communication, and the envy and resentment they arouse is a major obstacle to the acceptance of the legitimacy of an upper class by the rest of society.

Vigorous controversy has developed in sociological circles over the question of whether social-class stratification is useful as an efficient means of role allocation. Some claim that society requires a variety of occupational roles, and that one's social-class background gives one the attitudes desirable for his occupational function. The following is a typical statement of this viewpoint:

Social inequality is an unconsciously evolved device by which societies insure that the most important positions are filled by the most qualified persons. Hence every society, no matter how simple or complex, must differentiate persons in terms of both prestige and esteem, and must therefore possess a certain amount of institutionalized inequality. (*Kingsley Davis and Wilbert Moore, "Some Principles of Stratification,"* American Sociological Review, *10:242–249, April, 1945.*)

This position has been sharply criticized on the grounds that social-class conditioning and role ascription may make it difficult for the individual to make the best use of his potential abilities. The brilliant man from a lower-class background may have neither the objective opportunities to prepare himself for an important career nor the value system which will encourage him to pursue long years of education apprenticeship. Conversely the upper-class moron may be kept from useful service by family privilege and may lack completely the attitudes which enable unskilled laborers to adjust to their occupational roles. These and other criticisms have been made by Tumin [1953] who suggests that social class may be dysfunctional, i.e., it hinders social adjustment, whereas a better system of allocating occupational roles could be devised.

This is another form of the argument over ascribed versus achieved roles. A plausible summation is suggested by Gordon [1958, pp. 166–173], who points out that, while an equalitarian society might be ideal, such a society has never existed. Some system of differential reward always develops, and men do seek to transmit their advantages to their children. The resulting class system has a major influence in the allocation of occupational roles. It is not a perfect system, but is only seriously wasteful of talent when a "closed" system develops which does not allow people to cross class lines. This is a topic we will take up in more detail in the following chapter, "Social Mobility."

Cultivating class ethnocentrism

There is an anecdote of a private tutor in a wealthy family who sought to teach her pupil about the life of the poor. Then the little rich girl wrote a story about the poor, beginning:

"Once upon a time there was a very poor family. Everybody was poor. The Papa was poor, the Mama was poor, the children were poor, the cook was poor, the maid was poor, the butler was poor, the gardener was poor— Everybody was poor."

Members of one class cannot help judging members of other classes in terms of their own class expectations and values. The middle class scorns upper-class snobbishness, but strives desperately to raise its own children in a "good" neighborhood. People at every class level tend to see those above themselves as effete, snobbish, and pretentious, and those beneath as either disgusting or pathetic, as either good-for-nothing or "awfully pushy." At all intermediate status levels one tends to attribute one's own status to personal achievement, the status of those above to luck, and that of those beneath to inability and laziness. Miller suggests that, of all forms of ethnocentrism, class ethnocentrism is one of the most difficult to restrain:

It is considerably easier to manifest "tolerence" for the ways of the Zulu, Navaho, or Burmese than to achieve emotional acceptance of features of lower-class culture in our own society; in the former case it is relatively easy to recognize that disapproved or exotic behavior is a direct product of the group's culture and to accept such behavior on the grounds that it is "their way" of doing things, a way which is different from ours. In the case of lower-class culture, however, there is an almost automatic tendency to view certain customary behaviors in terms of right and wrong and to explain them as blameworthy deviations from accepted moral standards rather than as products of a deep-rooted cultural tradition. It is not too difficult to view the device of polygamous marriage and the mother-centered household among the Zulus as one alternative arrangement for meeting the problem of marriage and child-rearing; it is much harder to see the practice of serial mating and the female-based household in our own society as social forms which may constitute a practical or effective adaptation to the milieu in which they are found. . . .

The basic values and emphases of lower-class culture produced a vast army of woodsmen, construction workers, cattlemen, Indian fighters, frontier women, and many others without whose labors our country would never have achieved its present strength. . . . It is precisely these qualities and abilities which constitute the major emphases of lower-class male culture and which, in fact, comprise the basic set of qualities and skills learned and practiced in the "gang." (*Walter B. Miller, "Implications of Urban Lower Class Culture for Social Work,"* Social Service Review, 33:232–234, September, 1959. Copyright, 1959, by The University of Chicago.)

Defining the conventional morality

The social classes do not merely differ in etiquette; they also differ in moral judgments. The term "loyal worker" has one meaning in the union hall, another at the chamber of commerce. Kinsey [1948, pp. 375–379] has shown how sex mores differ between the classes. The lower-class emphasis is upon naturalness, not upon chastity; thus premarital sex experience is viewed rather tolerantly, since it is "natural"; but the lower classes strongly condemn as degenerate and "unnatural" the adolescent masturbation which the middle classes view

more tolerantly, or the elaborate love play which the middle-class marriage manuals recommend. On almost every point of moral conduct, class-typed mores differ.

Middle-class mores, however, tend to become the conventional mores. The church, the school, and the welfare and "uplift" agencies are middle-class institutions, staffed and run by middle-class persons, and dedicated to the cultivation of middle-class values. Political candidates must be models of middle-class virtue; stupidity is forgivable, but not immorality. The laws are written by middle-class legislators and enforce middle-class values. Thus the middle-class mores tend to become the official or conventional morality of the society.

This tendency creates certain strains for the lower-class person. He often finds that behavior which is normal and acceptable in his class subculture is condemned and punished when he steps outside this subculture, as he must do at school and in nearly all his dealings with persons in positions of authority. A good deal of resentment and class antagonism accumulates among the lower classes who feel that they are constantly being prodded, scolded, and "pushed around" by middle- and upper-class people.

In the "permissive" atmosphere of today, the lower-class person is likely to find the middle-class model somewhat confusing. The casual dress and casual sex relations which are part of the current "youth image" bear a deceptive and misleading similarity to lower-class clothing and sexual behavior traits. The youth revolt against middle-class ambition may well be a passing phase for middle-class youth, but one cruelly deceptive to the lower-class boy who seeks to rise in class status. The differences between classes still exist, and the blurring of distinctions presents an added hazard to lower-class youth who aspire to move into the middle class.

Explaining many other group differences

Many other kinds of group differences—racial, religious, regional—are really class differences. For example, almost any black-white comparison will prove to be very flattering to whites. Blacks have proportionately more crimes, more venereal disease, more illegitimate births, more drunkenness, more desertions, more broken families, and proportionately more people on relief. Their record of dereliction is due largely to the fact that discrimination and lack of opportunity have kept most blacks in the lower class. When blacks and whites are compared as racial groups, therefore, we are comparing an overwhelmingly lower-class group with another group having vastly larger middle- and upper-class segments.

Variations in the class composition of religious groups affect comparisons between them. One would expect Baptists and Catholics to have a higher rate of juvenile delinquency than Episcopalians and Congregationalists simply because juvenile deliquency usually is more frequent in lower-social-class groups. For the same reasons, exclusive residential suburbs of Long Island will have lower death rates than slum districts in New York City. Therefore, whenever data for two groups are compared, the critical observer will always wonder, "Are these groups comparable in class composition?" If not, some very misleading conclusions may be drawn.

Shaping life-adjustment patterns

The way people handle life situations varies with social class, as is illustrated in the following incident, reported to one of the authors by a perceptive student.

I was in a small two-man garage on a Saturday morning, making small talk with the proprietor as he worked on my car. He pointed to another car parked nearby. "How much do you think that car is worth?" he asked. I studied it a moment, and ventured, "Oh, perhaps $600." "I bought it a few minutes ago for $300," he remarked. "Now, I wonder why a fellow would sell his car so cheaply," I mused. He paused a moment, and said, "Oh, . . . you wouldn't understand." Suddenly I did understand. The proprietor was thinking "You, in your sheltered middle-class world of careful plans, long-term goals, and wisely rationed puritan pleasures, are unable to understand how a fellow would turn his car into quick cash to gratify a pressing impulse. Perhaps his eye is on something he can't wait to buy, or he needs money to finance a big weekend or to gain a new girl friend's gratitude. In his world, these may be more important than protecting his capital investment."

Social class affects the way people deal with virtually every aspect of reality. As space forbids examining them all, let us describe just two areas of life in which class background appears to produce contradictory tendencies: political attitudes, in which the lower classes appear to be more liberal (some would say "radical"), and social attitudes, in which the lower classes appear to be more conservative. (The terms, "liberal" and "conservative" are here used to describe differing degrees of receptivity to social change.)

Social class and political attitudes If social class influences the basic outlook of people, we should expect people to support the party and candidates closest to their class interests. Several surveys [Centers, 1949, chap. 5] seem to confirm this expectation in showing that the lower classes are more favorable toward government welfare benefits and services and government regulation of business than are the other classes. Since 1936 the electorate has divided quite sharply along class lines, and in recent decades "every cross-section political survey ever conducted shows the inevitable pattern of low-income people being dominantly Democratic and upper-income people being Republican" [Harris, 1957]. In the 1956 campaign, the list of those who contributed over $5,000 to either political party numbered 269 Republican and 56 Democratic contributors [*New York Times*, Feb. 3, 1957, p. 52]. In 1952 and 1956, the immense personal appeal of Eisenhower made deep inroads into the normally Democratic labor vote: yet these voters did not change their *party* preference and continued voting Democratic for other offices. In 1964, Johnson captured many middle-class and upper-class voters, but they returned to their usual voting habits in 1966. In 1968, the emergence of the American Independent party with George Wallace as presidential candidate split the working-class vote.

Class interest is not the only factor in voter behavior, although it does appear to be an important factor. Whenever the political candidates are clearly identified with issues that appear to threaten or favor the welfare of a particular segment of the population, most members of that segment will vote accordingly. But other considerations may overrule class interest for some people, or they may fail to understand the issues and unwittingly vote against their own class interests. For example, many lower-class people favor a sales tax over an income tax, perhaps because of its more "painless" collection, or perhaps because they do not realize that a sales tax places a larger share of the tax burden upon the lower incomes.

Party alignment by social classes does not always follow a predictable pattern, for some members of a social class may be expected to vote differently from their class. For several decades the Democrats have captured most of the lower-class vote and Republicans most of the vote from higher social classes, but this tendency may be altered by many factors. The emergence of a popular leader in either party, the rise of third parties, and the appeal of

issues which cut across class lines are among the factors which may change traditional social-class political alignments. In spite of a differential class support, both major American parties attempt a "consensus" type of appeal which reaches across class lines. In many industrialized countries, the link between class status and voting behavior is stronger than in the United States. In a study of British voting behavior, Lenski [1970, p. 362] found that the spread between lower-class support and upper- and middle-class support for a particular party was 33 percent, as compared with 18 percent for the United States. This means that British voters divided along class lines in voting nearly twice as faithfully as American voters.

Social class and social attitudes The lower class tends to be liberal on economic questions but conservative in many other social attitudes. The lower class appears reluctant to accept new ideas and practices and is suspicious of the innovators. Changes in health practices, food usage, religious doctrines, family life, or educational procedures are likely to find their strongest opposition among lower-class groups. Their limited education, reading habits, and associations isolate the lower class from a knowledge of the reasons for these changes, and this ignorance, together with their class position, makes them suspicious of the middle- and upper-class "experts" and "do-gooders" who promote the changes.

A case in point is an experiment in the use of the Salk vaccine for the prevention of poliomyelitis [Deasy, 1956]. The experiment occurred in a suburban area near Washington, D.C., where a large-scale trial program of the vaccine was attempted before it was released for use in general. Parents were notified of the opportunity in a letter from the school asking permission to give a free vaccination to the child. A follow-up survey disclosed that proportionately twice as many parents of upper and middle socioeconomic status gave permission, as is shown in Table 14. The reasons for lower-class refusal were explored. Fewer of the lower-class mothers had read about the program in the newspapers or discussed it with friends, and more of them expressed worries over its possible dangers. Lower-class participation was inhibited by lack of confidence in scientific experts, a greater fear of the new and untried, and a tendency to be unconcerned about actions whose results would not materialize until a future date.

Social class largely determines which parts of the culture one will experience.

A cross-cultural confirmation of lower-class conservatism comes from a survey of the response of English housewives to a program of free dental care under the government health system. Table 15 reveals a considerable lower-class resistance to this type of dental care even when it is free of charge.

Many other examples of lower-class conservatism could be cited. "Contemporary" design in art and home furnishings is first found in the shops catering to the wealthy and later vulgarized for the lower-class tastes. The lower class is last to feel the trend

toward the democratic family, permissive child-training practices, and birth control procedures [Bossard, 1954, chap. 15]. It does not follow that *all* social changes filter downward from the top, but a pattern of lower-class conservatism does seem to apply to many activities and interests.

Social class and social participation Social class largely determines which parts of the culture one will experience—opera, country club, and cotillion, or jukebox, tavern, and brawl. This is illustrated by class differences in degree of social participation. In general, the lower the social class, the fewer are the associations and social relations of the individual. Lower-class people belong to fewer organizations of any kind—clubs, civic groups, or even churches—than do middle and upper-class people [Foskett, 1955; Axelrod, 1956; Stone, 1960; Hyman and Wright, 1971]. We might assume that this lack of organized sociability is compensated by more numerous informal contacts, but we find that these also diminish as we go down the class continuum. Lower-class people have fewer acquaintances, fewer friends, gossip with and about fewer other people, and do less informal visiting [Shuval, 1956].

TABLE 14

Percent of respondents who gave consent for their child to participate in poliomyelitis vaccine trial

	Socioeconomic status		
	Highest (N-42) percent	Middle (N-44) percent	Lowest (N-44) percent
Gave consent	86	84	43
Did not give consent	14	16	57
Total	100	100	100

Source: Leila Calhoun Deasy, "Socio-economic Status and Participation in the Poliomyelitis Vaccine Trial," American Sociological Review, 21:185–191, April, 1956.

TABLE 15

Class attitudes to filling permanent teeth

Responses to filling permanent teeth	Class as measured by job and dwelling	
	Clerical, private housing	Unskilled, public housing
For	91.0%	53.0%
Against	6.3	40.3
Don't know	2.7	6.7
Total	100.0	100.0
$n =$	140	140

Source: Stewart Dickson, "Class Attitudes to Dental Treatment," British Journal of Sociology, *19:207, June, 1968.*

The age of mass communication cuts across class lines, and while the lower classes read and travel less than other classes, they spend more time with radio, television, and movies [Bogart, 1958, p. 91]. This greater audio-visual exposure is still a selective process, since lower-class listeners shun "serious" programs and stick as far as possible to entertainment, which in turn is shaped along stereotypes already accepted in lower-class culture. Mass communication undoubtedly speeds the acceptance of new gadgets, but other than this, its influence on lower-class listeners would appear to be mainly to intensify their social conservatism. In substance then, the lower-class person has only limited participation in any kind of social interaction which might lead to the rapid acceptance of new ideas.

Some of the patterns of behavior related to social class are indicated in the following digest of class attitudes toward governmental, religious, and educational institutions. All these propositions are supported by research findings, although the evidence for some is far more conclusive than for others. Some are documented elsewhere in this chapter; documentation for the rest is omitted because of space limitations.

A SUMMARY OF SOME CLASS ATTITUDES TOWARD SOCIAL INSTITUTIONS

Attitudes toward governmental institutions

Upper class Appreciate effect of government on own affairs; know leading officials and are interested in politics. Majority will regard governmental regime as basic to their own security and will resist any type of drastic change. A minority will take their own security for granted and work energetically for an "efficient" or "humanitarian" regime. Some youth in both upper- and middle-class circles are "disenchanted" and work for the overthrow of "materialistic" society.

Middle class Conscious of duty to be "good citizens." Responsive to appeals for "clean" or "honest" government, but for the most part will resist major change.

Lower class Many are completely indifferent to government since it seems remote and evidently has little effect on them. Some view it as the dispenser of petty favors such as minor jobs and possible payments for votes. A few may be consciously discontented with status and work for a revolutionary change that promises them greater benefits.

Attitudes toward religious institutions

Upper class Often take positions of leadership in lay movements and like to be considered "patrons" of the church. Some are critical of church dogma, but interested in the aesthetic aspects of religion. Some feel above the need for religion and show little interest except when custom demands their attendance on special occasions.

Middle class Apt to be responsive to appeals on a moral or intellectual basis. Somewhat uncertain about attitude toward traditional church dogmas. Highly critical of religious practices that seem to be excessively emotional.

Lower class Responsive to emotional services with (among Protestants) little ritual. Protestant groups often accept highly puritanical dogma which is often evaded in practice. Readily accepts reports of modern miracles. Some feel that the church is an upper-class institution and are either indifferent or openly hostile. Many join "storefront" churches that stress emotional expression and informal association.

Attitudes toward economic institutions

Upper class Take superior position and high standard of living for granted. Normally believe the traditional economic system is the best possible arrangement. Sometimes morally uneasy because of special privileges and seek to compensate by charity or civic service. Small minority

may worry about "social injustice" and promote social reforms.

Middle class Laud virtues of thrift, ambition, and "decent" living. Torn between desire to improve status by saving money and need to prove their importance by expensive living. Tend to accept prevailing system, but hope to rise within it. In time of prosperity some middle-class (and upperclass) youth will take their own prosperity for granted and, via the "hippie" life style, flee the competitive race for money and "material goods."

Lower class Usually take inferior position for granted. Have little real hope of improvement. Little chance for thrift, and occasional windfalls are used for immediate consumption. Some have acquired middleclass aspirations and seek rise in status through thrift and increased educational attainments. A few resent inferior position and hope for change through revolution and different type of economic structure.

Attitudes toward educational institutions

Upper class Many assume that their children will attend fashionable private schools and will make acceptable but not necessarily outstanding records. Education is regarded as a means of securing social acceptance and enriching cultural values rather than of preparation for earning a living. They support private schools generously, but some oppose raising taxes for public education. Others send their children to public schools in fashionable neighborhoods and to the major state universities. These parents are "patrons" of the schools and use their influence to increase community support of public education.

Middle class Life adjustment, vocational preparation, and opportunity for meeting suitable marriage partners are major aspects sought in higher education. Parents are concerned about standards of public education, join parent-teacher associations, and generally support higher school taxes. Children are expected to have a good school record. Some view the degree or certificate as more important than the content of education. Such parents refuse to be involved in maintaining educational standards and may resist increases in taxes. These parents are anxious that students graduate but not greatly concerned about high marks.

Lower class In an earlier period many considered the school as not very important or even a nuisance. Today, education is recognized as a prestige symbol; and polls show high aspirations for children's education. Although educational credentials are regarded as desirable, there is little commitment to study by either parents or children and school taxes are often defeated in lower-class neighborhoods. A minority, however, especially among upper-lower, become "middle-class converts" and will make great sacrifices for children's education.

THE FUTURE OF SOCIAL CLASSES: FROM "PROLETARIAT" TO "STATUS SEEKERS"

Karl Marx, in the volumes entitled *Das Kapital* and in the *Communist Manifesto*, probably did more to emphasize the importance of social class than any other thinker in history. In the Marxian view, conflict between social classes has been continous since the dawn of history, and the rise and fall of various social classes offer the key to the understanding of history. Prior to the industrial revolution, the top social class was a landed aristocracy which owned great estates by virtue of inheritance and noble rank. This class was forced to share top status with the manufacturers, traders, and financiers, whose wealth and prestige were greatly increased by the expansion of business since the time of the industrial revolution. Marx prophesied that the ultimate struggle would take place between the proletariat (wage workers) and the bourgeoisie (capitalists) and would end in the inevitable triumph of the proletariat, who would in turn establish a classless society under the banner of communism. This interpretation of history gave to communists a sort of "messianic hope" which enabled them to believe that, in spite of present obstacles, history was on their side and their final triumph was certain. For many years discussion of social class centered on the validity of the Marxian analysis.

The current opinion among social scientists is that Marx was only partly correct and that the class struggle is not proceeding on the lines he predicted. Marx predicted, for example, that classes would grow farther apart as industrialization advanced. Hence the lower class would become more conscious of its distinct interests and more hostile to the upper class, while the middle classes would gradually be pushed down into the proletariat. Actually the exact opposite seems to have taken place; classes are coming closer together both in possessions and in attitudes. The middle class is stronger than ever in Western societies, and the lower class is gaining a stake in the society which Marx wanted them to overthrow. Marx had predicted that communism would follow industrialization and that the most advanced countries would be ripe for communism under the influence of revolutionary urban wage earners. Since the writing of Marx, communism has spread in many places, but not in the manner that Marx predicted. The industrial countries have not developed Communist parties strong enough to take over the government (both Russia and China were primarily agricultural at the time of their Communist revolutions in 1917 and 1949), and expansion has come either through Chinese or Russian military conquest or by movements in agricultural areas led by the urban intellectuals with the support of a landlord-hating peasant population.

Skepticism about the Marxian prediction of an eventual classless society has also been strengthened by the difficulties of eliminating social class in Communist-controlled countries. The Soviet Union made an early attempt to abolish class privileges and insure equal opportunities to those of humble social origin. But it is clear that by the 1950s, the Communist party officers, factory managers, government officials, professional men, scientists, and artists in the Soviet Union formed a distinct self-perpetuating social class with special privileges and a distinct style of life with appropriate attitudes [Inkeles, 1950; Feldmesser, 1953]. A strong statement on the development of social-class lines in Communist society comes from the pen of Milovan Djilas, formerly vice-president of Tito's government in Yugoslavia, who was later thrown into prison for making statements such as this:

The establishment of the ownership of the new class was evidenced in the changes in the psychology, the way of life, and the material position of its members, depending on the position they held in the hierarchical ladder. Country homes, the best housing, furniture, and similar things were acquired; special quarters and exclusive rest homes were established for the highest bureaucracy, for the elite of the new class. The party secretary and the chief of the secret police in some places not only became the highest authorities but obtained the best housing, automobiles, and similar evidences of privilege. Those beneath them were eligible for comparable privileges depending upon their position in the hierarchy. . . . More than anything else, the essential aspect of contemporary Communism is the new class of owners and exploiters. (*Milovan Djilas, The New Class, Praeger Publishers, Inc., New York, 1957, pp. 57–58.*)

Far from achieving a classless society, the Communists have set in power a new class, based on the possession of nearly absolute power, which is even more rigid in its composition and more differentiated from the masses in its privileges than the upper class of capitalist societies. The dreams of the new freedom have given way to a regimentation more rigid than the old slavery. Judged by its creed, Communist society is the enemy of class privilege; judged by its results, it is class privilege's newest and strongest bastion. Some idea of the range of inequality in the Soviet Union is provided by Table 16, which gives earnings in the steel industry, but this table greatly underestimates the range of income, since it does not include the highest-paid scientists or party officials and omits such extremely important fringe benefits as bonuses, free housing, official cars, and other favors enjoyed by the Soviet officials. In non-Communist societies the possibilities of a Marxian-style class struggle for the control of society seem to be diminishing, but we are becoming increasingly aware of class struggle of a different type—the pursuit of status. This struggle is the main theme of Vance Packard's *The Status Seekers* [1959] and *The Pyramid Climbers* [1962], best-selling works of "popular sociology." Packard is not a professional sociologist, and his work has been criticized, among other reasons, for depicting class lines as a recent development when, in reality, they have long been present on the American scene [Lipset, 1959]. There is no doubt, however, that he has correctly identified the desire for social mobility as the major class concern in the United States today. Instead of seeing life as a struggle between classes with a fixed membership, the average American today sees it as a contest in which the reward is individual advancement from a lower- to a higher-class status.

Although desire for individual advancement is the aim of a great many Americans, an increasing number, drawn mainly from the ranks of the more affluent, have sought

TABLE 16

Remuneration in the Soviet steel industry

	1959*	1965
Director of scientific institute	600	600
Director of steel plant	400	400
Elevator operator, janitor, watchman	55	60
Typist, secretary	41	60

Rubles per month
Source: Murray Yanowitch, "The Soviet Income Revolution," Slavic Review, 22:693, December, 1963. (1965 figures are a projection of earlier plans.)

a more egalitarian society. They argue that the goal is not just to eliminate dire poverty but to secure a larger proportionate share for the bottom 20 percent of the population [Miller and Roby, 1970, pp. 3–20]. Still others disdain interest in material goods and are recruits for a hippie life style in which a voluntary type of poverty is at least a temporary requirement for participation. So far, the hippie group is a conspicious and powerless minority, but its very existence is a challenge to the prevailing economic values.

Changes in relative class status

One reason for lack of revolutionary fervor among workers is that many of the changes that Marx, Debs, and others worked for have now taken place without revolution. Such commonplace arrangements as legalized collective bargaining through labor unions, minimum wage laws, old-age pensions, and vacations with pay, which would have been considered fantastic dreams in the 1920s, are now taken for granted by most industrial workers. The result is that those who have usually been placed in the lower class now have many of the privileges of the middle class.

The essence of the Marxian appeal for class warfare was the belief that with the passing of time the rich would become increasingly wealthy and the poor increasingly miserable. This is not exactly what has been happening. All income levels have shared in the increasing productivity of our society and have gained in *absolute* standard of living; yet not all have shared equally in our growing prosperity. As shown in Figure 8, the share of our national income received by the top fifth has diminished very slightly, the middle-income receivers' share has grown somewhat, and the poorest fifth are better off in absolute terms, but relatively as poor as ever.

There is a widespread impression that taxes and welfare expenditures go a long way to redistribute income more equally. This is doubtful, possibly entirely false. Contrary to popular opinion, lower-income families pay a *higher* fraction of their income in taxes than more prosperous families.[3] Most of the very rich avoid the maximum income tax rates by taking advantage of the many tax loopholes thoughtfully provided for them. Although some government welfare programs benefit mainly the poor,

[3]According to The Tax Foundation, the percentage of income collected in taxes of all kinds rises steadily as income falls below $10,000, from 23.9 percent at $10,000 to 28.3 percent at $1,450. See *Allocation of the Tax Burden by Income Class*, The Tax Foundation, New York, 1960, p. 12.

others benefit mainly the prosperous and the rich—government expenditures for airports and air terminals, yachting facilities, interstate highways, irrigation projects which turn owners of desert wasteland into millionaires, and business subsidies of many kinds, to give a few examples. Whether the subsidies of the rich to the poor are greater or less than the subsidies of the poor to the rich has not been exactly determined. The following anecdote, related by a friend of one of the authors, is a case in point

As my host guided his 55-foot yacht toward its slip, he applauded the decision of a [Florida] city commission to cancel an urban renewal project, largely federally financed, which would benefit mainly the city's Negro slum area. As he expanded on the "taint" of federal funds to solve "local" problems, he tuned in on a weather report from a federally operated weather station, waved at the captain of a federally operated coast guard vessel which stood ready to rescue him if he got into trouble, carefully noted the position of the federally placed bouys and channel markers, nosed down a channel dredged with federal funds, and entered a marina financed partly from federal funds and tied up to a federally subsidized dock, concluding his lecture on the evils of government welfare programs with the sage observation, "We coddle people too much. People should stand on their own feet and pay their own way."

Although class privileges and obligations differ, all classes make useful contributions to society, and all types of class environments produce individuals who are problems to themselves and to society. Whether a class system is the best means of assigning different social functions is probably a question of only academic interest, since all modern societies follow the system. Ethical interest focuses on two questions: First, should the privileges and responsibilities of different classes be modified in the direction of minimizing differences between them? And second, can, or should, we promote the opportunities for individuals to change their class levels? Most societies are now more or less seriously committed to a

FIGURE 8

Who gets richer in the United States?

Percentage of national personal income, before taxes, received by each income fifth, 1910–1970.

Source: Adapted from data presented in Gabriel Kolko, *Wealth and Power in America*, Frederick A. Praeger, Inc., New York, 1962, p. 14; *Statistical Abstract of the United States*, 1970, p. 323.

program of curtailing upper-class privileges and improving levels of living for the lower class. The possibilities of individual movement between classes will be explored in a later chapter on social mobility.

SUMMARY

Social classes arise from division of labor and the consequences which follow from a division of labor. A social class is made up of people of similar social status who regard one another as social equals. Each class is a subculture, with a set of attitudes, beliefs, values, and behavior norms which differ from those of other classes. Social class is based on total social and economic position in the community, including wealth and income, occupation, education, self-identification, hereditary prestige, group participation, and recognition by others. Class lines are not clearly drawn but represent points along a continuum of social status. The exact size and membership of a given class is difficult to establish.

Social class is an important social reality. Social class largely determines one's life opportunities and colors one's personality development. Social class assigns privileges and responsibilities to individuals and thereby helps to get necessary work accomplished. Social-class subcultures breed a highly subtle and tenacious class ethnocentrism, which prevents classes from fully understanding one another. It is mainly the standards of the middle class that are written into law and sanctioned by the conventional morality. Many differences ordinarily assigned to race, religion, ethnic group, or to some other kind of group difference, are actually class differences; confusion arises from the fact that racial, religious, and other groups may be unevenly distributed along the class continuum.

Social class molds the life-adjustment patterns of the individuals; the lower class tends to be liberal in political action connected with economic benefits and conservative in accepting other social changes, while the opposite tends to be true of the upper class. This is partly explained by the fact that the lower the class level, the more limited tends to be the participation of the individual in social and community life.

Current scientific interest in class has shifted from the Marxian theory of class warfare to the struggle for individual social mobility and a lessening of the amount of inequality between classes. Current technological, economic, and governmental changes are increasing the relative size of the middle classes and bringing us closer to a middle-class society.

Questions and projects

1. Distinguish among *evaluated participation, status characteristics,* and *self-identification* as methods of determining social-class status. Which method do you think is best? Why?

2. Is there a culture of poverty? Can you explain the recent decrease in the number of the poor by a change in their culture?

3. How can social classes really be subcultures when children of all class levels attend school together?

4. Given unlimited money, to what degree could a government or a community provide children with complete "equality of opportunity"?

5. Is there a relation between the problems of health and education and the attitudes engendered by lower-class life? Explain.

6. How does class affect political attitudes? When a college student switches from his father's political party, does he do so because of increased knowledge, parental rebellion, or social mobility? Outline each possibility.

7. When a college student from a wealthy family takes a summer job working in a factory, how much does he learn from the "working class"?

8. What is meant by the "messianic hope" of Marxism? Have recent developments supported the Marxian theory of social class?

9. Do you feel that social-class stratification is harmful or beneficial to society as a whole? Why?

10. Is the United States primarily a middle-class country? Defend your answer.

11. Make a chart of officers in your senior high school class (or some other organization you know well). From which social-class level does each come? Are the officers proportionately representative of the social class present in the organization? Do members from different social classes view the group in the same way? Wherein, and why, do they differ?

12. Read and analyze the treatment of social class in one of the following novels: *Kitty Foyle* by Christopher Morley, *Marjorie Morningstar* by Herman Wouk, *Studs Lonigan* by James T. Farrell, *The Forge* by Thomas S. Stribling, *Mansfield Park* by Jane Austen, *The Age of Innocence* by Edith S. Wharton, *Fraternity* by John Galsworthy, *Tobacco Road* by Erskine Caldwell, *Hunky* by Thomas R. Williamson, *Babbitt* by Sinclair Lewis, *So Little Time* or *B. F.'s Daughter* by John P. Marquand.

Suggested readings

Baali, Fuad, and Clifton D. Bryant (eds.): *Introductory Sociology: Selected Readings for the Campus Scene*, Rand McNally & Company, Chicago, 1970. This collection of interesting readings has several articles dealing with aspects of social class which affect the campus. These include: **Ira L. Reiss,** "Social Class and Campus Dating"; **Delbert C. Miller,** "Town and Gown: The Social Status of a University Town"; **Richard Flacks,** "The Liberated Generation: An Exploration of the Roots of Student Protest"; **J. Ross Eshleman** and **Chester L. Hunt,** "Social Class Influences on Family Adjustment Patterns of Married College Students."

Brunswick, Ann F.: "What Generation Gap: A Comparison of Some Generational Differences among Blacks and Whites," *Social Problems*, 17: 358–370, Winter, 1970. An indirect commentary on social-class influence, since it finds that differences in education are as influential in determining attitudes as differences in age.

Coleman, Richard P., and Bernice L. Neugarten: *Social Status in the City*, Jossey-Bass, Inc., Publishers, San Francisco, 1971. A lucid analysis of the social-class structure of Kansas City, Missouri.

Hamilton, Richard F.: "The Marginal Middle Class: A Reconsideration," *American Sociological Review*, 31:192–199, April, 1966. A discussion of the class status of white-collar employees.

Lenski, Gerhard E.: *Power and Privilege: A Theory of Social Stratification*, McGraw-Hill Book Company, New York, 1966. A sophisticated statement of the theory that social stratification is based upon the functioning of distribution processes; concentrates more on the causes of social stratification than on the consequences.

Martineau, Pierre: "Social Classes and Spending Behavior," *Journal of Marketing*, 23:121–130, October, 1958; also, "Social Class and Its Very Close Relationship to the Individual's Buying Behavior," in **John S. Wright** and **Daniel S. Warner** (eds.), *Speaking of Advertising*, McGraw-Hill Book Company, 1963, pp. 147–153. Shows class influences on buying habits.

Miller, S. M., and Pamela A. Roby: *The Future of Inequality*, Basic Books, Inc., Publishers, New York, 1970. Argues the viewpoint that the notion of poverty as any fixed level of living is out of date and the current problem is not only to raise absolute levels, but also the relative position of the bottom 20 percent of the population.

Mitchell, Robert Edward: "Class-linked Conflict in Liberalism-Conservatism," *Social Problems*, 13: 418–427, Spring, 1966. A research study of contrasts in social-class attitudes on the national and local levels as seen in Berkeley, California.

*Shostak, Arthur B., and William Gomberg: *New Perspectives on Poverty*, Prentice-Hall, Inc., Englewood Cliffs, N. J., 1965. A series of articles devoted to the culture of poverty and to methods by which the lower class might absorb some elements of middle-class standards.

Warner, W. Lloyd, and Paul S. Lunt: *The Social Life of a Modern Community*, Yale University Press, New Haven, Conn., 1941, chap. 7, "Profiles of a Yankee City." A long chapter, reading like a novel, in which the attitudes and behavior of the different classes are dramatized.

*Winter, J. Alan (ed.): *The Poor: A Culture of Poverty or a Poverty of Culture?* Wm. B. Eerdmans Publishing Co., Grand Rapids, Mich., 1971. A collection of essays debating the idea of the culture of poverty.

Wrong, Dennis H.: "Social Inequality without Social Stratification," *The Canadian Review of Sociology and Anthropology*, 1:5–16, February, 1964. A discussion of the relationship between social class and the rise of a meritocracy.

From the time he was 2 until he reached 17, the witness told the Senate Finance Committee, his family was on welfare and he became a school dropout.

But today, at age 43, he pays taxes on $100,000 worth of real estate and on income of $40,000. His mother lives in an exclusive suburb, his son is in a preparatory school for Yale, his brother is a United States congressman and he is mayor of the nation's eighth largest city.

This was Cleveland's Democratic Mayor Carl B. Stokes speaking, and his plea was for Congress to place its priorities on people instead of things.

Stokes said he escaped dependency because he had a mother who instilled values in him, and after Army service, he was able to take advantage of the G. I. Bill of Rights and state-subsidized higher education. (The Washington Post, *Wednesday, Sept. 2, 1970, p. A-6.*)

This brief sketch concerns a poor boy who made good, moving in one generation from the bottom to one of the upper strata in American life. Two features stand out in the story: the social provision of channels for educational preparation, and his mother's success in instilling a mobility-oriented value system. He doubtlessly had ability; but without education and a driving ambition, this ability might never have been demonstrated. Ability, education, and ambition—without these, few men rise much above their social origins.

THE NATURE OF SOCIAL MOBILITY

No doubt talented persons are born into all class levels. If there were no barriers to social advancement, we could expect a great deal of mobility as some persons climbed while others slipped. But obviously barriers of many sorts block men's progress upward. One great barrier springs from the fact that *social classes are subcultures which fit children for participation in the class subculture to which they have been socialized.* The aver-

Social mobility

age lower-class child is less likely to have the vocabulary, the study habits, and the mannerisms most helpful in "school adjustment" and his chance of movement into the middle-class world is less because he has had little chance to learn them in his subculture. The middle-class child has this chance; meanwhile, he is shielded from the habits and learnings which would be appropriate for a lower-class world. The process of growing up in a class subculture thus sets forces in motion which tend to hold one in the same class position.

Another great barrier to mobility—possibly the greatest of all—is the "stratification of opportunity." The grandson of Henry Ford and the grandson of an Alabama tenant farmer did not have the same opportunity to become a corporation executive. Despite our efforts to equalize opportunities, it is clear that they are far from equal. It has been widely believed that a lack of ambition or motivation for advancement was the main reason why the poor remained poor. But recent research raises doubts whether this is true. Wilson [1966] and Underhill [1967] report evidence that, when environmental influences (such as family size, broken homes, quality of school) are controlled, the motivation among the poor and the more prosperous is very similar, while Irelan [1968] finds evidence that the aspiration to raise one's socioeconomic level may be even stronger among the poor than among the nonpoor. Reissman [1969] studied the levels of aspiration of 1,500 heads of households in New Orleans and found that the black poor expressed even greater aspirations for upward mobility than the white poor, but that both the white and black poor lacked the kind of "modern" attitudes needed for adjustment to a modern, urban, industrial economy. Thus, while it is by no means certain that aspiration for mobility is lacking in the lower class, it is undeniable that opportunities for social mobility are unequal. In addition to the obvious in-

equalities, such as housing, nutrition, family background, neighborhood influences, school quality, and access to higher education, there are many more subtle inequalities. For example, the middle-class youth who aspires to be a doctor or a scientist already knows, or can easily discover, the necessary steps to take; to the lower-class youth, these rather elementary facts may be paralyzingly remote. As one ghetto high school boy said, "I think I'd like to be a scientist, but . . . Hell, I've never even *seen* a scientist." Many such inequalities may add up to a "stratified opportunity" structure which some sociologists [Schiller, 1970] believe to be the greatest barrier to mobility.

Social mobility runs both ways—up and down. Some people fail to maintain the social-class rank into which they were born. Loss of wealth or income, acceptance of a lower-status occupation, and settling into a lower-status pattern of life are both the symptoms and the processes of downward mobility. Consider this case, supplied by a student of one of the authors.

Peter Wilson's father was a successful small-town lawyer who lived modestly but comfortably and was a pillar of small-town respectability. Peter was always a "different" child, obstinate and selfish; his parents indulged his whims and excused his shortcomings. Peter flunked out of two colleges in prompt succession and evaded two shotgun marriages as quietly as his father's legal skill could arrange. At this point his father gave up hope and moved to another locale.

For several years Peter clung to the edges of the lower-middle class. He held a succession of lower-middle-class jobs—cashier in a garage, inspector in a furniture factory, timekeeper on a construction project—but never held them for long. Nor did he ever get a very good job, for he lacked both education and dependability. Also, he never looked clean, and every suit he wore promptly assumed a slept-in look.

He finally drifted into a semiskilled factory job which he has now held for over a dozen years. He earns average wages, buys the food for the family, and spends the rest of his wages and most of his time with his cronies who work at the same factory. His father is still paying the rent, and his wife does housework to pay for other family needs.

The older sons have finished high school and hold semiskilled jobs. Both have married daughters of unskilled or semiskilled workers. The third generation now appears firmly fixed in the upper-lower or "working" class.

Such a spectacular drop from upper-middle to upper-lower or lower-lower class is unusual but not impossible. Lack of ability, lack of emotional stability, or possibly misfortune may prevent one from holding a suitable occupation and living the life appropriate to one's parental status. Some may *choose* downward mobility, rejecting the "rat race" and either seeking low-status occupations or avoiding any occupation whatever. Many of today's hippies and dropouts have made this choice.

Individual downward mobility of the kinds described above should be distinguished from *group downward mobility,* in which an entire group or category suffers a loss of social status. Jews in Hitler's Germany, the Asian merchant class in the new independent states of Africa, American farmers during the agricultural depression of the 1920s and the "dust bowl" of the 1930s, people in the coal-mining districts of Appalachia, skilled workers whose skills are made useless by technological change—all these are examples of a group downward mobility which individual choices or actions cannot influence. History provides many examples where, through neither fault nor prowess of their own, certain groups are degraded and others elevated in status.

CLASS AND CASTE

Some societies have developed structures which greatly hamper any kind of social mobility; in others, people are relatively free

to rise or fall. An *open-class* society would be one in which people move up or down in the social structure strictly on the basis of personal effort and ability; a *closed-class* society would be one in which position is fixed at birth and cannot be changed by individual achievement. As with all ideal types, perfect examples are hard to find, but the frontier society of early America is often regarded (not entirely correctly) as a society in which inherited prestige was of little importance, while the classic representation of the closed society is the caste system of ancient India. *Caste* refers to a social system in which position is based on ancestry regardless of achievement, is sustained by strict rules of endogamy prohibiting intermarriage with lower castes, and is often fortified by religious beliefs. In India, the barriers between castes were rigid, and exceptions were practically unknown. Caste specified type of occupation, place of worship, use of separate roads for travel, and separation to the greatest possible degree in all social relationships. The Brahmin in the upper caste was likely to be a person of wealth and education, but even if he were bankrupt and illiterate he still retained his caste status. The "untouchable," whose position was so low that he was outside the framework of the caste system, could not raise his status by individual accomplishments. Even if he was able to overcome his handicaps and acquire wealth and fame, he still retained his lowly social status in the eyes of the members of the regular castes [Hocart, 1950; Ryan, 1953; Marriott, 1955; Gardner, 1968; Gupta, 1968].

Recent legislation has attacked caste discrimination in India, but it is deeply rooted in the mores and difficult to change [Tripathi, 1967; Rosenblum, 1968]. The caste system is sanctioned by Hindu religious beliefs and regarded as the will of the gods by members of both the higher and lower castes. The only escape mechanisms are a very limited possibility of changing caste through adoption and the hope that one may have a higher status in his next incarnation. The Hindu believes in a prolonged round of rebirths; if he is unfortunate in his present life, he may be more favored in the next. This religious sanction of caste is not unchallenged, however, for some of the most prominent Hindus, including the late Mahatma Gandhi, have attacked caste barriers as a perversion of the essence of true Hinduism.

Although individual mobility in the caste system of India is not possible, it is sometimes possible for a whole group to alter its status. One method is through "Sanskritization" in which a group pulls out from a lowly caste with which it had been linked, claims higher status for itself, and copies the behavior of higher castes while tabooing all contact with those who have the lowly status it is trying to escape. Another method is to use the castes as political blocs and to demand government action to secure such privileges as job quotas or temple access [Olcott, 1944].

Race relations in the United States in the past have resembled a caste system, since many aspects of social status were determined by racial ancestry. Individual blacks who have achieved distinction might be treated respectfully but were still subject to the general rules of segregation. One contrast is that while Hindu religion supported the caste system, American religious bodies have generally denounced it. Perhaps the most influential book ever published in the United States on racial relations was *The American Dilemma* [Myrdal, 1944]. It developed the thesis that castelike segregation was fundamentally a violation of American spiritual and political ideals.

Features of American society which resembled the caste system included an etiquette in which blacks always filled a servile role, the restriction of housing, education, and jobs on the basis of race, and a legal prohibition of racial intermarriage in many states. The United States thus had a mixed caste-class system in which some statuses were open to achievement within a more or less open class system, while certain other statuses were closed to blacks as part of a caste system. For example, a wealthy black might have a chauffer-driven Cadillac and an expensive home, but he could not build this home in a white neighborhood, join the country club, or be buried in a white cemetary.

In recent years there have been many assaults on the castelike aspects of American society. Laws forbidding intermarriage have been declared unconstitutional, while federal legislation and court decisions have forbidden discrimination in employment and segregation in education, housing, and public facilities. Racial feelings of superiority and inferiority still persist, but the public answer to the "dilemma" of segregation versus democratic ideas has been that segregation had to go. Blacks and whites eat in the same restaurants, sleep in the same hotels, travel in the same conveyance without racial sections, and even intermarry without public interference. All of these practices were forbidden in the castelike segregated society, and their presence indicates that social caste practices in American society are on the way out.

Present-day racial tensions are more highly related to class than to caste. Centuries of discrimination and segregation have left a disproportionate number of blacks in lower-class status where they are denied access to many of the benefits of an affluent society, not primarily because they are black, but primarily because they are poor. The current trend of black-white relationships from a caste to a class context makes a great deal of difference to the rapidly growing group of middle-class blacks who are now competing successfully in an achievement society. But their success only increases the bitterness of those left behind in rural and urban slums. These people see

TABLE 17

*Blacks receiving welfare in
Greater Cleveland in 1964 constituted:*

84.5% of all families receiving aid to
    dependent children

74.3% of all families receiving city relief

64.3% of all families receiving county relief

58.8% of all persons receiving aid to the disabled

54.6% of all persons receiving aid for the blind

Source: Data compiled in a report by L. C. Schaller and C.
W. Rawlings, Race and Poverty, *Office of Race and Religion, cited in Sidney M. Peck, "The Economic Status of
Negro Labor" in Steven E. Deutsch and John Howard,
Where It's at: Radical Perspectives in Sociology, Harper
& Row, Publishers, Inc., New York, 1970, pp. 325–347.*

little change in their lives. The extent of their inequality is indicated by Table 17, showing the high proportion of blacks among welfare clients in Greater Cleveland where blacks constituted only 16.3 percent of the population.

Open and closed classes

No society has an absolutely open or a completely closed class system. Even in societies such as the United States, which lays great stress on individual initiative, family position plays a great role, since it prevents men from having the type of equal start in life that would be necessary for a completely open society. In every society, no matter how democratic or equalitarian its ethos may be, the successful parents will find ways to help their children hang on to the status and privileges the parents have enjoyed. This makes complete equality of opportunity impossible. The children of the most successful will inherit not only some of their parents' prestige, but also a better chance to acquire a good education, a driving ambition, and a chance to begin their working life with a fair supply of capital. In every society unsuccessful parents will, helpless-

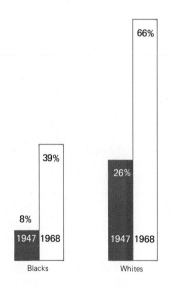

FIGURE 9
Percent of families receiving $7,000 or more in 1947 and 1968 (figures in 1968 dollars).

66%

39%

26%

8%

1947 | 1968

1947 | 1968

Blacks

Whites

Source: Based on data in *The Social and Economic Status of Negroes in the United States, 1969,* Bureau of Labor Statistics, Report No. 375, Current Population Reports, series P-23, no. 29.

ly and unwittingly, handicap their children in their competition for status. The children of the poor have to live down their parents' lowly status, have more trouble in acquiring a good education, and have great difficulty in obtaining the capital needed for business success. Unlike the untouchables of India, however, if they can overcome these obstacles, they will then be able to rise in status.

While "caste" and "closed-class system" mean approximately the same things, the concept of open and closed classes is more useful than the concept of caste, because it can be used as a measure of the amount of mobility in different societies. If a society has many individuals who came from lowly homes and rose to high positions, along with others who fell from the high status of their parents, then we say there is a high degree of social mobility and an approximation of the open-class society. A society in which only a few rise or fall from their parental status is closer to the caste system. The variations in rates of mobility are due both to the general rate of occupational improvement—the number of higher-status jobs appearing in the society—and the barriers against mobility within the society. Regardless of the attitude of the society toward social mobility, not many people will find an opportunity to improve their lot unless the society is making rapid economic advance.

One of the methods often used to analyze social mobility is a comparison of the occupations of sons with that of their fathers. A sharp difference in the nature of occupations followed by different generations indicates social mobility. Table 18 shows that in the United States the majority of sons find themselves in an occupation different from that of their fathers, and in most cases, the move was from a category of lesser prestige to one of greater prestige. Changes which have promoted this type of social mobility include a rapid decline in the number of farmers and unskilled workers and an increase in the number employed in white-collar and professional occupations. To a considerable degree the United States is an open-class society. Evidence from available studies shows no indication that social mobility has decreased in the last half century, while there may have been a slight increase [VanderZanden, 1970, p. 235].

A fairly open class system seems to be typical of most industrialized countries and one would assume that the rapid changes coming with industrialization also promote the chances of new occupational roles. Using the transition from manual to nonmanual occupations as a measure of social mobility, Lenski estimates that in industrialized countries approximately 30 percent have made this transition as shown in Table 19.

Social mobility in underdeveloped countries is not simply a matter of reaching a higher level within an established status system. It also generally involves a shift from being a part of a traditional farming culture to becoming a participant in a modern plantation or industrial economy. The

TABLE 18

Upward and downward occupational mobility in the U. S.

Occupation in 1962	Percent who have:		
	Moved up	Moved down	Not changed
Professionals	88.5	0.0	14.5
Managers	84.9	6.4	8.7
Clerks	77.7	17.8	4.5
Factory laborers	40.1	54.0	5.9
Farmers	2.9	15.1	82.0
Farm laborers	0.0	85.5	14.5

Note: From a national survey based on a sample of 20,700 males showing proportions of persons in each occupation who have moved up, moved down, or stayed at the same occupational level as their fathers.
Source: Adapted from Peter M. Blau and Otis Dudley Duncan, The American Occupational Structure, *John Wiley & Sons, Inc., New York, 1967, table 2.8, p. 39.*

individual leaves the water buffalo, the rice paddy, and a system of farming ruled by tradition and family authority, and enters the world of the tractor, time sheet, and rational agricultural techniques decreed by a remote and strange authority. It is not too difficult to recruit enough unskilled laborers, but competent skilled workers, technicians, and supervisors are scarce. In underdeveloped countries, the low status of manual labor tends to extend, to some degree, to the engineers and technicians, since they are also engaged in getting manual labor accomplished. The high-status occupations are those completely removed from manual labor—law, government, teaching, writing, and the like. The campaign for national independence in colonial areas has also focused the attention of ambitious young people on law and government. The results are that the underdeveloped society quickly accumulates many lawyers and civil service clerks, while independent businessmen, mechanics, and engineers will be in short supply for some time. Even though government employment may expand tremendously, it is still unable to take care of all who seek a career, while agricultural and

industrial development languishes, partly because of a lack of competent personnel [Van der Kroef, 1956; Hunt, 1966].

ETHNIC AND RELIGIOUS FACTORS IN MOBILITY

In most societies there is a tendency for national, racial, and religious groups to be distributed differently among the various social-class levels. Usually the social status of an ethnoeconomic group is determined by a combination of the following factors: (1) the length of time the group has been in the country; (2) the circumstances under which it entered the country; (3) the success of members of the group in improving their economic status; (4) stereotypes about the status of the group which may be widely believed, either by outsiders or by members of the group themselves; and (5) "visibility," or the ease with which outsiders can identify members of the group.

Table 20 illustrates the relationship between ethnic background and occupation in Canada. This table indicates the differential participation in various occupations by ethnic group. The English have twice the expected number of professional and financial posts in proportion to the size of the English population, while the French have about half the expected number of such posts. Scandinavians, who are mostly immigrants attracted to Canada by the prospect of cheap land, have ten times the expected number of farmers, while largely urbanized Jews have less than one-eleventh of their expected number of farmers.

A similar study made in a New England village by Warner in 1941 found that the upper class was entirely composed of Protestants of Anglo-Saxon background, although more recent immigrants of Catholic or Jewish faith were making a rapid rise [Warner,

TABLE 19

Upward mobility in industrialized countries

Country	Percent moving from manual to nonmanual occupations
United States	*34*
Sweden	*32*
Great Britain	*31*
Denmark	*30*
Norway	*30*
France	*29*
West Germany	*25*
Japan	*25*
Italy	*22*

Source: *Gerhard E. Lenski,* Power and Privilege, *McGraw-Hill Book Company, 1966, p. 411 (Data drawn from various studies).*

TABLE 20

Ethnic representation in occupational categories

	British	French	Ger-man	Italian	Jew-ish	Dutch	Scandi-navian	East Euro-pean	Other Euro-pean	Asian	Indian and Eskimo	Total male labor force
Professional and financial	+2.0	−1.9	−1.8	− 5.2	+ 7.4	− .9	− 1.9	−1.2	−1.1	+ 1.7	− 7.5	8.6
Clerical	+1.3	− .2	−1.8	− 3.2	− .1	− 1.7	− 2.4	−1.7	−2.0	− 1.5	− 5.9	6.9
Personal service	− .9	− .2	− .7	+ 2.9	− 2.4	− .5	− 1.1	+ .9	+5.1	+19.1	+ 1.3	4.3
Primary and unskilled	−2.3	+2.8	−2.1	+11.5	− 8.9	− 2.0	− .2	0.0	+1.8	− 3.6	+34.7	10.0
Agriculture	−1.5	−1.4	+8.8	− 9.5	−11.7	+10.3	+10.6	+6.9	+ .6	−6.5	+ 6.9	12.2
All others	+1.4	+ .9	−2.4	+ 3.5	+15.7	− 5.2	− 5.0	−4.9	−4.4	− 9.1	−29.5	58.0
Total	0.0	0.0	0.0	0.0	0.0	0.0	0.0	0.0	0.0	0.0	0.0	100.0

*A +2.0 sign indicates that the ethnic group has twice as much as its proportionate share of a given occupation, whereas a −2.0 sign indicates that the ethnic group has only one-half as much as its expected occupational quota, considering the ethnic group's size in proportion to the total population.

Source: Adapted from presentation in John Porter, The Vertical Mosaic, University of Toronto Press, Toronto, Canada, 1965, p. 87.

1941]. While occupation was only one of the traits considered by Warner in ranking social class, his findings were similar to those that would be expected on the basis of the Canadian data, thus indicating that the social mobility tendencies of a specific ethnic group may be similar in two different nations. An analysis of 1960 census data in the New England area indicated that the differential found by Warner in 1941 between the "old" and the "new" immigrant stock still persisted in 1960. That is, second-generation immigrants of German and English origin had a higher ranking in education and occupation than second-generation immigrants of Italian origin [Aho, 1969, pp. 512–526].

Most religious groups are highly conscious of how they differ from other groups in religious doctrines and in practices, but are less aware that they also differ in social class, nationality, racial, and religious background. In these respects, the Protestant denominations not only differ from Catholics and Jews, but also from each other, as

seen in Table 21. National data of this sort are seldom available, and Table 21 is limited to a sampling survey in Northern California and may not be typical of the nation as a whole. However, these are the most recent data available and are similar to the results of earlier national studies in 1957 [Lazerwitz, 1964] and in 1945–1946 [Pope, 1958]. In the other studies, Methodists were below the Presbyterians and Episcopalians in the proportion of upper-class members. The position of Roman Catholics is consistently below most Protestant bodies in all surveys yet published, but there are many indications of rapid mobility among Catholics since World War II [Kosa, 1962, pp. 361–371], and it may be that Table 21 does not accurately represent Catholic status in the nation as a whole.

Differences in class background greatly influence a group's adjustment to economic life, and it is not surprising that ethnoreligious groups differ in their rate of social mobility. Jewish immigrants to the United States came from urban European back-

TABLE 21

Annual family income of California church members, 1964

	$10,000 and up	$7,000– $9,000	$5,000– $6,000	$4,000 or less	No response
Congregationalists	64%	15%	10%	6%	5%
Methodists	53	26	10	5	7
Episcopalians	47	23	13	10	7
Presbyterians	48	24	11	12	5
American Lutheran	44	24	16	7	7
American Baptist	39	28	16	10	7
Roman Catholics	34	28	23	9	6
Southern Baptist	26	33	17	14	10

Source: *Survey of a random sample of church members in four northern California counties reported in Charles Y. Glock and Rodney Stark,* Patterns of Religious Commitment, *University of California Press, Los Angeles, 1968, p. 97.*

grounds; they adapted easily to our urbanized, industrialized society and rapidly developed traits of upward mobility, although discrimination has made it difficult for them to reach the topmost rungs of the ladder. On the other hand, distinctive racial groups such as the Negroes and American Indians, along with distinctive cultural groups such as the French Canadians and the economically impoverished Southern whites, are retarded in social mobility. These groups are handicapped both by discrimination and by a background in a subsistence type of agriculture which has not developed the traits required for success in urban economic competition.

Both the successful climber and the derelict member of the "best" family are exceptions to the general association between group affiliation and class status. Top-status groups often feel that such persons are a threat to their group status, and react to this threat by a concerted effort to keep their members on top and to resist the advance of those from lower levels. For example, in exclusive Grosse Pointe, Michigan, the Grosse Pointe Property Owners' Association and the local real estate brokers had in operation for many years an elaborate screening program for new residents. Such items as occupational status, way of living, American-sounding name, swarthy complexion, flashy dress, and many others were measured on a 100-point scale. Prospective purchasers needed a minimum score of 50 to pass. Southern Europeans had to score 65, and Jews, 85, with no passing scores at all for Negroes and Orientals [*Time,* April. 25, 1960; *New York Times,* Apr. 24, 1960]. Ironically, several of Detroit's leading gangsters had "passed," although it is unlikely that Jesus Christ would have been acceptable. Probably Grosse Pointe was only doing systematically what most other exclusive residential areas did informally.

When the high-status group is comparatively small in numbers, it may make a vigorous effort to see that all its members either play upper-class roles or else are removed from public view. Thus, during the American control of the Philippines, American citizenship conferred high social status, since Americans had political, economic, and educational prestige. Some Americans, however, were either unable or unwilling to play the role expected of an upper-class group; they became itinerant laborers who were often involved in petty crime and alcoholism and, most disturbing of all, often associated with lower-class Filipinos on an equal-status basis. Such Americans were encouraged to accept free transportation back to the United States, where they would not disturb the status image of Americans abroad.

All upper-class groups find their popular image threatened by members whose downward social mobility has made them **déclassé**. At times an upper-class group may be able to conceal their black sheep from public view. In parts of South and Central America or the Pacific Island areas where living is inexpensive and pleasant, the "remittance man" has long been a familiar figure. He was usually a European who had failed to fill the upper-class role acceptably and who was sent a monthly income by his family on condition that he get lost. He is is fading today, but a visit to an overseas American Express office suggests that emmigré hippies may be his replacement.

Just as the status of a group is diluted by the downward mobility of its members, so it is weakened by the upward mobility of outsiders. If the Brahmin must share high occupational status with those of lower caste, then the importance of being a Brahmin is no longer so great as when his group had a monopoly of high-status occupations. In a static society the caste rules made it exceedingly difficult for the low-cast members to enter prestige occupations. High-prestige occupations were reserved for the upper castes, just as American society has had Negro jobs and white jobs. It is good for the lower-status person to be hard-working; but when he gets "out of his place," he threatens the status of those who regard the top levels as their private preserve.

When an ethnoreligious group is forced to share high economic status with a different group, it may still resist the entry of the newcomers into other upper-class rela-

tionships. Thus Jews often find that entry into exclusive clubs is denied them because, although they have enough money, they belong to the wrong ethnic group. Or the New England Yankees may be forced to share economic and political leadership with Irish and Italians but still maintain social events from which these out-groups are excluded. The out-group member finds that certain economic advantages usually go to members of the in-group; and if he is successful in circumventing these barriers to economic advance, he still finds a lack of complete social acceptance in the upper strata. If the differences between the group affiliations of the new rich and those already established are slight, they eventually become assimilated in upper-class society. When the differences are based on sharply variant cultural practices or on recognizable physical features, then a well-established ethnoreligious group may be able to block the complete acceptance of the new recruits for a long time.

THE PROCESS OF SOCIAL MOBILITY

The American dream tells each young person to hope for a higher status and a better life than his parents. The emphasis seems to be on higher status more than upon money, for many a skilled workman takes pride in a son who enters schoolteaching at a salary less than he would earn as a skilled workman. This accent on status is revealed in a classic study of workers in automobile factories, which described them as prosperous but dissatisfied [Chinoy, 1952]. In terms of income and possessions they had done far better than their parents would have thought possible. The parents of many of them had lived either in slum tenements or in rural shacks, while these men lived in neat suburban cottages with all the usual modern conveniences. The pay was good and supplemented by fringe benefits such as pensions, insurance, and medical-care plans. Their dissatisfaction was not directed at their compensation, but grew from a feeling that they had no chance to escape the category of semiskilled workers.

In other words, the lower class had been upgraded; but the American dream also implies that one has a chance to rise to higher-class status, and for these men that possibility seemed remote. Some protected their egos by exaggerating the significance of minor promotions within the plant, while others daydreamed about someday leaving the factory and starting their own businesses, In neither case, however, was there any real chance of a significant rise in occupational status. In another era an intelligent workman who had mastered mechanical skills might be steadily promoted through supervisory levels until he reached a position in top management; or if these roads were blocked, he might use his mechanical skills to start a shop of his own. Today's workers find that supervisory positions above the level of foreman are usually filled by college-trained specialists, and that routine assembly-line work does not even give them mechanical skills which may be used elsewhere; in fact, it usually provides no mechanical skill at all. This situation represents a "break in the skill hierarchy," meaning that one may move from unskilled to skilled labor and eventually become a foreman, but that beyond that point lie barriers which are difficult to pass without the proper educational qualifications. Thus we have not one occupational ladder, but two: One stops with foreman; the other begins with a college diploma and a job in the "executive-development program" and ends with the presidency. To leap from the top rung of the first to the bottom rung of the second is rarely possible.

Another form of break in the skill hierarchy lies in the elimination of skilled jobs and their replacement by assembly-line operations. This means that the apprentice system within the factory has been diluted, the older workers robbed of distinction, and the younger workers deprived of a skilled model which they might copy [Warner and Low, 1946, p. 33].

While the break in the skill hierarchy has largely destroyed the stock-boy-to-president route, there are other roads to upward mobility. Education is more necessary to occupational mobility than before, but education is also more readily available than ever before in the United States. Scholarships and other institutionalized aids to the talented youth are available in considerable number. Yet as recently as 1966, it was found that "only 40 percent of highest-ability males from low-status origins attend four year colleges, as compared with 87 percent of those with the same ability but high-status origins" [Schiller, 1970, p. 437]. More recently, however, a considerable number of poor youths have been deliberately recruited and supported in college careers.

Although large-scale manufacturing may offer the poor boy few chances for promotion from within, the multiplication of the service industries—sales and service, retail trade, recreation, resort industry, and many others—do offer opportunities to persons with talent and ambition, even though they may lack college degrees.

In some occupations, the status of the occupation itself has changed. Farming has historically included a very few upper-class planters or plantation owners, a moderate number of fairly prosperous middle-status farm owners, and a large number of marginal farmers and tenant farmers of low income and low status. Today we have fewer farmers, but the average farm is larger and more prosperous, its owner is better educated, and his status and living standards compare more favorably with those of urban residents. Between 1940 and 1964 the number of tenant-operated farms declined from 39 to 17 percent of all farms. These tenant farmers have moved to town or city [Smith, 1969]. Those who remain farmers today are likely to have higher status and income than farmers a generation ago, while many of those who have left the farm have found a job of higher status than the one they left. Other occupations have shown a similar change in the nature or grade of work involved and the status of the occupation.

Prospects for social mobility

The prospects for social mobility depend upon the total number of openings in higher-status occupations and upon the barriers to their attainment by the lowly born. The need for an increasing number of individuals in higher-status occupations depends on changes in society which create more upper-class jobs and on the extent to which the upper-class parents produce enough children to fill these places. The need for personnel in high-status occupations in the United States has been growing, as shown in Figure 10. Meanwhile the high-income groups have had until recently a birth rate too low to replace themselves. This makes room for a good deal of upward occupational mobility. The development of automation is decreasing the demand for unskilled and semiskilled workers and for fine craftsmen, and is at the same time calling for a greater number of technicians capable of maintaining and coordinating complicated automatic machinery. This development is opening up a still larger number of higher-status positions, while still further decreasing the openings for the man who has little education or training. There will be a rapidly growing number of openings for specialists of many sorts and for technicians with at least a high school or junior college education plus specialized technical training. Meanwhile the openings for unskilled laborers will continue their long-term decline. The youth who does poorly at school can no

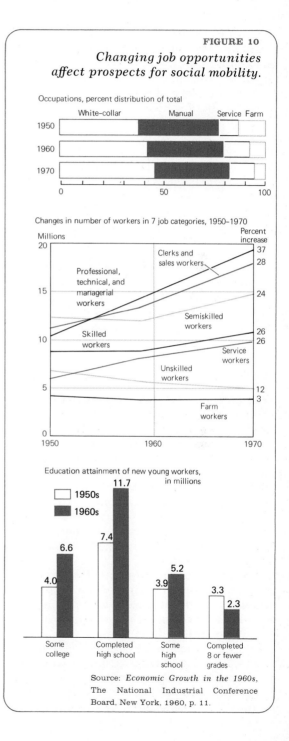

FIGURE 10

Changing job opportunities affect prospects for social mobility.

Source: *Economic Growth in the 1960s,* The National Industrial Conference Board, New York, 1960, p. 11.

longer drop out and easily get a job. Conant [1961, p. 34] has commented on the social dynamite in slum neighborhoods where as high as 70 percent of the boys and girls between the ages of sixteen and twenty-one are both out of school and out of work.

Social mobility probably is increasing.

We already have noticed that the route to skilled work via the apprentice system is yielding a shrinking number of openings. Even now, apprenticeship in many crafts is closed to all but the sons or protégés of union members. The fact has prompted Conant [1961, p. 47] to remark: "It is far more difficult in many communities to obtain admission to an apprenticeship program which involves union approval than to get into the most selective medical school in the nation."

For many people the prospects for mobility are considerably brighter than they may appear to the frustrated automobile assembly-line workers cited a few pages earlier. Direct promotion from laborer to management may be blocked by educational requirements for managerial jobs, but a larger percentage of Americans than ever before is receiving advanced education and anticipating the possibilities for occupational advancement that may follow. While the frontier is gone and the number of farmers is diminishing, the expansion of business and the increase of technical and professional services are giving a chance for upward mobility to millions of Americans. Blind alleys have appeared in some lines and new hurdles to advancement have developed, but new opportunities have opened up along with opportunities for training. The net result of these changes would seem to be some increase in mobility, with the United States probably a more nearly open-class society today than it has been for a long time.

One measure of mass social mobility is the extent to which Americans have been able to move above the poverty level of living. This level is defined as the minimum amount required by a nonfarm family of four. In 1959, 8⅓ million families were below the poverty level of $2,973; by 1968, when the poverty dividing line had risen to $3,553, the families below this level had fallen to 5 million. Even 5 million families living in poverty in the world's wealthiest country may be far too many, but this represents a removal of over 3 million families from poverty in nine years, one of the greatest instances of mass social mobility on record.

Channels of social mobility

The availability of routes for social mobility depends both on the individual and on the structure of the society in which he lives. Individual ability is of little consequence when society allocates its rewards on the basis of ascribed status. On the other hand, an open society is of little help to the individual who is not equipped for a competitive struggle. Jews in the United States found barriers against many types of economic activity, but small business and the professions proved relatively open and have allowed this group to attain quickly an above-average prosperity. Irish immigrants found that their growing political power gave them opportunities for government jobs and that experience in construction work provided the knowledge essential for success in the contracting business. At an earlier date, immigrants found that the free land in the West offered opportunities more open than those they could discover in the relatively closed urban communities. In traditional European and Latin American society, the hierarchy of the Roman Catholic Church and sometimes the army provided upward mobility for the poor but ambitious youth. In Spain, to become a rich and famous bullfighter is every poor boy's dream. Some competitive sports (professional boxing, football, baseball, basketball, but *not* polo, tennis, or golf) have usually been open to talented youth regardless of ethnic or social-class status and have usually been neglected by men from the more favored social strata.

In some societies the ambitious youth may find only one or two possible channels of mobility open to him; in others there may literally be hundreds of possible routes to higher social status. Some channels may be closed to the individual because of ethnic or social-class discrimination; others he may fail to perceive because of the limitations of his background, or may be unable to use because his abilities have not been properly developed.

Techniques of social climbing

For the boy who wishes to elevate his social-class status, the prime essential is an education and an occupation which fit his class ambitions. For the girl, either a prestige occupation or a higher status husband are needed for upward mobility. As already indicated, education, occupation, and income are the main factors which, operating over a period of time, will lift one's class status.

There are, however, many ways for a skillful climber to speed up the mobility process.

Change in standard of living It is not enough merely to get and spend more money, for what one buys is more important than the amount one spends. To gain acceptance at a new status level, one must assume a material standard of living appropriate to that level. This means moving to an appropriate neighborhood, decorating one's house in an appropriate manner, driving a car which is neither too humble nor too ostentatious, and so on. The outward appearances must fit. After one is solidly established, he may ignore some of the appearances, especially at the upper-class level. The person whose secure upper-class status is beyond question can afford to drive a nondescript car and dress with a casual unconcern for fashion. But those who are on the way up must be careful about conformity to the pattern.

Cultivation of class-typed behavior The mobility-oriented person will not be fully accepted into a higher class until he has absorbed the behavior patterns of that class well enough to follow them without glaring errors over a considerable period of time. The time can be shortened by deliberate effort. The aspirant can study books on etiquette, read the magazines on home decoration, and consciously watch and copy the manners of those whose acceptance he craves. Patterns of dress, vocabulary and diction, recreational activities, reading interests—these can be overhauled and polished. The children can be given music and dancing lessons, and be sent to carefully chosen private schools and summer camps. It is true that not all aspects of a class subculture can be acquired through deliberate study and conscious imitation, but such efforts can speed up the process of acceptance.

Manipulation of associations If opportunities for social climbing were removed,

FIGURE 11

The community is a network of overlapping associations.

Class in community	Memberships in associations and organizations						

The community is a network of associations or organizations whose membership may include persons at different class levels. Thus the organization helps persons to make social contacts across class lines. For the skillful manipulator, these associations are ladders of upward mobility, but few will climb more than one rung during a single lifetime.

Order of Patriotic Veterans   The Altruists

Angler's Club   Lowell Club

The Badgers   Mast Club

Civic League   Sword and Shield Club

Source: Adapted from descriptive materials in W. Lloyd Warner and Paul S. Lunt, *The Social Life of a Modern Community,* Yale University Press, New Haven, 1941, chap. 7.

many church organizations, civic associations, welfare societies, and other local associations would suffer a calamitous loss of membership. For how is the mobile person to meet and cultivate those who are a notch above him in social status? The very rich can engage a social secretary, part of whose task is to help them in the intricate art of social gamesmanship [Zorbaugh, 1929, pp. 55–56]. The new rich can even engage a professional service which is in the business of training the new rich in old rich behavior [Wakefield, 1961]. But the most useful device for social climbing is the association whose membership overlaps two or more class levels. The mobile person cultivates the highest-status members of an organization. Then he uses these friendships as levers to get himself into other higher-status organizations in which these friends are also members. Thus they climb, dropping out of the lower-status organizations as they gain admission to those of higher status [Chambers, 1954, pp. 384–406; Meeker, 1949, pp. 130–148]. The mobile Catholic can move to a better part of town, and thus transfer from a parish of lower-class members to a more aristocratic parish. The mobile Protestant may do likewise, or he may even switch to another denomination in which middle- or upper-class members are more numerous—from Church of God to Methodist, or from Methodist to Presbyterian. Church and welfare organizations are always in need of voluntary workers. A determined climber can easily find some whose members are worth cultivating. The informal clique, though perhaps harder to get into, is extremely useful because of its intimacy.

This, then, is the standard technique of the successful climber—to cultivate the upper-status members of one's cliques and associations, and use them to gain entrée into status groups in which one is not yet accepted. It takes a good deal of finesse to play this game. One must be socially perceptive, must learn quickly, and probably must have a certain amount of charm. Those who can play the game successfully achieve rapid mobility.

Marriage People on the way up must be careful whom they marry. At the very least, they must choose a mate whose social finesse and learning abilities will not be a drag. At best, a "good" marriage is a priceless asset. By marrying into a family a notch or two above his, an ambitious youth gets a better opportunity to use his talents. He may get financial backing to complete an education or launch a business; he gets good connections and valuable introductions; he gets a wife who already fully understands the class culture he must absorb; he gets a powerful motive to "succeed" and prove himself worthy of his wife's confidence in him. A girl who "marries up" is not automatically accepted into her husband's social class, especially if the jump up has been a long one. Such marriages, however, are very rare. The upper-class college boy may romance the tavern maid, but he rarely marries her. Interclass marriages are generally between persons at adjacent class levels. Where the wife has the social finesse and learning ability to absorb the class culture quickly, she is likely to be accepted into her husband's social class with little difficulty.

When a woman "marries down," does she lose her class status? That depends upon him. If he soon gains the education, occupation, and income, and absorbs the class culture of her class level, he generally becomes accepted at her class level. But if he retains lower-status education, occupation, income, and behavior, she is likely to find that her old associates are forgetting her.

The celebrity: a special status

How about the famous baseball star or prizefighter who gets more newspaper space than all the nation's scientists combined? How about the singer or actor who zooms to wealth and fame, complete with swimming pool, press agent, and hordes of worshipful fans? What is his social-class status?

Celebrity status is a special kind of status, based on spectacular achievement (or sometimes skillful press agentry), not upon one's total activities and behavior. The celebrity has a national public who follow his actions without ever knowing or interacting with him as a person. His social-class status would be measured by the status of those who would accept him, as a person, as their social equal, apart from his fame as a celebrity. President Roosevelt was clearly upper-class and President Truman just as clearly middle-class. Raymond Massey and Sir Cedric Hardwicke were members of the upper class before they became famous actors, and remained so after they retired; many other famous actors and actresses came from lower-class backgrounds, and have never been accepted as upper-class, however much they have been feted as celebrities.

Since there are many wealthy celebrity chasers, the celebrity meets many upper-class persons at charity balls, house parties, and other occasions. But when he ceases to be a celebrity and becomes a "has-been," which people will accept and entertain him as a social equal? This selective treatment tells his true social-class status. Ex-Presidents and war-hero generals may always remain celebrities, but many other kinds of celebrities lose their claim to fame and descend to a humble status.

SOCIAL MOBILITY AND DEFERRED GRATIFICATION

So many aspects of life are determined by one's attitude toward social mobility that certain mobility-oriented attitudes have been grouped under the term *deferred grati-*

fication pattern (abbreviated, DGP). This is simply the pattern of postponing immediate satisfactions in order to gain some later goal. You readers who are now studying this textbook, instead of playing poker or "goofing off," are practicing the DGP. The DGP may be described as a series of behavior tendencies of one who realizes that social mo-

A deferment of present satisfactions.

bility, either upward or downward, is a real probability in his life. Consequently, his attitudes and actions are guided by their supposed effect on his chances for upward social mobility.

In this type of planning, any activity today is viewed from the question of its consequences for tomorrow. Marriage may be postponed until one has finished school and secured a job. Education is considered neither a luxury nor a bore but an investment in future prospects. Thrift will lay the basis for eventual economic power, and emotional control will permit eventual emotional satisfaction. Time is used for self-improvement instead of aimless relaxation. A good description of this pattern has been given by Schneider and Lysgaard.

Deferred gratification evidently refers to postponement of gratifications or satisfactions. . . . It
may be contended that it does indeed fall into a *pattern*, characteristic of the so-called "middle-class," members of which tend to delay achievement of economic independence through a relatively elaborate process of education, tend to defer sexual gratification through intercourse, show a relatively marked tendency to save money, and the like. . . . [An] important point is the *normative* character of the deferred gratification pattern. Middle-class persons feel that they *should* save, postpone, and renounce a variety of gratifications. There are very probably also normative elements in the "lower-class" pattern of non-deferment. Thus, Whyte notes that one of the important divergences between the social mobility pattern and the corner-boy activity pattern in Cornerville appears in matters involving expenditure of money. The college boys save money for educational purposes or to launch business or professional careers. But the corner boys must share their money with others and avoid middle-class thrift. Should a corner boy have money and his friend not have it, he is expected to spend for both. The corner boy may be thrifty, but, if so, he cannot hope to hold a high position in the corner gang. (*Louis Schneider and Sverre Lysgaard, "The Deferred Gratification Pattern: A Preliminary Study,"* American Sociological Review, *18:142–149, April, 1953.*)

Evidence that the DGP really exists is found in several research reports [Rosen, 1956; McArthur, 1955; Kluckhohn, 1950; Kahl, 1953; Straus, 1962; Phillips, 1966]. Thus in a study of 2,500 high school students who classified themselves as "middle-class" or "working class," the middle-class students showed many traits of the DGP. For the working-class youth, physical violence both among themselves and in adult associations was more common, occupational goals were lower, more youth expected to leave school before completing high school, and both the youth and their parents gave less emphasis to saving money [Schneider and Lysgaard, 1953]. Other studies have shown a relationship between the postponement of sexual gratification and middle-class status. Kinsey, in his study of the sex life of the American male, came to the conclusion that early sexual intercourse was a routine part of growing up for the lower-class male but a breach of the mores for the males of higher social status. In fact, he concluded that the lower-class boy who had not had sex relations by the age of sixteen was either a physical or mental defective or a middle-class convert "earmarked for moving out of his community and going to college" [1948, p. 381]. Lower-class youth also marry at earlier ages than middle- or upper-class youth [Glick and Landau, 1950]. In all areas of life the lower-class emphasis is on immediate satisfaction rather than waiting for the rewards of a doubtful future.

Why does the lower class so seldom defer gratification? Possibly because the insecurity of the lower-class world places so much pressure for immediate survival that deferring gratification now for the sake of rewards in the future seems both futile and difficult. Allison Davis describes the pressures of lower-class life:

The actual daily pressure of 5 to 10 hungry stomachs to fill, backs to clothe, and feet to cover forces the working-class parent to reduce his ambitions to the level of subsistence; to lower his sights as far as long-term planning and studying for better jobs and for finer skills are concerned; to narrow, limit, and shorten his goals with regard to the care, nutrition, education and careers of his children.

This terrible pressure for physical survival means that the *child* in the average working-class family does not learn the "ambition," the drive for high skills, and for educational achievement that the middle-class child learns in his family. The working-class individual usually does not learn to respond to these strong incentives and to seek these difficult goals, because they have been submerged in his family life by the daily battle for food, shelter, and for the preservation of the family. In this sense, ambition and the drive to attain the higher skills are a kind of luxury. They require a minimum *physical security*; only when one knows where his next week's or next month's food and shelter will come from, can he and his children afford to go in for the long-term education and training, the endless search for opportunities, and the tedious apple polishing that the attainment of higher skills and occupational

status require. (*Allison Davis, "The Motivation of the Underprivileged Worker,"* in *William F. Whyte (ed.),* Industry and Society, *McGraw-Hill Book Company, New York, 1946, p. 89. See also S. M. Miller and Frank Riessman, "The Working Class Subculture: A New View,"* Social Problems, 9: 86–97, Summer, 1961.)

This excerpt shows how the lower classes have so few resources that there is very little that they can defer! Furthermore, most lower-class people have little feeling of control over their destiny. In other words, they do not feel that they can do anything that will make any difference in what happens to them. They accept unemployment, illness, poverty, and endless pregnancy as a "fate" beyond their control. Middle-class people are highly critical of what they perceive as the "laziness, shiftlessness, and immorality" of the lower class. In their class ethnocentrism, these middle-class critics fail to recognize that these lower-class patterns are practical, intelligent, and functionally useful adjustments to the realities of lower-class life. Just as the middle-class person is wise to read a book or take a nap instead of fussing and stewing when his plane is late, the lower-class person is acting intelligently when he fails to "save" because he will be laid off or on relief next month or next fall, anyway. Thus *the life style of the poor is a sensible adjustment to their lack of opportunity and resources.* Recent efforts by radical organizers to rouse the poor to organized protest have had some success, but most of the poor remain in apathetic resignation.

The middle class has the most to gain by practicing the DGP. The upper class has little need to defer gratifications, for they need only to retain a position already gained. Most lower-class people see little prospect that the deferment of immediate gratifications will be rewarded with any real change in their lives, so deferment would be only a pointless self-denial. It is true that the recent poverty and job-training programs have opened somewhat wider the door of opportunity for some of the poor, and some school dropouts and "hard-core" unemployed have obtained decent jobs for the first time in their lives. But these programs reached only a fraction of the poor, while many of those who had climbed painfully out of poverty in the late 1960s were dumped back into poverty during the 1970 recession. Such people have so few resources and so little experience in surviving such a reversal that it is questionable how many of them maintain their morale and "try again."

The hippie life style is a total rejection of middle-class values, of the DGP, of status mobility, and of the traditional work ethic. The hippie in the commune may occasionally work very hard at making handmade furniture or growing an organic garden, but totally rejects the idea of work to accumulate possessions, new clothes, or to gain social status, or because one "ought" to work [Andrews, 1970]. The hippie elevates immediate satisfactions over future concerns, feeling over reason, "freedom" over obligation, and a euphoric state of consciousness (often drug induced) as the ideal condition of existence. The hippie complex is puzzling to middle-class parents whose children disdain the opportunities their parents struggled and sacrificed to provide. Lower-class people are often angry and hostile toward hippies who reject the opportunities they never had.

There are many pseudohippies, who affect hippie dress and grooming, but are fairly conventional in values and life goals, although somewhat more relaxed in pursuing them. For some of those who take the full "hippie trip," it is only a temporary retreat from conventionality. But for those who remain for long, downward mobility is likely. As yet, there is no reliable research on the later life of hippies, but it seems likely that a decade or more of immersion in the hippie subculture would permanently impair both one's employability and one's capacity to fill conventional occupational roles. The long-term hippie may find that the middle-class life style which he rejected is no longer an option.

INDIVIDUAL COSTS OF SOCIAL MOBILITY

The idea that social mobility is good is part of our democratic ethos. We argue that a closed-class society thwarts the fulfillment of individual personality and deprives society of the contributions of many talented people.

Whether a society suffers because of limited mobility may depend upon its level of complexity. In a somewhat more simple society, such as existed in eighteenth-century Europe or America, very few roles could not be adequately filled by anyone of average ability, providing he were identified and prepared for his role from early childhood. Likewise, in a stable, unchanging society, the leadership roles, which consist mainly in carrying out the traditional rites and procedures, call for careful training rather than outstanding ability. A closed-class system is probably an asset to the simpler, more stable societies. It guarantees that most roles will be filled adequately, without wasting any talent really needed by the society.

A rapidly changing society, however, requires more of its leaders than an ability to preside over the traditional rituals. And a technologically advanced society requires vast numbers of highly intelligent, highly educated professionals, technicians, and experts. Such a society is less able to afford the waste of any of its brains. A fairly open class system may, therefore, be a necessity for "modern" society. Necessary though it may be, the open-class system has its penalties. In several ways, it exacts its price from those who compete within it.

Status insecurity

The medieval cobbler had little chance of rising but little danger of falling. He could be comfortable as a cobbler, free from the prod of ambition or the sting of failure. He could find fulfillment in his work without indignity or shame, and could enjoy his humble possessions and simple comforts without coveting the luxuries he was not encouraged to long for.

An open-class system grants man a chance to rise but charges him with the fear of failure. He cannot blame society for his lowly status but must shoulder this responsibility himself. There is no guarantee that he will not drop below his ancestral status, but even if he retains it, the retention does not mean that he has fulfilled his social obligations. His obligation is not merely to maintain his status but to improve it. Other men of lowly origin have reached high status. Why doesn't he?

This status anxiety is greatest in the middle class. The upper class has no need to struggle for higher status, and no great fear of losing it. At the lowest class level, few see much hope of status gain, and few struggle to climb. But those at some intermediate status level feel a stronger desire for further status gain, and a greater fear of status loss.

Some men in an open-class society respond to the challenge and make rapid advancement; some are so demoralized that they seek escape in drink, narcotics, sex, or other distraction. Many try to protect themselves by supporting institutional arrangements to limit free social mobility. Perhaps the best example of this is seen in trade union, civil service, and business policies which place a premium on seniority as a basis for promotion. As long as one conforms to minimum standards and "keeps his nose clean," he is in line for a gradual advancement which depends less upon his own ability than upon the health of the man ahead of him and the number of new openings created by the growth of the enterprise. Funeral by funeral, he works his way up the seniority ladder. Some men chafe under the restrictions of the seniority system, but many prefer a slower rate of promotion if it will blunt the rigors of open competition.

Strain of new role adjustments

Upward mobility not only carries new privileges; it also carries new responsibilities and restrictions. Occasionally a man declines an offered promotion because he shrinks from the added responsibilities it carries. "Nervous break-downs" among recently promoted executives are not uncommon.

Occasionally a man declines an offered promotion.

Since social classes are subcultures, upward mobility requires the unlearning and relearning of a great many minor role adjustments. An interminable list of patterns of speech, dress, food preference, table manners, etiquette, recreation, and so on must be revised to fit one's new class status. One study [Hacker, 1962] reports a 50 percent higher rate of heart symptoms among a group of young executives of working-class origin, as compared with a control group of young executives of middle-class origin. The strain of such adjustments is seldom appreciated by one who has not needed to make them.

Disruption of primary-group relationships

Among the student readers of this book will be many mobility-oriented students who are already becoming estranged from their parents. If their parents are working-class people of limited formal education, these students find that they are moving into a different social and intellectual world. On their successive visits home, they are finding fewer and fewer topics on which they can talk comfortably with their parents. Many parents sacrifice to help their children rise above their own position, only to watch sadly as their children become strangers to them. For both, the experience is painful.

Another point of strain comes from the tendency of social mobility to be correlated with geographic mobility. Contrary to the adage that "a rolling stone gathers no moss," the person who remains in his hometown is less apt to reach the top of any occupational pinnacle [Blau and Duncan, 1967, pp. 243–275]. The life story of ambitious persons usually includes migration to another location for education or apprenticeship and then perhaps several more moves among metropolitan areas as he gains experience and begins to assume major responsibilities. At another level, the man on a run-down farm in New England, the laborer in a Puerto Rican village, or an Arkansas hill dweller must move to more industrialized areas if he wishes to improve his opportunities.

This frequent movement means that it is difficult to develop roots in the neighborhood and that one is constantly changing the circle of family friends and making new arrangements with schools, churches, and local business establishments. The old family home, the familiar neighborhood, the friends of one's childhood—all these give way to a moving equilibrium of adjustment to new roles, new friends, and new places. The gain is excitement, novelty, and stimulation. The loss is reflected in brittle and temporary relationships which often lead to an ultimate loneliness and isolation. Indeed, one study [Hollingshead et al., 1954] suggests that mental illness may sometimes be the price for either upward or downward social mobility, and another [Ellis, 1952] finds an abnormally high rate of psychosomatic disorders among a group of upwardly mobile career women.

Downward mobility also takes its toll in mental illness. A study of schizophrenics found that the high representation of this group in the lower class was due to downward mobility of the schizophrenic from his father's social class status [Turner and Wagenfeld, 1967].

Even the marriage of the mobile couple is sometimes threatened. Often the two mates are not equally interested in mobility, or they may differ in their ability to learn the new role adjustments. One mate resents the implied insult of being constantly prodded, polished, and improved; the other resents his mate's lack of cooperation. The successful man who sheds the wife of his youth for a more cultivated partner is a familiar figure among the status seekers.

Other primary-group associates may also be sacrificed. One's easy camaraderie with his friends and fellow workers is threatened when he gains greater authority and income with the prospect of still further promotions. The wife of a major general recently remarked to the author, "I don't know who my friends are any more." Her friendships are now polite and correct, rather than relaxed and genuine. Many enlisted men in the army made no effort to gain officer status for fear it would alienate them from their "buddies" in the ranks; factory workmen sometimes hesitate to become foremen for similar reasons. Friendship under such circumstances may become "status-adulterated," in that those beneath him bootlick him while he bootlicks his superiors. In such a setting all motives become suspect, and genuine friendship may be a dim memory of the happier days before one had begun to climb the ladder of occupational success.

The other side of the picture is that upward mobility not only disrupts established social relationships but it may select those most willing to see such relationships disrupted. The person who leaves his hometown, his friends, and his family in pursuit of fortune is often one who is dissatisfied with his primary-group associations and feels a need to escape from the surroundings of his childhood [Warner and Abegglen, 1955, pp. 80-81]. In this sense the boy who makes good is a social deviant who has left behind the attitudes and the associations he might normally have been expected to form in the process of growing up. Such a revolt against the standards of the social class of one's family may even be stimulated by parents who pass on to their children the standards they value but have been unable to attain. The father who left school in the middle of the eighth grade may urge his son to prepare himself for a professional career, and the mother who married early may encourage her daughter to complete college before marrying. Apparently there are two types of mobility-oriented children: those who identify with mobility-oriented parents and those who reject their static or downwardly mobile parents [Reusch, 1953]. In any case, the "middle-class convert" will experience a shift of attitudes and associations which will probably be even more drastic than that

involved in the process of religious conversion or of changed citizenship. The fact that many social-class differences are subtle rather than pronounced makes the process all the more difficult, since the individual must be sensitive to nuances which are not easily recognizable. The shift from one class to another is a socially disruptive process which is easier for those who are already disenchanted with their pattern of life and anxious to make a complete break with the past.

Is a high rate of social mobility worth the cost? If a complex, changing society does not permit upward mobility to the talented and ambitious, it runs the risk of turning them into rebels and revolutionaries. The historic weakness of radical and revolutionary movements in the United States has generally been attributed to our open-class system; if one has good prospects for self-advancement within the existing social order, why overthrow it? Thus a high rate of social mobility may tend to stabilize a social order by providing mobility opportunities to talented youths who are dissatisfied with their social status. Today's young revolutionaries, unlike many earlier ones, are not so much protesting a lack of mobility opportunity in the society as they are attacking the basic values of the society along with its entire status system. They get relatively little support from lower-class and lower-middle-class youths, who seek upward mobility within the present system instead. If the mobility aspirations of the latter were to be widely frustrated, then they might listen more attentively to revolutionary rhetoric.

It is also possible that a high rate of social mobility may tend to undermine traditions and develop a cranky conservatism among older people. It may lead to a contempt for "honest toil" and a drive for the "fast buck," and lead to anomie for persons who move rapidly through a succession of statuses and roles [Tumin, 1957]. But the question of whether mobility is good or bad is irrelevant, for a relatively open class system appears to be necessary and inevitable in a rapidly changing, technologically advanced society.

SUMMARY

Social mobility refers to movement up or down in social status. This usually involves a change in occupation. Differential reproduction rates and expanding industry offer a continuous chance for occupational advancement and social mobility; they are probably at least as great in the United States now as in earlier years. Some European countries also have considerable social mobility; in others the rate has been held down by the fact that a slower trend toward industrialization leaves a larger part of the population in rural areas. The underdeveloped countries are entering a period of industrialization which increases social mobility, but the amount of mobility in these countries is still less than in more industrialized areas. Mobility in the United States has been hampered by the imposition of rigid educational requirements for many higher-level jobs but has been accelerated by the rapid growth in the number graduating from high school and college.

Both societies and ethnic groups vary in the number of channels of mobility open to their members. Channels may be restricted by the limited technological development of the society, discrimination against an ethnic or social-class group, failure of perception, and lack of development of the necessary personal qualities.

A society in which people are ranked strictly according to individual ability and performance is known as an *open-class* society; one in which status is theoretically based strictly on heredity is known as a *closed-class* or *caste* society. No class system is entirely open or closed. Modern industrial societies tend toward the open-class system; traditional agricultural societies may develop caste systems which restrict social mobility. Ethnic and religious membership to a certain extent still affects class position. Black-white relationships in the United States are often cited as a caste situation, although the attacks on segregation and discrimination in recent years make racial differences more clearly a matter of class than of caste barriers.

While a change in occupation is the crucial step in social mobility, the process may be speeded by: (1) revising one's standard of living, (2) cultivating class-typed modes of behavior, (3) manipulating associational memberships, or (4) a strategic marriage. The celebrity enjoys a special kind of status which gains him admittance to upper-class groups as long as he remains a celebrity.

Upward mobility is aided by a time perspective, most often found in the middle class, known as the *deferred gratification pattern*. The lower class, along with the middle-class hippie, tends to reject this pattern in favor of immediate gratification, whereas the upper class has a continuing status security that makes the deferment of gratification seem unnecessary. Lower-class norms are often regarded as immoral or pathological by middle-class critics, but have value in helping individuals adjust to the insecurities of life in the lower-class environment. Mobility brings new opportunities and greater outlets for potential ability, but it also brings emotional strains and threatens patterns of friendship, residence, and family ties. Those who are not firmly integrated into the social-class setting of their parental home appear to be most adaptable to the changes which make mobility possible. While bringing strain into the life of individuals, a high rate of social mobility may stabilize the social order, since discontented individuals may turn their energies to seeking personal advancement rather than to social revolution.

Questions and projects

1. Why is it that persons at the very top of the status ladder often spend less freely and put up less "front" than many persons who are a level or two beneath them?

2. Distinguish between caste and class. Is there any caste aspect to social stratification in the United States?

3. What advantages and disadvantages does a closed-class system hold for a society? For the individual? Do you know of any deliberate attempts to decrease competition for status in the United States?

4. What advantages and disadvantages does an open-class system hold for a society? For the individual? What makes absolute equality of opportunity impossible?

5. Do you consider yourself to be highly mobility-oriented? What factors do you think explain your own mobility orientation?

6. It is often said that the hippies can always drop back into middle-class roles if they wish. Is this true?

7. Assume that higher education should become completely free of all costs and that all jobs were filled strictly on merit without regard to family connections. Would you expect the same proportion of lower- and middle-class youth to reach high-status positions? Why or why not?

8. Why do upward-mobile persons usually drift away from their relatives and old friends? Is the tendency due to snobbishness?

9. Is marriage while in college an aid or a threat to the student's prospects for social mobility? Will his social mobility become a threat to his marriage?

10. Read *A Tree Grows in Brooklyn*, by Betty Smith. What factors account for Francie's rejection of the slum subculture and her desire to escape it? Did she escape through luck or through her own efforts?

11. Analyze a pledge list in a fraternity or sorority in terms of those you would label socially mobile as contrasted to those who are simply maintaining the family status. Describe any contrasts between the personality traits of the socially mobile and the stationary pledges.

12. Describe the groups in your community characterized by the most rapid and least rapid rate of upward mobility. On the basis of present trends in both of these groups, attempt to predict their relative position fifty years hence.

Suggested readings

Ellis, Evelyn: "Upward Social Mobility among Unmarried Career Women," *American Sociological Review,* 17:558–563, October, 1952. A discussion of some of the effects of social mobility on personality.

Hollingshead, A. B., R. Ellis, and E. Kirby: "Social Mobility and Mental Illness," *American Sociological Review,* 19:577–584, October, 1954. Analysis of the strains of social mobility and their effect on mental health.

Kosa, John: "Patterns of Social Mobility among American Catholics," *Social Compass,* 9:361–371, 1962. Reprinted in **William T. Liu and Nathaniel J. Pallone,** *Catholics, U.S.A.,* John Wiley & Sons, Inc.,

New York, 1970, under title, "The Emergence of a Catholic Middle Class," pp. 15–24. Documents and interprets recent rapid social mobility among American Catholics.

Miller, S. M., and Pamela Roby: *The Future of Inequality,* Basic Books, Inc., Publishers, New York, 1969. Deals with efforts to promote a general upward movement of the bottom 20 percent of the population.

Phillips, Derek L.: "Deferred Gratification in a College Setting: Some Gains and Costs," *Social Problems,* 13:333–343, Winter, 1966. A college study which may be distorted by the fact that most college students probably practice some degree of deferred gratification.

Schneider, Louis, and Sverre Lysgaard: "The Deferred Gratification Pattern: A Preliminary Study," *American Sociological Review,* 18:142–149, April, 1953; The Bobbs-Merrill Company, Inc., Indianapolis, reprint S-250. The classic statement of the DGP.

Smelser, Neil and Seymour Martin Lipset (eds.): *Social Structure and Mobility in Economic Development,* Aldine Publishing Company, Chicago, 1966. A series of papers dealing with the mutual interaction between social mobility and economic development.

*****Sorokin, Pitirim:** *Social and Cultural Mobility,* Harper & Row, Publishers, Inc., New York, 1927. A monumental study of social mobility in a variety of social systems and time periods.

Straus, Murray A.: "Deferred Gratification, Social Class and the Achievement Syndrome," *American Sociological Review,* 27:326–335, June, 1962. A study of the relationship between social class and acceptance of the deferred-gratification pattern.

Tumin, Melvin J.: "Some Unapplauded Consequences of Social Mobility in a Mass Society," *Social Forces,* 36:21–37, October, 1957; The Bobbs-Merrill Company, Inc., reprint S-294. Argues that social mobility imposes many personal and social costs upon a society.

Warner, W. Lloyd, and Paul S. Lunt: *The Social Life of a Modern Community,* Yale University Press, New Haven, Conn., 1941. Description of social class and social mobility in a New England factory town. Chap. 7, "Profiles of Yankee City," is again especially recommended.

Wilensky, Harold, and Hugh Edwards: "The Skidder," *American Sociological Review,* 24:215–231, April, 1959. Analysis of the social attitudes of the downwardly mobile.

Social interaction

Part Four describes some of the characteristic ways in which people treat one another. Chapter 14, "Social Processes," describes some fairly standardized types of interaction which appear in some form in most societies. Chapter 15, "Social Power," delineates the types of power and its use by different social groups. Chapter 16, "Race and Ethnic Relations," shows how facts and feelings about race enter into people's treatment of one another. Chapter 17, "Collective Behavior in Mass Society," analyzes a variety of forms of behavior in which the element of group encouragement and protection is especially important.

The background of partition [of India and Pakistan] is long and involved. It was the culmination of more than a century of dual struggle—the struggle for national independence against England, and the struggle for power inside India between Hindu and Moslem. . . .

And in those early days of uncertainty and confusion people became panicky. Whatever the animosity had been between Hindu and Moslem before Independence, the people had managed to live side by side. With partition, however, millions of people suddenly became jittery and insecure. A Hindu who lived in a city near the border like Lahore wondered what was to happen to him now that Lahore was to become a part of Pakistan. A Moslem who lived on the outskirts of Calcutta wondered what was to happen now that there would be a separate Moslem government in Pakistan that did not include him. The insecurity and confusion became multiplied as millions of people decided to move in order to be governed by their own group.

Then came violence. At first there were only sporadic incidents. A Moslem in Dacca, for example, would smash the shopwindows of a clothing store owned by a Hindu, claiming he had heard that Hindus were looting Moslem shops in Calcutta or Delhi. A Hindu in Calcutta would set fire to a Moslem home, in open view of a crowd, yelling that he had heard that Moslems were burning homes of Hindus who remained behind in Dacca or Karachi. Some Hindus or Moslems would try to take advantage of the national turmoil by seizing business properties or homes.

Each incident, of course, fed on rumors and begat even greater rumors. Outrages were carried out in the name of retaliation. Soon a civil war without battle-lines or armies raged throughout the sub-continent. People rushed through the streets with sticks or torches or whatever could be used to kill a man. (*Norman Cousins, "Where Violence Begins,"* Saturday Review, *Jan. 18, 1954, pp. 22ff.*)

Social processes

Here we have an example of conflict—one of the social processes. What are social processes, and what is their importance?

THE NATURE OF SOCIAL PROCESSES

The term social processes refers to *repetitive interaction patterns of behavior which are commonly found in social life*. One of the most extensive treatments of social process is found in Park and Burgess, *Introduction to the Science of Sociology* [1921]. This highly influential textbook of an earlier period is primarily devoted to the classification and analysis of social processes. In recent decades sociologists have become less interested in social processes and more interested in the intensive analysis of behavior in specific institutional and cultural settings. Yet it still remains important for the student to be aware of the major social processes to be found in all groups and all societies. The most frequent classification of the major social processes is in terms of *cooperation, competition, conflict, accommodation, assimilation, and amalgamation*. These social processes apply to both individuals and groups. We also include two other social processes which apply only to groups— *boundary maintenance and systemic linkage*.

Social processes and value judgments

In the first part of the twentieth century, scholars engaged in heated arguments over the relative importance of cooperation and competition in the natural world. Those who said that competition was the law of the universe often quoted Darwin's statement that evolution had been determined by a struggle for existence in which the strongest survived while the weaker were eliminated. Taking the name of "Social Darwinists," they argued that human life was also perfected by struggle and that philanthropy worked against the perfection of the race by allowing the unfit to survive [Simpson, 1959]. This theory was in turn attacked by Kropotkin [1925] in his book *Mutual Aid*.

Kropotkin used the works of Kessler as his rationale for arguing that even the animal world was not one of unlimited conflict and that if humans were looking for biological analogies, they could find significant examples of cooperation in the realm of nature.

I obviously do not deny the struggle for existence, but I maintain that the progressive development of the animal kingdom, and especially of mankind, is favored much more by mutual support than by mutual struggle. . . . All organic beings have two essential needs: that of nutrition and of propagating the species. The former brings them to a struggle and mutual extermination, while the needs of maintaining the species bring them to approach one another and to support one another. But I am inclined to think that in the evolution of the organic world—in the progessive modification of organic beings—mutual support among individuals plays a much more important part than mutual struggle. (*Statement of Kessler in* Memoirs of the St. Petersburg Society of Naturalists, *cited in Peter Kropotkin*, Mutual Aid, *Alfred A. Knopf, Inc., New York, 1925, p. 16.*)

Kropotkin added that while struggle exists between species, within species the dominant social process is cooperation, as is seen in flocks of birds, herds of buffalo, colonies of ants, and other group formations in the animal world. Hence he argued that those species which have survived are precisely those which have developed the process of mutual aid to the highest degree.

Today the philosophical argument about the relative merits of cooperation and conflict has somewhat subsided. Few people are interested in abstract arguments about the superiority of the cooperative or the competitive way of life. But today all face the difficulties of cooperation in a society dominated by secondary groups and the perils of conflict in an age threatened by atomic destruction. The new problems may have renewed men's interest in the sociological analysis of these topics. In fact, one recently founded magazine bears the title, *Journal of Conflict Resolution*.

COOPERATION

Cooperation is derived from two Latin words, *co* meaning *together* and *operari* meaning *to work*. Cooperation may be found in groups as small as the dyad (group of two persons) and as large as the United Nations. Forms of cooperative endeavor in primitive societies are usually traditional and are acted out without any conscious design. Trobriand Islanders do not "decide" to fish cooperatively; they just go fishing as their fathers always did. The more technologically advanced cultures often carry out elaborate plans for deliberate cooperative activities. Cooperation implies a regard for the wishes of other people and is often regarded as unselfish, but men may also find that their selfish goals are best served by working together with their fellows.

Deliberate primary-group cooperation

Cooperation by members of small groups is so common in every society that the life history of most individuals may be written largely in terms of their attempts to become a part of such groups and to adjust to the demands of cooperative group life. Even the most ardent individualist will find that much of his life satisfaction arises from the give and take in the family, recreation groups, and work groups. The need for cooperation in these activities is so much taken for granted that we sometimes forget that the enjoyment of a stable group experience depends largely upon one's ability to enter comfortably into cooperative relationships. The person who cannot cooperate easily and successfully is likely to be isolated and perhaps maladjusted.

Not only is primary-group cooperation important in itself, but it is closely related to secondary-group cooperation. Most large organizations are networks of smaller primary groups in which cooperation functions on a face-to-face basis involving many highly personal relationships.

Deliberate primary-group co-operation.

Deliberate secondary-group cooperation

When we think of cooperation, we often have in mind the kind engaged in deliberately by secondary groups. Consumer and producer cooperatives are an example. Consumer cooperatives are organizations of consumers which operate wholesale and retail stores. One form of consumers' cooperative, the credit union, pools the savings of members to form a loan fund handled on a similar basis. Members are paid the going rate of interest for their savings and are able to borrow funds at a set rate of interest, with rebates being divided among borrowers when a margin is available. Producers' cooperatives are most frequently used in the marketing of agricultural produce. Groups of farmers hope to eliminate the profits made by commercial middlemen through establishing their own warehouses and selling channels. Neither consumer nor producer cooperatives try to "undersell" other business concerns; they do business at competitive prices, then distribute profits (usually called "patronage dividends") among the members in proportion to their purchases from, or sales to, the cooperative.

In the Scandinavian countries and in England, such cooperatives do a major proportion of the total business in the country. In the United States they handle only a small fraction of the total business but are highly important in dairy and fruit farming, and consumer co-ops are strong in some areas. Scandinavian immigrants have carried this pattern with them to the United States, and cooperatives became strongest where a cohesive ethnic group regarded them as a traditional part of the culture [Kercher et al., 1941].

As is true of all types of social interaction, the success of cooperatives seems to depend to a great degree on the culture of the area. Oddly enough, the most fertile ground for cooperatives seems to be a society in which there has already been a strong development of private business. In these areas cooperatives have often survived both capitalist competition and governmental discouragement. Cooperatives in underdeveloped areas have had great difficulty despite the fact that they have often received governmental help [Hart, 1955]. In these areas the conduct of business is totally outside the experience of most of the people, and the middleman is usually an alien who is barred from participation in cooperative activity. As a result, even when the cooperative has had a government subsidy, it often has failed through corruption, mismanagement, or inability to repay loans. Cooperatives can succeed without governmental encouragement, but they rarely succeed unless the culture has familiarized the people with the practices essential to carrying on economic life in a market economy. This may explain why recent efforts to promote consumer cooperatives among ghetto poor and college students have not been very successful.

These "cooperatives" are but one of many forms of large-scale cooperative activity. The desire of people to work together for common goals is expressed through governments, fraternal bodies, religious organizations, and a host of special-interest groups. Such cooperation not only involves many people in the local community but also extends to a network of organized cooperative activity involving state, regional, national, and international relationships. Problems in such cooperation include decisions as to the geographical extent of cooperation, obtaining a consensus on the ends to be pursued and the means of reaching them, conflicts with other cooperative groups, and the inevitable difficulty of reconciling the conflicting claims of individuals and the subgroups with which they are associated.

Government may be taken as an example of such deliberate organized cooperation. When North America was first settled, it consisted of colonial regimes ruled by rival European nations. After a period of conflicts, the English achieved dominance, but soon the colonists revolted in order to gain the freedom to make their own cooperative arrangements. With independence, Americans organized state and national governments. The difficulty of reconciling the claims of state and national governments led to a civil war that, to some extent, established a pattern which has been followed since that time. Another type of cooperative adjustment has been the development of regional units such as the Federal Reserve Banks, now organized in twelve regions cutting across state lines. Our need for organized cooperation across national lines has led to the organization of the United Nations, and determining the proper roles to be followed by the constituent members of that body is a major problem of our time.

Impersonal and symbiotic cooperation

The world of nature is sometimes pictured as a world of conflict. Yet the concept of universal strife is contradicted by animals who hunt in packs, by insects who work together to maintain colonies, and even by the cooperation of dissimilar organisms.

Darwin, in his description of the nexus between cats and next year's clover crop, provided the now classic illustration of the network of vital linkages which bind different organisms together. Humble-bees alone, his observations disclosed, visit the red clover; other bees and insects cannot reach the nectar. But the number of humble-bees in an area depends in a great measure on the number of field mice, since these latter invade the nests of humble-bees and rob them of their food stores. Cats, in turn, are the natural enemies of mice and hence control their numbers. In areas adjacent to villages the nests of humble-bees were found to be more numerous than elsewhere owing no doubt to the number of cats there. An increase in the cat population, it may be inferred, is followed by a decrease in the number of mice thus permitting an increase of humble-bees and, consequently, a more widespread fertilization of red clover. Creatures that, to all outward appearances, are "remote in the scale of nature" are found to be linked together in a chain of relations. The deeper the analysis of the "web of life" is pushed the more meaningless becomes such a word as "independent." (*Amos H. Hawley*, Human Ecology, A Theory of Community Structure, *The Ronald Press Company, New York, 1950, pp. 33–34. The reference to Darwin is from* The Origin of Species.)

This cooperative interdependence of different species or orders upon one another is known in biology as *symbiosis*. Symbiotic relationships are not planned or deliberately established; they grow, as though by accident, from the efforts of organisms to survive. A great part of human cooperation may be said to be on the symbiotic level since it unites people in a mutual interdependence although they may have made no deliberate choice to cooperate. The marketplace draws men into a network of cooperation even though each wishes only to buy or sell for his own needs. The farmer, for instance, produces for the market which will give him the greatest net profit, but in this process he cooperates with many people about whom he neither knows nor cares. Most of our economic life is organized on the principle of pursuing self-interest by selling one's labor or goods at the highest price he can get. Although the goal is self-interest, the effect is to maintain a network of cooperative relationships in which men work to furnish goods and services desired by other men.

Even the dislocations of economic life may be viewed as furthering cooperation. If no one will buy a person's labor or his products, their refusal encourages him to shift into some type of labor or product that people will buy. The process is so painful that such market interferences as price supports, subsidies, and unemployment insurance have become common. Nevertheless, Western society may be said to rely to a great extent on mutual aid, which is no less effective because it is motivated by individualistic concerns. The main ideological controversies are not between those who reject cooperation and those who exalt it, but between the proponents of differing types of cooperation. The classical economists believed that the most effective integration of efforts would be ensured by a laissez-faire policy allowing men to be governed entirely by their pursuit of self-interest in the marketplace. Other men advocate various forms of deliberate cooperation, ranging from the consumers' cooperative to the enforced overall planning of the Soviet Union. Americans have generally followed the laissez-faire principle but have modified it by many types of cooperation undertaken deliberately either through government or through private associations.

COMPETITION

Competition is the struggle for possession of rewards which are in limited supply —money, goods, status, power, love—anything. It may be formally defined as *the process of seeking to obtain a reward by surpassing all rivals*. It is based on the inexorable fact that all people can never satisfy all their desires. It flourishes even in circumstances of abundance; rivalry is still keen for top jobs during periods of full employment. Regardless of the sex ratio, we find in many societies a bitter contest within each sex for the attentions of certain partners. Competition may be personal, as when two rivals contest for election to office; or it may be impersonal, as in a civil service examination in which the contestants are not even aware of one another's identity. Whether personal or impersonal, competition is conducted according to standards which focus attention on the surpassing rather than on the elimination of rivals.

American business sometimes seems to be in a flight from competition even as it praises its virtues. The antitrust laws represent an effort to keep competition effective when many businessmen would rather modify or eliminate it. Monopoly, division of markets, price fixing, and "fair trade" laws are techniques for reducing business competition. In some instances these practices are fought by government, in others they are supported. In transportation and in such public utilities as light and telephone service, government regulation restricts competition by setting rates and assigning territories.

Competition: a culturally patterned process

While competition is present to some degree in all societies, it differs greatly in degree from society to society. The fiercely competitive Kwakiutl and the relatively noncompetitive Zuni offer a striking contrast. The Kwakiutl work very hard to accumulate wealth which is used primarily to establish status rather than to provide material comfort. The competition for status reaches its height at the famous "potlatch," in which the chiefs and leading families vie with each other to see how much they can give away or

destroy [Murdock, 1936, pp. 242-248]. A family may spend a lifetime accumulating wealth, then bankrupt themselves in a single potlatch, thereby establishing the social status of their children. Members of a family who persisted in keeping their wealth would be criticized for their unwillingness to "do anything" for their children. The Zuni, on the other hand, disdain any emphasis on the accumulation of wealth or the demonstration of individual skill. Most wealth is owned by the entire community, and it is bad form to demonstrate individual superiority of any kind. Thus the Zuni child does not grow up believing that he should make the most money, get the highest grades, or run the fastest race.

Even such strong encouragement of competition as is found among the Kwakiutl does not mean that cooperation is completely absent. As the anthropologist Margaret Mead points out:

Nevertheless, no society is exclusively competitive or exclusively cooperative. The very existence of highly competitive groups implies cooperation within the groups. Both competitive and cooperative habits must exist within the society. There is furious competition among the Kwakiutl at the one stratum of society—among the ranking chiefs—but within the household of each chief cooperation is mandatory for the amassing of the wealth that is distributed or destroyed. (*Margaret Mead*, Cooperation and Conflict among Primitive Peoples, *McGraw-Hill Book Company, New York, 1937, p. 360.*)

Sometimes, too, it is hard to distinguish competition from cooperation, for a variation in form may disguise a similarity in process. Jessie Bernard [1960] comments on the Hopi, another "noncompetitive" society: "The Hopi girls who attempt to outdo one another in lack of skill are just as competitive as the Kwakiutl chiefs who attempt to outdo one another in the potlatch. The difference lies in the thing being tested, not in the process itself." Far from being two mutually distinct processes, competition and cooperation overlap in various ways, while both may go on simultaneously, as is true of the group whose members cooperate with one another while the group competes with another group.

Competition in American society

In its competitive emphasis, the United States is probably closer to the Kwakiutl than to the Zuni; yet this competition is sharply limited by many factors. Enactment of minimum wage laws works toward a situation in which men are not competing for a bare existence, and a growing emphasis on seniority as a basis of promotion means that many occupational goals cannot be reached by direct competitive efforts. In fact, the following description of the control of the competitive impulse in an American factory setting comes close to the Zuni practice:

Worker: "There's another thing; you know the fellows give the fast workers the raspberry all the time. Work hard, try to do your best, and they don't appreciate it at all. They don't seem to figure that they are gaining anything by it. It's not only the wiremen, the soldermen don't like it either. . . . The fellows who loaf along are liked better than anybody else. Some of them take pride in turning out as little work as they can and making the boss think they're turning out a whole lot. They think it's smart. I think a lot of them have the idea that if you work fast the rate will be cut. That would mean that they would have to work faster for the same money. I've never seen our rate cut yet, so I don't know whether it would happen or not. I have heard that it has happened in some cases though. . . . " (*F. J. Roethlisberger and William J. Dickson,* Management and the Worker, *Harvard University Press, Cambridge, Mass., 1939, p. 418.*)

Such practices modify but still do not eliminate the generally competitive pattern of American life. Athletics, politics, and business offer many competitive spectacles such as the World Series, the national presidential campaigns, and the struggle of the "independents" against the giants of the automobile industry. American men are encouraged to "make good," and neither the advantage of wealthy parents nor the drawback of being reared on the wrong side of the tracks completely absolves them from the pressure to get into the race for success. Women cannot rely on matchmaking parents to find a husband, and the sexual competition does not entirely cease when they are married since other women are still potential rivals. Even religion, often held to be the integrating force in society, functions on a competitive basis as numerous denominations compete for converts. In spite of efforts to moderate or limit the struggle, the average American is enmeshed in competitive activities from the time his mother purchases his first layette until he is buried in an expensive casket under an impressive headstone.

Effects of competition

Competition functions as one method of allocating scarce rewards. Other methods are possible. We might ration goods on some basis such as need, age, or social status. We might distribute scarce goods by lottery, or even divide them equally among all people. But each of these methods creates difficulties. Needs are highly debatable; any system of priorities will be disputed, for no group is likely to feel that another group is more deserving. Equal rewards to people who are unequal in needs, effort, or ability are certain to be disputed. Competition may be an imperfect rationing device, but it works and it eliminates a lot of arguments.

Another effect of competition is to shape the attitudes of competitors. When persons or groups compete, they normally develop unfriendly and unfavorable attitudes toward one another. Experiments have shown that when the situation is devised so that persons or groups cooperate in pursuit of a common goal, friendly attitudes are encouraged. When they meet under conditions which they consider competitive and frustrating, unfavorable attitudes and unflattering stereotypes appear [Sherif, 1958]. It has often been observed that when racial or religious groups compete, racial and religious prejudices appear and flourish [Berry, 1965, pp. 304–309]. Competition and cooperation differ sharply in the social attitudes they foster in the individual.

Competition is widely praised as a means of ensuring that each person will be stimulated to his greatest achievement. This belief was confirmed some years ago by many studies which show that wherever competition is culturally encouraged, it usually increases productivity although it sometimes lowers the quality [Murphy et al., 1937, pp. 476–495]. This generalization seems to apply to organizations as well as to individuals. It is often noted that while the competition of many different religious denominations in the United States may have produced many sects and congregations too small to support their programs efficiently, this competition has also promoted a greater alertness and aggressiveness in American religious institutions. Visitors to Europe often comment on Europe's impressive but empty churches, and evidence shows that Americans attend church and participate in church activities in far higher proportion than do Europeans [Isambert, 1964; Gustaffson, 1965]. In universities, too, competition seems beneficial. A careful study of medical education concludes that competition has stimulated scientific productivity [Ben-David, 1960] This study compares the universities of France and England, where university education was highly centralized, with those of Germany, where the development of independent regional universities led to an intense competition for scientific prestige, favoring the rapid development of new discoveries. This finding is consistent with the experience of the Russians, who found

that competition between factories has increased production even though all the factories are part of the total Communist system. The Soviet Union has recently resurrected the profit system as a stimulus to productive efficiency, although the profits are not distributed to stockholders as they are in a capitalist system.

The stimulus of competition is, however, limited in at least three respects. First, people may decline to compete. Since competition requires that some must lose while all remain somewhat anxious and insecure, people try to protect themselves from its rigors. Businessmen develop monopolistic practices, set prices, and engage in collusive bidding; unions set work quotas, enforce promotion through seniority, and limit union membership; farmers want price protection; teachers want seniority salary schedules; practically every group promotes many competition-limiting arrangements.

Furthermore, many persons simply withdraw from competition whenever they lose too regularly. In singing the praises of competition, many people overlook the important fact that although competition stimulates those who win fairly often, it discourages those who nearly always lose. The slow learner in the classroom, the athletic "dub" on the playground, the adolescent who fails to draw the interest of the opposite sex—such persons usually quit trying, for the pain of repeated failure becomes unendurable. They withdraw from competition in these areas, having decided that the activity isn't worthwhile. There is even experimental evidence that repeated failures not only dampen one's willingness to compete, but may even impair one's actual ability to compete [Hurlock, 1927; Vaughn, 1936; Winslow, 1944]. It appears that repeated failures will fill a person with such a sense of incompetence and such an overwhelming expectation of failure that he is unable to use his abilities to good advantage. Success or failure become self-perpetuating. There is ample experimental evidence that feelings of self-confidence and expectations of success will improve performance [Schwartz and Tangri, 1965; Coleman, 1966, pp. 319–325]. Even the expectations of other people have been found to affect one's ability to perform well [Rosenthal and Jacobson, 1968]. It is not surprising that repeated failures destroy both the willingness and the ability to compete. It may be that for every genius whom competition has stimulated to great achievement, there are a hundred or a thousand shiftless failures whom competition has demoralized.

A second limitation is that competition seems to be stimulating in only some kinds of activity. Where the task is simple and routine, competition is followed by the greatest gains in output; as the task becomes more intricate and the quality of work more important, competition is less helpful. In intellectual tasks, not only is the production of the cooperative group greater, but their work is of higher quality than that of the group whose members are competing with one another [Deutsch, 1949]. The nature of work in today's world is steadily shifting away from the kinds of work where competition between individuals is most beneficial. Competition between groups in technical or intellectual tasks seems to be stimulating, but within the group, cooperation appears to be more stimulating than competition.

A third limitation upon competition is its tendency to turn into conflict. To accede peacefully while a coveted reward is claimed by a more skillful competitor is not easy, and the rules of competition are often breached by a resort to conflict.

CONFLICT

The conflict process is little praised but widely practiced. It develops whenever a person or group seeks to gain a reward not by surpassing other competitors, but by preventing them from effectively competing. It is formally defined as the process of *seeking to obtain rewards by eliminating or weakening the competitors*. A murder or beating, a threat, a law passed to injure a competing group, a "gentleman's agreement" to exclude Jewish or black home buyers—these are a few of many conflict devices. In its most extreme form, conflict leads to the total annihilation of opponents as when the Romans destroyed Carthage and exterminated its inhabitants, or as when American settlers exterminated many tribes of American Indians. In less violent forms, conflict may be directed toward displacing an opponent from effective competition by getting him fired, getting the building inspector to condemn his place of business, smearing his reputation, or any one of many devices men use to get their competitors out of the way.

Group interest rather than personal relationships determines conflict alignments.

In recent years intellectual competition between differing schools of thought has been replaced by conflict on many university campuses. Strikes have been declared, buildings occupied, administrators held hostage, and bombs thrown in an effort to force acquiescence to the protester's point of view. There are even a few instances where professors have led students in shouting down a campus speaker or where academic conferences were paralyzed by a faction's refusal to allow scheduled speakers to be heard. This tendency to replace brain power with lung power is one more illustration of the tendency for competition to turn into conflict

Conflict between individuals may involve intense personal animosities, while group conflict, the type of greatest interest to sociologists, is highly impersonal. By this we mean that group loyalties and needs take precedence over individual feelings. Failure to understand this distinction often leads to the mistaken assumption that peace between nations is simply the result of good feeling between the individuals who compose the nations. Many Norwegians were shocked to see that some German children whom they cared for as refugees after World War I repaid their generosity by returning as German conquerors in World War II. Actually the apparent ingratitude should not have been a surprise since the German invasion of Norway was the result of conflict between nations in which individual feelings were irrelevant. This observation is borne out by the frequent shifts in power alignments in international conflict. Germans and Italians were enemies in World War I and allies in World War II, not because personal feelings had changed but because the national interest was differently defined. Group interests rather than personal relationships determine conflict alignments, as is shown by the speed with which our German and Japanese enemies in World War II became our allies when the "cold war" with the Soviet Union began. Friendships across boundary lines may help to promote joint activities, but it is a mistake to regard personal relationships as the solution to problems of world peace. Individuals usually find their role in group conflict by reference to the groups to which they belong. When conflict breaks out—a war, a strike, a boycott, a legislative battle—the individual either fights for his group or is branded as a traitor. In such a situation his feelings about friends on the other side have less weight than his obligations to his group.

It can even be argued that conflict is so constant a part of the social fabric as to be a "normal" pattern which is a part of the expected way of life. Thus a study of Italian peasant communities [Lopreato and Salzman, 1968] argues that it is a mistake to assume that the prevailing pattern is one of harmony. Rather than studying these communities according to a consensus model emphasizing social integration, attachment to the soil, personal contentment, and restraint, Lopreato and Salzman argue that one could just as well use a conflict model emphasizing social conflict, dislike of the land, and jealousies and resentments between individuals. They see conflict—sometimes open and active and sometimes hidden and temporarily dormant—as a normal aspect of social interaction.

The cumulative nature of conflict

Once begun, the conflict process is hard to stop. Since each aggressive act inspires a still more hostile retaliation, the conflict process tends to grow more bitter as it proceeds. Grievances are told and retold within each group and hostile attitudes are intensified. Each group develops a set of moral sanctions which justify a chain of even more savage retaliations.

The atrocities in conflict are often mistakenly attributed to the sadism or brutality of the individuals who commit them. Yet most of the atrocities in group conflict are committed by ordinary people in an extraordinary situation. The conflict process often places people in roles where they *must* be brutal. Steinbeck's *The Moon is Down* [1942] pictures an intelligent, humane German commander of forces occupying a Norwegian town, who is forced into brutal acts of reprisal to keep the town under control. Under some battle conditions prisoners who can't be cared for must be slaughtered. In an earlier era of labor-management warfare, the union would not allow strikebreakers to "lose" the strike for them, while management would not allow strikers to close down the plant. Each, in fulfilling his role, was forced into acts of brutality and violence.

But the extremes of conflict cannot be understood unless we recognize that the individual, committing the most indescribable acts of brutality, is supported by his group. He sees his act, not as wanton inhumanity, but as a moral necessity. During the range wars of the American West, the cattlemen who harassed, threatened, burned out, and in some cases murdered the settlers did not see themselves as greedy tyrants, withholding land from its legal claimants; they saw themselves as embattled patriots who had fought Indians, drought, and plague to build up a country and a way of life which a horde of greedy scum and conniving politicians wished to steal from them [Dale, 1930, chap. 9; Wellman, 1939, chaps. 35 and 36; Smith, 1967]. To understand why normal people can commit gruesome atrocities in conflict, we must understand how the group provides the sense of righteousness which sanctions such actions.

Conflict defines issues

Until the Supreme Court outlawed racial segregation in the public schools, there was much talk about brotherhood but no real decision as to whether black people were to have equal rights in American society. Since the Supreme Court decision, conflict has developed in many formerly peaceful areas and has increased the social distance between whites and blacks. The issue can no longer be buried under platitudinous talk; conflict forces us to face issues and make decisions. The immediate effect of the conflict unleashed by the court decision may have been to shatter many peaceful relationships. The long-run effect, sociologists

suspect, will be to reduce both discrimination and prejudice and eventually increase cooperative relationships between whites and blacks in our society.

In this respect group conflict may be compared to the effect of fever in the human body—costly and dangerous, but calling attention to deep-seated tensions which must be relieved if health is to be maintained. Just as the treatment of fever goes beyond symptoms to the cause of the difficulty, so the effective handling of conflict goes beyond merely maintaining order and seeks to treat the basic disturbance. Any tendency to ignore controversial issues or to paper over differences might be compared to the tendency to ignore such symptoms of ill health.

Conflict forces a facing of social issues and polarizes our attitudes towards them. The moderates are pushed, distrusted, and attacked by both sides and eventually forced to make a choice. The end result of the conflict is that the issues are resolved, at least for a time, in a fairly definite manner. The fact that the moderate is forced to take a definite position means that he has to assume responsibility instead of simply standing on the sidelines and deploring violence. At the end of the Middle Ages when men were being slaughtered because of religious differences, the moderates who piously deplored fanaticism were driven to a definite program—the separation of church and state—so that religious differences might be tolerated. In present racial controversies the moderate is pushed into active support of integration because of his commitment to orderly legal processes. One sociologist cites an example arising from the school desegregation conflict in Little Rock, Arkansas:

A distinguished religious leader from that community said to me this summer, "You know, while it was bad, maybe it was not a total loss. There is much more intelligent understanding of the responsibilities of citizenship now. People of the moderate or middle group have come to realize that they do not have the privilege of sitting on the sidelines and letting the radicals at the two ends determine the outcomes. They had to learn that ultimately they had to get in there and get their hands dirty with the problem. They had to see that they were being made the testing place for the whole South, and that when the chips were down they had to choose between the law and chaos. Maybe," he said, "we had to learn that, and it took the crisis to teach it to us." (*Dan W. Dodson, "The Creative Role of Conflict Re-examined,"* Journal of Intergroup Relations, *1:5–12, Winter, 1959–1960.*)

The disintegrative effects of conflict

Conflict disrupts social unity Conflict is a highly disturbing way of settling issues. Strikes may idle thousands of men and acres of costly machinery; marital conflicts wreck many families; racial and religious conflicts may prevent communities from facing their problems in a united spirit; universities have been so disrupted and public support so eroded by recent conflicts that some scholars fear that the survival of the university may be threatened [Nisbet, 1971]. As the ultimate example, atomic war now threatens the total destruction of humanity. Even when conflict achieves a new equilibrium, the price may be very great. The Thirty Years' War, 1618 to 1648, established the principle of religious toleration among German states, but it also reduced the German population by at least one-third, and much of the cultivated land became wilderness.

Internal conflict disrupts group unity Conflict within a group makes it hard for members to agree on group goals or to cooperate in pursuit of them. At any moment, in several of our states, one of the major political parties is split into warring factions, giving the other party a fine chance to win the next election. It was often claimed that France fell to Germany so easily in 1940 be-

cause the French people were so divided into conflicting factions that they were unable to unite against the enemy. Hitler confidently expected that the United States, with its heterogeneous population, would also be so riven with internal conflicts as to be unable to wage a united battle. This was one of his more costly misjudgments!

The integrative effects of conflict

Internal conflicts are sometimes ultimately integrative A limited amount of internal conflict may indirectly contribute to group interaction. Interests and viewpoints within a group shift from time to time; new policies and new leadership may be needed. An occasional contest within a group may keep its leadership alert and its policies up to date, whereas a suppression of internal conflicts may allow disastrous lags and explosive discontents to accumulate. Coser analyzes the role of conflict in promoting unity as follows:

In loosely structured groups and open societies, conflict, which aims at a resolution of tension between antagonists, is likely to have stabilizing and integrative functions for the relationship. By permitting immediate and direct expression of rival claims, such social systems are able to readjust their structures by eliminating the sources of dissatisfaction. The multiple conflicts which they experience may serve to eliminate the causes for dissociation and to reestablish unity. These systems avail themselves, through the toleration and institutionalization of conflict, of an important stabilizing mechanism. (*Lewis A. Coser,* The Functions of Social Conflict, *The Free Press of Glencoe, Ill., Chicago, 1956, p. 153.*)

External conflict tends to integrate the group Conflict with another group provides the members with an external outlet for their hostilities and resentments, and thus siphons off a lot of internal tensions. External conflict compels each member either to cooperate loyally or to get out. Simmel, a very perceptive early analyst of social conflict, defines the alternatives in these words:

If a political party which unifies many different directions of interest is pushed into a decisive and one-sided position of conflict, an occasion for secession results. In such situations, there are only two alternatives—either to forget internal counter currents or to bring them to unadulterated expression by expelling certain members. . . . The group in a state of peace can permit antagonistic members within it to live with one another in an undecided situation because each of them can go his own way and avoid collisions. A state of conflict, however, pulls the members so tightly together and subjects them to such a uniform impulse that they must completely get along with or completely repel one another. This is the reason why war with the outside is sometimes the last chance for a state ridden with inner antagonisms to overcome these antagonisms, or else to break up definitely. (*Georg Simmel,* Conflict, *tr. by Reinhard Bendix, The Free Press of Glencoe, Ill., Chicago, 1955, pp. 92–93.*)

External conflict also unifies the group through the imposition and acceptance of tighter controls than are normally accepted. The nation at war allows its business life to be completely directed toward national objectives in a way that would be unendurable in time of peace. The labor union gives "no-strike" pledges and accepts work rules which it would resist in peacetime. All groups tend to build bureaucratic structures and to centralize authority when faced by the need to organize resistance to an enemy.

While external conflict separates a group from its enemies, it also promotes federations or alliances with other groups. The phrase, "politics makes strange bedfellows," expresses the tendency to seek out allies in times of conflict even though they might be unacceptable in time of peace.

Effects of conflict

Integrative effects

Defines issues
Leads to a resolution of issues
Increases group cohesion
Leads to alliances with other groups
Keeps groups alert to members' interests

Disintegrative effects

Increases bitterness
Leads to destruction and bloodshed
Leads to intergroup tension
Disrupts normal channels of cooperation
Diverts members' attention from group
  objectives

Internal conflict disrupts group unity.

Our disdain for communism did not keep us from being effective allies with Russia in World War II; when the cold war developed, our rapid rapprochement with Germany and Japan showed that alliance is based on mutual interest, not mutual affection. Wars and threats of war have unquestionably encouraged the growth of political states and governmental institutions from the earliest tribal alliance to the United Nations. War forces a nation into coordinated activity, stimulates inventions, and inspires heroic sacrifices. Wars have settled issues: Through war the Italian peninsula became a unified nation; the Mexican War ended controversy over American colonization of the Southwest; World War II appears to have ended efforts for territorial expansion of

Japan and Germany. By settling issues, wars often clear the way for cooperative action. Conflict thus performs an associative as well as a divisive function and may be considered in some ways an integrative factor in social life.

ALTERNATIVES TO CONFLICT

The conflict process may fulfill useful functions, but at so great a cost that man often seeks to avoid it. Conflict is often avoided through some form of three other processes, *accommodation, assimilation,* and *amalgamation.*

Accommodation

It really threw me when my folks got a divorce right after I was graduated. I never thought much about my parents' love life; I guess I just took them for granted. Our home always seemed to me about like most others. At graduation, they came and beamed, gave me graduation gifts, met my friends, and all that. Then Dad took me aside and said that he and Mom were calling it quits. He said that they had bugged each other for years but had stuck it out to give me a proper home. Now that I would be on my own, they were going to separate.

Looking back on it now, I can remember little things that they let slip, but at the time I never noticed anything. They kept it pretty well covered up.

The above story, adapted from a student's life history in the authors' files, is an example of accommodation, a *process of developing temporary working agreements between conflicting individuals or groups.* It develops when persons or groups find it necessary to work together despite their hostilities and differences. Accomodation may be short-lived, or it may persist for centuries. No real settlement of issues is reached; each group retains its own goals and viewpoints, but

arrives at an "agreement to disagree" without fighting and perhaps to resume peaceful interaction. It is what Sumner [1907] called "antagonistic cooperation."

Accommodation replaces conflict with peaceful interaction without fully settling basic issues, but it allows hostilities to subside while more friendly attitudes may grow from this peaceful interaction. This is illustrated in a Gallup poll showing that, whereas in 1942, the adjectives which Americans most frequently picked to describe Germans were "war-like," "hard-working," "cruel," "treacherous," and "intelligent," by 1961 the list had changed to "hard-working," "intelligent," "progressive," "practical," and "brave"—a much more favorable list [Associated Press, Apr. 26, 1961]. The accommodation process obviously affects people's attitudes and behavior. Accommodation takes a number of forms. Some are deliberately planned and formally negotiated; others arise as unplanned products of group interaction.

Displacement Displacement is the process of suspending one conflict by replacing it with another. A classic example is the use of war or the threat of war to end internal conflicts and bring national unity. It is a standard stratagem of dictators and not unknown among democracies.

Finding a scapegoat is a favorable displacement technique. The term refers to an ancient Hebrew ceremony in which the sins of the people were symbolically heaped upon a goat which was driven into the wilderness. Unpopular minorities often become scapegoats. Anti-Semitism has long been used to deflect criticism and to unite conflicting groups in blaming Jews for all the ills of the society. In the newly independent countries, all the nation's problems may be blamed upon the remaining "colonial influences." The true powers and actions of the scapegoat are of little consequence; what matters is that a ruling group may be able to avert a possible attack upon itself by diverting popular hostility to the scapegoat.

Institutionalized release of hostility In many societies there are some institutionalized provisions for release of hostilities and tensions. Some primitive tribes regulated combat in a manner designed to express aggression, maintain "honor," and yet avoid destructive warfare. Warner [1931] describes an elaborate pattern of ritualistic warfare wherein Murngin tribes in Australia went through involved ceremonial combat in which, though nobody actually got hurt, a lot of hostility could be worked off. Then these rituals closed with a joint ceremonial dance expressing the renewed union and solidarity of the tribes. The Royal Copenhagen Procelain Works, instead of junking the imperfect pieces, takes them to the Tivoli amusement park, where it collects a fee from people who are willing to pay for the privilege of smashing the rejects. It seems that "busting things up" serves to release hostility and tension.

Perhaps our spectator sports, especially the contact sports like football, hockey, boxing, and wrestling would be examples of opportunities for the institutionalized release of hostility in our society. Ceremonials and feast days, orgies and religious experiences of various kinds may also serve to release tensions or provide catharsis for hostilities and thus ease the pressures toward conflict. Karl Marx was quite correct in holding that believers in a biblical devil, heaven, and Christian forgiveness would be slow to join in class warfare.

Superordination In some families one member totally and ruthlessly dominates the others. Some group conflicts end in the total defeat and submission of one group to the other. A war may "end" with the defeated people continuing resistance through guerilla warfare, assassination, sabotage, and noncooperation, thus continuing the con-

flict. Or they may accept defeat, submit, and make the best of it, as did Germany and Japan after World War II.

Superordination is likely to be accepted only when the parties are so unequal in power that resistance seems useless or impossible. When the subordinate group gains more power, the superordinate group must either relax its rule or risk a revolt. As Germany and Japan recovered from wartime devastation, the United States relaxed its rule rather than face growing resistance, while Russia's stern rule over conquered peoples provoked revolts in East Berlin, Hungary, and Poland, and seething resentment throughout her "colonies."

Conflict between two parties may sometimes be ended by their forced submission to a third party. History is crowded with instances. After Athens and Sparta had exhausted themselves, Macedonia conquered both. Only English rule brought peace between the Scottish clans. Most empires grew by picking off neighbors who were fighting among themselves.

Today the collapse of empires and the end of colonial rule in many areas is followed by the reappearance of local conflicts. The Near East peoples resumed ancient conflicts after the disintegration of the Ottoman (Turkish) Empire. Revolts, conflicts, and tribal war have plagued many African states since their independence. It is uncertain how soon stable national governments will be possible for such areas.

Compromise When all the parties are powerful enough so that none of them relish the prospect of conflict, they may compromise their differences. Compromise is a form of accommodation in which each party accepts less than its full goal in order to avoid or end conflict. Each normally makes concessions according to its relative power, with the more powerful party making the fewer concessions.

Since a compromise leaves all parties

somewhat dissatisfied, the compromise agreements are likely to be honored only so long as the respective power balance remains unchanged. As soon as either group gains in respective power, it is likely to press for a revision of the compromise, threatening renewed conflict if its demands are refused. During prosperous times, when the employer can scarcely fill his orders, the union will press for a more favorable contract; during a recession, when orders are fewer and stockrooms are full, the employer seizes the strategic moment to seek the revisions he desires. Politics may be seen as a continual round of shifting power positions and changing compromises. Politicians are often accused of dishonesty because of their compromising; yet without such compromises between the conflicting demands of many voting groups, democracy would become chaos.

Frequently the conflict has been so bitter and feelings so hostile that the parties are unable to reach a compromise. Several third-party techniques are often helpful in breaking such deadlocks.

Third-party roles in compromise The techniques of conciliation, mediation, and arbitration use the services of a third party to help reach a settlement. *Mediation* and *conciliation* are essentially the same, with the third party encouraging the disputants to keep talking, suggesting solutions, and using his own powers of persuasion. In *arbitration*, a third party hears their arguments and makes a decision, knowing that the contestants have already agreed to accept it. The third party may offer suggestions which the disputants could not offer without losing face, and he may be able to find new approaches to end a deadlock. Even if he is given the power of arbitration, his success depends mainly on his ability to gauge the relative power positions and suggest settlements fairly close to what might be obtained through all-out conflict.

Toleration In some conflicts victory is either impossible or unbearably costly, and compromise is unendurable; some values may be too deeply cherished to compromise. In these circumstances the participants sometimes discover that agreement may not be absolutely necessary. In toleration, people accept each other's right to differ without demanding a settlement. Toleration is an agreement to disagree peaceably. Religious conflict is a classic example of this situation. In Europe at the time of the Reformation, both Protestants and Catholics were positive that they had the "true" version of the Christian faith which should be accepted by all men. Neither group was willing to compromise, and in spite of severe conflict, neither group could destroy the other. Adjustment has been made on the basis of toleration; each church ceases to persecute other churches while continuing to hold that these other churches are in error.

Why was religious toleration so long in developing? Partly because toleration requires a frame of mind in which people are willing to grant others the right to be different; ethnocentrism is the enemy of toleration. Furthermore, toleration is possible only for those matters on which agreement is not absolutely necessary. As long as church and state were combined, rejection of the established church automatically became treason to the state; not until their separation could one worship as he pleased and still be a loyal citizen. Catholic and Protestant neighbors may disagree on many religious questions without the disagreement impairing their interaction as neighbors, friends, or fellow workers. If they intermarry, some religious differences may still be open to toleration, but their interaction as husband and wife will absolutely require agreement upon a number of issues. Our rather wide use of toleration today rests not only upon a considerable readiness to tolerate differences but also upon a social structure in which many areas of peaceful interaction are open to groups who differ bitterly upon other matters.

Assimilation Whenever groups meet, some mutual interchange or diffusion of culture takes place. Even groups who strenuously seek to prevent such diffusion, such as the modern Amish or the ancient Hebrews, do not fully succeed in protecting their culture from all cultural interchange. The Old Testament is filled with exhortations to avoid contact with the "heathen" peoples, and of their failures to heed this warning. The story of Samson was an object lesson on the folly of involvement with foreign women.

This process of *mutual cultural diffusion through which persons and groups come to share a common culture* is called *assimilation*. It is always a two-way process with each group contributing varying proportions of the eventual blend, depending upon respective group size, prestige, and other factors.

The assimilation process is nicely illustrated in the Americanization of our European immigrants. Arriving in great numbers between 1850 and 1913, many of them settled in immigrant colonies in the Northern cities. Within these "ethnic colonies"—Little Italy, Little Poland, and so on—they practiced much of their native European culture while absorbing some of the American culture. The immigrant parents often sought to transmit their European culture to their children, while the children generally sought to become American as rapidly as possible. These children very often rejected the "old world" patterns as bluntly and emphatically as possible. This conflict often caused parental anguish, family disorganization, and loss of parental control, so that many second-generation immigrants became confused, rebellious, and delinquent. As the third generation matured, the assimilation difficulties generally subsided; Americanization became fairly complete,

and the ethnic colony disappeared as the descendants scattered over city and suburb [Thomas and Znaniecki, 1927].

The third and following generations are now secure, and can afford to remember their ethnic history. Thus there is a "third-generation return," in which these fully assimilated Americans recall with pride their ethnic heritage and join in recording and preserving some parts of it [Hansen, 1952; Bender and Kagiwada, 1968].

Assimilation reduces group conflicts by blending differing groups into larger, culturally homogeneous groups. The bitter riots against the Irish and the discriminations against the Scandinavians in the United States [Higham, 1955] have disappeared as assimilation has erased the group differences and blurred the sense of separate group identity. Anything which binds people into a larger group will tend to reduce rivalry and conflict between them. This is strikingly illustrated by an experiment which involved the experimental formation of different groupings at a summer camp [Sherif and Sherif, 1953]. The boys were all from the same community and were similar in religion, social-class status, age, and national background. For the first experimental period ("integrative") they were treated as a single group, and they showed no signs of incipient social conflict. In the second experimental ("segregative") period they were divided into two groups who were housed separately and encouraged to develop separate programs of activities. The groups took the names of "Red Devils" and "Bull Dogs." Group antagonisms quickly developed, and physical violence between the groups reached the point where it had to be suppressed by the adult leaders. Personal relationships followed the patterns of group division, as is shown in Table 22.

This experiment is often taken to indicate that conflict tends to develop whenever group identity is recognizable. Perhaps a better interpretation is that conflict and

TABLE 22

Choices of friends at end of integrative period and at end of segregative period in an experiment on groups and conflict

Choices made by		Choices received by	
		in-group, percent	out-group, percent
End of integrative period	*Eventual Red Devils*	35	65
	Eventual Bull Dogs	35	65
End of segregative period	*Red Devils*	95	5
	Bull Dogs	88	12

Interpretation: When, at the end of the first phase of the experiment (the "integrative" period—see text), the boys were divided into Red Devil and Bull Dog groups, the boys in each group chose 35 percent of their friends from among their own group and 65 percent from the other group. At the end of the second ("segregative") phase of the experiment, during which the boys interacted only with members of their own group, they were again asked to select their friends. This time they selected most of their friends (95 percent and 88 percent) from within their own group, and very few (5 percent and 12 percent from the other group.
Source: Adapted from Muzafer Sherif and Carolyn Sherif, Groups in Harmony and Tension, *Harper & Row, Publishers, Inc., New York, 1953, p. 268.*

separation are likely whenever differences are emphasized. Japanese-Americans, by contrast, are a group which have become highly assimilated although physical differences are easily recognizable. Their acceptance of American middle-class values and their dispersion away from ethnic enclaves have operated to make their cultural similarity to other Americans more important than their physical differences.

Cultural assimilation removes many of the stimuli for conflict even when recognizable physical differences are present. Conversely, as in the case of Catholics and Protestants in Northern Ireland, physical similarity will not insure peace when groups cherish deep-seated cultural antagonisms exacerbated by present clashes of economic and political interests [Holden, 1969; Elmen, 1971].

Marginality The concept of *marginality* was first developed by Park in the course of his study of the assimilation process. He defined the *marginal man* as "a cultural hybrid, a man living and sharing intimately in the cultural life and traditions of two dis-

tinct peoples. . . . He was a man on the margin of two cultures and two societies. . . ." [1928, p. 892]. The second-generation immigrant is the classic example, described in detail in Stonequist's *The Marginal Man* [1937]. In 1940, Cuber suggested extending the term to cover any people "who occupy a peripheral role between any two differentiated but largely exclusive institutions, culture complexes or other cultural segments" [1940, p. 58]. Shibutani further defined the concept in 1961 in saying that "some men are marginal in that they stand on the border between two or more social worlds, but are not accepted as full participants in either" [1961, p. 275]. A great many people—the immigrant, those who are rapidly mobile in status, the children of overseas American personnel, the children born of a racial or ethnic intermarriage, the converts to (or from) a dogmatic religious faith—are to some degree marginal. Marginality generally carries feelings of confusion and anxiety, greater possibilities of deviation from group norms, and perhaps an "identity crisis" for the individual. In a society with numerous subcultures, practically everyone is a core member of some subcultures while marginal to some others [Arnold, 1970]. Marginality in any kind or degree is a measure of incomplete assimilation to a particular group or culture.

Amalgamation *Amalgamation* is the biological interbreeding of two groups until they have become one. Thus ended the conflicts of the Angles with the Saxon invaders and later, of the Anglo-Saxons with the Norman invaders. When it is a limited and disapproved interbreeding between racial groups, it is called *miscegenation*, a value-laden word implying an improper mixing of genes. Whenever racial or ethnic groups meet, some degree of "miscegenation" nearly always follows, often with painful consequences for the persons born from these unions. An incomplete amalgamation generally creates a status system where status is measured by blood "purity" as in Central America and parts of South America, where Spanish descent carries status value. When amalgamation becomes wholesale, the separate groups and their attendant group conflicts soon disappear.

Boundary maintenance

The importance of assimilation and amalgamation rests primarily in their elimination of boundary lines as two groups, formerly distinct, assume a common identity. Such boundary lines are a major aspect of social life, and we devote a great deal of energy to their establishment, maintenance, and modification. Questions such as the following are concerned with boundaries: Can a true believer attend services in another church? Do good girls have premarital sexual relations? Can a college athlete play semiprofessional baseball during the summer? Should foreign students be allowed to pursue an occupation in the United States?

Can laymen conduct church services? Is racial integration really desirable?

Any answer to these and similar questions will either enlarge or restrict the mem-

Sometimes existing boundary devices may be challenged.

bership of specific social groups and hence is a "boundary line" type of issue. National states indicate their territorial boundaries by markers, fences, and other evidence of the extent of their claims. Social groups without territorial limits face the necessity of establishing some type of social boundary lines which will separate their members from the rest of the society. For many groups a language, dialect, or specialized argot serves as a boundary which separates the members from outsiders: "If he doesn't speak our language, he certainly can't be one of us." Uniforms are also a device for separating members of one group from the rest of society, a practice found among clergy, policemen, nurses, and soldiers, among others. Sometimes formal identifying insignia such as the Indian caste marks are utilized. Frequently there is no overt indication of group membership, and only a subtle sense of "belonging," related to group standards of conduct, is all that separates the in-group from the outsiders.

Groups need not only to establish definite

boundaries but also to convince their members that the boundaries are important. Ethnocentrism usually develops and assists in this task by reassuring us about the virtue of our group and the shortcomings of others. Intense nationalistic indoctrination may build a patriotism which says that any weakening of national sovereignty through international agreements would be fatal. Or a religious body may seek to convince its members that it is the only true church. On a less formal basis, small suburbs may support a myth about the vices and high taxes of the big city as compared with the virtue and low cost of the suburb—a myth which has increasingly little basis in fact.

Loyalty to group boundaries is supported by sanctions which reward those loyal to the group, punish members who deviate from group boundary norms, and keep out those the group wishes to exclude. Rewards may include access to employment through union membership, the prestige of membership in an exclusive club, the congenial companionship of a friendship clique, and many others. Punishments, or negative sanctions, consist largely of the denial of the rewards of group membership. One cannot hold certain jobs without joining the union; one who persists in bringing "inappropriate" guests to the club may be asked to resign; a friend who betrays confidences soon receives none.

People wishing to hurdle the boundaries into a group often seek to lower the boundaries, while those already safely inside are intent upon maintaining them. For example, generations of graduate students have complained about the relatively useless foreign-language requirement for the Ph.D. degree, while those holding the degree have been slow to allow candidates to earn the degree any more easily than they themselves did. The power of exclusion is one of the rewards of group membership. By keeping others out, we assert our own superior status as

social arbiters and emphasize the gulf which separates us from those of less esteem. Whatever the basis used for acceptance or rejection, it quickly becomes a trait which distinguishes one group from another. Those rejected by the dominant group establish their own sense of identity and utilize their own epithets to stigmatize those who have excluded them. Thus to the gentile the Jew is a "kike" or a "yid," but the Jew may retaliate by referring to gentiles as "goy" or "shkotzim" or may use uncomplimentary phrases like "shicker as a goy" (drunk as a gentile). Such epithets set boundaries, since they convey a notion of relative status as well as of difference.

Social boundary lines are constantly shifting and often complex. Is a factory worker with a home in the suburbs lower class or middle class? If a man leaves Judaism for Presbyterianism, is he still regarded as Jewish? Is the Filipino a Westerner or an Asiatic? Is the black army officer defined in terms of military rank or racial status? These and countless similar boundary definitions are constantly being reformulated as groups strive to increase their rewards, avoid penalties, and place themselves in a favorable position. Sometimes boundary determination is accomplished through formal means, as in the case of naturalization requirements or initiation ceremonies. In other cases there is a more informal process of acceptance and rejection which indicates group boundary lines in terms which are definite even though not defined in written documents. Sometimes the existing boundary maintenance devices may be challenged. Many current radicals consider it "oppressive" to demand the cultivation of middle-class speech and conduct norms as the price of admission into the middle class [Kampf, 1970]. Boundary maintenance devices may change, but boundary establishment and modification is a continuous social process [Mack, 1965].

SYSTEMIC LINKAGE

Just as nations need both territorial limits and international trade, so other groups which require boundaries also need some type of linkage with the rest of society. The absence of boundaries means that the group is swamped by the larger society, but the absence of relationship with other groups leads to isolation, stultification, lack of growth, and the attempt to perform functions for which the group itself is not fitted. Even bitterly hostile primitive tribes have sometimes recognized this fact by instituting a system of "silent barter" with their enemies. Since personal relationships were too bitter, no face-to-face contact took place, but each group would leave trade articles at a mutually understood spot and pick up the articles left by the other tribe.

Systemic linkage is defined by Loomis [1961, p. 16] as "the process whereby the elements of at least two social systems come to be articulated so that in some ways and on some occasions they may be viewed as a single system." Even the Amish, a relatively isolated group, are linked to the rest of society by education, agricultural marketing, and the payment of taxes. For other groups the linkages are usually far more numerous. The rural village is linked to the urban metropolis by the market economy, by an educational system which sends teachers into the community and takes advanced students out, by churches and lodges which maintain contact with parent organizations, and by many other links. Like the Amish, some groups try to reduce systemic linkage to the minimum because they see in it a threat to boundary maintenance. Other groups promote such linkage deliberately, such as the church which belongs to an ecumenical organization, the labor union which sends a lobbyist to the capitol, and the chamber of commerce which looks for new markets for local industries. The methods vary, but even as groups seek to protect their separate identity by boundary maintenance, they are also impelled to seek links by which they can establish a relationship to the rest of society.

Boundary maintenance and systemic linkage use all the other social processes we have described and in this sense are in a different category. They are included in this chapter because the operation of conflict, cooperation, accomodation, assimilation, and amalgamation always influences both the boundaries which separate us and the links by which we are connected to others.

SUMMARY

Earlier scholars argued over the inherent superiority of competition, cooperation, or conflict; sociologists today study the manner in which these and other social processes contribute to social life. These processes are found in all societies, although there is great variation in emphasis. *Cooperation* may be personal or impersonal, deliberate or symbiotic in character. Primary groups demand highly personalized cooperation; secondary-group cooperation is found in many organized social groups as well as in a network of economic relationships which use the motive of individual gain to draw men into essentially cooperative activities.

Competition serves the function of allocating scarce rewards among the competitors. It has the additional function of stimulating both individual and group activity in a manner to increase the total productivity of the competitors, but it also discourages the further efforts of those who regularly fail. Experimental studies show that both cooperation and competition are related to the values of the culture. When the culture legitimizes competition, a competitive system often, but not always, increases the rate of productive activity while quality of work often suffers. Competition is unstable and frequently yields either to cooperation or to conflict.

Conflict develops when attention shifts from the contest itself to an effort to eliminate rivals. Group conflict may take place even when the members of the groups involved lack any personal animosity toward members of the opposing factions. Social conflict is frequently costly and disruptive, but it also has integrative functions. Conflict helps to define issues and bring about a new equilibrium of contending forces. Conflict between groups promotes unity within each group as members unite against the common enemy, and group conflict may lead to expanding alliances with other groups. Conflict may be ended in several ways. Conflicts may be *displaced* and the aggression directed at a new enemy. Conflicts may sometimes be ended or avoided through an *institutionalized release* of hostilities and aggressions through mock combat, festival and orgy, and other emotional outlets. Conflicts may be relieved, at least temporarily, through *accommodation,* which

takes several forms. *Superordination* consists in establishing uncontested rule over a weaker group. *Compromise* involves a limited surrender by all groups in order to end or avoid conflict. *Conciliators, mediators,* and *arbitrators* often aid in arranging compromises. Where compromise is unacceptable yet agreement not absolutely necessary, groups may use *toleration* as an alternative to conflict. Finally, when two groups have become *assimilated,* so that they share a common culture and common goals, they normally disappear as separate groups unless some visible indentification remains as a focus for conflict. *Marginality* applies to individuals who participate to some extent in two contrasting groups or cultures without being completely identified with either. *Amalgamation* is a biological fusion between two groups resulting in the elimination of distinctive physical characteristics.

Boundary maintenance is the process of preserving lines of distinction between groups and applies to every action which marks one either "in" or "out" of a specific group. *Systemic linkage* denotes the process by which groups avoid isolation while maintaining their separate identities.

Questions and projects

1. Are cooperation, competition, and conflict natural, instinctive, or automatic human responses, or must they be culturally acquired?

2. Why do you think the consumer cooperative has had such limited success in the United States? Will it succeed among the urban poor?

3. What examples of impersonal or symbiotic cooperation can be observed on the campus?

4. Discuss this proposition: "It is man's nature to want more than his fellows; competition is therefore firmly rooted in human instinct."

5. Under what conditions is competition an encouragement? When does it inhibit effort?

6. Why does competition often turn into conflict? Does social conflict always involve physical violence?

7. To what extent do friendly personal relations and mutual understanding serve to prevent conflict?

8. How is knowledge of the effects of conflict upon group solidarity sometimes used in international relations? In labor-management relations?

9. When homesteaders invaded the land of the cattlemen, conflict developed. Was there any practical possibility of avoiding that conflict?

10. Do decent and humane people ever take part

in atrocities? Why? How would most Americans, had they been socialized in Germany, have felt about the massacre of the Jews?

11. Why is accommodation always an unstable arrangement? What happens when the power balance shifts?

12. Why could toleration not have been used to avoid the Civil War, the cold war, or present racial conflicts?

13. What would be the problems or difficulties in solving the present racial crisis by amalgamation?

14. What boundary lines are maintained between those associated with a college and other residents of the local community? What types of systemic linkage exist between them?

15. What effect will the modernization of the garb of Roman Catholic nuns have on their group cohesion? Would the same comments apply to distinctive uniforms for students in girls' schools?

16. Find an example of a major disagreement on the campus or in a community. Trace the history of this controversy to the achievement of some accommodation pattern which resolved the crisis. What type of accommodation developed?

Suggested readings

Bender, Eugene L., and George Kagiwada: "Hansen's Law of Third-generation Return and the Study of American Religio-Ethnic Groups," *Phylon*, 29:360-370, Winter, 1960. Describes the tendency of the third generation to rediscover pride and interest in the ancestral culture.

Berry, Brewton: *Race and Ethnic Relations*, Houghton Mifflin Company, Boston, 1965. A very readable textbook in race relations using a social-process approach and with a good treatment of amalgamation and assimilation.

Bogardus, Emory S.: "The Long Trail of Cooperation," *Sociology and Social Research*, 31:54-62, September, 1946. A natural history of the process of cooperation.

*****Coser, Lewis A.:** *The Functions of Social Conflict*, The Free Press of Glencoe, Ill., Chicago, 1956. A study of the conflict process by a sociologist who believes it has functional values.

*****Gordon, Milton M.:** *Assimilation in American Life*, Oxford University Press, Fair Lawn, N.J., 1964. A sociological analysis of recent trends in the assimilation process together with a typography of various categories of assimilation.

International Sociological Association, in collaboration with **Jessie Bernard, T. H. Pear, Raymond Aron, and Robert C. Angell:** *The Nature of Conflict*, UNESCO, Paris, 1957. A sociological study of the conflict process, mainly with reference to war and international relations.

Lippit, Ronald: "The Process of Utilization of Social Research to Improve Social Practice," *American ·Journal of Orthopsychiatry*, 35:663-669, 1965. Reprinted in modified form in *****Arthur B. Shostak,** *Sociology in Action*, The Dorsey Press, Homewood, Ill., 1966, pp. 276-280. Discusses the relation of social research to social processes.

Mack, Raymond W.: "The Components of Social Conflict," *Social Problems*, 12:388-397, Spring, 1965. An eloquent statement from a sociologist who holds that conflict arises inevitably from the nature of social life, while boundary maintenance is a continuous social process.

Park, Robert E., and H. A. Miller: *Old World Traits Transplanted*, Harper & Brothers, New York, 1921. A classic treatment of the assimilation process.

Rosenthal, Robert and Lenore Jacobson: "Teacher Expectations for the Disadvantaged," *Scientific American*, April, 1968, pp. 16ff. Describes the effect of teacher expectations on academic performance.

Rubenstein, Richard E.: *Rebels in Eden*, Little, Brown and Company, Boston, 1970. A readable description of the history of violent conflict in American development.

*****Simmel, Georg:** *Conflict,* tr. by **Reinhard Bendix,** The Free Press of Glencoe, Ill., Chicago, 1955. A pioneer German sociologist's classic treatment of the functional nature of conflict.

Social power

I was assigned by a national magazine to do a story on the [Talmadge-George] campaign, but I soon discovered there wasn't going to be one. One of Senator George's supporters explained the situation to me:

"We used to re-elect the Senator every six years by getting in touch with about 100 of the right people in Georgia. When we did it this time, we discovered that those people had swung to Herman [Talmadge]. All that remains is for us to figure out who is going to give the bad news to Senator George." *(George E. McMillan,* Look, *July 5, 1960, p. 25.)*

Social power and power contests provide much of the drama of modern life. Every political campaign and every congressional debate is an exercise in the use of power. Every newspaper contains dozens of examples. Nearly every novel has a power contest of some sort as its theme. What is power and how it is manipulated?

THE NATURE OF SOCIAL POWER

Although social power has been variously defined by Weber [1946], Simmel [1959], Bierstedt [1950], Goldhamer and Shils [1939], Parsons [1963], and others, all definitions carry the idea of control over others. Power might be formally defined as the *ability to control the actions of other people, regardless of their wishes.* Power has at least three components: force, authority, and influence.

Force is the *use or threat of physical coercion.* It is illustrated by an invading army, by the ability of organized crime to prevent victims and witnesses from making complaints or giving testimony, or by the ability of bullying gangs to terrorize citizens or even fellow school children.

Authority is *an established right to make decisions and order the actions of others.* Sociologists have discussed the various types of authority. Weber, for example

[1946, pp. 196-252], sees three main types of authority: (1) *bureaucratic authority*, resting on formal office or rank (general, foreman, civil service officer); (2) *traditionalist authority*, resting on a belief in sacred norms and traditions which one must obey (husband, father, prince, priest); and (3) *charismatic authority*, the authority of an extraordinary person who is obeyed because of his charisma—his image of remarkable wisdom, saintliness, or invincibility (Christ, Joan of Arc, Napoleon, Franklin D. Roosevelt, Hitler). Authority and force are sometimes combined, as in a police force, army, or prison.

Influence is *the ability to affect the decisions and actions of others beyond any authority to do so.* The professor has authority to command certain work assignments and to assign grades; he has no authority to compel students to accept his opinions, but possibly he can influence them to do so. Influence rests partly upon respect, prestige, and affection and partly upon one's control over "facilities" which affect others. A newspaper publisher can be a valuable friend or a dangerous enemy; the corporation executive, school superintendent, or high-ranking officer can speed or slow down one's promotions; a member of the local aristocracy has "contacts" which can open many doors for a favored protégé. Great influence generally rests upon some combination of engaging personal qualities and a position from which one can affect the destiny of other people.

Authority and influence interact in reinforcing the position of the powerful; or one may undercut the other in reducing a person's power. Brim [1954] found that mothers who attributed high prestige to the role of doctors were more likely to follow the doctor's advice. Strodtbeck [1951] studied authority roles in the family by setting up situations in which the members have a difference of opinion and by then recording the interaction. He found that Navajo wives won 46 arguments to their husbands' 34, while Mormon wives lost 29 to 42. These figures show the differing roles of authority and influence of wives in these two subcultures.

Social power is easier to define than to measure. Sociologists have used three different models in an attempt to locate and measure social power [Rossi, 1957]. First, there is *potential power*—the power which is assumed to go with certain positions or situations in the community or the society. This is the "power elite" thesis of C. Wright Mills [1956]. The mayor presumably has more power than the city-hall janitor, and the chamber of commerce more than the teacher's club. Second, there is *reputed power*—the power ascribed to certain persons and groups by those who know the community [Form and Sauer, 1960; Preston, 1969]. Reputed power is determined by asking the question, "Who really runs things in this town?" of a number of people who know the town well. Finally, there is *decisional power*, as shown by observation of the decision-making process in operation [Fox, 1969; Bouma, 1970]. Observation of a power struggle as it takes place, with a detailed account of who did what and when, may reveal who is really in control of the situation.

Power has many degrees and forms, ranging from the tantrums of the small child to the armed mobilization of a great nation. This chapter will explore social power of five sorts: that of powerful individuals who are said to form an elite, of organized groups, of unorganized masses, of disruptive protest, and of law.

POWER OF THE ELITE

The power elite is composed of men whose positions enable them to transcend the ordinary environments of ordinary men and women; they are in positions to make decisions having major consequences. . . . For they are in command of the major hierarchies and organizations of modern society. They rule the big corporations. They run the machinery of the state and claim its prerogatives. They direct the military establishment. They occupy the strategic command posts of the social structure in which are now centered the effective means of the power and the wealth and the celebrity which they enjoy. (*C. Wright Mills, The Power Elite, Oxford University Press, Fair Lawn, N.J., 1956, pp. 3-4.*)

Every complex society has a quite small number of persons who are believed to have great power. Such a controlling group is called an *elite*. Membership in the elite is often inherited, but in some societies it may be acquired. Its bases vary. In ancient China, the elite was headed by the scholars who were experts in the Confucian classics, plus the large landowners and military leaders. In medieval Europe the elite was composed of the higher clergy and the landowning nobility. After the industrial revolution these elite were increasingly displaced by the business entrepreneurs whose rapidly growing wealth gained them entree into the elite group. In Soviet Russia, where the possessions of the landlords and the businessmen were confiscated and the clergy largely deprived of influence, a new elite has arisen composed of the artists, intellectuals, engineers, scientists, and top officials and administrators. In England when one speaks of "the Establishment," he refers to a few thousand persons of wealth and influence, mostly of noble or gentle birth, and educated mainly at Eton or Harrow and at Oxford or Cambridge. In the United States, "the Establishment" refers to the conventional society with all of its maintenance personnel (officials, legislators, judges, police, school administrators, and others who keep conventional society in operation).

The wealthy as an elite

One of the best-known efforts to describe an American elite is Ferdinand Lundberg's study [1937] of *America's 60 Families,* followed by *The Rich and the Super Rich* [1968]. Lundberg assumed that wealth brings power, usually exercised indirectly. While members of the sixty wealthiest families occasionally occupy important posts, most of their influence is wielded through their ability to appoint and control those who actually fill the offices. This power of the purse places business managers, politicians, college presidents, and bishops under the sway of the holders of great wealth. Corporations are controlled through the ownership of stock; contributions and benefactions keep the foundations, churches, and universities under control. Occasionally the great families quarrel, but through intermarriage and close social contact they usually develop a common viewpoint and act as a more or less unified group. Thus, according to Lundberg, wealth rules.

This picture, which may have been approximately true at the end of the nineteenth century, is almost certainly less true today. Great wealth today is often invested in many scattered investments and administered by professional experts rather than by the owners themselves. Political parties and philanthropic organizations are steadily growing less dependent upon a few large contributors as they cultivate a mass of small contributors.

A study of American wealth by *Fortune* magazine located 155 Americans worth $50 million or more, and estimated that there were about another hundred whom it failed to locate [Smith, 1957]. As one indication that these persons were powerful, this study noted that Philadelphia pursued a vigorous program of urban renewal while Boston for a time continued to decay; they attributed this contrast to a difference in attitude on the part of the two cities' millionaires. No doubt wealthy persons have disproportionate power; but the exact degree of this power is not easy to determine.

The knowledge elite

According to some scholars, there is a *knowledge elite*—a few dozen economists, political scientists, historians, sociologists, and free-lance intellectuals who are widely read by the decision makers in the United States [Kadushin, 1971]. Occasionally, they also reach a mass audience and exert a real influence upon events. An example of how much influence one knowledgeable person may have is seen in the changes adopted by the automobile industry after the publication of Ralph Nader's popular book *Unsafe at Any Speed* [1965]. A few irrefutable facts, effectively presented, led to a new federal law, with a new federal agency; and forced one of America's major industries to make substantial concessions. At this writing, he is bringing the same pressure to bear on government by subjecting the work of government bureaus to critical examination by a research staff known as "Nader's Raiders." One obscure young attorney, John Banzhaf, by getting his facts together and taking advantage of existing laws and rulings, forced the television industry to devote millions of dollars of free time to anticigarette messages. Beginning with no finances, authority, or influence, he worked "within the system" to effect significant change [Johnson, 1969; Page, 1970]. Individuals or groups who have the capacity to make effective factual analyses and to make strategic use of laws, rulings, courts, and publicity, can wield a very real power in society. Strategies are outlined in books such as Johnson's *How to Talk Back to Your Television Set* [1970]. The success with which a comparative handful of intellectuals aroused the nation to concern over the environment is an illustration that knowledge is power.

The executive elite

Another theory of the American elite concludes that strategic position is the prime source of power [Burnham, 1941; Mills, 1956]. According to this view, the structure of our society is based on a complex divison of labor which must be coordinated by a corps of expert managers. These highly paid executives are responsible for the smooth functioning of wealth-producing organizations, but they are not usually the principal owners of the enterprise they manage. Similarly, although they are responsi-

With a few exceptions, executive skill is transferable.

ble for supervising the services of scientists and technicians, they are not usually scientists themselves. Their skill lies in mastering the handling of organizations which channel the contributions of many different types of individuals toward a common goal. So strategic is their position that they often control the groups of which they are the nominal servants. Thus the typical great corporation is managed by a group of executives who own only a tiny fraction of the corporation's stock. While theoretically controlled by the stockholders who elect them, the managers tend in practice to become a self-perpetuating group whose actual control is unchallenged by stockholders as long as the flow of dividends is uninterrupted. Likewise, the most successful university president or foundation director is one who is able to "handle" his board of directors.

Executive skills are regarded as relatively independent of the context in which they operate; very different organizations may require the same type of coordination. With a few exceptions, executive skill is transferable. The same individual may rotate among responsible positions in military, political, industrial, or educational organizations. Governments often "draft" corporate executives for top executive posts, and business recruits many of its executives from government or university people. These executives associate together, move from one field to another, and generally select their own successors.

The executive elite have undoubted authority in the detailed control of their enterprises, while their influence is buttressed both by their strategic position and by personality traits which have caused them to be respected. Their power, however, is restricted by limitations on their right to determine policy and the requirement that they operate within institutional norms. The "rubber stamp" board of trustees may quickly dump an executive when a business starts to lose money, a school arouses public criticism, or a church suffers a fall in membership.

Mills viewed the corporation as either the base from which the executive elite originate or the goal toward which they are moving. He felt that their power meant that society becomes dominated by men primarily committed to a view of life expressed by a prominent executive in the immortal words, "What's good for General Motors is good for the country."[1] Mills made a strong case for the theory that executives who have had similar training, association, and outlook are often found in positions which involve decision making. There is no doubt that a profes-

sional managerial class has developed in the United States.

But many social scientists argue that the case for a ruling elite with a virtual monopoly of social power has not been proved [Rossi, 1956; Reissman, 1956; Dahl, 1958; Bell, 1958; Lowry, 1965, pp. xviii, xix; Miller, 1970, pp. 202, 275, 276]. These social scientists prefer to work in the more restricted field of local community studies and observational studies of the decision-making process, feeling that by accumulating a number of studies of these kinds they can eventually build a theory of power with a convincing factual foundation.

The community influentials

In recent years several sociologists have attempted to identify the people with unusual influence in particular American communities.[2] The usual technique is to select a group of people presumed to be well acquainted with a community and ask them for a list of the persons who are influential in that community. The people on the list are then interviewed in an attempt to narrow the field to a small number who appear to have the greatest power in community decision making. The final list is loaded with corporation executives, wealthy individuals of established social standing who are active in civic affairs, and lawyers associated with business interests. Politicians are seldom mentioned unless they are also prominent businessmen. Other professionals such as

---

[1]C. Wright Mills, *The Power Elite*, Oxford University Press, Fair Lawn, N.J., 1956, p. 168. For the context of Charles Wilson's statement, see "Conflict of Interest," *Time*, Jan. 26, 1953, p. 70.

[2]The major pioneer work in this field is Floyd Hunter, *Community Power Structure*, The University of North Carolina Press, Chapel Hill, 1953. A brief summary and analysis of these studies is found in Richard A. Schermerhorn, *Society and Power*, Random House, Inc., New York, 1961, pp. 88–92. A comparison of international elites is found in Delbert C. Miller, *International Community Power Structures: Comparative Studies of Four World Cities*, Indiana University Press, Bloomington, 1970. A general review of the role of elites in decision making is the focus of a series of articles edited by Terry N. Clark, *Community Structure and Decision-making: Comparative Analyses*, Chandler Publishing Co., San Francisco, 1968.

physicians, ministers, and educators form a tiny fraction of the total number of leaders and are usually classified toward the bottom of the list on a ranking of comparative influence. Labor leaders, mentioned in some communities and ignored in others, never form a substantial proportion of the community influentials.

The community influentials are thought to be the top of a power pyramid which determines whether any given project will receive community support. In some communities the survey evidence suggests that the fate of all major community proposals depends on the reaction of the same small group of influentials. Other communities may contain several power pyramids, including different individuals who are effective in different areas. The support of one group might be vital for a hospital-fund drive, of another group for passing a school-bond issue, and of still another group for the success of an urban redevelopment program [McKee, 1953; Kahn, 1970].

Community power appears to be exercised through determining the policies of community organizations. Organizational activity is a time-consuming process, and influentials often feel they have to struggle in order to limit their community participation so that they will have some time available for attention to their own business. The following description of the community participation of an "influential" in Lansing, Michigan is similar to that found in other cities:

On the average he now belongs to more than thirteen organizations: 3.9 business organizations, 2.4 professional organizations, 2.9 civic and welfare organizations, 0.8 service organizations and 3.5 social organizations. He has held the top appointive or elected offices in almost all of the organizations in which he has become actively involved. Almost all of the leaders belong to a common core of organizations: the Chamber of Commerce, Rotary, Country Club, a leading church, and the Community Chest. (*William H. Form and Warren L. Sauer,* Community Influentials in a Middle-sized City, *Institute for Community Development, Michigan State University, East Lansing, Mich., 1960, p. 4.*)

Community influentials usually operate through their influences in organizations. In most communities, no one organization is strong enough to bring about important changes by itself, so the ability to produce coordinated action by several groups is especially important. One recent study of a community of 50,000 people found eight men who held office in three or more important organizations and who were well acquainted with each other [Perruci and Pilisuk, 1970]. Such men would seem to have an obvious ability to influence organizational action and were regarded by important people in the town as being the core of the leadership group.

The actual leadership offices in voluntary organizations are more likely to be held by those who are in the process of reaching the status of "community influentials" than by those who have already arrived. The established leader is apt to operate by remote control through junior executives who perform the endless chores of office holding. The established influential, however, keeps in touch with developments and may take office himself when some type of emergency seems to demand top-level leadership. His advice is sought on matters considered important, and even when not holding organizational office he is able to exercise a veto power on projects he considers of doubtful merit. New programs have a good chance of success when the influentials lend their support. Fund-raising drives usually get a major portion of their total from small contributors, but influentials add the large gifts that make the difference between success and partial failure, while their endorsement sets a good example of civic virtue.

With occasional exceptions, the community influentials are seldom office holders in local government and consider this kind of activity not very attractive. The influentials recognize the importance of government but dread the prospect of controversies that may be "bad for business" and shrink from direct involvement in "dirty" politics [Hunter, 1953, pp. 151–170; Form and Sauer, 1960, p. 11; Miller, 1970, p. 197]. The community influentials are interested in seeing that government provides the services needed by business without either burdensome regulation or excessive taxation. In addition, as civic leaders they feel that good schools, reliable police protection, efficient public health services, and adequate sewage and water resources help to maintain a community which can attract both customers and employees.

In spite of their limited political participation, community influentials affect the policies of government through campaign contributions and through maintaining a liaison with office holders. When the community influentials are agreed among themselves, they can usually persuade local government and community groups to act as they wish. Yet the community influentials appear to be more powerful in some types of situations than in others. In some cases organized groups appear to be powerful only when their aims are supported by the community elite. In other cases the balance is reversed, and the community elite are helpless unless organized groups are firmly in agreement. Rossi summarizes this situation in the following statement:

Who has power over whom? Perhaps the clearest distinction here is between the two areas of community life—local government and the voluntary community associations. For local government officials who are ultimately brought before the bar of public opinion on election days, the leaders of solidary [highly unified] groups normally on their side carry the most weight. Insofar as wealth and the mass media are seen as potential influencers of public opinion they too are powerful. Within the voluntary community associations which depend largely on the bounty of large con- tributors, wealth and its control play the major role.

Another distinction must be drawn as to types of issues. An issue which divides the community (or which potentially might divide the community) can be moved to a decision point only by solidary groups. I have in mind in this connection such issues as integration in public housing or public schools. Projects which can be achieved without striking deeply at the gains of one particular group are perhaps best moved by the elite of wealth and status. Thus the best way to get a hospital drive underway is to get together a group of prominent citizens, but the best way to get an FEPC [Fair Employment Practices Commission] ordinance is to prove that some significant part of the electorate is for it. (Peter H. Rossi, "Theory, Research and Practice in Community Organization," in Charles R. Adrian, Peter H. Rossi, Robert A. Dahl, and Lloyd Rodwin, Social Science and Community Action, Institute for Community Development, Michigan State University, East Lansing, Mich., 1960, p. 13.)

The community influentials undoubtedly feel that they are far more successfully in control of things at the local than at the state or national level [Form and Sauer, 1960, p. 11; Clark, 1968, p. 96]. Their complaints about the "unfavorable business climate" in Washington and the state capital are frequent and bitter. Even the great businesses they run are subject to changes beyond their control. A decrease in demand or the shift of public interest from one product to another may ruin an industry which completely dominates the local scene. Many business establishments are minor parts of national corporations, and vital decisions are made by those living in other communities. Local politicians, labor leaders, and association executives are easier to deal with than those on the national scene who are responsible to a larger group. Even if one grants the theory that the executive type has major influence on the national scene, this does not necessarily strengthen the position of the community influentials. National leaders who come from the same general social background as the community leaders may still disregard their opinions on specific matters. The community is inextricably linked to the larger world, and a group apparently powerful in the locality may find its influence checkmated by decisions made elsewhere. In many communities the most powerful influentials may be the officers of absentee-owned corporations. They announce decisions meaning life or death for the community, but these decisions have been made elsewhere by corporate managers who may have little concern for the welfare of the local community [Pellegren and Coates, 1956]. Thus the true power in many communities lies outside, and is not with their own leaders.

ORGANIZATIONAL POWER

The struggle for power often appears to be largely a contest between organizations. The John Birch Society attempts to elect conservative candidates to public office, while the Americans for Democratic Action supports liberals. The AFL-CIO calls for a higher minimum wage, and the National Chamber of Commerce assails high wages as the cause of inflation. The Teamster's Union demands that railroads be prohibited from "piggyback" shipments of trucks, and the railroad association urges higher taxes on truck operations. All these and many other items in the daily press suggest that the power of highly organized groups is checked only by the opposition of other groups.

Sources of organizational power

Wealth, numbers, and specialized facilities The obvious advantage of organization is that it brings together the efforts of a large number of people along with a great deal of wealth. When an organization repre-

sents millions of veterans, church members, unionized workers, businessmen, farmers, or any other groups, it has at least a potential claim to speak for a considerable fraction of the population. An organization can accumulate a large treasury from the dues and small contributions of many members. By joining together, even the poor and unknown may gain some of the attributes of power often attributed to the elite, as seen in the recent appearance of the National Welfare Rights Organization and its local chapters.

The specialized facilities of the organization also increase its influence. The individual, far from any seat of government, may make his views known through the activities of the organizational lobbyist, who is constantly in contact with those who make government decisions. The special magazines or pamphlets put out by the organization help to keep the membership informed, while newspaper advertisements and radio and television programs carry the organization's program to the general public.

Coordinated membership response The major source of organizational power lies in the ability to enable many people to take *planned, concerted action* to affect social decisions. In a democracy this action may be accomplished by organizing blocs of voters who will cast their ballots in a way designed to assist organizational objectives. Even a small group may have some political influence if it will vote as a bloc. Many elections are decided by small margins, and a shift of 1 or 2 percent in votes may mean the difference between victory and defeat. If a comparatively small group can organize a united bloc of voters, it may be effective.

Organizations often launch a campaign in which each member is urged to write, wire, or see his congressman. A flood of several thousand individually worded letters from his constituents has a sobering effect upon the most daring congressman.

The American Medical Association has occasionally sought to have each congressman approached by his own personal physician in support of the association's legislative objectives. The effectiveness of such efforts is hard to determine. Apparently, if a measure is earnestly sought by a small but determined group, and if no active or organized opposition appears, its passage is generally assured. Where there is organized opposition, a more prolonged power contest usually follows.

Factors affecting group power

Size and organizational power While large groups are not always effective, a large membership does give them a large power potential. The lethargy and inertia of many large groups continue only so long as society is friendly to their basic values. Members of Protestant churches are notoriously reluctant to follow the lead of their clergy on many matters [Glock and Ringer, 1956; Hadden, 1970], but raised a mighty opposition when President Truman's proposal to send an ambassador to the Vatican appeared to threaten their traditional concept of separation of church and state. Veterans are relatively indifferent to the supernationalistic policies often adopted by their organizations, but if our elaborate system of veterans' benefits and bonuses were seriously threatened, the organizations representing twenty million veterans would become marvelously energetic! Large organizations become highly active and powerful when their vital interests are threatened.

Cohesiveness and action orientation Solidary groups which can unite their members in a given program have a great advantage over loosely structured organizations which must seek agreement through an education and discussion process and may seldom be able to count on a concerted response from their members.

Large religious groups, veterans' organizations, and political parties usually include individuals with a wide variety of views. Members do not consider themselves bound by the actions of governing bodies of such groups and may ignore or even oppose official views of the organization. By contrast, small organizations in which the leadership can make decisions binding on the members may have an influence greater than their size would indicate. This is borne out in a rather striking fashion by the success of real estate boards in determining the action of municipal government. The typical board of realtors requires its members to list all properties for sale, splitting the commission between the firm making the listing and the firm completing the sale. The board of realtors also receives a proportion of the commissions on listed property, which gives it a source of income apart from its membership assessments. The board normally has an executive committee with power to make policy decisions binding on all the members. A recalcitrant member can be suspended, which means that he is not allowed to make any sales from the board list during his suspension although other firms may sell off his listings.

Such an organization has power much greater than its limited size and the intermediate social status of its members would indicate. In several cities the board of realtors, although seldom regarded as a power organization or pressure group, has been highly effective in influencing community decision making. In one Midwestern city of about 250,000 population the board of realtors first defeated a school-bond issue which was supported in a spirited campaign by a great many of the civic organizations; then two years later the board reversed its stand and helped carry to victory a bond issue larger than the one originally rejected. In a public housing campaign in this city, the board of realtors persuaded the voters to reverse a unanimous city commission by referendum although the housing proposal adopted by the commission had the support of both political parties, both daily newspapers, the council of churches, and many social welfare organizations, labor unions, and leading citizens [Bouma, 1962a, 1962b]. A nearby city repeated this experience on two different occasions and in almost identical detail [Bouma, 1962c; 1970]. While other power factors are also involved, the board of realtors is a prime example of the power potential of small, cohesive, disciplined organizations.

Perceived role as a power factor The members of an organization have an image of what kinds of activities are proper for the organization, and this image limits the areas in which it can exercise power. Labor union members will usually support their leadership in wage negotiations even to the point of costly strikes, but have repeatedly shown that their union leaders cannot dictate their voting behavior [Marshall, 1961]. If union leaders could really "deliver" the votes of the membership, their political power would be enormously increased. Most church members expect the church to "stay out of politics," and occasional church efforts to control voting behavior have generally failed. A good example was found in Puerto Rico in 1960, where Archbishop Davis attacked the incumbent administration on birth control and other issues and organized a Catholic party in opposition. Puerto Rico is about 85 percent Catholic, and the church leaders threatened to excommunicate anyone supporting the administration; yet the administration was overwhelmingly reelected while the Catholic party got less than 10 percent of the votes [*U.S. News and World Report*, 1960].

For many years teachers' organizations were handicapped in seeking salary increases because their members' perception of

the role of a professional organization kept them from threatening to strike [Stiehm, 1961]. In recent years the members' perceived role of their organization has changed and teachers' organizations are using conventional strike tactics in seeking economic gains. Whether or not collective bargaining really boosts employees' compensation above the level they would otherwise receive is a moot question on which economists have long disagreed [Ross, 1947; Schultz and Meyers, 1950]. From our viewpoint, however, the essential point is that the teachers' perceived role of their organization limited the tactics it could use in power struggles.

Perceived role.

The power of an organization is also limited by the role assigned to it by the community. To many people the chamber of commerce is an organization dedicated to community welfare, while labor unions are considered selfish and "too powerful." The chamber of commerce is expected to speak out on taxes and other political issues, but the unions are scolded for doing the same thing. Businessmen in government are applauded; labor officials in government are feared; and college professors in government are often ridiculed. Many consider it proper for medical associations to resist outside pressures for changes in medical practice but think it arrogant for teachers' organizations to resist outside pressures for changes in teaching methods. Thus the public's perceived role of an organization or group limits its social power by determining the public support its actions will receive.

Organizational alliances Some of the advantages of large size may be won if several smaller groups join in united action. This alliance is simplified when the organizations involved are led by interlocking directorates. Most of the directors of corporations and community organizations also hold several other directorships in other corporations or organizations. Today the board of directors of the City National Bank hold a director's meeting, tomorrow three of them meet again at the community chest luncheon, and the next day one is elected to the official board of the First Methodist Church, and so on. Thus an overlapping network of membership links the organizations together, making for easy cooperation and vesting control of many organizations in a very small group of persons.

An alliance between entirely separate groups may be forged when their interests converge. The socialized-medicine controversies of recent years have found the American Medical Association allied with the Chamber of Commerce, the National Association of Manufacturers, the American Farm Bureau Federation, and many other organizations in opposing certain medical-care proposals, while many labor unions, public health and welfare organizations, and social-work organizations have been united in support. An alliance between farm organizations and business organizations has helped to persuade many state legislatures to pass "right to work" laws which outlaw the closed shop. Labor organizations have sometimes attempted to form an alliance with

farm organizations, but without much success. Farm organizations seem to feel a greater convergence of interest with business than with labor, especially as farming itself is becoming more commercialized. Some student leftists have romantic dreams of a student-worker alliance, but a more improbable alliance is difficult to imagine.

Countervailing power The opposite tendency of organized groups—to oppose each other rather than to cooperate—has been given the name of *countervailing power* [Galbraith, 1952]. This theory states that the exercise of great power by one organized group soon inspires an opposing power. Other groups may organize for effective opposition, or they may persuade the government to intervene. In the past, large-scale business enterprise eventually resulted in the appearance of the large labor union, and exploitation of farmers by milling interests and other middlemen produced the farm cooperatives. Large buyers such as chain stores limit the power of large manufacturers to set prices, while in turn the voluntary chains (associations of independently owned stores) enable the independent retailer to compete with the chain stores. Thus the power of one economic group is balanced by the power of another and none can entirely dominate the economy. While the concept of countervailance is most often applied to economic groups, this game of reciprocal checkmate tends to be true of all groups in society. The tendency of great power to inspire the organization of opposing power usually keeps any one group from gaining complete control in a democratic society. In a dictatorship, countervailance cannot freely operate.

Coercion and disruption Not all decisions are reached through the political processes of debate and persuasion. Groups are likely to resort to coercion, either when their political system is unresponsive to majority opinion, or when a particular group lacks majority support and refuses to accept the majority decision.

Forceful coercion is normally a monopoly of government, but it is also used by other groups. Fascist and communist governments have normally become established after a determined, ruthless minority party bullied and shot its way into power. Political kidnappings are a recent device for revolutionary parties to coerce the release of prisoners or payment of ransom.

Nonviolent coercion has a long history [Gregg, 1966; Hare and Blumberg, 1968]. It consists of nonviolent ways of making a policy so costly and painful to others that they will change it. The use of *economic coercion* through strikes, lockouts, and boycotts is far from new, but still useful. Another common technique is for a protesting group to place itself in a position where the dominant group must either make a concession or take violent action against the protestors. This technique is variously called *nonresistance, passive resistance,* or *nonviolent resistance.* The object is to arouse public sympathies and to shame the dominant party into making concessions. In the late 1950s and early 1960s, groups of blacks entered segregated restaurants, parks, and other public accommodations, waited patiently for service and submitted peacefully to verbal assault and arrest [Maybee, 1961; Peck, 1962]. This emotionally moving spectacle helped change public attitudes and led to desegregation of public facilities. The technique of nonresistance, passive resistance, or nonviolent resistance is the historic weapon of the underdog, for it can be used by the totally powerless. Its use by American blacks has declined as they developed a greater sense of "black power."

Civil disobedience is the open and public defiance of the law because of conscience or moral belief [Smith, 1968; Cohen, 1969]. It is a technique of nonviolent coercion, resting on the powerful appeal of the spectacle of people who are willing to suffer for a moral belief. Punishment is therfore willingly accepted rather than evaded, in order to publicize and dramatize their belief that the law is immoral. This technique can be highly effective in some situations, but requires great self-discipline lest its practitioners turn to violence.

Disruption is a form of coercion which is highly variable in both means and goals. It includes many ways of interrupting and paralyzing the normal day-to-day activities of a social system. Sometimes the goal is to force acceptance of the protester's demands; sometimes it is to dramatize a general atmosphere of protest; sometimes the motive appears to be the exhilarating experience itself with the goals either nonexistent or inconsequential. Offices may be thronged and closed, university classes disrupted, speakers heckled or shouted down, deans and college presidents held hostage, and buildings seized and occasionally bombed or burned. Off campus, streets may be "trashed," buildings damaged, and stores looted. Disruptions remain nonviolent only if no one attempts to restrain the disrupters or if everyone ignores them and proceeds with normal activities. Very often the disruption escalates into violence, as at Kent State and elsewhere [President's Commission on Campus Unrest, 1970].

Disruption is a technique whereby a small group can gain a great deal of attention without the arduous work, discipline, or patience which building a reform movement would entail. It especially appeals to the malevolent, the immature, and the irresponsible; and in some instances, has few roots beyond egoistic destructiveness. It is a denial of democratic processes and of the rights of majority rule. But whenever a minority feels that its legitimate grievances are not being "listened to," i.e., dealt with fairly by the majority, and that all legitimate channels of redress are blocked, disruption is likely.

The term *demonstration* is often used to refer to any of the forms of persuasion, coercion, or disruption. At least one prominent sociologist believes that demonstrations have become a permanent feature of the American political system [Etzioni, 1971]. Many of these demonstrations are certain to be violent. Proponents of violence claim that this is an inherent part of the American tradition. They cite the American Revolution, lynchings and vigilante law in the Old West, the Civil War, and the Klu Klux Klan as evidence [National Commission on the Causes and Prevention of Violence, 1969; Rubenstein, 1970]. Defenders of the democratic process view American history as a gradual evolution from violent disruption to orderly settlement of disputes through democratic means and cite the successful attainment of many basic reforms as evidence. Examples would include the egalitarian division of Western lands under the Homestead Act, the coming of the welfare state, the rapid, recent changes in the status of black people, and the rapid arousal to action to protect the environment.

Just when violence is a successful technique is uncertain. Some victories are won, but each may leave a legacy of bitterness which makes future victories more difficult. Majorities may arise against violence in a wave of law-and-order repression that results in minority groups becoming more powerless than ever.

SOCIAL POWER OF UNORGANIZED MASSES

Mass man in mass society

In the folk society the individual lives in a world of rather small, highly integrated local groups whose behavior is closely governed by custom and tradition. In the mass society one's life is increasingly dominated by large, impersonal, secondary groups. Social change is rapid, and custom and tradition provide no sure guide to behavior. In the mass society few people can be leaders. The important decisions are often made by a handful of leaders gathered in the great metropolitan centers. For example, no more than a few dozen people will actually share in deciding whether steel prices shall be increased next year. Not only are most people cut off from any direct share in such decision making; they are not even able to understand the basis on which industrial and governmental decisions are made. It is true that newspapers and newscasts bring reports of what has happened, along with an interpretation offered to justify these decisions. But the mass media cannot provide a real forum with a chance for interaction between audience and speaker, or any way for the masses to share in the actual making of most important decisions.

Under ancient despotisms, decisions were made by a few leaders, but these decisions were based upon a traditional morality and custom which the masses could understand and support. The actions of the ancient despot reflected the social values learned in the family and the church and reinforced by the general moral consensus of the community. Today the masses no longer live in a traditional society and are no longer embedded in a protective coating of time-honored customs and institutions. Instead, our "mass man" lives in an era in which change is the norm, in which older customs cannot be trusted, and in which changes that he has no part in bringing about may transform his life for better or for worse. Men live in communities of people like themselves, as isolated fragments of a varied and complex world. Lacking an opportunity for understanding, they inevitably substitute stereotyped images for social analysis and fads for tradition. In these circumstances the mass media become primarily a route of escape rather than enlightenment.

The student should recall that in describing groups the text distinguished between gemeinschaft and gesellschaft relationships. The gemeinschaft social relationships were of a personal, traditional type that applied to the entire society. The gesellschaft scrapped tradition in favor of a realistic (hard-boiled), impersonal, and highly specialized approach to various aspects of life. While the gesellschaft frees society from older restraints, it also cuts the roots of traditional culture and transforms the individual into the "mass man," helplessly and unknowingly swept along by current fads and fancies.

We once had faith that public education and the universal right to vote would prepare the ordinary man to become involved in the public issues of the day and to exercise his influence in a society geared to meet his problems. To some extent, this has happened. Politicians, educators, labor leaders, and business advertisers all gear their appeal to mass consumption. The appeal, however, is usually for the passive acceptance of decisions already made, not an invitation to share in making them. Both the world of political action and that of participation in voluntary associations are closed to the average mass man. Usually he votes, if at all, only in the highly publicized presidential elections. Either he belongs to no voluntary association or he is a nominal member who attends few meetings, has only a vague idea of the purposes and problems of the group, and feels himself cut off from the inner circle who really run things.

The expression of mass power

From this discussion of mass society, it might appear that mass man is totally powerless to affect his destiny. Individually, possibly yes. But collectively, no! The unorganized masses can exert a decisive power over social developments through several avenues.

The power of mass markets In a democratic society the masses exert influence through their choices of what goods to buy, what papers to read, what television programs to watch, and so on. This power is not unlimited, for the consumer is susceptible to some degree of manipulation, as motivation research has demonstrated [Packard, 1957; Dichter, 1971]. But in a competitive market economy such as ours, the consumer's preferences are rarely disregarded for very long. Courting his favor may produce a gaudy vulgarity in product design and shoddy escapism in television programs, but it unquestionably attests to the power of the mass market.

Mass veto power through noncooperation Some decisions can become effective only through mass cooperation. Public health programs, mass-immunization campaigns, and voluntary blood banks are successful only if a great many people cooperate. The American civil-defense effort limped through over a decade of monumental public indifference. In many places a regional shift of labor would be economically sensible, as in many coal-mining regions where mechanization of mines has produced much permanent unemployment; but any plans for their economic rehabilitation must begin with the fact that the miners simply do not want to move [Francois, 1961]. Government can compel the installation of auto seat belts, but cannot compel the people to use them. Wherever a decision cannot be effective without mass cooperation, the veto power of the masses must be considered.

Direct political power of masses In a democracy the ultimate power of the masses rests in their franchise to "throw the rascals out." Sometimes, it is true, this power is empty because both candidates hold the same values and serve the same interests. But whenever there is widespread mass discontent with the way things are going in a democracy, some party or candidate will appeal to this discontent, focus it on certain issues, and propose changes. Deep mass discontent almost guarantees change; either a new party pledged to change replaces the old, or the old party introduces changes as the price of continued power. The elite cannot always veto changes sought by the masses. The reforms of Roosevelt's New Deal era, established over the opposition of most of the elite, attest to the power of the skillfully focused discontent of the masses.

In a democracy the masses can compel changes opposed by the elite or veto changes sought by the elite. The history of fluoridation controversies provides an example of mass veto of elite decisions. The addition of small amounts of fluoride to the water supply was shown years ago to be an effective and apparently harmless method of greatly reducing tooth decay [Muhler and Hine, 1959]. Virtually every responsible scientific organization in the country has endorsed it, including the American Dental Association, the American Public Health Association, the American Medical Association, and many others. The scientific consensus is so complete that, according to one noted nutritionist, ". . . those who continue to oppose it are misinformed, stupid, or dishonest."[3] But in most cities where fluoridation was proposed, a bitter controversy developed. Opponents charged that it was a Communist plot to poison the water and an invasion of personal freedom and attributed a variety of preposterous evils to it. As soon as the announced date for the beginning of fluoridation had passed in this author's home town of Kalamazoo, the water department began receiving complaints that the water tasted bad, smelled foul, and caused headaches, nausea, and other ills, although, because of some mechanical difficulties, the actual addition of fluoride did not begin until several weeks later. In a majority of the cities where fluori-

[3]Frederick J. Stare, Chairman, Department of Nutrition, Harvard University, before Florida Dietetic Association; reported by Associated Press, Nov. 11, 1961.

dation was decided by popular vote, it was defeated, and the spread of fluoridation had virtually ceased by the end of the 1950s [McNeil, 1957; Attwood, 1958]. By the middle 1960s, however, fluoridation apparently had lost its appeal as a rallying point for discontented citizens, and elections began to be more favorable; yet mass opposition had delayed its introduction in many cities for nearly a generation.

This rejection of fluoridation was a clearcut victory of the masses over the elite, since the voters were rejecting the decisions of their administrative officials, the authority of science, and the leadership of most of their community influentials. Research studies found that opposition centered among the less-educated and lower-income citizens [McNeil, 1957; Plaut, 1959; Mausner and Mausner, 1955]. A tabulation of communities voting on fluoridation showed that the greater the proportion of people voting, the greater was the possibility that the measure would be defeated. The correlation with the large turnout implies that the fluoridation issue drew to the polls many voters who are chronically uninterested in, or distrustful of government. A large number of poorly educated, lower-class people seem to be chronically distrustful of government, suspicious of science and intellectuals, and resentful of the dominant role of the elite. When some issue such as fluoridation or a school-bond election offers a focus for their discontents, they unhesitatingly bury the decision makers in a flood of opposition votes [Thompson and Horton, 1960; Rosenthal and Crain, 1966].

Another striking example of mass veto of elite decisions occurred in Kalamazoo, Michigan, one of the first cities to install a downtown mall. In 1963 the city commission presented for voter approval an urban redevelopment program, financed largely by federal funds. For once, the Chamber of Commerce, the Board of Realtors, and the labor unions were on the same side, united to support the project along with the Council of Churches and many other organizations. No local organization opposed the proposal. Of several dozen community influentials, only one announced opposition. The newspaper lent editorial support and generous news coverage. Advocates launched an intensive informational campaign to build popular support. No organized opposition whatever appeared, although one city commissioner opposed the program. The newspaper carried letters to the editor on both sides. The only opposition publicity was an ungrammatical, abusive handbill distributed the night before election. With no organized opposition and the local power system solidly in support, the program's passage seemed assured. Yet it was defeated by a 3 to 2 majority [*Kalamazoo Gazette*, July and August, 1963]. Obviously, the power elite, even when in almost unanimous agreement, cannot dictate all decisions.

Important as the power of veto may be, it does not altogether dispel the picture of the lowest income group of society as one which is essentially without the power to affect decisions concerning it. Alinsky [1965] argues that the poor can utilize power and must be able to do so if their position is to be ameliorated. He argues that the deliberate organization of the poor, stressing whatever grievances are most keenly felt, can lead to positive action. Through demonstrations, boycotts, and bloc voting, the poor can become one of the pressure groups in the community. He believes that as they achieve power, they can prevent exploitation, formulate positive programs for their own welfare, and replace a helpless apathy with a sense of being able to control their environment. Although Alinsky-type programs seem to have been effective in some localities, there is disagreement concerning their value. Some hold that organizing efforts of this type simply hamper cooperation between different groups without leading to effective participation by the poor. Others argue that the poor can be better served by organizations including members of all classes than by

organizations of their own. Efforts to involve the poor in policy making and administration of the poverty programs of the late 1960s were not very successful for a variety of reasons, including fears and opposition of local political structures [Kramer, 1969; Moynihan, 1969].

The comments on the poor as having a sense of helplessness because of their isolation from the instruments of power applies almost equally well to blacks. Table 23 shows that blacks had only 5 percent of the political positions in Chicago in 1965, although comprising over one-fourth of the population. In the private sector they fared even worse, since a survey of leading positions in business, labor unions, voluntary organizations, and universities gave blacks only 2 percent of the offices [Baron et al., 1968, p. 144]. This low participation in the power structure supports other findings that individuals whose sense of grievance is combined with a feeling of powerlessness are most inclined to endorse violence [Ransford, 1968, p. 197]. No group in society is entirely powerless; but when any group is glaringly short of its proportionate number of power leaders, it is likely to develop feelings of helplessness and resentment.

Who, then, holds the reins of power in our society? No single group, for power is of several kinds and is diffused among many groups. The paradox of power in the twentieth century is that although our society is largely controlled by highly organized groups dominated by an elite leadership, this leadership may be blocked by the action of normally unorganized and apathetic masses of men whose basic attitudes toward life are often sharply different from those of the influentials who normally set the pace. Even this pace-setting function of the elite is restricted by the need to draw in the participation of the masses as consumers, workers, and participants in large-scale programs affecting public health and welfare. The gloomy predictions of a society doomed to mediocrity by the power of the most igno-

TABLE 23

*The exclusion of Negroes from government-policy-making
positions in the Cook County public sector (1965)*

	Policy-making positions	Positions held by Negroes	Percent
1. ELECTED OFFICIALS			
U.S. House of Representatives	13	1	8
State legislature	120	10	8
Cook County-nonjudicial	34	3	9
Chicago-nonjudicial	59	7	12
Cook County-judicial	138	8	6
Total	364	29	8
2. APPOINTIVE SUPERVISORY BOARDS			
Total	77	10	13
3. LOCAL ADMINISTRATIVE POSITIONS			
City of Chicago	156	2	1
Chicago Board of Education	72	7	9
Metropolitan sanitary district	7	0	0
Cook County government	13	1	8
Total	248	10	4
4. FEDERAL GOVERNMENT			
Civil service	368	8	2
Presidential appointments	31	1	3
Total	399	9	2
Grand total:	1088	58	5

*Source: Harold M. Baron, Harriet Stulman, Richard Rothstein, and Rennard Davis,
"Black Powerlessness in Chicago," Trans-action, November, 1968, p. 28. Copyright ©
November, 1968, by Trans-action, Inc., New Brunswick, New Jersey.*

rant have not been altogether borne out, but no student of social power can ignore the role of those who seldom sit in the seats of the mighty.

THE SOCIOLOGY OF LAW

Law as legitimized power

Power may be either legitimate, that is, socially sanctioned, or illegitimate. The power of the underworld crime syndicates [Cressey, 1969] is very real and very great, although not legitimate. Neither law nor our approved value system authorizes the acts of crime syndicates. Power is legitimate when it is sanctioned by society, and legal authority represents the formal legitimization of power. Most sociologists seem to agree with Roscoe Pound's definition of law as "social control through the systematic application of the force of politically organized society."[4] But this force is not always applied directly, in the form of the club-wielding policeman. As Hertzler [1961, p. 421] comments, "... the law in effect structures the power (superordinate-subordinate) relationships in the society; it maintains the status quo and protects the various strata against each other, both in governmental and non-governmental organizations and relationships."

The law "structures power relationships" by stating who may do what to whom. Before the passing of the National Labor Relations Act in 1935, employers were legally entitled to fire and blacklist employees who joined unions. This law established workers' legal right to join unions and prohibited employers from penalizing workers for union activity. While this law was not fully enforced in all areas, it greatly aided unions in organizing workers and was largely responsible for the great growth of union power from 1935 to 1945. By 1947, union power had grown enough to disturb many people. The somewhat restrictive Taft-Hartley Act was passed, and many state legislatures passed "right to work" laws which outlawed the closed shop. These laws hampered unions' organizing efforts and slowed the growth of union membership. In this way law "structures the power relationships" of a society and legitimizes the power of those whose power has the society's sanctions.

Some authorities view law as primarily designed to protect the interest of the power structure [Quinney, 1970]. While law expresses the society's concept of justice, this concept is usually defined in ways which are in harmony with the maintenance of the existing social structure [Guillote, 1968]. Such a statement, however, does not mean either that the law is rigid or that it expresses the viewpoint of only one group. The power structure is usually a coalition of several groups and exists only through compromises which include the acceptance of a certain amount of change [Scoble, 1961, pp. 140–141].

Law as expression of the mores

As was stated in our chapter on social control, law is a means of enforcing the mores in a complex, secondary-group society where informal group controls are less effective. Some laws are morally neutral and merely seek to establish a dependable procedure for doing something, such as, for example, writing an enforceable contract. But a great many laws deal with right and wrong behavior as determined by the values and experience of the society.

When a law expresses the moral consensus of the society, it will be effectively enforced. Comparatively few people in our society are murdered or forcibly raped. It is true that many murderers and rapists go unpunished, but their acquittal is largely due to the technical difficulties of legally establishing guilt "beyond a reasonable doubt." A law is effectively enforced when violations are comparatively infrequent and known violators may reasonably expect to be punished.

When a law is backed by no firm moral consensus, effective enforcement is less likely. The classic illustration is the Eighteenth Amendment, which prohibited the manufacture, sale, or transportation of alcoholic beverages in the United States. Whether this law reflected the mores of the majority of citizens at that time has been debated. Certainly there was no moral consensus. Many people considered good liquor a part of the good life and soon located a source of supply. Laws against gambling and prostitution are other examples of poorly enforced laws which are supported by no clear moral consensus. Perhaps the best current example of often unenforced laws are those forbidding marijuana use, which

[4]Roscoe Pound, in George Gurvitch and Wilbert E. Moore, *Twentieth Century Sociology,* Philosophical Library, Inc., New York, 1945, p. 300.

have been termed "the New Prohibition" [Kaplan, 1970].

Law often creates "crimes without victims" [Schur, 1964], meaning that the only persons injured, if any, are the ones who commit the act. Many of the laws regulating drug use and sex acts are of this sort. Many such laws are under attack as either unenforceable or as an unjust intrusion of the state into private behavior. When enforcement is attempted, the results are often more destructive to society than the crimes themselves [Haddon, 1969]. One writer suggests that it would be equally rational to punish obesity, which kills more people than drugs or murderers [Geis, 1968].

It is sometimes stated that a law *cannot* be enforced unless backed by a clear moral consensus. This generalization is not necessarily true, for it overlooks the great variation in the types of situations in which laws may be applied. Laws regulating gambling can be enforced only through the detailed supervision of the individual actions of a large number of people. On the other hand, laws requiring a handful of manufacturers to install safety equipment in automobiles can be enforced with comparative ease. Even though a law may have majority support, if this majority is apathetic and if enforcement requires tremendous individual supervision, the prospects for its enforcement are doubtful at best. But when the people supporting the law are keenly interested in its enforcement and when this can be done through inspection at a limited number of checkpoints, then even laws which do not rest on a clear consensus may be effective.

Law as molder of the mores

In a changing society the mores are constantly changing. Law is one of the forces which change the mores. The law states the approved moral code and makes social policy; thus it functions as an educator [Litwak,

1956]. It is not always necessary to wait for a moral consensus before passing a law; the enactment and enforcement of the law help to create a moral consensus. Child labor laws and compulsory school attendance laws were passed at a time when there was by no means a moral consensus to support them. A considerable fraction of the people sharply disagreed. But important pressure groups, including labor unions and some business groups, found it to their economic advantage to support these laws. Today virtually all are agreed that full-time child labor is bad and that compulsory school attendance is good. Law had helped to create a moral consensus where none existed.

Today law is being used effectively to change the mores dealing with race relations in the United States. Many people recite the cliché, "You can't legislate against prejudice," ignoring the fact that it is discrimination, not prejudice, which is the subject of legislative concern. Most Americans may be unaware that, to a great extent, "social patterns of segregation were created by law, and not the other way around."[5] Blacks and whites in the prewar South were not generally segregated; they lived in close intimacy, although without equality. The Civil War and Reconstruction destroyed the traditional racial arrangements. Some years later, "Jim Crow" laws were passed, requiring the separation of the races in railroads, waiting rooms, theaters, and other public accommodations [Woodward, 1957]. Law imposed upon all people a pattern of segregation which had not existed in the past and was not yet being uniformly practiced. Beginning about twenty-five years ago, the Union of South Africa reversed a mild trend towards race integration with a series of "apartheid" laws requiring strict segregation of the races [Nakasa, 1961].

[5]Jack Greenberg, *Race Relations and American Law,* Columbia University Press, New York, 1959, p. 5. See also Comer Vann Woodward, *The Strange Career of Jim Crow,* Oxford University Press, Fair Lawn, N.J., 1957.

Within recent years, a number of United States Supreme Court decisions have overthrown many state segregation laws and have interpreted the Constitution to forbid many kinds of segregation practices. In addition, many types of discrimination and segregation are now prohibited by civil rights legislation. Segregation, established with the help of law, is now being destroyed with the help of law. Segregation will not be ended easily or quickly, but the trend is unmistakable.

Under what conditions does law succeed in molding the mores? First, the law must operate with, and not against, the forces of change in the society. Attempts to stem the tide of change by law are foredoomed to failure. American marriage and divorce laws in the first two-thirds of the twentieth century steadily grew more stringent and restrictive; yet the divorce rate continued to rise. Law failed to prevent increasing divorce in a society whose values were growing increasingly tolerant of divorce.

When law is in harmony with the processes of change, it accelerates and institutionalizes changes. Compulsory segregation laws played an important role in establishing patterns of segregation in the South after the end of legal slavery created a desire for some other means of keeping Negroes under white control. They were thus in harmony with the trends of the time. Today it is the other way around. Discoveries by natural and social science have destroyed the intellectual respectability of theories of innate white superiority. Economic changes have made segregation increasingly costly and wasteful. The trend of change today is toward a greater equality of rights, opportunities, and rewards for black citizens. Antidiscrimination laws and court rulings are, therefore, working with the direction of social change in our society.

Second, if a law is to have any effect upon the mores, it must be actively enforced. In some Northern states, laws forbidding discrimination in restaurants and public accommodations were unenforced for many years. Negroes were too intimidated or apathetic to demand enforcement, and apparently few whites were interested. Most law enforcement begins when a citizen makes a complaint to the police or prosecutor, charging someone with a specific violation of law. Unless someone signs a complaint and will testify in court, the law may not be enforced. Today many blacks and sympathetic whites are prepared to demand enforcement of antidiscriminatory legislation.

Law can prevent him from carrying his attitude into action.

Whether a law will be obeyed will depend partly upon the costs and inconveniences of continued disobedience. As this is written, the white officials in many Southern communities have desegregated their schools, even though most of them were opposed to the measure. After years of opposition, it became clear to the responsible community leadership that they must either accept some degree of desegregation or abandon the public school system. Thus law can force people to act in opposition to some of their customs and mores by creating a situation where it is unbearably costly for them to do otherwise.

The effects of law upon attitudes, prejudices, and mores are indirect. Law cannot forbid a person to hold an attitude, but it can prevent him from carrying his attitude into action. Law can bring behavior changes and restructure the kinds of contacts groups have with each other, and these can in turn bring changes in attitudes and mores. That law functions indirectly to change mores is no longer a theory; it is now an established fact. We are, however, not yet certain of the exact circumstances under which a particular law or an administrative edict will change mores and practice in the desired direction, or will simply intensify opposition. The question cannot be answered without further research.

To sum up, law is powerless to change the mores of an entire people, or to reverse the direction of changes. But where the mores are conflicting, laws can mold conduct and eventually the mores. Laws can impose the behavior patterns of certain groups upon other groups in the society. Law is unenforceable if it is greatly in advance of, or greatly behind, the trends of change in the society, but law can somewhat accelerate or retard those changes in the mores which other changes in the society are encouraging.

SUMMARY

Power is the ability to control the actions of others. It includes *force*, the use or threat of physical coercion; *authority*, a recognized right to give orders to others, and *influence*, an ability to affect others' actions apart from authority. Influence rests both upon personal qualities and upon one's control over rewards which others desire.

The *power elite* includes those with great wealth, the top executives in business and other institutions, and the community influentials. The degree to which a power elite

actually rules in our society is a matter of dispute among social scientists.

Organizations wield great power, which stems from their ability to mobilize the wealth and specialized skills of a great many people in a coordinated program of action. The degree of an organization's power is affected by its size, its cohesiveness, its role as perceived by members and outsiders, its alliances with other organizations, and countervailing opposition from other organizations and groups.

Coercion and *disruption* have become techniques of minority groups seeking policy change in the United States. Coercion may be *forceful* or *nonviolent*. *Nonviolent coercion* includes *civil disobedience* and several techniques variously known as *nonresistance, passive resistance*, or *nonviolent resistance*. *Disruption* is often used by very small groups to seek concessions from the majority. All of these can be loosely included in the term *demonstration*, a fairly common and possibly permanent feature of our political life. Demonstrations are dangerous weapons, which sometimes gain victories but which often debase democratic processes and may conceivably provoke a repressive reaction.

Unorganized masses possess a great and often unused power, especially in democratic societies. Man may be individually powerless in mass society; yet as "mass man," he may be collectively decisive. Mass power is expressed through the mass market, which determines what products, designs, and entertainment forms shall predominate; it is expressed in the mass veto of elite decisions through mass noncooperation; it is expressed directly through the voting power of the masses, who thus determine which social policies shall prevail.

Law is a major instrument of social power, for law legitimizes the use of force by certain groups for certain ends. Most laws are an expression of the moral consensus of the society. In a complex society, law enforcement supplements informal primary-group controls as a means of social control.

Law also molds the mores of a society. Law institutionalizes the mores of certain groups and imposes these mores upon the remainder of society. The power of the law to change the mores is not unlimited. Law cannot change mores or behavior in a direction opposed to the other forces of change in the society. Law can accelerate or retard changes in mores or behavior in the direction in which they are already moving in response to other changes and pressures in the society. The effects of the law are indirect; by changing behavior and restructuring the contacts between groups, attitudes and mores are eventually modified. Law both expresses and makes social policy; it is both a conservative and a creative force in society.

Questions and projects

1. Distinguish between force, influence, and authority. Which is most characteristic of the dean of women in a college? Of a greatly admired university professor? Of an ex-President of the United States?

2. Is there a "power elite" among the student body on your campus? If so, upon what positions or characteristics is it based? Are there some reputed power structures which have little real power? Would these differ from campus to campus?

3. In your institution, what persons or groups do you believe would dominate the decision making in each of these issues: whether to drop intercollegiate athletics; whether to add a school of engineering to the institution; whether to dismiss a popular professor who has become "controversial"; whether to approve a student government charter sought by student leaders? Having formulated your answers, now answer the question: Who do you think really runs your institution?

4. Why do business executives apparently have greater community power than professionals?

5. Why does violence appeal to some campus militants? Is violence a legitimate activity on the campus?

6. Why is an effective alliance between radical students and workers highly unlikely?

7. Very often the policy statements of the official spokesman for organized groups are not carried into action. What are some reasons for this inaction?

8. Do you know of any recent or current social changes which are undermining the power position of labor unions? Of farm organizations?

9. Must power be organized? Are there any ways for unorganized masses to express real power? Of all power expression in our society, how much is carried out by organizations?

10. What is meant by the statement that "law structures the power relationships" of a society? Can you think of any recent changes in power relationships which have been brought about (at least in part) by law?

11. What is the normal relationship between law and the mores in civilized societies? Is it ever possible to enforce a law which is not backed by a firm moral consensus?

12. Under what conditions can law change the mores? How greatly?

13. Make a brief study of campus influentials by the *reputed-power* approach. Query a few faculty members to see whether they perceive the campus power system in the same way as the students.

Suggested readings

Adrian, Charles R., Peter H. Rossi, Robert A. Dahl, and Lloyd Rodwin: *Social Science and Community Action,* Michigan State University Press, East Lansing, 1960. A study of community power with special reference to community organization and the role of the planner.

Aiken, Michael, and Paul E. Mott: *The Structure of Community Power,* Random House, Inc., New York, 1970. A series of readings drawn from research articles on the bases of social power in a community.

Baron, Harold M., with Harriet Stulman, Richard Rothstein and Rennard Davis: "Black Powerlessness in Chicago," *Trans-action,* November, 1968; reprinted in *Charles A. Anderson: Sociological Essays and Research: Introductory Readings,* The Dorsey Press, Homewood, Ill., 1970. An analysis of the distribution of blacks in power positions in the Chicago area.

Bouma, Donald H.: "Issue-Analysis Approach to Community Power: A Case Study of Realtors in Kalamazoo," *The American Journal of Economics and Sociology,* 29:241-252, July, 1970. An analysis of the power of a cohesive organization, with some reflections on the issue-oriented versus the reputational approach to organizational and individual power.

*Coleman, James S.:** *Community Conflict,* The Free Press of Glencoe, Inc., New York, 1957. A brief, readable analysis of power conflicts in the community.

*Etzioni, Amitai:** *Demonstration Democracy,* Gordon and Breach Science Publishers, Inc., New York, 1971. An analysis of a series of demonstrations and of their current role in political life.

Form, William H., and Delbert C. Miller: *Industry, Labor, and the Community,* Harper & Row, Publishers, Inc., New York, 1960. A research study of community organizations and community influentials, with special attention to the role of organized labor.

*Garrison, William A.:** *Power and Discontent,* The Dorsey Press, Homewood, Ill., 1968. A brief but sophisticated examination of the exercise of authority and influence.

*Hacker, Andrew:** "Power To Do What?" in **Irving Louis Horowitz,** *The New Sociology,* Oxford University Press, Fair Lawn, New Jersey, 1964, pp. 134-147. Comments on the limits of the power of the managerial elite.

*Hunter, Floyd:** *Community Power Structure: A Study of Decisionmakers,* The University of North Carolina Press, Chapel Hill, 1953. A pioneering study of the organization of power in an American city.

Kahn, Si: *How People Get Power: Organizing Oppressed Communities for Action,* McGraw Hill Book Company, New York, 1970. An author with extensive community-organization experience outlines strategies to use in helping poor people gain power.

*Mills, C. Wright:** *The Power Elite,* Oxford University Press, Fair Lawn, New Jersey, 1956. A persuasive development of the thesis that our society is run by a small group of power wielders. See also the critical review by **Daniel Bell,** "The Power Elite—Reconsidered," *American Journal of Sociology,* 64:238-250, November, 1958.

Miller, Delbert C.: *International Community Power Structures: Comparative Studies of Four World Cities,* Indiana University Press, Bloomington, 1970. Report of an investigation of the composition and effectiveness of community power elites in Seattle, Bristol, Lima, and Cordoba.

*Moynihan, Daniel P.:** *Maximum Feasible Misunderstanding: Community Action in the War on Poverty.* The Free Press, New York, 1969. An analysis of the difficulties which arose when the poverty programs of the federal government tried to provide for "maximum feasible participation" of the poor.

Race and ethnic relations

In New Mexico, a fiery chicano activist named Reies López Tijerina, 43, has mustered a local following behind what amounts to a secessionist scheme aimed at giving Mexican-Americans their own land. Tijerina, who enjoys a reputation as something of a romantic revolutionary as a result of a 1967 shoot-out at the Rio Arriba County courthouse in Tierra Amarilla, is now serving a two-year prison term for assaulting two forest rangers. Undaunted by a stretch in prison, he has laid claim to millions of acres originally owned by Mexican settlers under Spanish land grants that were conveniently lost, destroyed or ignored by the Anglo authorities. At stake are New Mexico, Arizona, Nevada, Utah, Texas, parts of Colorado, at least half of California and a slice of Wyoming. Most historians concede Tijerina's point—that the land was wrested illegally from the original Mexican owners after the Mexican-American war. But the issue has yet to be taken up by Congress or the courts, and the chance that the land will ever be parceled out to the heirs of the original owners is all but nonexistent.

Tijerina's quixotic crusade—designed, among other things, to give Mexican-Americans pride in their heritage—has found an echo in Denver. There, another local chicano leader, Rodolfo (Corky) Gonzáles, 41, has called for chicanos to "unite in a new nation [on] the land that once belonged to us." (Newsweek, *June, 29, 1970, p. 27. Copyright © Newsweek, June 29, 1970.*)

This account highlights one of the many problems of intergroup relations in a changing world. In some countries throughout the world, people of different races are working together in industry, studying in school, deliberating in legislative bodies, worshiping in churches, and carrying on jointly all the many types of interaction which make up social life. In many cases, the terms of the interaction make no reference to race but only to individual abilities. Thus the colored man may be a general, and the white man a private, or vice versa; either may occupy a superordinate or a subordinate status without any implication of racial inferiority or superiority.

But the social structure of many countries

is largely determined by race. One's race largely controls the residential area, the governmental rights, the type of job and amount of compensation, the social groups in which one is accepted, and a host of other patterns of social interaction. Many group alignments are on the basis of function (what one does), such as labor unions or professional societies; or of interest, such as stamp collectors, athletic fans, music

Those who are different we often reject.

lovers, etc. But much of the world is still separated by what Giddings, an early American sociologist [1913, p. 17], called a "consciousness of kind." People who are "like us" we welcome; those who are "different" we often reject. The basis of similarity is some feeling of group identity, which may be based upon nationality, religious affiliation, economic status, language usage, or regional habitat, as well as race. Of all these criteria, race is one of those most widely used as a basis for group identity, and often "race relations" is considered a subject by itself.

THE CONCEPT OF RACE

"Race" is a troublesome concept, for it has no generally agreed meaning. In popular usage, "race" may mean all of mankind (the

"human race"), a nationality (the "German race"), or even a group which is mixed in nearly all respects but socially designated as different (the "Jewish race"). Almost any kind of category of people may be called a "race."

Even social scientists have not fully agreed in defining the term [Hunt, 1951]. Some have defined a race as a group of people separated from other groups by a distinctive combination of physical characteristics. As will be seen later, this poses certain difficulties because of intermixing, overlapping, and the gradual shading of physical characteristics (e.g., skin color) along a continuum without definite separations. Therefore, a "race" is not a biologically distinct grouping of people, yet many people think and act as though it were. Race is a socially significant reality, for people attach great importance to one's assumed racial identity. The scientist's fondness for neat scientific precision must be tempered by his need to deal with a tremendously important social reality. Perhaps an acceptable definition might read: *a race is a group of people somewhat different from other groups in its combination of inherited physical characteristics, but race is also substantially determined by popular social definition.*

Some historic theories of race

The ancient world was not much bothered by the question of race differences for the ancient world was not highly race-conscious. Slavery was not based on color, and the slave in pagan Rome had far brighter prospects than a slave in the American South. Intense race consciousness among European peoples did not develop until the colonial expansion, when white men needed a handy rationalization to justify their rule over nonwhite people. Then a succession of ingenious theories arose, all of which confirmed the white man's superiority and sanctified his rule.

One such theory, still widely held, is the theory of the Hamitic curse, holding that the blacks are the sons of Ham, cursed by God to be servants [Genesis 9:18–25]. The Bible records that Noah (not God) laid the curse upon Canaan (not upon Ham); the Bible does not state that God accepted and enforced Noah's curse, nor does the Bible say from whom the blacks are descended; but these are biblical oversights which believers in this theory are happy to correct. When the work of Darwin popularized evolutionary theories, it was not long before such theories were applied to racial origins. These held that blacks were either products of a separate evolution or were an intermediate offshoot, and therefore were a primitive, half-animal form of human being [Carroll, 1900]. A variety of geographic theories were given a racial twist; for example, the superior qualities of the white race were attributed to the climate it lives in. All these theories accomplished their purpose, which was to provide a plausible rationale for white rule at a time when science was unable to say much about race differences.

Most scientists today are agreed that all races are of one species, the product of a single evolution,[1] and all races are about equally "close" to the other animals. For example, the blacks more closely resemble the apes in skin color, nose form, and facial slant; but the whites more closely resemble the apes in lip form, hair texture, and amount of body hair.

The contemporary view of race

Scientists seek to classify races as groups of people with distinctive combinations of physical traits that set them off from other groups. Skin color is the principal trait used

[1]For a dissenting view which advocates the theory of a multiple origin of races see C. S. Coon, *The Origin of Races*, Alfred A. Knopf, Inc., New York, 1962. For a critique of Coon's approach, see T. Dobzhansky, "The Origin of Races," *Scientific American*, 208:169–172, 1963.

FIGURE 12

The races of mankind.

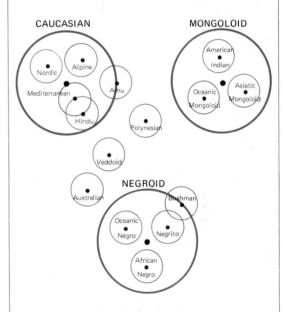

Distance between the centers of circles indicates the closeness of relationship. For example, Kroeber shows both the Polynesians and the Australians (native) as outside all three major racial stocks but shows the Australians as closer to the Negroid races than are the Polynesians.

Source: A. L. Kroeber, *Anthropology*, Harcourt, Brace & World, Inc., New York, 1948, p. 10.

in classifying races, although hair color, hair texture, amount of body hair, eye fold, shape of nose and lips, head contour, and body build are also used.

How many races are there? No objectively correct number can be given. Whether there are three, six, or fifty races depends upon which physical features we consider significant and upon the degree of similarity in physical appearance we demand of the members of a race. Dobzhansky comments on this confusion:

Boyd has recognized five, and Coon, Garn, and Birdsell nine or thirty or thirty-two races. Does it follow that some of these classifications are necessarily wrong? No, all may be right; it should always be kept in mind that while race differences are objectively ascertainable facts, the number of races we choose to recognize is a matter of convenience. (*Theodosius Dobzhansky,* Mankind Evolving: The Evolution of the Human Species, *Yale University Press, New Haven, Conn., 1962, p. 266.*)

It is conventional to divide the human species into three main racial stocks—the Mongoloid (yellow and brown), the Negroid (black), and the Caucasoid (white). Most groups can be placed in one of these three categories, as is shown in Figure 12. This figure also shows that the racial placement of some groups is uncertain because their physical characteristics overlap. For example, the Asian Indians have Mongoloid skin color but Caucasoid facial features; the Ainu of Northern Japan have Caucasoid skin color and hair with Mongoloid facial features. A further complication arises from the fact that the races have been busily interbreeding for thousands of years so that nearly all racial groups are considerably intermixed. Some groups, like the Jews, are not properly racial at all yet form a definite social entity and are often treated as though they were a race.

Physical anthropologists in searching for an objective basis for racial classification are now placing emphasis on genetic composition as indicated by blood types. Cur-

rently, there is an attempt to combine bloodtype data with more easily observable differences such as color, stature, hair form, nasal index, etc. Dobzhansky [1962], for instance, has suggested a tentative classification of thirty-four racial groups which he hopes is neither so broad that it obscures vital differences nor so numerous that it is unwieldy. Such research and attempts at sound classifications may be expected to provide much useful information about the various branches of Homo sapiens. The student should remember, however, that at the present time there is no generally accepted pattern of classification and that whenever one sees comment on "racial" differences, it is necessary to know what groups are involved. In the following sections of this chapter "racial" usually refers to "Negroid" and "Caucasian" and to members of these races found in the North American continent.

At this point a comment on terminology is in order. There is a growing tendency to refer to Americans with "Negroid" ancestry as *blacks* rather than *Negroes*. There really is not much linguistic difference, since *Negro* is a Spanish word meaning black. In this textbook, we have generally used the term *black*, except when reproducing quotations and statistical or historical materials.

THE SCIENTIFIC VIEW OF RACE DIFFERENCES

It is clear that the races differ in some inherited physical characteristics. May they also vary in their inborn intellectual and emotional characteristics? This is a reasonable logical possibility. Is it a fact?

Physical race differences are unimportant

Physically, all races are approximately alike in every important characteristic. With a few exceptions (such as that a dark skin is useful under tropical sun), the differences are ornamental, not functionally important. The physical differences within the human species are very modest compared with the differences within many species—dogs or horses, for example.

Intellectual and emotional race differences are hard to measure

Intellectual and emotional characteristics cannot be measured directly but must be inferred from some kind of performance. Here a difficulty arises. Many things can affect performance—native ability, experience, motivation, self-confidence, physical health, testing situation, and still others. The importance of any one of these factors can be measured accurately only if all others are held absolutely constant. How can comparative racial ability be measured? Only by comparing the performance of two racial groups where all these other factors are held constant. Does the evidence usually offered meet this test? Two kinds of evidence of racial inequality are usually offered: differential racial achievement and intelligence-test scores.

Differential racial achievements If all races have equal innate abilities, why have they not made equal achievements? This question is deceptively ethnocentric. It really asks, "If they are as smart as we are, why don't they do what we do as well as we do it?" Meanwhile, another people may be asking the same question about us. Obviously, if we define achievement purely in terms of our culture's values, we cannot lose. As with the discussion about the superiority of the temperate climate, the proof for superiority of racial achievement is only convincing when one ignores changes over a time span. Suppose achievement is defined as the building of a great civilization. Does this identify the superior races? Superior at what moment in history? By this test, the super-

ior "races" 5,000 years ago would be the Egyptians and the Semitic peoples of Asia Minor; 3,000 years ago, these plus the Indians and the Chinese; 2,500 years ago, the Greeks and the Persians; 2,000 years ago, the Romans; and so it goes. Why, then, did the Nordic whites spend four-fifths of human history hovering about campfires and wiping their greasy fingers on their thighs? The cultural-achievement test of racial superiority works out most nicely if it is confined to the last thousand years of history.

But, one may ask, when have the blacks built a great civilization? Doesn't their lack of creativity show inferiority? It is true that the blacks built no very impressive civilization in the tropical jungles or arid grasslands where many of the blacks lived. Neither did anybody else. But in other parts of black Africa, great trading cities arose which by the fourteenth century were the equal of any of the cities of Europe [Davidson, 1959, 1965]. Later, the history of African civilizations was forgotten or intentionally buried, after the slave trade began to hasten their destruction.

The leading early civilizations were river-valley civilizations. Not until the development of modern technology was it possible to plant civilization in the tropical jungle, where its permanence is still uncertain. The great early civilizations arose in Egypt, Asia Minor, and Southern Asia. Some of their builders were, at least in part, Caucasian; others were entirely Mongolian. But all of them built great civilizations when the northern Europeans were illiterate stone-age savages.

Cultural achievement is a product of many variables—geography and climate, contacts with other peoples, dominant values of the culture, the level of preexisting technology, and, possibly, racial ability. Since we know no satisfactory way to hold these other variables constant, we have no scientific way to measure the factor of racial ability in cultural achievement.

A different sort of cultural achievement is

a group's success in absorbing and using an advanced culture with which it comes into contact. By this test, the Nordic whites came off rather poorly. Falling heir to Roman civilization, they kicked it to pieces and sat on the remnants for hundreds of years. The nonwhite races of the world today, by comparison, are doing rather well.

Intelligence-test findings are inconclusive
Almost the only scientific attempts to measure comparative racial abilities have been through intelligence testing. There have been dozens, almost hundreds, of comparative studies of racial intelligence, usually black-white comparisons. Almost without exception they show a consistent degree of white superiority. The first large-scale test was run during World War I, when all servicemen took intelligence tests as part of army induction procedures. The average scores of whites were consistently higher than those of blacks. Two qualifications, however, are important: Many individual blacks had higher scores than many individual whites; and when the scores were broken down by states, blacks in the top three Northern states had higher average scores than whites in the bottom three Southern states —as is shown in Table 24.

TABLE 24

Intelligence test scores of Southern whites and Northern Negroes by states: Army recruits, World War I

Whites		Negroes	
State	Median score	State	Median score
Mississippi	41.25	*New York*	45.02
Kentucky	41.50	*Illinois*	47.35
Arkansas	41.55	*Ohio*	49.50

Source: Otto Klineberg, "What Psychological Tests Show," in Bernhard J. Stern and Allain Locke (eds.), When Peoples Meet, *Progressive Education Association, New York, 1942, p. 449.*

Why should Northern blacks have made higher scores than Southern whites? Selective migration—a tendency for the talented blacks to migrate northward—is a possible answer, but the evidence for the tendency is not very convincing and certainly would not provide a complete explanation [Klineberg, 1935; Shuey, 1958, chap. 9]. A more probable explanation is that these black groups came from a more favorable environment, and that this advantage was reflected in their performance on intelligence tests. The average white man in these Southern states lived a poverty-striken life in an area with poor schools and little social stimulation of any kind. The Northern blacks, although subject to many types of discrimination, probably had better schools and a more intellectually stimulating environment than many of the Southern whites.

Nearly all intelligence-test studies which compare unselected groups of whites and blacks show the whites to be superior; yet some black groups are superior to some white groups. Among the earlier intelligence-test studies, almost all heavily Catholic groups made rather low average scores [Klineberg, 1944, p. 35]. Does this mean that Catholics have less native intelligence than Protestants? The heavily Catholic groups tested at that time were from urban slum areas, densely populated by immigrants of southern European background; thus, these children were a disadvantaged group. The lowest test scores of all have been made by the isolated mountain people of the Southern highlands, the hillbillies, who are entirely Protestant, and are the most nearly pure Anglo-Saxons in the country. It is clear that we cannot predict a group's test score from its religion or racial origin, but we can make a quite accurate prediction of a group's intelligence-test score if we know its cultural environment.

This relationship of scores to environment should be no surprise, once we recognize that the intelligence test is misnamed. *Intelligence* tests *do not* measure *inborn in-*

tellectual capacity; they measure *intellectual performance.* The two differ widely; inborn intellectual capacity is inherited, but intellectual performance is affected by many variables of experience. When the intelligence test is used to compare two persons of similar background, motivation, learning experience, health, and familiarity with tests and test situations, it will quite reliably select the one with the greater intellectual capacity. When it is used to compare the inborn intellectual capacity of persons or groups who differ in these other respects, the intelligence test is worse than useless, for it gives false measurements. Most blacks in the United States are from a lower-class background. Among the factors which keep their test scores low are poor health, poor living conditions, an educationally impoverished home background, and often a poor school adjustment—the same factors which handicap most lower-class white children. Added to these are some special handicaps imposed by race—a drummed-in sense of racial inferiority and frequently an uncertain rapport with a white teacher or test administrator [Eells et al., 1969]. We cannot be certain how white and black achievements would compare under conditions of equal opportunity and reward, for nowhere are they fully equal. Not until whites and blacks have competed under conditions which are equal in all respects—and for two or three generations of time so that the legacy of past discrimination and failure is overcome—can we make a final judgment concerning their respective racial abilities. Meanwhile, practically all social scientists are prepared to assume that all races have a potential capacity equal to the demands of our society, as is indicated in this resolution of the American Anthropological Association:

The American Anthropological Association repudiates statements now appearing in the United States that Negroes are biologically and in innate mental ability inferior to whites, and reaffirms the fact that there is no scientifically established evidence to justify the exclusion of any race from the rights guaranteed by the Constitution of the United States. The basic principle of equality of opportunity and equality before the law are compatible with all that is known about human biology. All races possess the abilities needed to participate fully in the democratic way of life and in modern technological civilization. (*Resolution unanimously adopted by the Council of Fellows of the American Anthropological Association, Nov. 17, 1961.*)

From time to time a scientist with respectable academic credentials publishes a defense of inherited racial differences in intellectual capacity [McGurk, 1956; Shuey, 1958; Jensen, 1968, 1969]. These scholars review a wide range of intelligence tests and other test data, and conclude that blacks probably average somewhat below whites in innate intellectual capacity. Jensen writes with appropriate scientific caution, stating that hereditary racial differences in ability have been neither proven nor disproven and recognizing that group tests tell nothing about particular individuals; yet he concludes that "it is not an unreasonable hypothesis that genetic factors are strongly implicated in the average Negro-White intelligence difference" [1969, p. 82]. A storm of scientific criticism greeted both Shuey [Pettigrew, 1964, pp. 100–136] and Jensen [Bereiter, 1969; Brazziel, 1969; Crobach, 1969; Crow, 1969; Elkind, 1969; Hunt, 1969; Kagan, 1969], charging that they had interpreted test scores too literally and had not given proper weight to all the social and cultural factors which have inhibited black performance.

Emotions run high on this question because of the implication that if any differences in average innate racial ability are conceded, this might justify racial discrimination. We should note that two questions are involved: (1) are there any genetically based, hereditary, innate racial differences in ability? (2) are any such differences, if they exist, great enough to justify differential treatment for different races? The first of these questions has no indisputable answer, for most scientists are agreed that, while such differences are possible, none have yet been established. For the second question, we note that even if Jensen's conclusion of an average eleven-point IQ difference between whites and blacks [Jensen, 1968, p. 81] were to be accepted *as an innate, genetic* difference, this is no greater than the average IQ difference between different children in the same family. Furthermore, an eleven-point difference in *average* scores for the two racial groups would still leave many persons in the "inferior" group well above the average for the "superior" group, and many individuals in the "superior" group would rank below the average for the "inferior" group. Any system of unequal opportunities, based upon such an overlapping range of ability, would be difficult to justify.

It is also possible that any genetic differences between groups may be impermanent. The discovery of the genetic alphabet by Nirenberg and Korana [*Science News*, Jan. 11, 1969] and other imminent genetic discoveries open the possibility that we may before long find it easier to alter man's genetic characteristics than to change his social environment. It is conceivable that men in the future will be less involved in arguments over genetic differences than in actually changing both genetic inheritance and social environment in ways which may make current racial concepts obsolete.

Group differences in behavior are learned

Sometimes the "all men are alike" theme is distorted into a caricature of the facts. It is true that all groups appear to be alike in most of their inherited capacities. It is also true that groups differ greatly in their learned behavior. It is a fact that, as compared with whites in the United States,

blacks *average* lower in income, education, and occupational status and have higher rates of crime and delinquency, venereal disease, illegitimacy, desertion, and practically every other unflattering index. White resistance to school integration arises, in considerable part, from the fact that genuine school integration (racial balance) would expose many middle-class white children to the conduct norms and academic achievement levels of lower-class black children.

How should we interpret such facts? To some, they serve as an excuse for a continued denial of equal opportunity to blacks. The more perceptive observer sees that these unflattering facts are the *products* of unequal opportunity and will persist as long as opportunities and rewards are unequal. The perceptive observer also notes that averages do not apply to individuals; many blacks rank far above many whites in achievement.

The social scientist recognizes that many *very real* group differences exist in personality, behavior, and achievement. There is no convincing evidence that any of these differences are rooted in anything inborn; in fact, the evidence strongly indicates that all or nearly all *major group differences in personality, behavior, and achievement are entirely learned;* they are rooted not in heredity, but in group tradition, opportunity, and reward. One aspect of this situation is summed up in the concept of the "self-fulfilling prophecy," discussed earlier on page 136. The supposedly impartial observer notes that blacks have a more unfavorable record than whites in many kinds of social pathology, so he acquiesces in a system whereby blacks have inferior housing, more limited schooling, and more restricted job opportunities, thus producing the very results he had predicted. Why, then, do blacks excel in music, dancing, and athletics? Not because of any special ability, but because these fields are more open to blacks. Why do Jews pursue trade and avoid farming? For over a thousand years, trade was the only occupation gentiles would let them engage in. If scientists wish to understand special behavior traits of any group, they do not study the group's heredity; they study the conditions under which the group has lived and worked and interacted with other groups throughout its history.

Group averages tell nothing about individuals

On almost any uncontrolled comparison of whites and blacks in the United States, blacks will show a consistent inferiority. Many blacks, however, will rank above many whites. This fact raises some interesting policy questions. For example, when Dallas, Texas, gave a "readiness-for-learning" test to its first-grade pupils, it found the distribution shown in Table 25. This table and many similar pupil comparisons clearly show the average present *academic* superiority of white pupils. It also shows that many blacks were above many whites, since 31 percent of the whites were placed below average, while 26 percent of the blacks were average or above. If these children are divided according to race for school experience, nearly one-third of the whites will receive certain experiences which are denied to the one-fourth of the blacks whose "readiness for learning" is greater. Racial discrimination involves not only "the unequal treatment of equals"; it always goes beyond this to deny to the superior black the privileges enjoyed by the inferior white. Just how to reconcile this practice with the democratic ethos is a persistent problem for the supporters of a caste society.

To summarize the scientific facts about race differences, we may say that all theories of *inborn* race differences in ability, personality, or behavior are unsubstantiated by scientific evidence. While these characteristics cannot be exactly measured, it appears

TABLE 25

Readiness for learning among Dallas first-grade pupils

Percent	Negro	White
In below-average grouping	74	31
In average grouping	18	32
In above-average grouping	8	37

Source: A. D. Albright, *"What are Standards?"* Southern School News, *June, 1958, p. 1.*

that all major groups are alike in their average inheritance of everything that is important for social behavior or learning. Any average differences in innate abilities, if they exist, are very small, are clouded by great overlapping, and are insignificant in effect when compared with differences in learning opportunity. There are, however, great differences in the present average behavior and personality of racial and other groups, but these differences are largely or entirely due to group differences in tradition, opportunity, and reward. Wherever the total behavior conditions are alike, behavior eventually becomes alike.

PATTERNS OF ETHNIC RELATIONSHIPS

We often hear people speak of the "Jewish race" or the "German race." These peoples are not races in the usual scientific use of the term; yet they are often thought of and treated as races. Sociologists use the term *ethnic group* to refer to any kind of group, racial or otherwise, which is socially differentiated to an important degree and has developed its own subculture [Gordon, 1964, p. 27]. In other words, an ethnic group is one recognized by society and by itself as a definite group. Although the distinction is associated with a particular set of ancestors, its identifying marks may be language, religion, relationship to a geographic locale, nationality, physical appearance, or any combination of these. The term is properly applied whenever the group differences are considered socially significant enough to set off the group clearly from others. Thus in the United States the name "Catholic" by itself would not be considered an ethnic label, but "French Canadian Catholic" would call up an image of a group with a definite character both in its own eyes and in those of the rest of society. Although we find some pattern of ethnic arrangements in every complex society, we find also a great variety in the way different groups have arranged to live together. We shall look at these briefly under the headings "Racist Patterns" and "Equalitarian Patterns." The term *racist* refers to a society which is frankly dominated by one group; *equalitarian* refers to a society in which an effort is made to treat all groups equally. The following analysis is taken in part from Berry [1965, chaps. 7–12].

Some racist patterns of ethnic relationships

In spite of some moves toward equalitarian intergroup living, the main trend of the twentieth century has been toward racist solutions of intergroup problems. Never in the world's history has there been so much mass slaughter, expulsion of minorities, and division of territory along ethnic lines as in the twentieth century.

Annihilation The effort to completely exterminate a people by killing all of them is called *annihilation*. It is ironic that the greatest annihilation in recorded history was conducted by a highly civilized Christian state. Between 1933 and 1945, the German Nazis killed about 4.5 million European Jews [Reitlinger, 1968, p. 546], marching many of them into gas chambers with a systematic bureaucratic efficiency. (The frequently cited figure of 6 million was based upon early estimates which were hastily prepared for the Nuremberg trials in 1946. Subsequent research has produced a somewhat lower estimate, which nonetheless still documents a monumental example of man's inhumanity to man.) Other cataclysms in history may have produced more deaths, but we have no comparable example of such a deliberate, premeditated mass slaughter carried out as a government policy. Several instances of mass slaughter have transpired since then, perhaps the greatest of which accompanied the Hindu-Moslem clashes in India and Pakistan in 1948. Others include the slaughter of the Ibos in Northern and Western Nigeria in 1966 and of the Communists in Indonesia after their unsuccessful attempt to seize power in 1965.

Until recent years annihilation or near-annihilation was the price primitive peoples often paid for their contact with those from an advanced technological culture. To some extent the annihilation occurred through deliberate slaughter, following the American pioneer philosophy that "the only good Indian is a dead Indian." Usually, though, group decline was a result of more indirect effects of culture contact. These included the greater deadliness of tribal wars with the introduction of firearms, the spread of diseases such as tuberculosis, syphilis, and smallpox, limitations of the food supply through the loss of lands, and the disorganization of society through the ravages of alcohol and the weakening of tribal authority. Sometimes disease was deliberately used to decimate a native people. A native would be caught and held in a white settlement until he developed measles, whooping cough, or some such disease; then he would be released to join his people, who were highly susceptible to the new disease. Often one-half or three-fourths of them would die within a few weeks.

One example of complete annihilation took place in Tasmania, an island south of

Australia in which the aboriginal population was completely wiped out by English settlers, some of whom hunted the natives for sport and for dog meat [Murdock, 1936, pp. 16–18]. The Maoris in New Zealand, who are now fairly well accepted and have amalgamated to some extent with the whites, dropped from a population estimated at 200,000 in 1800 to 40,000 in 1897 [Winiata, 1958]. In the United States the Indians declined from an estimated population of 1½ to 2 million at the time of the Pilgrims to less than 400,000 [Kallen, 1958]. Even in Hawaii, which the Westerners entered in a relatively benign manner, the number of Hawaiians of native stock dropped from 300,000 in 1778 to 57,000 in 1872 [Berry, 1965, p. 140].

The effort to eliminate an ethnic group either through annihilation or through attempts to destroy its culture so that the group loses its identity is legally known as *genocide*, a practice which is now outlawed by the United Nations Convention on Genocide.

The prospects of native peoples are now changing. The reduction of disease through mass immunization promises to swell their numbers higher than before contact with the white man. This new demographic development is a mixed blessing, since it may be impossible for a society with a traditional culture to sustain an unchecked population increase in the limited territory available.

Expulsion and partition The idea that a nation should be composed of those who share a similar ethnic background has been especially popular in recent years. A mass shifting of population has resulted from an effort to make political boundary lines coincide with ethnic groupings—a shift which has frequently upset the patterns of centuries. People whose families have lived in certain areas for hundreds of years suddenly find themselves declared undesirable aliens and are forced to move to a land which

to them is new, strange, and terrifying, even though it may be populated by persons of the same race, nationality, or creed.

An early example of this practice is told in Longfellow's *Evangeline*, a story based on the forcible removal of a colony of French settlers from Nova Scotia. Other examples include the expulsion of Greeks from Turkey and of Turks from Greece, the partition of the land of Palestine into a Jewish state and an Arab state, the division of Ireland under which the heavily Protestant area around Belfast remains a part of the British Empire while the Catholic part of Ireland is an independent country, and the partition of India between Moslems and Hindus. Proof that no group is secure against the effects of such a policy is seen in the fate of the Germans living outside the boundaries of Germany. After World War II, Czechoslovakia, Poland, Yugoslavia, Bulgaria, Rumania, and Hungary all feared that the presence of a German minority might some day lead to claims on their territory by another strong German government. The answer to this problem seemed simple—eliminate the minority from the territory. Consequently over 10 million Germans were ordered to leave areas in Central and Eastern Europe where their families had lived for centuries.

During World War II both Russia and the United States forced ethnic groups to move from one part of the country to other areas. The Russians broke up the semiautonomous Volga German Republic and transported its inhabitants to Siberia; the United States placed thousands of West Coast Japanese in detention camps located hundreds of miles from their homes. Little is known of the ultimate fate of these Volga Germans whose ancestors had been invited to Russia by Peter the Great. The United States eventually reversed its policy and allowed the Japanese to live where they wished.

Segregation and discrimination Another type of racist solution, which is less brutal than those just described, is even more widespread. In a great many countries the attitude toward the members of subordinate groups is that they should be allowed to function only in a way that serves the interest of the dominant group; in other words, *discrimination*. The essence of discrimination in this sense is *a practice that treats equal people unequally*, in that members of different ethnic groups do not have the same opportunities to compete for social rewards. Discrimination often means that the duty of the subordinates is simply to do the work which the dominants are either unable or unwilling to perform.

The practice of *segregation* implies that contacts between the subordinates and the dominant group will be confined to those which are essential for the direction of the subordinates in their labors. Subordinates may come into intimate contact with the dominant group as household servants or as laborers in farm and industry. However, purely social contacts are greatly restricted, or if possible, altogether eliminated. If people eat together or sit down together, the association implies equality and tends to undermine the basic assumptions which underlie the system of discrimination. Intimacy but not equality of contact is permitted; dominant and subordinate may meet in bed as master and concubine, but not as husband and wife.

The segregation-discrimination pattern is probably most perfectly developed in the traditional caste society of India, in which the occupations that people might perform were carefully defined, intermarriage was taboo, and separation was the rule in most social relations. In terms of deliberate government policy, segregation and discrimination have been carried furthest by the Union of South Africa's policy of *apartheid*, which translates approximately as "separate development." Under this policy, South Africa has sought to reverse the slight progress of earlier years toward integration and

to separate the races absolutely except for employment, where jobs and pay are determined by color, with whites getting favored treatment. Some logical consequences of this system are that whites never work under the direction of blacks, that blacks receive less money than whites when they are employed in the same capacity, and that service and educational facilities for blacks are separate from those used by whites [Frye, 1968; Ballinger, 1970; MacCrone, 1970].

For many years the United States was committed to segregation and discrimination, with several states enforcing such policies by state laws. Currently the federal government and many state and local governments are working toward integration, but in many respects, the heritage of segregation still lingers.

Colonialism and discrimination At one time nearly half of the world's population and territory was included in the colonial empires of a few great powers. When this situation was at its height, the social, political, and economic dominance of the white man was frankly recognized. Perhaps a few native puppets might be kept in luxurious impotence; the rest of the native inhabitants could serve in menial positions or minor clerical occupations but could never hope to be given important executive posts. They might live in or near the houses of whites as servants, but strictly residential dwellings were usually segregated—the Europeans living in a compound cut off from the rest of the population. Native women might serve as mistresses for white men, but legal marriage was rare. The system was somewhat modified in practice by the need to use native personnel in the development of the country. This led to the limited training of a number of natives and to the opening of opportunities in higher education for a few (much more so in some colonies, such as British India, than in some others, such as the Belgian Congo). Eventually, as colonialism began to retreat, the social barriers of discrimination and segregation also tended to be eased; greater political power was granted to the native populations and social relationships reached more nearly a level of equality. This process has culminated in many countries in the end of foreign rule and the creation of independent governments.

With the coming of independence the tendency is to reverse the process of segregation and discrimination. Thus, the Europeans who once were dominant were, in some cases, forced out of the country. Most of the Dutch were compelled to leave Indonesia, while those who remained soon found that their activities were definitely restricted and their status changed from that of dominance to one of bare toleration. Europeans were shut out of many lines of business activity, and even missionaries and educators now find that their work takes place under the critical supervision of native governments.

Some equalitarian patterns of ethnic relationship

Integration The term "integration" has several different meanings. *Cultural integration* was discussed in Chapter 3 and *personality integration* is a concept in social psychology. *Racial integration,* or *ethnic integration,* refers to equal opportunity for all racial or ethnic groups to participate in all of the activities of a society. Yinger describes an integrated society as

One in which the members regardless of race, religion, or national origin, move freely among one another, sharing the same opportunities and the same public facilities and privileges on an equal basis. (*J. Milton Yinger, A Minority Group in American Society, McGraw-Hill Book Company, New York, 1965, p. 38.*)

This is a basically different process from assimilation (see Chapter 14), although the two processes may take place together. Immigrants from Europe typically became integrated while the process of assimilation was under way. With the second or third generation, they were both integrated and assimilated. With non-Caucasian immigrant groups, whose racial origin remains a visible sign of group difference, assimilation may be fairly complete, while integration is far from perfect. The American black population is assimilated but not fully integrated.

One indication of both past discrimination and present progress is found in comparative income figures for the two races. There is no reason for assuming there would ever be a perfect match between the incomes of any two groups in the society, but major disparities may be taken to indicate a definite lack of integration. Figure 13 shows that the "nonwhites" (mostly blacks) are 2½ times as likely to live in poverty as whites and less than half as likely to have a family income of over $15,000 a year. These data also show that, while the ratio of blacks to whites among the poor has been relatively constant, the ratio at all income levels above the poverty line shows great relative improvement for black families. Thus, between 1947 and 1968, the proportion of black families with an income over $15,000 rose about three times as fast as the proportion of white families. Yet, while the rise from poverty by both whites and blacks has been substantial, as shown in Figure 14, the gap between whites and blacks still remains a large one. At the earliest, it will not be closed until all discrimination has been eliminated and a generation of blacks has come to maturity free of racial handicaps [Kain, 1969; Thurlow, 1969].

Every kind of enforced segregation in the United States is now forbidden by law. Most segregation and discrimination *based directly upon race itself* is ended, but much effective segregation and discrimination remain. Wherever access depends upon geographic address, income level, or ability to pass qualifying examinations, the black people are at a disadvantage because of past inequalities. It is largely due to these kinds of incidental segregation that two-thirds of the nation's black children were still attending virtually all-black schools in 1970 [Associated Press, Jan. 5, 1970]. Similarly, despite open housing and fair-employment legislation, the majority of blacks live in urban ghettos and work in low-status jobs. Integration is encouraged by the legal attack on discrimination and segregation and by the fact that an industrial society seems to promote an open-class system. But the persistence of earlier prejudiced attitudes among both blacks and whites, the rise of separatist sentiments among some militant groups, the cumulative effect of unequal educational opportun-

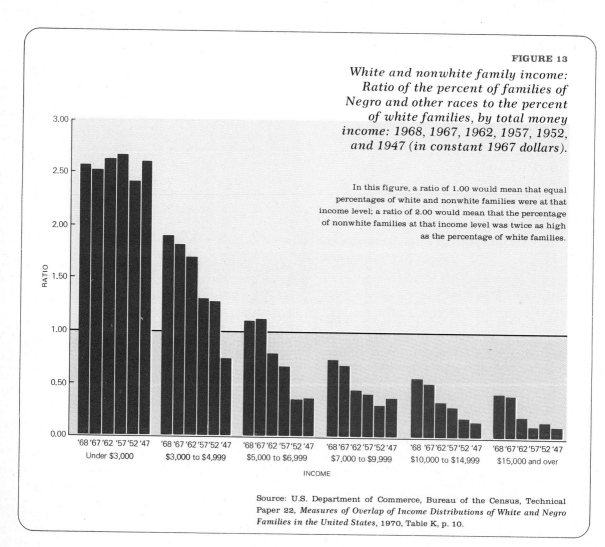

FIGURE 13

White and nonwhite family income: Ratio of the percent of families of Negro and other races to the percent of white families, by total money income: 1968, 1967, 1962, 1957, 1952, and 1947 (in constant 1967 dollars).

In this figure, a ratio of 1.00 would mean that equal percentages of white and nonwhite families were at that income level; a ratio of 2.00 would mean that the percentage of nonwhite families at that income level was twice as high as the percentage of white families.

Source: U.S. Department of Commerce, Bureau of the Census, Technical Paper 22, *Measures of Overlap of Income Distributions of White and Negro Families in the United States*, 1970, Table K, p. 10.

ity, and the heavy concentration of the black population in urban ghettos all contribute to discourage integration. On balance, the trend seems to be toward a more open society in which racial inequalities are decreasing. This movement toward a racially open society, however, is neither as rapid nor as consistent as its advocates might desire.

Cultural pluralism Cultural pluralism is a form of accommodation in which ethnic groups retain their distinct cultural differences and traditions, while cooperating peacefully and relatively equally in political, economic, and social life. The standard example of cultural pluralism is Switzerland, a country which maintains a high degree of national unity although it has no national language and is religiously divided. In Switzerland, Protestants and Catholics have been able to live agreeably under the same government, while speaking German, French, or Italian. Since the Swiss citizen does not feel that either his religious loyalty or his ethnic identification is threatened by other Swiss, he is free to give a complete allegiance to the Swiss nation as a common government which allows for the tolerance of distinctly different cultural groups. Canada, with the division between the French and the English, and Belgium, with a division between the French- and the Flemish-speaking population, are other examples of cultural pluralism (not, however, without some ethnic conflict). The different groups who make up a pluralistic society in these nations frequently engage in a struggle for influence, but the essential idea is that national patriotism does not require cultural uniformity, and that differences of nationality, religion, language, or even race do not preclude loyalty to a common national government.

Cultural pluralism does not seem to attract the newly independent nations of Asia and Africa, although many of them have established governments in areas including

FIGURE 14

Poverty and affluence in the United States, white and black, 1947 and 1968. Figures are in 1968 dollars. Poverty is defined as below $3,000 and affluence as above $10,000.

Families below poverty level

Families in affluence

Black White — 1947
Black White — 1968
Black White — 1947
Black White — 1968

60% / 23% / 23% / 9% / 3% / 11% / 21% / 42%

Source: *The Social and Economic Status of Negroes in the United States*, 1969, BLS Report No. 275, Current Population Report series P-23, no. 29, U.S. Government Printing Office, Washington, D.C., 1970, p. 16.

a number of language and tribal groups which never before in history were recognized as one nation. Instead of assuring the various groups of their cultural autonomy, the usual trend has been a drive toward uniformity. This includes the establishment of a national language and a general push toward a high degree of cultural unity in following the patterns of the dominant group.

The Saxon invasion of the sixth century soon produced the Anglo-Saxon type.

The United States has also been cool toward the concept of cultural pluralism as applied to racial and nationality groups, where most Americans have preferred either integration or discrimination and segregation as a solution. Indians and Mexican-Americans constitute practically the only large ethnic groups in the United States which have expressed some desire for cultural pluralism [Deloria, 1970; Grebler, et al., 1970; Debo, 1970]. Their preference may be explained by the fact that they were in the United States before the Anglo-Americans had arrived and, in spite of considerable pressure, have been able to maintain some degree of cultural identity.

Our religious divisions are one area of intergroup relations where some observers [Herberg, 1960] believe cultural pluralism is an essential and valuable feature of American life. For other ethnic groups, it may be that cultural pluralism is only a transitional stage. Gordon [1964, pp. 243–245] argues that one has to accept and have pride in the group of his origin before he is ready to accept assimilation into the larger society. Thus immigrants and their children may gain a sense of security and identity when encouraged to talk about the contributions which their ethnic cultures have made to American society. Similarly, black students may profit from knowing that Africa has been an historic crossroads of civilization, not merely the locale of primitive tribes.

Although integration has been espoused by most American black leaders, policies similar to cultural pluralism have a persistent appeal. With the advent of legal desegregation, the appeal of these pluralistic policies has been reinforced by the realization that many blacks have difficulty entering the main stream of American society at a favorable level. Since middle-class status is often seen as "white middle-class," the Black Muslims and some other "black power" advocates recommend that blacks work separately to build their own society. This "black nationalist" proposal is discussed later in this chapter.

Amalgamation While assimilation refers to a blending of two cultures, *amalgamation* means a biological interbreeding of two peoples of distinct physical appearance until they become one stock. Although distinct physical types have seldom entirely disappeared, enough interbreeding has taken place so that it is difficult to find any large group of individuals who form a "pure" racial type, if, indeed, there ever have been any. England has practiced amalgamation on a grand scale. The Saxon invasion of the sixth century soon produced the Anglo-Saxon type, to be blended again with the

Normans in the eleventh century. Hawaii includes the descendants of the original inhabitants of the islands, plus a large number of Caucasian settlers, Chinese, Japanese, Filipinos, and Koreans. All these have intermarried quite freely, the highest rates being in groups which have more males than females. Many of the leading families of the islands trace their ancestry back to a union of early European or American traders with the Hawaiian nobility.

In the United States the conditions of slavery favored the amalgamation of white and black. Although intermarriage was illegal in the Southern states, concubinage was widespread. Sexual access by white males to black females was usually regarded as one of the privileges of the caste system. The system emphasized the dominant position of the white male, since he was in a position to possess black females at will and to prohibit such relationships between black males and white females. Mere association with white females, however willing, would subject a black male to charges of rape, and hundreds of black men have been lynched or legally executed on this charge. No white man has been lynched for a similar offense against a black woman, and only in recent years have white men been legally prosecuted for raping black women.

Amalgamation in the United States has greatly declined during the past century, for a variety of reasons: the end of slavery, the decline of the plantation, the diminishing number of white households with black servants, the rising status of blacks, a growing mutual disapproval of interracial sex contacts, and possibly the spread of contraception. But while extramarital amalgamation has declined, has interracial marriage increased? The limited evidence on this question is mixed and inconclusive. Hawaii for many years has had a fairly high rate of intermarriage, involving white and colored, as well as marriage between members of various oriental groups. In other parts of the United States the interracial marriage rate has fluctuated at a relatively low level, and no definite trend is discernible. In Boston, one of the few places where records are available over a period of time, an average of 3.9 percent of all Negro marriages between 1914 and 1938 involved a white partner, while between 1900 and 1904, mixed marriages accounted for 13.6 percent of all Negro marriages [Simpson and Yinger, 1965, p. 371]. For the years between 1955 and 1965, data on Negro-white marriages were gathered by the state of Michigan as shown in Table 26; these show a gradual rise in Negro-white marriages as a percentage of all marriages involving Negroes, from less than 1 percent in 1955 to 3 percent in 1965. Data for the years 1963 to 1967 are obtainable for thirty-five states, including about half of the marriages which take place in the country, as shown in Table 27. These data indicate that interracial marriages comprise less than 1 percent of all marriages, with no clear indication of change in either direction.

TABLE 26

Percent of Negro marriages involving whites in Michigan, 1955–1965

Year	1955	1956	1957	1958	1959	1960	1961	1962	1963	1964	1965
Percentage	0.80	0.89	0.76	0.94	1.01	1.01	1.13	1.20	1.56	2.85	3.02

Source: David M. Heer, "Negro-White Marriage in the United States," Journal of Marriage and Family Living, 28:265, August, 1966. 1964 and 1965 data from Center For Health Statistics, Michigan Department of Health.

TABLE 27

Negro-white marriages in the United States, 1963–1967

Year	Numbers of states reporting race*	Total marriages+	All interracial marriages‡	Interracial marriages as % of all marriages	Negro-white marriages		
					Total	White bride, Negro groom	Negro bride, white groom
1963	33	796,827	3,444	.0043	1,033	776	257
1964	36	952,018	4,631	.0048	1,484	1,130	354
1965	37	1,057,054	6,370	.0060	2,649	1,730	919
1966	35	898,193	4,880	.0054	1,804	1,274	530
1967	35	932,091	5,489	.0058	2,219	1,772	447

*Includes some states in which major areas did not report race (Cook County, Ill., in 1964–1967 and New York in 1965).
+Excludes marriages of couples for which race was not stated on the marriage certificate.
‡Includes marriages of white or Negro to nonwhite other than Negro.
Source: U.S. Department of Health, Education, and Welfare, Vital Statistics, "Notes on Interracial Marriage." (Mimeographed, undated.)

Summarizing these statistics, we can say that the proportion of interracial marriages is very low and that, while the Michigan data show a slight upward trend, the total involved is still too small to determine whether we are seeing long-term trends or minor fluctuations.

Whether there will eventually be a complete blending of the races is by no means certain. At present, it is estimated that 21 percent of the Americans classified as white have some black ancestry, while nearly three-fourths of blacks have some white ancestry [Stuckert, 1958; Burma, 1946]. In all societies the choice of mates is affected by forces which make for endogamy and by counterforces working for exogamy. At present the marriage rate in the United States between those of different European stocks as well as between Protestant and Catholic is high, whereas the rate of Jewish-gentile intermarriage is low and that between black and white is still lower. Legal equality along with increased contact between members of different races may bring a high rate of intermarriage. It is possible, however, that our great-grandchildren may be bound by our preferences in mate selec-

tion about as tightly as we are bound by those of our great-grandfathers. So many factors are involved that it is extremely difficult to predict future intermarriage trends.

MINORITY REACTIONS TO DOMINANT GROUPS

The patterns of ethnic relations which a society follows are mainly those imposed by the dominant group. Therefore, if ethnic relations become a problem, the dominant ethnic group has created it. American whites have not been lynched by blacks; gentiles have not been led to gas chambers by Jews; and Asian and African nationals have not been legislated out of business by the overseas Chinese and Indians. Since the most powerful group in a society dictates the patterns of the society, it would be more correct to speak of a white problem than a black problem, or of a majority problem than a minority problem. Yet the minority groups are not entirely passive. Each group plays a role in the interaction. What are some of the minority responses?

Submissive manipulation

Flattery is the historic weapon of the weak. Harriet Beecher Stowe's *Uncle Tom's Cabin* shows a submissive slave whose adjustment was characterized by faithfulness to his master and deference to white people in general. Through dogged loyalty, flattery, and submissiveness he assumed that he would gain his white master's favor and protection. To many whites, such a black is a "good nigger"; that is, he accepts his caste position. But other blacks may contemptuously call him an "Uncle Tom."[2] In a period when discriminatory patterns are completely dominant, the Uncle Tom posture will help the subordinates to gain the favor of the dominants and also enable them to become acquainted with the culture of a technologically advanced group. As acculturation proceeds to reduce the cultural differences between the two groups, the Uncle Tom posture fades. The subordinates become less willing to assume the role, while the dominants grow less omnipotent in their ability to dispense penalties and rewards.

Marginal adaptation

Marginal adaptation is an effort to cultivate fields where the majority offers the least resistance. Booker T. Washington, a prominent Negro leader in the period between 1880 and 1910, urged that Negroes should seek to develop their skills in agriculture and craftsmanship. He promoted vocational education as a step in this direction. The

[2]There are few characters, either in fiction or in real life, who have been as misrepresented as Harriet Beecher Stowe's Uncle Tom. It is true that he did use flattery as a means of manipulation, but there were also occasions when he boldly resisted the slave owners. His name not only connotes a submissive attitude but also indicates how the process of stereotyping takes place by emphasizing one trait and neglecting others. Today the term "Uncle Tom" is an epithet which is hurled at any black person who is not as aggressive toward whites as some other black person thinks he should be.

success of his program, however, has been limited by technological trends and white resistance. Mechanization of agriculture and industry restricted the number of people who could make a livelihood as artisans, while both farmers and craftsmen were hostile to black competition. Blacks were welcomed as unskilled laborers or field hands but found resistance when they attempted to become independent farmers or highly skilled artisans.

Various groups have sought adaptation as marginal trading peoples through finding business opportunities neglected by the majority. This has been true of Jews, overseas Indians and Chinese, Syrians, Armenians, and some Arab traders. Such business is often profitable, but the minority group's initial success in this adaptation has often aroused the resentment of the majority group, which replies by instituting various forms of discrimination against them.

In general, the effort of a minority to find an outlet in fields neglected by the majority group is successful only when the field is highly specialized and the minority group is small in numbers. Thus a small number of American Chinese have found a role in hand laundries and in the souvenir shops and restaurants of Chinatowns, and gypsies have been successful as fortune tellers and carnival operators; but no large ethnic group has been able to escape discrimination through marginal adaptation.

Withdrawal and self-segregation

Withdrawal has been most characteristic of small religious groups such as the Amish, who deliberately limit their interaction with the rest of society; but it may be found to some extent in other types of groups as well. One mark of this tendency is the development of ethnic colonies in which an ethnic group sponsors schools, churches, social agencies, and recreational establishments catering primarily to an ethnic clientele. While particular institutions of this type, such as national or racial churches, may persist for many years, it is difficult for the group to maintain the cohesion needed to resist the impact of the larger society. Over a period of time members of such groups find themselves increasingly involved with outsiders and tend to become absorbed in the general community, if they are not readily identifiable by their physical characteristics. As they become aware of the opportunities in the society, they discover that often the best economic openings are in businesses serving the general community, the most attractive houses are outside of the ethnic area, and the education best adapted to social mobility is found in schools not dominated by the ethnic group. Unless the ethnic colony is held together by a strong religious tie and is either replenished by a constant supply of new members or bitterly ostracized by the rest of society, it does not last very long.

This type of segregation does offer a small number of careers which are protected from the competition of outsiders. Ethnic schools, churches, and newspapers afford a chance for the employment of clergymen, teachers, and journalists, and the political power of an ethnic bloc may also guarantee a few government jobs. Businesses such as funeral homes, insurance companies, and restaurants may cater to a market ignored by concerns operated for the general society. Such segregated opportunities are necessarily limited in scope, and while they may provide an outlet for a few members of the ethnic colony, they cannot meet the economic aspirations of very many.

The oppression psychosis

When one is treated in a special manner because of his ethnic identity he cannot easily separate this treatment from the things that happen for other reasons. A member of a minority group may develop a tendency to imagine discrimination even when it is absent. The personal antagonisms normal to any type of social life thus become group antagonisms, and every failure or frustration is attributed to discrimination, regardless of the real facts of the situation. Since an inability to distinguish a real from an imaginary environment is a part of many mental illnesses, this behavior in its extreme form may be considered a type of psychosis. Kardiner and Oversey [1951] traced the patterns of behavior discovered in blacks under psychoanalytic treatment and concluded that ethnic discrimination is often a factor in serious mental illness, since it produces tensions which some individuals are unable to resolve. Similar conclusions from a variety of data were also reached by Parker and Kleiner [1966].

Group self-hatred

Group self-hatred is another reaction which disturbs the mental equilibrium of some minority members. Since the subordinates are a part of the total society, it is difficult for them to reject unfavorable stereotypes that are a part of the general culture. When the black infers from almost everything that he reads, sees, hears, and experiences that he is inferior, he can hardly resist believing that he is. The current "black is beautiful" theme is a reaction against group self-hatred and an effort to build an acceptable self-image. The phenomenon of Jewish anti-Semitism is well-known, and some degree of similar feeling is hard for members of any minority group to escape. Since society rejects the individual because of the alleged shortcomings of his group, he sometimes concludes that the cause of his trouble is not the dominant group's prejudices, but the unworthy traits of his own group which justify this discrimination.

Some people who have internalized this

reaction are able to escape by "passing." The light-complexioned black may become "white"; the Jew or the immigrant may change his name and associate only with members of the dominant group. Passing, however, is not necessarily tied to group self-hatred, but may be motivated simply by a desire to escape from discrimination. For most people either marks of physical identification or close ties with the group make "passing" impossible. Enforced identification with a group he considers inferior makes it difficult for the individual to accept himself. Just as respect for parents aids a person in establishing self-respect, so respect for the group with which he is identified helps to establish the self-esteem necessary if one is to develop a secure personality. A rather striking example of this process was recounted to one of the authors by a social worker in Hawaii in connection with the local Filipino population. Filipinos were the last group to enter Hawaii in large numbers and held the poorest-paying jobs. Their status difficulties found expression in an attempt by Filipino children to deny their national origin and call themselves Japanese or Chinese, since these groups held a higher status in Hawaii. With the coming of independence for the Philippines in 1946 their attitude changed. Now they were identified with one of the first Asian colonial countries to gain independence, and their homeland occupied a prominent place in world affairs. They began to identify themselves as Filipino and, having reason to be proud of their ancestry, could accept it and enter into the process of assimilation without anxiety.

Nativism

A quite opposite type of reaction is found in the rejection of the culture of the dominant group and a zealous dedication to minority cultural patterns. Nativistic reactions have appeared in many parts of the world. The American Indians in the period around 1888 developed a "ghost dance" which symbolized the rejection of the white man's world and a hope that supernatural forces would push back the white man, return the buffalo, and restore the old life [Berry, 1965, pp. 398–399]. In 1918 Marcus Garvey organized the Universal Negro Improvement Association, whose aim was to lead American Negroes back to Africa. He attracted many followers, but his schemes foundered and eventually he was sent to prison on a charge of using the mails to defraud [Cronon, 1955]. Currently the Black Muslims and some other Black Power militants are preaching racial separation to American blacks [see Chapter 21].

A very different type of group, the racist Southern whites, might also be classed as nativistic since their attempts to block national efforts toward racial integration led to a states-rights movement with a vigorous rejection of all non-Southern influence. Nativistic movements elsewhere include the emphasis on "negritude" in central Africa [Balandier, 1955], the Dar Ul Islam movement in Indonesia, which strives to reject all Western influences and make Indonesia into a Moslem state [*Economist*, 1956], and a great variety of similar movements in many countries.

Nativistic movements often arouse a strong emotional response, but the conditions of life in the modern world make their chances of success rather dubious. In a time when the process of industrialization is forcing all groups to certain common cultural adjustments, any group will find it difficult to turn its back on the rest of the world. Isolation and a return to the past will not solve the problems of today.

Antisocial behavior

Some ethnic minorities show very little antisocial behavior. For example, the Chinese in the United States, though frequently poor and often discriminated against, have a proud cultural tradition, a clear sense of identity, a strong family system—and a low crime rate. Among America's poor blacks, however, poverty and discrimination are joined by a confused sense of identity, a weak family system, and a widespread feeling of outrage. Antisocial behavior is one result. Some forms of delinquency and adult crime are ways of striking back at an unjust society. Escape into drugs or alcohol provides a temporary haven for those who find reality too bleak to confront. Irresponsible sexual adventures give a sense of masculine achievement or of feminine fulfillment to those whose other routes to these emotional rewards are blocked. Gambling brings a daily ray of hope into a world where hope is a rare visitor. Antisocial behavior of various kinds is widespread among most ethnic minorities who suffer strong feelings of outrage, powerlessness, and despair.

Riots and collective violence

Many riots, lynchings, massacres, or pogroms have been launched by dominant groups for any of many reasons—to divert hostilities upon a scapegoat, to express hatreds, to intimidate or punish a minority, to eliminate a competitive threat, to dispel monotony and boredom—the list is a long one. But minorities as well as majorities also relish the catharsis which collective violence provides. Such violence does not need a definite aim and may not even be directed at those most responsible for minority oppression. Thus, most of the rioting in American cities since 1964 took place within black districts, and property destruction was done either to black-owned property or to other property serving blacks, so that one result was an increase in property insurance rates and retail prices, making life more difficult than before the riots took place. Similarly the riots were not related to specific de-

mands, and the incidents which triggered the violence were often mere pretexts rather than obvious wrongs [Locke, 1969; Gordon, 1971].

What did the rioters gain then? Sometimes the violence aroused community concern which resulted in improvement programs, although this was countered by a "white backlash" which often increased resistance to any kind of civil rights progress. More to the point, the riots provided an immediate sense of power to those who felt society had ignored and mistreated them. Tomorrow they might resume their misery in the ghetto, but tonight they could burn, attack, and pillage in ways that arouse fear in an entire city. Sporadic violence by a minority does very little, if anything, to improve their lot, but such violence is apt to be a part of the price society pays for the frustration of minority citizens.

Movements of reform and revolt

While the nativistic movements attempt to reestablish the supremacy of a dying culture, most of the current minority protest movements are an effort to secure for this minority group an acceptable status in the modern world. A number of reform and revolt movements are discussed in Chapter 21 of this text.

HOW ETHNIC PATTERNS CHANGE

Individual attitudes and community behavior

Since ethnic patterns are based upon prejudices, is it not useless to attack patterns of segregation and discrimination before prejudices are reduced? Until quite recently, even the social scientists shared the popular belief that "you can't legislate against prejudice." Like other people, we believed that those who wish to change ethnic relations must rely upon education and persuasion; then when persons have formed more tolerant attitudes, their actions will change and discrimination will disappear.

Social scientists now realize that these beliefs are based upon false assumptions. First, prejudice is not the cause of discrimination; it is far more nearly true to say that discrimination is the cause of prejudice. Discrimination separates groups so that they have only the inequality-type of contacts which create and feed prejudice. Second, we now know that our actions are not primarily determined by our individual attitudes. Current research indicates that probably the reverse is true—that our actions are determined by the pressures of groups of which we are a part and that our attitudes are largely determined by our group actions. This is to say that, over a period of time, our attitudes conform to the kind of action required by the community in which we live. Some of the implications of this approach may be found in a study of an integrated teamsters' local union [Rose, 1952]. The union had strongly stressed the idea of integration and had insisted that equal opportunities be given to the drivers regardless of race. Interviewers found that the great majority of white teamsters recognized and supported the policy of employment integration. But when they were asked their opinion about integrated housing, the white teamsters expressed a high degree of opposition. Judged by the standard of racial tolerance, these two attitudes seem to be inconsistent. Looked at from the standpoint of group patterns, however, the inconsistency disappears. The teamsters were members of a union which felt that following a policy of employment integration was vital to the success of the union; as union members they had been indoctrinated with this policy, and they supported it. They were also residents of neighborhoods which supported the practice of housing segregation, and as conventional members of the community they accepted community values. In both circumstances the teamsters were responding to the patterns of group expectations, and in neither case could their actions be attributed to purely personal attitudes.

Important as personal attitudes are, they do not exist in isolation. A campaign designed to diminish prejudice is more effective when it is tied to a definite attack on discrimination, just as a campaign of racial intolerance is more effective when linked to a specific pattern of segregation. The community patterns of ethnic behavior are somewhat influenced by personal attitudes, but they are more directly shaped by the public and private groups able to control crucial decisions. The real estate board deciding whether or not it is "ethical" to promote integrated housing, the labor union which may seek either to exclude or integrate, the corporation setting its promotion "ceiling" for blacks, the school board drawing school-district boundaries and hiring teachers, the courts in reaching decisions, and the legislative bodies passing laws which treat different ethnic groups in either an equal or a discriminatory fashion—these and countless other groups set the pattern of the community. If individuals who feel strongly about ethnic relations are able to influence group policy, their attitudes will have some effect. Otherwise their individual feelings will have little influence on the development of ethnic relationships [Blumer, 1956].

Technology changes social structure

Today all patterns of intergroup relationships are subject to controversy. While many persons and groups share in the debate, the real cause of change in intergroup relations may be the social changes—in population, in technology, in cultural values—

which set the stage for our intergroup relations. For example, the invention of the cotton gin made large-scale cotton plantations profitable and created a need for a large supply of cheap, docile labor. The cotton gin ended all Southern discussion of whether slavery was desirable. More recently, the mechanization of Southern agriculture has replaced unskilled labor with mechanical slaves. Many of the rural blacks moved to the city or to the North; they escaped from the paternalistic supervision of the planter and escaped also from some of the patterns of discrimination which could be rigidly enforced only in a rural setting where the white master knew everything that his colored hands were doing.

A caste society is best perfected in a static, unchanging system of relationships, sanctified by universally understood traditions. A growing, rapidly changing, dynamic society makes ancient caste rules quite unworkable; for example, a Brahmin in Calcutta today would soon starve if he ate only food upon which the shadow of no untouchable had fallen. A rapidly changing society tends either to reshuffle or to bypass crusty aristocracies and assign the important tasks and rewards according to individual merit rather than inherited privilege.

FACTORS DETERMINING ETHNIC PATTERNS

Relationships between ethnic groups are seldom static for very long, although the causes of change are often complex and intertwined. Many attempts have been made to construct an ethnic-relations cycle of stages through which such relationships will pass [Bogardus, 1930; Brown, 1934; Park, 1949; Glick, 1955; Edgerton, 1965]. Usually such cycles mention a stage of initial discovery in which the chief interest of the groups in each other is one of novelty or curiosity, followed by casual trading contacts which

in turn result in friction leading to conflict. Conflict results in the defeat of the technologically backward group, which then undergoes a period of subordination until it has learned enough of the culture of the superordinate power to free itself from domination. Cycle theory emphasizes the changing character of ethnic relationships and does give a rough idea of developments which may be expected. However, the relationships which they describe are so complex and the potential patterns of ethnic relationships are so varied that cycle theory has only a very limited predictive value. Few sociologists, for example, expected that during the 1960s any significant number of black Americans would turn from integration to separatism as a goal.

Ethnic relationships are subject to change because ethnic groups are continually engaged in the types of interaction described in the chapter on social processes. This interaction is constant, but the circumstances and the relative power of different groups is in a constant state of change. For instance, individuals from different ethnic groups are in a continuous state of competition, but the competition changes when a stable rural society enters a period of industrialization. Two major factors influence ethnic interaction. One is deliberate, planned change in the structure of society, which we will label *enacted* change, and the other is the gradual movement of society, unplanned and nondirected, which we will label *crescive* change. "Crescive" is defined in the dictionary as "increasing" or "growing" and implies change that develops out of the existing order without conscious design.

Enacted change

Occasionally governments or other social institutions decree certain patterns of relationships which have a far-reaching effect. The legalization of slavery is one such enacted measure which set the relative status of ethnic groups in extremely rigid form.

The legal definition of slaves in the United States as "property," while they were legally "persons" in Central and South America had great effects on their status. Central and South American slaves had certain rights guaranteed by law (to marry, hold property, buy their freedom, and others), but since property has no rights against its owners, slaves in the United States had no legal rights whatever [Silberman, 1964, chap. 4].

The acceptance of the idea of caste in Hindu religion is another type of enactment with persistent consequences. In the United States, the decision that the public lands would be reserved for homesteaders in 160-acre units prevented the rise of an agrarian landlord-tenant system in the West. Similarly the passing of a restrictive immigration act cut down support for cultural pluralism by limiting the number of immigrants to a number which could be assimilated with relative ease. After the Civil War, the "Jim Crow" laws of the Southern states made racial segregation legally mandatory in that area.

Currently, one of the leading types of enacted change is represented by the civil rights laws passed by the national Congress as well as by many of the individual states. These laws prohibit or restrict many types of racial segregation and discrimination. Civil rights laws have made many changes in American society, but no one would claim that they are completely effective. The limits of their effectiveness are very largely set by crescive changes which may work either for or against the aims of the law.

Crescive change

Most change in our society is not enacted by any legislature or the board of trustees of any organization but comes about without deliberate planning. Such unplanned, unintended changes are called *crescive*. No plan or decree is responsible for urbanization. No deliberative group brought forth the cotton gin which created a demand for cheap labor, or the mechanical cotton picker which later made this kind of cheap labor unnecessary. Nor did any legislative body produce the shift in scientific opinion which made a racist interpretation of human conduct untenable.

Policies of integration are favored by the general expansion of education, which makes it easier for members of a submerged minority to prepare themselves for social mobility. Conversely, they are hampered by the drift away from unskilled manual labor, which means that only the man with training is able to find a good job. Legislation can outlaw discrimination in employment, but this is of limited effect unless minority members are qualified for competition on a merit basis.

Enacted legislation has pretty well eliminated deliberate educational segregation in many areas, but de facto segregation continues to exist and may even expand because segregated housing produces segregated schools. Segregation in housing flourishes because a rapid black migration to the cities produces a massive demand for black housing, which means that integrated housing is often only a transitional phase until black demand takes up all the housing in districts that had been integrated.

In the Union of South Africa industrial development and the consequent demand for labor works against apartheid legislation enacted to push the nonwhite population into rural areas. In India the caste system has survived onslaughts against it, in part, because the castes have become a political force in claiming group preference from government bodies. In the United States a rising income for blacks has caused business firms to treat black customers with greater courtesy rather than in the demeaning fashion demanded by the traditional racial etiquette. Similarly the black movement to the cities makes political leaders more sensitive to the wishes of a constituency in which the "minority" grows larger.

These examples and many more indicate that crescive development may either accelerate or retard enacted programs of change in ethnic relations. This does not mean that ethnic relations are determined by the unconscious processes of history which man is powerless to control. Rather it means that to be effective without great cost and disruption enacted change must be in harmony with the relevant trends in society. If industrial changes are in process, we must consider how these changes will affect the present and prospective situation of members of ethnic groups. If population is moving from the farm to the city and we desire residential integration, then positive steps must be taken to make the central city more attractive to the majority and also to enable racial minorities to enter the suburbs. If limited education or unstable family life prevent the minority from acquiring the skills and attitudes needed for social mobility, then steps can be taken to stabilize family life and improve the schools. In other words, effective enacted change must do more than simply endorse a desirable pattern of ethnic relationships. It must either relate the enacted change to crescive development or seek to change the course of this development.

THE NEW SEPARATISM

As outlined earlier, segregation and discrimination came under legal, administrative, and social attack in the mid-twentieth century. As shown in Table 28, America's black population has made rapid gains in almost every respect. Much to the surprise

and dismay of many whites, however, these gains did not earn any gratitude from blacks; instead, they were accompanied by an outburst of black resentment and hostility.

This should have been no surprise. When a long-oppressed group is partly freed from its oppression, the result is likely to be not gratitude but *anger*—anger that they had to wait so long, and anger that they still are only partly free. The remaining injustices seem more outrageous than ever. Although the proportion of nonwhite families in poverty was cut by almost two-thirds between 1947 and 1968 [Figure 14] and by one-half between 1959 and 1970 [Silberman, 1970], this still leaves almost one-fourth of black families in poverty, compared with one-eleventh of white families. These gains serve as a reminder of the inequalities still remaining, as Raymond Mack states:

> **The present friction in American race relations stems less from black Americans' being "kept in their place" than from the fact that so many of them in the present generation have managed to work their way out of what has traditionally been "their place." It is precisely because black Americans have achieved so much in the past twenty years that so many of them are so dissatisfied. Real access to real equality of opportunity no longer seems absolutely impossible. Perhaps worse, it seems frustratingly delayed.** (*Raymond Mack, "Riot, Revolt, or Responsible Revolution: Of Reference Groups and Racism,"* Sociological Quarterly, *10:151, Spring, 1969.*)

Black college students—that group of blacks who have probably had the greatest gains—are the most militant and discontented. As illustrated in Figure 15, black college students feel that opportunities are still far from equal and Northern students, the ones with the greatest degree of integration, are the most critical of the white establishment.

For such reasons, many of the younger and more aggressive black people have

TABLE 28
Black and white progress in the United States

Category	Year	Blacks	Whites
Percent above poverty level	*1959*	*43.8*	*81.9*
($3,743 in 1969)	*1969*	*69.0*	*90.5*
Median for married man of	*1960*	*$3,993*	*$5,877*
blue-collar income	*1969*	*$5,746*	*$7,452*
Increase in median income of			
married blue-collar workers	*1960–1969*	*$1,753*	*$1,575*
Percent gain in number of married men			
in blue-collar jobs	*1960–1969*	*40*	*10*
Median black income as percent			
of white income	*1965*	*54*	
	1969	*64*	
Percent with family income $10,000 and over (1968 dollars)	*1947*	*3*	*11*
	1960	*8*	*24*
	1968	*21*	*42*
Percent with 4 years high school	*1959*	*25*	*52.6*
	1965	*37.5*	*60.0*
Percent with 4 years college	*1959*	*4.0*	*10.3*
	1965	*7.0*	*12.2*
Median years of school completed	*1959*	*8.6*	*12.1*
	1969	*11.3*	*12.4*

Source: Based on data reported in The Negroes in the United States: Their Economic and Social Situation, *U.S. Dept. of Labor Bulletin 1511, June, 1966; Charles E. Silberman, "Negro Economic Gains Impressive but Precarious," Fortune, 82:74–78, July, 1970; U.S. Census Bureau Special Report, 1970.*

turned from integration to separatism as a goal. They were frustrated by the slowness of progress toward integration and by a suspicion that whites would never allow integration to become complete. Also, they claimed that complete integration, if granted, would carry the price of denial of black identity—that blacks would have to become "black white men" [Browne, 1968]. This was accompanied by the call for blacks to unite under black leadership to seek power—

Black Power—to redress their wrongs [Wagstaff, 1969; Henderson and Ledebur, 1970]. As Carmichael and Hamilton state:

Black Power. . . is a call for black people in this country to unite, to recognize their heritage, to build a sense of community. . . .*Before a group can enter the open society it must first close ranks. By this we mean group solidarity is necessary before a group can operate effectively from a bargaining position of strength in a pluralistic society.* (*Stokely Carmichael and Charles V. Hamilton,*

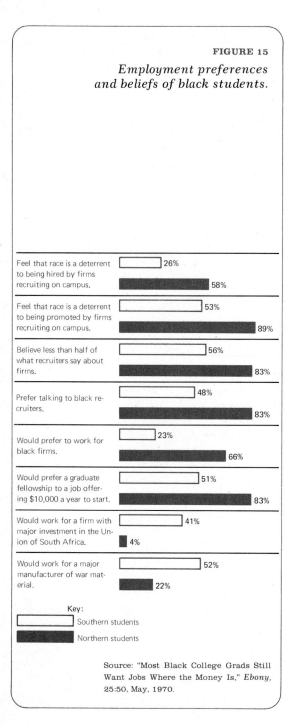

FIGURE 15

Employment preferences and beliefs of black students.

	Southern students	Northern students
Feel that race is a deterrent to being hired by firms recruiting on campus.	26%	58%
Feel that race is a deterrent to being promoted by firms recruiting on campus.	53%	89%
Believe less than half of what recruiters say about firms.	56%	83%
Prefer talking to black recruiters.	48%	83%
Would prefer to work for black firms.	23%	66%
Would prefer a graduate fellowship to a job offering $10,000 a year to start.	51%	83%
Would work for a firm with major investment in the Union of South Africa.	41%	4%
Would work for a major manufacturer of war material.	52%	22%

Key:

☐ Southern students

■ Northern students

Source: "Most Black College Grads Still Want Jobs Where the Money Is," *Ebony*, 25:50, May, 1970.

Black Power, *Random House, Inc., New York, 1967, p. 44.*)

Black separatism is a call for cultural pluralism. It includes the "black is beautiful" theme, with cultivation of black art, literature, poetry, and drama. Black art is seen as basically different and not to be evaluated by the same criteria as "white art." Black separatism includes black control of business, schools, police, and government in predominantly black areas.

Black nationalism includes all that black separatism does, in addition to a geographic separation of the country into independent white and black states [Blake, 1969]. While only a minority of blacks appear to support black separatism and black nationalism, these issues have the support of many of the most vocal and newsworthy blacks. To the integrationist leaders, separatism appears to be a sellout to those who would keep the blacks in second-class citizenship. Roy Wilkins of the National Association for the Advancement of Colored People states:

There are individuals (millions of them) and organized forces in the nation itching to respond to the disruptive clamor of Negroes themselves for separation. One day it will be separate, all-black studies centers. The next it will be not only a quota system on jobs, but one on the types of jobs in separate black buildings under black bosses. Then it will be separate (and inferior) schools and residential areas (like South Africa) and the completely separated elective offices so that the impact of a black bloc within a white party will be nil. If Negro youth will think beyond their understandable frustration. . . they will surely realize that they must not commit suicide by opening Pandora's box of racial separatism. (*Roy Wilkins, Des Moines Register and Tribune, March 30, 1969.*)

Many sociologists fear that black separatism would leave black people in neglected, poverty-ridden enclaves and that reduced contacts with whites would intensify and perpetuate prejudices and would set back the cause of equal opportunities and rewards for the races [Pettigrew, 1969].

Separatism and territorially based minorities

Most examples of cultural pluralism are found in countries where each ethnic group is concentrated in a particular territory. In Canada the French are centered in Quebec; in each of the fifteen republics of the Soviet Union, a single ethnic group is generally dominant; each of the cantons of the Swiss Confederation is composed principally of one of three nationalities— German, French, or Italian. But in the United States, each immigrant group was generally scattered rather than concentrated in a single region, and this favored assimilation and integration rather than cultural pluralism. The two major ethnic groups in the United States which do have somewhat of a territorial base—the American Indians and the Mexican-Americans— have shown considerable resistance to assimilation.

The American Indians In agriculture at least, the Europeans assimilated Indian culture rather than the reverse. Much of the success of the European colonization was due to the colonists' adoption of the planting of corn, potatoes, tobacco, peanuts, cocoa, rubber, and several other crops. But conflict soon developed, and the colonists adopted a policy of genocide which exterminated most of the coastal and Eastern woodlands tribes. After genocide became unfashionable, the surviving Indians were herded onto reservations provided by treaties, all of which the whites eventually violated. This policy of isolation on reservations foundered on the difficulty of finding any land so worthless that no white man wanted it. Repeated white invasions of reservation lands would be followed by the inevitable succession of incidents, "massacres," and finally an army campaign such as at the Little Bighorn where Custer earned his ignominious reward. Even in those instances where the Indians had successfully assimilated white culture, the white man's relentless land hunger destroyed this adjustment. For example, the Cherokees of northern Georgia had a stable agriculture, had developed a written language and conducted a publications program, and eagerly adopted new technology. But rumors of gold whetted white appetites, and President Jackson, violating solemn treaty obligations and in open disregard of a decision of the United States Supreme Court, ordered the army to move the Cherokees to Oklahoma along the notorious "trail of tears," where 4,000 of them perished. Even after their arrival in Oklahoma, where they again tried to build a modern society, the Cherokees were yet again frustrated by white land hunger [Wilkins, 1971]. This sordid story, repeated in many variations, constitutes the history of our "generosity" to the Indians [Deloria, 1970; Debo, 1970]. Of the 138 million acres which Indians held by treaty in 1887, only 52 million acres remained by 1934; and to retain even this requires a constant battle against efforts to "free" the Indian from his remaining land [Wax, 1971, p. 54].

Insofar as the whites had a program for Indians, other than pushing them out of the way, it was a policy of disrupting communal tribal life and encouraging cultural assimilation, sometimes with cash payments for loss of lands. Some who received these payments had as little as one-fourth Indian ancestry and had lost any real connection with tribal life. But even the payments to genuine tribal members brought no benefits beyond a momentary splurge. Accustomed to a cooperative tribal life, they individually lacked the land base, the economic opportunities, and the managerial experience to use these payments as capital to finance their economic self-improvement.

The overall results of Indian policy have been dismal: a failure to assimilate the Indians and to integrate them into American cultural and economic life, but a considerable success in breaking down their traditional tribal life, leaving many of them anomic and demoralized. While many Indians have left the reservations, most of these live in squalid urban slums. Assimilation has largely failed for two reasons: (1) it demanded that the Indian stop being an Indian and sacrifice his tribal culture; but (2) while demanding that the Indian become assimilated, the whites often blocked his successful assimilation by resisting the kind of cooperative communal ventures which might have proven profitable, while discriminating against Indians in many ways which parallel the discrimination

The queer people.

against blacks. Some Indians have indeed become integrated into the mainstream of American life and achieved middle-class status, but many more have reached only a sort of half-way assimilation which combines the worst of both worlds. After the expenditure of more public funds upon each Indian than upon each member of any other minority, the Indians remain the minority with the greatest poverty, the most ill health, and probably the greatest personal demoralization of any major group in American life.

In 1934 anthropologist John Collier became Commissioner of Indian Affairs and reversed the historic policy of encouraging tribes to disband and assimilate. He proposed that the Indians be assisted to survive as tribal units and preserve their tribal culture [Wax, 1971, p. 57]. Government policy since then has vacillated between "termination" (disbanding and enforced assimilation, usually with disastrous results), "preservation" (half-heartedly promoted and usually frustrated by local Indian Service personnel), and "relocation" in cities with federal help (with mixed results, depending upon whose evaluation is accepted) [Deloria, 1970]. The Indians themselves are divided between the "traditionalists" who wish to preserve tribal life and customs, and the "progressives" who promote assimilation and industrial development. Recently a spirit of militant activism has arisen, somewhat similar to the Black Power movement among black Americans, urging that Indians reject "Euroconformity" and preserve Indian language, crafts, and religion, and demanding that Indians control their own schools and economic life [Steiner, 1968, pp. 268–289; Wax, 1971, p. 176].

Four hundred years of contact with whites has left the Indian culture battered but still surviving. A few Indian tribes, such as the Hopi, have strictly controlled outside contacts and have succeeded both in preserving their own culture and in maintaining a viable economy at a modest subsistence level; others have lost most of their culture and live a life of poverty and apathy on the fringes of white society. And even the Hopi face the possible destruction of their economic base through the pumping out of the ground-water supply of the Black Mesa by coal mining operators who use several million gallons of water each day to carry the coal slurry through the pipelines to power plants that provide the white man's electricity [Ashton, 1971]. It seems that every viable economy the Indians establish is eventually sacrificed to white needs. Can the Indian survive only be ceasing to be an Indian? The answer is uncertain.

The Mexican-Americans About 70,000 Mexican-Americans, a mixture of Spanish and Indian stocks, were added to the American population as a result of the war with Mexico. These Mexicans were already established in village communities before the "Anglos" arrived, bringing with them a strong sense of racial, religious, and cultural ethnocentrism which expressed itself in a condescension and contempt for everything Mexican. These circumstances produced little Anglo pressure for assimilation, and little Anglo opposition to the retention of the ancestral Mexican culture. While some cultural interchange followed, the eventual accommodation was a cultural pluralism in which cross-cultural contacts were minimal. Natural increase and immigration have increased the Mexican-American population to slightly over five million in 1970, heavily concentrated in the Southwest where migrants can join existing communities and where proximity to Mexico permits easy visiting.

While much of the traditional Mexican culture survived, the agricultural land base was soon destroyed as the Mexicans lost most of their land to the Anglos. As indicated in the excerpt which opens this chapter, the ancient Spanish land grants, sometimes lost and often accompanied by incomplete records of intervening title changes, were promptly set aside by Anglo courts, presided over by Anglo judges interpreting newly enacted Anglo land laws before Anglo juries. Again, patterns of discrimination arose with the usual dreary consequences. Today, the Mexican-Americans are heavily concentrated in the unskilled jobs with low pay and frequent unemployment. The Mexican-American children begin school later and leave earlier; in Texas, adults with Spanish surnames average 4.7 years of school, compared with 8.1 for blacks and more than 10 for the

entire population, while in California, median years of school completed are 8.6 for Mexican-Americans, 10.5 for blacks, and 12.2 for Anglos [U.S. Commission on Civil Rights, 1970, p. 23]. Although some use of Spanish is fairly common in the Southwest and the state of New Mexico is officially bilingual, it is only recently that schools have begun to use Spanish for instruction in some of the classes. Recently a Governor's Committee on Public Education completed a three-year study of ways to improve public education in Texas—without consulting any Mexican-American parents and without consulting a single prominent Mexican-American educator [U.S. Commission on Civil Rights, 1970, p. 27]. The Roman Catholic Church, useful as an assimilation bridge and mobility ladder for many European immigrants, has played no such role for the Mexican-Americans, who found themselves in parishes which were almost exclusively Mexican, for very few Anglos in the Southwest were Catholics. Thus land deprivation, discrimination, language barriers, and isolation from equal-status contacts kept most Mexican-Americans poor and unassimilated despite an official policy of promoting assimilation.

While some Mexican-Americans have achieved education and prosperity, far more of them feel powerless and alienated. Today many are rejecting assimilation and integration in favor of separatism and militant protest. The term *chicano* is sometimes applied to all Mexican-Americans and sometimes only to the activist ones, while *chicanismo* is a protest against the "cultural genocide" which they feel has robbed them of a proper appreciation of their Mexican heritage [Moore, 1970, pp. 149-156]. They stress group social values over individual achievement and recommend confrontation and disruption when ordinary political action fails. While "race" is perhaps an inaccurate term to apply to Mexicans, there is much rhetoric of race pride and of *la raza*, a term which refers to Mexican cultural heritage rather than to biological origin. Under chicano impetus, it is possible that any tendencies toward continuing assimilation may be reversed, and that a territorial ethnic base coupled with a militant ideology may produce a viable and enduring parallel society among the Mexican-Americans.

These brief sketches of the Indians and the Mexican-Americans are grossly abbreviated, yet they reveal certain similarities between these two groups and the American blacks. Although historical settings and details differ, discrimination has had much the same consequences upon them all—widespread poverty, ill health, personal demoralization, and, recently, the rise of a militant activism which rejects assimilation and integration as goals [Cabrera, 1969; Burma, 1970; Grebler, et al., 1970; Serrin, 1970]. Much the same may be said of the Puerto Ricans in the United States [Senior, 1965; Howard, 1970; Fitzpatrick, 1971]. Even American Jews, who have sought complete acceptance into American society, nonetheless harbor fears that complete assimilation would end their survival as an ethnic group [Gans, 1965; Glazer and Moynihan, 1970, pp. 159-165]. While every subjugated ethnic minority in the United States today is aggressively casting off the chains of subordination, the old "melting pot" vision of assimilation is widely rejected; and it is difficult to predict whether the ultimate outcome will be a fairly complete assimilation and integration or some form of cultural pluralism.

Not only in the United States but throughout the world, ethnic groups are divided between the security that results from separatism and the expanding opportunities that may accompany integration. To some, separatism means a voluntary return to the limitations imposed by segregationist majorities. To others, separatism means individual and group fulfillment and an escape from competition with an entrenched majority. Both viewpoints are valid, and social science offers few guidelines that give a reliable indication of the future course of intergroup relations. It is evident that onesided discrimination is on the way out, but it is uncertain whether this means integration into large societies or fragmentation into a number of ethnic enclaves.

SUMMARY

A *race* is defined either as a group of people who share common physical characteristics or as a group whose boundaries are set by social definition, with no common agreement on usage. Race differences are biologically trivial, but culturally important. As far as scientific investigation has determined, it seems probable that all racial groups inherit about equal amounts and kinds of potential ability; differences in group personality patterns, behavior, or achievements seem to be due to differences in learning situations.

The term *ethnic* is used to designate groups defined by common ancestry and culture. Ethnic relationships involve both cooperation and conflict between distinctive social groups, which often exist within the same national boundaries. Bloody persecution, violent revolution, rigid and exploitative segregation, and a fragmenting of political units along ethnic lines have been the principal trends of ethnic relationships in the twentieth century. Other trends include cultural pluralism, which emphasizes the rights of societies rather than of individuals, and integration, which ignores group identification in favor of individual rights. Minority reactions to domination include submissive adjustment, marginal adaptation, withdrawal and self-segregation, the oppression psychosis, group self-hatred, nativism, protest movements, escape through antisocial conduct, and "passing" into the majority group.

Although great emotion may accompany ethnic attitudes, the actual pattern of behavior is found to be dependent on group pressure while individual behavior usually conforms to community pressures. Community behavior patterns are not always consistent with widespread ethnic attitudes, and the community that supports integrated behavior in one sphere such as employment may support segregated practices in another such as housing. Amalgamation has been practiced on a large scale in the past but seems to be relatively limited in the United States at the present time. Cycles of ethnic relationships interpret behavior of the past but are of limited value in predicting future trends.

Factors affecting the course of ethnic relations include *enacted* change set in motion by deliberate decision of organized groups and *crescive* changes, which occur through the unplanned growth and development of society.

Opposing pressure for separatism and integration are in competition; and while one group leader demands that his group be enclosed by rigid boundary lines, another is seeking systemic linkage with the rest of society. Recent trends both in the United States and in most other countries have been toward greater equality between ethnic groups. Progress toward equality, however, leads to greater impatience with the obstacles and inequalities which still remain. Sharp intergroup conflicts and disagreements about both goals and means make it difficult to make firm predictions about future patterns of ethnic relations.

Questions and projects

1. Why is the term "ethnic" used in preference to "race" throughout most of this discussion?

2. Is the world tending toward greater contact and cooperation between members of different ethnic groups or toward segregation and conflict?

3. The United States government has supported a program for relocating American Indians from their reservations to cities. What are the arguments for and against such a program?

4. Is education the best way to change racial patterns?

5. Which occupational group has done more to change the pattern of ethnic relations—engineers or government officials?

6. Distinguish between segregation and cultural pluralism.

7. If all ethnic discrimination were ended, would all groups produce equal proportions of highly successful men and women?

8. The first reports of the reaction of the American armed forces to integration were favorable from all concerned. Now there are increasing reports of black discontent and conflict in the army. How would you account for this development?

9. Has amalgamation been greatest in a discriminatory or an egalitarian society?

10. What is the interrelationship between enacted and crescive change in promoting changes in ethnic relationships?

11. Read Richard Wright's *Black Boy,* Harper & Row, Publishers, Inc., New York, 1945. How do you think Richard's socialization was affected by race? Why did he become intensely ambitious?

12. Read Thomas F. Pettigrew, "Racially Separate or Together," *Journal of Social Issues,* 25:43–69, January, 1969. Do you feel his conclusions are sound? List the factors which might lead some people to reject his viewpoint.

13. If there are dormitories at your institution, how are black and white students housed? Separate dormitories, separate dormitory sections, or integrated? Are roommates assigned at random, or are blacks paired as roommates? What can be said for or against each arrangement?

14. What can be said for and against having certain classes or college curricula in which enrollment is open only to black students?

Suggested readings

*Alex, Nicholas: *Black in Blue: A Study of the Negro Policeman*, Appleton-Century-Crofts, New York, 1969. A survey of the status of the Negro policeman, one of today's marginal men.

Boorstin, Daniel J.: *The Sociology of the Absurd*, Simon & Schuster, Inc., New York, 1970. A book which, in humorous vein, pushes the principle of merit by ethnicity to the limits of ultimate absurdity.

*Bouma, Donald H., and James Hoffman: *The Dynamics of School Integration: Problems and Approaches in a Northern City*, Wm. B. Eerdmans Publishing Co., Grand Rapids, Mich., 1968. Analyzes the conflict between the neighborhood school concept and a racially integrated school program.

Broom, Leonard, and Norval D. Glenn: *Transformation of the American Negro*, Harper & Row, Publishers, Inc., New York, 1965. A study of the adaptations necessary for blacks to move into the mainstream of American life.

Browne, Robert S.: "The Case for Two Americans—One Black, One White," *New York Times Magazine*, Aug. 11, 1968, pp. 12ff. A strong brief statement of the case for black separatism.

*Clark, Kenneth: *Dark Ghetto*, Harper & Row, Publishers, Inc., New York, 1965. A lucid presentation of some aspects of lower-class black culture based on an analysis of an antipoverty program in Harlem.

*Davidson, Basil: *Old Africa Rediscovered: The Story of Africa's Forgotten Past*, Victor Gollancz, Ltd., London, 1965; or *The Lost Cities of Africa*, Little, Brown and Co., 1959. Readable accounts of ancient African civilizations, which neither consign the continent to barbarism nor erect a romantic facade on a basis of dubious historical evidence.

*Glazer, Nathan, and Daniel P. Moynihan: *Beyond the Melting Pot*, Harvard University Press, Cambridge, Mass., 1970. A description of the interaction of ethnic groups in New York City.

*Grier, William H., and Price M. Cobbs: *Black Rage*, Bantam Books, Inc., New York, 1968. An impassioned discussion of the attitudes of American blacks.

*Herberg, Will: *Protestant, Catholic, Jew*, Doubleday & Company, Inc., Garden City, N.Y., 1960. A treatment of religious identity as a form of cultural pluralism replacing nationalism.

*Meier, August, and Elliott Rudwick (eds.): *Black Protest in the Sixties*, Quardrangle Books, Inc., Chicago, 1970. The rise and development of the black protest movement.

Pettigrew, Thomas: "Racially Separate or Together," *Journal of Social Issues*, 25:43–69, January, 1969. Reprinted under separate cover by Anti-Defamation League, 315 Lexington Avenue, New York, 10016. A presentation of the pitfalls of black separatism as seen by a distinguished social psycologist. Amplified in book form under the same title and published by McGraw-Hill Book Company in 1971.

Rainwater, Lee, and William E. Yancey: "Black Families and the White House," *Trans-action*, July –August, 1966, pp. 6–11. A popular presentation of the controversy accompanying the Moynihan report which pointed to family disorganization as a basic cause of black difficulty.

*Tumin, Melvin M. (ed.): *Comparative Perspectives on Race Relations*, Little, Brown, and Company, Boston, 1969. A series of brief reports on intergroup relations in a variety of countries.

*Wagstaff, Thomas: *Black Power: The Radical Response to White America*, Glencoe Press, Beverly Hills, 1969. A book of readings which includes excerpts from most of the writers on black power.

For descriptions of the problems and prospects of other American minorities (Indians, Mexican-Americans, Puerto Ricans), see the citations on pp. 377–380.

Collective behavior in mass society

I was there [at an address by Senator Joseph McCarthy] with a young lady, and we'd resolved that it would be the height of unwisdom to make any comment because the atmosphere at the conclusion of the meeting would undoubtedly be charged with tension. . . . We stood by and watched this particular performance.

Then a man next to me said, "Oh, I know that Wilbur Jerger [who had made anti-McCarthy comments]. He's a teacher in the Valley and a yid." To this the young lady with me said, "Well, he's got a right to speak." And then all my resolutions flew out the window. I said, "Yes, he's got a right to speak." And I said, "Everyone has a right to speak." And he said, "If you think everyone has a right to speak, you must be a Red." And I said, "Well, if believing that everyone has a right to speak makes me a Red, then I'm a Red!"

That was probably a very silly thing to have said, but I was defiant and this led to a call on his part, "Here's a Red, here's a Red, here's a Red." Well, from every direction they came. I was pretty terrified and looked about frantically for a wall or a fence—something to which I could put my back and at least fight in one direction. I was rendered completely inarticulate and frightened by the horde converging upon me. I felt I was surrounded in every direction. There must have been a hundred people in the group that came around me. They were throwing punches. And I was trying to protect the young lady, whose arms were catching the blows, and holding her with one arm and swinging the other as well as I could. . . .

The battle went on, it may have been a minute, it may have been two minutes—it would be absolutely impossible for me to estimate its duration. It seemed like hours while looking up at the fear-crazed faces of these people—elderly people for the most part. . . .

As they went on for, as I say, a minute or two, a young fellow came up. He must have been 18 or 19, tall, I think almost 7 feet tall. . . . He approached the group and said, "We don't want any violence on this church property. Violence on church property won't help our cause. We don't want violence on church property." This had an almost magical effect upon the group. The whole group dissolved just as rapidly as it had gathered. . . .

Then this young fellow came up to me and said, "Man, you're a fool. I'm not with these people. I'm here for the same purpose that you are, but I have better sense than to make any remark at all before these people. . . . You could have been killed." And without even stopping to take his name or thank him, because I certainly wasn't in possession of my faculties, I just let him go. (*Quoted in Ralph H. Turner and Lewis M. Killian,* Collective Behavior, *Prentice-Hall, Inc., Englewood Cliffs, N.J., 1957, pp. 149–150.*)

This is an example of collective behavior —an audience, momentarily a mob, finally calmed through a strategic leadership appeal. No topic in sociology is more fascinating than the study of collective behavior. Unfortunately, it is not easy to study scientifically. Mobs, riots, and panics do not often occur under the calm gaze of a visiting sociologist. Deliberately to provoke one, however studious our intent, would put us in jail. Besides, just how would a sociologist conduct an interview in the midst of a mob or panic? We are limited to eyewitness accounts by observers and participants, to police records, newspaper accounts, and other scattered data. Seldom can we locate a statistically adequate sample of participants for systematic study. A number of ingenious attempts have been made to duplicate crowd conditions of behavior in a laboratory for purposes of research, but relatively few types of crowd behavior can be so reproduced. Even with these limitations we have a good deal of descriptive information, together with some empirical research, from which we have developed certain insights into the various forms of collective behavior.

NATURE OF COLLECTIVE BEHAVIOR

All sociologists talk about "collective behavior," but few attempt to define it. When they do, the definitions are not very useful. Smelser's definition, "mobilization on the basis of a belief which redefines social action" [Smelser, 1963, p. 8] will probably not be very helpful to most students. Milgram and Toch [1969, p. 507] define collective behavior as "behavior which originates spontaneously, is relatively unorganized, fairly unpredictable and planless in its course of development, and which depends upon interstimulation among participants." Collective behavior includes such topics as crowds, mobs, panics, crazes, mass hysteria, fads, fashions, propaganda, public opinion, social movements, and revolutions. The last two of these topics are treated in a later chapter.

There are no fully satisfactory theoretical formulations of collective behavior. Perhaps this catchall term includes so many kinds of behavior that no framework of theory can encompass them all. One of the most provocative analyses is that of Smelser [1963, chap. 1] which, while perhaps imperfect [Wilkinson, 1970], may be as useful as any. Smelser lists the determinants of collective behavior as:

1. *Structural conduciveness.* Financial panics and fashion crazes do not plague simple, traditional societies. An urbanized society is more prone to mass phenomena than a scattered rural population. The rootless, anonymous, transient members of a highly mobile mass society are more given to extremes of behavior than those in a settled folk society.

2. *Structural strain.* Deprivation and fears of deprivation lie at the base of much collective behavior. The sting of injustice—real or fancied—prompts many to extreme action. Impoverished classes, oppressed minorities, groups whose hard-won gains are threatened, even privileged groups who fear the loss of their privileges—all these are candidates for extreme behavior.

3. *Growth and spread of a generalized belief.* Before any collective action, there must be a belief among the actors which identifies the source of the threat, the route of escape, or the avenue to fulfillment.

4. *Precipitating factors.* Some dramatic

event, or a report thereof, sets the stage for action. A cry of "police brutality" in a racially tense neighborhood may touch off a riot. One person starting to run may precipitate a panic.

5. *Mobilization for action.* All that remains now is for action to begin.

6. *Operation of social control.* At any of the above points, the cycle can be interrupted by leadership, police power, propaganda, legislative and government policy changes, and other social controls.

CROWD BEHAVIOR

A crowd is a *temporary collection of people reacting together to stimuli.* A busload of passengers, each buried in his own daydreams, is not a crowd; let the driver announce that he wishes to stop for a few drinks, and they promptly form a crowd.

Unlike most other groups, a crowd is temporary. Its members rarely know one another. Most forms of crowd behavior are unstructured with no rules, no traditions, no formal controls, no designated leaders, no established patterns for the members to follow. Crowd behavior may appear to be spontaneous and utterly unpredictable, but as we shall see, crowd behavior is not purely a matter of chance or impulse. Crowd behavior is a part of the culture. The kinds of crowds that form and the things a crowd will do and will not do differ from one culture to another. Crowd behavior can be analyzed and understood, and to some extent predicted and controlled.

Some characteristics of crowd behavior

Anonymity Crowds are anonymous, both because they are large and because they are temporary. The size of the group and the

nature of the interaction remove the sense of individuality from the members, even when they recognize acquaintances. They do not pay attention to other members as individuals and do not feel that they themselves are being singled out as individuals. Thus the restraints on a member of a crowd are reduced, and he is free to indulge in behavior which he would ordinarily control, because moral responsibility has been shifted from him to the group. At least one study [Festinger et al., 1952] claims to have confirmed these mechanisms through laboratory experimentation. Members of crowds seldom confess to any feeling of guilt after sharing in even the most outrageous atrocities, and this shift of moral responsibility to the group is part of the explanation.

Crowds are anonymous.

Impersonality Group behavior is typically impersonal. By this we mean that when groups interact with other groups, this interaction takes very little account of personal feelings or personal relations between members of different groups. The soldier bears no personal grudge against the enemy soldier he shoots, nor does it matter that the opposing football player is a personal friend. The impersonality of crowd behavior is revealed in race riots where one member of the enemy race is as good or bad as another.

We drove around for a long time. We saw a lot of colored people, but they were in bunches. We didn't want any of that. We wanted some guy all by himself. We saw one at Mack Avenue.

Aldo drove past him and then said, "Gimme that gun." I handed it over to him and he turned around and come back. We were about 15 feet from the man when Aldo pulled up, almost stopped and shot. The man fell and we blew.

We didn't know him. He wasn't bothering us. But other people were fighting and killing and we felt like it, too. (*Alfred M. Lee and Norman D. Humphrey*, Race Riot, *Holt, Rinehart and Winston, Inc., New York, 1943, p. 38.*)

It should be no surprise that peaceful passersby are attacked in race riots. If the other *group* is the enemy, then *any* member of the group is automatically a victim. When FLN terrorists in Algeria tossed a grenade, killing a guest in a hotel, Europeans surged into the streets and lynched the first two Moslems they found [*Time*, Aug. 11, 1961]. But if the group setting for behavior is destroyed, then the behavior changes. For example, in the Chicago race riot of 1919, one Negro outdistanced all but one of his assailants so that the two became separated from their groups and began to interact as individuals, whereupon they quit fighting [Chicago Commission, 1922, p. 22]. Removed from their groups, they realized that fighting was pointless. Group behavior is impersonal; when interaction becomes personal, it ceases to be group behavior and changes in nature.

Suggestibility Since crowd situations are normally unstructured, there are no designated leaders and no recognized behavior patterns for the members to carry out. Furthermore their individual responsibility has been shifted to the group. Often the situation itself is confused and chaotic. In such a state of affairs, people act readily and uncritically upon suggestion, especially if the suggestion is made in a decisive, authoritative manner. The "unpredictability" of crowds is just another way of saying that crowds are highly suggestible [Lang and Lang, 1961, pp. 221–225].

Social contagion The most dramatic feature of crowd behavior is the emotional buildup which crowd members give to one another. This communication of feeling is most impressive in mobs and riots, but is found in orderly crowds as well. The first one or two cheers at a pep rally normally fall flat; not until we hear the deep swell of voices around us will we cheer very lustily. Every professional speaker or entertainer knows that an audience thinly scattered over a large auditorium will be unresponsive. A well-filled smaller hall is far better. Above all, the audience must be seated close together, without many empty seats separating them. Every revivalist tries to move the audience down front so that they are close to him, and solidly packed, before he starts. The phenomenon he seeks has sometimes been called by the cumbersome title *interactional amplification* although the term *social contagion* is simpler. This is the process whereby the members of a crowd stimulate and respond to one another and thereby increase their emotional intensity and responsiveness. Contagion is increased by "milling" and "rhythm." The crowd, if unseated, may push and surge back and forth, carrying individuals along with it. The crowd may break into rhythmic clapping or shouting, with successive waves of sound carrying members to higher peaks of excitement. All these processes help to explain why crowd behavior sometimes goes farther than most of the members intended. Persons who came intending to be only onlookers get caught up in the process and find themselves joining in. Many campus confrontations start out in a partly serious, partly festive mood, but escalate through the stages of verbal abuse, rock-throwing, tear-gassing, beating and clubbing, and sometimes shooting.

Social contagion helps to explain the great suggestibility of a crowd, once it is tuned up for action. A person reading in solitude a hilarious scene from a popular comedy will not find it nearly so funny as when he sees it as a member of an audience. The "claque," a small organized group that starts and leads the applause for a star at the right moment, is a familiar fixture in the opera house. Since our own actions are reinforced by the action of others, it takes only a few to start a wave of laughter or applause.

When a crowd becomes emotionally aroused, it needs emotional release and may act upon the first suggested action which is in line with its impulses. Lynching mobs were not always concerned about which Negro they lynched; if the intended victim escaped, they might lynch any Negro who was handy. In Omaha in 1919, when the mayor refused to surrender a lynch victim, the mob attempted to lynch the mayor and very nearly succeeded [*Literary Digest*, Oct. 11, 1919]. In a Texas town in 1930, the victim was hidden in the vault of the courthouse; the mob burned the courthouse, then followed by wrecking the Negro part of town [Cantril, 1941, pp. 97–110]. The Civil War draft riots in New York City began as protests against the draft, but soon became full-fledged anti-Negro riots. Any suggested action, if it is in line with the established impulses and antagonisms of the members, is likely to be acted on by an emotionally aroused crowd [Lang and Lang, chap. 8].

These characteristics of crowd behavior explain why the crowd is more than a collection of individuals. Each individual member is to some degree different in the crowd from the person he is when alone. As Allport [in Lindzey, 1954, vol. 1, p. 28] remarks, "It used to be said in Germany that there is no such thing as a 'single Nazi.' Only with the support of a group does the peculiar subservience to the leader and his ideology take possession of the individual." We can never fully understand crowd behavior unless we understand that the crowd, like all groups, is more than merely a collection of individuals.

A crowd in action can be a terrifying thing. A factual account of everything said and done by an aggressive mob would be unprintable. To cite just one example, lynching victims were frequently burned alive, or slowly strangled and sometimes emasculated as well as being subjected to other inexpressible tortures [Raper, 1933, pp. 6–7, 144]. People will apparently do anything when caught up in the crowd. Is this true?

Limitations on crowd behavior

However irrational and unrestrained it may appear, crowd behavior is limited by at least four considerations: (1) the emotional needs of the members; (2) the mores of the members; (3) the leadership of the crowd; (4) the external controls over the crowd.

A crowd does only those things that most of its members would like to do.

Emotional needs of members Crowd behavior expresses the emotional needs, resentments, and prejudices of the members. People who led boring, monotonous lives, like the medieval European peasants, appreciated an occasional witch-burning to break the monotony of their lives. People who fear deprivation, like our second-generation immigrants who have struggled from the slum to a better neighborhood and who fear that black residents will "ruin" the neighborhood, need an outlet for their fears and anxieties. In a crowd situation people may do things they ordinarily would not do, but a crowd does only those things that most of its members *would like to do*. The emotional stimulus and protection of the crowd enables its members to express the impulses, hostilities, aggressions, and rages which they are restrained from expressing in calmer moments. Many of us, for example, like to break things, but we must restrain the impulse. People in a riot can shed restraints and can tear things up without guilt feelings. If blocked from its first objective, a mob generally shifts to another. The substitute, however, still represents the hated victim, or fulfills the frustrated wish.

Homogeneous audiences are the most responsive. Having the same interests and viewpoints, the members respond enthusiastically to the speaker. The political rally attracts mainly the party faithful. Its function is similar to that of a pep meeting before a football game—to arouse enthusiasm and dedication to the team. A crowd is most likely to take aggressive action when its members share a common set of prejudices and hostilities. Persons who do not share these feelings are likely to edge backward to the fringes, while the core of the crowd is made up of like-minded members.

Mores of the members Crowd behavior is limited by the mores of its members. The crowd rarely if ever does anything which does not claim a measure of moral approval. Lynchings did not occur in areas where the mores of most people strongly condemned

them. Lynchings took place only where a large proportion of the people felt that a lynching was morally justified, even necessary, under certain circumstances. The members of the lynching party normally considered themselves public benefactors, not guilty law breakers. Even the lynching party, then, was expressing, rather than violating, the mores of the members and probably the dominant mores of the region. We note, furthermore, that while the victim might have been killed, burned, and mutilated, he was never crucified, nor was his body ever eaten. The crowd's mores did not support these actions.

It is true that a crowd member may confess later that he shared in acts he realizes were morally wrong. Each person, like each group, holds a number of mutually inconsistent views, and at a given moment one or another of them is operative. It may seem very "right" to shout down a platform speaker whose ideas we see as wicked and immoral; but when the speaker for *our* side is silenced, then freedom and justice have been trampled in the dust. Our mores teach us that we should be loyal to family, friends, and fellow workers, and should do nothing that injures other people. When a strike is called in a vital industry, such as railroad transportation or telephone communication, should the worker loyally support his striking fellows and thereby inconvenience and possibly injure the public, or should he stay on the job and thereby injure his fellows? Rarely in a behavior situation does the individual have only *one* applicable moral judgment. Which of one's several sets of mores will operate in a particular situation will depend largely upon the group pressures surrounding him at that moment.

The function of crowd behavior is not to paralyze the moral judgments of its members; the function of the crowd is to isolate and neutralize some of one's moral judgments, so that certain others can find unrestrained expression. Thus a crowd is doing only those things for which the mores of the participants give considerable approval.

Crowd leadership The leadership profoundly affects the intensity and direction of crowd behavior. Given a collection of frustrated, resentful people, a skillful demagogue can convert them into a vengeful mob and direct their aggression at any "enemy" who is included among their antagonisms. Likewise, a leader can sometimes calm or divert a crowd by a strategic suggestion or command. In the illustration which opens this chapter, the young man stopped a mob by reminding them that they were on church property. These people were church members, and this reminder called into operation some mores which they had forgotten.

Since most crowd behavior is unstructured, with no designated leaders, leadership is "up for grabs." Anyone may be able to assume leadership by simply calling out suggestions and commands. The most unlikely persons sometimes assume leadership. In the panic of the *Lusitania* ship disaster, it was an eighteen-year-old boy under whose direction a few lifeboats were successfully filled and launched [LaPiere, 1938, p. 459]. In many crowd situations, the members, frustrated by confusion and uncertainty, *want* to be directed, and the first person who starts giving clear orders in an authoritative manner is likely to be followed. An impressive appearance is helpful, but the assured manner of one who knows what he is doing is essential. Let us see specifically what the crowd leader does.

1. *The leader must establish rapport.* By *rapport*, we mean a responsive trusting attentiveness such as any really successful speaker gets from his audience. One of your authors recalls observing a war-bond rally of workers in a large factory. A visiting dignitary first gave a speech which was a model of good speech construction and delivery, spoken in Harvard accents. It was received with polite applause. Then the plant manager began by holding out two ham-like paws and saying, "You guys see these hands? They didn't get that way pushing a pencil. They pushed a wheelbarrow for four years, and then they operated a drill press and a turret lathe and just about every damn machine in this place." With these few words, he established rapport. He spoke their language. Rapport is most easily established by a leader who has the same background as the members. He senses their wants, recognizes their antagonisms, speaks their language, and can predict their reactions.

2. *The leader builds emotional tensions.* For some types of crowds (mobs, riots, some audiences) he builds up their emotional tensions by an impassioned reminder of their problems and grievances. The revivalist convicts the sinners of their sins; the leader of the lynching mob arouses the men to defend the purity of their wives and daughters; the cheerleader focuses all history on the outcome of tomorrow's game. In some kinds of crowds (the panic, some audiences) the leader need not arouse emotional tension, for it already exists; he passes directly to the next function.

3. *The leader suggests action to release the tension.* The revivalist calls for repentance; the cheerleader demands victory and lights the bonfire; the campus demonstration leader cries, "Burn the R.O.T.C. building."

4. *The leader justifies the suggested action.* Seldom does a crowd respond instantly to suggestion (except perhaps in panic behavior). Generally the leader makes some effort to justify the suggestion. The revivalist pictures the new life of release from sin; the lynch leader warns, "It'll be *your* daughter next!" The repetition of the suggestion and its justifications permits social contagion to continue to operate, so that tension continues to mount and the need for release of tension continues to grow.

Leadership can function either to stimulate or to restrain a crowd, or to direct activity from one objective to another. Leadership is, therefore, one of the limiting factors in crowd behavior.

External controls Most mob behavior occurs in the summertime when people are normally standing around and gathering in large outdoor assemblies. Cold weather discourages mobs; so do hard thundershowers. Mob behavior is rare on army posts, where military discipline can be invoked to maintain order. Servicemen must release their tensions off the post—and do so at intervals!

The principal external controls on crowd behavior, however, are those exerted by the police. There are practically no instances of persons being lynched in spite of a really determined effort of law-enforcement officials to prevent the lynching. Most lynchings were preceded by either the open connivance of law-enforcement officials, or by their merely token resistance. The virtual disappearance of lynching in recent years stems in large part, not from any lack of persons who would enjoy a lynching, but from the determination of law-enforcement officials to prevent lynchings. Today, shootings and "disappearances" have replaced the classic lynchings.

Police have learned a great deal about the management of crowds. A sociologist, Joseph D. Lohman [1947], prepared a widely used handbook on the handling of potential riot situations, which summarizes in simple language what social science has learned about ways of directing crowd behavior. Among the procedures used in preventing small incidents from developing into riots are: (1) preventing crowd formation by promptly arresting and carrying off noisy troublemakers and ordering the onlookers to move on; (2) meeting threatened disorder with an impressive *show of force*, bringing enough police and equipment into the area so that a *use* of force is unnecessary; (3) isolating a riot area by throwing a police cordon around it and allowing people to leave but not to enter the area; (4) diminishing a crowd by directing the persons on the fringes to "break up and go home," thus stripping the crowd down to its core and depriving the core of its mass support; (5) emphasis in police training on the officer's duty to maintain the peace, so that the officer's own prejudices do not lead him into the fatal error of ignoring attacks on those whom he does not like.

With very few exceptions, serious riots are evidence of police failure. School integration disorders in the 1960s are an example. Where local police and public officials let it be known that no disorders would be tolerated, disorders were rare. Smelser [1963, pp. 261–268] cites many cases where hesitation and indecision of police and other officials, or even their open sympathizing with the rioters, has aided in riot development.

Some exceptions must be made to the proposition that police can control crowds if they wish. Small cities have no police reserves that can be shifted from place to place in an emergency. A local festival or celebration may bring people into a locality in numbers beyond the capacity of local police to handle. Rock festivals and motorcycle rallies have become difficult to schedule, for very few communities are willing to risk an unmanageable crowd of this sort. Campus demonstrations are especially difficult to control. Feeling that the campus is "theirs," campus crowds are difficult to disperse by the "peel down and send home" method. Many of the most active members of campus crowds are frequently drawn from the "nonstudent fringe," people who have neither fees, credits, nor jobs to lose. Sometimes the active leadership is provided by itinerant hardcore revolutionists who often materialize wherever demonstrations begin and who encourage the escalation of violence. They are rarely arrested, being expert in judging just when to flee. The presence of police on campus is generally resented by students, and university administrators have become loath to summon police to the campus.

Police control of civil disturbances poses a difficult problem. Failure to use firmness early in a demonstration may encourage the crowd to grow and the disorder to become unmanageable; yet a premature police presence or the use of force is likely to "radicalize" a crowd (or a student body) and provoke an escalation of disorder. Whatever the police do is likely to be judged an error! Obviously, the capacity of police force to control crowd behavior is not unlimited.

Some forms of crowd behavior

The audience An audience is a crowd with interest centered on stimuli outside themselves. The stimuli are mainly one-way. With the movie, radio, or TV audience, the stimuli are entirely one-way. Every instructor, however, realizes that any performer before a "live" audience is affected by the audience reaction. Dollard tells how he was stimulated by the responsive audience in a lower-class Southern Negro church which he was invited to address:

It was all I had expected and more too. Not familiar enough with the Bible to choose an opportune text, I talked about my own state, described the country through which I had passed in coming south, spoke of the beauty of their land, and expressed my pleasure at being allowed to participate in their exercises. Helped by appreciative murmurs which began slowly and softly and became louder and fuller as I went on, I felt a great sense of elation, an increased fluency, and a vastly expanded confidence in speaking. There was no doubt that the audience was with me, was determined to aid me in every way. I went on. . .

The crowd had enabled me to talk to them much more sincerely than I thought I knew how to do; the continuous surge of affirmation was a highly elating experience. For once I did not feel that I was merely beating a sodden audience with words or striving for cold intellectual communication. . .

Mine was a miserable performance compared to the many Negro preachers I have seen striding the platform like confident panthers; but it was exactly the intensive collective participation that I had imagined it might be. No less with the speaker than with the audience there is a sense of losing the limitations of self and of unconscious powers rising to meet the unbound, unconscious forces of the group. (*John Dollard*, Caste and Class in a Southern Town, *Yale University Press, New Haven, Conn., 1937, pp. 242–243.*)

Within an audience, then, there may be significant two-way stimulus and response, even though the audience situation discourages the communication. There is also a certain amount of communication between members, as they cheer, applaud, boo, whisper, mutter, doze, or snore. Social contagion still operates, usually at a more subdued level than in other crowds—highly subdued at a sedate church service, more freely expressive at a political rally or a sports event. Audiences may become unruly and may even become converted into a mob, as in the instance opening this chapter.

The mob A mob is an emotionally aroused crowd taking violent action. There are several types of mobs, differing in important respects.

1. The lynching mob. Lynchings were once popular in the South and the West, although they have occurred in all parts of the country. Unlike the riot, a lynching is a peculiarly American institution, rare in other parts of the world. It is a part of the vigilante tradition, wherein a self-appointed group of citizens seeks to preserve public order by punishing culprits. The nineteenth-century victims were both white and black; twentieth-century victims became predominantly black; 1,795 black and 195 white Americans have been lynched since 1900.

Lynchings were not all alike. Raper [1933, pp. 55ff.] and Cantril [1941, pp. 93–110] have distinguished between what they call the Bourbon and the proletarian lynching. The Bourbon lynching took place in Deep South areas of heavy black population. Rigid segregation prevented direct competition between whites and blacks, and the "poor whites" were less likely to see the blacks as a threat or to harbor a general bitterness toward blacks than in some other areas. A lynching was considered a deserved punishment of a specific person for a specific offense. It was carried out by leading citizens (or with their encouragement) and without serious interference from law-enforcement officials. The mob was small and orderly, as though conducting a legal execution. Other blacks were not molested, nor was black property destroyed.

The proletarian lynching took place where blacks were less numerous and their status less exactly defined. There was more direct competition between blacks and poor whites and much more poor-white hostility against blacks in general. The lynching was an outburst of white antagonism against the black group; its object was to punish the race, not just an individual. The lynching mob was large and emotional, made up mainly of poor whites, who were unconcerned with whether the victim was guilty or whether they had the right person. The lynching was generally accompanied by torture and mutilation and often followed by mistreatment of other blacks and destruction of black property. Community reaction tended to vary with social class; upper-class members and community leaders disapproved; lower-class members justified the lynching as necessary to keep the blacks in "their place." A lynching, then, may be a pseudolegal execution by community leaders, an impassioned emotional outburst of deprived whites against the black race, or some combination of both. In either case the individual lyncher is supported by the crowd in taking an action which is basically in accord with his mores.

Lynching today has virtually ceased; only six persons (one white and five blacks) were lynched during the 1950s, and none during the 1960s. Although now replaced by other techniques of intimidation or punishment, lynching remains of interest to social scientists as a dramatic form of group behavior.

2. *The riot.* A riot is the action of a violently aggressive, destructive mob. It may be a race riot, in which members of two races indiscriminately hunt down and beat or kill one another, as in Chicago in 1919 [Chicago Commission, 1922] or in Detroit in 1941 [Lee and Humphrey, 1943]. One study of the many race riots [Lieberson and Silverman, 1965] finds that they are usually precipitated by a report of a dramatic violence by one race against the other—rape, murder, assault, police brutality—in a society where race problems have not been—and perhaps cannot be—resolved by existing social institutions, and are most likely to occur in communities that have been unresponsive to black needs and appeals [Downes, 1968].

It may be a religious riot, as that between the Hindus and the Moslems in India in 1947 [Duncan, 1947; McGinty, 1947] or between Catholics and Protestants in Northern Ireland. It may be a nationality riot, like that between American servicemen and Mexicans in Los Angeles in 1943, or the so-called "zoot-suit" riot [Turner and Surace, 1956], or the many mob actions against European immigrants in the United States during the nineteenth and early twentieth centuries [Higham, 1955]. Race, religion, or nationality—no matter what the cause, the crowd behavior is much the same. A group is disliked because it is different; or it serves as a convenient scapegoat; or it is hated because it threatens competition. With suitable stimulating incidents and without effective police discouragement, persons who are individually frustrated and insecure start action; it builds and grows; the attacked group strikes back, and the riot is under way.

There are other kinds of riots. The protest riot, common in colonial countries, has the object of dramatizing grievances and wringing concessions from the governing powers. The black riots in many American cities beginning in 1965 were not conventional race riots—not primarily a clash between races—but protest riots. A decade of civil rights "victories" had brought few gains to lower-class blacks who remained outside the "affluent society." While skilled and educated Negroes were gaining, lower-class blacks were falling steadily farther behind, growing more frustrated than ever. Usually precipitated by reports of police brutality (often untrue) large-scale violence, burning, and looting exploded across the country [Moynihan, 1965; Blauner, 1966; Cohen and Murphy, 1966; Rustin, 1967; *Ebony*, special issue, August, 1967; National Advisory Commission on Civil Disorder, 1968; Boskin, 1969; Urban America, Inc., 1969]. Any riot provides the individual with the support of the crowd and a release from moral responsibility, so that he may express any impulse which seizes him. Most riots include all these elements—flaunting of authority, attack upon disliked groups, and looting and wrecking of property, especially property belonging to the hated group.

Some recent campus riots, notably at Berkeley, California, in 1964 and 1965, and at Kent State in 1970, caused many Americans to wonder what our students were coming to! As riots go, most of the student demonstrations were pretty tame affairs, involving only a small fraction of the students plus some nonstudents who hung around the larger campuses. Student disorders are, of course, as old as the university. A wave of them in the 1880s hit many colleges, with Amherst's rebellion led by Calvin Coolidge and (later Chief Justice) Harlan Fiske Stone (after Stone was thrown out of another college for demonstrating) [Feuer, 1966]. These nineteenth-century rebellions were staged by students who were alienated from their college administrations but who were not alienated from the society. Today's campus disorders have

typically been led by students and nonstudents who are deeply alienated from Establishment society and who will not be placated by anything less than major changes in contemporary social institutions [Knott, 1971].

3. *The orgy.* A revelous crowd which transgresses the normal mores is having an orgy. Like other mobs, the orgy releases tensions; but where the riot is mad with anger, the orgy is mad with joy. One cannot have an orgy by oneself; revelry must be shared or it falls flat. But a very creditable orgy may be promoted by anywhere from a handful of persons to a crowd of thousands. Exactly where "decent recreation" leaves off and the orgy begins is, perhaps, a value judgment. But to be effective in the release of tension, the orgy must involve behavior which exceeds the ordinary daily restraints and inhibitions.

In the orgy we see the factors which operate in all crowd behavior—leadership, social contagion, suggestibility, and transfer of moral responsibility to the group. Since it takes time for these forces to begin to operate, the party takes a while to get going. Before long, inhibitions are diluted, and interaction becomes less restrained. Thus many a motel party, after-the-game celebration, or convention get-together winds up as an orgy.

All societies create frustrations in their members, and all societies provide in some way for the release of tensions. In many societies the orgy is an institutionalized way for members to release their accumulated tensions. A great many primitive societies had periodic festivals or holidays in which ceremonial and orgiastic behavior were combined. Games, feasting, drinking, orgiastic dancing, and the suspension of some of the sex taboos were common features of primitive festivals. Among the Incas, for example,

Holidays might last for a day or for a week; there

might be public dancing, such as when hundreds of radiantly clothed "Chosen Women" danced with Huaschar's chain; there could be games and sports; there was always drinking, of a sort one writer calls "approved license." For the Indian [Inca] was expected to get drunk, which he did, quaffing immense quantities of fermented chìcha; for ritual drunkenness was as essential to a good festival as agriculture discipline to a good harvest.

Games at the festivals differed from those played by the Indian boy. . . . On the day fixed for the [December] feast, men and girls came to a predetermined place among the ripened fruit gardens, whose ripening they were to celebrate. Men and women were completely naked. At a given signal they started on a race, upon which bets were placed, toward some hill at a distance. Each man that overtook any woman in the race "enjoyed her on the spot." *(Victor W. VonHagen,* Realm of the Incas, *Mentor Books, New American Library of World Literature, Inc., New York, 1957, pp. 96–97. From the series,* The Ancient Sun Kingdoms of the Americas, *The World Publishing Company, Cleveland.)*

Students of revelry have assumed that the greater the accumulated tensions, the greater the temptation to find release through orgy. Casual observation would seem to support this thesis. Whenever men are isolated from female company and subjected to harsh discipline, monotonous work, and unsatisfactory living conditions for long periods of time, most of them promptly go on a spree at the first opportunity. Army camps, naval stations, construction camps, lumber camps, and mining camps are classic examples. Presumably, the greater the frustrations and tensions, the more riotous the release. Ernie Pyle [1943, p. 3], the perceptive war correspondent, observed that infantry men often endured mud, rain, and dirt, and continuous chaos and uncertainty even as to where they would eat and sleep, whereas sailors ordinarily had clean clothes, good food, and a ship to call home. He then remarked that ". . . sailors didn't cuss as much or as foully as soldiers. They didn't bust

loose as riotously when they hit town." One writer describes the emotional needs and outlets of the men who built the Hoover Dam during the early 1930s:

To men who have pushed concrete fifteen days, or nights, with no more emotional outlet than a pool table can absorb, Las Vegas becomes a natural and compelling magnet. The liquor is vile and no one trusts the wheels; but all drink and play furiously. It is payday, and it matters not what the night of the week. Where Sunday and Christmas are days like any others, traditional Saturday-night revels lose all significance. By ten-thirty things are well under way. By two everyone is drunk and begging for more. Rooms, as large as small auditoriums, are packed to bursting with sweating inebriates fighting for the edge of the gambling tables. *(Theo White, "Building the Big Dam,"* Harper's Magazine, *June, 1935, p. 118.)*

Today the automobile and the mobile home have largely destroyed the isolation of the construction camp, lumber camp, or mining camp, and the orgy has largely faded from their fringes. What no amount of moralizing could do, changing technology has accomplished. The armed services have attempted to make military life more comfortable and less frustrating, and the row of taverns, gambling places, and houses of prostitution in the nearest town may have shortened, but not entirely disappeared.

American society has many approved forms of recreation—dancing, movie-going, participation sports, spectator sports, and many others—which doubtless serve to release tensions. Our society has not, however, institutionalized the orgy as a legitimate release. In primitive societies, the orgy is a relatively safe outlet. In a nonmechanical society, drunkenness which is limited to an occasional socially designated experience is comparatively harmless. In a society with a consanguine family system, collective property ownership, and a serene unconcern with exact biological paternity, an occasional period of sexual license creates no problems. But in our society the price of an orgy may be a painful accident, a costly fire, or a scandalous pregnancy. Our society's inability to provide safe, harmless orgies, however, also carries a price tag. In a society which produces a great many tensions within individuals, these tensions must find release in one way or another. Blocking one dangerous outlet does not guarantee that the substitute outlet will be less offensive. LaPiere comments:

That the cause of the drunken spree lies in social circumstances which demand an occasional escape, rather than, as moralists assume, in the commercial provision of opportunities for such indulgence, is illustrated by the history of an attempt to check the week-end sprees of English industrial workers. Motivated, no doubt, by the best of intentions, the stringent closing of the "pubs" in the depressing East End of London some years ago had, however, such unanticipated consequences that it was soon found advisable to remove the harsh restrictions. Withholding alcohol from workers who were accustomed to a week-end drunk reduced drunkenness and disorderly conduct, but it caused a striking increase in the frequency of wife beating, murder, and suicide. (*Richard LaPiere,* Collective Behavior, *McGraw-Hill Book Company, New York, 1938, p. 484.*)

The persistent question of how to reconcile our appetite for revelry with our need for individual safety and social order is not likely to be settled in the forseeable future.

4. The panic. A panic is "a collective flight based on a hysterical belief" [Smelser, 1963, p. 131]. A panic involves the same elements of crowd behavior, blossoming suddenly under the stress of crisis. We have done little empirical research on panic, since we dare not produce panics to order for study. There are, however, many descriptive accounts and theoretical formulations [Strauss, 1944; Foreman, 1953; Smelser, 1963]. Panic appears to be most likely to seize a group which is fatigued by prolonged stress, although many panics have spread through perfectly relaxed groups. Smelser [1963, chap. 6] sees panic as likely when people feel in great danger with a very limited escape route; where there are ample escape routes, or no escape route whatever, panic is unlikely. Wherever they occur, a perceived crisis produces fear, uncertainty, confusion, and a lack of decisive leadership. The role of leadership is crucial in panic prevention, for panic spreads when members lose faith in organized, cooperative effort, and each takes individual defensive action [Mintz, 1951]. In a burning building, one person shouting "Fire!" or "Let me out!" may be enough to start a panic. When a crowd is leaving in orderly manner, if there is any interruption—if someone stumbles and momentarily blocks the aisle—somebody may break out of line in a dash and touch off a panic.

In panic prevention, a leader does at least two things: He organizes the crowd so that cooperative activity can proceed, and he relieves uncertainty by specific directions and reassurances. Marshall [1947, p. 130] has pointed out that when an army unit is under heavy fire, if the unit leader says, "Let's get out of here!" panic is likely; but if he says, "Follow me to that fence," panic is improbable. Once panic has spread, it generally continues until the crisis is past or the members are exhausted (or dead). Panic prevention depends upon a leader's assumption of authoritative direction quickly enough to organize cooperative action before some individual panics and touches off general panic.

MASS SOCIETY

While *society* is as old as man's social life, *mass society* is relatively new. A *mass* is not simply a lot of people, but "a relatively large number of persons, spatially dispersed and anonymous, reacting to one or more of the same stimuli but acting individually without regard for one another" [Hoult, 1969, p. 194]. As Blumer describes the mass:

It has no social organization, no body of custom and tradition, no established set of rules or rituals, no organized group of sentiments, no structure of status roles, and no established leadership. It merely consists of an aggregation of individuals who are separate, detached, anonymous, and thus, homogeneous as far as mass behavior is concerned. (*Herbert Blumer, in Alfred McClung Lee (ed.),* Principles of Sociology, *Barnes and Noble, Inc., New York, 1969, pp. 86–87.*)

Mass society would be a society in which the informal, primary-group, community-based, tradition-oriented relationships of the society have been replaced by contractual, secondary-group, utilitarian relationships. It is the final stage of the shift from *gemeinschaft* to *gesellschaft* relationships. Mass

The elite are no longer separated from the nonelite.

society is characterized by anonymity, mobility, specialization of role and status, and by individual choices relatively independent of traditional mores or values. Since informal, primary-group, and traditionally oriented relationships do remain important in modern societies, the "mass society" is an ideal type or model which actually exists nowhere, but whose features are increasingly predominant in most modern societies.

The traditional society was ruled by small elite groups which were well insulated from the rest of the people and ruled according to revered customs and traditions. In the mass society, tradition is an undependable basis for decision, and the elite is no longer insulated from what the nonelite are thinking and feeling. On the contrary, the elite can be influenced by the nonelite, through the ballot in democracies and through riots and noncooperation in all political systems. Because of this fact, various sections of the elite will attempt to propagandize, organize, and manipulate the nonelite in support of elite political goals [Kornhauser, 1959]. With the use of classified mailing lists and computers which can insert personal names and addresses at appropriate places in computer-written letters, it is possible for the propagandist or advertiser to create the illusion of a personal message in an impersonal mass mailing. Thus a Milwaukee nun was startled to receive a computer-written letter beginning: "Dear Mr. Mother Superior: How would you like to see a brand new Mustang parked outside P. O. Box 1043?"[1] In an increasingly impersonal mass society, the illusion of the "personal touch" has cash value!

Much of the writing about "mass society" and "mass culture" is a mournful lament for the loss of past virtues. In contrast to our supposedly rugged, high-principled ancestors, mass man is reviled as a rootless clod; of vulgar tastes, morbid or frivolous preoccupations, and having a pervasive disdain for reason and intellect [Zolla, 1968] While this may be an accurate description of a great many people, whether this is a new development can be questioned. Philip Wylie once ventured the opinion that, after all, "Most of the people always have been slobs." Intellectual interests and "cultivated" tastes have always been shared by relatively few of the people. Mass man is *different*

[1]Quoted from *Moneysworth,* January 25, 1971.

from his ancestors. Whether he is in any way inferior to them is uncertain.

MASS BEHAVIOR

Mass society is prone to some kinds of collective behavior called *mass behavior*. This term refers to *the unorganized, unstructured, uncoordinated, individually selected behavior of masses in a mass society*. It differs from crowd behavior in that crowd behavior is brief and episodic and is acted out by people as a group, whereas mass behavior is more enduring and arises from the sum total of many individual actions. Also, crowds are collections of people, whereas masses are scattered and in no direct, continuous contact with one another. Masses cannot mill and interact as crowds do. When many people, acting individually rather than as a group, move in the same direction, this is mass behavior. A flight of refugees or the spread of beards and long hair among young people would be a good example.

The rumor

A *rumor* is a rapidly spreading report unsubstantiated by authenticated fact. While rumors may arise in any kind of society, they are most characteristic of mass societies. They may be spread by mass media or by word of mouth. Much of our casual conversation consists of rumor mongering. Every topic, from our neighbor's morals to the fate of the nation, attracts interesting and disturbing rumors. Whenever there is social strain, rumors flourish. Wherever accurate and complete facts on a matter of public concern are not available or are not believed, rumors abound. Since rumors can ruin reputations, discredit causes, and undermine morale, the manipulation of rumor is a common propaganda device.

In the definitive work on rumor, Allport and Postman [1947, p. 46] point out that a great amount of rumor mongering springs from nothing more complicated than the desire for interesting conversation and the enjoyment of a salacious or unusual tidbit. A person is most likely, however, to believe and spread a rumor *if it will justify his dislikes or relieve his emotional tensions*. People who dislike Republicans, hate blacks, or despise hippies will remember and repeat damaging rumors about these groups. The rumor changes continuously as it spreads, for people unconsciously distort it into the form that most perfectly supports their antagonisms. People uncritically accept and believe a rumor if it fits in with their pattern of beliefs and dislikes, or if it provides an emotionally satisfying explanation of phenomena. Thus many bitter critics of the Roosevelt administration readily believed and repeated rumors to the effect that wartime rationing was unnecessary (rumors that warehouses and gasoline storage tanks were overflowing, that the government was wasting or destroying vast quantities, and so on). Such rumors were emotionally satisfying to critics of the rationing program, and justified the black-marketing of the many people who violated rationing restrictions [Clinard, 1952].

The fad or fashion

A *fad* is a trivial, short-lived variation in speech, decoration, or behavior. As this is written, the phrase, "Right on" is "in" on the campus. It will probably have passed by the time this manuscript fights its way through editors and publishers to the campus bookstores.

The fad apparently originates in the desire to gain and maintain status by being different, by being a leader, and dies out when it is no longer novel. Bogardus [1950, pp. 305–309] studied 2,702 fads over many years, finding that most of them deal with superficial accessories and gewgaws. They typically grow rapidly, have a two- or three-month plateau, and then decline, although some last longer, and a few become permanent parts of the culture.

Fashions are similar to fads, but change less rapidly and are less trivial. The hemlines of women's dresses go up, down, up, down, while men's beards luxuriate, wither, and luxuriate again! Fashion operates only in societies with a class system. In a homogeneous, undifferentiated society, distinction through fashion does not arise, since all act and adorn themselves alike. In a rigid caste society, fashion is unnecessary, for distinction is already firmly assigned [Blumer, 1969c, p. 117]. Yet fashions do not always originate among the elite and diffuse downward, but may originate at any social level. Fashions spread as people who wish to be up-to-date make their collective selections from many competing models [Blumer, 1969b].

Fashion may involve almost any aspect of group life—manners, the arts, literature, philosophy, even fields of science—but is most often seen in clothing and adornment. Fashions reflect the dominant interests and motives of a society at a particular time. In the eighteenth century, elaborate clothing reflected an ornate and decorative upper-class culture, and the confining styles of the Victorian era reflected Victorian prudishness [Flugel, 1930]. Fashion changes often reflect changes in tastes, attitudes, and values. The present trend towards reduced differentiation in sex roles [Winick, 1969] is accompanied by the trend towards unisex clothing [Stannard, 1971]. During the political conservatism and relative indifference to social problems of the placid 1950s, the popular song lyrics were trivial and romantic; as concern over social problems and competing life styles grew in the later 1960s, the popular song lyrics assumed a sharp tone of social criticism [Rosenstone, 1969]. Fashion is not entirely trivial, but often reflects the currents of change in a society.

There is much speculation, but little scientific research, on the possibility that fashion changes and choices arise from unconscious emotional needs and impulses. In one of the very few research studies, Becker [1971] concluded that those women who were first to wear miniskirts were women who had negative self-images, while the women who accepted the midiskirt craved attention so badly as to wear something ugly and sexless to attract it. Although unconscious motivation may be involved, fashion choices are not entirely irrational, for they meet genuine social needs as defined by social class, age and sex group, and other group affiliation. Fashion consciousness aids the middle-class social climber, and a distinct mode of dress or hair style fills the early teen-ager's need to "belong" in a private world not run by adults [Barber and Tobel, 1953]. Fashion changes may be deliberately manipulated by the apparel industry, but only to a limited degree, for there is evidence that consumers will not passively accept everything labeled "fashionable" [Jack and Schiffer, 1948; Lang and Lang, 1961, chap. 15]. Determined efforts of the women's wear industry to promote the midiskirt in 1970 met with very little success.

The craze

Where the panic is a rush away from a perceived threat, the craze is a rush toward some satisfaction. As Smelser observes [1963, chap. 7], the craze may be superficial (miniature golf, monopoly, hula hoops, celebrity fan clubs) or serious (war crazes, nomination of a president); it may be economic (speculative boom), political (bandwagons), expressive (dance steps), religious (revivals), to mention only a few types. Flagpole sitting, dance marathons, jugsaw puzzles, canasta, and chain letters have all had their moments.

The craze differs from the fad in that it becomes an obsession for its followers. The use of LSD became a craze among a minority of college students, with an estimated 5 or 6 percent having tried LSD at least once at the peak of the craze in 1967 [Meyer, 1969, p. 201]. With Dr. Timothy Leary as its high priest, LSD was to bring the world into a new nirvana of peace, love, and creativity. But a growing fear of LSD's hazards seems to have ended its craze and reduced its users to around 1 percent of college students [Meyer, 1969, p. 201].

Many crazes involve some kind of get-rich-quick scheme. The Holland tulip craze of 1634 bid up the price of tulip bulbs until their value exceeded their weight in gold. The Florida land boom of the 1920s pushed land prices to levels fantastically beyond any sound economic valuation. In the craze, the individual gets caught up in a mass hysteria and loses his caution. Speculators sell to one another at climbing prices until some bad news pricks the bubble or until so many susceptible persons have joined that no new money is entering the market; then confidence falters, and the market collapses in a frenzy to unload holdings [Mackay, 1932].

Since the craze is taken over by only a small fraction of the population and is a time-consuming preoccupation, it inevitably wears itself out quite quickly, soon to be replaced by another for those who are susceptible.

Mass hysteria

This is some form of irrational, compulsive belief or behavior which spreads among people. It can be a brief crowd phenomena, as when a wave of uncontrollable twitching spread through a Louisiana high school [Schuler and Parenton, 1943]. The *New York Times* [Sept. 14, 1952] reports that at a Mississippi football game, 165 teen-aged girls in a cheering section became excited and "fainted like flies." Or mass hysteria may extend beyond a single collection of people at a single moment in time. In one

town, dozens of people over several weeks reported being attacked by a "phantom anesthetist" who sprayed them with an unknown drug which caused paralysis and other symptoms [Johnson, 1945]. The Salem witchcraft trials are an interesting historical example of mass hysteria [Starkey, 1949]. Recurrent waves of flying-saucer reports, together with an elaborate pseudo-scientific literature on flying saucers, are a more modern example of mass hysteria [Hackett, 1948; Gardner, 1957, chap. 5]. From an analysis of the reports, it can be suspected that flying-saucer reports were the main cause of flying-saucer reports; that is, publicity about flying saucers was dependably followed by a series of new "sightings." While such mass delusions are interesting phenomena, we have not studied them closely enough to permit more than educated guesses as to why some people succumb while others resist. It is, of course, a scientific possibility that some of the "unidentified flying objects" are from outer space. As stated earlier, a negative proposition (e.g., "there are no flying saucers") is impossible to prove; but the evidence for them, at present, is most unconvincing [Condon, 1969].

Do we, then, have fully satisfactory explanations for collective behavior? Not entirely. All the forms of collective behavior herein discussed arise from some form of frustration or discontent. All serve to release tensions and provide some form of wish-fulfillment. We can venture some forecasts of when and where the more extreme forms of collective behavior are likely to appear and have some knowledge of how they may be controlled. With further study, we should know more.

PUBLICS AND PUBLIC OPINION

The term "public" is used in several senses. In popular use, "the public" is synonymous with "the people" or with practically everybody—not a very useful concept. Sociologists use the term in two senses: (1) A *public* may be defined as *a scattered number of people who share an interest in a particular topic.* There is a baseball public, an opera public, an investment public, a political-affairs public, and many others. (2) A *public* may be defined as *a number of people who are concerned over, divided upon, and in discussion about an issue.* Each important issue thus has its public, and there is no such thing as *the* public under these two definitions.

The members of a public are not gathered together like the members of a crowd. Each member of a public can communicate directly with only a handful of the other members. A public is reached mainly through the mass media. The titles of many magazines reveal the public for which each is published— *House and Garden, Field and Stream, Guns and Ammo, Western Horsemen, Cats Magazine, U.S. Camera, Stamps, Motor Trend, The Theater, Workbench, Audio, National Geographic Magazine, Holiday, Pacific Affairs,* and hundreds more. Since the members of a public can communicate effectively only through such mass media, it follows that those who control the media have considerable power to influence the opinions of that public.

Publics are created by cultural complexity. In a simple culture there would be few if any publics. A complex culture produces many interest groups with rival axes to grind and develops many issues over which people differ. For example, one group wishes to keep our national parks in their unspoiled condition with a minimum of development; another group wants to develop them into recreation centers with resorts, airstrips, and ski lifts; still other groups wish to hunt the game, log the timber, mine the minerals, graze the grassland, or dam the streams in the parks. Such interest clashes multiply as a culture becomes more complex.

Few issues arise in a simple, stable culture; that is, few situations develop which cannot be handled by following the traditional folkways and mores of the society. But in a complex, changing culture, issues are constantly arising. In other words, situations are constantly developing which our traditional folkways and mores either will not handle at all or will handle only in a way that leaves some groups dissatisfied. For example, should "hard" pesticides which remain poisonous for a long time (such as DDT) be banned in order to protect the environment, or are they necessary for food production and disease control? Tradition gives no clear answer.

In these ways a complex changing culture creates a great many publics, each concerned with an activity, interest, or issue. As the members of a public consider the issue, and form opinions concerning it, *public opinion* is developed.

Public opinion also has two definitions: (1) *an opinion held by a substantial number of people;* (2) *the dominant opinion among a population.* According to the first usage, there can be many public opinions; according to the second, public opinion refers to a public *consensus* upon an issue. Both usages are common in the literature, and the particular meaning must be inferred from the way the term is used.

Public opinion is a creation of the mass society and the mass media. In traditional societies, *gemeinschaft* relations predominate, while an elite rules according to established traditions without very much concern for anything such as public opinion. If the ordinary people had been questioned about current "issues," their usual response would have been one of bewilderment. True enough, there were differences of interest and viewpoint in earlier societies, but these were typically thrashed out *within* the elite without involving the ordinary people (except as they suffered the consequences). Public opinion depends upon having a mass whose opinions are important to the elite, whereupon different sections of the elite seek to propagandize and manipulate this mass in support of elite interests. Democracies differ from dictatorships in that in democracies different groups among the elite compete vigorously for mass support, whereas in a dictatorship some faction among the elite gains dominance, removes or neutralizes its competitors, and enjoys a monopoly of propaganda.

Dimensions of public opinion

Public opinion has at least three dimensions. *Direction* simply states whether an opinion is for or against a proposed course of action. A count of the "yes" and "no," or the "approve" and "disapprove" opinions measures the direction of opinion. *Intensity* refers to the strength with which an opinion is held. "Yes" may mean, "Yes, absolutely, whatever the costs," or it may mean, "Yes, I guess so." *Integration* refers to the way an opinion is tied in with one's total set of beliefs and values. Is this opinion an expression of a man's general outlook or an exception to it? For example, Mr. Smith favors national health insurance (sometimes called "socialized medicine") because he favors a welfare state wherein the government provides many social services to its citizens. Mr. Jones, less enthusiastic about the welfare state, supports national health insurance because after some study he believes that it is the only practical way to organize health services. Mr. Brown, strongly opposed to the welfare state, supports national health insurance because he dislikes physicians and wants to see their heads knocked together. Mr. Black supports it because his union tells him it is good. While identical in direction and perhaps intensity, these four opinions are basically quite different because of the way they relate to the mental context of their holders. The opinion which is well integrated with one's total value system is less easily changed by persuasion than the opinion which is divorced from or inconsistent with one's general system of beliefs and values.

Measurement of public opinion

The leaders of a group or a nation cannot lead wisely unless they know which way the people are willing to be led. The public-opinion poll is a recent invention for finding out what people are thinking. A poll is simple in concept but difficult to carry out because, as is shown above, an opinion is a rather complicated phenomenon. The pollsters prepare a set of questions on an issue, seeking to phrase the questions in such a way that the wording does not prejudice the informant's answer. Then these questions are offered to a small number of people (from a few hundred to a few thousand) so that each group or class in the total population is represented in the sample in its correct proportion. If all these preliminary arrangements are made without serious error, opinion is measured quite accurately. The Gallup Poll, for example, has predicted the vote on recent elections with an average error of less than 2 percent of the total population vote. But there are many pitfalls in public-opinion polling which a pollster must guard against if he is to attain this level of accuracy. One of the greatest is the tendency of people to state firm opinions on issues which they know nothing about, have not thought about, and really have no opinion upon. In 1959 a Los Angeles newspaperman asked a number of people the question, "Do you think the Mann Act deters or helps the cause of organized labor?" About one person in eight knew what the Mann Act is (it forbids the interstate transportation of women for immoral purposes) and realized that the question was unanswerable. But of the remainder who admitted that they knew nothing of the Mann Act, about one-half expressed decided opinions about its effects.

If the "opinions" of people who know nothing about an issue are included, a poll is not very accurate. Other pitfalls surround the wording of questions, the selection of the sample, and the weighing or interpreting of responses [Parten, 1950; B. Phillips, 1966]. Polling is no job for amateurs!

Manipulation of public opinion

The main emphasis in public-opinion research has been upon ways of manipulating public opinion [Albig, 1957]. *Propaganda* includes all efforts to persuade people to a point of view upon an issue; everything from Sunday school lessons to billboards are

Propaganda is not necessarily bad.

propaganda; advertising, sales promotion, and fund-raising drives are prime examples. The usual distinction between education and propaganda is that education seeks to cultivate one's ability to make discriminating judgments, while propaganda seeks to persuade one to the undiscriminating acceptance of a ready-made judgment. In practice, education often includes a good deal of propaganda. Teachers sometimes propagandize for their own opinions; interest groups seek

to get their own propaganda, disguised as "educational materials," into the school; society virtually forces the school to propagandize for the approved moral and patriotic values. To draw a clear distinction between education and propaganda is not always possible. And it should be repeated that propaganda is not necessarily "bad"; it is merely a term applied to *all* attempts to influence other peoples' opinions and actions. Most students, beginning perhaps with a ninth-grade course in civics, have seen descriptions of the techniques of propaganda in textbook after textbook. We shall not repeat them here. Good descriptions of propaganda techniques are easily available, should the student wish to consult them [Lee and Lee, 1939; Doob, 1948, 1966; Lasswell, 1951; Qualter, 1962, ch. IV].

Does the propagandist get the greatest opinion change when his propaganda diverges greatly, or only slightly, from the opinions already held by the receivers? An awareness of such divergence is known as *cognitive dissonance*. Some research studies find that when the degree of divergence from the original opinion is greater, so is the opinion change; other studies reach the opposite conclusion. Whittaker [1964] reconciles these contradictory findings, saying that when the issue is one upon which the receivers hold intense opinions with a deep personal involvement, opinion change diminishes as dissonance increases. Too great a dissonance even produces a "boomerang" cognitive effect; that is, the receiver rejects the propaganda with an even stronger loyalty to his original opinions. But when the issue is one on which the receiver has no intense opinions or deep personal involvement, increasing dissonance produces increased opinion change. For each receiver, there is an "optimal discrepancy" which will produce a maximum opinion change.

Limits of propaganda If the powers of propaganda were unlimited, the side with the most money and the best public relations agency would always win. Since this does not always happen, the power of propaganda must be limited in various ways.

1. Competing propagandas are probably the greatest limitation. Where the state has a monopoly of propaganda, as in totalitarian states, a citizen can hardly find any facts to use in arriving at opinions other than the officially approved ones. With a monopoly of propaganda, a propagandist can suppress and manufacture facts, and no effective rebuttal is possible. The mere *existence* of competing propagandas in a democratic state exerts a restraining influence both upon the propagandist and upon his receiver.

2. The credibility of the propagandist in the eyes of the receivers limits what they will accept. When his "facts" and opinions diverge from theirs, this creates tensions which the receiver can relieve either by changing his opinions or by downgrading the propagandist [Aronson et al., 1963]. Credibility is reduced where the propagandist is obviously grinding his own ax, so propaganda is often conducted under the name of a noble-sounding organization (Fundamental Freedoms Foundation, Tax Equality Association, Homeowners' Association) which conceals the selfish interests of the propagandists.

3. The sophistication of the receiver limits the effects of propaganda. In general, those who are well educated or well informed on the issue are less affected by propaganda than the poorly educated and the poorly informed.

4. The beliefs and values of the recipient limit the propaganda he will believe. Many people are fond of picturing themselves as open-minded, discriminating analysts of competing propagandas, but they are usually reacting mechanically to slogans and catchwords. Most people accept uncritically any propaganda which fits in with their established attitudes and values, and usually reject, equally uncritically, any which

conflicts. For this reason, a propagandist rarely tries to change the basic attitudes of his recipients; instead, he tries to get them to accept his definition of the issue, in terms of their attitudes. For example, a propagandist for banning the use of "hard" pesticides will define the issue as one of protection versus reckless destruction of the environment; the propagandist for continuing "judicious use" of pesticides will define the issue as "food for people" versus "birdies for bird-watchers." The propagandist's task is to get the people to accept a definition of the issue that will call up those attitudes and images which support the propagandist's cause. Communist propaganda has been ineffective in the United States because its pictures of the villainous businessman, the "oppressive" church, and a "proletariat" middle class simply struck no responsive note in the basic images, attitudes, and values of the American people.

5. Cultural drifts and trends limit the effectiveness of propaganda. A cultural drift is not stopped by propaganda. For this reason, all "back to the simple life," "white-supremacy," and "women's place is in the home" propagandas are doomed to futility. Propaganda may accelerate or retard a cultural trend, reinforce or weaken a value. But it is doubtful if propaganda in a democratic society can either initiate or halt a cultural trend, destroy a well-established value, or instill a new value which the culture is not already developing.

Psychological warfare

There is nothing new in the use of propaganda as a military weapon; only the great modern emphasis upon psychological warfare is new. Entirely too much was expected of psychological warfare in World War II. Propaganda intended to undermine the morale of the enemy had little effect, either upon enemy civilians or military units, so long as their primary-group structures remained intact (see page 159). Not until disruption of primary-group life was accomplished through separation, loss of communication, loss of leadership, interruptions of food and medical supplies, and other disruptions —not until then did morale and organized resistance crumble. Apparently psychological warfare has little effect upon an efficiently operating enemy; its main effect is to hasten the disintegration of the enemy after superior military force has begun his defeat [Shils and Janowitz, 1948].

The United States and the Soviet Union are both engaged in worldwide propaganda programs whose effects cannot be accurately predicted. The short-run effects of such propaganda campaigns seem to lie in strengthening people's present views and providing them with a rationale for their existing convictions rather than in changing their attitudes [Bogart, 1957; Qualter, 1962]. The long-run effects of a sustained propaganda program may be greater, since it may gradually build up a body of factual information among its recipients and thus effect gradual changes of attitude and opinion. This, at least, is the hope that motivates our "Voice of America" broadcasts.

SUMMARY

Collective behavior is a characteristic of complex cultures and is usually absent in simple societies. A *crowd* is a temporary gathering of people who are acting together. *Crowd behavior* is characterized by: (1) anonymity—the individual loses his customary restraints and sense of personal responsibility; (2) impersonality—only the group affiliation of the person is important; (3) suggestibility—crowd members act uncritically upon suggestions; (4) social contagion—crowd members build up one another's emotional involvement. Crowd behavior is limit-

ed, however, by: (1) emotional needs and attitudes of the members; (2) the mores of the members, who rarely do anything which is not condoned by certain of their mores; (3) crowd leaders, who must establish rapport, build emotional tensions, suggest action to relieve these tensions and justify this action; and (4) external controls, mainly the police, whose ability to control crowd behavior depends partly upon their skill and partly upon the nature of the particular crowd.

Crowd behavior takes many forms. The *audience* is largely, but not entirely, a one-way crowd responding to a single stimulus. The *mob* is a crowd in violent action. The *lynching mob* is an extralegal device for the enforcement of local mores, and takes different forms according to the local setting. In the *riot* the members of a violently aggressive mob are releasing accumulated hostilities. In the *orgy*, a good-natured mob enjoys itself through uninhibited indulgence. In the *panic*, people become a mob in sudden, disorganized flight from danger.

A *mass* is a separated number of people responding individually to the same stimuli. *Mass society* is a society in which traditional, primary-group, *gemeinschaft* relationships have been largely replaced by *gesellschaft* relationships, characterized by anonymity, mobility, specialization, and independence of traditional values. *Mass behavior* is the unorganized, unstructured, uncoordinated behavior of masses in a mass society. Forms of mass behavior include the *rumor*, a rapidly spreading report unsubstantiated by fact; the *fad* or *fashion*, temporarily popular variations in speech, manners, dress, or behavior; the *craze*, a short-lived mass preoccupation with a particular satisfaction; *mass hysteria*, some form of irrational compulsion which spreads among a people; and possibly others.

The term *public* is defined by sociologists both in terms of those people sharing a common interest and of those people sharing a common concern over an issue. *Public opin-*

ion includes both the different opinions held by substantial numbers of people and the consensus opinion held by most people. Public opinion is important in mass society, where elites are influenced by masses and seek to propagandize and organize these masses in support of elite interests. Individual opinions differ in direction, in intensity, and in integration, or the way they relate to the rest of one's thinking. Consequently, it is difficult to "add up" individual opinions and measure the sum of public opinion, but professional pollsters have developed techniques which can measure opinion with considerable accuracy.

Practically every interest group today is trying to manipulate public opinion so that propaganda, often called "public relations," is one of our largest businesses. Propaganda may be less powerful than it sometimes appears to be, for its effects are limited by competing propagandas, by the credibility of the propagandists, by the sophistication of its receivers, by the established beliefs and values of the receivers, and by the existing trends within the culture. Psychological warfare attempts to use propaganda to weaken an enemy and to project a favorable image of one's own country upon the world's people.

Questions and projects

1. When we say that crowd behavior is "unstructured," what do we mean? Of what importance is its unstructured character?

2. Why do mob members seldom feel guilty about their mob actions?

3. Are there any situations in our culture which contain elements of the institutionalized orgy?

4. Should we fully institutionalize the orgy in American society? What benefits might accrue? What differences would arise?

5. What caused the recent student disorders in colleges and universities? Are students generally becoming more restless, or less restless? Why?

6. How does mass society differ from traditional society? Why are propaganda and public opinion more characteristic of mass society?

7. Do you think you are immune to panic? To crazes? To mass hysteria? What makes you think so?

8. Can you think of any propaganda efforts or causes which have failed in the United States because they conflicted with our cultural values? With prevailing cultural trends?

9. Write up a description of a campus pep rally as an example of crowd behavior.

10. Try an experiment in rumor. Select a rumor (consulting with your instructor in finding a harmless rumor) and set it going by a specified number of tellings. Then record the time, frequency, and form in which it "comes back" to you as it spreads over the campus.

11. Recall and describe a crowd situation in which the behavior lagged dispiritedly for a time. Show how each of the characteristics of crowd behavior came into operation and kindled a proper enthusiasm in the members. Or, if you have the opportunity, attend and observe a crowd situation for your analysis.

12. Prepare a list of aggressive actions which you think you could engage in if placed in a suitably encouraging crowd situation. Prepare a list of actions in which you think you could not possibly share, no matter what the crowd situation. Give your reasons for each listing.

13. Run a campus public-opinion poll on a fictitious proposition such as "Do you favor or oppose the Hill-Wallerton proposal to pay college students a salary according to their point averages?" See how many will admit that they do not know of the proposal, and how many state firm opinions on it.

Suggested readings

Allport, Gordon W., and Leo Postman: *The Psychology of Rumor*, Holt, Rinehart and Winston, Inc., New York, 1947; or "The Basic Psychology of Rumor," in **Wilbur Schramm (ed.):** *The Process and Effects of Mass Communication,* The University of Illinois Press, Urbana, Ill., 1955, pp. 141–155. How and why rumors appear and circulate.

*Blumer, Herbert: "Collective Behavior," in **Alfred McClung Lee (ed.):** *Principles of Sociology,* Barnes and Noble, New York, 1969, chaps. 7–12. A classic treatment of this topic in one of the College Outline Series handbooks.

*Cantril, Hadley, *The Psychology of Social Movements,* John Wiley & Sons, Inc., New York, 1963, chap. 4, "The Lynching Mob." A vivid description of two lynchings, analyzed in terms of the people who performed them.

Katz, Daniel, Dorwin Cartwright, Samuel Eldersveld, and Alfred McClung Lee (eds.): *Public Opinion and Propaganda,* Holt, Rinehart and Winston, Inc., New York, 1954. A collection of readings covering many aspects of public opinion and propaganda.

*Knott, Paul D. (ed.): *Student Activism,* Wm. C. Brown, Publishers, Dubuque, Iowa, 1971. A brief collection of significant essays on student activism.

Lang, Kurt, and Gladys Engle Lang: *Collective Dynamics,* Thomas Y. Crowell Company, New York, 1961. A textbook on collective behavior, with interesting chapters on rumor, panic, crowd behavior, fashion, public opinion, and other topics covered in this chapter.

Lee, Alfred McClung, and Norman D. Humphrey: *Race Riot,* Holt, Rinehart and Winston, Inc., New York, 1943. A description and analysis of the Detroit race riot of 1941.

*Lipset, Seymour M., and Sheldon S. Wolin (eds.): *The Berkeley Student Revolt,* Anchor Books, Doubleday & Company, Inc., Garden City, N.Y., 1965. A collection of essays about this student disorder. For a brief account, see **Seymour M. Lipset and Paul Seabury,** "Lesson of Berkeley: Question of Student Political Activities," *Reporter,* Jan. 28, 1965, pp. 36–40.

Milgram, Stanley, and Hans Toch: "Collective Behavior: Crowds and Social Movements," in **Gardner Lindzay and Elliot Aronson (eds.):** *Handbook of Social Psychology,* Addison-Wesley Publishing Co., Reading, Mass., 1969, vol. IV, pp. 507–610. A systematic collection of research and theory, most of which (pp. 507–584) deals with the topics covered in this chapter.

Smelser, Neil J.: *Theory of Collective Behavior,* The Free Press of Glencoe, New York, 1963. Attempts to develop and apply a theoretical framework for analyzing collective behavior.

Turner, Ralph H., and Lewis M. Killian: *Collective Behavior,* Prentice-Hall, Inc., Englewood Cliffs, N.J., 1957, chaps. 3–13. An interestingly written textbook, about half of which is devoted to the topics covered in this chapter.

White, Theo: "Building the Big Dam," *Harper's Magazine,* June, 1935, pp. 112–121. An entertaining explanation of how and why construction-camp workers used to go on payday sprees.

Human ecology

Part Five describes the way people and institutions are distributed in space and the way they relate to the physical environment they occupy. Chapter 18, "Population," considers the factors in population change, migration, and composition. Chapter 19, "The Community in Mass Society," describes rural and urban communities and the emergence of a worldwide urban culture.

Population

Doubling times [for a population to double] in the underdeveloped countries range around 20-35 years. Examples of these times (from figures released by the Population Reference Bureau) are: Kenya—24 years; Nigeria—28; Turkey—24; Indonesia—31; Philippines—20; Brazil—22; Costa Rica—20; and El Salvador—19. Think of what it means for the population of a country to double in 25 years. In order to just keep living standards at the present level, the food available to the people must be doubled. Every structure and road must be duplicated. The amounts of power must be doubled. The capacity of the transport system must be doubled. The number of trained doctors, nurses, teachers, and administrators must be doubled. This would be a fantastically difficult job in the United States—a rich country with a fine agricultural system, immense industries, and rich natural resources. Think of what it means to a country with none of these.

Remember also that in virtually all UDCs, people have gotten the word about the better life it is possible to have. They have seen colored pictures in magazines of the miracles of Western technology. They have seen automobiles and airplanes. They have seen American and European movies. Many have seen refrigerators, tractors, and even TV sets. Almost all have heard transistor radios. They *know* that a better life is possible. They have what we like to call "rising expectations." If twice as many people are to be happy, the miracle of doubling what they now have will not be enough. It will only maintain today's standard of living. There will have to be a tripling or better. Needless to say, they are not going to be happy. *(Paul R. Ehrlich,* The Population Bomb, *Ballantine Books, Inc., New York, 1968, pp. 22-23. Copyright © 1968 by Paul R. Ehrlich. Reprinted by permission of Ballantine Books, Inc.)*

Human ecology is the study of the interrelationships of people with their physical environments. More simply, it is the study of how people and institutions are located in space. It includes both the study of population (demography) and the study of community and regional organization.

Demographers are interested in both the size and the composition of a population.

A small population with large natural resources and extensive territory will have limited economic growth and urban development. A dense population with limited natural resources will have difficulty in maintaining a high standard of living. On the other hand, a growing population offers increasing markets for housing, food, and similar commodities, whereas a declining population may reduce market demand. Sometimes a population will vary from the usual sex and age distribution with certain predictable social consequences. A population with a large number of children and old people leaves a smaller proportion of people in productive labor to support them. If the sex ratio is markedly unequal, many people will be unable to marry (if marriage is monogamous) and may seek companionship outside of the normal family relationships. In many ways, population statistics are reflected in the social life of a people.

One person per square foot of land surface in less than 800 years.

Population has been relatively stable throughout most of history. In the first 1,650 years after the birth of Christ, world population a little more than doubled. In the next 125 years it doubled again. World population is now estimated at over 3.5 billion [UN Demographic Yearbook, 1969], and is expected to reach 7 billion by the year 2000 [McCormack, 1970, p. 6]. World population now grows in about six years by as many persons as it grew in the first 1,650 years following the birth of Christ. The earth could support a population somewhere between 7.5 billion and 50 billion, depending upon whose estimate we accept; the higher figure, however, assumes that our technology will be able to produce the "things" we need from rocks, sea, and air, and that we shall be willing to live on food from "algae farms and yeast factories." At present rates of growth, we shall reach this 50-billion figure in less than 200 years. If present rates of growth were to be continued for 800 years, we should have one person per square foot of land surface of the earth [Hauser, 1960, p. 7]. One demographer [Knibbs, 1928, p. 49] has estimated that if the offspring from a single couple were to grow at the rate of 1 percent a year for 10,000 years, it would take 248,293,000 billion earths to hold the bodies of all these people. Yet our present rate of world population increase is 2.0 percent. India is growing at an annual rate of 2.5 percent, and Ceylon, Taiwan, the Philippines, Mexico, and some other areas are growing at a rate of over 3 percent. Obviously, such rates of population growth are a recent phenomenon and are certain, *one way or another,* to be temporary. Eventually either the birthrate will drop to replacement levels or the death rate will rise to eliminate the population the world is unable to support. Since no one advocates death as an answer to population problems, attention has been concentrated on reducing the birthrate. But birthrates have seldom responded to large-scale efforts at change either up or down, and the success of such efforts in the underdeveloped countries is by no means certain. So far only the Japanese have been substantially successful in deliberate national efforts to reduce the birthrate.

DEMOGRAPHIC CONCEPTS

In order to study population questions, one must understand the very definite meanings of demographic concepts. "Birthrate" and "death rate," for instance, are terms frequently used in demographic discussion. Usually they refer to the *crude* rate, which is the number of births or deaths per thousand people per year. Crude birthrates and death rates do give a picture of population trends, but they may be misleading because births and deaths are greatly affected by the age structure of the population. A population in which a large proportion of people are relatively old would show a high crude death rate even though health levels were very high. Similarly, a population with a high proportion of either the very old or the very young would have a low crude birthrate even though the women of childbearing age were producing children at close to their biological potential. To allow for this factor of age we frequently use *age-specific* rates, which give birthrates or death rates for specific age levels.

Standardized birthrates and death rates are rates which have been adjusted to account for differences between populations in some characteristic—age distribution, occupational distribution, rural-urban residence—which is believed to affect birthrates or death rates. For example, a birthrate standardized for age would be calculated as follows: First, some age distribution, often a life insurance "life table," is chosen as a "standard" age distribution; then, using age-specific birthrates for a population, the birthrate for that population can be calculated as if that population had the "standard" age distribution. In this way, the true fertility rate or death probability in various populations can be compared. For example, a retirement community like St. Petersburg, Florida, has a low birthrate and a high death rate, suggesting that it is a very unhealthy place to live. But the *standardized* birthrate and death rate for St. Petersburg would give an accurate comparison of the fertility of its young people and the death probability for people of all ages between St. Petersburg and other communities. Such comparisons of standardized birthrates and death rates reveal whether any differences between crude rates for different populations are due to the factor which has been standardized or to other factors. In Table 29, the crude birthrates of the two communities vary greatly; but since the age-specific birthrates are identical, the standardized birthrates would also be identical.

Sex distribution is also of interest to the demographer, for it affects the crude birthrate as well as many other social phenomena. Thus we speak of the *sex ratio*, which is the number of males per 100 females. A sex ratio of 100 indicates that the two sexes are found in equal number, one of 110 that there are 110 men to 100 women, and one of 90 that there are 90 men to 100 women.

Demographers often speak of *life expectancy*. This usually refers to the number of years of life the average infant may expect at birth, but it may also be age specific—for example, life expectancy at age sixty (average additional years of life to be expected after reaching an age of sixty).

Insurance companies use actuarial tables indicating the life expectancy at any given age. Life expectancy should be distinguished from *life span*, which refers to the length of life possible for a member of a particular species. In the last century life expectancy at birth has increased greatly, while the evidence indicates that our life span has changed little if at all.

The very elementary concepts which we have just described represent only a few of the tools used in demographic analysis, but they are probably adequate for an introductory treatment of the subject. Knowledge of the techniques of population-trend analysis is essential to those who plan business,

TABLE 29
Hypothetical birthrates as affected by age distribution

| Age category | Growthville | | | Resthaven | | |
	No. of persons	Age-specific birthrate	No. of births	No. of persons	Age-specific birthrate	No. of births
Children under 16	800	10	4	100	10	1
Young adults	1,000	150	75	300	150	23
Middle aged and elderly	200	1		1,600	1	1
Total	2,000		79	2,000		25
Crude birthrate	79÷2=39.5			25÷2=12.5		

Source: Adapted from Everett K. Wilson, Sociology, The Dorsey Press, Homewood, Ill., 1966, p. 311. For purposes of this illustration, it is assumed that all categories have equal sex ratios. The age-specific birthrate gives the births per thousand females at specified ages.

governmental, religious, or educational programs. Some students may wish, eventually, to pursue specialized courses in this field.

CHANGING POPULATION COMPOSITION

The composition of a population affects its social life. Washington, D.C., with its many female clerical workers, St. Petersburg with its retired people, and Columbus, Georgia, with nearby Fort Benning—these cities are different, in part, because of differences in the age, sex, and occupational composition of the population whose needs they fill.

As shown in Table 30, the age composition of the United States has been constantly changing. A high birthrate together with a relatively low death rate means that children will compose a large fraction of the total population and old people a relatively small fraction. The long-term decline in our birthrate, lasting until the 1930s, reduced the children's share of our population and increased the proportion of the aged. Meanwhile, a slight extension of the life expec-

tancy of the aged further increased the proportion of the aged. Then, in the 1930s the birthrate started back up, climbing from 17 births per 1,000 in 1933 to 27 in 1947; then it hovered around 24 during the 1950s, and fell to 17.6 by 1968, and rose slightly to 18.3 in 1970. This again increased the proportion of children, while the proportion of aged continued to rise.

We must remember that it is primarily changes in the birthrate, not in the death rate, which have changed the proportion of the aged in our population. This point is widely misunderstood by people who confuse *life span* with *life expectancy*. As stated earlier the life span measures the time which fortunate people live until carried off by "old age"; life expectancy is the mean number of years of life remaining at any given age. Life expectancy at birth has doubled in the last century and a half; life expectancy at age sixty has increased only a couple of years. In other words, infants today are far more likely to reach the age of sixty than infants a century ago, but people who have reached sixty today have only two more years of life remaining than those who reached sixty a century ago. Stated still differently, more people live to be old today, but old people today do not live much longer than old people used to live, as shown in Figure 16.

Life span and death rates, therefore, have played only a minor part in the increasing proportion of the aged. But if the proportion of children in a population increases, the *proportion* of the aged in the population is reduced. The rapid growth in the proportion of the aged at present is due to the fact that those now approaching old age were born during a period of high birthrates, whereas those now approaching middle age were born during a period of lower birthrates. If birthrates and death rates remained stable over a long period of time, the proportion of people at each level would stabilize.

TABLE 30

Changing age composition and dependents in the United States

Year	Dependents per 100 persons of working age (20-64)		
	Young and old	Young only (under 20)	Old only (over 64)
1820	153	146	7
1850	123	117	6
1900	94	86	8
1940	71	59	12
1950	72	58	14
	Dependents per 100 persons of working age (18-64)*		
	Young and old	Young only (under 18)	Old only (over 64)
1960	82	65	17
1966	83	66	17
PROJECTIONS: SERIES A **(1.6 to 1.8% GROWTH** **RATE)**			
1975	83	66	17
1980	85	68	17
1990	92	74	17
PROJECTIONS: SERIES D **(1.0 to 1.1% Growth Rate)**			
1975	73	56	17
1980	68	51	17
1990	71	53	18

*Note that definition of "working age" is changed for 1960 and later. In the "projections," Series A is the most rapid growth rate and Series D is the least rapid growth rate which the Census Bureau considered likely.
Source: Philip M. Hauser, Population Perspectives, *Rutgers University Press, New Brunswick, N.J., 1960, p. 71; Bureau of the Census,* Population Estimates, *ser. P-25, no. 381, Dec. 18, 1967, p. 9.*

The age-specific birthrate in the United States is likely to continue to fall during the 1970s, but the crude birthrate is likely to rise a little. This is because of the age composition of our population. The children born during the high birthrate years of the late 1940s and 1950s are now entering child-bearing age. This change in age composition may give us the odd combination of a declining age-specific birthrate and a climbing crude birthrate.

Changes in population have many social consequences. A change in the ratio of dependents to workers has great economic impact. It affects employment, living standards, and price levels. The proportion of the aged has important economic and political consequences, such as the drive for more generous pension plans, the promotion of more generous health and welfare services for old people, experimentation with retirement communities, and recreational programs. Such services for a steadily growing segment of our population are enormously costly. With each increase in the proportion of the aged in the population, there are also proportionately fewer people working and paying taxes. In other words, an increased proportion of the aged lays a heavier tax burden upon proportionately fewer people.

The scientific study of the aged is claiming increased attention. *Geriatrics* is a branch of medicine concerned with old age and its diseases and disabilities; *gerontology* is a more inclusive field embracing the entire subject of the aged and their problems. Interest in gerontology is stimulated both by the doubling of the proportion of the aged during the twentieth century and by the shift from a rural, agricultural society, which provided a far more comfortable environment for aged people than does the urbanized and specialized, mobile society of today. The fact that by 1990 man can expect three times as many years of retirement as in 1900 (Figure 17) makes gerontology an important field of study.

FIGURE 16

Life expectancy at various ages in the United States: 1789-1968.

Source: *Statistical Abstracts of the United States; Historical Statistics of the United States; Statistical Bulletin of the Metropolitan Life Insurance Co.*, August, 1970, pp. 9-11.

Important as these effects have been in the United States, they are dwarfed by comparison with the impact of changing population composition in the underdeveloped countries. A sharp reduction in the death rate in these countries, mainly in infancy and early childhood, has allowed a rapid population increase, which is reflected in a very high proportion of the population under fifteen years of age. In these countries the ratio of children under fifteen to total population varies from 35 to 50 percent, while in most western countries the ratio varies between 20 and 30 percent (see Figure 18).

This means that the poorest countries are also those with the largest proportion of children to raise and the smallest proportion of people of working age to support them. Education, for instance, is a major expense as all of the world's countries endeavor to produce a trained citizenry. The developing countries, however, often have twice as large a proportion of school-age children as the industrialized nations. Or, to put the matter another way, they could double the educational expenditures per child with no increase in the school budget if their population composition were the same as that of Western Europe.

One of the long-run consequences of a severe war is alteration of the population composition. The population picture in Berlin, Germany, in 1910 was similar to that of an American city, and the population pyramid for that year indicates a fairly "normal" age and sex distribution. In 1945, however, the German population as a whole had an estimated "surplus" of 8 million women of childbearing age, meaning that many German women at this time had no chance for marriage. Two world wars killed millions of Germans, and the fact that most of these casualties were men of marriageable age meant that these wartime losses altered the composition of German population for many years.

Changes in population composition are

FIGURE 17

By 1990, men at age sixty can expect three times as many years of retirement as in 1900.

LIFE EXPECTANCY OF MALE WORKERS, AGE 60

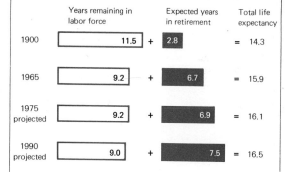

	Years remaining in labor force	Expected years in retirement	Total life expectancy
1900	11.5 +	2.8	= 14.3
1965	9.2 +	6.7	= 15.9
1975 projected	9.2 +	6.9	= 16.1
1990 projected	9.0 +	7.5	= 16.5

Source: 1961 White House Conference on Aging, Chart Book, Federal Council on Aging, Government Printing Office, Washington, D.C., 1961, p. 50; Bureau of the Census, *Current Population Reports,* "Population Estimates," series P-25, no. 381, Dec. 18, 1967, p. 39.

less dramatic than the recent spectacular spurts of population growth, but they are both the cause and the result of major changes in a society. Hence the demographer is constantly concerned with ascertaining changes in the sex ratio, the age composition, and the movement of population both within and between countries.

MIGRATION

The ancestors of the American Indians are thought to have come to the North American continent over a land bridge from Asia some time in the remote past. All other Americans trace their ancestry to relatively recent migrants. From the time of the Pilgrim fathers, some 30 million immigrants, mostly from Europe, settled in this country and changed it from a wilderness of food gatherers and hunters to the flourishing nation we know today. International immigration is now less important than in previous years, but a tremendous movement within the country leads to a constant redistribution of population.

Push, pull, and channels

The forces affecting migration may be grouped under three headings: (1) push, (2) pull, and (3) channels. *Push* relates to unfavorable conditions in the homeland which make people want to leave. In the 1840s a potato famine in Ireland made the United States seem attractive to many Irishmen, and the failure of the Revolution of 1848 caused many Germans to seek their fortunes in a land where immigrants were asked no questions about political beliefs. Sometimes the push comes from a catastrophe, sometimes from economic stagnation and lack of opportunity, sometimes from political or religious persecution. Today the shifts of national boundary lines after World War II and the rise of intolerant political

FIGURE 18

Effect of population composition on proportion of school-age children.

36 million total population, 13,724,000 school–age children

Philippines | 38% | 62%

50 million total population, 12,553,000 school–age children

France | 25% | 75%

In the Phillippines in 1968, 38 percent of a population of 36 million were between the ages of five and nineteen. The Philippines had slightly more school-age children than France, where 25 percent of a population of 50 million were between the ages of five and nineteen.

Source: *Demographic Yearbook, 1968,* The United Nations, New York, 1970.

movements, especially communism, have made life in their native lands intolerable for many people. In 1969 it was estimated that 17 million people had been forced to leave their ancestral homes and had not yet found a permanent place of residence [*World Refugee Report*, U.S. Committee For Refugees, 1969].

. . . except for the American Indians, they are all the descendents of immigrants.

Pull refers to the attractive features in the country receiving immigrants. Immigration proceeds toward the area of greater opportunities, as these are perceived by the individual. This perception is a cultural definition and not necessarily an objectively valid judgment. It is not the overall opportunity for economic development which is decisive, but the ease with which the individual can move into a situation with relatively little cultural readjustment. Alaska, for instance, is much more sparsely settled than California or New York and may have greater potential economic opportunities. Yet dozens of immigrants move to these states for every one who enters Alaska, simply because they seek an opportunity to make a living in an area where they believe they will be comfortable. Very few people seem to want the hardy life of the raw frontier. Indonesians

FIGURE 19

A population pyramid shows the age and sex distribution of a population.

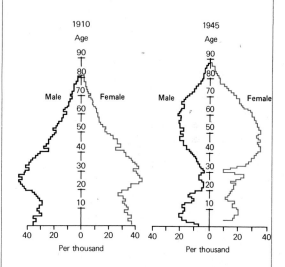

These two pyramids show the age and sex composition of Berlin in 1910 and 1945. In 1910, Berlin was growing rapidly through the migration of young adults, showing as a huge bulge above age twenty. In 1945, the pyramid shows the scars of two wars, with a relative shortage of men at all ages between twenty and sixty-five, and a spectacular shortage of infants.

Source: Reproduced by permission from Gustav Stalper's "Germany's Biological Destruction," *Fortune*, 37:93, May, 1948.

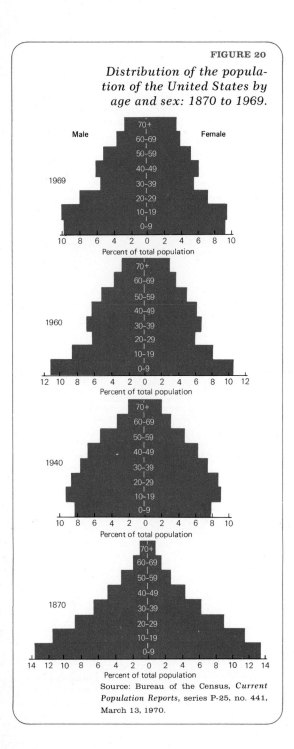

FIGURE 20

*Distribution of the popula-
tion of the United States by
age and sex: 1870 to 1969.*

Source: Bureau of the Census, *Current
Population Reports*, series P-25, no. 441,
March 13, 1970.

continue to move into heavily populated
Java, although sparsely peopled Sumatra
asks for settlers. In some parts of Central
and South America, good—but remote—land
lies unused, while people flock into the
miserable shanty-town slums which climb
the hills outside the major cities. Possibly
this picture may be changed by planned
economic development which brings both
jobs and cultural amenities to the more isolated areas. An extraordinary opportunity
for gain, such as a gold discovery or the presence of rich agricultural land with easy
access to markets, may exert a powerful
pull. Frequently though, the migration to
areas of supposedly rich potential is slow
until "social overhead"—towns, schools,
medical resources, roads, and stable governments—has been provided. An area becomes
attractive when the handicaps of a different
environment seem less significant than the
opportunity for more rapid social mobility
in a direction that does not seem to threaten
traditional cultural values.

Channels refer to the means of movement
from one area to another. They include the
availability of transportation, of information, of help in overcoming financial obstacles, and the presence or absence of barriers
in both the homeland and the receiving
country. The twentieth century has seen the
development of marvelous means of transport accompanied by severe restrictions of
immigration. Physically it was never easier
to move from one country to another.

Socially or politically, people find it harder
to make such a move now than they did in
the nineteenth century. Then they could
ordinarily move about without restrictions
of any kind. Even passports were seldom
required. Today we take it for granted that
countries will select the type and number of
immigrants they wish to receive and that
individuals will be unable to move unless
some governmental bureau has given permission. Among the early immigrants to
America were prostitutes, prisoners from

penal colonies, illiterates, adherents of
radical political movements, the diseased
and the physically deformed, none of whom
would be admitted today. Indeed, it is certain
that many of the early migrants whose memory is now enshrined by the Daughters of
the American Revolution and similar organizations would not be able to qualify
for entry under our present laws.

International migration

Increasing population and a developing
nationalism have combined to make governments wish to restrict immigration to the
type of immigrants they feel the national
culture can most easily assimilate and to
the number the nation can easily absorb into
its economy. In the United States we exclude
those with physical defects and certain other
personal disqualifications. Until 1968 we
also set a quota for each country, based upon
our population composition in 1920 and designed to favor the northwestern European
nations. We normally admitted no more than
170,000 immigrants from outside the Western hemisphere. While some additional immigration was allowed as an emergency
measure to help displaced persons after
World War II, the net effect of United States
immigration policy since 1921 has been to
make immigration a relatively unimportant
factor in the size and composition of the
American population.

Immigration patterns changed when new
immigration laws became effective in 1968.
The rigid national quota system (which
allowed only 100 immigrants a year from
most Asian and African countries) was replaced by a new system giving priority to
those with occupational skills useful to the
United States. Meanwhile, prosperity in
northwestern Europe made migration to the
United States less attractive than in the past.
The result is that the proportion of immigration from the United Kingdom and northern

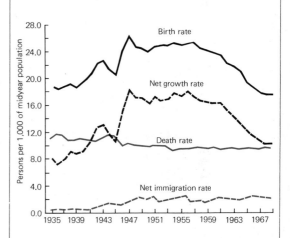

FIGURE 21

*Annual rates of net growth,
births, deaths, and net immigration in the United
States, 1935 to 1969.*

Source: Bureau of the Census, *Current
Population Reports*, series P-25, no. 442,
March 20, 1970.

Europe has sharply decreased and that from southern Europe and Asia has increased. For instance, immigration from the Philippines has increased tenfold and that from Portugal more than sixfold, while the proportion from Germany and the United Kingdom dropped by more than one-half between 1965 and 1970. Total immigration has increased slightly, moving from 296,697 in 1965 to 373,326 in 1970 [*Metropolitian Life Statistical Bulletin,* November, 1970, p. 9].

Most of the rest of the world, like the United States, has also followed selective or restrictive immigration policies. The countries which encourage immigration are those like Brazil, Canada, and Australia, which are considered underpopulated and welcome immigrants as a means of developing their resources. Since Australia and Canada restrict Oriental and African immigration, however, even those countries cannot be described as having a completely open immigration policy.

Internal migration

Although international migration is subject to increasing restrictions, a considerable shift of people is constantly going on within nations. In a normal year, one American family in five will move. In times past the American industrial labor force was recruited from European migrants and the agricultural force from African slaves and, until recently, from temporary Mexican migrants. Now that slavery has been ended and immigration reduced, the need for labor is met by movement of the American population. The past forty years have seen millions of people moving to the cities of the North and the West from the agricultural areas of the South and the Middle West; they have seen, too, a considerable movement of Puerto Ricans to the mainland.

While this internal migration is different in form from international migration, the consequences of the two shifts are much the same. The movement into a new region changes the population composition, provides new labor, and introduces a group of people ignorant of the local folkways, who have to make their adjustment to a strange cultural setting. Southern whites and blacks along with Puerto Ricans and others thus make many of the same contributions and experience many of the same problems as did the European immigrants of an earlier day.

SOCIAL AND CULTURAL ASPECTS OF POPULATION CHANGE

What causes a change in the rate of population growth? There is no evidence that groups differ in their biological capacity to reproduce and to survive, or that this capacity changes from time to time. Research on birthrates concerns both *fecundity*, the biological capacity to reproduce, and *fertility*, the actual rate of reproduction. Fecundity varies greatly between individuals, but we have no evidence of major differences between large population groups. In every population some individuals are either sterile or have limited fecundity, but the distribution of such persons is relatively constant. Fertility is based on fecundity, but no group reproduces at its biological maximum. Since our biological capacity to reproduce appears to be constant, social and cultural factors must explain most variations in birthrates and death rates.

Changes in death rates

Throughout most of history, both birthrates and death rates have been high, with only a small rate of natural increase. In the Bronze Age of ancient Greece, expectation of life at birth was an estimated 18 years. By the opening of the nineteenth century it had doubled to about 36 years. A century and a half later it has doubled again, standing at 70 years in the United States (specifically, 67.0 for white males, 74.2 for white females, 61.1 for nonwhite males, and 69.2 for nonwhite females in 1967). Between 1900 and 1970, our crude death rate fell by almost one-half, from 17.2 to 9.4 deaths per 1,000 people. What has caused such a sharp decline?

A great many factors, stretching backwards for hundreds of years, have contributed to the drop in the death rate. Improved transportation made it possible to transport a food surplus and to alleviate a local famine. Improvements in food preservation made it possible to preserve a food surplus. The growth of nationalism brought political institutions which were better able to cope with local crop failures and threatened famines. But medicine, sanitary engineering, and public-health measures were mainly responsible for the dramatic drops of the past century. After Pasteur and the germ theory of disease, many epidemic diseases quickly yielded to preventive measures. Pure food and water supply routed others. In the Western countries today, the great killers of the past—smallpox, cholera, diphtheria, typhoid, and scarlet fever—have become so rare that it is hard to find cases for medical students to observe.

The decline in the death rate began about 1750 in England and France and generally preceded any decline in the birthrate. A country with a falling death rate and a stationary birthrate will show an explosive rate of population increase. This is what explains the rapid population growth of recent centuries.

Age at marriage and marriage rate

One factor in the birthrate is the proportion of people who get married and the ages at which they marry (see Table 31). A study of fertility in Indianapolis found that women married under the age of seventeen had twice as many children as had women married at the age of twenty-six to twenty-eight (shown in Table 32). Early marriage not only increases the number of years of childbearing; early marriage is also associated with lower social-class background, together with attitudes and practices which favor large families.

The proportion of people who never marry varies greatly with different social conditions. In this connection, a comparison of the United States with Ireland is revealing. In 1964 the marriage rate (number of marriages per 1,000 people) was 6.8 in Ireland compared with 9 in the United States. The Irish simply don't marry as much, or as early, as the Americans.

The 1946 census showed that of all those [Irish] over thirty-five years of age, 46.6 of the men and 29.5 percent of the women in rural areas were unmarried; and 33.7 percent of the men and 34.8 percent of the women in urban areas. In the whole country more than two-thirds of the men between the ages of 20 and 44 were still single. The average marriage age for men is 35 and for women 29. About one fourth of the population never marries at all, compared to about one tenth in England.
(*Kevin Devlin, quoted in Paul Blanshard,* The Irish and Catholic Power, *Beacon Press, Boston, 1953, p.142*)

Yet Ireland is one of the rather poor, largely agricultural countries which usually have a high birthrate, and in addition, the laws of the country prohibit divorce and discourage the sale of contraceptives. Marriage is a serious business with no escape clause, and birth control is not seriously considered by most Irish families. Therefore many of the Irish either marry quite late or do not marry at all; the culture promotes fertility within marriage but discourages marriage itself. Emigration is high and the net population growth is less than in countries like the United States which encourage both marriage and birth control.

Proportion of persons married and median age at first marriage in the United States, 1890 to 1969

Year	Proportion married, 14 years old or older standardized for age		Median age at first marriage	
	Male, percent	Female, percent	Male	Female
1890	61.2	59.4	26.1	22.0
1900	59.9	58.7	25.9	21.9
1910	60.4	60.1	25.1	21.6
1920	61.3	60.4	24.6	21.1
1930	62.1	61.2	24.3	21.3
1940	62.8	61.0	24.3	21.6
1950	68.0	66.1	22.8	20.3
1955	69.3	67.4	22.6	20.2
1960	70.0	67.8	22.8	20.3
1965	67.9	63.9	22.8	20.6
1969	—	—	23.2	20.8

Source: Department of Commerce, Bureau of the Census, U.S. Census of Population, vol. 2, part 1, Current Population Reports, ser. P-20, nos. 96 (1960) and 105 (1965). 1969 data from Metropolitan Life Statistical Bulletin, November, 1970, p. 5.

The marriage rate is also related to the age and sex composition of the population. One would assume that usually the number of both sexes is approximately equal and that the age distribution is "normal"; but actually this is seldom true. In the United States female workers are attracted to well-established urban areas; Washington, D.C., in 1960 had a sex ratio of 88.3 (that is, 100 females for every 88.3 males). Areas of recent settlement attract more men; Alaska had a sex ratio of 132.3. Such unbalanced sex ratios reduce the marriage rate.

The recent American increase in the number of marriages in general and of early marriages in particular has been one of the unexpected developments of the last half century. People had often assumed that while marriage was a practical necessity in the rural setting, the city encouraged bachelorhood. They also assumed that in an agricultural society men could and should marry early, whereas in an urban society marriage would have to be postponed in order to gain an education. Again the rural society was associated with a system in which the work of women was largely restricted to the home, and it was assumed that as women became "emancipated" from restriction to a domestic life, they would postpone or avoid marriage for the sake of a career.

None of these assumptions has been borne out. Feminine emancipation, urbanization, and increased education have all been accompanied by a rush to the altar. It remains true that urban people and college-educated people still marry later than rural and less-educated people. But every group is marrying earlier than formerly, although the long-term decline in age at first marriage ended in the late 1960s.

Why, in the face of so many "logical" reasons for postponing marriage, has the age at marriage fallen so sharply? We are uncertain. Perhaps it is a natural consequence of the fact that parents permit and often encourage children to start "dating" and "going steady" at earlier ages than formerly. Perhaps it illustrates a growing unwillingness of young people to follow the deferred-gratification pattern and is an expression of the buy-now-pay-later pattern which characterizes a growing sector of our economy. At any rate, the fact of earlier marriage is indisputable, and one consequence has been accelerated population growth.

Cultural norms and family limitation

Since both governments and churches are often concerned about the birthrate, one might assume that the controlling cultural norms are of a political or religious charac-

TABLE 32

Wife's age at marriage and fertility

Children per 100 wives by age 44	Age at marriage							
	Under 17	17–19	20–22	23–25	26–28	29–31	32–34	35+
Catholic couples	394	351	331	227	191	165	—*	—*
Protestant couples	366	276	207	169	129	69	72	34

*Too few cases to be reliable.
Source: Pascal K. Whelpton and Clyde V. Kiser, "Social and Psychological Factors Affecting Fertility," Milbank Memorial Fund Quarterly, 21:232, 233, July, 1943. This study covers a sample of white families in Indianapolis, Ind.*

ter. Rulers of expanding countries usually oppose birth control and urge a high birthrate as the basis of military strength. There is a widespread conviction among American blacks, especially young males, that birth control is another form of white-imposed "genocide" [Darity et al., 1971]. On different grounds, the Roman Catholic clergy has been reluctant to approve the use of contraception and, until recent years, has tended to minimize the seriousness of population pressure. The Protestant clergy tend to accept contraception as a legitimate aspect of social adjustment. The governments of some overpopulated countries encourage birth control as necessary for population stabilization.

The evidence to date indicates that, with the exception of Japan, neither governments nor churches have been able to effect much change in the birthrate. Hitler and Mussolini had little success in the effort to stimulate a higher birthrate, and most of the current government efforts to reduce population increases have had disappointing results. Likewise, the endorsement of birth control by the Protestant clergy has had little effect in areas where the general social milieu favors large families, and the strictures of the Catholic clergy have not prevented a falling birthrate among urban Catholics. For a number of years, however, the Catholic clergy have discouraged the use of any

means of birth control except the rhythm method, one which is less effective than other techniques. Thus an analysis of the reproductive patterns of Catholics affords a case study of the effectiveness of the efforts of a religious group to influence family-limitation practices.

Comparisons of birthrates between United States cities which are heavily Catholic or Protestant and between different countries show no consistent trend—sometimes the predominantly Catholic area is higher,

TABLE 33

International Catholic-Protestant birthrate comparisons

Country	Crude birthrate	Birthrate order	Percent Catholic	Catholic rank order
Iceland	20.9	1	2	6
Netherlands	18.6	2	49	4
Norway	17.6	3	1	7
Italy	17.6	3	99	1
Austria	17.2	5	89	3
United Kingdom	17.1	6	9	5
Finland	15.7	7	1	7
Belgium	14.8	8	99	1

Source: Birthrate data from United Nations Demographic Yearbook, 1969; Catholic percentages derived from data in Statesman's Yearbook, 1970–1971.

sometimes the Protestant area is higher, as shown in Table 33 [Hunt, 1967]. One explanation is offered in a cross-national comparison of birthrates which found that in industrialized countries there was a tendency for Catholic areas to be higher when they were a minority of the population and lower when Catholics constituted a majority [Day, 1968]. Day believes that there can be a Catholic subculture which supports high natality, but this subculture only develops in a situation in which Catholics feel they are at a disadvantage in the society. A number of studies of Catholic and white Protestant birthrates in the United States do show that Catholics have some what higher birthrates than similarly situated non-Catholics [Whelpton and Kiser, 1943; Freedman et al., 1961; Harter and Roussel, 1969]. But the effects of this difference are reduced by the fact that Catholics in the United States are more heavily concentrated in urban areas where birthrates are relatively low. The total difference between Catholic and Protestant rates is relatively small. The Catholic rate is far less than an uncontrolled rate of increase, and is less than that of black Protestants [Lenski, 1961, p. 241].

On an ideological level, there is a sharp contrast between the condemnation of contraception in the official statements of the Roman Catholic Church and the acceptance of contraceptive techniques by most Americans. On the practical level of reproductive behavior, the difference is not so great, for a large proportion of Catholics have for some years been adopting the family-planning practices typical of the American population [Bogue, 1959, p. 696]. One survey found that over half of the American Catholic wives are practicing methods of contraception forbidden by the papal edict [Potvin et al., 1968]. The main support of an American fertility high enough to sustain rapid population growth is found more in the general attitudes of the society rather than in specific Roman Catholic influences.

In summary, the situation is well expressed by a Methodist minister: "The major obstacle to population control is not the Roman Catholic Church. The big obstacle is the middle-class American who wants more children." He blamed the "almost total unawareness of the fact that a three-child family means about a fifty percent increase in every generation," for the situation he believes presents the United States with its gravest crisis in history [Sharp, 1969]. A few religious groups whose faith is closely related to their general culture, such as the Amish and the Hutterites, continue to show a consistently high birthrate. For large groups whose members are not knit in a closely controlled culture, such as Protestants and Catholics, one can only say that their birthrate tends to follow general social trends; the religious factor is difficult to isolate from other variables.

Social status and the birthrate

The folk proverb that the "rich get richer and the poor get babies" describes fairly correctly the relationship between social status and the birthrate. In general, a low birthrate is more characteristic of urbanized, well-educated, and high-income groups, and a high birthrate is more apt to be found among rural, poorly educated, and low-income groups. Groups in which these characteristics are mixed usually have intermediate fertility rates.

The planning attitude and family limitation In rural areas a large family has labor value. In the modern city child labor is prohibited, and each additional child adds to the family expenses without increasing its income. Supposedly, in the city only the wealthier couples could afford large families, whereas the poor would find a large family a difficult burden. Such reasoning assumes that both the poor and the more well-to-do have the same tendency to plan their lives. In the discussion of the deferred-gratification pattern in the chapter on social mobility, we found that planning was not a typical lower-class pattern. Instead of trying to control their environment, lower-class people are likely to consider themselves creatures of fate, subject to forces beyond their control. Most of them do not *desire* larger families than middle-class people [Chilman, 1968] but they *get* larger families because they have neither strong motivation to limit family size nor easy access to birth-control techniques.

Recent studies show wide variation among lower-class people in their readiness to make use of contraceptive techniques. Apparently there are many who greatly prefer small families and will make use of contraceptive techniques when materials and information are made available by Planned Parenthood clinics or similar agencies [Jaffe and Polgar, 1968]. There are many others, however, who do not respond to even the most convenient clinical facilities. The diffusion of birth-control practices is limited by the lack of convenient, low-cost, well-publicized birth-control facilities in many areas. Birth control is limited even more greatly by the social factors which make a large family seem desirable to many people, or which inhibit some people from using effective birth-control techniques.

Just as the educated, urbanized section of the population showed the greatest birthrate declines in the 1920s and 1930s, this same group showed the greatest birthrate gains in the post–World War II period. Their birthrates are still somewhat below those of the uneducated and rural groups (see Figure 22) but are well above the rates required to replace themselves. There is no evidence that the urbanized, college-educated couples have abandoned family planning or birth control; they simply are planning three-child or four-child families and thus contributing to the population explosion. The

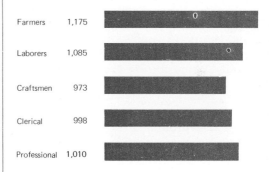

FIGURE 22

Occupation of husband and fertility in the United States; number of children born per 1,000 women aged twenty-five to twenty-nine in 1969.

Farmers	1,175
Laborers	1,085
Craftsmen	973
Clerical	998
Professional	1,010

Source: Bureau of the Census, *Current Population Reports*, series P-70, no. 205, July 22, 1970.

United States now has a birthrate which, although in considerable part planned, is high enough to produce the largest population increase per decade that the country has ever known.

Family limitation was known among the upper-class families of Greece, Rome, and some other classical civilizations and in some primitive societies, but only recently has family limitation become common in the Western world. It arose as an urbanized middle class saw a chance for economic advancement through the control of their environment and gradually shifted from a fatalistic to a planning approach. As time passed, the planned-family pattern has gradually been diffused to lower-income groups and rural areas. While the process has been accompanied by controversy, the spread of birth control seems due to cultural changes that prompted the adoption of the planning process rather than to the actual success of birth-control propaganda.

In general, the residents of a rural folk society have been indifferent to the possibilities of birth control.

Birthrates for blacks are generally higher than for whites, with a replacement index of 175 as compared to 142 for whites in 1969 [*Current Population Reports*, ser. P-20,

p. 203, July 6, 1970, p. 1]. Black birthrates have been dropping rapidly and are drawing closer to white birthrates in the United States, as shown in Table 34, but the differential is still great enough to affect our population composition for at least several decades. Currently, about 11 percent of our population is black, and it is estimated that this may rise to 14 percent by the year 2,000 [*Current Population Reports*, op. cit., p. 1].

National planning and family limitation

From the preceding discussion it appears that neither religious nor government institutions have been very successful in the effort to influence family size when their definition of the situation did not correspond to that of the bulk of the population. In general, the residents of a rural folk society have been indifferent to the activities of free birth-control clinics, and an urbanized middle class has resisted efforts of church and state to increase its fertility. Currently, the governments of many nations in the underdeveloped areas consider their unchecked population increase to be a major problem. They are considering government efforts to persuade their people to adopt practices of family limitation, and some have set up free or inexpensive birth-control clinics along with propaganda in favor of the use of contraception.

Efforts to popularize contraception in underdeveloped countries have not been total failures, but have not been highly successful [Berelson, 1966; Wolfers, 1969]. There is considerable recognition, among scholars and officials, of the need for birth control in such countries [Rao, 1967; Chang et al., 1969; Hock, 1969], but the success of present programs is not impressive. Most of the experimental programs dealt mainly with people who were either rural peasants or had recently emerged from that status. Some of these people showed a degree of interest in family limitation, but few fol-

TABLE 34

Own children under 5 years old per 1,000 women 15 to 45 years old,
by metropolitan-nonmetropolitan residence and labor status, 1969

	White:* own children under 5 years old per 1,000 women		Negro:* own children under 5 years old per 1,000 women	
	1960	1969	1960	1969
Total	466	345	525	358
Metropolitan	456	337	498	360
In central cities	409	318	487	351
Outside central cities	499	349	543	396
Nonmetropolitan	484	361	585	354
In labor force	202	188	334	295
Not in labor force	629	478	690	424

*White-Negro comparisons are affected by the larger proportion of Negro (12 percent)
than white (2 percent) children under 5 living apart from their mother, and hence not
classified as "own children."
Source: Current Population Reports, ser. P-20, no. 189, Aug. 18, 1969.

lowed a consistent pattern in the use of contraceptive practices. Apparently this type of birth control is congenial to a well-educated, urban, middle-class group but is contrary to the cultural norms of other types of population.

Taiwan and Hong Kong are among the most highly urbanized and industrialized areas in Asia, and it is significant that these are two of the few Asiatic areas (other than Japan) reporting some success in promoting birth control [Chang, 1969]. A recent comparative study finds that a substantial decline in the birthrate does not always follow modernization, but nowhere has the birthrate fallen in the absence of modernization [Weller and Sly, 1969]. Modernization is under way nearly everywhere, bringing with it both the conditions favoring rapid population growth and the conditions favoring the eventual acceptance of birth control.

Something about the dynamics of popula-

tion control may be learned from the Japanese experience. The Japanese population grew from 56 million in 1920 to 73 million in 1940. This increase alone would have populated Japan with 114 persons per square mile, a density exceeded by only twelve of the American states. Defeat in war and the loss of expanding empire made population pressure even more unmanageable. Following World War II, the government encouraged population restriction through legalized abortion and contraception. By 1953, it was estimated that about one-half of all conceptions were ended by abortion [Muramatsu, 1960]. The Japanese birthrate fell from 34.3 in 1947 to 17.2 in 1957, almost exactly one-half. This is the most precipitous intentional decline in a nation's birthrate known to history. The principal means has been abortion, but some Japanese sentiment favors a shift of emphasis to contraception and female sterilization as more desirable techniques.

Japan may be the first country in the world to end population growth. A 1969 report of the Japanese Population Council indicated that the birthrate had fallen to two children per Japanese woman and that, if the trend continued, population growth would end by 1983 [*Otago Daily Times*, Aug. 8, 1969, reprinted in *Population Bomb Press Clippings*, November, 1969]. Some Japanese fear a labor shortage which will slow Japanese industrial expansion, and advocate a change in population policy. Others think that a stabilized population is desirable and that Japan has reached its optimum population [Boffey, 1970].

A major reason for the Japanese success in population control as contrasted with its relative failure in most other countries is that the Japanese adopted a technique which most other countries have been reluctant to sanction. Abortion is morally repugnant to many people, but it is a technique which always works, is relatively simple and cheap, and does not require any change in sexual habits. The Japanese accepted abortion, and only gradually has a part of the population learned to practice contraception. Other countries have also found their people slow to accept contraception but have been reluctant to make either abortion or sterilization readily available. The result is that the Japanese are approaching a stable population while most other countries still have a rapidly growing population.

While the Japanese acceptance of abortion may be the chief reason for the success of their population control programs, other factors are also important. The government encountered little resistance to its population control program because the traditional values of Japanese society were not an obstacle. The Japanese traditional family system was more concerned with the well-being of the heir than with large numbers of offspring. Abortion and infanticide had long been occasional practices. Neither of the

dominant religions, Buddhism and Shintoism, objects to family planning. Japan is an urban industrial country with an efficient governmental bureaucracy and a literate population. All these circumstances made the task far simpler than in a country like India with wide-spread illiteracy, primitive village life, some religious hostility to family planning, and a different emphasis in the familistic system. In such a setting the average village Indian lacks either the means or the motivation for family planning. Just one anecdote will tell something of the problem facing family planners in many underdeveloped areas. In one district the literacy barrier was surmounted by a large poster showing a three-child native family in comfortable surroundings, contrasted with another larger family amid squalor. But the reaction was unexpected. Instead of admiring the greater comfort of the small family, the observers murmured, "That poor family—only three children!"

Puerto Rico has used the public-health services to make contraception available to its people, but like India and Japan, has had only limited success with this technique. Students of the situation report that contraception is often tried but seldom adopted as a lasting practice and consequently has had little effect on the birthrate. They also report that sterilization has become amazingly popular, although it is not officially encouraged, and many who want the operation may have difficulty in obtaining it [Hill et al., 1959, pp. 178–181; Wells, 1969, pp. 185, 404]. In India, where attempts to popularize contraception have not been very successful, a small but growing interest in sterilization is reported [Evans, 1961].

From the results of the attempts to popularize family limitation in Japan, Puerto Rico, and India, one would conclude that the adoption of contraception is not so much a matter of governmental or religious policy as of cultural adjustment. Recent studies from several Asiatic countries show that most couples in those countries *desire* families of about their present size [Ridker, 1969]. Consequently, a change in widespread social attitudes is necessary if birth control is to be widely used. Sociologists studying the birth-control program in Puerto Rico believe that a program stressing group discussion and aimed at overcoming cultural difficulties, for example, lack of communication between man and wife, might lead to a successful use of contraception [Hill et al., 1959, pp. 365–389]. Such a program is difficult to carry out because of the expense, the shortage of skilled personnel, and the possibility of opposition from elements of the community opposed to a birth-control program. It would seem more likely that effective population control in underdeveloped areas would depend upon either the official acceptance of methods such as abortion or sterilization which do not require a change in usual family habits, or upon the development of much simpler and more effective means of contraception than are now widely available.

To achieve effective family limitation, either a means of birth control must be developed which is consistent with the culture or the culture must be altered to provide encouragement for consistent planning. To some extent both developments are occurring. Increased urbanization and education are changing the culture of traditional peasant populations in a manner compatible with the adoption of consistent planning practices. The contraceptive pill has proved both popular and efficient in urban populations, but peasant groups in developing countries need some device which is less expensive and which does not require daily administration. One such device has been developed—the Lippes loop, an intrauterine device (IUD) which can remain in place for many months—and has been moderately successful among peasant groups [Potter et al., 1968], but the search for the ideal contraceptive continues. Eventually the combi-

nation of general cultural change and technical improvements in contraception should make effective family limitation practical for all population groups. The question is whether effective family limitation can be achieved before population increase becomes completely unmanageable.

Future population pressure

Urbanization and industrialization in Western countries have had twin effects upon population growth. The development of urbanization and industrialization was accompanied by changes in medicine and sanitation that produced a rapid drop in death rates and a great population growth. But urbanization and industrialization also unleashed forces which eventually led to a reduction of the birthrate. We have thus shifted from a society with high birthrates and death rates to a society with low death rates and medium birthrates, but with a higher rate of population growth than can possibly be sustained over any long time.

The non-Western world is now in the earlier stages of this demographic transition. Death rates have been plunging precipitously as non-Western lands gained epidemic control in the post-World War II years. For example, the death rate in Ceylon fell by one-half in a single decade [Morgan, 1956]. In such countries a rapidly falling death rate and an approximately stationary birthrate give a rate of population growth which soon becomes unmanageable (see Figure 23). The pressure of numbers may lead to effective means of population restraint or to an aggressively expansionist military policy. Over forty years ago, Thompson [1929] stated that population pressure was encouraging Japan's march toward war, and suggested ways of averting this consequence. His suggestions were not followed, and we all know the outcome. Will China and India repeat this story? Possibly so. But in

The trend

Billions of persons

WORLD POPULATION:
THE PICTURE IN 1969
AND A LOOK
TOWARD 2000

FIGURE 23

*World population: 1969
and 2000.*

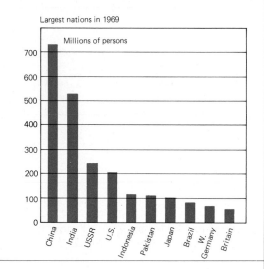

Largest nations in 1969

Millions of persons

China India USSR U.S. Indonesia Pakistan Japan Brazil W. Germany Britain

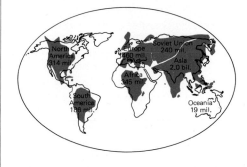

1969
Area of continents drawn in proportion to population
Total 3.56 billion

North America 314 mil. Europe 460 mil. Soviet Union 240 mil. Asia 2.0 bil. Africa 345 mil. South America 186 mil. Oceania 19 mil.

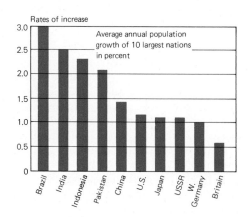

Rates of increase

Average annual population
growth of 10 largest nations
in percent

Brazil India Indonesia Pakistan China U.S. Japan USSR W. Germany Britain

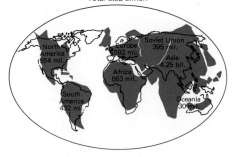

In year 2000
Area of continents in proportion to population
Total 6.92 billion

North America 554 mil. Europe 592 mil. Soviet Union 395 mil. Asia 4.25 bil. Africa 663 mil. South America 432 mil. Oceania 30 mil.

Source: *New York Times*, Dec, 22, 1963,
sec. 4, p. 8. © 1963 by the New York Times
Company. Reprinted by permission; data
for 1969 from *United Nations Demographic Yearbook*, 1969.

such a war, they might be less likely to lose [Organski and Organski, 1962].

Malthus on population

The argument about population pressure still swirls around the ideas of the Rev. Thomas R. Malthus, an English clergyman whose *Essay on Population* in 1798 called the world's attention to this topic. Malthus believed that the essential reason for poverty was the pressure of population growth on the world's resources. He reasoned that the effects of natural fertility were held in check only by such negative forces as famine, war, and pestilence. Thus, whenever an improvement in productive technology yielded an economic surplus, these products would soon be consumed by an expanding population. Malthus did not deny the possibility of increasing industrial and agricultural production, but he believed that the increase would be unable to keep up with population growth, and expressed his belief that population tends to multiply in geometric ratio (2, 4, 8, 16, etc.) while production can only increase in an arithmetic ratio (1, 2, 3, 4, etc.). Each increase in population becomes a basis for a further increase in the next generation, but each increase in the yield from an acre of land is not a basis for a still further increase the following season. Instead, having boosted the yield this year, producers will find it harder, not easier, to boost the yield still higher next year. Thus, people increase through multiplication whereas the food supply increases only by addition and is constantly being outrun by the growth of population. Malthus urged later marriages as a means of keeping down the birthrate, but he was pessimistic about the chance that this policy would be followed. He saw no practical possibility of averting hunger, famine, and pestilence. Organized charity and relief would only enable a few more to survive today so that they might starve

tomorrow. Because of these gloomy predictions of Malthus, economics became known as the "dismal science."

In the 1920s it was popular to believe that the events of the preceding century had disproved the Malthusian hypotheses. The world had seen the greatest population growth in its history, and at the same time the standard of living had improved rather than declined. Why did Malthus's gloomy predictions fail to materialize? One reason is that Malthus failed to foresee the widespread use of improved methods of contraception. The contraceptive devices of his day were so crude and inefficient that he and other writers paid little or no attention to them. Another reason was that Malthus could not be expected to foresee the magnitude of the industrial and agricultural revolution of the nineteenth and twentieth centuries. Great new land areas in North and South America and Australia were brought under cultivation. Improvements in agriculture rapidly boosted output per acre. For a time, birthrates in the Western world were falling so rapidly and production was rising so rapidly that Malthus began to sound like a gloomy scold instead of a gifted thinker.

Recently, however, Malthus has been restored to fashion by scholars known as the "neo-Malthusian school." The Western nations, while using family planning, now seem to be planning and raising families much larger than can possibly be maintained for very many generations. Pressure upon our water resources is already acute in some parts of the United States, and further pressures may be anticipated as our population figures continue to soar. Granted that the United States can provide a high standard of living for 250 million people, can we provide it for 400 million, or a billion, or 10 billion?

As indicated earlier, the United States has a post-World War II baby crop entering the childbearing ages. Even with a sharp drop in the birthrate, our population would increase for as many years as shown in Table 35. It is estimated that, if an average of 2.11 children were born per woman, the population would remain stable, once the age distribution became adjusted to this birthrate. Assuming that births dropped immediately to this level, instead of the present 3.06 children per woman by age thirty-five to thirty-nine, it would still be fifty years before the population would stabilize, and by then the United States would have a population of approximately 300 million [Barnett, 1970]. It is relevant to note that each American consumes more of the world's resources than a person in any other land. A noted population expert states:

A preliminary census report was recently released which indicates that the population of the United States may grow by "only" 75 million people by the end of the century.

Assume for a moment that the demographic projections, which have often been too low in the past, are accurate, and that in the year 2000 the population of the United States is "only" some 280 million people. What might that mean to us and to the world?

Each American has roughly 50 times the nega-

tive impact on the Earth's life-support systems as the average citizen of India. Therefore, in terms of eco-system destruction, adding 75 million more Americans will be the equivalent of adding 3.7 billion Indians to the world population. (*Paul R. Ehrlich*, New York Times, *Nov. 4, 1970, p. 47. Copyright © 1970 by The New York Times Company. Reprinted by permission*).

It is the underdeveloped areas of the world that offer the best illustrations of Malthus's chilling predictions. Here the "revolution of rising expectations" meets the population explosion. In these areas death control has been sensationally effective; birth control is difficult to popularize; and the expansion of agricultural and industrial production is a slow and complex process. In spite of considerable improvement, production in underdeveloped areas has done little more than keep up with the population increase, and in some places has actually fallen behind population growth. In spite of herculean efforts, the gap between the per capita income of the industrialized and the underdeveloped areas continues to increase.

It seems almost impossible that an unchecked population growth can take place

TABLE 35

Anticipated population growth in the United States

If average completed family size is:	Then the population of the United States in each of the following years will be (in millions of people):*			
	1980	1990	2000	2020
3.10 children per woman	237	277	321	440
2.78 children per woman	232	266	301	386
2.45 children per woman	228	255	281	336
2.11 children per woman	226	248	266	299

Table assumes a slight decline in the death rate and a net immigration of 400,000 per year.
Source: "Projections of the Population of the United States by Age and Sex (Interim Revisions): 1970–2020," Current Population Reports, ser. P-25, no. 448, August, 1970.

in even the next fifty years without a deterioration in living standards. A few years ago, predictions of impending world famine were pouring from the pens of demographers. But spectacular increases in food production are beginning in the underdeveloped areas of the world. This "green revolution" comes from the development of high-yield plant strains which are appropriate for modern fertilizer technology in the climates of the countries involved [Horsfall, 1970]. Some experts are predicting that India, for example, will be self-sufficient in food grain production by 1974–1975 [Satin, 1969]. The expected nightmare of world famine seems to have receded somewhat, but *any* productivity increases will bring only a temporary respite if population continues to multiply. It is also possible that environmental pollution, and not food shortage, may set the limits of world population.

But even if we can escape Malthusian doom, some people are asking if this kind of struggle is really worthwhile. Rapid population growth carries a price tag of many kinds. One scholar [A. Miller, 1960] claims that rapid population growth requires an increase in government controls of many kinds, promotes the bureaucratization of society, and reduces the range of individual liberties. Already in England, that historic citadel of individual liberty, the state will take away a farmer's land (with compensation) if he does not farm it efficiently; the national interest cannot allow a landowner the luxury of inefficient land use. In the Netherlands one is not permitted to build a one-story house; the land cannot be spared. Individual liberty in modern societies is a luxury which is gradually sacrificed as population pressure grows intense. How much of it should be sacrificed in order to feed more and more people? Some years ago Landis framed the issue in this manner:

Certainly individualized Western man has reached the point where he is unwilling to devote his full energies to food supply. The dream of luxuries, of leisure which comes from having plenty, has motivated him to cross oceans in quest of spices, and has led him to penetrate nature's deep secrets with microscope and telescope. He will not willingly settle for a life motivated primarily by a struggle for appeasement of hunger. He can hardly conceive of the fact that millions live on that level already.

The world now supports around 2.4 billion people [in 1950; increased to 3.5 billion by 1970]. It perhaps could sustain a maximum of somewhere between 5 and 10 billion, but to do so would require a maximum of free migration between continents and nations and the exertion of all human effort toward producing the maximum of food. Is man willing to devote all his energies to feeding the world, as will be required in a hundred to a hundred fifty years, assuming present rates of population growth? (*Paul H. Landis, "Is There Room for the Next 1,000,000,000 People?"* The Clearing House, 28:140–141, November, 1953.)

The study of population offers prime illustrations of cultural relativity and of how values change along with the changing needs and experiences of a people. In an agricultural society with high death rates and unchecked epidemic diseases, large families made sense. A century ago, the question, "How many children have you?" brought answers like, "Seven, four living." Today, the family picture showing the patriarch surrounded by a dozen children, scores of grandchildren, and two or three hundred great-grandchildren is beginning to be a source of embarrassment, not of pride. Today, the couple who insists upon their right to bear as many children as they wish are beginning to look like the passenger who tries to bring his luggage into a crowded lifeboat. The emergent values, reflecting current needs, are embodied in the "zero population growth" ideal—that no couple should bear more than two children and should seek adoption if they desire a larger family. It is clear that eventually zero population growth will be approached, either through voluntary choice, through compulsory birth control, or through Malthusian misery.

SUMMARY

Human ecolgoy is a study of the interrelationships of people with their physical environment. *Demography* is concerned with the age and sex composition of the population, its movement, both within and across national frontiers, and its rate of growth.

The *age* and *sex composition* of a population affects its social life in many ways. Changes in age composition are due mainly to changes in birthrates and death rates and are presently increasing the proportions of both aged and children in many populations. The increased proportion of youth is a major handicap to underdeveloped countries, since it increases educational costs while reducing the proportion of the population in productive labor. The permanent rise of a rather large group of old people has prompted the rise of *geriatrics* and *gerontology*, disciplines devoted to the problems of the aged.

Migration is affected by the *push* given to people by unsatisfactory conditions at home, by the *pull* of attractive opportunities elsewhere, and by the *channels* or means through which they are able to migrate. The United States received a constant stream of immigrants until the enactment of restrictive legislation in 1921. Since then immigration has been restricted not only by the United States but also by many other countries.

Most migration today is internal, especially from farm to city within a country. Political dislocations have produced record numbers of refugees, but although transportation is easy, social restrictions make refugee resettlement more difficult than ever before.

In the past three centuries a nearly stable world population has exploded into fantastic growth. Effective death control has cut the death rate in nearly all areas of the world, while only in some areas has the birthrate fallen appreciably, and in none has it fallen enough to restore a historic stability of population.

A society's birthrate is largely a result of the average age at marriage, the proportion of people who marry, and their use or non-use of birth control. Malthus dismissed the idea of the effectiveness of contraception and predicted inevitable overpopulation and misery unless people controlled population growth by postponing marriage. The rapid colonial expansion and industrial and agricultural development of the nineteenth century delayed the fulfillment of Malthus's predictions, but they now appear likely to be fulfilled in at least some parts of the world. Family planning is being used in some areas, but many cultural barriers impede its acceptance in the areas where the most unmanageable population explosions are likely to occur. Effective family planning apparently requires either a cultural base which the undeveloped societies may not have until after they have developed an urban industrial civilization, or the development of contraceptive techniques which do not require daily attention.

Questions and projects

1. What has been the rate of population growth throughout most of history? Why have world rates of population growth changed recently? How long will present rates of growth continue?

2. What factors other than birth control affect the rate of reproduction?

3. At the present time the prosperity of some

areas of the world might be favorably affected by population increase. Evaluate the prospects of migration from overpopulated areas to those considered underpopulated.

4. What were the ideas of Malthus? Do you feel that the passage of time has outdated or confirmed these ideas? Why or why not?

5. Is it true that the countries of Asia, Africa, and Latin America are now undergoing a population cycle similar to that experienced by the United States and Western Europe at an earlier date?

6. How would you explain the tendency of inhabitants of underdeveloped areas to react more favorably to the use of sterilization and abortion than to contraception?

7. Will it be necessary to use compulsory methods of birth control to control population increase? What reason is there for thinking voluntary methods will or will not be successful?

8. How would you explain the tendency toward an excess of females in American cities and an excess of males in the rural districts?

9. What is meant by "push," "pull," and "channels" in connection with immigration?

10. In recent years the United States has had an increase in the proportion of both children and aged in the overall population. What effects would you expect this change in population to have in social and economic relationships?

11. Do you believe that a couple has a "right" to bear as many children as they want and can provide for?

12. Using the most recent Statistical Abstract of the United States, compare the population growth of your state with others. What factors would appear to affect the relative position of your state? What adjustments do you feel your state will be required to make to meet the needs indicated by population changes?

13. Using the *United Nations Demographic Yearbook*, compare birth and death rates in the Philippines, India, and Mexico with those in Great Britain, France, and the United States. What conclusions would you draw about the probable future of population growth in these countries?

Suggested readings

Bogue, Donald J.: *Principles of Demography*, John Wiley & Sons, Inc., New York, 1969. A comprehensive textbook in population analysis.

Ehrlich, Paul, and Anne H. Ehrlich: *Population, Resources, Environment: Issues in Human Ecology*, W. H. Freeman and Company, San Francisco, 1970. An impassioned and scholarly plea for effective action to deal with the crisis in ecology.

Ford, Thomas R., and Gordon F. De Jong (eds.): *Social Demography*, Prentice-Hall, Inc., Englewood Cliffs, N.J., 1970. A series of readings indicating the manner in which population composition interacts with social structure.

*****Handlin, Oscar:** *The Newcomers*, Harvard University Press, Cambridge, Mass., 1959. A comparison of Puerto Rican adjustment in New York City with that of previous immigrants.

Hill, Reuben, J. Mayone Stycos, and Kurt W. Back: *The Family and Population Control*, The University of North Carolina Press, Chapel Hill, 1959. An intensive analysis of the Puerto Rican effort to popularize birth control.

Hunt, Chester L.: "Female Occupational Roles and Urban Sex Ratios in the United States, Japan, and the Philippines," *Social Forces*, 43:407–417, March, 1965. Analyzes why Japanese urban sex ratios differ from those in the Philippines and the United States.

Morris, Judy K.: "Professor Malthus and His Essay," *Population Bulletin*, 22:7–27, February, 1966. Background and current relevance of the Malthusian theory.

Mudd, Stuart (ed.): *The Population Crisis and the Use of World Resources*, W. Junk, The Hague, Netherlands, 1964. Describes the population problem in various countries and the attempts to popularize the use of birth control and the idea of optimal use of world resources.

Rainwater, Lee: *And The Poor Get Children,* Quadrangle Books, Inc., Chicago, 1960. A report of the fertility patterns of the poor as revealed by intensive interviews.

Spengler, Joseph J.: "Population and Economic Growth," in **Ronald Freedman (ed.),** *Population:*

The Vital Revolution, Doubleday & Company, Inc., Garden City, N.Y., 1964, pp. 56–69. An economist analyzes the relationship of population to economic development.

Zero Population Growth, National Reporter, Los Altos, California, 94022. A journal, published by the organization with the same name, presenting articles and news items supporting the idea that no couple should bear more than two children.

. . . if the anonymity New York grants us is a problem, it is also a blessing. In small towns it is natural and easy to be passing friendly with everyone nearby, and in small towns it works. But in New York there are too many people nearby. Just try to imagine walking down Madison Avenue and being friendly to everyone you meet there! Not only would you never get where you were going, but you would be making a nuisance of yourself to thousands of people with their own errands to run. The very multitude of people makes it necessary for us to stare through and beyond one another.

. . . were I living in an apartment house, I would not care to know who lives above me, below me, or in the next apartment on either side. I want to choose my friends: I do not care to have them thrust upon me by the rental agent. And I do not want people dropping in to borrow whatever people borrow, nor to chitchat whatever neighbors chitchat. . .

It *can* be lonely at times inside that anonymity, but let a small-town friendliness echo through those canyons and the future would be chaos forever, bumper to bumper and nose to nose from here to infinity. (*John Ciardi, "Manner of Speaking,"* Saturday Review, *Feb. 12, 1966, pp. 16–17.*)

The community in mass society

The social life people lead is affected by the kind of community in which they live. The community is as old as man—or even older, for our subhuman ancestors probably shared a community life. *A community is a local grouping within which people carry out a full round of life activities.* Defined in greater detail [Jonassen, 1959, p. 20; Hillery, 1955], a community includes (1) a grouping of people, (2) within a geographic area, (3) with a division of labor into specialized and interdependent functions, (4) with a common culture and a social system which organizes their activities, (5) whose members are conscious of their unity and of belonging to the community, and (6) who can act collectively in an organized manner. For it to qualify as a true community, its members must be able to experience all or nearly all aspects of the culture within its boundaries. The handful of houses in a hamlet do not form a community, for their occupants must travel elsewhere for many of their needs and relationships. While in strict correctness the term "community" refers to a grouping of people, and not to the territory they occupy, both usages are fairly common in sociological literature. The term is also loosely used to describe almost any subculture or category of people, whether geographical (Hickory Corners, New York City, the "world community") or social (the "community of scholars," the "black community," the "artistic community"), but these are not strictly correct sociological uses of the term.

It has been traditional to classify communities as rural or urban, depending upon whether their populations were small and agricultural, or larger and industrial or commercial. The classification was never entirely satisfactory, for it made no provision for the fishing village, the mining camp, the trading post, or many other special types of communities. Modern transportation has so eroded the boundaries between city and country that we actually have a gradual shading of one community into the other and not two distinct types of community. One analysis locates four types of community along the rural-urban continuum: the rural community, the "fringe" community, the town, and the metropolis [Arensberg and Kimball, 1965]. While these are ideal types and thus in a sense artificial, they are useful tools for analysis.

Community and mass society The concepts of community and mass society are, in a sense, contradictory. The concept of community emphasizes the unity of a settlement of people, their identification with one another, their ability to act together, and their common sharing of traditions, interests, and values. The concept of mass society poses an aggregation of separate, detached, anonymous individuals with a social organization based on contract instead of

kinship, where ties between persons are utilitarian instead of personal or sentimental, where there are no generally revered traditions and no established leadership elite (see p. 395). Thus defined, there could be no true community in a true mass society. But both concepts describe ideal types, and an ideal type is always an exaggeration of reality. The concept of mass society highlights certain features and trends which are, to a considerable degree, characteristic of modern societies. The concept of community describes some features of social organization which are true, to a considerable degree, of most local settlements of people. While perfect examples are difficult to find, the concepts are useful as starting points for study.

THE RURAL COMMUNITY

The physical and social conditions of urban and rural life are different. Consequently there are differences in the personality and behavior of urban and rural people. These differences have provided endless source material for the novelist and the playwright, and continue to interest the sociologist.

The folk society

Some sociologists have seen the concept of the folk society as a close parallel to rural life. This concept is somewhat reminiscent of the gemeinschaft described in Chapter 8. Redfield describes the folk society:

Such a society is small, isolated, nonliterate and homogeneous with a strong sense of group solidarity. The ways of living are conventionalized into that coherent system which we call a "culture." Behavior is traditional, spontaneous, uncritical and personal; there is no legislation or habit of experiment and reflection for intellectual ends. Kinship, its relationships and institutions, are the type categories of experience and the familial group is the unit of action. The sacred prevails over the secular; the economy is one of status rather than of the market. (*Robert Redfield, "The Folk Society,"* American Journal of Sociology, *52:293–308, January, 1947. Copyright, 1947 by The University of Chicago. For criticism and discussion of the folk-society concept, see Oscar Lewis,* Life in a Mexican Village, *The University of Illinois Press, Urbana, 1951; Horace Miner, "The Folk-Urban Continuum,"* American Sociological Review, *17:529–537, October, 1952.*)

The folk society is most perfectly illustrated by the primitive agricultural society—tradition-bound, informal, homogeneous, and unchanging. Its opposite is the mass society—large, impersonal, changing, and dominated by secondary contacts and mass communication processes—reminiscent of the gesellschaft. Much of the discussion of rural-urban differences is in terms of folk society—mass society contrasts.

Today, however, rural life is losing its folk-society flavor. What are the traditional features of rural life and how are they changing?

Traditional characteristics of rural life

Rural communities are not all alike. Edwards [1959] distinguishes at least five types of rural communities: the town-country community with farms scattered about a village center; the open-country community without any village center; the village community, whose subtypes include the fishing village, the mining village, and the mill village; the line village, with farm homes strung along the road at the ends of long, narrow farms; and the plantation. Yet certain characteristics are common to nearly all kinds of rural communities.

Isolation Perhaps the most conspicuous feature of American rural life in times past was its isolation. Throughout much of the world, rural people are clustered into small villages, within walking distance of the surrounding farmland. In the United States, the isolated homestead became the usual pattern of rural settlement, a pattern that was productively more efficient but socially isolating. Not only was the local group isolated from other groups but each family was isolated from other families. With a thinly scattered population, personal contacts were few. Each contact involved the perception of an individual as a complete person, not simply as a functionary. There were few impersonal contacts in folk or rural societies—no anonymous bus drivers, ticket sellers, grocery clerks, or policemen. Nearly every contact was with an acquaintance who was treated, not only in terms of his economic function, but also in terms of his total personality and all the many facets of his status in the community.

The hospitality pattern of the American frontier, wherein the traveler was welcome to spend the night at almost any farmhouse, was a practical response both to frontier needs—where else would the traveler stay?—and to frontier loneliness. The traveler brought news, contact with the outside world, and a break in monotony. Even today the hospitality pattern survives under conditions of extreme isolation. On the Alaska Highway the mores of the region require one to offer assistance to any stranded mororist; he may actually die if assistance is not given. The hospitality pattern is a perfect illustration of how customs and mores arise in response to social needs and change as these needs change.

Homogeneity Taken as a whole, American settlers were a quite heterogeneous lot. But within a given locality, the settlers were likely to be quite homogeneous in ethnic and cultural background. They showed a strong tendency to follow earlier migrants from their home communities, so that the settlers from a particular country and district tended to be clustered into rather homogeneous settlements. This homogeneity, together with the comparative isolation of settlements from one another, helped to encourage the conservatism, traditionalism, and ethnocentrism of American rural communities.

Agricultural employment Nearly all were farmers or hired hands, while even the minister, doctor, teacher, storekeeper, and blacksmith were deeply involved in an agricultural way of life. All faced common problems, performed common tasks, and shared a common helplessness before the awesome natural forces which man could not control.

Subsistence economy The traditional American homestead tried to produce nearly everything it consumed. The bulging smokehouse, the well-stocked fruit cellar, and the shelves sagging with home-canned goods were a source of pride to the farm family. In a rapidly expanding economy with a chronic shortage of money and credit, a subsistence-and-barter economy was a socially useful adaptation. Thrift was an honored value, and conspicuous consumption was seen as an urban vice. A farmer's status was measured by his lands, his herds, his barns, his crops, and the inheritance he could pass on to his children—and not by the name of his tailor or interior decorator.

Living within a subsistence rather than a market economy, rural people were inclined to be suspicious of intellectuality and "book learning." The farmer was most likely to see a piece of paper when some "city slicker" was trying to do him out of something. Distrust of city people and disapproval of urban life was a predictable rural attitude.

These are some of the influences which shaped American rural personality. Hospitable and cooperative, conservative and religious, hard-working and thrifty, ethnocentric and intolerant—these characteristics were products of the physical and social conditions of rural life in America. Today these conditions have vastly changed. And so has the social behavior of rural people.

The rural revolution

Reduced isolation Two generations ago the isolation of rural life could be measured by the contrast between the styles shown in the Sears, Roebuck catalog and those on the pages of a metropolitan newspaper. Today the styles are similar. The automobile and good roads have wrought a transformation of rural and village life which is difficult for the present generation of students to appreciate. Thousands of small villages have ceased to be true communities, as good roads have carried their trade, their storekeepers, their professional men, and their recreation to a nearby city. If close enough to the city, they have become suburbs; if too distant, they have become the half-empty shells of decaying houses and aging people, as are so many of the villages of America today. Transportation, plus the press, movies, radio, and television, have ended the social isolation of rural America. The true provincial today may be the urban slum dweller, who may spend years without venturing beyond his own set of canyons, or possibly the suburbanite living within the walls of his one-class, one-age-group, lily-white neighborhood.

Commercialization and rationalization of agriculture Without a revolution in agricultural productivity, there could have been little urban growth. In 1790 it required the surplus of nine farm families to support one urban family; today twenty nonfarm families are supported by each farm family. Farming used to be a way of life which called for no special knowledge beyond that which one absorbed unavoidably as he grew up. Today farming is a highly complex operation demanding substantial capital, specialized knowledge, rapid changes in productive technology, and continuous market analysis. The "average" American farm represents an investment of at least $70,000 in land and buildings, and this "average" includes many which are too small or ill-equipped to be efficient. This investment is rising rapidly. Most of the new harvesting machines for harvesting cherries, oranges, celery, and other crops cost from $20,000 to $40,000 each. Today's successful farm has become a roofless factory, using a variety of managerial skills comparable to those needed for many another business, and more often described as "agribusiness."

As farming has grown more demanding, the number of farm families has fallen precipitously—from 6.7 million and 22 percent of all American families in 1935 to 2.5 million and 4.8 percent of all families in 1970. Meanwhile the average size of farms has steadily increased from 143 acres in 1925 to 387 acres in 1970, and is expected to reach 700 acres by 1980.

Farms are growing larger because of changes in farm technology. Mechanization allows one farm family to handle more acreage, and more acreage permits a more efficient use of farm machinery. Consequently, larger farms are more efficient. Production costs per unit of production on small farms are more than twice as high as on larger farms [Tweeten and Schreiner, 1970, p. 43]. All these trends are still continuing at a rapid rate and would proceed even faster if they were not retarded by political programs intended to aid marginal farmers. Fewer than half of our farms produce 85 percent of our farm produce, and they could easily produce the remaining 15 percent if farm production were not deliberately restricted.

Because of these changes in agricultural technology, the farm population is rapidly shrinking. In 1790 the rural (farm and nonfarm) residents comprised 94.8 percent of the population. By 1920, when "farm" and "rural nonfarm" people were first separated in the census, farm people constituted 30.1 percent of the population; in 1970, only 5.1 percent, and they are still diminishing in number. We were once a nation of farmers. Today farmers are becoming one of the smallest of our major occupational groups. At present more than 1 million of our farm families are unnecessary for agricultural production and could leave the farm tomorrow without ever being missed. These are our "farm poor"—farmers with too little land, equipment, and capital, or too little energy or managerial skill to farm very profitably. One-third of our farms are part-time or postretirement operations. But of our full-time farm operations, one-fourth produce less than $5,000 of farm produce per year (and this is gross produce, not net income after expenses). These farms contribute little to our national farm product and do not provide a decent living to their operators. Yet an estimated three-fifths of the farm poor are too old, too handicapped, or too uneducated to transfer to other occupations, even if offered job training [Burchinal and Siff, 1964]. They steadily disappear from farming through retirement and rarely through transfer to other employment. As they retire, their lands are added to other farms. Thus the number of farmers shrinks, while the average size of farms increases. As the farm became part of the market economy, the attitudes appropriate to a subsistence economy have languished. Thrift, as an absolute value, seen as *good* in and of itself, is also a useful practice in a subsistence economy. In a market economy it becomes an anachronism. Farm people today appear to have as avid an appetite for new cars and color television sets as urbanites. After all, values grow out of the experience of the group. In a subsistence economy of limited productivity, where there is rarely enough of anything, especially money, the elevation of thrift to an absolute value is practical and sensible. With the development of a highly productive market economy, thrift becomes pointless as an end in itself. Instead, reasonable thrift becomes a means to an end, such as saving money on inessentials in order to afford the major purchase of a home or a new car. This and many other value changes have accompanied the technological revolution in American agriculture.

These processes are in operation throughout the Western world. In the six European Common Market countries, employment in agriculture has fallen by over one-third since 1955 [*New York Times*, Mar. 28, 1971, p. 6]. Germany, Holland, and Belgium have less than 10 percent of their labor force in agriculture, France about 15 percent, and Italy about 22 percent. Their rural areas face the same problems of farm unemployment and lack of training for other employment, while their cities have the same problems of congestion, housing, pollution, and taxation.

Urbanization of rural life It is no longer possible to identify a rural rustic by his outmoded dress or bucolic manner. Although there are still some differences between the modal personalities, life styles, and value systems of rural and urban dwellers, all the historic rural-urban differences are shrinking. To a high degree, rural life is becoming urbanized, as historically urban patterns have spread into rural areas. Taylor and Jones [1964] speak of the "urbanized social organization" of contemporary America, and every rural sociology textbook reflects this urbanization of rural life [Copp, 1964; Rogers and Burdge, 1972]. This process is widespread but uneven. Rural areas closer

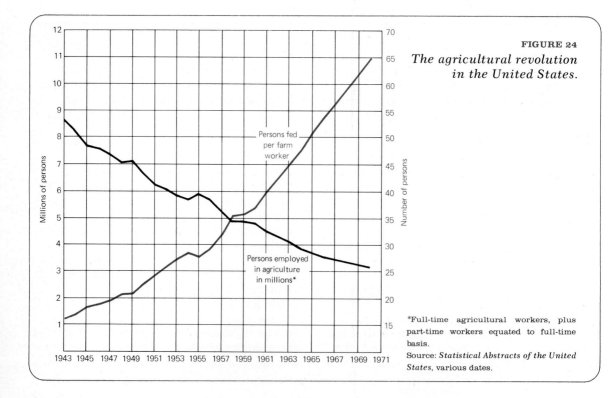

FIGURE 24

The agricultural revolution in the United States.

*Full-time agricultural workers, plus part-time workers equated to full-time basis.

Source: *Statistical Abstracts of the United States*, various dates.

to large cities and those where agriculture is most highly rationalized and commercialized show the highest degree of urbanization; more isolated areas and areas where farming practices are more traditional show fewer urban influences. But everywhere, the steady urbanization of rural society is evident.

There are many examples of urbanization. The electric pump and the septic tank have brought urban plumbing to the rural home. The rural birthrate has been dropping closer to the urban birthrate—77 percent higher in 1940, 40 percent higher in 1950, 34 percent higher in 1960, and 21 percent higher in 1969. Our population today is predominantly urban. In 1970, only 5.1 percent of our people lived on farms, with 69 percent in metropolitan areas and 25 percent living in smaller cities, towns, villages, and "rural nonfarm" homes. Most of these rural nonfarm people (unless retired) are urban commuters, who become a powerful urbanizing influence upon rural life. In many urban fringe areas, people are divided between farm and nonfarm employment, and any classification of such areas as either rural or urban is arbitrary. Recently the rather clumsy term "rurban" has been coined for these mixed areas which are neither urban nor rural. The term has not become very popular; but the phenomenon of the mixed urban-rural area is important, for this is a rapidly growing form of community in America.

THE URBAN COMMUNITY

The development of cities

In order for the primitive Stone Age village to overshoot its few dozen households and expand to a size of several hundred thousand, it had to have a food surplus, a water supply, and a transportation system. Since

a river valley provided all three, the first large cities arose six or seven thousand years ago in the valleys of the Nile, the Tigris, and the Euphrates. Surplus food to support an urban population was abundant in the fertile valley, and the slow-flowing rivers provided simple transportation. Although most ancient cities remained tiny by modern standards, a few reached a size of several hundred thousand, complete with problems of water supply, sewage disposal, and traffic congestion.

The growth of cities unleashed revolutionary changes. The primitive village was a folk society, organized on a kinship basis and guided by customary procedures. A number of conditions are necessary for a large city: (1) a division of labor into many specialized occupations; (2) social organization based upon occupation and social class rather than kinship; (3) formal government institutions based on territory rather than family; (4) a system of trade and commerce; (5) means of communication and record keeping; and (6) rational technology. These developments proceed steadily as small towns grow into large cities. Obviously the large city could not arise until the culture had made a number of necessary inventions; at the same time, the development of the city proved a great stimulus to the making and improving of such inventions as carts and barges, ditches and aqueducts, writing, number systems, governmental bureaucracies, and many others.

Towns and cities are of many kinds—temple towns, garrison towns, mining towns, political capitals, resort centers, industrial cities, trading centers, and others. The "company town" is a unique kind of community which has now nearly disappeared [Allen, 1966]. Most large cities are diversified, carrying on a number of kinds of activity. An early sociologist, Cooley [1894], noted that cities tend to grow wherever there is a "break" in transportation so that goods must be unloaded and reloaded for transshipment. Port cities like London, Montreal, and New Orleans are located up a navigable river at the point where large ocean vessels can go no further. Denver lies at the foot of a mountain range, Pittsburgh at the confluence of two rivers. The break-in-transportation theory does not necessarily apply to resort centers like Las Vegas, Aspen, or Monte Carlo, to political capitals like Washington or Brazilia, or to other specialized cities for which transportation was relatively unimportant, but the break-in-transportation theory still serves to explain the location of most cities.

In the Western world, urbanization has accompanied industrialization. Commercial and industrial development provided an urban "pull"; changing agricultural technology and high rural birthrates combined to provide a rural surplus of people. In many undeveloped countries today, however, urbanization is rushing along without a proportionate industrial development. Even with little prospect of finding jobs or housing, peasants over much of the world are deserting the village and flocking into the city. In Indonesia, for example, the population of the cities has doubled every ten to fifteen years without proportionate increase in either urban industrial output or agricultural productivity. The results seem to be an intensification of every type of problem:

Since the war the supplies of food to the cities of Java have diminished at the same time as the number of city people to be fed has increased. . . . The result is that much of the food consumed in the cities is now brought from abroad. . . . A city whose physical structure was designed for half a million is now the home of about six times that number. . . . There is a free movement of population and so the erection of housing facilities in the cities, improvement of roads, introduction of subsidized bus service—in short any alleviation of the discomforts of city life—will operate, along with subsidized rice, to draw people from the crowded countryside. . . . Efforts of town planning and house construction are frustrated; people are drawn to the cities faster than decent places for

them to live can be found. (*Nathan Keyfitz, "The Ecology of Indonesian Cities,"* American Journal of Sociology, *66:348–354, January, 1961. Copyright, 1961, by The University of Chicago.*)

The result of such urban growth is a type of slum practically unknown in the United States, the *suburban squatter slum.* Nearly every major city in Asia, Africa, and South America has on its outskirts a large area occupied by people living on land they do not own or rent, in flimsy shanties which they have built of scrap materials—shipping crates, scrap lumber, old signboards, flattened tin cans, old bricks, or anything else that can be scrounged. Generally there are no urban services—power, water, or sewers—and people live in a squalor which makes American slums look like castles by comparison. From one-fourth to one-half of the "urban" residents of much of the world—50 percent in Ankara, Turkey; 40 percent in Caracas, Venezuela—live in such wretchedness [Howton, 1967; Juppenlatz, 1970, p. 15].

Here the brutal consequences of the population explosion are evident. A falling death rate and a birthrate that remains high give a rate of population growth which exceeds the rate of expansion of the economies of the underdeveloped countries. Add to this, in most cases, a political system that is at best inefficient, and very often is both corrupt and inefficient, and human misery is the inevitable result.

The ecological pattern of cities

Most cities look as though they just happened—grew without plan or design—and they did. While a few major cities such as Washington, D.C., once had a plan, they have long since outgrown it. But while most city growth is not planned, neither is it entirely haphazard. Cities have structure, and there is some reason for the arrangement of their

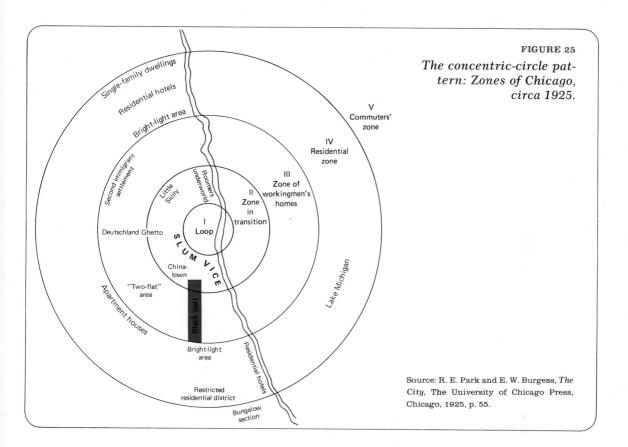

FIGURE 25
The concentric-circle pattern: Zones of Chicago, circa 1925.

Source: R. E. Park and E. W. Burgess, *The City*, The University of Chicago Press, Chicago, 1925, p. 55.

parts. Several sociologists have sought to discover the underlying pattern according to which a modern city develops.

Patterns of urban design Burgess's *concentric zone pattern*, shown in Figure 25, is one such attempt. Based upon his studies of Chicago in the early 1920s, it shows a central business district at the center, surrounded by a slum consisting of old buildings which are gradually being replaced by the expansion of the business district. This in turn is surrounded by zones of successively better-class residences.

Do real cities resemble the Burgess pattern? Each American city (with the possible exception of Los Angeles) has a central business district, partly or entirely surrounded by a slum. This surrounding zone contains the oldest buildings in the city, undesirable because of decay, dirt, and congestion. Housing quality tends to improve as one moves outward from this slum, and much of the choice residential area is located in the suburbs. However, these zones are not unbroken bands surrounding the city, nor are they circular in shape. Instead, the various grades of residence are rather irregularly distributed and often concentrated on one side of the city.

This observation led Hoyt [1933] to frame his *sector theory of city growth,* holding that a particular kind of land use tends to locate and remain in a particular sector of the city.

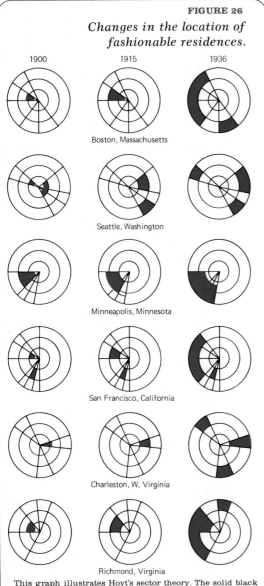

FIGURE 26

Changes in the location of fashionable residences.

1900　　　1915　　　1936

Boston, Massachusetts

Seattle, Washington

Minneapolis, Minnesota

San Francisco, California

Charleston, W. Virginia

Richmond, Virginia

This graph illustrates Hoyt's sector theory. The solid black spaces show how the fashionable residential areas shifted outward from the city center between 1900 and 1936.

Source: Homer Hoyt, *The Structure and Growth of Residential Neighborhoods in American Cities*, Federal Housing Administration, Washington, D.C., 1939, p. 115.

Figure 26 shows how this theory is borne out in several American cities over several decades. Thus industry tends to locate in one sector, upper-class housing in an opposite sector, and working-class housing in intermediate sectors; then as time passes, each of these sectors simply expands outward until some change in topography breaks up the pattern.

The *multinuclear theory* [Harris and Ullman, 1945] holds that a number of centers —business, shopping, manufacturing—and residential areas become located early in a city's history. Topography, cost, and historical accident all enter into these early choices. These concentrations tend to survive and fix the pattern of later city growth. Larger cities, which usually represent the growing together of once separate villages or communities, provide multiple nuclei. These three patterns are shown in comparison in Figure 27.

Still another pattern can be recognized— one so simple that it has not been dignified by being called a theory. It relates land use to topography. Railroads tend to follow the river valley; heavy industry locates along the railroad; upper-class residence seeks the highlands; and the intermediate levels of housing are scattered in between.

The existence of alternative theories shows that none of them is entirely satisfactory. None of them is perfectly illustrated by any American city, and many cities outside the United States will show very little resemblance to any of these patterns; for example, Calcutta stretches for some 35 miles along the Ganges River [Rose, 1967, chap. 11]. Each pattern is an idea which real cities more or less perfectly resemble. Since most American cities do show some resemblance to one of these patterns, the theories are helpful in revealing their prevailing structure.

City structure today is being revolutionized by transportation. In most cities the central business district has ceased to expand, and the commercial growth leapfrogs to the suburban shopping centers. A growing ring of decay is left surrounding the business district, as it no longer razes its fringe as it expands. An aging and decaying central city is soon trapped by declining tax sources and mounting tax expenditures. This is the basic reason why nearly every city in the country is caught in a financial crisis and has made some efforts at urban renewal.

Slums A slum is a deteriorated area of the city inhabited by poor people. As mentioned earlier, most Asian, African, and South American cities have large "shanty" slums on their outskirts. Slums in the United States are generally in the inner-city areas, the "area in transition" in Burgess' concentric zone pattern. The oldest housing in the city is generally found in this area separating the central business district from the newer residential districts. Old buildings, however, do not cause slums. Old buildings, when structurally sound, are sometimes remodeled into highly fashionable residential districts. *It is the low income of the residents which creates a slum* [Muth, 1969]. There are several steps in the conversion of old housing into slum housing: (1) older housing units are subdivided, often through illegal makeshift conversions, so that some units lack even the facilities for cleanliness (when three families share a bathroom, nobody cleans it); (2) with subdivision, there is an enormous increase in overcrowding and congestion, with buildings deteriorating through heavy use and lawns worn bare or turned into parking space; (3) building owners neglect maintenance, since they can rent slum housing regardless of condition; (4) people who have always been poor (perhaps for generations) and have always lived in old houses generally take poor care of property. Thus a vicious circle of cause and effect is maintained: slum landlords justify their neglect of property mainte-

FIGURE 27

Three patterns of city structure.

Concentric zone theory

Sector theory

KEY   DISTRICT
1 Central business district
2 Wholesale light manufacturing
3 Low-class residential
4 Medium-class residential
5 High-class residential
6 Heavy manufacturing
7 Outlying business district
8 Residential suburb
9 Industrial suburb
10 Commuters' zone

Multiple nuclei

Generalizations of internal structure of cities. The concentric-zone pattern is a generalization which Burgess proposed as an ideal type to apply more or less perfectly to all cities. The arrangement of the sectors in the sector theory varies from city to city. The diagram for multiple nuclei represents one possible pattern among innumerable variations.

Source: C. D. Harris and E. L. Ullman, "The Nature of Cities," *The Annals*, 242:13, November, 1945.

nance because slum tenants do not "take care" of property, while slum tenants typically have not developed habits of property care because they have never had any property worth taking care of.

Efforts to prevent slum deterioration by enforcement of housing codes do not work. Enforcement is exceedingly difficult. The owners are often concealed behind complexes of management companies and property corporations, and are difficult to locate and serve papers upon. Thus arises the cliché that the slum is a place "where the rats can't be fazed and the owners can't be found." Finally, even if enforcement were effective, there is no way to keep owners from abandoning a building which is no longer profitable. Taxes and mortgage payments may be unpaid, utilities are soon shut off, and the building is vacated and quickly vandalized. Entire blocks and even entire districts are today being abandoned to the rats, the vandals, and the squatters [*Business Week*, Apr. 4, 1970, pp. 57ff.; Rogin, 1971].

Programs of "slum clearance" which replace slum housing with office buildings and middle-income housing do not reduce slums; they just relocate them! To eliminate slums would require either mass housing subsidies or the elimination of poverty. Anything less is merely palliative.

In contrast to this analysis, an American political scientist has attracted considerable attention with his suggestion that slums exist because most slum people are shiftless and improvident, and that the "urban crisis" has developed because slum people have been encouraged to insist that they be lifted from the squalor which their own shiftlessness and improvidence create [Banfield, 1970]. He believes that slum dwellers' work habits, life style, and habits of property maintenance must be changed before "slum clearance" can succeed. He believes that public housing, poverty programs, and most other grants-in-aid are dysfunctional,

for they encourage the poor to look for handouts instead of seeking to work their way into respectability. He feels that the only solution is for urban blacks to achieve upward mobility as other ethnic minorities have done. Without taking space to assess his arguments, it may be said that most social scientists consider them to be little more than an updated version of the ancient argument that the poor deserve their wretchedness.

The slum is sometimes pictured as an area totally lacking in social organization. This is incorrect, for there is a pattern of social organization in the slum [Whyte, 1955; Suttles, 1968]. The slum is highly provincial, with people rarely venturing beyond the "turf" of their ethnic group. The overall pattern is one which Suttles calls "ordered segmentation" [pp. 225–227]. Each ethnic group has its boundaries, within which most social relationships are confined and socially controlled. Programs which disrupt these established boundaries therefore weaken the social controls of the area.

There are rural areas which are true slums in all but location. As described in Fetterman's *Stinking Creek* [1970], rural slum housing is equally dilapidated, has even fewer utility services, and room crowding may be equally great. Poverty and hopelessness are equally widespread, social services are even less adequate than in the urban slum, and "welfare" is the principal source of income. The rural slum is equally grim but receives even less attention than the urban slum.

Metropolitan areas and suburbs Modern transportation is responsible for the suburb and the metropolitan area. A "standard metropolitan statistical area" is defined by the census as a county or group of counties containing at least one city (or a pair of adjoining cities) with over 50,000 people. Adjacent counties are included if they are metropolitan in character, as measured by certain criteria. In 1970, some 69 percent of the nation's population lived in our 212 metropolitan areas.

The suburb is the fastest growing part of America. Between 1950 and 1960 the suburbs of our metropolitan areas grew by 49 percent, while our rural population was shrinking 0.8 percent and the central cities were growing by only 10.6 percent. Between 1960 and 1970, the central cities grew by only 1.5 percent while the suburbs grew by 33.5 percent. While this is a smaller percentage gain for the suburbs than in the preceding decade (since this percentage gain was computed on a larger base), the growth of the suburbs actually accelerated during the 1960s. The suburbs accounted for nearly two-thirds of the nation's population growth during the 1950s, but for more than three-fourths of the nation's population growth during the 1960s.

This explosion of the suburbs is a part of what has recently come to be known as *urban sprawl.* Vast strip cities are developing from Boston to Baltimore, another from Buffalo to Detroit, across Michigan and on through Chicago around to Milwaukee, and many others. These strip cities fit no traditional pattern of city structure. In time, new theoretical constructs will be developed to describe them. Urban sprawl and strip cities bring a host of problems with them [Whyte, 1958]. The existing structures of township, city, and county government are quite inadequate to organize this developing urban monstrosity. With over 1,400 separate political units in the New York metropolitan area, each with its vested interests to defend, any coherent overall planning becomes almost an impossibility. Some observers believe that the problems of these metropolitan areas are so difficult that they will not be solved, and that the largest metropolitan areas will go into a relative decline [Vernon, 1960]. Some other observers believe that bold planning *can* solve the problems of urban sprawl and urban blight [Jacobs, 1961;

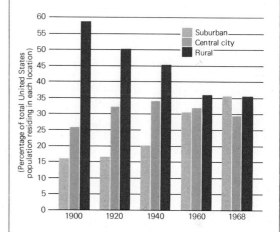

FIGURE 28

Shift of the United States population to the suburbs, 1900-1968.

Source: U.S. Department of Commerce, Bureau of the Census, *U.S. Census of Population: 1960, Selected Area Reports, Standard Metropolitan Statistical Areas,* Final Report DC(3)-ID: *Current Population Reports, Trends in Social and Economic Conditions in Metropolitan Areas,* series P-23, no. 27, February, 1969; and *Current Population Reports, Provisional Estimates of the Population of 100 Large Metropolitan Areas: July 1967,* series P-25, no. 441, December, 1968.

Gruen, 1964; Abrams, 1965; Erber, 1970].
Urban sprawl is not exclusively an American
problem; it is taking place all over the world,
even in the Soviet Union, despite official
efforts to stem the growth of the larger cities
[Anderson, 1966]. Urban growth proceeds
for much the same reasons and has much
the same consequences everywhere in the
world.

*Any coherent overall planning
becomes an impossibility.*

Changing racial structure Since 1940,
the black population of our central cities has
been growing rapidly while the white population has been fleeing to the suburbs. Between 1940 and 1950, while the white population of all central cities was growing by
3.7 percent, the black population grew by 68
percent; between 1950 and 1960, the figures
were 4.9 percent for whites and 49.8 percent
for blacks. Between 1960 and 1970, the
white population of the central cities declined by 5.4 percent while their black
population grew by 32.8 percent. Such figures suggest that within a few more years,
we might have central cities filled with the
black and the poor, surrounded by affluent,
lily-white suburbs. This might be expected
to intensify the historic clashes of interest
between the central city and the suburb.

In the late 1960s, however, these migration patterns began to change. The tiny
trickle of black migration to the suburbs
multiplied more than tenfold, as seen in
Table 36. While the black population of the
central cities was increasing by 32.8 percent
between 1960 and 1970, the black population of the suburbs was growing by 45.6 percent. The black proportion of the central
cities' population is still rising (from 17 percent in 1960 to 21 percent in 1970), but the
rate of growth is slackening.[1] The nightmare of a black central city locked in conflict with an all-white suburb no longer
appears to be a certainty. This does not mean
that residential segregation is disappearing,
for most of the new black suburbanites have
moved to predominantly black suburbs
[Farley, 1970]. But the concentration of
blacks in the central cities is slowing down,
and very few central cities are likely to have
black majorities. Instead, it appears that the
black population is beginning to break out
of its confinement into the dispersal which
other immigrant groups followed.

Urban ecological processes

Change is continuous in the American city.
The means through which the distribution
of people and institutions change are known
as *ecological processes.* To understand them
we must begin with the *natural area,* a collection of people and activities which are
drawn together in mutual interdependence
within a limited area. The single-men's district of flophouses and cheap hotels, cheap
restaurants, pawn shops, burlesque shows,
taverns, and missions, all catering to the
needs of low-income homeless men, is an
example of a natural area. Other natural
areas include the department-store section,
the entertainment area, the communities of

[1]Computed from data in *Current Population Reports,* P-23, no. 37,
June 24, 1971, p. 1.

recent immigrants, the rooming-house district, the college students' residential area, the warehouse district, and many others. Natural areas are unplanned. They arise from the free choices of individuals. Persons having similar needs and preferences are drawn together into an area where these are most easily fulfilled, and their association creates a natural area.

The *neighborhood,* unlike the natural area, may be either planned or unplanned. A neighborhood is an area where people neighbor, and not all areas are neighborhoods. There is very little neighboring in some areas, such as the rooming-house district, and more neighboring in the ethnic communities and family-residence areas. Some urban neighborhoods are consciously planned, with housing, communication, shopping, and recreation facilities deliberately arranged to encourage neighboring. More often the neighborhood is an unplanned product of people's need for social relations. Neighboring is greatest in family-residence areas where people face common problems of child rearing and crabgrass fighting. Neighborhoods and natural areas are constantly being formed, dissolved, and relocated through the urban ecological processes of *concentration, centralization, decentralization, segregation,* and *invasion* [Lee, 1955].

Concentration is the tendency for people and institutions to gather where conditions are favorable. It produces the growth of cities. *Centralization* is the clustering together of the economic and service functions within the city. People come together to work, to play, to shop, then return to other areas to live. The shopping district, the factory district, and the entertainment district are empty of people for a part of each day or night. The central business district is a prime example of centralization. *Decentralization* describes the tendency of people and organizations to desert the center of the city for outlying areas where congestion is less

and land values are lower. The automobile and motor truck and electric power have greatly encouraged residential, commercial, and industrial decentralization—a tendency which greatly complicates the task of anyone who seeks to diagram the pattern of the city.

Segregation refers to the concentration of certain types of people or organizations within a particular area. The "Gold Coast," the ghetto, and the black belt are examples, along with the hotel and banking districts, the theater district, and "used-car row." Segregation may be either voluntary or involuntary. Most immigrant groups voluntarily segregated themselves, for life was more comfortable this way. The ghetto in the large American cities was partly voluntary and partly involuntary [Wirth, 1928]. The black belt is an example of involuntary segregation, as low income, realtor practices, the threat of violence, and "neighborhood improvement associations" combined to limit black residence to restricted black areas [Abrams, 1955; Grier and Grier, 1960].

Invasion takes place when a new kind of people, organization, or activity enters an area. Residential areas may be invaded by business; a business area may be invaded by a new kind of business; residents of a different class level or ethnic group may move into a residential area. Generally the invasion is of a higher-status area by a lower-status group or activity. This direction of invasion is a normal outcome of the process of city growth and of aging. A once-exclusive residential area of homes which are no longer fashionable is invaded by people a class level below the present occupants. A generation later the same area may be invaded by persons still another class level lower, or by blacks or other ethnics, or by secondhand stores and other business houses. Occasionally the direction is reversed. Many large cities today contain some areas where dilapidated housing is being renovated or rebuilt into an upper-

TABLE 36

*Change in black and white populations of urban areas:
1960–1966 and 1966–1968*

Mean annual percentage change	1960-1966	1966-1968
CENTRAL CITIES		
White	−0.3	−1.0
Black	3.4	1.0
SUBURBS		
White	3.0	2.0
Black	0.7	8.0

Sources: U.S. Department of Commerce, Bureau of the Census, U.S. Census of Population: 1960, Selected Area Reports, Standard Metropolitan Statistical Areas, Final Report DC (3)-ID; Current Population Reports, Trends in Social and Economic Conditions in Metropolitan Areas, ser. P-23, no. 27, February, 1969; and Current Population Reports, Provisional Estimates of the Population of 100 Large Metropolitan Areas, July 1967, ser. P-25, no. 411, December, 1968.

class residential area. Many upper-income people have fled to the suburbs because attractive new housing is located there. Many would like to remain close to the city's center if satisfactory housing is available. Some areas have therefore traveled the complete cycle of upper-class residence to slum to upper-class residence. In all likelihood, the cycle will now be repeated.

Stages in the invasion cycle Several sociologists have sought to define the several stages of an invasion cycle [McKenzie, 1925, p. 25; Gibbard, 1938, pp. 206–207; Lee, 1955, pp. 257–260]. The *initial* stage brings a small number of people into the area and may not even be noticed for a time. When the old occupants become aware of an invasion, a *reaction* stage begins, whose intensity depends upon the cultural and racial characteristics of the invaders, the attitudes of the old residents, and the neighborhood solidarity. Opposition is most likely when the invaders are black. A common device is the "civic," "protective," or "neighborhood-improvement" association. This organization seeks to prevent residents from selling or renting to the invaders, and to discourage the invaders from seeking to

buy or rent in the area. Such associations are most effective when most of the homes are owned by their occupants. If the reaction fails to stop the invaders, then the *general influx* stage soon follows. When there are enough of the newcomers to make the old residents unwilling to remain, the "tip point" has been reached, and the old residents rapidly abandon the area to the newcomers. The *climax* is the complete replacement of the old residents with newcomers or with commercial or institutional land use. The final stage is *succession*, in which the area may remain in a disorganized and chaotic state, or may become well-organized around its new residents or land use.

This invasion cycle is continuously in operation in every American city. The processes of growth and aging make it inevitable. It is a costly process—costly in terms of human frustration and economic waste— but no one has suggested a practical alternative. Zoning is not an alternative—it is simply a technique for making invasion and succession more deliberate and orderly, and for protecting vested interests in the process [Babcock, 1966].

Incidentally, the black invasion is a perfect illustration of how the culture creates social conflicts. The black population of our major cities has been exploding, largely through the urban migration of blacks. As blacks are excluded from most new subdivisions, they can find room to live only by invading older white residential areas. If there were no discrimination, blacks would scatter themselves over the community according to income and preference, as other ethnic groups have eventually done. But because there *is* discrimination, blacks are continuously desperate for a place to live. Many whites would not object to a sprinkling of blacks in their neighborhood but will not live in a predominantly black district. Fearing a mass black invasion, they try to keep out all blacks. Their effort restricts black housing and makes a mass invasion more likely to follow an initial influx. Thus whites' attempts to keep blacks out ensure that when they do come to many neighborhoods, they will come in an overwhelming tide. This is another example of the self-fulfilling prophesy. The prediction that the first black family will bring a black flood causes white people to act in ways which guarantee exactly this result [Wolf, 1957]. Areas which have become integrated tend to become resegregated through the departure of the white population. Of all possible ways of providing housing for a growing urban black population, we seem to have hit upon the most inefficient and painful.

It is through these ecological processes that the city continues to change. City planners today are trying to control and direct the processes in order to make them less wasteful and painful.

Urban life and personality

The city is a place of contrasts. Cities are centers of learning, of the arts, of science and medicine, of excitement, glamor, and "progress," while rural areas have been charged with provincialism, superstition,

ignorance, and bigotry. Cities are also centers of vice and crime, of frivolous extravagance, of unbridled self-indulgence, and of insincere pretension. In short, the city reveals in vivid contrast most of the dominant characteristics of the culture, and has been a source of endless inspiration to artists and writers, as in this example:

For Manila is a city like all cities—changeless and changing. Giving and taking back. Harsh and yet tender as a child's caress. And unlike other cities, it is the east and the west meeting at last. It is the Malay and the Latin. The American and the Chinese. . . . The city of the strident voice and the brick and cement jungles, and the city with the hidden lullabies and the warm hand. Cankered by ugliness and evil, spiked with violence and sudden death, it has its moments of breathless beauty and primal innocence. And if a man could see his way clear through to the very core of the city, he might yet apprehend the final meaning which could be the germ of his fulfillment. (*Vicente Rivera, Jr., "This is Manila,"* Sunday Times Magazine (*Manila*), Nov. 20, 1953, pp. 9–10.)

A vacation is merely a change of scene for tightly scheduled activities.

Even though poetic rather than sociological, this description still carries a sense of the heterogeneity and contrast of the city. What are the dominant characteristics of the city, and how do they shape urban life and personality?

Speed and tension The city is always in a hurry. Work and play are timed by the clock as we proceed from deadline to deadline. Lunches become business appointments, or possibly the busy executive eats lunch at his desk, barking commands between bites, while even the most humble worker must catch the bus and punch the time clock. Genuine relaxation is impossible for many urbanites, and a vacation is merely a change of scene for tightly scheduled activities.

Anonymity The sheer pressure of numbers makes for anonymity. Of course there are groups within which the urbanite is known as a person, but much of his routine life is spent in the anonymous crowd—the *Lonely Crowd* of David Riesman [1950]. The heterogeneity of city life, with its mixture of people of all races, creeds, classes, occupations, and ethnic origins heightens this sense of anonymity. Differing interests separate people from any intimate acquaintance with others whom they meet in passing. Lee remarks:

Anonymity is a loss of identity in a city teeming with millions. Many urbanites live in a social void, or vacuum in which institutional norms are not effective in controlling or regulating their social behavior. Although they are aware of the existence of many institutional organizations and many people around them, they do not feel a sense of belongingness to any one group or community. Socially, they are poor in the midst of plenty. (*Rose Hum Lee*, The City, *J. B. Lippincott Company, Philadelphia, 1955, p. 454.*)

In the "skid rows" are the extremes of urban anonymity—the forgotten men and women of obscure past and uncertain future. They exist outside the pale of organized conventional living, their lives centered in the rooming- or flophouse, the cheap tavern, and perhaps the rescue mission. Here the deviants may cluster and pursue their deviation with a minimum of interference. They are the defeated refuse of our social system, resigned, and often contented with a social role which demands little and offers little [Bogue, 1963; Wallace, 1965].

Social distance City people are physically crowded but socially distant. Social distance is a product of anonymity, impersonality, and heterogeneity. Ethnic differences are one form of heterogeneity, dividing people into groups which often dislike or disdain one another. But occupational differences may be even more important sources of social distance. Unlike the agricultural community, the city has no common occupational focus which serves as a common interest for urbanites. Workers may follow any one of thousands of different occupations and have little understanding of, or interest in, other lines of work. The varieties of work attract people with a great range of education, skills, training, and temperament. This diversity of interests, backgrounds, and economic levels means that a man learns to reveal only the side of his personality which the other person can be expected to understand. This constant masking of one's true feelings adds up to a great lack of understanding. The great city which multiplies contacts also produces loneliness. From this loneliness a man often flees into a frantic effort to accommodate himself to changing popular tastes in order to prove to his blasé neighbors that he really "belongs" and thus merits at least a segment of their attention. The city is a place of outward conformity and inner reservations, of "front" and conspicuous consumption, of "keeping up with the Joneses." When people cannot know us for what we are, they must judge us by what they see. Hence the great importance of the well-tailored appearance, the impressive car, the occupational title, and the "good" address.

City people may have as many primary-group associates as rural people, and may see them more often. But whereas *most* of the rural person's daily contacts are primary, *most* routine social contacts in the city are impersonal, segmented, and correct. Formal politeness takes the place of genuine friendliness. The telephone and the printed checklist make it possible to contact people impersonally when necessary while keeping them at a distance. Urbanites become nigh-dwellers, not neighbors. Apartment dwellers may live for years without any acquaintance with many of the other occupants. Geography is a basis for grouping among rural farm people, both because of scarcity of neighbors and because of the community of interests which develops from their common problems and life styles. Urban dwellers have no such scarcity of neighbors, and one's immediate neighbors rarely share much community of interest with one. Instead, those persons with whom one shares a community of interest are likely to be scattered throughout the area. Thus common interest replaces geographic proximity as a basis for grouping in the city. Toward that great mass of people with whom one rubs elbows daily, but with whom one shares neither kinship nor common interest, one is formal and correct. The ability of urbanites to look past or through people without seeing them is quite disconcerting to many rural visitors.

Regimentation The pressure of numbers requires that urban life be highly regimented. Traffic lights control the flow of traffic; elevators and escalators move on schedule. The city dweller learns to work by the clock, under close supervision, often following the letter of his instructions without any effort to understand what he is doing or why. Changes in his routine are decreed from above and must be coordinated by the electronic computer, which places each human robot in the right spot at the right time performing the right function. Even recreation for children is organized, and the harried housewife races to get Junior to his club at 4:15 so that he will be on time for the period of "free play." Such control is sometimes irksome, but the true city dweller has learned to accept the idea that most of life is according to plan and to justify his subservience to regulation on the ground of efficiency.

What results do these conditions of urban life have on personality? Very little actual research has been done on this question, although it has attracted a great deal of sociological speculation. Sociologists suspect that urban life produces greater emotional tension and insecurity than does rural life, and some empirical evidence supports this conclusion. The rates of mental illness are higher in the city than in rural areas. It is, however, not clear whether the city causes more mental disorder, attracts the maladjusted person to the city, or merely locates and diagnoses more accurately the extent of mental illness in the population. One well-controlled study, however, finds that farm and small-town children show a higher level of personal adjustment than urban children, with greater self-reliance, a greater sense of personal worth, and fewer feelings of nonbelonging [Mangus, 1948]. Although insecurity and rejection are entirely possible in a rural setting, the heterogeneous and anonymous nature of the city probably increases insecurity and the sense of nonbelonging.

Segmentation of personality is a necessary technique for coping with the multiple human contacts of an urban area. Most routine urban contacts are of secondary-group rather than primary-group nature. Most contacts are instrumental; that is, we use another person as a necessary functionary to fulfill our purposes. We do not ordinarily interact with entire persons, but with people in terms of their formal roles as mailmen, bus drivers, elevator operators, salespersons, and other functionaries. We thus interact with only a segment of the person, not with the whole person. Such casual, superficial, short-lived relations with segments of people constitute a large part of the urbanite's social contacts, in contrast to the rural dweller, who has relatively fewer contacts with anyone whom he does not know well or with whom he fails to interact as a complete person [Sorokin and Zimmerman, 1929, pp. 48 –58]. Even the superficial camaraderie with the taxicab driver is not genuine informal social interaction, but is a standardized part of the service [Davis, 1959].

The worldwide urban culture

Is there an urban culture which is shared by cities everywhere, or are these conditions of urban life and personality unique to the Western world? The descriptions of cities, city life, and urban problems show a good deal of similarity, wherever the cities are located [Motwani, 1951; Miner, 1952, 1967; Abu-Lughod, 1961; Rose, 1967]. An urban society operates in roughly similar fashion wherever urbanization has taken place. Regardless of the cultural setting, urbanization brings certain inescapable consequences—population density, anonymity, impersonality, regimentation, and segmentation of personality. Urban people reveal certain differences from country people everywhere. All over the world, the rural village communities are changing, old traditions are crumbling, and new technologies and new patterns of work and social life are emerging [Halpern, 1967]. Meanwhile, subcommunities within all larger cities retain a culture with some elements of the folk society. These are products of urban migration and presumably will endure as long as the city is fed by a constant stream of migrants from rural areas. The higher rural birthrate and the shrinking need for rural labor as farming grows more efficient, make it likely that migration will endure for some time.

The antiurban bias

Ever since their earliest appearance, cities have been viewed with suspicion by rural peoples. The Old Testament prophets were rural men, denouncing the sins and vices of the wicked cities. Jefferson despised cities and felt that only a nation of freeholding farmers could possibly remain a democracy. Even many city people share the antiurban bias, which sees the city as a center of sin and crime, of trickery and hypocrisy, of political corruption, of frivolity and superficiality, and of vexing problems of all sorts. Meanwhile the country is assumed to be a haven of simple honesty and rugged integrity, where good things grow and God's own people dwell. The antiurban bias is revealed in the widespread assumption that the country or small town is a better place to raise children, that farming and raising food is more noble than other work, that "grass roots democracy" is more genuine and rural voters more trustworthy, and that rural life and rural people are simply "better" in nearly every way. Even social research follows the antiurban bias. Most urban research shows what a mess the city is in, while funded research on rural life is generally screened to avoid any data which would challenge the assumption that "the rural community is a good place to live" [Olson, 1964].

All of these assumptions are dubious, and many of them are demonstrably false. Urban and rural life are *different*, but whether one is better than the other is a question of values. The "goodness of life" in a community cannot be measured until we agree on what measures to use. If high health levels, high average incomes, higher educational levels, and many social amenities are the values chosen, then city life is better. If a quiet, less complicated life is preferred, then the country has the edge. Obviously, this is a philosophical question, not a scientific question, and it should be remembered that the assumption of rural (or urban) superiority represents a bias, not a fact.

RURAL AND URBAN CONVERGENCE

Although "rural" and "urban" are useful concepts, there has never been a sharp dividing line between them. Even before the suburban movement and the urbanization of rural life, the two life styles converged in the *town.*

The town

The town is intermediate between rural and urban communities. It is too large for all inhabitants to be acquainted with one another, yet small enough for informal relationships to predominate. Social behavior more closely resembles the rural than the metropolitan city pattern. There is no census definition for the town; the census classifies any settlement of over 2,500 persons as "urban" and all else as "rural." Sociological studies of the town have seldom bothered to define it, but the towns studied have never exceeded several thousand people.

Most towns are either county seats or rural trading centers. The county seat towns are usually stagnant, and the rural trading towns are usually declining as the rural farm population falls. A great many of the youth must migrate elsewhere for employment, giving the town an abnormal population distribution and a "dead" atmosphere. About the only towns showing growth are those close enough to cities to become commuter suburbs, or so located as to attract industry (having water supply, labor supply, transportation, and proximity to markets), or those where tourism and recreation are thriving.

The local autonomy of the small town has eroded under the impact of the mass society. Martindale and Hanson [1969, p. 6] find the townspeople divided between "locals" who would like to preserve local self-sufficiency and "cosmopolitans" who would orient local life to the national economy and the mass society.

The fading rural-urban distinction

Urban-rural differences of all sorts are rapidly shrinking in the Western world, and soon this will probably be true everywhere. The suburb is the most rapidly growing part of the United States, and suburbanites who sought to flee the racial tensions, congestion, pollution, and tax crises of the city are now finding these problems catching up with them. Even this difference is fading.

The rural-urban distinction has already become secondary to the occupational distinction in importance [Stewart, 1958; Dewey, 1960]. The distinctive rural pattern of life is more closely linked to an agricultural occupation than to mere residence in a rural area. A study of rural-urban differences in interpersonal relations found that farm people differed considerably from urban residents, while there was comparatively little difference between urban and rural nonfarm people [Reiss, 1959]. Clearly, occupation has become more important than rural or urban residence as a clue to one's personality and way of life.

Nor should it be assumed that urbanization *necessarily* brings anomie, disorganization, and a lack of informal primary-group relationships. Earlier observers of urbanism were impressed by these features of urban life [Park et al., 1925; Sorokin and Zimmerman, 1929]. But either the observers exaggerated these characteristics, or urbanites have changed. Some modern studies have found that anomie is no more widespread in highly urbanized than in less highly urbanized areas [Greer and Kube, 1959]. As urbanism increases, neighboring and participation in formal organizations decline, but primary-group relationships within kinship and friendship groups increase. When rural people migrate to the city, they do not enter a social vacuum but rely heavily upon relatives for social interaction [Blumberg and Bell, 1959]. Instead of the extended family declining in importance with urbanization, research finds that the extended family is an even more important unit in large cities than in rural areas [Key, 1961]. Apparently as urbanism increases and people tend to become anonymous members of the community, they rely more heavily upon close friends and relatives for intimate response, identity, and a sense of belonging. The rise of the proportion of secondary contacts with urbanism implies no absolute weakening of primary-group life.

THE FUTURE OF CITIES

Much of the popular literature on the "crisis of the cities" implies that the city is doomed. This is nonsense! Unless modern civilization disappears, the city will survive, because the large city is essential to modern civilization. True, the problems of the modern city are grave, but ways to solve or endure them will be found.

The new town movement

Within recent years over a hundred "new towns" have been launched in the United States. The endless expansion of existing large cities would be economically inefficient and aesthetically unpleasing. The new town movement seeks to siphon off some of our population growth into self-sufficient new planned communities. Instead of growing haphazardly into the costly, inefficient, ugly things that most large cities have become, the new towns are planned from the start, with residential areas, civic buildings, parks, shopping areas, and industrial districts located for both efficiency and beauty. Europe has pursued the new town idea more enthusiastically than the United States, with Tapiola, Finland, as a world-famous example of how a city can be both efficient and lovely.

While holding promise of a far more pleasant life for those fortunate enough to inhabit them, new towns are no cure for the problems of existing cities. They require a huge initial investment, and most of the new town developments in the United States are in

financial difficulty. In the United States, they generally have a "country club" atmosphere, excluding all who are not moderately prosperous. By design, the new towns are kept to a modest size, and cannot be the magnet for artists, intellectuals, power-seekers, and "happenings" which make the great city a less secure but more exciting place to live. Some residents of the new towns complain that life there is safe, efficient, and comfortable, but just a bit dull. Thus the new towns escape some urban problems while creating others; yet on balance, the new towns offer to some people a more civilized pattern of urban living than they now experience [*Business Week*, Nov. 22, 1969, pp. 130ff.; Canty, 1969; Schaffer, 1970].

City planning and urban renewal

One commonly recommended antidote for urban problems today is city planning. Practically every city has a city-planning board, although often it does little but decide upon the location of highways, public buildings, and upon zoning changes. Any comprehensive planning is certain to meet opposition from many vested interests. Yet without comprehensive planning and execution of these plans, the American city faces accelerating decay. Slums are spreading faster than they are being cleared. Uncoordinated, piecemeal development of the urban fringe and of the "strip" cities is certain to mean great waste and agonizing future problems. Sewers, water mains, and expressways, built *after* many homes and buildings are constructed, will require expensive demolition. One suburb will wind up with lots of children to educate, while another suburb will have the industrial properties which make up the tax base needed to finance good schools. Certain areas will begin to have costly floods when the development of adjacent areas alters the watershed. Quiet residential areas will become noisy thoroughfares because of developments in adjacent areas. Problems like these are the fruit of uncoordinated, unplanned regional development. There are, as yet, few planning authorities with power to make, let alone enforce, the execution of plans for an entire metropolitan area. Eventually, after the problems have become intolerable and most of the mistakes have already been made, we shall probably create the plans. One sociologist a few years ago outlined the problem in these terms:

If the cities, and especially their decaying centers are to be brought up even to a tolerable standard of life, they must be reconstructed by the square mile instead of the individual house or the city block. . . . Despite the blight which has crept outward from the heart of cities, there are in the blighted areas billions of wealth in the form of physical utilities to be salvaged by making these centers habitable and attractive for human living . . . . We have the beginnings of a new house-building industry and we can develop further the prefabrication of houses, the assembling of land, and the financing of community building all of which are still in embryo. We do not start with a clean slate. We shall not have the opportunity to build new cities as we did a century ago, but we shall have an unprecedented opportunity to reconstruct with new materials and new methods the old cities which were created in response to conditions which have ceased to exist. (*Louis Wirth, "Life in the City," in Leon Carnovsky and Lowell Martin,* The Library in the Community, *The University of Chicago Press, Chicago, 1944, pp. 21–22. Copyright 1944, by The University of Chicago.*)

This statement emphasizes the physical reconstruction of buildings; but other problems are attracting equal attention. They include the provision of adequate public facilities such as recreation centers, public-health units, and schools; the necessary supplies of clean air, light, and water, along with provisions for sewage disposal; the guidance and control of the restless youth of our cities; and finally the overwhelming problem of urban traffic. In some cases the unit of planning is an urban neighborhood, whereas other problems may demand state, regional, or even national attention.

Urban renewal programs are now a fixture of nearly every large American city. Congress in 1966 authorized a "model cities" program, administered by the Model Cities Administration of the Department of Housing and Urban Development. This was intended to show, in a few cities, what a coordinated attack on a city's multiple problems could accomplish. The success to date has not been impressive. Many new civic buildings, office buildings, and middle-income housing have been built. Slums have been shifted around. But in the meantime, urban problems have grown steadily more severe and urban discontent has multiplied. New Haven, Connecticut, had a most impressive series of urban renewal projects, designed to rescue the decaying areas of the city with reconstruction, to rescue disadvantaged groups with job training and other services, and, hopefully, to prevent the outbreak of riots and civil disorders. Yet all this did not prevent New Haven from having a riot in 1967. According to some critics, a failure to consult the poor, whom many of the "improvements" displaced rather than helped, was primarily responsible [Powledge, 1970]. Following the wave of urban riots of 1967, many cities launched new programs designed to ease urban tensions, but they have been more palliative than corrective, and have been, at best, no more than a modest success [Bayton, 1969; Marshall Kaplan, 1970].

The enormously difficult questions of how to arrest urban blight and reconstruct the social life of our cities are too complicated to be treated here. These problems fill other textbooks for other courses. Meanwhile, debate on the means and ends of urban planning and reconstruction continues [Bellush and Hausknecht, 1967; Catanese and Steess, 1970; Erber, 1970; Chartrand, 1971]. Cities are as old as recorded history, but only within the lifetime of living men have we begun to live in an urban society. And only within the memory of today's college undergraduates have we begun seriously to consider how man can organize an urban society for his comfort and contentment.

SUMMARY

A *community* is usually defined as the residents of an area within which all a group's life activities can be carried on. Rural and urban people are different because the physical and social conditions of life are different in urban and rural communities. The traditional rural community tended to be a folk society. Its isolation, homogeneity, agricultural occupation, and subsistence economy all tended to develop people who were thrifty, hard-working, conservative, and ethnocentric. Changing technology has brought a rural revolution, with reduced isolation, commercialized large-scale farming, and a way of life very similar in many respects to urban patterns.

Cities become possible when an agricultural surplus develops, together with improved means of transportation, and tend to locate at breaks in transportation. Attempts to explain the ecological pattern of American cities have produced the concentric zone, sector, and multiple-nuclei theories, none of which any city perfectly fits but which all cities somewhat corroborate. The most significant current developments in city structure are the *metropolitan area*, including the *suburb*, which now accounts for most of our current population growth.

The rapid growth of the black population of the central cities, together with the flight of whites to the suburbs, aroused fears of eventual conflict between black city and white suburb, but these migration patterns are now changing. Black migration to suburbs is growing, and eventual black dispersion is a possibility.

Slums are a product of the low income of slum residents, setting in motion a cause-and-effect circle of property neglect by landlords and property abuse by tenants. Urban renewal programs have, to date, shifted slums around but not reduced them. Only mass housing subsidies or the elimination of poverty will eliminate slums.

The city is a conglomeration of *natural areas*, constantly forming and shifting through the *ecological processes* of concentration, centralization, decentralization, segregation, and invasion. The *invasion cycle* has several stages: the initial influx, reaction, general influx, climax, and succession.

Urban life and personality are affected by the physical and social conditions of urban living—speed and tension, anonymity, social distance, and regimentation. These conditions produce impersonality, insecurity, and segmentation of personality, which appear to be universal characteristics of urbanization all over the world. The widespread assumption that these differences make rural life and rural people "better" is known as the *antiurban bias*. Today, urban and rural differences are rapidly shrinking in the Western world and will eventually do so elsewhere. The rural-urban distinction is already less important than occupational classification as a clue to one's personality and way of life. The *town* is an example of rural-urban convergence, with townspeople divided upon whether to seek to retain small-town self-sufficiency or to seek integration into the national economy.

The *new town movement* is an attempt to siphon people and industry into new planned communities. *Urban renewal* and *city planning* are an attempt—not yet highly successful—to grapple with the increasingly grave problems of the city.

Questions and projects

1. Why did prehistoric man build no cities?

2. To what extent does the folk society survive in rural America today? Where and why has it most completely disappeared from rural America?

3. How are the personality characteristics of rural and urban people a product of their physical and social conditions of life? What sort of problems are faced by rural migrants to the city?

4. What has produced the rural revolution? What has this done to rural-urban differences?

5. Why has "conspicuous consumption" been more of an urban than a rural pattern? Is this relation changing today? How or why?

6. Are the "rural nonfarm" people closer to the rural or to the urban pattern in personality and life style?

7. What causes city slums? What causes rural slums? How do rural slums resemble and differ from urban slums?

8. Why should urban planning be so difficult? Why can't planners devise a workable plan and carry it through?

9. Take the city you know best and apply each of the three theories of city structure. Which fits it best? How well does the theory describe the actual arrangement of this city?

10. Trace the stages of the invasion cycle for an area of the city you know best. Try to date each stage. How long did each stage last and how long did the entire cycle require? Was it a happy or painful period?

11. What factual data can you find to measure the "goodness" of life in rural and urban society? What values are used in this evaluation?

12. Read Edward T. Chase, "Jam on the Côte d'Azur," *Reporter*, Sept. 28, 1961, pp. 44–46, or Wilfred Owen, *Cities in the Motor Age*, The Viking Press, Inc., New York, 1959. Then prepare your answer to the question: Are automobiles an asset or a blight upon the modern city?

Suggested readings

Abrams, Charles: *The City Is the Frontier*, Harper & Row, Publishers, Inc., New York, 1965. A readable, optimistic analysis of urban planning, housing, and urban renewal.

Banfield, Edward C.: *The Unheavenly City: The Nature and Future of Our Urban Crisis*, Little, Brown and Company, Boston, 1968. A diagnosis of urban ills which is highly critical of all the remedies usually designated as "liberal."

Bell, Wendell, and Marion D. Boat: "Urban Neighborhoods and Informal Social Relations," *American Journal of Sociology*, 62:391–398, January, 1957; Bobbs-Merrill reprint S-14. Research data on the extent and intimacy of neighborhood contacts in the urban milieu.

Chase, Edward T.: "Jam on the Côte d'Azur," *Reporter*, Sept. 28, 1961, pp. 44–46. A popularly written article on traffic problems in European and American cities.

*Greer, Scott: *Urban Renewal and American Cities*, The Bobbs-Merrill Company, Inc., Indianapolis, 1965. A critique of urban renewal and a call for a different approach.

Gruen, Victor: *The Heart of Our Cities*, Simon & Schuster, Inc., New York, 1964. Discussion of urban redevelopment by America's best-known urban planner.

*Halpern, Joel M.: *The Changing Village Community*, Prentice-Hall, Inc., Englewood Cliffs, N.J., 1967. A brief description of the revolutionary changes in village life throughout the world.

*Jacobs, Jane: *The Death and Life of Great American Cities*, Random House, Inc., New York, 1961. An attack on conventional city planning and a call for a different approach.

Martindale, Don: "Prefatory Remarks: The Theory of the City," introduction to Max Weber, *The City*, The Free Press of Glencoe, Inc., New York, 1958. A penetrating review of sociological theory on the city.

*Michelson, William H.: *Man and His Urban Environment*, Addison-Wesley Publishing Company, Inc., Reading, Mass., 1970. An attempt to integrate signigicant theory and research on the relation between urban environments and man's social life. Advanced content written in simple language.

Rogers, Everett M., and Rabel J. Burdge, *Social Change in Rural Societies*, Appleton-Century-Crofts, Inc., New York, 1972. A textbook in rural sociology.

Taylor, Miller Lee, and A. R. Jones: *Rural Life and Urbanized Society*, Oxford University Press, Fair Lawn, N.J., 1964. A description of how rural society is becoming urbanized.

*Wallace, Samuel E., *Skid Row as a Way of Life*, Harper & Row, Publishers, Inc., New York, 1965. A readable but sociologically sophisticated analysis of vagrancy and the skid row subculture.

Wirth, Louis W.: "Urbanism as a Way of Life," *American Journal of Sociology*, 44:1–25, July, 1938; Bobbs-Merrill reprint S-320. A classic essay describing urban life and personality.

Social change and
social policy

Part Six deals with change and man's efforts to effect change. Chapter 20, "Social and Cultural Change," discusses the forces which encourage and resist change and the social consequences of change when it is accomplished. Chapter 21, "Social Movements," describes some more or less organized efforts of people to promote changes they desire or to resist changes they deplore.

Social and cultural change

Homouda Awadan's nights have been restless recently, mainly because his cow no longer sleeps in the same room with him.

Awadan is one of 2,000 peasants moved last summer from overpopulated mud-hut villages in Ibis, a modern village with brick houses, electric lighting, running water and special pens for cattle.

The operation is sponsored by the U.S. Point Four program and the Egyptian Agriculture Department.

Life in the modern village has posed many problems to the fellaheen [peasants], many of whom came from villages that have seen little change since the days of the pharaohs.

All his life Awadan has slept with his cow, his chief work animal and provider of milk, yogurt and white cheese. Keeping the animal inside the house kept his floor littered with animal refuse, but Awadan could not take a chance on the beast being stolen.

"For the past three nights I have been waking in the middle of the night to check on my cow down in the village," said Awadan, still not used to the separation from his most treasured possession.

Awadan often yearns for the uncomplicated life of the mud village, but he remembers the five acres of land the government gave him and decides to stay. He never owned land before. He had to rent it from a big landowner.

Sheikh Rashad, director of the co-operative union at Ibis village, said it took much convincing to move the fellaheen into the model village. They are not inclined to move, no matter how crowded, he said.

In spite of all preparations, unexpected situations arose, Rashad said. Stacks of dry wood soon began appearing on top of the houses, similar to the mud villages, he added. At Ibis they had special storage rooms for wood, but the fellaheen would not use them. (*Associated Press. Nov. 9, 1959.*)

All cultures are constantly changing—some rapidly and some very slowly. Even when it tries to do so, no society succeeds in exactly copying and transmitting the culture of its ancestors. This fluidity is most easily illustrated by language changes. English has changed so greatly that most students have their troubles with Shakespeare and are hopelessly lost in Chaucer. In 1755 Samuel Johnson published his dictionary in the hope that it would stabilize word meanings and stop language changes, but soon he confessed that he had failed. None of the historic efforts to preserve a culture without change has been more than temporarily and partially successful. Social change is continuous and irresistible. Only its speed and direction vary.

There is a distinction between *social change*—changes in the social structure and social relationships of the society—and *cultural change*—changes in the culture of a society. Some social changes might include changes in the age distribution, average educational level, or birthrate of a population; or the decline of informality and personal neighborliness as people shift from village to city; or the change in the relationship between workers and employers when unions become organized; or the change of the husband from the boss to a partner in today's democratic family. Cultural changes might include such things as the invention and popularization of the automobile, the addition of new words to our language, changing concepts of propriety and morality, new forms of music, art, or dance, or the general trend towards sex equality. Yet the concepts overlap. The trend towards sex equality involves both a changing set of cultural norms concerning male-female roles, and some changing social relationships as well. Nearly all important changes involve both social and cultural aspects. In practice, therefore, the distinction is seldom a very important one, and the two terms are often used interchangeably. Sometimes the term *sociocultural change* is used to include changes of both kinds.

There is an important distinction between social change and *progress*. The term "progress" carries a value judgment. Progress means change in a desirable direction. De-sirable as measured by whose values? Are faster automobiles, taller buildings, higher incomes, and greater acceptance of divorce and abortion desirable? Not all Americans are agreed. Since progress is an evaluative term, social scientists prefer the neutrally descriptive term "change."

There are a number of different theories of social and cultural change [Applebaum, 1970; Allen, 1971]. The equilibrium and conflict theories of change were discussed in Chapter 4. Cyclical theories of change are as old as Aristotle, and among many modern proponents of cyclical theories of change, those of a philosopher, Spengler [1918], an historian, Toynbee [1935-1961], and a sociologist, Sorokin [1941] are notable. But a study of the conflicting grand theories of change may be of less use to the introductory student than a study of the conditions and processes of change.

PROCESSES OF SOCIAL CHANGE

Discovery

A *discovery* is *a shared human perception of an aspect of reality which already exists.* Man discovered the principle of the lever, the circulation of the blood, and the conditioned reflex. A discovery is an addition to mankind's store of verified knowledge. A discovery adds something new to the culture because, although this aspect of reality may always have existed, it became part of the culture only after its discovery.

A discovery becomes a factor in social change only when it is put to use. A discovery may become part of the background of knowledge which people use in evaluating their present practices. Thus the recent discoveries of physiology and psychology that males and females are very much alike in their intellectual capacities did not *compel* men to alter their attitudes toward the status of women; but the discoveries made the nineteenth-century patriarch look ridiculous and certainly diluted men's determination to preserve traditional male dominance.

When new knowledge is used to develop new technology, vast changes generally follow. The ancient Greeks knew about the power of steam, and before A.D. 100 Hero of Alexandria had built a small steam engine as a toy, but steam power produced no social changes until it was put to serious use nearly 2,000 years later. Discoveries become a factor in social change when new knowledge is put to new uses.

Invention

An *invention* is often defined as *a new combination or a new use of existing knowledge*. Thus George Selden in 1895 combined a liquid-gas engine, a liquid-gas tank, a running-gear mechanism, an intermediate clutch, a driving shaft, and a carriage body, and patented this contraption as an automobile. None of these ideas were new; the only novelty was the combined use of them. The Selden patent was attacked and eventually revoked by the courts on the ground that he did not originate the idea of combining these items.

While existing elements are used in a new invention, it is the *idea* of combining them in a useful way that produces something which never before existed. Thus iron, with the addition of small amounts of other metals, became steel, a new metal with properties which no metal known at that time could equal. Likewise a round slice of tree log and a length of tree limb were not new, but the wheel and axle were new. The wheel did not exist until someone had, and carried to successful use, the idea of using a limb and a slice of a tree log in this manner.

Inventions may be classified as *material inventions*, such as the bow and arrow, telephone, or airplane, and *social inventions*, such as the alphabet, constitutional government, or the corporation. In each case, old elements are used, combined, and improved for a new application. Invention is thus a continuing process, with each new invention the last in a long series of preceding inventions and discoveries. In a popularly written book, Burlingame [1947] has analyzed a number of familiar inventions, showing how each began hundreds or thousands of years ago and passed through dozens of preliminary inventions and intermediate stages. Invention is not strictly an individual matter; it is a social process involving an endless series of modifications, improvements, and recombinations. As Gillin [1948, pp. 158–163] has pointed out, each invention may be new in *form, function,* and *meaning*. "Form" refers to the shape of the new object or the actions of the new behavior trait; "function" refers to what the invention does; "meaning" refers to the long-range consequences of its use. To these three, we might also add that an invention may be new in *principle,* that is, in the basic scientific law upon which it is based.

The jet engine and the piston engine use the same principle (expansion of burning gases) but differ in form (one uses expanding gases directly for thrust, the other to push a piston in a cylinder). The steam engine and the piston gasoline engine are similar in form but differ in principle (one creates expanding gases by boiling water, the other by burning gasoline). The bow and arrow differs in both principle and form from the primitive spear but has the same function and meaning. The wheeled cart was new in all respects (in principle, since the load was carried by wheel and axle instead of being dragged or packed; in form, since it was new in design; in function, since it carried both people and possessions; in meaning, since it made large-scale, long-distance overland transport possible). Very few inventions are new in all four respects.

The term *innovation* has sometimes been used to include both discoveries and inventions [Barnett, 1953, pp. 7-8]. In either case, something new has been added to the culture.

Diffusion

Even the most inventive society invents only a modest proportion of its innovations. Most of the social changes in all known societies have developed through *diffusion, the spread of culture traits from group to group.* Diffusion operates both within societies and between societies. Jazz originated among black musicians of New Orleans and became diffused to other groups within the society. Later it spread to other societies and has now been diffused throughout the civilized world.

Most of the content of any complex culture has been diffused from other societies.

Diffusion takes place whenever societies come into contact. Societies may seek to prevent diffusion by forbidding contact, as did the Old Testament Hebrews:

When the Lord thy God shall bring thee into the land whither thou goest to possess it, and hath cast out many nations before thee... thou shalt smite them and utterly destroy them; thou shalt make no covenant with them, nor shew mercy unto them; neither shalt thou make marriages with them.... For they will turn away thy son from following me, that they may serve other gods.... But... ye shall destroy their altars, and break down their images, and cut down their groves, and burn their graven images with fire. *(Deuteronomy 7:1-5.)*

Like most efforts to prevent intercultural contacts, this prohibition failed. The Old Testament tells how the Hebrews persisted in mingling and intermarrying with the surrounding tribes, adopting bits of their cultures in the process. Whenever cultures come into contact, some exchange of culture traits always takes place.

Most of the content of any complex culture has been diffused from other societies. Ralph Linton has written a famous passage which tells how the 100 percent American has actually borrowed most of his culture from other societies.

Our solid American Citizen awakens in a bed built on a pattern which originated in the Near East but which was modified in Northern Europe before it was transmitted to America. He throws back covers made from cotton, domesticated in India, or linen, domesticated in the Near East, or silk, the use of which was discovered in China. All of these materials have been spun and woven by processes invented in the Near East. He slips into his moccasins, invented by the Indians of the Eastern woodlands, and goes to the bathroom, whose fixtures are a mixture of European and American inventions, both of recent date. He takes off his pajamas, a garment invented in India, and washes with soap invented by the ancient Gauls. He then shaves, a masochistic rite which seems to have been derived from either Sumer or Ancient Egypt.

Returning to the bedroom, he removes his clothes from a chair of Southern European type and proceeds to dress. He puts on garments whose form originally derived from the skin clothing of the nomads of the Asiatic steppes, puts on shoes made from skins tanned by a process invented in ancient Egypt and cut to a pattern derived from the classical civilizations of the Mediterranean, and ties around his neck a strip of bright-colored cloth which is a vestigial survival of the shoulder shawls worn by seventeenth century Croatians. Before going out for breakfast he glances through the window, made of glass invented in Egypt, and if it is raining puts on overshoes made of rubber discovered by the Central American Indians and takes an umbrella, invented in southeastern Asia. Upon his head he puts a hat made of felt, a material invented in the Asiatic steppes.

On his way to breakfast he stops to buy a paper, paying for it with coins, an ancient Lydian invention. At the restaurant a whole new series of borrowed elements confronts him. His plate is made of a form of pottery invented in China. His knife is of steel, an alloy first made in southern India, his fork a medieval Italian invention, and his spoon a derivative of a Roman original. He begins breakfast with an orange, from the eastern Mediterranean, a cantaloupe from Persia, or perhaps a piece of African watermelon. With this he has coffee, an Abyssinian plant, with cream and sugar. Both the domestication of cows and the idea of milking them originated in the Near East, while sugar was first made in India. After his fruit and first coffee he goes to waffles, cakes made by a Scandinavian technique from wheat domesticated in Asia Minor. Over these he pours maple syrup, invented by the Indians of the Eastern woodlands. As a side dish he may have the egg of a species of bird domesticated in Indo-China, or thin strips of the flesh of an animal domesticated in Eastern Asia which have been salted and smoked by a process developed in northern Europe.

When our friend has finished eating he settles back to smoke, an American Indian habit, consuming a plant domesticated in Brazil in either a pipe, derived from the Indians of Virginia, or a cigarette, derived from Mexico. If he is hardy enough he may even attempt a cigar, transmitted to us from the Antilles by way of Spain. While smoking he reads the news of the day, imprinted in characters invented by the ancient Semites upon a material invented in China by a process invented in Germany. As he absorbs the accounts of foreign troubles he will, if he is a good conservative citizen, thank a Hebrew deity in an Indo-European language that he is a **100 percent American**. (*Ralph Linton*, The Study of Man, *Appleton-Century-Crofts, Inc., New York, 1936, pp. 326–327*.)

Diffusion is always a two-way process.

Traits cannot diffuse unless there is some kind of contact between peoples, and these contacts always entail some diffusion in both directions. Europeans gave horses, firearms, Christianity, and whisky to the Indians in exchange for corn, potatoes, tobacco, and the canoe. Yet the exchange is often lopsided. When two cultures come into contact, the society with the simpler technology generally does the more borrowing. Within societies, low-status groups generally borrow more than high-status groups. Slave groups generally absorb the culture of their masters, while their own is forgotten or deliberately extinguished.

Diffusion is a selective process. A group accepts some culture traits from a neighbor, at the same time rejecting others. We accepted much of the Indian's food but rejected his religion. Indians quickly accepted the white man's horse but long rejected the white man's cow.

Diffusion generally involves some modification of the borrowed element. As noted earlier, each cultural trait has *principle, form, function*, and *meaning*. Any or all of these may change when a trait is diffused. When Europeans adopted Indian tobacco, they smoked it in a pipe somewhat like the Indian pipe, thus preserving the form, although they also added other forms—cigars, ciagrettes, chewing tobacco, and snuff. But they entirely changed function and meaning. Indians smoked tobacco as a ceremonial ritual; Europeans used it first as a medicine, and later for personal gratification and sociability. The outward forms of Christianity have been diffused more readily than the functions and meanings. In missionary areas many converts have accepted the forms of Christian worship while retaining many of their traditional supernatural beliefs and practices. Non-Western peoples have put tin cans and other Western artifacts to a variety of uses, both utilitarian and aesthetic. American colonists accepted maize (corn) from the Indians unchanged; it traveled to Europe, where it was used as food for animals but not for people; it was then diffused to West Africa, where it became a favorite food and even an offering to the gods. Endless examples could be cited to show how traits are nearly always modified as they are diffused.

Sociologists and anthropologists have made many research studies of the diffusion process [Allen, 1971, chap. 12]. Most of our aid programs in underdeveloped countries, as well as those for "underprivileged" groups in our own country, are primarily efforts to promote diffusion. Consequently, it is one of the most important topics in sociology.

FACTORS IN THE RATE OF CHANGE

Discovery, invention, and diffusion are processes of change. But what causes them to happen? We cannot answer this question without first examining the meaning of the term *cause*. A cause is sometimes defined as a phenomenon which *is both necessary and sufficient* to produce a predictable effect. It is necessary in that we never have this effect without this cause, and sufficient in that this cause, alone, always produces this effect. Thus defined, very few causes have been established in social science. Does drunkenness cause divorce? Many long-suffering souls put up with a drunken mate, while others divorce mates who are bone dry. Obviously, drunkenness is neither a necessary nor a sufficient condition to produce a divorce. Most causation in social science is multiple—that is, a number of factors interact in producing a result. What factors interact in producing a social change?

First of all, we note that the factors in social change are predominantly social and cultural, not biological or geographic. Not everyone accepts this view. Some people would attribute the rise and fall of great civilizations to changes in the biological characteristics of nations. Often these theories have a racial twist; a great civilization is said to arise from a vigorous, creative race, and falls when the race mixes with lesser breeds and dilutes its genius. According to an opposite version, a great burst of creativity follows a fortunate intermixture of races and dies out as the hybrid strain runs out. Most scientists reject all such theories. There is no convincing scientific evidence that any race differs from any other race in its biological basis for human learning, or that man's biology has changed significantly during the last twenty-five thousand years or so. During the period of recorded history, man's biological attributes appear to have been a constant, not a variable, in his behavior.

Physical environment

Major changes in the physical environment are quite rare, but very compelling when they happen. The desert wastes of North Africa were once green and well populated. Climates change, soil erodes, and lakes gradually turn into swamps and finally plains. Social life is greatly affected by these changes, although they sometimes come about so very slowly that the changes in social life may be largely unnoticed. True, man may speed up these changes through his land use; he can accelerate or retard soil erosion through conservation practices. But in this instance, the causes are still social and cultural, for it is the actions of men which set in motion these environmental changes.

Much more common in human history is a change of a group's physical environment through migration. Especially in primitive societies, whose members are very directly dependent upon their physical environment, migration to a different environment brings major changes in culture. Civilized man can more easily transport his culture and practice it in a new and different environment. The British colonial in the jungle outpost often persisted in taking afternoon tea and dressing for dinner. Yet no one would suggest that he was unaffected by the jungle environment; even civilized man's culture is affected by a change of physical environment.

Population changes

A population change is itself a social change, but also becomes a causal factor in further social and cultural changes. When a thinly settled frontier fills up with people, the hospitality pattern fades away, secondary-group relations multiply, institutional structures grow more elaborate, and many other changes occur. A rapidly growing population must either migrate or improve its productive techniques. Great historic migrations and conquests—of the Huns, the Vikings, and many others—have arisen from the pressure of a growing population upon limited resources. Migration encourages further change, for it brings a group into a new environment, subjects it to new social contacts, and confronts it with new problems. No major population change leaves the culture unchanged.

Isolation and contact

Societies located at world crossroads have always been centers of change. Since most new traits come through diffusion, those societies in closest contact with other societies are likely to change most rapidly. In ancient times of overland transport, the land bridge connecting Asia, Africa, and Europe was the center of civilizing change. Later, sailing vessels shifted the center to the fringes of the Mediterranean Sea, and still later to the northwest coast of Europe. Areas

of highest intercultural contact are the centers of change.

Conversely, isolated areas are centers of stability, conservatism, and resistance to change. Almost without exception, the most primitive tribes have been those who were the most isolated, like the polar Eskimos or the Aranda of Central Australia. Even among civilized peoples, isolation brings cultural stability. The most "backward" American groups have been found in the inaccessible hills and valleys of the Appalachians [Sherman and Henry, 1933; Surface, 1970].

Leyburn [1935] has shown how European groups who migrated to remote, isolated frontiers often retained many elements of their native culture long after they had been discarded by their parent society. Thus by the nineteenth century, the social life of the Boers in the Transvaal resembled the life of the late seventeenth-century Dutch more than that of their contemporaries in the Netherlands.

Ethnic enclaves, whose isolation is social and voluntary rather than geographic, show a similar conservatism, whether it be Americans in Spain [D. Nash, 1967], Amish in America [Hostettler, 1964], or Tristan Islanders in England [Munch, 1964, 1970]. Isolation invariably retards social change.

Structure of society and culture

The structure of a society affects its rate of change in subtle and not immediately apparent ways. A society which vests great authority in the very old people, as classical China did for centuries, is likely to be conservative and stable. A society which stresses conformity and trains the individual to be highly responsive to the group, such as the Zuñi, is less receptive to change than a society like the Ileo who are highly individualistic and tolerate considerable cultural variability [Ottenberg, 1959]. When a culture is very highly integrated, so that each element is tightly interwoven with all the others in a mutually interdependent system, change is difficult and costly. Among a number of Nilotic African peoples, such as the Pakot, Masai, and Kipsizis, the culture is integrated around the cattle complex. Cattle are not only a means of subsistence; they are also a necessity for bride purchase, a measure of status, and an object of intense affection [Schneider, 1959]. Such a system is strongly resistant to social change. But when the culture is less highly integrated, so that work, play, family, religion, and other activities are less dependent upon one another, change is easier and more frequent. A tightly structured society, wherein every person's roles, duties, privileges, and obligations are precisely and rigidly defined, is less given to changes than a more loosely structured society wherein roles, lines of authority, privileges, and obligations are more open to individual rearrangement.

The structure of American society is highly conducive to social change. Our individualism, our lack of rigid social stratification, our relatively high proportion of achieved statuses, and our institutionalization of research all encourage rapid social change. Today tens of thousands of workers are systematically employed in finding new discoveries and inventions. This exploration is something new in the world's history. Our dazzling and sometimes upsetting rate of change is one consequence.

Attitudes and values

To us change seems normal, and most Westerners pride themselves upon being progressive and up to date. By contrast, the Trobriand Islanders off the coast of New Guinea had no concept of change, and did not even have any words in their language to express or describe change [Lee, 1959a, pp. 89–104]. When Westerners tried to explain the concept of change, the Islanders could not understand what they were talking about. Societies obviously differ greatly in their general attitude toward change. A people who revere the past, worship their ancestors, honor and obey their elders, and are preoccupied with traditions and rituals will change slowly and unwillingly. When a culture has been relatively static for a long time, the people are likely to assume that it should remain so indefinitely. They are intensely and unconsciously ethnocentric; they assume that their customs and techniques are correct and everlasting. A possible change is unlikely even to be seriously considered. Change in such a society occurs mainly when it is too gradual to be noticed.

A rapidly changing society has a different attitude toward change, and this attitude is both cause and effect of the changes already taking place. Rapidly changing societies are aware of social change. They are somewhat skeptical and critical of some parts of their traditional culture and will consider and experiment with innovations. Such attitudes powerfully stimulate the proposal and acceptance of changes by individuals within the society. There may be variations between localities in attitude towards change. One study finds that farmers' acceptance of agricultural innovations is affected by their impression of their local community's receptivity to the idea of change [Flinn, 1970].

Different goups within a locality or a society may show differing receptivity to change. Every changing society has its liberals and its conservatives. The Amish subculture in the United States has been notably resistant to change of every kind except, sometimes, in farming techniques. And a group may be highly receptive to change of one kind but highly resistant to changes of other kinds. Thus we can enter many churches of strikingly modern architecture and hear a sermon basically unchanged since the days of Luther.

Attitudes and values affect both the amount and the direction of social change. The ancient Greeks made great contributions to art and learning but little to technology. Work was done by slaves; to concern oneself with a slave's work was no proper task for a Greek scholar. No society has been equally dynamic in all aspects, and its values determine in which area—art, music, warfare, technology, philosophy, or religion—it will be inventive.

Perceived needs

A society's rate and direction of change are greatly affected by the needs its members perceive. "Needs" are subjective; they are real if people feel that they are real. According to our values, half the world needs to discard ancient systems of landholding and consolidate tiny, scattered parcels into more efficient units. But unless people feel such a need, nothing changes; only the perceived needs of a society count.

Some practical inventions languish until the society discovers or develops a need for them. The zipper fastener was invented in 1891 but ignored for a quarter century. The pneumatic tire was invented and patented by Thompson in 1845 but was ignored until the popularity of the bicycle created an awareness of need for it; then it was reinvented by Dunlop in 1888.

It is often stated that changing conditions create new needs—genuine, objective needs, not just subjectively "felt" needs. Thus, urbanization created a need for sanitary engineering; the modern factory system created a need for labor unions; and the high-speed automobile created a need for superhighways. A culture is integrated, and therefore any changes in one part of the culture create a need for adaptive changes in related parts of the culture.

It is doubtless true that failure to recognize an objective need may have unpleasant consequences. For centuries, sickness and death were the price of man's failure to recognize that urban growth made sanitary engineering a necessity. A more recent failure to recognize that death control creates a need for birth control has brought half the world to the brink of starvation. All this does not alter the fact that it is only those "needs" which are perceived as necessary which stimulate innovation and social change.

Necessity, however, is no guarantee that the needed invention or discovery will be made. At present, we perceive that we need cures for cancer and for the common cold, a pollution-free power source, and an effective protection against radioactivity. There is no certainty that we shall develop any of these. Necessity may be the mother of invention, but invention also needs a father —a cultural base to provide the necessary supporting knowledge and technique.

The cultural base

The cave man could make exceedingly few material inventions, for he had very little to work with. Even the bow and arrow combines a number of inventions and techniques—notching the bow ends, tying the bowstring, hafting and pointing the arrow, plus the idea and technique of shooting it. Not until these components were invented was it possible to invent the bow and arrow. By the *cultural base*, we mean *the accumulation of knowledge and technique* available to the inventor. As the cultural base grows, an increasing number of inventions and discoveries become possible. The invention of the geared wheel provided a component which has been used in countless inventions. The discovery of electromagnetism and the invention of the vacuum tube provided necessary components for hundreds of more recent inventions.

Unless the cultural base provides the necessary preceding inventions and discoveries, an invention cannot be completed. Leonardo da Vinci in the late fifteenth century sketched many machines which were entirely workable in principle and detail, but the technology of his day was incapable of building them. His drawings for the aerial bomb, hydraulic pump, air-conditioning unit, helicopter, machine gun, military tank, and many others were clear and workable, but the fifteenth century lacked the advanced metals, the fuels, the lubricants, and the technical skills necessary to carry his brillant ideas into practical reality. Many inventive ideas have had to wait until the supporting gaps in knowledge and technique were filled in.

When all the supporting knowledge has been developed, the appearance of an invention or discovery becomes almost a certainty. In fact, it is quite common for an invention or discovery to be made independently by several persons at about the same time. Ogburn [1950, pp. 90–102], a sociologist who specialized in the study of social change, listed 148 such inventions and discoveries, ranging from the discovery of sun spots, independently discovered by Galileo, Fabricius, Scheiner, and Harriott, all in 1611, to the invention of the airplane by Langley (1893–1897), Wright (1895–1901), and perhaps others. In fact, disputes over who was first with an invention or a scientific discovery are common and sometimes acrimonious [Merton, 1957c]. When the cultural base provides all the supporting items of knowledge, it is very probable that one or more imaginative persons will put these items together for a new invention or discovery.

Cross-fertilization The great importance of the cultural base is revealed by the principle of *cross-fertilization*, which states that discoveries and inventions in one field became useful in an entirely different field. Pasteur's germ theory of disease grew out of his efforts to tell France's vintners why their wine turned sour. The vacuum tube, developed for radio, made possible the electronic computer, which now aids research in nearly everything from astronomy to zoology. Certain radioactive materials, byproducts of the search for more deadly weapons, are now invaluable in medical diagnosis, therapy, and research. Stouffer's studies [1949], designed to show the armed services how to get more effective fighting men, also provided knowledge that was useful to students of group dynamics, race relations, and several other fields of sociology.

The exponential principle This principle states that, as the cultural base grows, its possible uses tend to grow in a geometric ratio. To illustrate: If we have only two chemicals in a laboratory, only one combination (A-B) is possible; with three chemicals, four combinations are possible (A-B-C, A-B, A-C, and B-C); with four chemicals, ten combinations; with five chemicals, twenty-five, and so on. As the size of the cultural base grows by addition, the possible combinations of these elements grow by multiplication. This helps to explain today's high rate of discovery and invention. A vast accumulation of scientific technical knowledge is shared by all the civilized societies, and from this base new inventions and discoveries flow in a rising tide.

RESISTANCE TO AND ACCEPTANCE OF SOCIAL CHANGE

Not all proposed innovations are accepted by the society. A process of *selective acceptance* operates as some innovations are accepted instantly and some only after long delay; some are rejected entirely; and others are accepted in part. Thus we accepted completely the Indian's corn, accepted and modified his tobacco, accepted in a very small, highly modified way his totemic clans (Boy Scout "beaver" and "wolverine" patrols), and totally rejected his religion. Acceptance of innovations is never automatic and is always selective according to a number of considerations.

Specific attitudes and values

Aside from its general attitude toward change, each society has many specific attitudes and values which cling to its objects and activities. When government agents introduced hybird corn to the Spanish American farmers of the Rio Grande Valley a few years ago, they readily adopted it because of its superior yield; but within three years, they had all returned to the old corn. They didn't like the hybrid corn because it didn't make good tortillas [Apodaca, 1952]. People's established likes and dislikes are important factors in social change.

If an object has a purely utilitarian value —that is, if it is valued because of what it will do—change may be accepted quite readily. Thus a recent study [Fliegel and Kivlin, 1966] of the acceptance of new farm practices by American farmers finds that those which are perceived as most profitable and least risky are most readily accepted. If some feature of the traditional culture is valued intrinsically—valued for itself, aside from what it will do—change is less readily accepted. To the American farmer, cattle are a source of income, to be bred, culled, and butchered whenever most profitable. But to many of the Nilotic peoples of Africa, cattle represent intrinsic values. The owner recognizes and loves each cow. To slaughter one would be like killing one of the family. A Pakot with a hundred cattle is rich and respected; one with only a dozen is poor; the man with no cattle is ignored as though he were dead. Efforts of colonial officials to get such peoples to manage their herds "rationally"—to cull their herds, breed only the best, and stop overgrazing their lands—have generally failed.

The average American, who usually takes a coldly rational, relatively unsentimental view of economic activities, finds it hard to appreciate the sentiments and values of non-Western peoples. He is irritated by the Biaga of Central India, who refused to give up their primitive digging sticks for the far superior moldboard plow. Why? The Biaga loved the earth as a kindly and generous mother; they would gently help her with the digging stick to bring forth her yield, but could not bring themselves to cut her "with knives" [Elwin, 1939, pp. 106–107]. The American is annoyed by the Ettwah Indians' unwillingness to adopt green manuring (plowing under a crop of green sanhemp as fertilizer). But to this Indian, "green manuring involves a very cruel act of plowing under the sanhemp leaf and stalk before they are ripe. This act involves violence." [Mayer, 1958, p. 209.] Yet is there any basic difference between these illustrations and an American's refusal to eat horse meat because it conflicts with his values? What is the basic difference between the Cambodian farmer who rejects inorganic fertilizer because it is an interference with nature and the many Americans who reject contraception because it is an interference with nature? How about those American groups who reject divorce, or alcoholic beverages, or movies, or card playing because these would conflict with their values? To each of us, it seems entirely logical and right to reject any innovation that conflicts with our mores or values; when another group does likewise, their refusal often impresses us as stubborn ignorance. Such is ethnocentrism!

Demonstrability of innovations

An innovation is most quickly accepted when its usefulness can be easily demonstrated. The American Indians eagerly accepted the white man's gun, but still have not fully accepted the white man's medicine, whose superiority is less easily demonstrated. Many inventions are so inefficient in their earlier stages that general acceptance is delayed until they are perfected. During the automobile's first three decades of development, public scorn was expressed by the derisive advice to "get a horse!" Early imperfections delay, but rarely prevent, the eventual acceptance of workable inventions.

An innovation is most quickly accepted when its usefulness can be easily demonstrated.

Some innovations can be demonstrated quite easily, on a small scale; others cannot be demonstrated without costly, large-scale trials. Most mechanical inventions can usually be tested in a few hours or days, and at modest cost. Most social inventions such as the corporation, social organization based on role rather than on kinship, or world government, are not easily tried out in the laboratory or testing bureau. Many social inventions can be tested only through a long-term trial, involving at least an entire society. We hesitate to adopt an innovation until we have been shown how it works; yet we can determine the practical value of most social inventions only by adopting them. This dilemma slows their acceptance.

Compatibility with existing culture

Innovations are most readily accepted when they fit in nicely with the existing culture. The horse fitted easily into the hunting culture of the Apache, as it enabled them to do better what they were already doing. Not all innovations mesh so well. Innovations may be incompatible with the existing culture in at least three ways.

First, *the innovation may conflict with existing patterns.* In some parts of Asia and Africa, Islam now appears to be spreading faster than Christianity, perhaps because Christianity conflicts with native polygamy while Islam does not. We have already pointed out how it would be difficult for American society to institutionalize premarital sex experience. Not only does it conflict with some of our mores and sentiments; it also conflicts with our family structure and our property institutions, neither of which makes any very satisfactory provision for children born out of wedlock.

When an innovation conflicts with existing culture patterns, there are at least three possible outcomes: (1) It may be rejected, just as most Americans have rejected communism; (2) it may be accepted, and the conflicting cultural traits may be adjusted to it, as we have altered our child-labor practices to permit compulsory public education; (3) it may be accepted and its conflict with the existing culture may be concealed and evaded by rationalization, as in those areas (including France and, until recently, five of the United States) where contraceptives are freely sold "for prevention of disease," although the sale of contraceptives is forbidden by law. While not always decisive, conflict with the existing culture discourages acceptance of an innovation.

Sometimes an apparent conflict can be avoided by role compartmentalization. As an example, the Kwaio of the Solomon Islands have chiefs every Tuesday! Their social organization included no chiefs, but it became necessary to invent some to handle dealings with white officials after World War II. To avoid conflict between these new "chiefs" and the traditional holders of authority and influence, they simply agreed that the chiefs would "reign" only on Tuesdays when the white officials called [Keesing, 1968]. In this way, a potentially disruptive innovation was insulated from the rest of the culture.

Second, *the innovation may call for new patterns not present in the culture.* The American Indians had no patterns of animal husbandry into which the cow could be fitted. When they were first given cows by government agents, they hunted them as game animals. A society generally tries to use an innovation in old, familiar ways. When this fails, the society may develop new ways of making effective use of the new element. Thus we have disguised each new building material to make it look like an old, familiar material. Early concrete blocks were faced like rough-finished stone; asphalt and asbestos shingles were finished to look like brick or wood; aluminum siding is still made to look like wood. Then, after some years, each of these materials begins to be used in designs and ways which make full use of its own properties and possibilities. Most innovations call for some new patterns in the culture, and it takes time to develop them.

Third, *some innovations are substitutive, not additive,* and these are less readily accepted. It is easier to accept innovations which can be added to the culture without requiring the immediate discard of some familiar trait complex. American baseball, jazz, and the "western" movie have been diffused throughout most of the world. Each could be added to almost any kind of culture without requiring surrender of any native traits. But the approximate equality of the sexes, democracy, or rational business enterprise have diffused more slowly; each requires the surrender of traditional values and practices. Many non-Western peoples have readily accepted the procedures and materials of scientific medicine—inoculations, antibiotics, analgesics, and even surgery—for these could coexist with their traditional folk medicine. The ill Navaho could swallow the government doctor's pill while the Navaho healing dance continued. But often these peoples neither understand nor accept the scientific foundations of medicine, such as the germ, virus, and stress theories of disease, or the rest of the medical subculture, for these conflict with their traditional belief system [Gould, 1965; Wolff, 1965; J. Nash, 1967]. Whenever the nature of the choice is such that one cannot have *both* the new and the old, the acceptance of the new is usually delayed.

Costs of change

Change is nearly always costly. Not only does change disrupt the existing culture and destroy cherished sentiments and values, but it also involves some specific costs.

Technical difficulties of change Very few innovations can simply be added to the existing culture; most innovations require some modification of the existing culture. Only recently did England replace an awkward and clumsy monetary system with a decimal currency, while the United States has been debating and postponing a switch to the metric system of measures for over a century. Why have such clumsy systems been retained for so long? Because the changeover is so difficult. England's switch to a decimal currency in 1967 proved to be far more complicated than simply learning a new system. Changes in cash registers, coin machines, bookkeeping records, standardized merchandise sizes, and arguments over pound fractions were all involved. Learning the metric system would be very simple, but the task of making and stocking everything from window frames to nuts and bolts in both size ranges for a half century or so is overwhelming. Railroads would be more efficient if the tracks were a foot or two farther apart to permit wider cars; but the cost of rebuilding the tracks and replacing the rolling stock is prohibitive. Our city streets are far too narrow for today's traffic, but street widening is unbearably costly after the streets are lined with skyscrapers. New inventions and improved machines often make present machinery obsolete and destroy the market for technical skills which workmen have spent years in developing.

Vested interests and social change The costs of social change are never evenly distributed. The industry which is made obsolete and the workmen whose skill is made unmarketable are forced to bear the costs of technical progress, while others enjoy the improved products. Those to whom the status quo is profitable are said to have a *vested interest.* Communities with an army post or navy yard nearby find that all this government money is good for business, so these communities have a vested interest in retaining these military establishments. Students attending state universities have a vested interest in tax-supported higher education. Nearly everyone has some vested interests—from the rich with their tax-exempt bonds to the poor with their welfare checks.

Most social changes carry a threat, real or imaginary, to some vested interests who then oppose these changes. Examples are almost endless. In 1579 the Council of Danzig, acting in response to pressure from weavers, ordered the strangulation of the inventor of an improved weaving machine; and the spinsters of Blackburn, England, invaded Hargreave's home to destroy his spinning jennies [Stern, 1937]. The early railroads were opposed by landowners who didn't want their lands cut up, and by canal owners and toll-road companies; and then in turn the railroads became vigorous opponents of the automobile and helped to block construction of the St. Lawrence Seaway. In 1922, the major automobile manufacturers launched a massive advertising campaign against four-wheel brakes, claiming that they would injure passengers, damage tires, and cause cars to overturn. Employer opposition to the organization of labor unions was long and bitter, and still continues in some places, while many unions resort to "featherbedding" in the effort to retain jobs made unnecessary by technical change. The radio industry bottled up FM radio as long as possible, and more recently the television industry and the motion-picture-theatre operators have done their best to block pay television and cable television. Each group is an ardent advocate of progress in general, but seldom at the expense of its own vested interests.

Vested interests, however, appear as promoters of change whenever they believe the proposed change will be profitable to them. American corporations spend billions of dollars each year to develop new products which they can sell profitably. Many business groups in the Great Lakes area energetically supported the St. Lawrence Seaway proposal. Such government enterprises are normally denounced as socialism by vested interests which are not enriched thereby, while those vested interests whom the proposal benefits will find other terms to describe it. (Apparently, *socialism* operates when the government spends money to benefit *you*, not me!) Business interests have sought and obtained many kinds of government regulation and "interference" when it seemed in their interest to do so. Labor unions have been most eloquent supporters of laws to limit child labor. The great Chicago fire of 1871 showed the weakness of competing private fire-fighting companies, and, more important, imposed such heavy losses upon fire insurance companies that they threw their support behind the proposal for tax-supported municipal fire departments. Many social reforms have finally been secured, after long agitation, because powerful vested interests came to redefine their interests and decided that the reform would benefit them.

Role of the change agent

Who proposes a change and how does he go about it? The identity of the originator greatly affects acceptance or rejection. Any proposal of the Communist Party in the United States is doomed to certain defeat. Opponents of all sorts of proposals often label them Communist in order to defeat them. Innovations which are first adopted by persons at the top of the prestige scale and power system are likely to filter downward quite rapidly; those first adopted by low-status persons are likely to percolate upward more slowly, if at all.

Successful change agents often seek to make the change appear innocuous by identifying it with familiar cultural elements. King Ibn Saud introduced radio and telephone to Saudi Arabia by quoting the Koran over them. Franklin D. Roosevelt's leadership rested partly upon his ability to describe significant reforms in terms of homespun American sentiments and values.

The change agent must know the culture in which he works. When American officials sought to combat communism through posters contrasting pictures of great religious leaders with those of Communist leaders, the campaign failed among the Moslem Indonesians, who felt it irreverent and offensive to display a picture of Mohammed. Government attempts to settle Navajo Indians as individual families on irrigated land were unsuccessful, for the Navajo were accustomed to work land cooperatively along extended kinship lines. An amusing illustration of how ignorance and ethnocentrism handicapped a change agent is found in Micronesia, where an American labor relations expert sought to recruit Palauan workers for a mining operation. He first demanded to see the "chief"—a request which posed a problem since they had no chief in their social structure. Finally they produced a person with whom the American expert sought to establish rapport by throwing an arm around his shoulders and laughingly tousling his hair. In Palauan culture this was an indignity roughly equivalent, in our culture, to opening a man's fly in public [Useem, 1952]. Needless to add, this expert was not very successful.

Sometimes a change agent succeeds in promoting a change, only to find that the results are an unhappy surprise. In one South African area the Western workers noticed that the native mothers were exhausted by nursing their babies for two years; they successfully introduced bottle feeding. The innovation had the effect of evading the native taboo upon sexual relations during lactation, so that instead of bearing a child every three or four years, the women now bore a child every year or so, and were more exhausted than ever [Lee, 1959*b*]. Change agents must thoroughly understand the interrelations of the culture if they are to be able to predict the consequences of a particular change. At this moment, when thousands of American representatives are functioning as change agents in nearly every underdeveloped country of the world, we might remind ourselves of the necessity for change agents to be observant students of the society they wish to help, if they are to avoid unhappy consequences.

The efforts of the change agent are not always appreciated. The inventor is often ridiculed; the missionary may be eaten; and the agitator or reformer is usually persecuted. Radicals are likely to be popular only after they are dead, and organizations (like the Daughters of the American Revolution) dedicated to the memory of dead revolutionists have no fondness for live ones. Those who sought to change the segregated racial patterns of American society may become heroes in the history books, but they faced jail and physical violence during their lifetime. The record of a black minister active in the civil rights struggle of the 1950s is revealing:

Christmas, 1956, Shuttleworth home bombed and completely demolished; winter 1957, Bethel Baptist Church dynamited by racists; late 1957, Shuttleworth and wife mobbed, beaten, and stabbed; jailed eight times—four times during the Freedom Rides; sued for three million dollars by state officials of Alabama; automobile and personal property sold at public auction; driver's license revoked for a whole year; three Shuttleworth children illegally arrested and beaten in Gadsden (Alabama). . . is currently involved in twenty-seven criminal and civil actions. (*SCLC Newsletter (Southern Christian Leadership Conference), September, 1961.*)

Change agents are often hated and despised, especially when they attack attitudes and values which other people cherish.

The deviant as change agent Many change agents are deviants of some sort. The nonconformist may unwittingly launch a new fashion, speech form, or dance step. Inventors are people who love to tinker; they are more excited by the challenge of a new idea than by the possibility of riches [Barnett, 1953, pp. 150-156]. Social reformers are necessarily people who are disenchanted with some aspect of the status quo. Without deviants, there would be many fewer social changes.

SOCIAL AND PERSONAL DISORGANIZATION

Social effects of discovery and invention

No social change leaves the rest of the culture entirely unaffected. Even an "additive" innovation draws time and interest away from other elements of the culture. Some innovations are shattering in their impact. When the missionaries passed out steel axes to the Yir Yoront of Australia, the gift appeared to be an innocuous gesture, but the stone ax was so tightly integrated into the culture that a chain reaction of disruption spread through the social structure [Sharp, 1952]. The stone ax was a symbol of adult masculinity. It might be lent to women and to youths, and the lines of ax borrowing were very important features of the social organization. When superior steel axes were passed out indiscriminately, and owned by women and youths, the symbol of authority was so undermined that authority itself became clouded, relations were confused, and reciprocal obligations became uncertain. The stone for the axes was quarried far to the south, and traded northward along trade routes through an established system of trading partners, who also shared in important ceremonials. With the substitution of the steel ax, trading relationships languished, and this rich ceremonial sharing was lost. Deep and serious disturbance of Yir Yoront culture is traced to the single innovation of the steel ax. The illustration is dramatic; but have the effects of the automobile or the radio upon American culture been less far-reaching? Ogburn [1933, pp. 153-156] has complied a list of 150 social changes which he attributes to the radio; and television has brought still more.

Ogburn distinguishes three forms of the social effects of invention. (1) *Dispersion, or the multiple effects of a single mechanical invention*, is illustrated by the many effects of the radio, or by the automobile, which shortens travel time, supports a huge manufacturing and servicing industry, provides a market for vast quantities of gasoline and oil, steel, glass, leather, and other materials, requires a massive road-building program, alters courtship and recreational behavior, promotes suburbs and shopping centers, and has many other consequences. (2) *Succession, or the derivative social effects of a single invention,* means that an invention produces changes, which in turn produce further changes, and so on. The invention of the cotton gin (a) simplified cotton processing and made cotton more profitable; this result (b) encouraged the planting of more cotton; and the planting (c) required more slaves; the increase in slavery and growing Southern dependence upon cotton export (d) helped to provoke the Civil War, which (e) greatly stimulated the growth of large-scale industry and business monopoly; these in turn (f) encouraged antitrust laws and labor unions; and the chain still continues. While these developments were not entirely due to the cotton gin, it helped to produce them all. (3) *Convergence, or the coming together of several influences of different inventions,* may be variously illustrated. The six-shooter, barbedwire fencing, and the windmill facilitated the settlement of the great American plains. The automobile, the electric pump, and the septic tank made the modern suburb possible. Nuclear warheads, intercontinental missiles, and radar detection system have, in the opinion of many military theorists, made total war obsolete.

Much has been written about the social effects of invention. It does not matter whether the new trait has been invented within the society or diffused into it; the social effects are equally great from either method. Guns "made all men the same size" and ended the power advantage of the horsed knight in armor; cannons ended the relative impregnability of the medieval castle and strengthened the king at the ex-

pense of the provincial nobility. A diffused trait often finds a society quite unable to cope with it successfully. For example, primitive societies which brew their own alcoholic beverages generally have cultural controls over their use, but primitive societies which have received alcohol from white men have had no such controls, and the effects have been generally devastating [Horton, 1943]. To cite one instance, the Eskimo of St. Lawrence Island, when first introduced to alcohol, promptly went on a month-long drunk and missed the annual walrus migration; the following winter most of them died of starvation [Nelson, 1899]. Innovations, whether discovered, invented, or diffused, can be equally disruptive.

Unequal rates of change

Since a culture is interrelated, changes in one aspect of the culture invariably affect other aspects of the culture. The affected traits will usually be adapted to this change, but only after some time has passed. This time interval between the arrival of a change and the completion of the adaptations it prompts is called *cultural lag,* a concept developed by Ogburn [1922, pp. 200–213]. As an illustration, he pointed out that about 1870, workers in large numbers began entering factories where they were often injured in unavoidable accidents. But not until another half century had passed did most states get around to enacting Workmen's Compensation laws. In this instance, the cultural lag was about fifty years.

A cultural lag exists wherever any aspect of the culture lags behind another aspect to which it is related. Probably the most pervasive form of cultural lag in present Western societies is the lag of institutions behind changing technology. For example, in most states the size of a county was based upon the distance one could travel to the county seat and return in the same day; despite improved transportation, the county unit still remains at its old size, inefficient for many of its functions. The metropolitan area sprawls over a hodgepodge of many different state, county, city, and township units, so that efficient area planning, government, and law enforcement become an impossibility. At least a half century ago, advancing technology had tied the civilized world into an interdependent whole; but it took a second world war to jolt the United States out of its complacent isolationism. For a full centry, urbanization and industrialization were destroying the possibility for the individual worker to ensure the security of his family by depending upon himself, his relatives, and his neighbors; yet only after the Great Depression of the 1930s dramatized this fact did we establish social security, unemployment insurance, and other welfare measures.

Some cultural lags involve the lag of one part of the material culture behind a related part of the material culture. A quarter century after cars are built to cruise at high speeds, we get started on a superhighway system. Most airports are too small to accommodate the latest types of aircraft. For a quarter century after we replaced the horse with the automobile, we continued to build the garage out behind the house, back where the smelly stables used to go. Sometimes the material culture lags behind changes in the nonmaterial culture. For example, educational research has long since discovered that movable classroom furniture aids in organizing learning activities; yet thousands of classrooms still have inflexible rows of desks screwed to the floor. Finally, one aspect of the nonmaterial culture may lag behind other related aspects of nonmaterial culture. For example, millions of dollars are spent on quack practitioners and patent medicines which medical science has repeatedly shown to be useless, while dozens of communities reject measures like fluoridation which science has shown to be effective and harmless. Our hesitant

and halfhearted support for birth control is lagging many decades behind our monumental support for death control. The population explosion is perhaps our most catastrophic cultural lag.

The concept of cultural lag applies to differing rates of change *within* a society, not to rates of change between societies. It describes the disharmony between related parts of a single culture, produced through unequal rates of change. Cultural lags are most numerous in a rapidly changing culture. They are symptoms, not of a backward society, but of a highly dynamic and increasingly complex society. But even if all people were wise, objective, and adaptable, they would still need some time to discover what adaptations a new change would require, and more time to work out and complete those adaptations. Most of us, however, are pretty ignorant about matters outside our specialty, are prejudiced and swayed by vested interests, and are not nearly so adaptable as we like to imagine. Cultural lags are numerous and persistent.

Social change and social problems

A social problem is a condition which many people consider undesirable and want to correct [Horton and Leslie, 1970, pp. 3–6]. A perfectly integrated society would have no social problems, for all institutions and behavior would be neatly harmonized and defined as acceptable by the values of the society. A changing society inevitably develops problems. Either the conditions themselves change and become unacceptable (population growth, soil erosion, and deforestation create a conservation problem), or the society's changing values define an old condition as no longer tolerable (child labor, poverty, racism, or lack of education). Social problems are part of the price of social change. The detailed analysis of social problems, however, belongs in another textbook and another course.

Disorganization and demoralization

As has been repeatedly suggested in this chapter, all new elements disrupt the existing culture to some extent. If a culture is well organized, with all its traits and institutions fitting closely together, change in any one of them will disorganize this arrangement.

When a culture becomes highly disorganized, the people's sense of security, morale, and purpose in life is damaged. When people are confused and uncertain, so that their behavior is also inconsistent, hesitant, and contradictory, they are described as *personally disorganized*. If their disorganization proceeds until they lose their sense of purpose in life and become resigned and apathetic, we describe them as *demoralized*. They have lost their morale, and often their behavior controls are lost as well. A demoralized people is likely to suffer population decline, through a lowered birthrate, a higher death rate, or both. The capacity of a thoroughly demoralized people simply to die out has attracted the attention of a number of anthropologists [Rivers, 1922; Maher, 1961].

The extermination of the buffalo demoralized the American Indians of the Great Plains [Lesser, 1933; Wissler, 1938; Sandoz, 1954; Deloria, 1970]. The buffalo provided food, clothing, and shelter; in all, over fifty separate parts of the buffalo carcass were used by the Indians. The buffalo hunt provided the principal object of the Indian's religious cermonials, the goal of his maturing, and a road to status and recognition. His other avenue to status—warfare—was also dependent upon an ample supply of dried buffalo meat. When the government exterminated the buffalo in order to pacify the Indians, it demoralized them as well. The integrating and status-giving functions of the war party and the buffalo hunt were lost. Religious ceremonials were now empty and meaningless. The hunting economy was totally destroyed, and the Indians lived, and sometimes starved, on government handouts. The traditional goals and values which gave zest and meaning to life were now unavailable, and to substitute the white man's goals and values was an almost impossible task of learning. In the few instances where Indians did successfully adopt the white man's economy, this, too, was soon destroyed by the white man's hunger for the Indians' land [Collier, 1947, pp. 199–219; Foreman, 1932; Deloria, 1970]. Suffering from the destruction of their own culture, denied access to the white man's culture, ravaged by the white man's diseases, and corrupted by his alcohol, many Indian tribes became deeply demoralized. Depopulation was almost universal, and only in recent decades has Indian population begun to rebuild. This story of devastatingly disruptive social change, disorganization of the culture, and personal disorganization and demoralization of the people has been repeated hundreds of times in the world's history.

Not all native peoples, however, have been demoralized by their contacts with Western societies. The Palauans of Micronesia have worked out an interdependent blend of traditional culture and Western commercialism. They happily drive trucks and pound typewriters to earn money to buy the traditional clan gifts, and use motor launches to carry their sweet potatoes to traditional festivals [Mead, 1955, p. 128]. Whether change disrupts a society to the point of demoralization depends upon the nature of the changes, the way they are introduced, and the structure of the society upon which they impinge.

Is change least painful when it comes slowly? Not necessarily. Since culture involves interrelations, it is generally easier to accept a cluster of related changes than to accept them one at a time. For example, if a primitive people acquires cotton clothes without soap, then filth and disease are predictable; if given clothes without irons and sewing machines, then they will be clothed in tatters. With mud floors to sit upon, and no place to store clothing and these other artifacts, filth and clutter are a certainty. But if all these elements—clothes, soap, irons, sewing machines, and floored houses with shelves and closets—are adopted together within a single generation, these changes can be made far more easily than if they are spaced over several generations.

Western cultural diffusion generally converts the native village into a depressing slum, not because the people adopt too many new traits but because they adopt too few. It may even be psychologically easier to make a lot of changes than a few. As Margaret Mead [1956, pp. 445–446] has observed, "A people who choose to practice a new technology or enter into drastically new kinds of economic relationships will do this more easily if they live in different houses, wear different clothes and eat different, or differently cooked, food." Much of the social disorganization which accompanies social change stems from the fact that a people who are willing to adopt new trait complexes are blocked from doing so. Sometimes they are blocked by their own limited resources and sometimes by the unwillingness of the dominant whites to admit them into full participation in Western civilization. The Mau Mau terrorism in Kenya in the 1950s was largely attributable to the frustration of the Kikuyu's intense desire to share in Western civilization [Bascom and Herskowitz (eds.), 1959, p. 4].

We need, therefore, to revise the notion that slow change is necessarily more comfortable than rapid change. In some situations, the rapid wholesale change of a way of life may be infinitely less disturbing than piecemeal changes, as Mead [1956, chap. 18] has shown in her study of the Manus, who moved from the Stone Age into Western civilization in a single generation. The reason may be that slow change allows cultural lags to accumulate, not to be corrected until they become painful. Rapid change may actually produce fewer lags, because many of the related items of the culture may be changed at the same time.

Change has come with dazzling speed upon contemporary Western societies. Within a few short generations, the Western peoples have shifted from life in rural, agricultural folk societies to life in an immensely complex urban, industrial, impersonal mass society. Are contemporary Western societies disorganized? Certainly! Cultural lags are numerous at every point. The school is constantly straining to prepare children for a society which changes even before they become adult. The church carries a doctrine stated largely in the language and context of an agricultural society; much of it is irrelevant to the needs and problems of our impersonal, secondary-group world; yet the effort to restate its message in modern terms has riven the church into warring factions. A century ago husband and wife could each assume a quite clearly defined role; today no bride can be at all sure what she will be expected to be and do in her marriage. Every level of government is struggling with tasks which few of our grandfathers would have guessed it would ever assume. Disputes over the privileges and responsibilities of corporations, unions, and other economic groups now occupy the center of the political arena. Although the traditional informal controls of the folk society are failing to regulate the behavior of individuals in this impersonal urban world of ours, we are still hunting for effective substitutes.

There is national consensus upon neither goals nor means in our society. The supporters of the "counterculture" reject the traditional goal of individual material advancement through work as selfish and destructive. They reject the idea that corrective social changes should be sought only through democratic precedures and justify the activist techniques of confrontation and disruption as means of promoting social change.

These are symptoms of social disorganization—failure of traditional controls, role confusions and uncertainties, conflicting moral codes, lack of consensus upon goals or means of social action, experimentation and change in institutional behavior. In such a disorganized society, people are affected. Many fail to internalize a coherent system of values and behavior controls. A smaller number become seriously disorganized and grow so erratic and contradictory in behavior that they are diagnosed as mentally ill and in need of psychotherapy. Whether those who embrace the hippie life style are simply personally disorganized or are well organized around a deviant life organization is a question which is impossible at this time to answer.

If our society is so badly disorganized, why are we not all mentally ill? Despite our accelerating rate of social change during the past century, the available evidence indicates that the frequency of mental illness has not significantly increased [Goldhamer and Marshall, 1953]. More persons are diagnosed and treated than formerly, but this proves only that more cases of mental illness are being located and treated. Measuring the frequency of mental illness, either present or past, is a difficult research problem [Manis et al., 1964; Phillips and Clancy, 1970]. It is possible that there is no more mental illness today because we have become able to develop personalities that are adaptable to social change [Mead, 1947]. Children in our society are socialized to anticipate and appreciate change. The strain of change may be considerably reduced by a socialization which seeks to prepare persons to adapt themselves. Since adult roles

are uncertain, we seek to socialize and educate children to function successfully in several roles, not just in one. Finally, we have developed social case work and psychiatry for persons who cannot work out an effective life pattern by themselves. All over the world today, the rate of social change is accelerating. Whether man can adapt himself as rapidly as his social life is changing is still a moot question.

The organization-disorganization-reorganization cycle

What eventually happens to a society disorganized by social change? Some primitive societies died out, but most larger societies eventually succeed in reorganizing their culture to accommodate the social changes.

Children in our society are socialized to anticipate and appreciate change.

The horse disorganized the Plains Indians' cultures; but very quickly the people adapted their culture to the changes the horse made possible. They developed new skills of caring for horses and making gear, developed a status system around horse ownership, and greatly increased their class distinctions. The Sioux and the Comanche changed from sedentary agriculturalists to nomadic hunters in a very dramatic example of a rapid and successful integration of a new culture complex. The hunting tribes like the Crow, Blackfeet, and Apache were able to hunt buffalo more effectively than before and transport a larger supply of preserved food. Their warfare became more mobile and more lethal. They developed an elaborate horse complex including at least 119 items [Ewers, 1955], and the richness and comfort of their lives was greatly increased.

The culture of the American people has been extensively reorganized to integrate the automobile. Garages are now attached to our houses. Parking facilities are planned and provided along with new buildings. The layout of cities and suburbs and the location of schools, shopping areas, and factories all reflect our dependence upon the automobile. Most of these developments gained momentum only in recent decades —one-third of a century after the automobile became common—another instance of cultural lag. And today, having integrated the automobile into our culture, we are beginning to wonder if we should not reduce our dependence upon the automobile.

When social changes arrive slowly, there is time to integrate one change before the next arrives. Today, however, all the major societies of the world and most of the minor societies are changing at a breakneck pace. Before one change can be integrated, a dozen more have arrived. *Change has now become the norm.* The static, integrated society which sociologists used to pose as a model, as a starting point for analysis, is only an intellectual construct, not a concrete reality. Used in this way—as a starting point for study—the model of the static society has some intellectual usefulness. But we must remember that, except for a few isolated bands of primitives, all societies are changing rapidly and that change is now the norm all over the world. Disorganization and

reorganization are a continuous process all over the world. All major societies are in a race to see whether adaptive reorganization can proceed fast enough to avoid the accumulation of intolerable lags and irreconcilable social tensions.

SOCIAL PLANNING: CAN CHANGE BE DIRECTED?

Is it possible to control and direct social changes so that they will be less painful and costly? Social scientists disagree. Some feel that social change is caused by social forces beyond man's effective control. For example, when the necessary supporting knowledge is developed, an invention will be made by someone, even if this invention is most troublesome to man. The atom bomb is an example. Although we fear it may destroy us, we go on advancing it because others will do so anyway. Could the Indian wars possibly have been avoided? The Indians had land we wanted for our growing population, and our advance was certain to destroy the Indian's way of life. The many unnecessary brutal episodes were merely the symptoms, not the cause, of a conflict which was unavoidable, given these groups with their respective needs and cultural backgrounds. Practically any great social change can be thus described in terms of blind social forces, so that we conclude that what *did* happen was about the only thing that *could* happen in that situation.

At least one contemporary scholar has hit the best-seller lists with a popular book which questions our ability to direct or adjust to our hurtling pace of social change. Alvin Toffler in *Future Shock* [1970] gives the term "future shock" to the social disease of excessive social change. He maintains that a large and steadily growing number of people are disoriented and baffled by social change which is so rapid that much of their learned attitudes and behavior is ineffectual or even dysfunctional. He expects future shock to grow steadily more widespread and severe, and is not optimistic about our ability to relieve it.

Some social scientists, however, believe that we can exert *some* influence over the course of social change. They believe that some degree of social planning is possible. *Social planning* is defined [Himes, 1954, p. 18] as "a conscious interactional process combining investigation, discussion, agreement, and action in order to achieve those conditions, relationships, and values that are regarded as desirable." More simply, social planning is an attempt at the intelligent direction of social change [Adams, 1950; Riemer, 1947; Gross, 1967; Bennis, et al., 1969, chap. 1]. In his *The Active Society* [1968], Etzioni argues that, rather than drifting aimlessly, a society can guide social change to achieve humane social goals. He sees this social guidance, not as a pattern imposed by a ruling elite, but as a result of the efforts of active-minded publics who mobilize to demand changes in accord with their needs and interests. But just how the conflicting wishes of different publics are to be reconciled would remain a perplexing problem.

Elite direction of social planning is characteristic of the Communist societies. Decision making has been highly centralized, and plans have been exceedingly intricate and detailed. The present tendency in Communist societies is toward some decentralization of decision making, with less attempt to specify all possible details [Shaffer, 1968; Smolinski, 1968]. Planning which attempts to program practically all the activities of a society is less successful than planning that is limited to only one, or a small number, of activities or goals. This kind of social planning is an old American tradition. When the framers of our Constitution rejected primogeniture (the European provision that the lands pass intact to the eldest son) and entail (the provision that prevents him from selling them), these American planners were seeking to construct a society of small, landowning farmers instead of a society of landed estates. This purpose was reinforced by the Homestead Act of 1862, which gave public lands in small parcels to individual farmers instead of selling it in large blocks to the highest bidders. Zoning ordinances, building codes, public education, and compulsory school attendance laws are examples of social planning. Some problems which call for planning at the national or international level include the use of the world's water resources [Kalinen and Bykov, 1969], use of mineral resources under international waters, and many others.

A critic of planning would contend that such planning efforts do not really change anything, but are merely a slightly more orderly way of carrying out changes that are inevitable anyway. The comment perhaps sums up the matter. Certainly, no social planning will prevent or reverse a change which present knowledge and longtime trends are creating. There is, for example, no way of returning to the "simple life," nor is it possible by planning to steer social change in a direction contrary to most people's wishes and values. The major social changes are probably uncontrollable, but social planning may be able to reduce the delays and costs of integrating them into the culture.

SUMMARY

All societies change continuously. New traits appear through *discovery* and *invention*, or through *diffusion* from other societies.

The rate of social change varies enormously from society to society and from time to time. In rare instances, certain *geographic changes* produce great social change. More often, *migration* to a new environment brings changes in social life. *Changes in population size or composition* always produce social changes. Since *isolation* retards change and cross-cultural contacts promote change, physically or socially isolated groups show fewer changes. The *structure of the society and culture* affect change: A highly conformist, authoritarian society or a highly integrated culture is less prone to change than the individualistic, permissive society or the less highly integrated culture. A society's *attitudes and values* greatly encourage or retard change. The *perceived needs* of a people affect the speed and direction of change. Perhaps most important of all, the *cultural base* provides the foundation of knowledge and skill necessary to develop new elements; as the cultural base expands, the possibilities of new combinations multiply in an *exponential* manner, while knowledge in one area often *cross-fertilizes* other areas of development.

Not all innovations are accepted. The attitudes and values of a group determine what kind of innovations a group is likely to accept. If an innovation's usefulness can be demonstrated easily and cheaply, the proof is helpful; but many social inventions cannot be tested except through a complete acceptance. Compatible innovations are more readily accepted than those which clash with important features of the existing culture. Technical difficulties of fitting a change into the existing culture often cause great economic cost and personal inconvenience. Vested interests normally oppose change, but they occasionally discover that a proposed change is to their advantage. The change agent's ingenuity and social position affect his success in introducing changes. Unless the change agent knows the culture very well, he may fail in his efforts, because he generally miscalculates the consequences of his changes.

Social and personal disorganization are costs of social change. Discoveries and inventions, as well as diffused new traits and complexes, often set off a chain reaction of change which disrupts many aspects of the culture. The different parts of the culture, interrelated and interdependent though they are, do not change at the same rate of speed. The time interval between the appearance of a new trait and the completion of the adaptations it forces is called *cultural lag*. All rapidly changing societies have many cultural lags and are somewhat *disorganized*. In a disorganized society, persons who may have greater difficulty in finding a comfortable behavior system become themselves disorganized. When they lose hope of finding a rewarding way of conducting their lives and cease trying, they have become *demoralized* and may actually die out as a group. Changing societies are in a constant process of disorganization and reorganization, since change is now the norm in all modern societies. In an effort to speed and simplify this process and reduce the costs and wastes of social change, *social planning* is increasingly being attempted. Social scientists are not agreed upon the degree of success to be expected from the direction of social change by social planning.

Questions and projects

1. Why are social scientists hesitant to use the term "progress"?

2. Is knowledge of the diffusion process likely to reduce ethnocentrism?

3. Have any recent American attempts been made to prevent diffusion or to limit contacts of Americans with other cultures?

4. What are some of the change-promoting fea-

tures of American society? What are some of its change-resisting features?

5. Is the rate of invention likely to continue rising, or to fall off? Why?

6. Is our fondness for European art inconsistent with our fear of certain European ideas?

7. Why will a person who insists upon the latest cars, fashions, and gadgets often be entirely satisfied with ancient social philosophies?

8. How many of those persons whom we now consider "great" were noncontroversial during their lives? How many achieved greatness by promoting changes and how many by preventing changes?

9. Is it possible for a change agent to promote a major change without arousing violent hostilities?

10. What are some recent social changes in our society which you consider undesirable? Some which you consider desirable? What values are you using in making these judgments?

11. Why should social change be so difficult? Why can't people simply get together, decide what changes are desirable, and then promote them?

12. Evaluate this statement: "The more successfully we progress, the fewer cultural lags and social problems we shall have."

13. Is our high divorce rate a symptom of social disorganization or reorganization? How about our rather widespread practice of premarital sex relations? The popularity of very youthful marriages?

14. If it is assumed that racial integration in the United States is desirable, would acceptance of integration be easier if we proceed slowly, step by step, or rapidly integrated all activities and services at the same time?

15. Can social planning ever change "human nature"? Must it, in order to succeed?

16. Read one of the following novels, which describe Americans operating as change agents in other societies, and explain the agents' successes or failures in that capacity: Ronald Hardy, *The Place of the Jackals*; Graham Greene, *The Quiet American*; James Ullman, *Windom's Way*; Kathryn Grondahl, *The Mango Season*; Margaret Landon, *Never Dies the Dream*; Thomas Streissguth, *Tigers in the House.*

Suggested readings

Adams, E. M.: "The Logic of Planning," *Social Forces*, 28:419–423, May, 1950. A brief outline of the principles of social planning in a democracy.

Allen, Francis R.: *Socio-cultural Dynamics: An Introduction to Social Change*, The Macmillan Company, New York, 1971. A textbook on theories of social and cultural change.

*Applebaum, Richard P.: *Theories of Social Change*, Markham Publishing Co., Chicago, 1970. A concise summary of current sociological thought on social change.

*Barnett, H. G.: *Innovation: The Basis of Cultural Change*, McGraw-Hill Book Company, New York, 1953. An anthropologist's analysis of the development and acceptance of innovations.

*Bascom, William R., and Melville J. Herskovits (eds.): *Continuity and Change in African Cultures*, The University of Chicago Press, Chicago, 1959. Two essays—Simon Ottenberg, "Ibo Receptivity to Change" (pp. 130–143), and Harold K. Schneider, "Pakot Resistance to Change" (pp. 144–167) —seek to explain the opposite reactions of two societies to social change.

Bennis, Warren G., Kenneth D. Benne, and Robert Chin: *The Planning of Change*, Holt, Rinehart and Winston, Inc., New York, 1969. A comprehensive textbook on social planning and social change.

Coleman, James S.: *Resources for Social Change: Race in the United States*, John Wiley & Sons, Inc., New York, 1971. Seeks to show how powerless groups in the United States, especially poor black people, can gain more power to obtain "equality of opportunity."

Etzioni, Amitai: *Demonstration Democracy,* Gordon and Breach Science Publishers, Inc., New York, 1971. An analysis of the technique of promoting social change by confrontation and disruption.

Lee, Dorothy: "The Cultural Curtain," *Annals of the American Academy of Political and Social Science,* 323:120–128, May, 1959. An interesting article showing, with many illustrations, the need for change agents to understand the culture in which they promote change.

Maher, Robert F.: *The New Men of Papua: A Study in Culture Change,* The University of Wisconsin Press, Madison, 1961. A primitive society, described several decades ago by anthropologists, is restudied to evaluate the impact of culture change.

*__Mead, Margaret:__ *Cultural Patterns and Technical Change,* UNESCO, 1955; Mentor Books, New American Library of World Literature, Inc., New York, 1955. Studies the impact of modern technology on five traditional societies, with discussion of how to proceed in bringing modern technology to traditional societies.

*__Ogburn, William F.:__ *Social Change,* The Viking Press, Inc., New York, 1922. The classic study of social change.

*__Spicer, Edward H.__ (ed.): *Human Problems in Technological Change,* Russell Sage Foundation, New York, 1952. A casebook describing a number of societies where important changes were introduced, showing the process of adoption and the social consequences of these changes.

Last night I told Jim: "I been working in the same factory as you 10 years now. We go in at the same time, come out at the same time. But I do all the shopping, get the dinner, wash the dishes and on Sunday break my back down on the kitchen floor. I'm real tired of doin' all that. I want some help from you." Well, he just laughed at me, see? Like he done every time I mentioned this before. But last night I wouldn't let up. I mean, I really *meant* it this time. And you know? I thought he was gonna let me have it. Looked mighty like he was gettin' ready to belt me one. But you know? I just didn't care! I wasn't gonna back down, come hell or high water. You'll just never believe it, he'd kill me if he knew I was tellin' you, he washed the dishes. First time in his entire life." (*Quoted from Vivian Gornick, "Consciousness,"* New York Times Magazine, *Jan. 10, 1971, p. 22. Copyright © 1971 by The New York Times Company. Reprinted by permission.*)

A woman must have alternative modes of self-expression and self-esteem beyond the prescribed female sex role. As Betty Friedan, Simone de Beauvoir and others have described it, this traditional role labels the female as inherently passive, weak-willed, frivolous, irrational, emotional, intellectually and physically inferior and dependent. With these imputed characteristics, self-fulfillment can only come with nurturing, motherhood and domesticity. The "traditional woman" gives of herself to the exclusion of personal ambition, desire or need. The potential convert to Women's Liberation must recognize that there are other alternatives to self-fullment than this. (*Anita Lynn Micossi, "Conversion to Women's Lib,"* Trans-action, *November-December, 1970, p. 83. Copyright © December, 1970, by Trans-action, Inc., New Brunswick, New Jersey.*)

To radical feminists, Betty Friedan is the albatross they would like to shed. Sally Kampton puts it this way: "She misrepresents the case for feminism by making people believe that reform is the answer. The problem is more fundamental. The entire society has to be upended." (*Paul Wilkes, "Mother Superior to Women's Lib,"* New York Times Magazine, *Nov. 29, 1970, p. 150. Copyright © 1970 by The New York Times Company. Reprinted by permission.*)

Social movements

These few phrases introduce one of the most recent, and yet one of the oldest, of our social movements. What are social movements? Why do they appear? What are the conditions under which they succeed or fail?

NATURE AND DEFINITION
OF SOCIAL MOVEMENTS

Early sociologists saw social movements as efforts to promote change. More recent sociologists view social movements as efforts either to promote or to resist change. For example, Turner and Killian [1957, p. 308] define a social movement as *"a collectivity acting with some continuity to promote or resist a change in the society or group of which it is a part."*

This definition covers a wide range of movements: religious movements like Moral Rearmament, Youth for Christ, or the growing interest of young people in psychedelic and occult experience [Lidz and Rothenberg, 1968]; reform movements like the civil rights movement or the abortion reform movement; revolutionary movements like the Communist Party or the New Left; and many others.

Social movements are not institutions. Social institutions are relatively permanent and stable elements of a culture, whereas social movements are highly dynamic and have an uncertain life span. Institutions hold institutional status; that is, nearly everyone regards them as necessary and valuable aspects of the culture. A social movement lacks institutional status, for vast numbers of people view it with indifference or hostility. If a movement gains general or nearly universal support, its work is done and its active life, as a movement, is over.

Social movements are also distinguished from associations. An association is generally a formal organization, with members, officers, and a written constitution. A social movement often comes to include one or more associations, but usually includes many supporters who are not members of these supporting associations, while some movements are almost totally unorganized. Furthermore, the association is typically engaged in carrying out the customary behavior of the society, while the social movement is concerned with some change in behavior forms. The fact that a movement which has reached the stage of formal organization may call itself the "so-and-so association" should not blur the distinction between association and movement.

Social movements sometimes act as pressure groups, but most pressure groups are not social movements. Most pressure groups merely want the existing norms and values of the society to be interpreted to their benefit. But social movements are primarily and consciously concerned with promoting or resisting actual changes in these social norms and values. Occasionally, but only occasionally, do social movements function as pressure groups.

Sociologists and other social scientists are much interested in the scientific analysis of social movements. They study them in several ways, including: (1) participant-observer studies, in which the sociologist joins the movement to observe it from the inside [Festinger et al., 1955; Lincoln, 1961; Ilfeld and Lauer, 1964]; (2) historical or longitudinal studies, combing published accounts, historical documents, newspaper files, and other sources [Edwards, 1927; Gusfield, 1955; Blake, 1969; O'Neill, 1969]; (3) comparative-membership studies, analyzing a sample of members or leaders (a) statistically, according to age, sex, class, occupation, education, and other characteristics in an effort to find out who joins and why [Lipset, 1950; Almond, 1954; Flacks, 1967; M. Lee, 1968], or (b) through interviews and biographical accounts, in an effort to discover their common feelings and motives [Crossman, 1949; Ernst and Loth, 1952; Kerpelman, 1969; Wilkes, 1970]; (4) content analyses of a movement's statements and propaganda [Lasswell and Blumenstock, 1939].

SOCIAL SITUATIONS FAVORING SOCIAL MOVEMENTS

Social movements do not "just happen." They arise wherever social conditions are favorable, and these conditions will have produced many people who are ready and willing to promote them. What kinds of social conditions are favorable to the appearance and spread of social movements?

Cultural drifts

Gradual, broad, sweeping changes in values or behavior are constantly going on in all civilized societies today (and in most primitive societies as well). Such changes are called *cultural drifts*. The concept originated with Herskovits [1949, p. 581], who describes it as a process "where minor alterations slowly change the character and form of a way of life, but where the continuity of the event is apparent." In the course of a cultural drift most of the people develop new ideas of what society should be like and how society should treat them. The long development of democratic society is an example of cultural drift. Some other examples include the emancipation of women, the accent on materialism, the changed attitude toward leisure and recreation, and the higher evaluation of education. At present, the trend among the majority of younger people is away from materialism and toward the hippie life style. It is too early to say whether this is a momentary bit of fashion or the beginning of a long-term shift of values.

Each cultural drift arises through the interaction of many causative factors. Each is far too extensive to be produced by any one social movement, although one or more movements may be involved in the change process. Cultural drifts thus often provide an opportunity for social movements to prod and hasten developments already under way. For the past century, a cultural drift has been running toward more nearly equal rights for all kinds of groups—age, sex, religious, political, racial, or ethnic. This cultural drift makes it almost a certainty that present social movements seeking social equality for racial minorities with whites will eventually succeed, while present movements to resist such changes will eventually fail. Thus do cultural drifts aid or doom a social movement.

Social disorganization and social movements

"I took away their despair," said Nasser to explain his devoted following in the Arab world. Before a man can be a leader, there must be people ready to be led. Few such people are found in stable, well-integrated societies. The members of a well-integrated society are generally complacent and secure, feel no discontent, and have no interest in change. They rarely join social movements. It is the changing society—simple or complex—in which social movements flourish.

A changing society is always to some extent disorganized. As we outlined in the last chapter, societies differ greatly in the speed with which they change and in the degree to which a particular change disorganizes the culture. Social disorganization brings confusion and uncertainty to a society's members, since their traditions no longer form a dependable guide to behavior. In a disorganized society, individuals tend to become rootless and anomic. Leo Srole has drawn up an anomie scale which reveals some of the characteristics of the anomic frame of mind. In ascending order of intensity, these characteristics are: (1) a feeling that the community leaders are indifferent to a man's needs; (2) a feeling that little can be accomplished in a society which he sees as basically unpredictable and disorderly; (3) a feeling that his life goals are slipping out of reach; (4) a general sense of futility; and (5) a conviction that he cannot count on his personal associates for social and psychological support [Merton, 1957a, pp. 164–169].

Another concept which describes the individual's imperfect integration with his society is the concept of *alienation*. This is more inclusive than anomie, for it includes the components of *powerlessness, normlessness,* and *social isolation* [Nettler, 1957; Dean, 1961]. It is, therefore, an almost complete emotional separation from the society.

Once-honored rules no longer seem to be binding.

Alienation and anomie become widespread states of mind in a disorganized society. Their symptoms are insecurity, confusion, restlessness, and suggestibility. Once-honored rules no longer seem binding and once-cherished goals no longer attainable, while no other rules or goals seem worth the

effort. Such a confused and frustrated setting is ideal for the appearance and growth of social movements.

The spread of the Ghost Dance among the American Indians illustrates the relationship between social disorganization and social movements [McKern and McKern, 1970]. This was a dance which, if performed properly, was supposed to bring the end of the white man and the return of the buffalo. It originated among the North Paiutes of Nevada and spread in two great waves in 1870 and 1890. However, it spread only among those peoples whose tribal life was seriously disrupted, mainly by the destruction of the buffalo [Lesser, 1933]. Each tribe participated in Ghost Dance ceremonials with an intensity roughly proportional to the amount of deprivation they suffered through the disruption of their tribal life [Nash, 1937]. The Sioux, flushed with recent victories and favorable treaties under Red Cloud ignored the Ghost Dance in the 1870s; but by 1890, wretched and dispirited on a reservation, they eagerly adopted it. The Navaho, who remained prosperous and comfortable throughout this period, greeted the Ghost Dance with an amused and tolerant indifference; but when the Great Depression of the 1930s brought acute distress to the Navaho, aboriginal ceremonials had a remarkable revival [Kluckhohn, 1938].

Frustration and confusion, rather than poverty and misery, spawn social movements. People can be emotionally secure and contented at a miserable level of bare subsistence, *if* their value system defines this deprivation as a necessary and proper condition of life. Corruption, social inequality, and social injustice do not necessarily doom a social system. Many social systems have remained stable and unshakable for centuries, despite grinding poverty, rampant corruption, and gross exploitation. Such a social order can survive as long as most members can attain the goals they have been encouraged to pursue. Man is so pliable and educable that almost any kind of social system will appear good to him, if it has a fair degree of internal consistency and if he is properly socialized to live within it. Therefore, traditional societies are often highly stable until they once begin to change; once the traditional customs and values are questioned, the people may experience a tremendous inflation of wishes, sometimes called a "revolution of rising expectations." Revolutions are most likely to occur, not when a people are most miserable, but after things have begun to improve [Brinton, 1938, pp. 40-44; Street and Street, 1961]. What apparently happens is that, although people have begun to live better, their scale of wants expands so much more rapidly that they are more frustrated than ever. Revolutions and other uprisings are especially likely to break out after a downturn has interrupted a period of improvement, creating an intolerable gap between rising expectations and falling realizations [Davies, 1962; Geschwender, 1968].

Social discontent

Social discontent is a widespread general dissatisfaction with the existing society. It has at least three roots: relative deprivation, perception of injustice, and status inconsistency.

Relative deprivation The concept of *relative deprivation*, proposed by Stouffer [1949], means that one *feels* deprived according to the gap between what one has and what he feels he should have. Farmers in the National Farm Organization felt deprived when they compared their income and working hours with those of factory workers [Morrison and Steeves, 1967]. The greatest discontent and protest among college students in the 1960s arose, not at the inferior colleges with a conformist atmosphere and little student freedom, but at the finest and most liberal schools, where student expectations were high. Consequently, schools where the students had the least objective cause for complaint were nonetheless the schools with the greatest gap between student expectations and institutional realities [Keniston, 1969, p. 238]. Wherever hopes and expectations rise faster than realizations, feelings of relative deprivation increase.

Relative deprivation is increasing throughout most of the underdeveloped world. The traditional folk societies are being disorganized at a rapid rate. All over the world, the impoverished peoples are getting the notion that poverty, hunger, and illness are not necessary after all. They are beginning to long for bicycles, radios, refrigerators, and all the other things that glitter along the slope of endlessly ascending desires. They hunger for these treasures but have little real understanding of what it takes to produce them. Therefore, even where people are beginning to get some of the things they covet, the satisfactions come with a tantalizing and unbearably frustrating slowness. A weakening of traditional and tribal controls generally accompanies this enormous inflation of desires. It will be a remarkable achievement if the underdeveloped areas are able to carry through an orderly program of economic and social development. Meanwhile, the population explosion in the underdeveloped countries, combined with limited rural opportunity, is sending hordes of peasant peoples to the cities, where they huddle in squalid suburban slums, as described on page 444. Uneducated and untrained, many are unemployed and often come to share the "culture of poverty" which Oscar Lewis has so eloquently described [1959, 1963a, 1963b, 1965, 1966]. Cut off from the extended family and village life which formerly made their poverty bearable, and unable to enter successfully into the urban culture, these rootless, alienated unfortunates are the potential shock troops for tomorrow's revolutionary movements.

Perception of injustice Social injustice is not an objective social fact; it is a subjective value judgment. Is it just or unjust that one man should have ten times, or ten thousand times, as much wealth as another? This depends upon one's beliefs and values. In a number of countries the masses live in abject poverty while the rich live in Sybaritic splendor, pay virtually no taxes, and block all attempts at social reform. Is such a social system unjust? Most readers will probably think so; but whether a social system is unjust is not the crucial question. It is when a social system is *perceived* as unjust by its members that they become frustrated and alienated. Perceived social injustice thus provides both a desire for change and a moral justification for breaking heads, if necessary, to get it [Turner, 1968].

A sense of injustice is not limited to the miserable poor. Any group, at any status level, may come to feel itself the victim of social injustice. A wealthy class, firmly believing that its wealth and privileges are just and proper, may suffer an intense and righteous sense of injustice when faced with "confiscatory" taxes or land-reform policies intended to benefit others. Whether such policies are "objectively" just is impossible to establish, since "justice" is a matter of values. But a *feeling* of social injustice provides fertile soil for social movements, equally among the rich, the poor, and the in-betweens.

Status inconsistency *Status inconsistency*, described on pages 112–113, develops when one's several statuses are not equally ranked [Lenski, 1954; Goffman, 1957; Malewski, 1966]. People who have a strong feeling of status inconsistency are likely to feel deprived and improperly recognized and rewarded.

These three factors—relative deprivation, perception of injustice, and status inconsistency—when all are present in the same person, make for a discontent and readiness to join social movements.

Structural preconditions for social movements

In a provocative synthesis, Stockdale [1970] suggests five preconditions for the appearance of collective action: (1) *social discontent;* (2) *structural blockage* (barriers in the social structure which prevent people from removing the sources of their discontent); (3) *contact* (interaction between the discontented); (4) *efficacy* (the probability that proposed action will relieve discontent); and (5) *ideology* (a body of beliefs which justify and support the proposed action). When all these are present, collective action is almost inevitable. Table 37 shows Stockdale's application of this synthesis to several recent social movements. A synthesis of this sort, if sound, should enable us to predict which groups are likely to spawn active social movements in the near future. A longitudinal study would be needed to test Stockdale's propositions.

PERSONAL SUSCEPTIBILITY TO SOCIAL MOVEMENTS

In a stable, well-integrated society with very few social tensions or alienated groups, there are few social movements and few people who are interested. Contented people rarely join social movements. Those who are at peace within themselves and with their society are likely to be fully absorbed in their own activities. They generally view social movements with either amusement, indifference, or hostility. But in a changing, continuously disorganized society, the fully contented person is a rarity. More people in such a society believe they perceive social injustice and become dissatisfied or alienated. It is the dissatisfied who build social movements. The frustrated and misplaced, the restless and rootless, those who putter in boredom, those who seethe with hostility, and those who are oppressed by the futility of their present lives—these are the material of which most social movements are built. Let us note some of the circumstances apparently associated with such states of mind.

Mobility

People on the move have little chance to put down roots and become integrated into the life of the community. Their mobility not only weakens the community's control over them; it also deprives them of the emotional satisfactions of really belonging to the local group. California, whose population doubled in less than a generation, seems to be the birthplace of more movements, cults, and sects than any other several states combined, while in low-mobility states like Vermont, an agitator can address his largest crowds in a whisper.

When mobility is forced upon people by changing circumstances, they are even more in need of a social movement as an emotional refuge. Cohn's [1957] study of European millenarian movements in the Middle Ages found that millenarian fantasies were strongest among the uprooted peasants who were forced off the land to become urban workers or beggars and unemployed. They suffered the effects of geographic mobility and downward social mobility combined. But mobility of either sort almost always produces social movements.

We should remember, of course, that this is a joint cause-and-effect relationship. That is, many people are mobile because they are rootless, and many people are rootless because they are mobile. No matter what the circumstances, high-mobility groups gener-

ally provide more than their share of a movement's converts.

Marginality

Persons who are not fully accepted and integrated into a group are termed *marginal*. The concept of marginality is more fully explained on page 320. Marginal persons are likely to feel uneasy and insecure, anxious for acceptance and resentful that it has been withheld. Stated differently, they are aware of a discrepancy between their self-image and the public image of them, and the inconsistency is frustrating.

Contented people rarely join social movements.

Marginality often seems to produce overconformity, as is shown by the fierce patriotism of the newly naturalized citizen, the tireless zeal of the new religious convert, or the meticulous etiquette of the new-rich. But sometimes marginal people give up this search for acceptance and join an unpopular social movement, as though to say, "Here, at least, *someone* appreciates me!" In fact, much of the membership and leadership of many social movements seems to have come from marginal groups in society [Lasswell and Blumenstock, 1939, pp. 277–300; Hoffer, 1951]. This does not mean that only marginal people join movements. In the case of the Cooperative Commonwealth Federation, a socialist political movement in Saskatchewan, the established leaders among the farm people became active CCF members; yet among the town businessmen, mainly the marginal persons joined [Lipset, 1950]. Since the CCF reflected basic changes in the value system of rural Saskatchewan, the opinion leaders among the farmers were among the first to join. But since the movement did not reflect the dominant values of the business community, it attracted those businessmen whose marginal acceptance had prevented them from fully internalizing the values of the business group.

Most movements draw many of their early members and leaders from the marginal persons and groups in the society. Marginal people are more susceptible because they are anxious for acceptance somewhere and are less firmly wedded to the norms and values of the groups which have only partly accepted them. But until a movement succeeds in also attracting the leaders and decision makers of the group it aims at, it generally remains weak and ineffectual.

Social isolation

Considerable research shows that persons and groups who are isolated from the community are more alienated and are more receptive to mass movements than groups whose status and work integrates them into the community. Kornhauser [1959, p. 159] says that ". . . free-lance intellectuals appear to be more disposed toward mass movements than intellectuals in corporate bodies, especially universities." The worker groups who are most receptive to social movements, especially to violent movements, are those whose work cuts them off from the larger society, such as miners, maritime workers, and longshoremen [Kornhauser, 1959, chap.

12]. Because of either geographical location or social structure, these workers have few social contacts with other groups in the society. They rarely belong to the mixed-membership voluntary associations which thrive among other groups. They have few opportunities to participate in the formal and informal life of the community; their ties to the established order are weak, and they are more easily mobilized to overthrow it.

Changing social status

No evidence shows that activity in social movements is more intense at one class level than another, but evidence does show that a *change* of status increases susceptibility. Upward mobility brings a person into new class groupings in which his position is marginal and where he is somewhat insecure. But a loss of social status, or threatened loss, is still more unsettling. There is a good deal of evidence that those who feel they are suffering downward mobility are abnormally hostile toward other groups and are more often violent and authoritarian in their social attitudes [Bettelheim and Janowitz, 1950, pp. 55ff; Srole, 1956; Kaufman, 1957], and are good candidates for social movements [Geschwender, 1968]. In Germany the farmers who voted most heavily for Hitler between 1932 and 1934 were neither the rich nor the poor, but were the commercial-type farmers who were most vulnerable to market changes [Loomis and Beagle, 1946; Heberle, 1951, pp. 222–236]. In other words, the farmers who feared that they might become poor turned Nazi more regularly than did those who were already poor. But all the observers of Nazism agree that the strongest support before the Nazis gained power came from the lower-middle-class shopkeepers, tradesmen, and artisans who, having lost their savings in the postwar inflation, were now being squeezed between the gains of organized labor and

TABLE 37

Structural preconditions for the emergence of collective action: Four examples

...mple	VARIABLES				
	Discontent (Inequity)	Structural blockage	Contact	Efficacy	Ideology
...tto riots	High level of discontent. Inputs of education, skills and energy tend to be inequitably rewarded—low levels of income, cultural deprivation.	Individual efforts to improve situation blocked by discrimination in jobs, housing, etc.	High level of contact among alienated ghetto dwellers. Critical mass of potential partisans.	Costs of collective action high, although individuals may perceive low potential personal costs. Chances of removing original source of discontent low.* Probable satisfaction in acting against the system.	Legitimacy of the present system questioned on both local and societal levels. Whites and "black bourgeoisie" depicted as colonial exploiters.
...ano grape ...ke	High level of discontent. Inputs of physical effort and skills receive lower returns than could be obtained in off-farm employment.	Individual unable to improve situation by increased effort, skills or negotiation. Discrimination.	Migrants in Delano area less geographically mobile than migrants in other sections of the country. Greater contact for longer time periods.	Costs of participation low relative to potential outcomes.+ Collective bargaining has been successful in industry.	Growers are depicted as greedy affluent capitalists who exploit migrants. Acceptance of collective bargaining.
...dent pro- ...(active)	High levels of discontent. Students object to being "processed" through an impersonal bureaucratic system and "channeled into an unjust society." Many altruistically concerned with inequity situations of minorities.	Individual efforts to "work through channels" usually ineffective.	Protests occur only when "critical mass" of dissatisfied students are in frequent contact.	Sanctions not generally severe in early cases of student protest.*	University depicted as an impersonal bureaucratic system which processes students and channels them into an unjust society.
...tional ...mers ...ganization ...O)	High level of discontent. Inputs of education, skills, capital and energy receive lower returns than could be earned in off-farm work.	Individual has almost no influence on prices received and only limited control of production costs.	Potential partisans are contacted by recruiters. Meetings are "rites of intensification."	Costs to participants low relative to potential outcomes.+ Collective bargaining has been successful in industry.	Processors and distributors of agricultural products depicted as exploiters of farmers. Acceptance of collective bargaining.

...r any given level of discontent, the emergence of collective action is generally positively related to the efficacy of collective action (in-
...sely related to severity of sanctions). Where the level of discontent is very great, collective action may occur even with the threat of ex-
...me sanctions.
...sts and potential payoffs to grape strikers and NFO members are principally economic. Leaders attempt to convince potential partisans
...t the probability of success is high and potential payoffs are great. The costs for specific individuals, however, may be high.
...rce: quoted by permission from Jerry D. Stockdale, "Structural Preconditions for Collective Action," paper presented at the 1970 annual
...ting of the Society for the Study of Social Problems.

the rationalization of production and distribution by the big corporations and department stores [Fromm, 1941, pp. 211-216; Mannheim, 1940, pp. 102ff.; Gerth, 1940]. The same groups formed the core of the French Poujadist movement in the 1950s, a tax-revolt movement centered among the small shopkeepers who were threatened by big-business retailing [Heberle, 1956; Lipsedge, 1956]. The most violent reaction to Martin Luther King's demonstration marches came in Northern upper-working-class neighborhoods whose residents, often first- or second-generation immigrants, had clawed their way out of the slum and feared that black neighbors would recreate the slum they had escaped [Giles, 1967]. A recent study [Rother, 1967] of John Birch Society members found that, as compared with a control group of nonmembers, the John Birch Society members had experienced far more mobility, mostly downward, and the study concluded by attributing their political extremism to their status frustrations. Probably no development is more certain to inspire a social movement than a perceived threat to the economic security and social status of some segment of the society.

Lack of family ties

The advice, "Marry and settle down," is not just a piece of rhetoric; it actually happens. When a man gets a little home with a big mortgage and a wife busily presenting him with new mouths to fill and feet to cover, he may lose his urge to man the barricades! The more extremist and unpopular the movement, the more strongly do family ties discourage one's participation. Activity in a social movement is time-consuming and competes with family responsibilities.

A person with a warm, richly satisfying family life has no emotional need to find a cause to fill the emotional void in his life,

which is seen as the main reason people join social movements [Hoffer, 1951]. Membership studies of social movements have generally found a disproportionate share of members who either have no families or are estranged from their families. This is especially true with the more radical movements. Thus Ernst and Loth's [1952, pp. 1-15] study of former American Communist Party members found that most of them joined the party during their late teens or early twenties, while still unmarried, and while engaged in bitter emancipation conflicts with their parents. During the 1930s, a youth with a strong emotional need to tell his devout-Baptist-Republican-businessman father, "You can't run *my* life!" often joined the Communist Party. Today, he can choose between "New Left" activism or "turning on" and "dropping out" as a hippie. One psychiatrist, after psychoanalytic interviews with a sample of campus revolutionists, concludes that most of them came from homes which superficially appeared to be permissive, but in which parents withdrew from and emotionally abandoned their children. He asserts that their parents' failure to provide reassurance and guidance left these children immature and lacking in the confidence and ability to pursue conventional life goals [Hendin, 1971]. But there is not yet enough research to permit psychiatric generalization about campus revolutionists. Are campus revolutionists unstable persons who are displacing their own emotional conflicts upon the society? Or are they fearlessly unmasking the hypocrisy and exploitation of an unjust society? It is possible that both propositions are in some measure correct.

Since a stable, tightly knit family life discourages activity in social movements, most revolutionary movements, from early Christianity to the Communist Party, have attacked the family. The Apostle Paul counseled Christians to remain single and undistracted if they were able to. One of the first moves of the new Communist government of China was to launch a vigorous, calculated attack upon the family, aiming to undermine family authority, sever the lines of family obligation, and transfer personal loyalties and emotional moorings from the family to the Communist Party [Chandrasekhar, 1959; Yang, 1959]. But a new regime, after it is firmly established, supports and uses the family as a conservative and stabilizing force. Thus the early Communist regime in Russia attacked the family, endorsed free love, ridiculed parental authority, and encouraged postcard divorce; in Russia today, parental authority is supported, divorce is exceedingly difficult, public morals are puritanical, and affectionate family life is officially encouraged [Alt and Alt, 1959; Kharchev, 1961]. There is no inconsistency in this about-face. It merely reveals a revolutionary movement at different stages in its career.

Personal maladjustment

In the preceding pages we have repeatedly hinted that the maladjusted are especially susceptible to social movements. Those who have failed to find a satisfying life role and a comfortable, secure status are very likely, consciously or unconsciously, to be shopping for something to bring purpose and meaning to their lives. In a perceptive discussion, Hoffer [1951, pp. 45–46] has distinguished the temporary from the permanent misfits. The temporary misfits are "people who have not found their place in life but still hope to find it." Adolescent youth, unemployed college graduates, demobilized veterans, and new immigrants are examples. Restless, frustrated, and fearful that opportunity may elude them, they are good fodder for movements but are not very dependable. As rapidly as the society can offer rewarding jobs and statuses to them, they are likely to lose interest in so-

cial movements. The permanent misfits are those who. because of limited talent or some impassable social barrier, are forever blocked from the role and status they crave. The unsuccessful artist or writer, the middle-aged craftsman whose trade is destroyed by automation and who must compete as an unskilled laborer, the single woman who desperately wants husband, home, and children but has no hope of finding them—all are permanent misfits, since there is little prospect of their ever finding a life role and status rewarding enough to absorb their interests. They remain frustrated and in emotional need of something to fill the aching void in their lives.

Are social movements, then, only a refuge for the homeless failures and misfits of society? Do such people join a movement in a sort of emotional reflex, and not as an act of intellectual judgment? Yes, to some extent. Heberle [1951, p. 113] remarks, "The neurotic, maladjusted, unbalanced or psychopathic seem to be attracted not so much by the ideas [of a movement] as by the sense of oneness, of belonging, which appeases their feelings of insecurity, of helplessness, of isolation." Certainly there are both rational and nonrational factors in movement membership, and the nonrational factors are more important than we sometimes admit. Members of the more extreme movements often shift from one movement professing one set of beliefs to another movement professing an opposite set of beliefs with very little intellectual difficulty. Thus, "Hitler looked on the German Communists as potential National Socialists. . . [Nazi] Captain Roehm boasted that he could turn the reddest Communist into a nationalist in four weeks. On the other hand, [Communist] Karl Radek looked on the Nazi Brown Shirts (S.A.) as a reserve for future Communist recruits" [Hoffer, 1951, p. 17]. Later history showed all these men to be correct. While it is dangerous to generalize about motives, such evidence lends support

to the belief that people join extremist movements to satisfy their emotional compulsions, while the rational programs of these
movements are unimportant so long as the
members' emotional yearnings are fulfilled.

Are the less extreme movements equally
nonrational? Probably not. When a movement expresses a developing consensus
of opinion among the more influential
members of the society, as the temperance
movement did in the nineteenth century
[Gusfield, 1955], as the Cooperative Commonwealth Federation did in Saskatchewan
[Lipset, 1950], or as the civil rights movement did in the 1950s, such a movement
attracts the responsible leaders of the community, not the misfits. Probably most of
the members of a movement find some element of emotional compensation in their
activity, as nearly all of us find it in our own
behavior. But the evidence would not justify
a conclusion that movements arise solely
from the people's need to scratch their emotional itch.

All the above conditions help to prepare
people who are receptive to the appeal of a
social movement. The circumstances do not
"cause" important mass movements. Unless
there is deep and widespread social discontent, any movement growing purely from
the misfits' hunger for a crusade will have
no future. But when social unrest is intense
and alienation and anomie become normal,
then the homeless, the status cliff-hangers,
and the misfits become the shock troops of
mass movements which can set an entire
nation on fire. The ultimate consequences
depend upon the actions of the responsible
leaders of the society. If they perceive social
injustices in need of correction and social
tensions in need of resolution, assume leadership, and channel this mass protest into
constructive social reforms, the main features of the social system may be conserved.
But if they seek to block social reforms
which are passionately sought and long
overdue, as did the eighteenth-century

French or the early twentieth-century Russian aristocrats, they guarantee the eventual
destruction of the social system.

TYPES OF SOCIAL MOVEMENTS

To classify social movements is not always
easy, for sometimes a movement is intermediate or mixed in nature, or is different
at different stages of its career. As always,
the categories below are "ideal types," into
which actual movements more or less perfectly fall.

Migratory movements

At the close of the Civil War, about ten thousand Southerners left the country rather
than endure the Yankee Reconstruction and
established colonies in Mexico and Brazil
[Nunn, 1956; Ross and Kerner, 1958].
Sometimes discontent with present circumstances, together with the lure of a greener
distant pasture, leads large numbers of people to migrate. The mere fact that a lot of
people migrate does not create a migratory
social movement, nor is one created purely
by the number of people who move, each for
private and widely varied reasons. We have
a migratory social movement when there is
a common focus of discontent, a shared purpose or hope for the future, and a widely discussed and shared decision to move to a new
location, regardless of whether they migrate
as an organized group or as individuals and
families. The northward migration of Southern Negroes began to assume the proportions of a social movement about the time
of World War I and only today is beginning
to subside. A more spectacular example is
the Irish migration in which over 750,000
of the Irish people, already economically
distressed and politically discontented, left
their country in the five years following the
great potato-crop failures beginning in 1845

[Morehouse, 1928]. In the seventeen years before the Berlin Wall was built in 1961, over 4 million East Germans fled the dull grey monotony of the German Democratic Republic. This was over one-fourth of that country's population, making this one of the greatest mass migrations in history [Gilroy, 1961; Bailey, 1961].

Zionism: a contemporary migratory social movement For over 2,000 years, Jews have dreamed of a return to the "Promised Land." A succession of self-styled messiahs following the end of the middle ages stimulated much excitement, but no solid accomplishments. Yet interest remained, and Theodore Herzl fanned this impulse into a political movement at the first Zionist congress in 1897. But the attractions of the Zionist movement paralleled the degree of Jewish persecution throughout the world. Migration to Palestine (now Israel) during the 1920s was limited by the British Government, which ruled Palestine under a League of Nations mandate, and allowed only a trickle of immigrants. During the 1930s, migration multiplied greatly as Jewish persecution in Europe mounted, much of this migration in violation of British regulations. By 1948, when the United Nations attempted to resolve the Arab-Jewish question by partitioning Palestine into separate states, the Jewish population of Palestine was only 35 percent native-born. Jewish immigration continued at a high rate, with the native-born fraction of the Jewish population of Israel falling as low as 25 percent in 1951, then rising to 37 percent in 1960.

Arab opposition to Jewish migration and to the establishment of the state of Israel led to wars in 1947, 1956, and 1967, and this conflict remains unresolved. Many accounts sympathetic to the Israeli cause are available [Hurewitz, 1968; Eckhardt and Eckhardt, 1970; Segre, 1971], an occasional critical account is found [Lilienthal, 1965], and, rarely, an Arab point of view appears in

English [Abu-Lughod, 1970]. Meanwhile Jewish migration to Israel continues, and the future rate of migration will be as greatly determined by what happens to Jews elsewhere as by what happens in Israel.

Expressive movements

When people are bottled up within a confining social system from which they cannot flee and which they feel powerless to change, the result generally is an expressive social movement. In the expressive movement the individual comes to terms with an unpleasant external reality *by modifying his reactions to that reality*, not by modifying the external reality itself. Through some kind of activity—dreams, visions, rituals, dances, games, or other forms of emotional expression—he finds enough emotional release to make life bearable. Often the expressive movement is millenarian. Dozens of movements have helped people to ignore a miserable present by fixing their gaze upon a glorious millennium that is about to dawn [Cohn, 1957].

Most millenarian movements are purely escapist in that they occupy people with happy dreams while the existing realities remain unchanged. Yet the millenarian movement may pave the way for eventual reform or revolt because it cuts ties to the past, and may function as a unifying and arousing force in a previously passive population. Thus it may serve as a connecting link between prepolitical and actively political movements [Talmon, 1962].

Expressive movements are many and varied. The medieval flagellants sought a release from their sense of sin and personal unworthiness (and possibly gratified other compulsions) by masochistic orgies [Cohn, 1957, chap. 6]. A modern religious movement like Youth for Christ, which concentrates upon changing persons, not upon changing the society, is an expressive movement. Some scholars would include crazes, fads, and fashions as expressive movements [Blumer, 1969a, pp. 114–119], but the present writers consider them too trivial to be social movements and have discussed them in Chapter 17, "Collective Behavior."

The cargo cult: a contemporary expressive movement The native peoples of Melanesia, like most primitive peoples everywhere, considered the white man's social system inferior to theirs but the white man's goods highly desirable. They noted that the white men apparently did not work; only the natives worked. Yet shiploads of wonderful cargo kept appearing over the horizon. Since they already believed that the Europeans were spirits of their dead ancestors, sent to bring these things to them, it was only a small step to believe in the myth that a vast cargo, temporarily diverted by the whites, would some day arrive in ships and planes along with the spirits of their ancestors. The cargo would arrive when they had successfully performed the proper rituals and completed the right preparations to receive and store it. Then the whites would be driven away, and the cargo would revert to its rightful owners. These beliefs arose among various Melanesian peoples, becoming widespread in the 1920s. They led to a little violence in some places and to government attempts at suppression, but the movement was mainly nonviolent. Faith was not diminished by failure of the cargo to arrive, and cargo cults still remain active in the area. Cargo cults are understandable as the response of people who have developed an intense desire for European goods but have very limited means for getting them. Like all millenarian movements, they are the effort of a confused and frustrated people to make new adjustments to situations of social crisis for which their traditional culture has no satisfactory answers [Worsley, 1957; Firth, 1955].

Utopian movements

Ever since Sir Thomas More wrote his *Utopia*, the term has meant a society of such perfection that it can be found only in man's imagination. Many other writers had a try at describing a perfect society, from Plato in his *Republic* to B. F. Skinner in *Walden II*. Many attempts to create such a perfect society were made in the eighteenth and nineteenth centuries when utopian movements were popular [Nordhoff, 1875; Davis, 1930, chap. 2]. Since these idealists were never able to experiment with an entire society, the utopian movement was an attempt to create an ideal social system within a small community of dedicated followers; later this system might expand to include the entire society. Many of the utopian communities which were strongly religious survived longer because they did not have to "pay off" in personal happiness or material well-being. The payoff was in following the will of God. But other utopian communities, like Brook Farm and the Oneida Community, were secular in ideology. They were based on a conception of man as basically good, cooperative, and altruistic, needing only a favorable setting to unlock these virtues. Most of the religious and all of the secular utopian movements failed, either because of inner contradictions and impracticabilities or because of conflict with the external society [Burton, 1939; Halloway, 1951; Bestor, 1950, 1970].

The utopian ideal, however, remains very much alive. Skinner's *Walden II* [1948] is possibly the best-known example of contemporary utopian literature, but there are many other modern utopians [Kateb, 1971]. It is likely that people will never cease trying to imagine a more perfect society.

The commune: a contemporary utopian social movement The commune, described briefly on page 216, is spreading among those who are variously called hippies, dropouts, freaks, or members of the "alternative society." While some of the members are obvious misfits who could not "make it" under any social system, many are highly talented, well educated, and appear to be emotionally stable. All share a conviction that conventional society is hypocritical, exploitative, destructive of human values, decadent, and hopelessly doomed by its own contradictions. They see their alternative society as an answer to loneliness, alienation, exploitation, and social injustice.

While rejecting the orthodox churches as either hypocritical or simply irrelevant, most communards are highly religious. Some are "Jesus freaks," who reject "hard" drugs and sexual promiscuity, and seek to live the simple communal life of the early New Testament Christians. Many have a sympathetic interest in the Eastern religions (Hindu, Buddhist) and a wide range of mystic and occult beliefs [Lidz and Rothenberg, 1968].

In some communes the members hold regular jobs; but in many, the main source of funds is welfare, plus some income from odd jobs, occasional work, sale of handicraft objects, and contributions from parents. The nonworking commune is thus parasitic upon the society, and therefore cannot serve as the utopian model for the entire society to copy. If the alternative society of the commune is to be generally accepted, the commune in which most people work will need to be the model.

The alternative-society movement, like all utopian movements, faces the scorn and opposition of conventional people. Reports of police harassment are common, and some rural communes have been literally "run off" by local residents who, among other objections, may have feared the commune's attraction for their own youth. Since communards are typically rather gentle people without weapons or much inclination to

fight, they have been prey to thievery and to the bullying of motorcycle toughs, for whom terrorizing a commune is a favorite sport.

To date, communards have been drawn mainly from white, middle- or upper-class youth. Will the commune spread among the black and the poor, many of whom have long practiced a semi-communal sharing of their meager resources [Davis, 1946]? Possibly, but it is also possible that the commune appeals only to those who have experienced the comfortable, conventional life style of the middle and upper classes and found it unsatisfying.

Reform movements

The reform movement is an attempt to modify some parts of the society without completely transforming it. Reform movements are impossible in an authoritarian society whose rulers tolerate no criticism. Reform movements can operate only in a democratic atmosphere where people have considerable freedom to criticize existing institutions and may secure changes in them when the majority wishes.

American history is crowded with reform movements—abolition, feminism, prohibition, and many others. In the past month one of your authors has received fund appeals from at least two dozen reform movements and organizations, all seeking some reform in American law or public practice—several seeking equal rights for blacks, and one or more concerned with wildlife conservation, ecological destruction, wilderness preservation, national parks' protection, birth control and population policy, sharecroppers, American Indians, nuclear policy, and one from the "Defenders of Furbearers," seeking to outlaw the "cruel" steel trap—besides several appeals from groups who wish to reform other parts of the world. One of the most recent reform movements is the

Gay Liberation Movement, in which many homosexuals have "come out of the closet" and organized to demand acceptance of homosexuality as a legitimate alternative life style [Miller, 1971]. Our democratic atmosphere, our Judeo-Christian values, and our tradition of voluntarism have combined to make reform movements a conspicuous feature of past and present American history.

Women's Liberation: a contemporary reform movement The feminist movement of the nineteenth and early twentieth centuries, after considerable dispute over goals and tactics, finally united upon the goal of woman suffrage, and soon dissolved after this goal was won [O'Neill, 1969]. Today's Women's Liberation Movement found its ideology in books such as Simone de Beauvior's *The Second Sex* [1953], Betty Friedan's *The Feminine Mystique* [1963], and Kate Millet's *Sexual Politics* [1970]. But the spark which ignited the movement was the condescending treatment of women in the New Left [Piercy, 1970], whose attitude was epitomized in Stokely Carmichael's famous dictum that "the only position for women in S.N.C.C. is prone" [*Time*, Nov. 21, 1969, p. 54]. As one woman reports, "Suddenly women found themselves *serving*, as secretary, mother and concubine, while men did all the speaking, writing and negotiating—and these were men who professed to reject the 'oppressive' ritual machinery of their society" [Gottlieb, 1971, p. 27].

While pique may have thrown the spark, it fell upon the tinder of undeniable sex discrimination and the recent decline in the status of women in American society (see pages 217–220 for documentation and a brief description of the philosophy and goals of Women's Lib). The movement consists of hundreds of local groups, many of which are affiliated with a national organization. The National Organization of Women (NOW) is

the largest and probably the most conservative, whose goal is to "bring women into full participation in the mainstream of American society now, exercising all the privileges and responsibilities thereof in truly equal partnership with men" [Wilkes, 1970, p. 143]. Some other groups are more radical, such as Women's International Terrorist Conspiracy From Hell (WITCH) or Women's Radical Action Project (WRAP), and a continuous reshuffling of organizational structures can be expected. The more radical members of Women's Lib are generally ardent New Leftists, who see the liberation of women as merely one aspect of a total revolution in the society.

Reliable membership studies are not available, but a casual inspection of Women's Lib groups shows that the members are predominantly white, educated, middle-class, and relatively young. One sociologist-member claims that conversion to Women's Lib requires that a woman have: (1) means and resources to pursue some alternative to the traditional female sex role; (2) a political sophistication about the uses of power; (3) a sense of achievement discrepancy between her potentials and her accomplishments; and (4) a long-term pattern of defiance of traditional values, with practically all members being religious unbelievers, sexually "emancipated," and illegal drug users or experimenters [Micossi, 1970]. The main conversion technique is the "consciousness-raising" session, in which a group of ten or fifteen women, under a leader, are encouraged to examine and discuss their personal experiences in the light of "sexism" (the ascribing of subordinate roles to women) and "male chauvinism" (patronizing condescension to women) [Gornick, 1971]. Consciousness-raising sessions are devoted to arousing an awareness of the many subtle ways in which women's subordinate role is maintained.

Is Women's Lib a rational response to the culture lag between our democratic egalitarian ethos and our patterns of sex discrimination? Or is it a displacement of the emotional problems of unhappy, neurotic women? Are they unhappy and neurotic because of cultural lags in the status and treatment of women, or because of emotional difficulties which would make them unhappy and neurotic in any cultural setting? While reliable evidence is lacking, it is likely that all these propositions are in considerable part true. At the least, the relatively moderate goals of NOW are no more than are required by the democratic ethos and the Civil Rights Act of 1964. It is also likely that, as with most social movements, the more active members—the "true believers" Hoffer describes [1951]—derive their commitment from their own emotional discontents. Journalistic biographical sketches of a few leaders and members show a high proportion who have a history of marital failure, and of frustration and dissatisfaction with female sex roles [Wilkes, 1970; Gornick, 1971]. Some members reveal an aggressive hostility toward men and would much prefer a karate black belt to a wedding ring. So, while it is likely that Women's Lib attracts a high proportion of frustrated, hostile people, this is true of many movements, and does not necessarily invalidate a movement's claims. While the more radical goals of Women's Lib may never be attained, the movement appears to have revived a cultural drift towards sex equality which had been stalled for decades.

Revolutionary movements

A *revolution* is *a sudden, usually violent, and relatively complete change in a social system.* It is distinguished from the coup d' etat, or palace revolt, which replaces the individuals who rule, but leaves the institutions and the power system of the society unchanged. The term is sometimes applied to gradual, sweeping, peaceful changes such as the industrial revolution or the "sexual revolution," but this is a different usage of the term. The revolutionary movement seeks to overthrow the existing social system and replace it with a greatly different one. Unlike the reformer who wants to correct some imperfections in the present social order, the revolutionist considers the system not worth saving. The reformer is, therefore, the revolutionist's worst enemy, for social reforms may drain off the discontent upon which the revolutionist wishes to build his revolution.

A democracy is poor soil for revolution. A revolutionary movement must be rooted in a tremendous social discontent; but in a democracy, social unrest generally leads to social reform, and reform indefinitely postpones the revolution. But where authoritarian government blocks the popular wish for reform, the reformer must then attack the government, and he becomes a revolutionist. Revolutionary movements flourish where reform is blocked so that the revolutionary movement is the people's only alternative to their present misery. It is no accident that the Communist Party is weakest in the thoroughly democratic countries like the United States, England, and the Scandinavian countries, and is far stronger in countries with a tradition of repressive government, or where government is nominally democratic, yet is so structured as to be an ineffective instrument of the popular wish for reform. In France and Italy, many people despair of reform and turn to revolutionary parties [Cantril, 1958].

Edwards [1927] and Brinton [1938] have independently arrived at a practically identical sequence of stages which they believe to be typical of most successful revolutions: (1) an accumulation of deep unrest, stretching over many years; (2) the defection of the intellectuals, who grow increasingly critical of the status quo; (3) the emergence of an economic incentive for revolt and a social myth or set of beliefs to justify it; (4) the revolutionary outbreak, aided by the hesitation and weakness of the ruling group; (5) the rule of the moderates, who soon fail to control the various groups among the revolutionists or to satisfy the aroused passions of the populace; (6) the rise of the radicals or extremists, who gain power and begin to exterminate all opposition; (7) the reign of terror; (8) the return to normality, as moderates regain power, consolidate the achievements of the revolution, and restore some aspects of the prerevolutionary society. This outline is based largely upon the French and Russian revolutions; the more recent Mexican revolution has followed this course fairly closely. How closely the Chinese and Cuban revolutions will follow the pattern remains to be seen.

Sometimes it is difficult to classify a movement as clearly reform or clearly revolutionary, since the supporters cover a broad spectrum ranging from moderate reformers to violent revolutionists. Women's Lib is an example. The Black Panther Party is revolutionary in goals and tactics, at least as it affects black people, although it would leave white society in much its present condition [Foner, 1970].

The New Left: a contemporary revolutionary movement The spirit of protest among mainly the younger people also ranges from reformist to revolutionary. The young reformers and the young revolutionists are in considerable agreement in their indictment of the present society as unjust, exploitative, and destructive of humanity, but they differ in their prescription. The reformers work "within the system" to effect change, using nonviolent demonstration and political activity as means. Reformers admire "Nader's Raiders," the team working with Ralph Nader, while revolutionists consider such efforts irrelevant or even counterproductive. The New Left is especially contemptuous of the liberal. One observer reports that "All New Leftists agree

on *liberal*. He is universally defined as a hypocritical, selling-out vacillator, a guilt-ridden moralist unable to act decisively because he sees all sides of an issue; a picker at tiny parts of a problem who thereby fails to solve any of it; an immoral man" [Romm, 1970, p. 247].

There are numerous published descriptions of the revolutionary New Left. Some are critical [Feuer, 1968; Gerberding and Smith, 1970; Kelman, 1970], some are neutrally descriptive and analytical [Cohen and Hall, 1971], and some are sympathetic [Hoffman, 1968; Lynd, 1969; Oglesby, 1969]. Some are compilations of New Left statements, handbills, posters, and other material [Berke, 1969; Romm, 1970].

Like most revolutionists, many New Leftists are at times undemocratic in seeking to impose their views, even when they are minority views, upon the majority by any means considered effective. Sometimes they are ruthlessly intolerant of dissent [Kelman, 1970], shouting down public speakers whom they wish to silence and disrupting meetings they wish to paralyze, as described in a New Left news release:

To the consternation of many liberal professors and students, radical activists have shown their unwillingness to adhere to the niceties of bourgeois civil libertarianism when it comes to persons associated with war crimes, U.S. Imperialism, and reactionary and racist domestic policies.

Saigon's ambassador to the U.N., Nguyen Huu Chi, was draped in a Nazi flag and doused with water by student radicals as he attempted to speak at New York University recently. The demonstrators found James Reston of the *New York Times* speaking elsewhere in the building and disrupted his talk too, chanting, "Bourgeois press eats shit!"

A representative of the U.S. Agency for International Development, Joseph Mendenhall, didn't get through his speech at Northwestern University in Chicago recently. Mendenhall was speaking on "American Non-Military Commitment in Southeast Asia" when the lights went out and a small guerrilla band got him in the face with two piepans of whipped cream.

A University of Southern California professor was giving a speech about urban development at El Camino College near Torrance, Calif., recently, when a militant student group called Human Education Power, disrupted the meeting to present ten demands to the administration. The speaker was not allowed to finish his talk, as the students said his remarks had racist overtones. *(Allen Young, "Bourgeois Civil Libertarianism," Liberation News Service, New York, Dec. 14, 1968.)*

The New Leftists' belief that "the end justifies the means" in their case is illustrated by their conviction that:

Severe means are necessary and appropriate techniques for destroying all or substantial parts of the American political system *because that system is undemocratic and illegitimate.* **They refuse to abide by the "rules of the game" because they do not approve of the "game" and they want to create a new one. They contend that their ends—fundamentally reordering the American political system and its social, economic and educational underpinnings—justify their means.** *(William P. Gerberding,* The Radical Left, *Houghton Mifflin Company, Boston, 1970, pp. 312–313. Reprinted by permission of the publisher.)*

The historical revolutionary idea that anything is right if it promotes the revolution is carried to its logical conclusion in Abbie Hoffman's *Steal This Book* [1971], a detailed instruction manual in how to steal, cheat, and defraud and thus to overthrow the established order by making normal business operations impossible to conduct.

The New Left's intellectual mentors are Fanon [1961], Marx, Marcuse [1964; 1969], and Reich [1970]; its heroes are Mao, Castro, and Che Guevera. The New Left is nonprogrammatic in that it concentrates largely upon attacking the established order but gives very little attention to the blueprints for the society which should replace it. Many of the revolutionists seem to be more attracted by the process of disruption than by any set of goals (as suggested by Abbie Hoffman's *Revolution for the Hell of It* [1968]).

While their ideology draws heavily from Marxian social thought, with much admiration of China and Cuba, the New Left despises Russia and the Communist Party of the United States, seeing them as traitors to the cause of humanity. No ideological pigeonhole perfectly fits the New Left, but *anarchism* is the most appropriate label.

The future of the New Left is difficult to foresee. Most current youth protest is reformative, not revolutionary. Whether a movement becomes and remains reformative or revolutionary depends heavily upon the response of the society [Shaskolsky, 1968]. Reformers turn revolutionist when reforms are blocked. As this is written, the campuses are quieter than for several years past, the Students for a Democratic Society has splintered into factions, and the Black Panther Party is in disarray, with some leaders dead and most of the rest in jail or exile, busily reading one another out of the party [*New York Times*, Mar. 7, 1971, p. 26]. But the revolutionary movement is far from extinguished, and it will flourish in proportion as discontents accumulate.

Resistance movements

The revolutionary movement arises among people who are dissatisfied because social change is too slow. The resistance movement arises among those dissatisfied because change is too fast. The resistance movement is an effort to block a proposed change or to uproot a change already achieved. The Ku Klux Klan is perhaps our best-known resistance movement, organized in the South after the Civil War to keep Negroes "in their place" by terror and intimidation [Brown, 1902, part 4; Mecklin, 1924], and reborn in the North after World War I as a nativistic movement [VanderZanden, 1960; Alexander, 1965]. The nativistic movement is an attempt to protect the purity of the group and its culture from new or foreign intrusions [Higham, 1955; Friedman, 1967]. The Native American party and the Know-Nothing movements of the 1830s and 1840s were anti-immigrant and anti-Catholic, and coincided with an increase of Irish and German immigration to the United States. As in most resistance movements, there was a large element of scapegoating in the focusing of frustrations arising from many sources upon the immigrant, who was blamed for practically all troubles.

In a democratic society, all periods of rapid change will stimulate resistance movements. The New Deal era of reform produced a large number of them [Schlesinger, 1960, vol. 3, chap. 1]. Some, like the Committee for Constitutional Government and the American Liberty League, were largely fund-collecting offices for the distribution of anti-New Deal propaganda. Others like the Silver Shirts, the Black Legion, and the Christian Americans were would-be mass movements which united opposition to New Deal reforms with anti-Semitism, isolationism, and antiforeign sentiments in a fascist-type organization [Lowenthal and Guterman, 1949; Carlson, 1943, 1946]. More recently the movement of extreme resistance to liberalism, internationalism, and welfare statism has come to be known as the "radical right" [Bell, 1963]. Recently the "New Right" has appeared, differing slightly from the radical right in being less preoccupied with anti-communism, and favoring a thorough and consistent return to laissez faire economics and minimum government activity [Lipset, 1968; Lehr and Rossetto, 1971]. The most "far-out" resistance movement of all is the Minutemen, a secret network of small groups who collect arms and train to prepare an armed resistance to an expected communist seizure of power [Jones, 1968].

Over ninety resistance organizations appeared in the wake of the Supreme Court's school desegregation decision in 1954. The most successful was the White Citizens' Councils, which claimed 65 chapters and 80,000 members in Mississippi alone [VanderZanden, 1959; Routh and Anthony, 1957; Cater, 1956]. The councils applied economic sanctions to any person, white or Negro, who supported desegregation. The councils included many prominent politicians and business leaders, and were able to exert enough influence so that desegregation supporters were likely to be dismissed from their jobs, evicted from rented properties, have credit withdrawn, and suffer other economic penalties. Uncooperative businessmen might be boycotted by wholesalers and have their loans called and their insurance canceled. The White Citizens' Councils apparently succeeded, at least temporarily, for there was practically no school desegregation in large areas of the South where the councils were most active. While their greatest strength remains in the Deep South, they have spread into border and northern states as the segregation controversies have moved northward [Baker, 1970].

The John Birch Society: a contemporary resistance movement The John Birch Society is perhaps the most influential of the long list of organizations resisting most of the social reforms of the past half century [Barrett, 1961; Mosk and Jewel, 1961; Grove, 1961; Buckley, 1966; Freedman, 1966; Epstein and Forster, 1967; Anti-Defamation League, 1969]. The society was founded in December, 1958, by Robert Welch, Jr., a retired businessman who describes democracy as government by "mobocracy," and has branded the late President Eisenhower as a "dedicated, conscious agent of the communist conspiracy" (although some members think this is going a little "too far"). Mr. Welch's book, the *Blue Book of the John Birch Society* is a quite remarkable volume which tells how nearly all of America's recent leaders have been pro-Communist, and how even most of the anti-communist organizations are secretly communist. While avowedly anti-communist, Mr. Welch and his followers concentrated mainly upon attacking American moderates like the late President Eisenhower, Chief Justice Earl Warren, and the late Mrs. Eleanor Roosevelt. Mr. Welch's prime immediate objective was the impeachment of Chief Justice Warren as long as he remained in office. The movement thus falls into the standard pattern of recent American resistance movements in opposing social reforms by calling them communistic.

The movement began to grow more rapidly after the press "exposed" it, showing that there were many people ready to join an organization with its purposes. Membership figures are secret but are known to include a number of present or former congressmen and other prominent persons. It reported an annual income of around 4 million dollars a year during the late 1960s, considerably larger than the known income of any other conservative-membership organization [Baker, 1969]. The organization is semisecret and under completely authoritarian control at all levels. Mr. Welch determines its policies, handles funds without the necessity of accounting for them to its members, and is authorized to expel members at his discretion. Activities are centered upon recruiting members and denouncing "pro-Communists." Techniques include infiltrating and assuming control if possible of political parties, PTAs, and other organizations, writing campaigns, and, occasionally, telephone harassment of the society's critics and opponents.

Meanwhile other resistance movements are currently active, such as the Christian Anti-Communist Crusade, the National Education Program, the Christian Crusade, and dozens of other organizations. As some die, others are born. Wherever there is change and reform, people who are unhappy over them will organize in protest. Often these opponents use anticommunism as a vehicle for their resentment, labeling as "communist" everything and everybody they dislike. This group felt betrayed and

abandoned when the Eisenhower administration failed to dismantle the New Deal. Movements like the John Birch Society and the Christian Anti-Communist Crusade are their response.

LIFE CYCLE OF SOCIAL MOVEMENTS

No two movements are exactly alike; yet different movements have much in common. Most completed movements pass through much the same set of four stages —of unrest, excitement, formalization, and institutionalization, first suggested by W. E. Gettys [Dawson and Gettys, 1934, pp. 708 –709], who applied them to his study of the Methodist movement in England. A few accomplish their purpose without needing to enter the later stages. Other life cycles suggested by Zald and Ash [1966] and by Blumer [1969a, pp. 103–114] are quite similar, differing only in details.

Agitators seem to pop up everywhere.

The unrest stage

All movements are rooted in social unrest. When people grow bored and restless, or develop a sense of social injustice, or when some change has disrupted an established way of life, they develop an unstable volatility which we call social unrest. When they confront situations that their traditional ideology cannot explain, they are frustrated. For example, the Great Depression of the thirties brought actual destitution to millions of workers who had been socialized to believe that there must be something wrong with a man who cannot support his family. The emotional experience was shattering for most unemployed men, many of whom agonized painfully about accepting relief when it was offered. Social change, social disorganization, and social unrest are inseparable. This stage may be very prolonged, lasting as many as several generations.

The excitement stage

Unrest is vague, generalized, and unfocused. When it becomes focused on certain conditions, and when certain "causes" of misery are identified so that proposals for action fill the air, the excitement stage has come. During this stage it is easy to gather an audience, and agitators seem to pop up everywhere. Many fledgling movements are launched, mostly to founder on the rocks of clumsy leadership or ineffective appeals. Sometimes a magnetic agitator, working on people whose needs have made them receptive, can rouse a huge following almost overnight. To convert such a mass into an effective movement requires a skillful organizer. The excitement stage is typically brief, leading quickly either to action or to a loss of interest.

The formalization stage

Some of the migratory and expressive movements may be able to operate without formal organization, but those which seek to mod-

ify the society must become organized. An excited mass of followers will drift away unless their enthusiasms are ordered and directed. In the formalization stage, a chain of officers is worked out, fund raising is systematized, and the ideology of the movement is clarified. The ideology reminds people of their discontents, identifies the villians, states the movement's objectives, outlines the strategy and tactics for attaining the stated purposes, and provides the moral justification for all these actions. Formalization converts an excited mass into a disciplined membership and a vague cause into a practical enterprise. This, too, is a brief phase leading quickly into institutionalization.

The institutionalization stage

Institutionalization eventually overtakes most movements if they last long enough. The movement crystalizes into a definite pattern, including traditions to uphold and possibly vested interests to defend. Efficient bureaucrats replace zealous agitators as leaders, and members feel themselves supporters of a worthy organization rather than campaigners in a sacrificial crusade. The acquisition of elaborate office suites or buildings (as by labor organizations in recent years) is evidence that the institutionalization of the movement is complete. This stage may last almost indefinitely.

The dissolution stage

Most scholars end the movement's cycle with the institutionalization stage. But this is not really the end, for different movements come to different conclusions. A movement may die at any stage in its career. Some movements achieve their objectives and then disappear, like the movement for women's suffrage. The officers of a movement which is killed through success may attempt to switch the movement to a new objective, as the National Foundation did after polio was conquered. Such a change of direction is rarely successful. Some movements, however, do undergo a transition in which the movement comes to pursue objectives quite different from the original ones. As an example, the Townsend movement for liberal old-age pensions lost most of its members when returning prosperity and the growth of other pension plans undercut its program, but the Townsend clubs survived for quite a number of years as recreational groups of older people who were only mildly interested in the pension plan [Messinger, 1955]. A movement may shrink into a sectlike band of followers, doggedly pursuing an objective which is probably forever unattainable, such as the prohibitionist movement embodied in the Women's Christian Temperance Union [Gusfield, 1955]. Some movements achieve full institutional status and make a contribution to the institutions of the society. This progress is illustrated by the many religious sects which have completed the transition into denominations.

APPRAISAL

Do social movements do more good than harm? That is like asking if wind does more good than harm. Social movements are one of the ways a society changes itself. The changes, though often painful, would not occur unless some social force produced them.

Are the members emotionally sick people finding outlet for their compulsions, or are they generous humanitarians seeking to alleviate human suffering? Some of each! Some movements have more of one than of the other characteristic, but most move-ments have both, just as each person may have some of both within his own personality.

Will there be more new movements in the future? Yes, for social movements inevitably accompany rapid social change. What kinds? This we cannot predict. Authoritarian society encourages migratory, expressive, and perhaps revolutionary movements. An optimistic era like the eighteenth century abounds in utopian and reform movements, while, as Stephan Runciman [1956, p. 14] notes, "a disillusioned age turns to religion, as an escape from the uncertainties of the world." We can be certain only that social movements will continue to express people's dissatisfaction with the society in which they find themselves.

SUMMARY

Social movements are collective attempts to promote or resist change, either in the society or in its members. Broad cultural drifts provide a favorable setting for social movements pushing in the same direction as the cultural drift. Social change and social disorganization produce the frustration, alienation, anomie, and confusion which make people more receptive to social movements. Perceived social injustice provides both the desire for change and the moral justification for a movement's actions. Mobility, marginality, social isolation, changing social status, lack of family ties, and personal maladjustments all tend to make persons more receptive.

Movements are of several types: *migratory*, wherein people physically flee a frustrating society; *expressive*, wherein they modify themselves rather than the society and find emotional outlet through expressive behavior; *utopian*, wherein a small band seeks to create a perfect society in miniature; *re-

form, wherein a group seeks to persuade a democratic society to correct its imperfections; *revolutionary*, wherein people seek to replace the existing social system with a new one; and *resistance*, wherein conservatives seek to block or uproot social changes they dislike.

Sociologists and historians seek to describe a "typical" life cycle which movements may approximate: an *unrest* stage of widespread but unfocused discontent; an *excitement* stage, during which discontent is increased and focused; a *formalization* stage, when mass excitement is organized into effective action; an *institutionalization* stage, when the movement crystallizes into a bureaucracy, and a *dissolution* stage, when an active movement receives one of several kinds of funerals. While not always rational and sometimes annoying, social movements help a democratic society to take up cultural lags and remain passably integrated.

Questions and projects

1. How is a social movement distinguished from an institution, association, or pressure group?

2. How do cultural drifts affect social movements? Considering present cultural drifts, what do you think will be the eventual success of the prohibitionist movement? Of the John Birch Society? Of the Women's Liberation Movement? Of the movement to legalize abortion?

3. Why are social movements most likely to arise after a society begins to improve its material conditions rather than when it is in abject poverty?

4. Compared with other Western countries, has the United States had few or many social movements? Why?

5. What factors affect a person's receptivity to social movements?

6. Among the several types of social movements, which are the most numerous in present American society? Why?

7. Can you think of any social movements in the United States not mentioned in this chapter? In which classification would you place each?

8. What determines a person's decision to support one of several movements? Is it pure chance? The ideas and goals of the particular movement? The emotional needs it fills? Or what?

9. Is a movement likely to appeal to different kinds of people at different stages in its career? Why?

10. Some movements seem to attract mainly misfits and neurotics, while others attract the solid "respectables" of the community. Why? Sometimes a movement attracts the opinion leaders of one group and the misfits of another group. How do you explain this phenomenon?

11. Applying Stockdale's synthesis in Table 37, what predictions would you make about the prospects that the Women's Liberation Movement will inspire "collective action" on a mass scale?

12. How do you explain the failure of the Communist Party to build a mass movement in the United States?

13. If it should be shown that most of the leaders of a particular movement are psychologically maladjusted persons, how should this effect your evaluation of the movement? Apply your answer to Women's Liberation, the New Left, the radical right, and student protest movements.

14. Suppose you were a promoter, seeking a favorable area in which to launch a social movement. What statistics would you use in finding a receptive location?

15. Do you know anyone who has a long history of involvement in "far-out" causes or movements? What kind of person is he? Do you know another person with a long activity in more moderate movements and organizations? How does he contrast with the other person?

16. Take three or four students whom you know

very well and estimate, according to the information in this chapter, the receptivity of each one to social movements. How about yourself? Are you a good or poor prospect for membership? In what kind of movement? Would your judgments be scientific conclusions or subjective impressions?

Suggested readings

Annals of the American Academy of Political and Social Science, "Protest in the Sixties," vol. 382, March, 1969. A collection of theory and research on social movements.

Barber, Bernard: "Acculturation and Messianic Movements," *American Sociological Review*, 6:663–669, October, 1941; Bobbs-Merrill reprint S-332. Shows how messianic movements arose among American Indian peoples as a reaction to the disorganization of their tribal life.

Blumer, Herbert: "Social Movements," in **Alfred M. Lee (ed.),** *Principles of Sociology*, College Outline Series, Barnes & Noble, Inc., New York, 1969, pp. 99–120. A concise outline of the field of social movements.

Foner, Philip S. (ed.): *The Black Panthers Speak*, J. B. Lippincott Company, Philadelphia, 1970. A collection of statements by Black Panther Party leaders, plus some other commentary.

Gerberding, Willian P., and Duane E. Smith: *The Radical Left: The Abuse of Discontent*, Houghton Mifflin Company, Boston, 1970. A collection of commentary on the New Left movement.

Green, Arnold W., and Eleanor Melnick: "What Has Happened to the Feminist Movement?" in **Alvin W. Gouldner (ed.),** *Studies in Leadership*, Harper & Row, Publishers, Inc., New York, 1950, pp. 277–302. A detailed account of how a movement was affected by victory, defeat, and social change. Should be read in conjunction with recent sources on the Women's Liberation Movement.

Gusfield, Joseph R. (ed.): *Protest, Reform, and Revolt: A Reader in Social Movements*, John Wiley & Sons, Inc., New York, 1970. A collection of research and theory on social movements.

*Kelman, Stephen: *Push Comes to Shove: The Escalation of Student Protest*, Houghton Mifflin Company, Boston, 1970. A Harvard student's account of the student strike at Harvard.

*Knott, Paul D.: *Student Activism*, Wm. C. Brown Company, Publishers, Dubuque, Iowa, 1971. A brief, readable collection of commentary on the student protest movement.

Kornhauser, William: *The Politics of Mass Society*, The Free Press, New York, 1959, especially part 3, "Social Composition of Mass Movements." A readable analysis of social movements as a result of discontinuity and alienation in mass society.

Lang, Kurt, and Gladys Engel Lang: *Collective Dynamics*, Thomas Y. Crowell Company, New York, 1961, chaps. 16, 17. Two detailed and perceptive chapters on social movements, in a textbook on collective behavior.

*Lincoln, C. Eric: *The Black Muslims in America*, Beacon Press, Boston, 1961. A participant-observer study of this movement by a black sociologist.

*Morgan, Robin (ed.): *Sisterhood Is Powerful: An Anthology of Writings from the Women's Liberation Movement*, Random House, Inc., New York, 1970. A series of trenchant statements of the Women's Lib ideology.

McLaughlin, Barry (ed.): *Studies in Social Movements: A Psychological Perspective*, The Free Press, New York, 1969. A collection with emphasis upon motivation and interaction in social movements.

Oglesby, Carl: *The New Left Reader*, Grove Press, Inc., New York, 1969. A collection of statements by various New Left leaders.

VanderZanden, James W.: "The Klan Revival," American Journal of Sociology, 65:456–462, March, 1960; Bobbs-Merrill reprint S-299. A membership study of the revived Ku Klux Klan, showing social backgrounds and possible motivations of current members.

Van Leeuwen, Arend Theodor: *Development Through Revolution,* Charles Scribners' Sons, New York, 1970. A scholarly analysis of revolution as a process of social change.

Worsley, Peter: *The Trumpet Shall Sound: A Study of "Cargo" Cults in Melanesia,* MacGibbon & Kee, London, 1957. Reviewed in *American Journal of Sociology,* 64:324–325, November, 1958. A comprehensive study of millenarian cults in New Guinea.

Bibliography

Abrahamsen, David: *Crime and the Human Mind,* Columbia University Press, New York, 1944.

Abrams, Charles: *The City Is the Frontier,* Harper & Row, Publishers, Incorporated, New York, 1965.

Abu-Lughod, Ibrahim (ed.): *The Arab-Israeli Confrontation of June 1967: An Arab Perspective,* Northwestern University Press, Evanston, Ill., 1970.

Abu-Lughod, Janet: "Migrant Adjustment to City Life: The Egyptian Case," *American Journal of Sociology,* 65:22–32, 1961.

Adams, E. M.: "The Logic of Planning," *Social Forces,* 28:419–423, 1950.

Adorno, T. W., Else Frenkel-Brunswick, D. J. Levinson, and **R. N. Sanford:** *The Authoritarian Personality,* Harper & Row, Publishers, Incorporated, New York, 1950.

Aho, William R.: "Ethnic Mobility in Northeastern United States: An Analysis of Census Data," *Sociological Quarterly,* 10:512–526, Fall 1969.

Albig, William: "Two Decades of Opinion Study: 1936–1956," *Public Opinion Quarterly,* 21:14–22, 1957.

Aldous, Joan: "Wives' Employment Status and Lower-class Men as Husband-Fathers: Support for the Moynihan Thesis," *Journal of Marriage and the Family,* 31:469–476, August 1969.

Alexander, Charles C.: *The Ku Klux Klan in the Southwest,* University of Kentucky Press, Lexington, 1965.

Alinsky, Saul D.: "The War on Poverty—Political Pornography," *Journal of Social Issues,* 21:41–47, January 1965.

Allen, Francis R.: *Socio-Cultural Dynamics: An Introduction to Social Change,* The Macmillan Company, New York, 1971.

Allen, James B.: *The Company Town in the American West,* University of Oklahoma Press, Norman, 1966.

Allport, Gordon W., and **Leo Postman:** *The Psychology of Rumor,* Holt, Rinehart and Winston, Inc., New York, 1947.

Almond, Gabriel A. et al.: *The Appeals of Communism,* Princeton University Press, Princeton, N.J., 1954.

Alsop, Stewart: "The American Class System," *Newsweek,* June 29, 1970, p. 88.

Alt, Herschel, and **Edith Alt:** *Russia's Children,* Bookman Associates, Inc., New York, 1959.

Altus, W. D., and **T. T. Tabejian:** "MMPI Correlates of the California E-F Scale," *Journal of Abnormal and Social Psychology,* 48:145–149, 1953.

Anderson, Raymond H.: "Soviet Urban Sprawl Defies Official Efforts to Curb the Growth of Cities," *New York Times,* Nov. 13, 1966, p. 122.

Anderson, Scarvia B. et al.: *Social Studies in Secondary Schools: A Survey of Courses and Practices,* Princeton University Press, Princeton, N.J., 1964.

Andrews, Lewis M.: "Communes and the Work Crisis," *Nation,* 211:460–463, Nov. 9, 1970.

Apodaca, Anadeto: "Corn and Custom: The Introduction of Hybrid Corn to Spanish American Farmers in New Mexico," in Edward H. Spicer (ed.), *Human Problems in Technological Change,* Russell Sage Foundation, New York, 1952, pp. 35–39.

Appelbaum, Richard P.: *Theories of Social Change,* Markham Publishing Company, Chicago, 1970.

Ardrey, Robert: *The Territorial Imperative,* Atheneum Publishers, New York, 1966.

Arensberg, Conrad M., and **Solon T. Kimball:** *Culture and Community,* Harcourt, Brace and World, Inc., New York, 1965.

Argyris, Chris: "We Must Make Work Worthwhile," *Life,* May 5, 1967, pp. 56ff.

Arnold, David O. (ed.): *The Sociology of Subcultures,* The Glendessary Press, Berkeley, 1970.

Arnold, Thurman: *The Folklore of Capitalism,* Yale University Press, New Haven, Conn., 1937.

Aronson, Elliot, et al.: "Communicator Credibility and Communication Discrepancy as Determinants of Opinion Change," *Journal of Abnormal and Social Psychology,* 67:31–36, 1963.

Asch, S. E.: "Effects of Group Pressure upon the Modification and Distortion of Judgments," in Heinz Guetzkow (ed.), *Groups, Leadership, and Men,* U.S. Office of Naval Research, Carnegie Press, Carnegie Institute of Technology, Pittsburgh, 1951.

Attwood, William: "The Fluoridation Controversy," *Look,* June 4, 1958, pp. 9–23.

Axelrod, Morris: "Urban Structure and Social Participation," *American Sociological Review,* 21:13–18, 1956.

Babcock, Richard F.: *The Zoning Game: Municipal Practices and Policies,* University of Wisconsin Press, Madison, 1966.

Bach, George R.: "The Marathon Group: Intensive Practice of Intimate Interaction," *Psychological Reports,* 118:995–1002, 1966.

Bailey, George: "The Disappearing Satellite," *Reporter,* Mar. 16, 1961, pp. 20–23.

Bain, Read: "Our Schizoid Culture," *Sociology and Social Research,* 19:226–276, 1935.

———: "The Self- and Other-words of a Child," *American Journal of Sociology,* 41:767–776, May 1936.

Baker, Charles R.: "Survey of Extremism," *Homefront,* July–August 1969. Reprinted in Paul B. Horton and Gerald R. Leslie (eds.), *Studies in the Sociology of Social Problems,* Appleton Century Crofts, 1971, pp. 512–520.

———: "White Citizens' Councils Fight for Segregation Now," *Homefront* [newsletter of the Institute for American Democracy, Washington, D.C.], January 1970.

Balandier, George: "Race Relations in West and Central Africa," in Andrew W. Lind (ed.), *Race Relations in a World Perspective,* University of Hawaii Press, Honolulu, 1955.

Bales, Robert F.: "Small-group Theory and Research," in Robert K. Merton, Leonard Broom, and Leonard S. Cottrell, Jr. (eds.), *Sociology Today: Problems and Prospects,* Basic Books, Inc., Publishers, New York, 1959, pp. 293–308.

Ballinger, Margaret: *From Union to Apartheid: A Trek to Isolation,* Frederick A. Praeger, Inc., New York, 1970.

Baltzell, E. Digby: *Philadelphia Gentlemen: The Making of a National Upper Class,* The Free Press of Glencoe, Inc., New York, 1958.

Banfield, Edward C.: *The Unheavenly City,*

Little, Brown and Company, Inc., Boston, 1970.

Barber, Bernard: *Social Stratification*, Harcourt, Brace & World, Inc., New York, 1957.

——— and Lyle S. Tobel: "Fashion in Women's Clothes and the American Social System," *Social Forces*, 31:124–131, 1953.

Barnes, C. A.: "A Statistical Study of the Freudian Theory of Levels of Psychosexual Development," *Genetic Psychology Monographs*, 45: 105–174, 1952.

Barnett, H. G.: *Innovation: The Basis of Social Change*, McGraw-Hill Book Company, New York, 1953.

Barnett, Larry: "Population Pressure: How Many Children?" *ZPG National Reporter*, II, (9)18, 1970.

Baron, Harold M., with **Harriet Stulman, Richard Rothenstein,** and **Kennard Davis:** "Black Powerlessness in Chicago," *Transaction*, 6:27–33, November 1968.

Barrett, George: "Close-up of the Birchers' Founder," *New York Times Magazine*, May 14, 1961, pp. 13ff.

Barth, Alan: "Report on the 'Rampageous Right,'" *New York Times Magazine*, Nov. 26, 1961, pp. 25ff.

Bascom, William R., and **Melville J. Herskovitz** (eds.): *Continuity and Change in African Cultures*, University of Chicago Press, Chicago, 1959.

Bavelas, Alex: "Communication Patterns in Task-oriented Groups," in Dorwin Cartwright and Alvin F. Zander (eds.), *Group Dynamics*, Harper & Row, Publishers, Incorporated, New York, 1953, pp. 493–494.

Bayton, James A.: *Tension in the Cities: Three Programs for Survival*, Chilton Book Company, Philadelphia, 1969.

Becker, Howard S.: *Outsiders*, The Free Press of Glencoe, Inc., New York, 1963.

———: "Whose Side Are We On?" *Social Problems*, 14:239–247, Winter 1967.

Becker, John: Research note in *Behavior Today*, Feb. 22, 1971, p. 2.

Bell, Daniel: "The Power Elite—Reconsidered," *American Journal of Sociology*, 64:238–250, 1958.

——— (ed.): *The Radical Right: The New American Right, Expanded and Updated*, Doubleday & Company, Inc., Garden City, N.Y., 1963.

Bell, Inge Powell: "The Double Standard," *Trans-action*, November–December 1970, pp. 75–80.

Bell, Robert R.: *Premarital Sex in a Changing Society*, Prentice-Hall, Inc., Englewood Cliffs, N.J., 1966.

Bellush, Jewel, and **Murray Hausknecht** (eds.): *Urban Renewal: People, Policies, and Planning*, Doubleday & Company, Inc., Garden City, N.Y., 1967.

Ben-David, Joseph: "Scientific Productivity and Academic Organization," *American Sociological Review*, 25:828–843, 1960.

Bender, Eugene L., and **George Kagiwada:** "Hansen's Law of 'Third Generation Return' and the Study of American Religico-Ethnic Groups," *Phylon*, 2:360–370, Winter 1968.

Benedict, Ruth: *Patterns of Culture*, Houghton Mifflin Company, Boston, 1934.

———: "Continuities and Discontinuities in Cultural Conditioning," *Psychiatry*, 1:161–167, 1938.

Bennis, Warren G., Kenneth D. Benne, and **Robert Chin:** *The Planning of Change*, Holt, Rinehart and Winston, Inc., New York, 1969.

Bereiter, Carl: "The Future of Individual Differences," *Harvard Educational Review*, 39: 310–318, Spring 1969.

Berelson, Bernard (ed.): *Family Planning and Population Programs*, Basic Books, Inc., Publishers, New York, 1969.

——— et al.: *Family Planning and Population Programs: A Review of World Development*, The University of Chicago Press, Chicago, 1966.

Berger, Bennett et al.: "Child-rearing Practices of the Communal Family," in Arlene S. Skolnick and Jerome H. Skolnick (eds.), *Family in Transition*, Little, Brown and Company, Boston, 1971, pp. 509–523.

Berke, Joseph (ed.): *Counter-Culture*, Peter Owen, Ltd., London, 1969.

Bernard, Jessie: "Autonomic and Decisive Competition," *The Sociological Quarterly*, 1:25–38, January 1960.

————: "Women, Marriage, and the Future," *The Futurist*, 4:41–43, April 1970.

Bernstein, Basil: "Elaborated and Restricted Codes: An Outline," *Sociological Inquiry*, 36: 254–261, Spring 1966.

Bernstein, Morey: *The Search for Bridey Murphy*, Doubleday & Company, Inc., Garden City, N.Y., 1956.

Berry, Brewton: *Race and Ethnic Relations*, Houghton Mifflin Company, Boston, 1965.

Bestor, Arthur E., Jr.: *Backwoods Utopias: The Sectarian and Overnite Phases of Communitarian Socialism in America: 1663–1829*, University of Pennsylvania Press, Philadelphia, 1950, 1970.

Bettelheim, Bruno, and **Morris Janowitz:** *The Dynamics of Prejudice*, Harper & Row, Publishers, Incorporated, New York, 1950.

————: "Does Communal Education Work? The Case of the Kibbutz," *Commentary*, 33:117–125, February 1962. Reprinted in Edwin M. Schur (ed.), *The Family and the Sexual Revolution*, Indiana University Press, Bloomington, 1964, pp. 293–307.

————: *The Children of the Dream*, The Macmillan Company, New York, 1969.

Biderman, Albert D.: "Social-Psychological Needs and 'Involuntary' Behavior as Illustrated by Compliance in Interrogation," *Sociometry*, 23:120–147, 1960.

————: *March To Calumny*, The Macmillan Company, New York, 1963.

Bierstedt, Robert A.: "An Analysis of Social Power," *American Sociological Review*, 15: 730–738, December 1950.

————: *The Social Order*, McGraw-Hill Book Company, New York, 1963.

Biller, Henry B.: "Father Absence and the Personality Development of the Male Child," *Developmental Psychology*, 2:181–201, April 1970.

Birch, Herbert G., and **Joan Dye Gussow:** *Disadvantaged Children: Health, Nutrition, and School Failure*, Harcourt, Brace & World, Inc., New York, 1970.

Blake, J. Herman: "Black Nationalism," *The Annals of the American Academy of Political and Social Science*, 382:15–25, Mar. 1969.

Blau, Peter Michael, and **W. Richard Scott:** *Formal Organizations: A Comparative Approach*, Chandler Publishing Company, San Francisco, 1962.

———— and **O. Dudley Duncan:** *The American Occupational Structure*, John Wiley & Sons, Inc., New York, 1967.

Blauner, Robert: "Whitewash over Watts," *Trans-action*, 3:3–9, March–April 1966.

Bliven, Bruce: "The Revolution of the Joneses," *New York Times Magazine*, Oct. 9, 1960, pp. 28ff.

Blood, Robert A., and **Donald M. Wolfe:** *Husbands and Wives*, The Free Press of Glencoe, Inc., New York, 1960.

Blood, Robert O., Jr., and **Donald M. Wolfe:** "Negro-White Differences in Blue-Collar Marriages in a Northern Metropolis," *Social Forces*, 48:59–64, September 1969.

Bloodworth, Dennis: "How Mao Rides the Dragon," *The Observer* (London), Sept. 11, 1966; reprinted in *Current*, October, 1966, pp. 48–50.

Bloom, B. S.: "The Thought Process of Students in Discussion," in Sidney J. French (ed.), *Accent on Teaching*, Harper & Row, Publishers, Incorporated, New York, 1954.

Blumberg, Leonard, and **Robert R. Bell:** "Urban Migration and Kinship Ties," *Social Problems*, 6:328–333, Spring 1959.

Blumer, Herbert: "Social Science and the Desegregation Process," *Annals of the American Academy of Political and Social Sciences*, 304:137–143, 1956.

————: "Collective Behavior," in Alfred McClung Lee (ed.), *Principles of Sociology*, Barnes & Noble, Inc., New York, 1969 (a), pp. 65–122.

————: "Social Movements," in Alfred M. Lee (ed.), *College Outline Series: Principles of Sociology*, Barnes & Noble, Inc., New York, 1969 (b), pp. 99–120.

————: "Fashion: From Class Differentiation to Collective Selection," *Sociological Quarterly*, 10:275–291, Summer 1969 (c).

Boffey, P. M.: "Japan: A Crowded Nation Wants to Boost Its Birthrate," *Science*, 167:960–962, Feb. 13, 1970.

Bogardus, Emory S.: "A Race Relations Cycle,"

American Journal of Sociology, 35:612–617, 1930.

——: *Fundamentals of Social Psychology,* Appleton Century Crofts, New York, 1950.

——: "Racial Distance Changes in the United States During the Past Thirty Years," *Sociology and Social Research,* 43:127–135, 1958.

——: "Racial Reactions by Regions," *Sociology and Social Research,* 43:286–290, 1959.

Bogart, Leo: "Measuring the Effectiveness of an Overseas Information Campaign: A Case History," *Public Opinion Quarterly,* 21:475–498, 1957.

——: *The Age of Television,* Frederick A. Praeger, Inc., New York, 1958.

Bogue, Donald J.: *The Population of the United States,* The Free Press of Glencoe, Inc., New York, 1959.

——: *Skid Row,* The Community and Family Study Center, Chicago, 1963.

Boodish, Hyman M.: "Liberal Arts Training for Engineers and Scientists," *The Social Studies,* 48:31–33, 1957.

Boskin, Joseph: "The Revolt of the Urban Ghettos," *Annals of the American Academy of Political and Social Science,* 382:1–14, March 1969.

Bossard, James H. S.: *The Sociology of Child Development,* Harper & Row, Publishers, Incorporated, New York, 1954.

Bouma, Donald H.: "The Analysis of the Social Power Position of a Real Estate Board," *Social Problems,* 10:116–128, Fall 1962 (a).

——: "The Legitimation of the Social Power Position of a Real Estate Board," *American Journal of Economics and Sociology,* 21:383–392, October 1962 (b).

——: *Why Kalamazoo Voted No,* W. E. Upjohn Institute for Employment Research, Kalamazoo, Mich., 1962 (c).

——: *Kids and Cops,* Wm. B. Eerdmanns Publishing Co., Grand Rapids, Mich., 1969.

——: "Issue-analysis Approach to Community Power: A Case Study of Realtors in Kalamazoo," *The American Journal of Economics and Sociology,* 29:241–252, July 1970.

Bouma, Gary D.: "Assessing the Impact of

Religion: A Critical Review," *Sociological Analysis,* 31:172–179, Winter 1970.

Bovard, Everett W., Jr.: "Group Structure and Perception," *Journal of Abnormal and Social Psychology,* 46:398–405, 1951.

Brady, Thomas F.: "French Worker-Priests Must Abandon Politics," *New York Times,* Jan. 31, 1954, sect. 4, p. 7.

Braungart, Robert: Research note in *Behavior Today,* Nov. 9, 1970, p. 3.

Brazzeil, William F.: "A Letter from the South," *Harvard Educational Review,* 39:348–356, Spring 1969.

Brim, Orville G., Jr.: "The Acceptance of New Behavior in Child-rearing," *Human Relations,* 7:473–491, 1954.

Brinton, Crane: *The Anatomy of Revolution,* W. W. Norton & Company, Inc., New York, 1938.

Broom, Leonard, and **F. Lancaster Jones:** "Status Consistency and Political Preference: The Australian Case," *American Sociological Review,* 35:989–1001, December 1970.

Bronfenbrenner, Urie, with the assistance of **John C. Condry, Jr.:** *Two Worlds of Childhood: U.S. and U.S.S.R.,* Basic Books, Inc., Publishers, New York, 1970.

Brown, Judith K.: "A Note on the Division of Labor by Sex," *American Anthropologist,* 72:1073–1078, October 1970.

Brown, Roger W.: "Determinants of the Relationship between Rigidity and Authoritarianism," *Journal of Abnormal and Social Psychology,* 48:469–475, 1953.

Brown, William G.: *The Lower South in American History,* The Macmillan Company, New York, 1902.

Brown, William O.: "Culture Contact and Race Conflict," in E. B. Reuter (ed.), *Race and Culture Contacts,* McGraw-Hill Book Company, New York, 1934.

Browne, Robert S.: "The Case for Two Americas—One Black, One White," *New York Times Magazine,* Aug. 11, 1968, pp. 12ff.

Brunswick, Ann F.: "A Generation Gap? A Comparison of Some Generational Differences between Blacks and Whites," *Social Problems,* 17:358–371, Winter 1970.

Bruyn, Severyn T.: *The Human Perspective in*

Sociology: The Methodology of Participant Observation, Prentice-Hall, Inc., Englewood Cliffs, N.J., 1966.

Buckley, Thomas: "When Good Birchers Get Together," *New York Times,* June 5, 1966, pp. 48ff.

Burchard, Waldo: *The Role of the Military Chaplain,* University of California Press, Berkeley, 1963.

Burchinall, Lee G., and **Hilda Siff:** "Rural Poverty," *Journal of Marriage and the Family,* 26:399–405, November 1964.

Burgess, Ernest W., and **Harvey J. Locke:** *The Family: From Institution to Companionate,* American Book Company, New York, 1953.

Burlingame, Roger: *Inventors behind the Inventor,* Harcourt, Brace & World, Inc., New York, 1947.

Burma, John H.: "The Measurement of Negro Passing," *American Journal of Sociology,* 52: 18–22, 1946.

——— (ed.): *Mexican Americans in the United States, A Reader,* Schenkman Publishing Co., Inc., Cambridge, Mass., 1970.

Burnham, James F.: *The Managerial Revolution,* The John Day Company, Inc., New York, 1941.

Burton, Arthur (ed.): *Encounter: The Theory and Practice of Encounter Groups,* Jossey-Bass, Inc., San Francisco, 1969.

Burton, Katherina: *Paradise Planters: The Story of Brook Farm,* David McKay Company, Inc., New York, 1939.

Cabrera, Arturo Y.: *Emerging Faces: The Mexican Americans,* William C. Brown Company, Publishers, Dubuque, Iowa, 1971.

Canty, Donald (ed.): *The New City,* Frederick A. Praeger, Inc., New York, 1969.

Calvin, A. D., and **Wayne H. Holtzman:** "Adjustment to the Discrepancy between Self-Concept and the Inferred Self," *Journal of Consulting Psychiatry,* 17:39–44, 1953.

Campbell, Donald T., and **Thelma H. McCormack:** "Military Experience and Attitudes toward Authority," *American Journal of Sociology,* 62:482–490, 1957.

Cantril, Hadley: *The Psychology of Social*

Movements, John Wiley & Sons, Inc., New York, 1941.

———: "Identification with Social and Economic Class," *Journal of Abnormal and Social Psychology,* 38:74–80, 1943.

———: *The Politics of Despair,* Basic Books, Inc., Publishers, New York, 1958.

Canty, Donald (ed.): *The New City,* Praeger Publishers, New York, 1969.

Caplow, Theodore: *The Academic Marketplace,* Basic Books, Inc., Publishers, New York, 1958.

Carlson, J. R.: *Under Cover,* E. P. Dutton & Co., Inc., New York, 1943.

———: *The Plotters,* E. P. Dutton & Co., Inc., New York, 1946.

Carothers, J. C.: "A Study of Mental Derangement in Africans, and an Attempt to Explain Its Peculiarities, More Especially in Relation to the African Attitude of Life," *Journal of Mental Science,* 93:548–597, 1947. Summarized in James C. Coleman, *Abnormal Psychology and Modern Life,* Scott, Foresman and Company, Chicago, 1956, pp. 256–259.

Carroll, Charles: *The Negro a Beast, or, In the Image of God,* American Bible and Book House, St. Louis, Mo., 1900.

Cartwright, Dorwin, and **Alvin F. Zander** (eds.): *Group Dynamics: Theory and Research,* Harper & Row, Publishers, Incorporated, New York, 1960.

Catanese, Anthony J., and **Alan W. Steess:** *Systematic Planning: Theory and Application,* D. C. Heath and Company, Boston, 1970.

Cater, Douglas: "Civil War in Alabama's Citizens' Councils," *Reporter,* May 17, 1956, pp. 19–21.

Centers, Richard: *The Psychology of Social Classes,* Princeton University Press, Princeton, N.J., 1949.

Chambers, Rosalind C.: "A Study of Three Voluntary Organizations," in D. V. Glass (ed.), *Social Mobility in Britain,* The Free Press, Glencoe, Ill., 1954, pp. 384–406.

Chandler, Michael: Research note in *Behavior Today,* Dec. 14, 1970, p. 2.

Chandrasekhar, S.: "Mao's War with the Chinese Family," *New York Times Magazine,* May 17, 1959, pp. 21ff.

Chang, M. C., T. H. Liu, and L. P. Chow: "Study by Matching of the Demographic Impact of an IUD Program," *Milbank Memorial Fund Quarterly*, 47:137–167, April 1969.

Chartrand, Robert Lee (ed.): *Hope for the Cities*, Spartan Books, New York, 1971.

Chicago Commission on Race Relations: *The Negro in Chicago*, The University of Chicago Press, Chicago, 1922.

Chilman, Catherine S.; "Fertility and Poverty in the United States: Some Implications for Family-Planning Programs, Evaluation and Research," *Journal of Marriage and the Family*, 30 (2):207–227, May 1968.

Chinoy, Ely: "The Tradition of Opportunity and the Aspirations of Automobile Workers," *American Journal of Sociology*, 57:453–459, 1952.

Christensen, Harold T., and Christina F. Gregg: "Changing Sex Norms in America and Scandinavia," *Journal of Marriage and the Family*, 32:616–627, November 1970.

Clark, Terry N.: "Community Structure, Decision-Making, Budget Expenditures, and Urban Renewal in 51 American Communities," *American Sociological Review,* 33:576–593, August 1968.

Clausen, Connie: *I Love You Honey, but the Season's Over*, Holt, Rinehart and Winston, Inc., New York, 1961.

Clinard, Marshall B.: *The Black Market: A Study in White Collar Crime*, Holt, Rinehart and Winston, Inc., New York, 1952.

———: *Sociology of Deviant Behavior*, Holt, Rinehart and Winston, Inc., New York, 1968.

Cohen, Albert K.: *Delinquent Boys: The Culture of the Gang*, The Free Press of Glencoe, Ill., Chicago, 1955.

Cohen, Jerry, and William S. Murphy: *Burn, Baby, Burn*, E. P. Dutton & Co., Inc., New York, 1966.

Cohen, Marshall: "Civil Disobedience in a Constitutional Democracy," *Massachusetts Review*, 10:211–216, Spring 1969.

Cohen, Mitchell, and Dennis Hale (eds.): *The New Student Left*, The Beacon Press, Boston, 1967.

Cohen, Nathan E.: *The Citizen Volunteer: His Responsibility Role and Opportunity in Modern Society*, Harper & Row, Publishers, Incorporated, New York, 1960.

Cohn, Norman: *The Pursuit of the Millennium*, Essential Books, Fair Lawn, N.J., 1957.

Coleman, James C.: *Abnormal Psychology and Modern Life*, Scott, Foresman and Company, Chicago, 1964.

Coleman, James S.: *The Adolescent Society*, The Free Press of Glencoe, Inc., New York, 1961.

——— et al.: *Equality of Educational Opportunity*, U.S. Department of Health, Education and Welfare, Washington, D.C., 1966.

Coleman, Richard P., and Bernice L. Neugarten: *Social Status in the City*, Jossey-Bass, San Francisco, 1971.

Collier, John: *Indians of the Americas*, W. W. Norton & Company, Inc., New York, 1947.

Compte, August: *Positive Philosophy.* Translated by Harriet Martineau, C. Blanchard Company, New York, 1855.

Conant, James B.: *Slums and Suburbs: A Commentary on Schools in Metropolitan Areas*, McGraw-Hill Book Company, New York, 1961.

Condon, Edward U.: "UFO's I Have Found and Lost," *Bulletin of the Atomic Scientists*, 35: 6–8, December 1969.

Cooley, Charles Horton: "The Theory of Transportation," *Publications of the American Economic Association*, vol. 9, no. 3, 1894.

———: *The Nature of Human Nature*, Charles Scribner's Sons, New York, 1902.

———: "A Study of the Early Use of Self Words by a Child," *Psychological Review*, 15:339–357, 1908.

Cooper, David: *The Death of the Family*, Pantheon Books, a division of Random House, Inc., New York, 1970.

Copp, James H. (ed.): *Our Changing Rural Society: Perspectives and Trends*, The Department of Publications, State University of Iowa, Iowa City, 1964.

Cortéz, Juan B., and Florence M. Gatti: "Physique and Propensity," *Psychology Today*, October 1970, pp. 42ff.

Coser, Lewis: *The Functions of Social Conflict*, Free Press of Glencoe, Ill., Chicago, 1956.

——— and Bernard Rosenberg: *Sociological*

Theory, The Macmillan Company, New York, 1969.

Craig, John G., and **Edward Gross**: "The Forum Theory of Organizational Democracy, Structural Guarantees as Time Variables," *American Sociological Review*, 35:19–33, February 1970.

Creed, E. R.: "Genetic Adaptation," in J. Rose (ed.), *Technological Injury: The Effects of Technological Advances on Environment, Life, and Society*, Gordon and Breach Science Publishers, London, 1969, pp. 119–134.

Cressey, Donald R.: *Theft of a Nation: The Structure and Operations of Organized Crime in America*, Harper & Row, Publishers, New York, 1969.

Cronbach, Lee J.: "Heredity, Environment, and Educational Policy," *Harvard Educational Review*, 39:338–347, Spring 1969.

Cronon, Edmund D.: *Black Moses*, The University of Wisconsin Press, Madison, 1955.

Crossman, Richard (ed.): *The God That Failed*, Harper & Row, Publishers, Incorporated, New York, 1949.

Crow, James F.: "Genetic Theories and Influences: Comments on the Value of Diversity," *Harvard Educational Review*, 39:301–309, Spring 1969.

Cuber, John R.: "Marginal Church Participants," *Sociology and Social Research*, 25:57–62, September 1940.

Dahl, Robert A.: "A Critique of the Ruling Elite Model," *American Political Science Review*, 52:463–469, 1958.

Dahrendorf, Ralf: "Conflict Groups, Group Conflicts and Social Change," *Class and Industrial Society*, Stanford University Press, Stanford, Calif., 1959, pp. 202–223.

———: "Towards a Theory of Social Conflict," in Amitai and Eva Etzioni (eds.), *Social Change*, Basic Books, Inc., Publishers, New York, 1964, pp. 100–123.

Dai, Bingham: "Obsessive-Compulsive Disorders in Chinese Culture," *Social Problems*, 4:313–321, 1957.

Dale, Edward Everett: *The Range Cattle Industry*, University of Oklahoma Press, Norman, 1930.

Darity, William A., Castellano B. Turner, and **H. Jean Thiebaux**: "Race Consciousness and Fears of Black Genocide as Barriers to Family Planning," paper presented at Ninth Annual Meeting of the National Association of Planned Parenthood Physicians, Kansas City, Missouri, 1971; reprinted in *Population Reference Bureau*, Selection No. 37, June, 1971, pp. 5–12.

Darwin, Charles: *On the Origin of the Species*, Introduction by Ernst Mayer, Harvard University Press, Cambridge, Mass., 1964.

Davidson, Basil: *The Lost Cities of Africa*, Little, Brown and Company, Boston, 1959.

Davidson, Bill: "Combat Soldiers Fail to Shoot," *Colliers*, Nov. 8, 1952, pp. 16–18.

Davidson, Sara: "Open Land: Getting Back to the Communal Garden," *Harper's*, June 1970, pp. 91–102.

Davies, James C.: "Toward a Theory of Revolution," *American Sociological Review*, 27:5–19, 1962.

Davis, Allison: "The Motivation of the Underprivileged Worker," in William F. Whyte (ed.), *Industry and Society*, McGraw-Hill Book Company, New York, 1946, pp. 84–106.

———: *Social-class Influences on Learning*, Harvard University Press, Cambridge, Mass., 1952.

——— and **Robert J. Havighurst**: "Social Class and Color Differences in Child-rearing," *American Sociological Review*, 11:698–710, 1946.

Davis, Ethelyn: "Teen-aged Attitudes towards Work: A Challenge to the Protestant Ethic?" *Proceedings of the Southwestern Sociological Association*, 19:226–230, April 1969.

Davis, Fred: "The Cabdriver and His Fare: Facets of a Fleeting Relationship," *American Journal of Sociology*, 65:158–165, 1959.

Davis, Graham H., and **J. Robert Curr**: *National Commission on the Causes and Prevention of Violence: Violence in America*, U.S. Government Printing Office, Washington, D.C., 1969.

Davis, Jerome: *Contemporary Social Movements*, Appleton Century Crofts, Inc., New York, 1930.

Davis, Kingsley: *Human Society*, The Macmillan Company, New York, 1949.

Dawson, Carl, and **W. E. Gettys**: *Introduction to Sociology*, The Ronald Press Company, New York, 1934, 1948.

Day, Lincoln H.: "Natality and Ethnocentrism: Some Relationships Suggested by an Analysis of Catholic-Protestant Differentials," *Population Studies*, 22:22–50, March 1968.

Dean, Dwight G.: "Alienation: Its Meaning and Measurement," *American Sociological Review*, 26:753–758, 1961.

Deasy, Leila Calhoun: "Socio-Economic Status and Participation in the Poliomyelitis Vaccine Trial," *American Sociological Review*, 21:185–191, 1956.

de Beauvoir, Simone: *The Second Sex*, Alfred A. Knopf, Inc., New York, 1953.

De Bell, Garrett: *The Environmental Handbook: Prepared for the First National Environmental Teach-in, April 22, 1970*, Ballantine Books, New York, 1970.

Debo, Angie: *A History of the Indians of the United States*, University of Oklahoma Press, Norman, 1970.

Deloria, Vine, Jr.: *Custer Died for Your Sins: An Indian Manifesto*, The Macmillan Company, New York, 1970.

Demerath, N. J.: "Schizophrenia among Primitives," *American Journal of Psychiatry*, 98:703–707, March 1942.

Dempsey, David: "What It's Like to Live with Genius," *New York Times Magazine*, Oct. 5, 1958, pp. 36ff.

Deutsch, Morton: "An Experimental Study of the Effects of Cooperation and Competition upon Group Process," *Human Relations*, 2:199–231, 1949.

Dewey, Richard: "The Rural-Urban Continuum: Real but Relatively Unimportant," *American Journal of Sociology*, 66:60–66, 1960.

Diamond, Stephen: *What the Trees Said: Life on a New Age Farm*, Delacourte Press, Dell Publishing Co., Inc., New York, 1971.

Dichter, Ernest: *Motivating Human Behavior*, McGraw-Hill Book Company, Inc., New York, 1971.

Dittes, James E., and **Harold H. Kelley:** "Effects of Different Conditions of Acceptance upon Conformity to Group Norms," *Journal of Abnormal and Social Psychology*, 53:100–107, 1956.

Dobzhansky, Theodosius: *Mankind Evolving: The Evolution of the Human Species*, Yale University Press, New Haven, Conn., 1962.

Dodson, Dan W.: "The Creative Role of Conflict Re-examined," *Journal of Intergroup Relations*, 1:5–12, 1959.

Dollard, John, et al.: *Frustration and Aggression*, Yale University Press, New Haven, Conn., 1939.

Doob, Leonard: *Propaganda*, Holt, Rinehart and Winston, Inc., New York, 1948.

——: *Public Opinion and Propaganda*, Archon Books, The Shoe String Press, Inc., Hamden, Conn., 1966.

Douglas, Jack D. (ed.): *The Relevance of Sociology*, Appleton Century Crofts, New York, 1970.

Douvan, Elizabeth: "Employment and the Adolescent," in F. Iven Nye, *The Employed Mother in America*, Rand McNally & Company, Chicago, 1963, pp. 142–164.

Downes, Bryan T.: "The Social Characteristics of Riot Cities: A Comparative Study," *Social Science Quarterly*, 49:504–520, December 1968.

Doyle, Bertram W.: "The Etiquette of Race Relations—Past, Present, and Future," *Journal of Negro Education*, 5:191–208, April 1936, Bobbs-Merrill reprint, 136–339.

Draper, Theodore: "The Psychology of Surrender," *Atlantic Monthly*, 176:62–65, 1945.

Drury, Allen: *Advise and Consent*, Doubleday & Company, Inc., Garden City, N.Y., 1959.

Dubois, Cora: *The Peoples of Alor*, The University of Minnesota Press, Minneapolis, 1944.

Duncan, David Douglas: "In the Middle of an Indian Massacre," *Life*, Oct. 6, 1947, pp. 6ff.

Dunham, H. Warren, and **S. Kirson Weinberg:** *The Culture of the State Mental Hospital*, Wayne State University Press, Detroit, 1960.

Durkheim, Emile: *Le Suicide: étude de Sociologie*. Translated by J. A. Spaulding and G. Simpson, The Free Press, Glencoe, Ill., 1951.

East, Marjorie: "Family Life by the Year 2000," *Journal of Home Economics*, 62:13–19, January 1970.

Ebenstein, William: *Today's Isms: Communism, Fascism, Capitalism, Socialism*, Prentice-Hall, Inc., Englewood Cliffs, N.J., 1970.

Eckhardt, Alice, and **Roy Eckhardt:** *Encounter with Israel: A Challenge to Conscience*, Association Press, New York, 1970.

Edgerton, Robert B.: "Some Dimensions of Disillusionment in Culture Contact," *Southwestern Journal of Anthropology*, 21:231–243, Autumn 1965.

Edwards, Allen A.: "Types of Rural Communities," in Marvin B. Sussman (ed.), *Community Structure and Analysis*, Thomas Y. Crowell Company, New York, 1959.

Edwards, Lyford P.: *The Natural History of Revolution*, The University of Chicago Press, Chicago, 1927.

Eels, Kenneth, Allison Davis, Robert J. Havighurst, Virgil E. Herrick and Ralph N. Tyler: *Intelligence and Cultural Differences: A Study of Cultural Learning and Problem Solving*, University of Chicago Press, Chicago, 1951.

Egan, Gerard: *Encounter Group Processes for Interpersonal Growth*, Wadsworth Publishing Company, Inc., Belmont, Calif., 1970.

Eggan, Dorothy: "The General Problem of Hope Adjustment," *American Anthropologist*, 45:357–373, July 1943.

Ehrlich, Paul R.: *The Population Bomb*, Ballantine Books, New York, 1968.

Ehrmann, Winston: *Premarital Dating Behavior*, Holt, Rinehart and Winston, Inc., New York, 1959.

Elkind, David: "Piagetian and Psychometric Conceptions of Intelligence," *Harvard Educational Review*, 39:319–337, Spring 1969.

Ellis, Evelyn: "Social Psychological Correlates of Upward Social Mobility among Unmarried Career Women," *American Sociological Review*, 17:558–563, 1952.

Elmen, P.: "Focus on Ireland: A Land Where Faith Matters," *Christian Century*, Feb. 3, 1971, pp. 88–170ff.

Elwin, Varrier: *The Biaga*, John Murray (Publishers), Ltd., London, 1939.

Epstein, Benjamin R., and Arnold Forster: *The Radical Right: A Report on the John Birch Society and Its Allies*, Vintage Books, New York, 1967.

Erber, Ernest (ed.): *Urban Planning in Transition*, Grossman Publishers, New York, 1970.

Ernst, Morris, and David Loth: *Report on the American Communist*, Holt, Rinehart, and Winston, Inc., New York, 1952.

Etzioni, Amitai: *The Active Society: A Theory of Societal and Political Processes*, The Free Press, New York, 1968.

——: *Demonstration Democracy*, Gordon and Breach, Science Publishers, Inc., New York, 1971.

Eulan, Hans: "Identification with Class and Political Role Behavior," *Public Opinion Quarterly*, 20:515–529, 1956.

Evans, Rowland, Jr.: "India Experiments with Sterilization," *Harper's Magazine*, November 1961, pp. 78–88.

Ewers, John C.: *The Horse in the Blackfeet Culture*, Bureau of American Ethnology, Bulletin no. 159, Washington, 1955.

Fairchild, Henry Pratt (ed.): *Dictionary of Sociology*, Philosophical Library, Inc., New York, 1957.

Fanfani, Amintore: *Catholicism, Protestantism and Capitalism*, Sheed & Ward, Inc., New York, 1955.

Fanon, Franz: *The Wretched of the Earth*, Paris, 1961. Translated by Constance Farrington, Grove Press, Inc., New York, 1968.

Faris, R. E. L.: "The Alleged Class System in the United States," *Research Studies of the State College of Washington*, vol. 22, June 1954.

Farley, Jennie: "Maternal Employment and Child Behavior," *Cornell Journal of Social Relations*, 3:58–71, Fall 1968.

Farley, Reynolds: "The Changing Distribution of Negroes within Metropolitan Areas: The Emergence of Black Suburbs," *American Journal of Sociology*, 75:512–529, January 1970.

Fast, Julius: *Body Language*, M. Evans distributed in association with Lippincott, New York, 1970.

Feldmesser, Robert A.: "The Persistence of Status Advantages in Soviet Russia," *American Journal of Sociology*, 59:19–27, 1953.

Festinger, L., A. Pipestone, and T. Newcomb: "Some Consequences of Deindividuation in a Group," *Journal of Abnormal and Social Psychology*, 47:382–389, 1952.

——, Henry W. Riecken, and Stanley Schachter: *When Prophecy Fails*, The University of Minnesota Press, Minneapolis, 1956.

Fetterman, John: *Stinking Creek: A Portrait of a Small Community in Appalachia*, E. P. Dutton & Company, Inc., New York, 1970.

Feuer, Lewis S.: "The Risk is 'Juvenocracy,'" *New York Times Magazine*, Sept. 18, 1966, pp. 56ff.

———: *The Conflict of Generations*, Basic Books, Inc., Publishers New York, 1968.

Fey, Harold E.: "Let Us Possess the Land," *Christian Century*, 71:757–759, 1954.

Firth, Raymond: "The Theory of Cargo Cults: A Note on Tikopia," *Man*, 55:130–132, 1955.

Fitzpatrick, Joseph P.: *Puerto Rican Americans: The Meaning of Migration to the Mainland*, Prentice-Hall, Inc., Englewood Cliffs, N.J., 1971.

Flacks, Richard: "Liberated Generation: An Explanation of the Roots of Student Protest," *Journal of Social Issues*, 23:52–75, July 1967.

Fletcher, Joseph F.: *Situation Ethics: The New Morality*, The Westminster Press, Philadelphia, 1966.

Fliegel, Frederick C., and **Joseph E. Kivlin:** "Attributes of Innovation as Factors in Diffusion," *American Journal of Sociology*, 72:235–248, November 1966.

Flinn, William L.: "Influence of Community Values on Innovativeness," *American Journal of Sociology*, 75:983–991, May 1970.

Flugel, J. C.: *The Psychology of Clothes*, The Hogarth Press, Ltd., London, 1930.

Foner, Philip S. (ed.): *The Black Panthers Speak*, J. B. Lippincott Company, Philadelphia, 1970.

Foreman, Grant: *Indian Removal*, University of Oklahoma Press, Norman, 1932.

Foreman, Paul B.: "Panic Theory," *Sociology and Social Research*, 37:295–304, 1953.

Form, William H., and **Warren L. Sauer:** *Community Influentials in a Middle-sized City*, Institute for Community Development, The Michigan State University Press, East Lansing, 1960.

Fortune, R. F.: *The Sorcerers of Dobu*, E. P. Dutton & Co., Inc., New York, 1932.

Foskett, John M.: "Social Structure and Community Participation," *American Sociological Review*, 20:431–438, 1955.

Fox, Douglas M.: "The Identification of Community Leaders by the Reputational, and Decisional Methods: Three Case Studies and an Empirical Analysis of the Literature," *Sociol-*

ogy and Social Research, 54:94–103, October 1969.

Fox, Ruth: "The Alcoholic Spouse," in Victor W. Eisenstein (ed.), *Neurotic Interaction in Marriage*, Basic Books, Inc., Publishers, New York, 1956, pp. 148–167.

Francois, William: "Where Poverty Is Permanent," *Reporter*, Apr. 17, 1961, pp. 38–39.

Frederichs, Robert W.: *A Sociology of Sociology*, The Free Press, New York, 1970.

Freedman, D. X.: "On the Use and Abuse of LSD," *Archives of General Psychiatry*, 18:330–347, 1968.

Freedman, Janet: "The Birch Tree Grows," *Library Journal*, 91:625–628, Feb. 1, 1966.

Freedman, Ronald, Pascal K. Whelpton, and **Arthur A. Campbell:** *Family Planning, Sterility, and Population Growth*, McGraw-Hill Book Company, New York, 1959.

———, ———, and **John W. Smit:** "Socio-Economic Factors in Religious Differentials in Fertility," *American Sociological Review*, 26:608–614, 1961.

Freeman, Howard E.: "Attitudes toward Mental Patients among Relatives of Former Patients," *American Sociological Review*, 26:59–66, 1961.

Friedan, Betty: *The Feminine Mystique*, W. W. Norton & Company, Inc., New York, 1963.

Friedman, Norman L.: "Nativism," *Phylon*, 28:408–415, Winter 1967.

Fromm, Erich: *Escape from Freedom*, Holt, Rinehart and Winston, Inc., New York, 1941.

———: "Individual and Social Origins of Neurosis," *American Sociological Review*, 9:380–384, 1944.

———: *The Art of Loving*, Harper & Row, Publishers, Incorporated, New York, 1956.

Frye, William R.: *In Whitest Africa: Dynamics of Apartheid*, Prentice-Hall, Englewood Cliffs, N.J., 1968.

Galbraith, John Kenneth: *American Capitalism: The Concept of Countervailing Power*, Houghton Mifflin Company, Boston, 1952.

Gallup, George, and **S. F. Rae:** *The Pulse of Democracy*, Simon & Schuster, Inc., New York, 1940.

Gans, Herbert J.: "Sociology of New Towns,"

Sociology and Social Research, 40:231–239, March 1956.

Gardner, Martin: *Fads and Fallacies in the Name of Science*, Dover Publications, Inc., New York, 1957.

Gardner, Peter M.: "Toward a Componential Model of Indian Caste," *Journal of Social Research*, 11:37–48, March 1968.

Geis, Gilbert: "The Fable of a Fatty," *Issues in Criminology*, 3:211–214, Spring 1968.

——: "Rejoinder to Geis," *Issues in Criminology*, 3:215, Spring 1968.

Gerberding, William P., and Duane E. Smith (eds.): *The Radical Left: The Abuse of Discontent*, Houghton Mifflin Company, Boston, 1970.

Gerth, Hans: "The Nazi Party: Its Leadership and Composition," *American Journal of Sociology*, 55:517–541, 1940.

Geschwender, James A.: "Explorations in the Theory of Social Movements," *Social Forces*, 47:127–135, December 1968.

Gibb, Cecil A., in Gardner Lindzey (ed.): *Handbook of Social Psychology*, Addison-Wesley Publishing Company, Inc., Reading, Mass., 1954, vol. 2, pp. 884–889.

Gibbard, Harold: "Residential Succession: A Study in Human Ecology," unpublished Ph.D. dissertation, University of Michigan, 1938.

Giddings, F. H.: *The Principles of Sociology*, The Macmillan Company, New York, 1913.

Giles, Robert H.: "How to Become a Target City," *The Reporter*, June 15, 1967, pp. 38–41.

Gillin, John P.: *The Ways of Men*, Appleton Century Crofts, New York, 1948.

Gilroy, Harry: "Flight from East Germany: The People," *New York Times*, Aug. 13, 1961, sect. 4, p. 4.

Glazer, Nathan, and Daniel P. Moynihan: *Beyond the Melting Pot: The Negroes, Puerto Ricans, Jews, Italians and Irish of New York City*, The M.I.T. Press, Cambridge, Mass., 1970.

——: "The Culture of Poverty: The View from New York City," in Alan Winter, *The Poor: A Culture of Poverty or a Poverty of Culture?*, William B. Eerdmans, Publishers, Grand Rapids, Michigan, 1971, pp. 20–48.

Glick, Clarence: "Social Roles and Types in Race Relations," in Andrew W. Lind, *Race Relations in World Perspective*, University of Hawaii Press, Honolulu, 1955.

Glick, Paul C., and Emanuel Landau: "Age as a Factor in Marriage," *American Sociological Review*, 15:517–529, 1950.

——: *American Families*, John Wiley & Sons, Inc., New York, 1957.

Glock, Charles Y., and Benjamin B. Ringer: "Church Policy and the Attitudes of Ministers and Parishioners on Social Issues," *American Sociological Review*, 21:148–156, April 1956.

Glueck, Sheldon, and Eleanor Glueck: *Predicting Juvenile Delinquency and Crime*, Harvard University Press, Cambridge, Mass., 1959.

Goffman, Irvin W.: *Where the Action Is: Three Essays*, Doubleday & Company, Inc., Garden City, N.Y., 1967.

Goffman, Erving W.: *Presentation of Self in Everyday Life*, Social Science Research Center, University of Edinburgh, 1956. Reprinted by Anchor Books, Doubleday & Company, Inc., Garden City, N.Y., 1959.

——: "Status Consistency and Preference for Change in Power Distribution," *American Sociological Review*, 22:275–281, April 1957.

Goldhamer, Herbert, and Edward A. Shils: "Types of Power and Status," *American Journal of Sociology*, 45:171–182, September 1939.

—— and Andrew Marshall: *Psychosis and Civilization: Two Studies in the Frequency of Mental Illness*, The Free Press, Glencoe, Ill., 1953.

Goldner, Fred H.: Review of Vance Packard: *The Pyramid Climbers*, *American Journal of Sociology*, 69:197, September 1963.

Goldthorpe, John H., and David Lockwood: "Affluence and the British Class Structure," *Sociological Review* (New Series), 11:133–163, July 1963.

Golembiewski, Robert T., and Arthur Blumberg (eds.): *Sensitivity Training and the Laboratory Approach*, F. E. Peacock Publishers, Inc., Italsca, Ill., 1970.

Gordon, Leonard: *A City in Racial Crisis*, Arizona State University Press, Temple, 1971.

Gordon, Milton: *Social Class in American Society*, The Duke University Press, Durham, N.C., 1958.

———: *Assimilation in American Life: the Role of Race, Religion and National Origins*, Oxford University Press, New York, 1968.

Gornick, Vivian: "Consciousness," *New York Times Magazine*, Jan. 10, 1971, pp. 22ff.

Gottlieb, Annie: "Female Human Beings," *New York Times Book Reviews*, Feb. 21, 1971, Part II, pp. 1ff.

Gould, Harold A.: "Modern Medicine and Folk Cognition in Rural India," *Human Organization*, 24:201–208, Fall 1965.

Gouldner, Alvin: "Cosmopolitans and Locals: Towards an Analysis of Latent Social Roles," *Administrative Science Quarterly*, 2:281–292, December 1957.

———: "Anti-Minotaur: The Myth of a Value-Free Sociology," *Social Problems*, 9:190–213, Winter 1962.

———: "Toward the Radical Reconstruction of Sociology," *Social Policy*, May–June 1970, pp. 18–25.

Grebler, Leo, Joan W. Moore, and **Ralph C. Guzman** et al.: *The Mexican Americans: The Nation's Second Largest Minority*, The Free Press, New York, 1970.

Greenwald, Harold: *The Call Girl*, Ballantine Books, Inc., New York, 1959.

Greer, Scott, and **Ella Kube:** "Urbanism and Social Structure: A Los Angeles Study," in Marvin B. Sussman (ed.), *Community Structure and Analysis*, Thomas Y. Crowell Company, New York, 1959.

Gregg, Richard B.: *The Power of Nonviolent Resistance*, Schocken Books Inc., New York, 1966.

Greely, Andrew M.: "The Protestant Ethic: Time for a Moratorium," *Sociological Analysis*, 25:20–33, Spring 1964.

Grier, Eunice, and **George Grier:** *Discrimination in Housing*, Anti-Defamation League, New York, 1960.

Griffin, John H.: *Black Like Me*, Houghton Mifflin Company, Boston, 1961.

Gross, Bertram M. (ed.): *Action under Planning: The Guidance of Economic Development*, McGraw-Hill Book Company, 1967.

Gross, Edward: "Some Functional Consequences of Primary Group Controls in Formal Work Organizations," *American Sociological Review*, 18:368–373, 1953.

Grove, Gene: *Inside the John Birch Society*, Fawcett Publications, Inc., Greenwich, Conn., 1961.

Gruen, Victor: *The Heart of Our Cities*, Simon & Schuster, Inc., New York, 1964.

Guillote, V. V.: "Power and Law," *Human Mosaic*, 2:113–120, Spring 1968.

Gupta, Shiva Kumar: "On Caste Stratification in a Village of Uttar Pradesh," *Eastern Anthropologist*, 21:87–94, January-April, 1968.

Gusfield, Joseph R.: "Social Structure and Moral Reform: A Study of the Women's Christian Temperance Union," *American Journal of Sociology*, 56:221–232, 1955.

Gustafsson, Berndt: "The State of Sociology of Protestantism in Scandinavia," *Social Compass*, 12:359–365, 1965.

Hacker, Andrew: "The Boy Who Doesn't Go to College," *New York Times Magazine*, June 24, 1962, pp. 11ff.

Hackett, Herbert: "The Flying Saucer," *Sociology and Social Research*, 32:869–873, 1948.

Hadden, Jeffrey K.: *The Gathering Storm in the Churches*, Doubleday & Company, Inc., Garden City, N. Y., 1969.

Haddon, Tom: "Making People Good by Law," *New Society*, 13:79–81, January 1969.

Hall, Edward T.: *The Silent Language*, Doubleday & Company, Inc., Garden City, N.Y., 1959.

———: "Our Silent Language," *Americas*, 14:5–8, February 1962.

Hall, Florence Turnbull, and **Marguerite Paulsen Schroeder:** "Effects of Family and Housing Characteristics on the Time Spent on Household Tasks," *Journal of Home Economics*, 62:23–29, January 1970.

Halloway, Mark: *Heavens on Earth: Utopian Communities in America, 1680–1880*, Library Publishers, New York, 1951.

Halpern, Joel: *The Changing Village Community*, Prentice-Hall, Inc., Englewood Cliffs, N.J., 1967.

Hamersma, Richard: Research note in *Behavior Today*, Nov. 23, 1970, p. 3.

Hamilton, Richard F.: "The Marginal Middle

Class: A Reconsideration," *American Sociological Review*, 31:192–199, April 1966.

Hammer, Richard: *One Morning in the War: The Tragedy at Son My*, Coward McCann, Inc., New York, 1970.

Hansen, Marcus L.: "Third Generation in America: The Problem of the Third Generation Immigrant," *Commentary*, 14:492–500, November 1952.

Hare, Paul, and **Herbert H. Blumberg** (eds.): *Nonviolent Direct Action, American Cases: Social-Psychological Analyses*, Corpus Books, Washington, D.C., 1968.

Harlow, Harry F., and **Margaret K. Harlow:** "A Study of Animal Affection," *Natural History*, 70:48–55, 1961.

Harris, C. D., and **E. L. Ullman:** "The Nature of Cities," *Annals of the American Academy of Political and Social Science*, 242:7–17, 1945.

Harris, Louis: "Election Polling and Research," *Public Opinion Quarterly*, 11:111, 1957.

Hart, Donn V.: "The Philippine Cooperative Movement," *Far Eastern Survey*, 24:27–30, 1955.

Harter, Carl, and **Janice Roussel:** "The Fertility of White Females in New Orleans: A Comparison of Protestants and Parochial and Secular Educated Catholics," *Milbank Memorial Fund Quarterly*, 47:39–53, January 1969.

Hartnagel, Timothy F.: "Father Absence and Self-Conception Among Lower-class White and Negro Boys," *Social Problems*, 18:152–163, Fall 1970.

Harvey, Jesse: Unpublished doctoral dissertation. Reported in *Science News Letter*, Dec. 5, 1953, p. 360.

Hauser, Phillip M.: *Population Perspectives*, Rutgers University Press, New Brunswick, N.J., 1960.

Havighurst, Robert J., and **Allison Davis:** "A Comparison of the Chicago and Harvard Studies of Social Class Differences in Child-Rearing," *American Sociological Review*, 20: 438–442, 1955.

Hayanagi, Tadashi: "The Mother's Child-Rearing Attitudes and her Child's Socialization—A Clinical Aspect in Child Socialization," *Journal of Educational Sociology*, 23:110–123, October 1968.

Heberle, Rudolf: *Social Movements*, Appleton Century Crofts, New York, 1951.

————: Review of *Stanley Hoffman: Le Mouvement Poujade* (Librairie Armand Colin, Paris), in *American Journal of Sociology*, 63:440–441, 1956.

Hedgepeth, William: *Communal Life in America*, The Macmillan Company, New York, 1970.

Heisel, Dorelle: "What Is Your Concept of Masculine and Feminine?" unpublished research study, University of Cincinnati, 1970.

Helfer, Ray E., and **C. Henry Kempe** (eds.): *The Battered Child*, The University of Chicago Press, Chicago, 1968.

Helfrich, Harold W., Jr.: *The Environmental Crisis: Man's Struggle to Live with Himself*, Yale University Press, New Haven, Conn., 1970.

Henderson, William Leroy, and **Larry C. Ledebur:** *Economic Disparity: Problems and Strategies for Black America.* The Free Press, New York, 1970.

Hendin, Herbert: "A Psychoanalyst Looks at Student Revolutionaries," *New York Times Magazine*, Jan. 17, 1971, pp. 16ff.

Herberg, Will: *Protestant, Catholic, Jew*, Doubleday & Company, Inc., Garden City, N.Y., 1960.

"Here's Where Church Tried to Swing an Election: With Text of Pastoral Letter," *U.S. News and World Report* 49:59–61, Nov. 7, 1960.

Herskovitz, Melville J.: *Man and His Works*, Alfred A. Knopf, Inc., New York, 1949.

Hertzler, J. O.: *American Social Institutions*, Allyn and Bacon, Inc., Boston, 1961.

Herzog, Elizabeth: *Children of Working Mothers*, Children's Bureau Publication no. 382, U.S. Department of Health, Education, and Welfare, 1960.

Heussenstamm, F. K.: "Bumper Stickers and the Cops," *Trans-action*, February 1971, pp. 32–34.

Higham, John: *Strangers in the Land: Patterns of American Nativism, 1860–1925*, Rutgers University Press, New Brunswick, N.J., 1955.

Hill, Reuben, J. Mayone Stycos, and **Kurt W. Back:** *The Family and Population Control*, The University of North Carolina Press, Chapel Hill, 1959.

Hillery, George A.: "Definitions of Community: Areas of Agreement," *Rural Sociology,* 20:111–123, 1955.

Himelhock, Jerome: "Generational Conflict and Youth Culture: Myth or Reality." Paper read at American Sociological Association, Washington, D.C., 1970.

Himes, Joseph S.: *Social Planning in America: A Dynamic Interpretation,* Doubleday & Company, Inc., Garden City, N.Y., 1954.

Hocart, Arthur M.: *Caste: A Comparative Study,* Methuen & Co., Ltd., London, 1950.

Hock, Saw Swee: "Family Planning Attitudes in West Malaysia," *South-East Journal of Sociology,* 2:59–61, May 1969.

Hodge, Robert W., and **Donald J. Treiman:** "Class Identification in the United States," *American Journal of Sociology,* 73:535–547, March 1968.

Hoebel, E. Adamson: *Man in the Primitive World,* McGraw-Hill Book Company, New York, 1949.

Hoffer, Eric: *The True Believer,* Harper & Row, Publishers, Incorporated, New York, 1951.

Hoffman, Abbie: *Revolution for the Hell of It,* The Dial Press, Inc., New York, 1968.

———: *Steal This Book,* Pirate Editions, New York, 1971. Distributed by Grove Press, Inc., New York.

Hoffman, Lois W.: "Research Findings on the Effects of Maternal Employment on the Child," in F. Ivan Nye and Lois W. Hoffman (eds.), *The Employed Mother in America,* Rand McNally & Company, Chicago, 1963, pp. 190–212.

Holden, David: "A Bad Case of Troubles Called Londonderry," *New York Times Magazine,* Aug. 3, 1969, pp. 10–11–29.

Hollingshead, August B.: *Elmtown's Youth,* John Wiley & Sons, Inc., New York, 1949.

——— and **Fredrich C. Redlich:** "Social Stratification and Psychiatric Disorders," *American Sociological Review,* 18:163–169, 1953.

——— and ———: *Social Class and Mental Illness: A Community Study,* John Wiley & Sons, Inc., New York, 1958.

Holzman, Mathilda, Zella Luria, and **Herbert Sherman:** "Adolescent Subculture: Endover, New England," *School Review,* 76:231–245, June 1968.

Hook, Sidney: "War against the Democratic Process," *Atlantic,* 223:45–49, April 1969.

———: "Real Crisis on the Campus," *Readers Digest,* 95:41–45, August 1969.

Hooton, E. A.: *Crime and the Man,* Harvard University Press, Cambridge, Mass., 1939.

Hopper, Janice A.: "Sociologists in the 1964 National Register of Scientific and Technical Personnel," *The American Sociologist,* 7:71–78, February 1966.

Horney, Karen: *The Neurotic Personality of Our Time,* W. W. Norton & Company, Inc., New York, 1937.

Horowitz, Irving Louis (ed.): *The New Sociology: Essays in Social Science and Social Theory in Honor of C. Wright Mills,* Oxford University Press, Fair Lawn, N.J., 1964.

Horsfall, James G.: "The Green Revolution: Agriculture in the Face of the Population Explosion," in Harold W. Helfrich, Jr., *The Environmental Crisis,* Yale University Press, New Haven, Conn., 1970, pp. 85–98.

Horton, Donald: "The Functions of Alcohol in Primitive Societies," *Quarterly Journal of Studies on Alcohol,* 4:293–303, 1943.

Horton, Paul B., and **Donald H. Bouma:** "The Sociological Reformation: Immolation or Rebirth?" *Sociological Focus,* 4:25–41, Winter 1970–1971.

——— and **Gerald R. Leslie:** *The Sociology of Social Problems,* Appleton Century Crofts, New York, 1970.

Horton, Philip: "Revivalism on the Far Right," *Reporter,* July 20, 1961, pp. 25–29.

Hostettler, John A.: "Persistence and Change Patterns in Amish Society," *Ethnology,* 3:185–198, April 1964.

Hoult, Thomas Ford: *Dictionary of Modern Sociology,* Littlefield, Adams and Company, Totowa, N.J., 1969.

Houriet, Robert: *Getting Back Together,* Coward-McCann & Geoghegan, New York, 1971.

Howard, John R. (ed.): *The Awakening Minorities: American Indians, Mexican Americans, Puerto Ricans,* Aldine Publishing House, Chicago, 1970.

Howton, F. William: "Cities, Slums, and Acculturative Process in Developing Countries," *Buffalo Studies,* 3:21–42, December 1967.

Hoyt, Homer: *One Hundred Years of Land Values in Chicago*, The University of Chicago Press, Chicago, 1933.

Huang, L. J.: "Some Changing Patterns in the Communist Chinese Family," *Marriage and Family Living*, 23:137–146, May 1961.

Huff, Darrell: *How to Lie with Statistics*, W. W. Norton & Company, Inc., New York, 1954.

Hunt, Chester L.: "The Treatment of 'Race' in Beginning Sociology Textbooks," *Sociology and Social Research*, 35:277–284, 1951.

———: *Social Aspects of Economic Development*, McGraw-Hill Book Company, New York, 1966.

———: "Catholicism and the Birth Rate," *Review of Religious Research*, vol. 8, Winter 1967, pp. 67–80.

Hunt, J. MCV.: "Has Compensatory Education Failed? Has It Been Attempted?" *Harvard Educational Review*, 39:278–300, Spring 1969.

Hunter, Floyd: *Community Power Structure*, The University of North Carolina Press, Chapel Hill, 1953.

Huntington, Ellsworth: *The Character of Races as Influenced by Physical Environment, Natural Selection and Historical Development*, Charles Scribner's Sons, New York, 1924.

Hurewitz, J. C.: *The Struggle for Palestine*, Greenwood Press, Publishers, New York, 1968.

Hurley, John R., and **Donna P. Palonen:** "Marital Satisfaction and Child Density Among University Student Parents," *Journal of Marriage and the Family*, 29:483–484, August 1967.

Hurlock, Elizabeth B.: "The Use of Group Rivalry as an Incentive," *Journal of Abnormal and Social Psychology*, 22:278–290 (1927).

Huxley, Aldous: *Brave New World*, Doubleday & Company, Inc., Garden City, N.Y., 1932.

———: *Brave New World Revisited*, Harper & Row, Publishers, Incorporated, New York, 1958.

Hyman, Herbert H., and **John Shelton Reed:** "'Black Matriarchy' Reconsidered: Evidence from Secondary Analysis of Sample Surveys," *Public Opinion Quarterly*, 33:346–354, Fall 1969.

——— and **Charles R. Wright,** "Trends in Voluntary Associational Memberships of American Adults: Replication Based on Secondary Analysis of National Sample Surveys," *American Sociological Review*, 23:191–206, April 1971.

Ilfeld, Fred, Jr., and **Roger Lauer:** *Social Nudism in America*, College and University Press Services Inc., New Haven, Conn., 1964.

Inkeles, Alex: "Social Stratification and Mobility in the Soviet Union: 1940–1950," *American Sociological Review*, 15:465–479, 1950.

———: "Industrial Man: The Relation of Status to Experience, Perception, and Value," *American Journal of Sociology*, 66:1–31, 1960.

Irelan, Lona M. (ed.): *Low Income Life Styles*, Publication 14, U.S. Welfare Administration, Washington, D.C., 1968.

Isambert, Francois-Andre: "Is the Religious Abstention of the Working Classes a General Phenomenon?" in Louis Schneider, *Religion, Culture, and Society*, John Wiley & Sons, Inc., 1964, pp. 400–402.

j (pseud.): *The Sensuous Woman*, Lyle Stuart, New York, 1970.

Jack, Nancy Koplin, and **Betty Schiffer:** "The Limits of Fashion Control," *American Sociological Review*, 13:730–738, 1948.

Jacobs, Jane: *The Death and Life of Great American Cities*, Random House, Inc., New York, 1961.

Jaffe, Frederich S., and **Stephen Polgar:** "Family Planning and Public Policy: Is the Culture of Poverty the New Cop-out?" *Journal of Marriage and the Family*, 30:228–235, May, 1968.

Jensen, Arthur R.: "Social Class, Race, and Genetics: Implications for Education," *American Education Research Journal*, 5:1–42, January 1968.

———: "How Much Can We Boost IQ and Scholastic Achievement?" *Harvard Educational Review*, 28:1–123, Winter 1969.

The John Birch Society, 1969, factsheet #R285, The Anti-Defamation League of B'Nai B'Rith, New York, n.d.

Johnson, Donald M.: "The 'Phantom Anesthetist' of Mattoon: A Field Study of Mass Hysteria," *Journal of Abnormal and Social Psychology*, 40:175–186, 1945.

Johnson, Nicholas: "What You Can Do to Improve TV," *Harper's Magazine*, 238:14–20, February 1969.

——: *How to Talk Back to Your Television Set*, Little, Brown and Company, Boston, 1970.

Jonassen, Christen T.: "Community Typology," in Marvin B. Sussman (ed.), *Community Structure and Analysis*, Thomas Y. Crowell Company, New York, 1959.

Jones, Howard W., and **William W. Scott**: *Hermaphroditism, Genital Abnormalities, and Related Endocrine Disorders*, The Williams & Wilkins Company, Baltimore, 1958.

Jones, J. Harry, Jr.: *The Minutemen*, Doubleday & Company, Inc., Garden City, N.Y., 1968.

Jost, Hudson, and **Lester W. Sontag**: "The Genetic Factor in Autonomic Nervous-System Function," *Psychosomatic Medicine*, 61:308–310, 1944.

Juppenlatz, Morris: *Cities in Transformation: The Urban Squatter Problem of the Developing World*, University of Queensland Press, St. Lucia, Queensland, Australia, 1970.

Kadushin, Charles: "How and Where to Find the Intellectual Elite in the United States," *Public Opinion Quarterly*, 35:1–18, Spring 1971.

Kagan, Jerome S.: "Inadequate Evidence and Illogical Conclusions," *Harvard Educational Review*, 39:274–277, Spring 1969.

Kahl, Joseph A.: "Educational and Occupational Aspirations of 'Common Man' Boys," *Harvard Educational Review*, 23:186–203, 1953.

Kahn, Si: *How People Get Power: Organizing Oppressed Communities for Action*, McGraw-Hill Book Company, New York, 1970.

Kain, John F.: *Race and Poverty—The Economics of Discrimination*, Prentice-Hall, Inc., Englewood Cliffs, N.J., 1969.

Kalinen, G. P., and **V. D. Bykov**: "The World's Water Resources: Past, Present, and Future," *Impact of Science on Society*, 19:135–140, April–June 1969.

Kallen, Horace M.: "On Americanizing the American Indian," *Social Research*, 25:469–473, 1958.

Kallman, Franz J.: "The Genetic Theory of Schizophrenia," *American Journal of Psychiatry*, 103:309–322, November 1946.

Kampf, Louis: "The Trouble With Literature," *Change Magazine*, May–June, 1970, pp. 27–34.

Kandel, Denise B., and **Gerald S. Lesser**: "Parental and Peer Influences on Educational Plans of Adolescents," *American Sociological Review*, 34:213–223, April 1969.

Kaplan, Bert: *A Study of Rorschach Responses in Four Cultures*, Papers of the Peabody Museum of American Archeology and Ethnology, vol. 42, no. 2, Harvard University, Cambridge, Mass., 1954.

—— and **Thomas F. A. Plaut**: *Personality in a Communal Society: An Analysis of the Mental Health of the Hutterites*, University of Kansas Press, Lawrence, 1956.

Kaplan, John: *Marijuana—The New Prohibition*, Harcourt Brace & World, Inc., New York, 1970.

Kardiner, Abram, and **Lionel Oversey**: *The Mark of Oppression: A Psychosocial Study of the American Negro*, W. W. Norton & Company, Inc., New York, 1951.

Kateb, George (ed.): *Utopia*, Aldine-Atherton Press, New York, 1971.

Katz, Daniel A., and **Robert L. Kahn**: "Open Systems Theory," *The Social Psychology of Organizations*, John Wiley & Sons, Inc., New York, 1966, pp. 14–29.

Kaufman, Walter C.: "Status, Authoritarianism, and Anti-semitism," *American Journal of Sociology*, 52:379–382, 1957.

Keesing, Roger M.: "Chiefs in a Chiefless Society: The Ideology of Modern Kwaio Politics," *Oceania*, 38:276–280, June 1968.

Kellogg, W. N., and **L. A. Kellogg**: *The Ape and the Child*, McGraw-Hill Book Company, New York, 1933.

Kelley, Dennis K., and **William J. Chambliss**: "Status Consistency and Political Attitudes," *American Sociological Review*, 31:375–382, June 1966.

Kelman, Herbert C.: "Deception in Social Research," *Trans-action*, 3:20–24, July–August 1966.

Kelman, Stephen: *Push Comes to Shove: The Escalation of Student Protest*, Houghton Mifflin Company, Boston, 1970.

Keniston, Kenneth: "The Sources of Discontent," in Walt Anderson (ed.), *The Age of Protest*, Goodyear Publishing Company, Pacific Palisades, Calif., 1969. Originally published in Kenneth Keniston, *Young Radicals: Notes on Committed Youth*, Harcourt, Brace & World, Inc., New York, 1968.

Kephart, W. M.: *Family, Society, and the Individual*, Houghton Mifflin Company, Boston, 1966.

Kercher, Leonard, Vant W. Kebker, and **Wilfred C. Leland, Jr.:** *Consumers' Cooperatives in the North Central States*, The University of Minnesota Press, Minneapolis, 1941.

Kerpelman, Larry C.: "Student Political Activism and Ideology: Comparative Characteristics of Activists and Nonactivists," *Journal of Counseling Psychology*, 16:8–13, 1969.

Kerr, Clark: "Industrial Conflict and Its Mediation," *American Journal of Sociology*, 60:230–245, November 1954.

Key, William H.: "Rural-Urban Differences and the Family," *Sociological Quarterly*, 2:49–56, 1961.

Keys, Ancel: "Experimental Induction of Neuropsychoses by Starvation," in Milbank Memorial Fund, *Biology of Mental Health and Disease*, Harper & Row, Publishers, Incorporated, New York, 1952, pp. 515–525.

Kharchev, A. G.: "The Nature of the Russian Family," *Voporosy Filosofia*, no. 1, translated and abridged in *Soviet Review*, 2:3–19, 1961.

Kinsey, Alfred C., Wardell B. Pomeroy, and **Clyde E. Martin:** *Sexual Behavior in the Human Male*, W. B. Saunders Company, Philadelphia, 1948.

—— et al.: *Sexual Behavior in the Human Female*, W. B. Saunders Company, Philadelphia, 1953.

Kirkendall, Lester A.: *Premarital Intercourse and Interpersonal Relations*, Julian Press, New York, 1961.

Kitagawa, Evelyn M., and **Philip H. Hauser:** *Education and Income Differentials in Mortality, United States, 1960*, University of Chicago Population Center, Chicago, 1967.

Klausner, Samuel Z.: *On Man in His Environment*, Jossey-Bass, Inc., San Francisco, 1971.

Klineberg, Otto: *Negro Intelligence and Selective Migration*, Columbia University Press, New York, 1935.

Kluckhohn, Clyde: "Participation in Ceremonials in a Navaho Community," *American Anthropologist*, 40:359–369, 1938.

Kluckhohn, Florence: "Dominant and Substitute Profiles of Cultural Orientation: Their Significance for an Analysis of Social Stratification," *Social Forces*, 28:376–393, 1950.

Knibbs, George Handley: *The Shadow of the World's Future: Or the Earth's Population Possibilities and Consequences of the Present Rate of Increase of the World's Inhabitants*, Ernest Benn, Ltd., London, 1928.

Knott, Paul D. (ed.): *Student Activism*, Wm. C. Brown Company, Publishers, Dubuque, Iowa, 1971.

Knudson, Dean D.: "The Declining Status of Women: Popular Myths and the Failure of Functionalist Thought," *Social Forces*, 48:183–193, December 1969.

Koenig, Robert P.: "An American Engineer Looks at British Coal," *Foreign Affairs*, 26:285–286, 1948.

Kohn, Melvin, "Bureaucratic Man: A Portrait and an Interpretation," *American Sociological Review*, 36:461–474, June 1971.

Kornhauser, William: *The Politics of Mass Society*, The Free Press of Glencoe, Inc., New York, 1959.

Kosa, John: "Patterns of Social Mobility among American Catholics," *Social Compass*, 9:361–371, December 1962. Reprinted in William T. Liu and Nathaniel J. Pallone, *Catholics/U.S.A. Perspectives on Social Change*, John Wiley & Sons, Inc., New York, 1970, pp. 15–24.

Kramer, Ralph M.: "Participation of the Poor," *Comparative Community Case Studies in the War on Poverty*, Prentice-Hall, Inc., Englewood Cliffs, N.J., 1969.

Kretschmer, Ernest: *Physique and Character*, Harcourt, Brace & World, Inc., New York, 1925.

Krout, Maurice A.: *Introduction to Social Psychology*, Harper & Row, Publishers, Incorporated, New York, 1942.

Kuhn, Manford H., and Thomas S. McPartland: "An Empirical Investigation of Self-Attitudes," *American Sociological Review*, 19:68–75, February 1954.

Kuo, Zing Yang: "Genesis of Cat's Responses in Rats," *Journal of Comparative Psychology*, 11:1–35, 1931.

Lander, Bernard: *Toward an Understanding of Juvenile Delinquency*, Columbia University Press, New York, 1954.

Landis, Paul H.: *Social Control*, J. B. Lippincott Company, Philadelphia, 1956.

——: *Making the Most of Marriage*, New York: Appleton Century Crofts, New York, 1970.

Lang, Kurt, and Gladys Engel Lang: *Collective Dynamics*, Thomas Y. Crowell Company, New York, 1961.

LaPiere, Richard T.: *Collective Behavior*, McGraw-Hill Book Company, Inc., New York, 1938.

——: *A Theory of Social Control*, McGraw-Hill Book Company, New York, 1954.

Laserwitz, Bernard: "Jews in and out of New York City," *The Jewish Journal of Sociology*, 3:254–260, December 1961.

Lasswell, Harold D.: "The Strategy of Soviet Propaganda," *Proceedings of the Academy of Political Science*, 1951, vol. 24, pp. 214–226.

—— and Dorothy Blumenstock: *World Revolutionary Propaganda*, Alfred A. Knopf, Inc., New York, 1939.

Lasswell, Thomas E.: *Class and Stratum*, Houghton Mifflin Company, Boston, 1965.

Lazerwitz, Bernard: "Religion and Social Structure in the United States," in Louis Schneider, *Religion, Culture and Society*, John Wiley & Sons, Inc., New York, 1964, pp. 426–435.

Lee, Alfred M.: *Multivalent Man*, George Braziller, Inc., New York, 1966.

—— and Elizabeth Briant Lee: *The Fine Art of Propaganda*, Harcourt, Brace & World, Inc. and the Institute for Propaganda Analysis, New York, 1939.

—— and Norman D. Humphrey: *Race Riot*, Holt, Rinehart and Winston, Inc., New York, 1943.

Lee, Dorothy: *Freedom and Culture*, Prentice-Hall, Inc., Englewood Cliffs, N.J., 1959 (a).

——: "The Cultural Curtain," *Annals of the American Academy of Political and Social Science*, 323:120–128, 1959 (b).

Lee, Ming T.: "The Founders of the Chinese Communist Party: A Study in Revolutionaries," *Civilizations*, 18:113–127, 1968.

Lee, Rose Hum: *The City*, J. B. Lippincott Company, Philadelphia, 1955.

Lehr, Stan, and Louis Rossetto, Jr.: "The New Right Credo—Libertarianism," *New York Times Magazine*, Jan. 10, 1971, pp. 24ff.

Lemert, Edwin M.: *Social Pathology*, McGraw-Hill Book Company, New York, 1951.

Lenski, Gerhard: "Status Crystallization: A Non-vertical Dimension of Social Status," *American Sociological Review*, 19:405–413, June 1954.

——: *The Religious Factor*, Doubleday & Company, Inc., Garden City, N.Y., 1961.

——: "Status Inconsistency and the Vote: A Four Nation Test," *American Sociological Review*, 32:298–301, April 1967.

——: *Human Societies: A Macrolevel Introduction to Sociology*, McGraw-Hill Book Company, New York, 1970.

——: "The Religious Factor in Detroit: Revisited," *American Sociological Review*, 36:48–50, February 1971.

Leon, Dan: *The Kibbutz: A New Way of Life*, Pergamon Press, New York, 1970.

Leslie, Gerald R.: *The Family in Social Context*, Oxford University Press, Fair Lawn, N.J., 1967.

Lesser, Alexander: "Cultural Significance of the Ghost Dance," *American Anthropologist*, 35:108–115, 1933.

Levy, Marion J.: *The Family Revolution in Modern China*, Harvard University Press, Cambridge, Mass., 1949.

————: "Social Patterns (Structures)," in Wilbert E. Moore and Robert M. Cook (eds.), *Readings on Social Change*, Prentice-Hall, Inc., Englewood Cliffs, N.J., 1966.

Lewis, Oscar: *Five Families: Mexican Case Studies in the Culture of Poverty*, Basic Books, Inc., Publishers, New York, 1959.

————: *The Children of Sanchez: Autobiography of a Mexican Family*, Vintage Books, Random House, Inc., New York, 1963 (a).

————: *Life in a Mexican Village: Tepoztlan Revisited*, with drawings by Alberto Beltram, The University of Illinois Press, Urbana, 1963 (b).

————: *Village Life in Northern India: Studies in a Delhi Village*, with the assistance of Victor Barnouw, Vintage Books, Random House, Inc., New York, 1965.

————: *La Vida: A Puerto Rican Family in the Culture of Poverty, San Juan and New York*, Random House, Inc., New York, 1966 (a).

————: "Culture of Poverty; with Biographical Sketch," *Scientific American*, 215:19–25, October 1966 (b).

Lewis, Sinclair: *Babbitt*, Harcourt, Brace & World, Inc., New York, 1922.

Leyburn, James G.: *Frontier Folkways*, Yale University Press, New Haven, Conn., 1935.

Lidz, Theodore, and **Albert Rothenberg:** "Psychedelism: Dionysus Reborn," *Psychiatry*, 31:116–125, May 1968.

Lieberman, E. James: "The Case for Small Families," *New York Times Magazine*, March 8, 1970, pp. 86–89.

Lieberson, Stanley, and **Arnold R. Silverman:** "Precipitants and Conditions of Race Riots," *American Sociological Review*, 30:887–898, December 1965.

Liebow, Elliot: *Tally's Corner: A Study of Negro Streetcorner Men*, Little, Brown and Company, New York, 1967.

Lief, Harold I.: Research note in *Behavior Today*, December 1970, p. 1.

Lilienthal, Alfred M.: *The Other Side of the Coin: An American Perspective of the Arab-Israeli Conflict*, The Devin-Adair Company,

Inc., New York, 1965.

Lincoln, C. Eric: *The Black Muslims in America*, Beacon Press, Boston, 1961.

Lindesmith, Alfred E.: "Social Problems and Sociological Theory," *Social Problems*, 8:98–102, 1960.

Lindzey, Gardner (ed.): *Handbook of Social Psychology*, Addison-Wesley Press, Inc., Cambridge, Mass., 1954.

Linton, Ralph: *The Study of Man*, Appleton Century Crofts, New York, 1936.

Lipsedge, M. S.: "The Poujade Movement," *Contemporary Review*, 189:83–88, 1956.

Lipset, Seymour M.: "Leadership and New Social Movements," in Alvin W. Gouldner (ed.), *Studies in Leadership*, Harper & Row, Publishers, Incorporated, New York, 1950, pp. 342–362.

————: "Vance Packard Discovers America," *Reporter*, July 9, 1959, pp. 32–33.

————, **A. Throw** and **James S. Coleman:** *Union Democracy: The Internal Politics of the International Typographical Union*, The Free Press of Glencoe, Ill., Chicago, 1956.

————: "George Wallace and the U.S. New Right," *New Society*, 12:477–482, October 1968.

Litwak, Eugene: "Three Ways in which Law Acts as a Means of Social Control: Punishment, Therapy, and Education," *Social Forces*, 34:217–223, 1956.

Locke, Hubert G.: *The Detroit Riot of 1967*, Wayne State University Press, Detroit, 1969.

Lohman, Joseph D.: *The Police and Minority Groups*, Chicago Park District, Chicago, 1947.

Lombroso, Cesare: *Crime, Its Causes and Remedies*. Translated by H. P. Horton, Little, Brown and Company, Boston, 1912.

Loomis, Charles P., and **J. Allan Beagle:** "The Spread of German Nazism in Rural Areas," *American Sociological Review*, 11:724–734, 1946.

———— and **Zona Kemp Loomis:** *Modern Social Theories*, D. Van Nostrand Company, Inc., Princeton, N.J., 1961.

Lopreato, Joseph, and **Janet E. Salzman:** "Descriptive Models of Peasant Society: A Reconciliation from Southern Italy," *Human Organization*, 27:132–142, Summer 1968.

Lorenz, Konrad: *On Aggression*, Harcourt, Brace & World, Inc., New York, 1966.

Lowenthal, Leo, and **Norbert Guterman:** *Prophets of Deceit*, Harper & Row, Publishers, Incorporated, New York, 1949.

Lowie, Robert H.: *Introduction to Cultural Anthropology*, Holt, Rinehart and Winston, Inc., New York, 1940.

Lowry, Ritchie P.: *Who's Running This Town? Community Leadership and Social Change*, Harper & Row, Publishers, Incorporated New York, 1965.

Luft, Joseph: *Group Processes: An Introduction to Group Dynamics*, National Press, Palo Alto, Calif., 1970.

Lumley, Frederick E.: *Means of Social Control*, Century Company, New York, 1925.

Lundberg, Ferdinand: *America's Sixty Families*, Vanguard Press, Inc., New York, 1937.

————: *The Rich and the Super Rich: A Study in the Power of Money Today*, Lyle Stuart, Inc., New York, 1968.

Lynch, Frank: *Social Class in a Bicol Town*, Philippines Studies Program, University of Chicago, Chicago, 1959.

Lynd, Robert S., and **Helen M. Lynd:** *Middletown*, Harcourt, Brace & World, Inc., New York, 1929.

———— and ————: *Middletown in Transition*, Harcourt, Brace & World, Inc., New York, 1937.

Lynd, Staughton: "The New Left," *Annals of the American Academy of Political and Social Science*, 382:64–72, March 1969.

McArthur, Charles: "Personality Differences between Upper-Class Harvard Freshmen (Private School Graduates) and Middle-Class Harvard Freshmen (Public School Graduates)," *Journal of Abnormal and Social Psychology*, 50:247–254, 1955.

McClosky, Herbert, and **John H. Schaar:** "Psychological Dimensions of Anomy," *American Sociological Review*, 30:14–40, February 1965.

McGinty, Alice B.: "India: A House Divided," *Current History*, 13:288–289, 1947.

McGothlin, William H., and **David O. Arnold:** "LSD Revisited: A Ten-Year Follow-up of LSD Medical Use," *Archives of General Psychiatry*, 24:35–49, January 1971.

MacCrone, Ian: *The Price of Apartheid*, South African Institute of Race Relations, Johannesburg, South Africa, 1970.

Mack, Dolores E.: "Where the Black-Matriarchy Theorists Went Wrong," *Psychology Today*, January 1971, pp. 24ff.

Mack, Raymond W.: "The Components of Social Conflict," *Social Problems*, 12:394–397, Spring 1965.

Mackay, Charles: *Extraordinary Popular Delusions and the Madness of Crowds*, L. C. Page & Company, Boston, 1932.

McCormack, Arthur: *The Population Problem*, Thomas Y. Crowell Co., New York, 1970.

McGurk, L. M.: "Psychological Tests: A Scientist's Report on Race Differences," *U.S. News and World Report*, Sept. 21, 1956, pp. 92–96.

McKee, James B.: "Status and Power in the Industrial Community: A Comment on Drucker's Thesis," *American Journal of Sociology*, 58:364–370, 1953.

McKenzie, R. D.: "The Ecological Approach to the Study of the Human Community," in Robert E. Park, E. W. Burgess, and R. D. McKenzie (eds.), *The City*, The University of Chicago Press, Chicago, 1925, pp. 63–79.

McKern, Sharon S., and **Thomas W. McKern:** "The Peace Messiah," in Raymond Friday Locke (ed.), *The American Indian*, Mankind Publishing Company, Los Angeles, 1970, pp. 147–176.

McNeil, Donald R.: *The Fight for Fluoridation*, Oxford University Press, Fair Lawn, N.J., 1957.

McVay, Frank L.: "The Social Effects of the Eight Hour Day," *American Journal of Sociology*, 8:521–530, January 1903.

Maher, Robert F.: *The New Man of Papua: A Study in Cultural Change*, The University of Wisconsin Press, Madison, 1961.

Malewski, Andrzej: "The Degree of Status Incongruence and Its Effects," in Reinhard Bendix and S. M. Miller (eds.), *Class, Status, and Power*, The Free Press, New York, 1966, pp. 303–308.

Malinowski, Bronislaw: *Crime and Custom in*

Savage Society, Routledge & Kegan Paul, Ltd., London, 1926.

Maliver, Bruce L.: "Encounter Groupers Up against the Wall," *New York Times Magazine*, Jan. 3, 1971, pp. 4ff.

Mangus, A. R.: "Personality Adjustment of Rural and Urban Children," *American Sociological Review*, 13:566-575, 1948.

Manis, Jerome G., and **Bernard N. Meltzer:** "Attitude of Textile Workers to Class Structure," *American Journal of Sociology*, 60:30-35, 1954.

——— and ———: "Some Correlates of Class Consciousness among Textile Workers," *American Journal of Sociology*, 69:177-184, September 1963.

Manis, Jerome, G., Milton J. Brawer, Chester L. Hunt, and **Leonard C. Kercher:** "Estimating the Prevalence of Mental Illness," *American Sociological Review*, 29:84-89, February 1964.

Mann, Richard D., Graham S. Gibbard, and **John J. Hartman:** *Interpersonal Styles and Group Development*, John Wiley & Sons, Inc., New York, 1967.

Manheim, Karl: *Man and Society in an Age of Reconstruction*, Harcourt, Brace & World, Inc., New York, 1940.

Marcuse, Herbert: *One-dimensional Man*, Beacon Press, Boston, 1964.

———: *An Essay on Liberation*, Beacon Press, Boston, 1969 (a).

———: "Student Protest Is Nonviolent Next to the Society Itself," *New York Times Magazine*, p. 137, May 4, 1969 (b).

Marriott, McKim (ed.): *Village India*, The University of Chicago Press, Chicago, 1955.

Marshall Kaplan, Gans, and **Kahn:** *The Model Cities Program: The Planning Process in Atlanta, Seattle, and Dayton*, Frederick A. Praeger, Inc., New York, 1970.

Marshall, Ray: "Labor in the South," *Antioch Review*, 21:80-95, 1961.

Marshall, S. L. A.: *Men under Fire*, William Morrow & Company, Inc., New York, 1947.

Martindale, Don, and **R. Galen Hanson:** *Small Town and the Nation: The Conflict of Local and Translocal Forces*, Greenwood Publishing Company, Westport, Conn., 1969.

Marx, Karl, and **Frederic Engels:** *Basic Writings on Politics and Philosophy*, ed. by Lewis S. Feuer, Doubleday & Co., Inc., New York, 1959.

Masters, William H., and **Virginia E. Johnson:** *Human Sexual Response*, Little, Brown and Company, Boston, 1966.

——— and ———: *Human Sexual Inadequacy*, Little, Brown and Company, New York, 1970.

Mausner, Bernard, and **Judith Mausner:** "A Study of the Anti-scientific Attitude," *Scientific American*, 192:35-39, 1955.

Maybee, C.: "Evolution of Non-Violence," *Nation*, 193:78-81, 1961.

Mayer, Albert J., et al.: *Pilot Project: India*, University of California Press, Berkeley, 1958.

Mead, George Herbert: *Mind, Self and Society*, The University of Chicago Press, Chicago, 1934.

Mead, Margaret: "The Implications of Culture Change for Personality Development," *American Journal of Orthopsychiatry*, 17:633-646, 1947.

———: *Cultural Patterns and Technical Change*, UNESCO, Mentor Books, New American Library, Inc., New York, 1955.

———: *New Lives for Old*, William Morrow & Company, Inc., New York, 1956.

———: *Culture and Commitment: A Study of the Generation Gap*, Natural History Press, New York, 1970.

Mecklin, John H.: *The Ku Klux Klan*, Harcourt, Brace & World, Inc., New York, 1924.

Meeker, Marcia: "Status Aspirations and the Social Club," in W. Lloyd Warner (ed.), *Democracy in Jonesville*, Harper & Row, Publishers, Incorporated, New York, 1949, pp. 130-148.

Merrill, Francis E.: "The Self and the Other: An Emerging Field of Social Problems," *Social Problems*, 4:200-207, January 1957.

Merton, Robert K.: "Social Structure and Anomie," *American Sociological Review*, 3:672-682, 1938.

———: "Bureaucratic Structure and Personality," in *Social Theory and Social Structure*, The Free Press, Glencoe, Ill., 1949, pp. 151-160.

——— et al. (eds.): *Reader in Bureaucracy*, The Free Press, Glencoe, Ill, 1952.

————: *Social Theory and Social Structure*, The Free Press of Glencoe, Inc., New York, 1957 (a).

————: "Manifest and Latent Functions: Toward a Codification of Functional Analysis in Sociology," in *Social Theory and Social Structure*, The Free Press of Glencoe, Inc., New York, 1957 (b) pp. 19–84.

————: "Priorities in Scientific Discovery: A Chapter in the Sociology of Science," *American Sociological Review*, 22:635–659, December 1957 (c).

Messinger, Sheldon L.: "Organizational Transformation: A Case Study of a Declining Social Movement," *American Sociological Review*, 20:3–10, 1955.

Meyer, Marshall W.: "Expertness and the Span of Control," *American Sociological Review*, 33:944–951, December 1968.

Meyer, Roger E.: "LSD: The Conditions and Consequences of Use and the Treatment of Users," in *Proceedings of the Rutgers Symposium on Drug Abuse.* Compiled and edited by J. R. Wittenborn et al., Charles C Thomas, Publisher, Springfield, Ill., 1969, pp. 199–208.

Michel, Andree, and **Francoise Lautman Feyrabend:** "Real Number of Children and Conjugal Interaction in French Urban Families: A Comparison with American Families," *Journal of Marriage and the Family*, 31:359–363, May 1969.

Michels, Robert: *Political Parties: A Sociological Study of the Oligarchial Tendencies in Modern Democracy.* Translated by Eden and Cedar Paul, The Free Press, Glencoe, Ill., 1949.

Michener, James A: *Kent State: What Happened and Why*, Random House, Inc., New York, 1971.

Micossi, Anita Lynn: "Conversion to Women's Lib," *Trans-action*, November–December 1970, pp. 82–90.

Milgram, Stanley, and **Hans Toch:** "Collective Behavior: Crowds and Social Movements," in Gardner Lindzey and Elliott Aronson (eds.), *Handbook in Social Psychology*, Addison-Wesley Publishing Company, Inc., Reading, Mass., 1969, vol. IV, pp. 507–610.

Miller, Arthur S.: "Some Observations on the Political Economy of Population Growth," *Law and Contemporary Problems*, 25:614–632, 1960.

Miller, Daniel C., and **Guy E. Swanson** et al.: *Inner Conflict and Defense*, Holt, Rinehart and Winston, Inc., New York, 1960.

Miller, Delbert C.: *International Community Power Structures: Comparative Studies of Four World Cities*, Indiana University Press, Bloomington, 1970.

Miller, Merle: "What It Means to Be a Homosexual," *New York Times Magazine*, Jan. 17, 1971, pp. 9ff.

Miller, S. M., and **Elliot G. Mishler:** "Social Class, Mental Illness, and American Psychiatry," *Milbank Memorial Fund Quarterly*, 37: 174–199, 1959.

———— and **Frank Riessman:** "The Working Class Subculture: A New View," *Social Problems*, 9:86–97, Summer 1961.

———— and **Pamela A. Roby:** *The Future of Inequality*, Basic Books, Inc., Publishers, New York, 1970.

Miller, Walter B.: "Lower Class Culture as a Generating Milieu of Gang Delinquency," *Journal of Social Issues*, (3) 14:5–19, 1958.

Millet, Kate: *Sexual Politics*, Doubleday & Company, Inc., Garden City, N.Y., 1970.

Mills, C. Wright: *The Power Elite*, Oxford University Press, Fair Lawn, N.J., 1956.

Mills, Theodore M.: *The Sociology of Small Groups*, Prentice-Hall, Inc., Englewood Cliffs, N.J., 1967.

Miner, Horace (ed.): *The City in Modern Africa*, Frederick A. Praeger, Inc., New York, 1952, 1967.

Mintz, Alexander: "Non-adaptive Group Behavior," *Journal of Abnormal and Social Psychology*, 46:150–158, 1951.

Mitchell, Robert Edward: "Methodological Notes on a Theory of Status Crystallization," *Public Opinion Quarterly*, 28:315–325, 1964.

Mittelbach, Frank C., and **Joan W. Moore:** "Ethnic Endogamy—The Case of Mexican Americans," *American Journal of Sociology*, 74:5–62, July, 1968.

Miyamoto, S. Frank, and **Sanford M. Dornbusch:** "A Test of Interactionist Hypothesis of

Self-conception," *American Journal of Sociology*, 61:399–403, 1956.

Monroe, Keith: "The New Gambling King and the Social Scientists," *Harper's Magazine*, January, 1962, pp. 35–41.

Montagna, Paul D.: "Professionalization and Bureaucratization in Large Professional Organizations," *American Journal of Sociology*, 74:138–145, September 1968.

Montagu, Ashley: *Man: His First Million Years*, Mentor Books, New American Library, Inc., New York, 1958.

———: *Sex, Man and Society*, G. P. Putnam's Sons, New York, 1969.

Moore, Joan W., with **Alfred Cuellar:** *Mexican Americans*, Prentice-Hall, Inc., Englewood Cliffs, N.J., 1970.

Moore, W. E.: *Industrial Relations and the Social Order*, The Macmillan Company, New York, 1947.

———: *Social Change*, Prentice-Hall, Englewood Cliffs, N.J., 1963.

Morehouse, Frances: "The Irish Migration of the 'Forties,'" *American Historical Review*, 33:579–592, 1928.

Moreno, J. L.: "Psychodramatic Treatment of Marriage Problems," *Sociometry*, 3:2–23, 1940.

Morgan, Theodore: "The Economic Development of Ceylon," *Annals of the American Academy of Political and Social Science*, 305:92–100, 1956.

Morris, Desmond: *The Naked Ape*, McGraw-Hill Book Company, New York, 1968.

Morrison, Delton E., and **Allan D. Steeves:** "Deprivation, Discontent, and Social Movement Participation," *Rural Sociology*, 32:414–434, December 1967.

Mosk, Stanley, and **Howard H. Jewel:** "The Birch Phenomenon Analyzed," *New York Times Magazine*, Aug. 20, 1961, pp. 12ff.

Motwani, Kewal: "The Impact of Modern Technology on the Social Structure of South Asia," *International Social Science Bulletin*, 3:783–793, Winter 1951.

Moynihan, Daniel P.: "Behind Los Angeles: Jobless Negroes and the Boom," *The Reporter*, Sept. 9, 1965 (a), p. 31.

———: *The Negro Family: The Case for National Action*, U.S. Department of Labor, Washington, D.C., 1965 (b).

———: *Maximum Feasible Misunderstanding: Community Action in the War on Poverty*, The Free Press, New York, 1969.

Muhler, Joseph Charles, and **Maynard K. Hine** (eds.): *Fluorine and Dental Health: The Pharmacology and Toxicology of Fluorine*, Indiana University Press, Bloomington, 1959.

Munch, Peter A.: "Culture and Super-Culture in a Displaced Community: Tristan de Cunha," *Ethnology*, 3:369–376, October 1964.

———: *Crisis in Utopia* Thomas Y. Crowell Company, New York, 1970.

Muramatsu, Minoru: "Effect of Induced Abortion on the Reduction of Births in Japan," *Milbank Memorial Fund Quarterly*, 38:153–166, 1960.

Murdock, George P.: *Our Primitive Contemporaries*, The Macmillan Company, New York, 1936.

———: *Social Structure*, The Macmillan Company, New York, 1949.

———: "Sexual Behavior: A Comparative Anthropological Approach," *Journal of Social Hygiene*, 36:133–138, 1950.

Murphy, Gardner, Lois Murphy, and **Theodore M. Newcomb:** *Experimental Social Psychology*, Harper & Row, Publishers, Incorporated, New York, 1937.

Muth, Richard F.: *The Spatial Pattern of Urban Residential Land Use*, The University of Chicago Press, Chicago, 1969.

Myers, Jerome and **Lee L. Bean** in collaboration with **Max P. Pepper:** *A Decade Later: A Follow-up of Social Class and Mental Illness*, John Wiley & Sons, Inc., New York, 1968.

Myrdal, Gunnar: *An American Dilemma*, Harper & Row, Publishers, Incorporated, New York, 1944.

———: *Rich Lands and Poor*, Harper & Row, Publishers, Incorporated, New York, 1957.

Nader, Ralph: *Unsafe at Any Speed: The Designed-in Dangers of the American Automobile*, Grossman, New York, 1965.

Nakasa, Nathaniel: "The Human Meaning of

Apartheid," *New York Times Magazine*, Sept. 24, 1961, pp. 42ff.

Nash, Dennison: "The Fate of Americans in a Spanish Setting: A Study of Adaptation," *Human Organization*, 26:157–163, Fall 1967.

Nash, June: "The Logic of Behavior: Curing in a Maya Town," *Human Organization*, 26:132–140, Fall 1967.

Nash, Philleo: "The Place of Religious Revivalism . . . ," in Fred Eggan (ed.), *Social Anthropology of the North American Tribes*, The University of Chicago Press, Chicago, 1937.

National Academy of Sciences: *The Behavorial and Social Sciences: Outlook and Needs*, Prentice-Hall, Inc., Englewood Cliffs, N.J., 1969.

National Advisory Commission on Civil Disorders: *Report*, Washington, D.C., 1968; Bantam Books, Inc., New York, 1968.

Nelson, Edward W.: "The Eskimo about Bering Straits," *18th Annual Report, Bureau of American Ethnology*, Washington, 1899, part 1, pp. 268–270.

Nelson, Jack, and **Jack Bass:** *The Orangeburg Massacre*, The World Publishing Company, Cleveland, 1970.

Nettler, Gwynn: "A Measure of Alienation," *American Sociological* Review, 22:670–677, 1957.

Nichols, Lee: *Breakthrough on the Color Front*, Random House, Inc., New York, 1954.

Nimkoff, Meyer F., and **Russell Middleton:** "Types of Family and Types of Economy," *American Journal of Sociology*, 66:215–225, 1960.

Nisbet, Robert A.: "The Decline and Fall of Social Class," *Pacific Sociological* Review, 2:11–17, Spring 1959.

——: "The University Had Better Mind Its Own Business," *Psychology Today*, 4:22–37, March 1971.

Nordhoff, Charles: *The Communistic Societies of the United States* (1875), Schocken Books Inc., New York, 1965.

Nunn, W. C.: *Escape from Reconstruction*, Leo Potishman Foundation, Ft. Worth, 1956.

Nye, F. Ivan: "Adolescent-Parent Adjustment: Age, Sex, Sibling Number, Broken Homes, and Employed Mothers as Variables," *Marriage and Family Living*, 14:327–332, November 1952.

——: *Family Relationships and Delinquent Behavior*, John Wiley & Sons, Inc., New York, 1958.

——: "Maternal Employment and the Adjustment of Adolescent Children," *Marriage and Family Living*, 21:240–244, August 1959.

—— and **Lois M. Hoffman:** *The Employed Mother in America*, Rand McNally & Company, Chicago, 1963.

——, **John Carlson,** and **Gerald Garrett:** "Family Size, Interaction, Affect, and Stress," *Journal of Marriage and the Family*, 32:216–226, May 1970.

O'Connor, Patricia: "Intolerance of Ambiguity and Abstract Reasoning Ability," *Journal of Abnormal and Social Psychology*, 47:526–530, 1952.

Odum, Howard W.: *Understanding Society*, The Macmillan Company, New York, 1947.

Ogburn, William F.: "The Influence of Invention and Discovery," in President's Research Committee on Social Trends, *Recent Social Trends*, McGraw-Hill Book Company, New York, 1933, pp. 122–166.

——: *Social Change*, The Viking Press, Inc., New York, 1922, 1950.

——: "The Wolf Boy of Agra," *American Journal of Sociology*, 64:449–454, March 1959.

—— and **Meyer F. Nimkoff:** *A Handbook of Sociology*, Routledge & Kegan Paul, Ltd., London, 1964.

Oglesby, Carl (ed.): *The New Left Reader*, Grove Press, Inc., New York, 1969.

O'Hanlon, Thomas: "Anarchy Threatens the Kingdom of Coal," *Fortune*, 78–85, January 1971.

Olcott, Mason: "The Caste System of India," *American Sociological Review*, 9:648–657, 1944. Reprinted in H. Lawrence Ross (ed.), *Perspectives on the Social Order, Readings in Sociology*, McGraw-Hill Book Company, New York, 1968, pp. 405–413.

Olson, Philip: "Rural American Community Studies: The Survival of Public Ideology,"

Human Organization, 23:342–350, Winter 1964–1965.

O'Neill, William L.: *Everyone Was Brave: The Rise and Fall of Feminism in America,* Quadrangle Books, Inc., Chicago, 1969.

Orden, Susan R., and Norman M. Bradburn: "Working Wives and Marital Happiness," *American Journal of Sociology,* 74:392–407, January 1969.

Organski, Katherine, and A. F. K. Organski: *Population and World Power,* Alfred A. Knopf, Inc., New York, 1962.

Otten, Michael C.: *University Authority and the Student: The Berkeley Experiment,* University of California Press, Berkeley, 1970.

Ottenberg, Simon: "Ileo Receptivity to Change," in William R. Bascom and Melville J. Herskovitz (eds.), *Continuity and Change in African Cultures,* The University of Chicago Press, Chicago, 1959, pp. 130–143.

Packard, Vance: *The Hidden Persuaders,* David McKay Company, Inc., New York, 1957.

———: *The Status Seekers,* David McKay Company, Inc., New York, 1959.

———: *The Pyramid Climbers,* McGraw-Hill Book Company, New York, 1962.

———: *The Sexual Wilderness,* David McKay Company, Inc., New York, 1968.

Page, Joseph A.: "Law Professor behind ASH, SOUP, PUMP and CRASH," *New York Times Magazine,* Aug. 23, 1970, pp. 32ff.

Park, Robert E.: "Human Migration and the Marginal Man," *American Journal of Sociology,* 33:893, May 1928.

———: *Race and Culture,* The Free Press, Glencoe Ill., 1949.

Park, Robert E., and Ernest Burgess: *Introduction to the Science of Sociology,* The University of Chicago Press, Chicago, 1921.

———, ———, and R. D. McKenzie: *The City,* The University of Chicago Press, Chicago, 1925.

Parker, Seymour, and Robert J. Kleiner: *Mental Illness in the Urban Negro Community,* The Free Press, New York, 1966.

Parsons, Talcott: *Structure and Process in Modern Society,* The Free Press of Glencoe, Inc., New York, 1960.

———: "On the Concept of Political Power," *Proceedings of the American Philosophical Society,* 107:232–262, June 1963.

———: "Evolutionary Universals in Society," *American Sociological Review,* 29:339–357, June 1964.

Parten, Mildred: *Surveys, Polls, and Samples: Practical Procedures,* Harper & Row, Publishers, Incorporated, New York, 1950.

Pasley, Virginia: *21 Stayed,* Farrar, Straus & Co., New York, 1955.

Pavenstedt, Eleanor (ed.): *The Drifters: Children of Disorganized Lower-Class Families,* Little, Brown and Company, Boston, 1967.

Pearson, Karl: *The Grammar of Science,* A. & C. Black, Ltd., London, 1900.

Peck, James: *Freedom Ride,* Simon & Schuster, Inc., New York, 1962.

Pellegren, Roland J., and Charles H. Coates: "Absentee-owned Corporations and Community Power Structure," *American Journal of Sociology,* 61:413–419, 1956.

Perruci, Robert, and Marc Pilisuk: "Leaders and Ruling Elites: The Interorganizational Bases of Community Power," *American Sociological Review,* 35:1040–1057, December 1970.

Peters, John Fred: "Mate Selection among the Shirishna," *Practical Anthropology,* 18:19–23, January–February 1971.

Petersen, William: Review of *Vance Packard: The Status Seekers, American Sociological Review,* 25:124–126, February 1960.

Pettigrew, Thomas R.: *Profile of the Negro American,* D. Van Nostrand Company, Inc., Princeton, N.J. 1964.

———: "Racially Separate or Together?" *Journal of Social Issues,* 25:43–69, January, 1969.

Phillips, Bernard S.: *Social Research,* The Macmillan Company, New York, 1966.

Phillips, Derek L.: "Deferred Gratification in a College Setting: Some Gains and Costs," *Social Problems,* 13:333–343, Winter 1966.

——— and Kevin J. Clancy: "Response Bias in Field Studies of Mental Illness," *American Sociological Review,* 35:503–505, June 1970.

Piercy, Marge: "The Grand Coolie Damn," in Robin Morgan, *Sisterhood Is Powerful,* Random House, Inc., New York, 1970, pp. 421–438.

Plaut, Thomas F. A.: "Analysis of Voting Behavior on a Voting Referendum," *Public Opinion Quarterly*, 23:213–222, 1959.

Podalsky, Edward: "The Sociopathic Alcoholic," *Quarterly Journal of Studies on Alcohol*, 21:292–297, June 1960.

Pope, Liston: "Religion and the Class Structure," *The Annals of the American Academy of Political and Social Science*, 256:84–91, 1948.

Porterfield, Austin L.: *Youth in Trouble*, Leo Potishman Foundation, Fort Worth, Tex., 1946.

Potter, Robert G., Ronald Freedman, and **Lien-Ping Chow:** "Taiwan's Family Planning Program," *Science*, 160:848–852, May 24, 1968.

Potvin, Raymond, Charles F. Westoff, and **Norman B. Ryder:** "Factors Affecting Catholic Wives' Conformity to their Church Magisterium's Position on Birth Control," *Journal of Marriage and the Family*, 30:263–272, May 1968.

Powledge, Fred: *Model City, A Test of American Liberalism: One Town's Efforts to Rebuild Itself,* Simon & Schuster, Inc., New York, 1970.

Preston, James D.: "The Search for Community Leaders: A Re-examination of the Reputational Technique," *Sociological Inquiry*, 39:39–47, Winter 1969.

"Protecting Man From Man: Setting Limits to Genetic Engineering," *Science News*, 95:31–33, Jan. 11, 1969.

Prothro, E. Terry: "Ethnocentrism and Anti-Negro Attitudes in the Deep South," *Journal of Abnormal and Social Psychology*, 47:104–108, January 1952.

Pyle, Ernie: *Brave Men*, Holt, Rinehart and Winston, Inc., New York, 1943.

Qualter, Terence H.: *Propaganda and Psychological Warfare*, Random House, Inc., New York, 1962.

Queen, Stuart A., Robert W. Haberstein, and **John B. Adams:** *The Family in Various Cultures,* J. B. Lippincott Company, Philadelphia, 1961.

Quinney, Richard: *The Social Reality of Crime*, Little, Brown and Company, Boston, 1970.

Rakstis, Ted J.: "Sensitivity Training: Fad, Fraud, or New Frontier?" *Today's Health*, January 1970, pp. 20ff.

Ransford, H. Edward: "Isolation, Powerlessness and Violence: A Study of Attitudes and Participation in the Watts Riot," *American Journal of Sociology*, 73:581–591, March 1968.

Rao, Mihir Kumar: "Family Planning a National Obligation," *Kurukshetra*, 15:11–13, February 1967.

Rao, P. Kodandra: *Bi-lingualism for India*, W. O. Judge, Bengal, India, 1956.

Raper, Arthur F.: *The Tragedy of Lynching*, The University of North Carolina Press, Chapel Hill, 1933.

"Rebels in Indonesia," *Economist*, 181:59, 1956.

Reckless, Walter C., et al.: "The Good Boy in a High Delinquency Area," *Journal of Criminal Law, Criminology and Police Science*, 47:18–25, May–June 1957.

"Red Torture Broke Few G. I.'s," *U.S. News and World Report*, August 8, 1955, p. 8.

Reich, Charles: *The Greening of America: How the Youth Revolution Is Trying to Make America Livable*, Random House, Inc., New York, 1970.

Reiss, Albert J., Jr.: "Rural-Urban Status Differences in Interpersonal Contacts," *American Journal of Sociology*, 65:182–195, 1959.

Reiss, Ira L.: *Pre-marital Sexual Standards in America*, The Free Press of Glencoe, Inc., New York, 1960.

——: *The Social Context of Sexual Permissiveness*, Holt, Rinehart and Winston, Inc., New York, 1967.

Reissman, Leonard: Rev. of *C. Wright Mills: The Power Elite*, *American Sociological Review*, 21:513–514, August 1956.

——: "Readiness to Succeed: Mobility Aspirations and Modernism among the Poor," *Urban Affairs Quarterly*, 4:379–396, March 1969.

Reitlinger, Gerald: *The Final Solution: The Attempt to Exterminate the Jews of Europe*, Thomas Yoselof, South Brunswick, N.J., 1968.

Reuben, David: *Everything You Always Wanted to Know about Sex and Were Afraid to Ask,* David McKay Company, Inc., 1968.

Reusch, Jurgen: "Social Technique, Social Status, and Social Change in Illness," in Clyde Kluckhohn and Henry A. Murray, with D. M. Schiender (eds.), *Personality in Nature, Society, and Culture,* 2d ed., Alfred A. Knopf, Inc., New York, 1953, pp. 123–136.

Ribble, Margaret A.: *The Rights of Infants,* Columbia University Press, New York, 1943.

Ridker, R. G.: "Desired Family Size and the Efficacy of Current Family Planning Programmes," *Population Studies,* 23:279–284, July 1969.

Riemer, Svend: "Social Planning and Social Organization," *American Journal of Sociology,* 52:508–516, 1947.

Riesman, David, with **Nathan Glazer** and **Reuel Denney:** *The Lonely Crowd: A Study in the Changing American Character,* Yale University Press, New Haven, Conn., 1950.

Rivers, W. H. R.: "On the Disappearance of Useful Arts," in *Festkrift Tillägnad Edward Westermarck,* Helsingfors, 1912, pp. 109–130. Summarized in A. L. Kroeber, *Anthropology,* Harcourt, Brace & World, Inc., New York, 1949, p. 375.

—— (ed.): *Essays on the Depopulation of Melanesia,* Cambridge University Press, London, 1922.

Roach, Jack L., and **Orville R. Gursslin:** "An Evaluation of the Concept of the Culture of Poverty," *Social Forces,* 45:383–392, March 1967.

Robinson, H. A., F. C. Redlich, and **J. K. Myers:** "Social Structure and Psychiatric Treatment," *American Journal of Orthopsychiatry,* 24:307–316, 1954.

Robinson, Ira, Karl King, Charles Indby, and **Frances Clune:** "Change in Sexual Behavior and Attitudes of College Students," *The Family Coordinator,* 17:119–123, April 1968.

Roby, Thornton: *Small Group Performance,* Rand McNally & Company, Chicago, 1968.

Rock, Ronald S., with **Marcus A. Jacobson** and **Richard M. Janopaul:** *Hospitalization and Discharge of the Mentally Ill,* The University of Chicago Press, Chicago, 1968.

Roebuck, Julian, and **S. Lee Spray:** "The Cocktail Lounge: A Study in Heterosexual Relations in a Public Organization," *American Journal of Sociology,* 72:388–395, January 1967.

Roethlisberger, F. J.: *Management and Morale,* Harvard University Press, Cambridge, Mass., 1949.

—— and **William J. Dickson:** *Management and the Worker,* Harvard University Press, Cambridge, Mass., 1939.

Rogers, Everett M., and **Rabel J. Burdge:** *Social Change in Rural Society,* Appleton Century Crofts, New York, 1972.

Rogin, Richard: "This Place Makes Bedford-Stuyvesant Look Beautiful," *New York Times Magazine,* Mar. 28, 1971, pp. 30ff.

Rogow, Robert T.: "Membership Participation and Centralized Control," *Industrial Relations,* 7:132–145, February 1968.

"Rome and New Orleans," *America,* Aug. 24, 1957, p. 518.

Romm, Ethel Grodzins: *The Open Conspiracy: What America's Angry Young Generation Is Saying,* Stackpole Books, Harrisburg, Pa., 1970.

Rose, A. J.: *Patterns of Cities,* Thomas Nelson, Ltd., Melbourne, Australia, 1967.

Rose, Arnold: *Union Solidarity: The Internal Cohesion of a Union,* The University of Minnesota Press, Minneapolis, 1952.

——: *Theory and Method in the Social Sciences,* The University of Minnesota Press, Minneapolis, 1954.

Rosen, Bernard: "The Reference Group Approach to the Parental Factor in Attitude and Behavior Formation," *Social Forces,* 24:137–144, 1955 (a).

——: "Conflicting Group Membership: A Study of Parent-Peer Group Cross-Pressure," *American Sociological Review,* 20:155–161, 1955 (b).

——: "The Achievement Syndrome: A Psychocultural Dimension of Social Stratification," *American Sociological Review,* 21:203–211, 1956.

Rosenblum, A. Leon: "Social Class Affiliation and Ethnic Prejudice," *International Journal* *of Comparative Sociology*, 8:245–264, Summer 1967.

———: "On Caste and Class in India: A Theoretical Aspect of Social Change," *Indian Sociological Bulletin*, 6:87–96, January, 1969.

Rosenstone, Robert A.: "'The Times They Are A-Changing': The Music of Protest," *The Annals of the American Academy of Political and Social Science*, 382:131–144, March 1969.

Rosenthal, Donald B., and **Robert L. Crain:** "Structure and Values in Local Political Systems: The Case of Fluoridation Decisions," *Journal of Politics*, 28:169–195, February 1966.

Rosenthal, Robert, and **Lenore Jacobson:** "Teacher Expectations for the Disadvantaged," *Scientific American*, 218:16ff, April 1968.

Ross, Arthur: "Wage Determination and Collective Bargaining," *The American Economic Review*, 37:793–822, December 1947.

Ross, Madeline, and **Fred Kerner:** "Stars and Bars along the Amazon," *Reporter*, Sept. 18, 1958, pp. 34–36.

Rossi, Peter H.: Review of *C. Wright Mills, The Power Elite, American Journal of Sociology,* 62:232–233, 1956.

———: "Community Decision Making," *Administrative Science Quarterly*, 1:415–443, 1957.

Roszak, Betty, and **Theodore Roszak:** *Masculine-Feminine: Readings in Sexual Mythology and the Liberation of Women*, Harper & Row, Publishers, Incorporated, New York, 1970.

Roszak, Theodore: *The Making of a Counter Culture: Reflections on the Technocratic Society and Its Youthful Opposition*, Doubleday & Company, Inc., Garden City, 1969.

Rother, Ira S.: "The Righteous Rightists," *Trans-action*, 4:27–35, May 1967.

Routh, Frederick B., and **Paul Anthony:** "Southern Resistance Forces," *Phylon*, 18:50–58, 1957.

Roy, Donald: "Efficiency and 'The Fix': Informal Intergroup Relations in a Piecework Machine Shop," *American Journal of Sociology,* 60:225–266, 1955.

Rubenstein, Richard E.: *Rebels in Eden: Mass Political Violence in the U.S.*, Little, Brown and Company, Boston, 1970.

Runciman, Stephen: *Byzantine Civilization*, Meridian Books, Inc., New York, 1956.

Rushing, William A.: "Two Patterns in the Relationship between Social Class and Mental Hospitalization," *American Sociological Review*, 34:533–541, August 1969.

Rustin, Bayard: "A Way Out of the Exploding Ghetto," *New York Times Magazine*, Aug. 13, 1967, pp. 16ff.

Ryan, Bryce F.: *Caste in Modern Ceylon*, Rutgers University Press, New Brunswick, N.J., 1953.

Rydon, Hope: "On the Trail of the West's Wild Horses," *National Geographic*, January 1971, pp. 94–109.

Sagarin, Edward: *Odd Man In: Societies of Deviants in America*, Quadrangle Books, Inc., Chicago, 1970.

Sahlins, Marshall D.: "Land Use and the Extended Family in Moala, Fiji," *American Anthropologist*, 59:449–462, 1957.

Sandoz, Mari: *The Buffalo Hunters*, Hastings House, Publishers, Inc., New York, 1954.

Santrock, John W.: "Paternal Absence, Sex Typing and Identification," *Developmental Psychology*, 2:264–272, April 1970.

Satin, Lowell R.: "Next Steps to Sustain the Agricultural Revolution," *International Development Review*, 11:20–21, March 1969.

Schachter, Stanley: "Deviation, Rejection, and Communication," *Journal of Abnormal and Social Psychology*, 46:190–207, 1951.

Schaffer, Frank: *The New Town Story*, Mac-Gibbon and Kee, Ltd., London, 1970.

Schein, Edgar H.: "Interpersonal Communication, Group Solidarity and Social Influence," *Sociometry*, 23:148–161, 1960.

Schiller, Bradley R.: "Stratified Opportunities: The Essence of the Vicious Circle," *American Journal of Sociology*, 76:426–442, November 1970.

Schindler, John A.: *How to Live 365 Days a Year*, Prentice-Hall, Inc., Englewood Cliffs, N.J., 1954.

Schlesinger, Arthur M., Jr.: *The Age of Roosevelt*, vol. 3, *The Politics of Upheaval*, Houghton Mifflin Company, Boston, 1960.

Schneider, Harold K.: "Pakot Resistance to Change," in William R. Bascom and Melville J. Herskovitz (eds.), *Continuity and Change in African Cultures*, The University of Chicago Press, Chicago, 1959, pp. 144-167.

Schneider, Louis, and **Sverre Lysgaard**: "The Deferred Gratification Pattern: A Preliminary Study," *American Sociological Review*, 18: 142-194, 1953.

Schuler, Edgar A., and **V. J. Parenton**: "A Recent Epidemic of Hysteria in a Louisiana High School," *Journal of Social Psychology*, 17:221-235, 1943.

Schultz, George, and **Charles Meyers**: "Union Demands and Unemployment," *The American Economic Review*, 40:362-380, June 1950.

Schuman, Howard: "The Religious Factor in Detroit: Review, Replication and Reanalysis," *American Sociological Review*, 36:30-48, February 1971.

Schur, Edwin M. (ed.): *The Family and the Sexual Revolution*, Indiana University Press, Bloomington, 1964.

Schutz, William C.: *Joy-expanding Human Relationships*, Grove Press, Inc., New York, 1967.

Schwartz, Michael, and **Sandra S. Tangri**: "A Note on Self-concept as an Insulator against Delinquency," *American Sociological Review*, 30:922-934, December 1965.

Scoble, Harry: "Leadership Hierarchies and Political Issues in a New England Town," in Morris Janowitz, *Community Political Systems*, Free Press of Glencoe, Inc., New York, 1961.

Sears, Robert R., Eleanor E. Macoby, and **Harry Levin**: *Patterns of Child Rearing*, Harper & Row, Publishers, Incorporated, New York, 1957.

Segre, V. D.: *Israel: A Society in Transition*, Oxford University Press, London, 1971.

Seligman, Daniel: "A Special Kind of Rebellion," *Fortune*, January, 1969, pp. 67ff., also, June 1959, p. 73.

Selznick, Philip: "An Approach to the Theory of Bureaucracy," *American Sociological Review*, 8:47-554, 1943.

Senior, Clarence: *Puerto Ricans: Strangers, Then Neighbors*, Quadrangle Books, Inc., Chicago, 1965.

Servin, Manuel P.: *The Mexican Americans: An Awakening Minority*, The Free Press, New York, 1970.

Sewell, William H.: "Infant Training and the Personality of the Child," *American Journal of Sociology*, 58:150-159, 1952.

Sexton, Patricia Cayo: *The Feminized Male: Classrooms, White Collars and the Decline of Manliness*, Random House, Inc., New York, 1969.

Shaffer, Harry G.: "New Winds in Soviet Planning," *Queen's Quarterly*, 75:402-409, August 1968.

Sharp, Lauriston: "Steel Axes for Stone Age Australians," in Edward H. Spicer (ed.), *Human Problems in Technological Change*, Russell Sage Foundation, New York, 1952, pp. 69-90.

Sharp, Rodney: Address reported in *Los Angeles Times*, Oct. 25, 1969. Reprinted in *Population Bomb* Clippings, March 1970.

Shaskolsky, Leon: "The Negro Protest Movement—Revolt or Reform?" *Phylon*, 29:156-166, Summer 1968.

——— and **M. E. Moore**: *The Natural History of a Delinquent Career*, The University of Chicago Press, Chicago, 1931.

———, **H. D. McKay,** and **G. F. McDonald**: *Brothers in Crime*, The University of Chicago Press, Chicago, 1938.

Sheldon, William H., and **S. S. Stevens**: *The Varieties of Temperament*, Harper & Row, Publishers, Incorporated, New York, 1942.

———: *Varieties of Delinquent Youth*, Harper & Row, Publishers, Incorporated, New York, 1949.

Shepard, Martin, and **Marjorie Lee**: *Marathon 16*, G. P. Putnam's Sons, New York, 1970.

Shepher, Joseph: "Familism and Social Structure: The Case of the Kibbutz," *Journal of Marriage and the Family*, 31:567-573, August 1969.

Sherif, Muzafer A.: "A Study of Some Social Factors in Perception," *Archives of Psychology*, no. 187, 1935.

——— and **Carolyn Sherif**: *Groups in Harmony and Tension*, Harper & Row, Publishers, Incorporated, New York, 1953.

————: "Superordinate Goals in the Reduction of Intergroup Conflict," *American Journal of Sociology*, 63:349–356, 1958.

Sherman, Mandell, and **Thomas R. Henry:** *Hollow Folk*, Thomas Y. Crowell Company, New York, 1933.

Shibutani, Tamotsu: *Society and Personality: An Interactionist Approach to Social Psychology*, Prentice-Hall, Inc., Englewood Cliffs, N.J., 1961.

Shils, Edward A., and **Morris Janowitz:** "Cohesion and Disintegration in the Wehrmacht in World War II," *Public Opinion Quarterly*, 12:280–315, 1948.

————: "Primary Groups in the American Army," in Robert K. Merton and Paul Lazarsfeld (eds.), *Continuities in Social Research: Studies in the Scope and Method of the American Soldier*, The Free Press, Glencoe, Ill., 1950.

Short, James F., Jr., and **Fred L. Strodtbeck:** *Group Process and Gang Delinquency*, The University of Chicago Press, Chicago, 1965.

Shostak, Arthur B. (ed.): *Sociology in Action: Case Studies in Social Problems and Directed Social Change*, The Dorsey Press, Homewood, Ill., 1966.

Shuey, Audrey M.: *The Testing of Negro Intelligence*, J. P. Bell Company, Lynchburg, Va., 1958.

Shur, Edwin F.: *Crimes without Victims: Deviant Behavior and Public Policy*, Prentice-Hall, Inc., Englewood Cliffs, N.J., 1965.

Shuval, Judith L.: "Class and Ethnic Correlates of Casual Neighboring," *American Sociological Review*, 21:453–458, 1956.

Silberman, Charles E.: *Crisis in Black and White*, Random House, Inc., New York, 1964.

————: "Negro Economic Gains, Impressive but Precarious," *Fortune*, 82:74–78, July 1970.

Simmel, Georg: *Conflict.* Translated by Reinhard Bendix, The Free Press of Glencoe, Ill., Chicago, 1955.

————: *Georg Simmel.* Translated and edited by Kurt Wolff, Ohio State University Press, Columbus, 1959.

Simmons, J. L.: *Deviants*, Glendessary Press, Berkeley, 1970.

Simon, William: Review of *Vance Packard: The Sexual Wilderness, American Sociological Review*, 34:605–606, August 1969.

Simpson, George E.: "Darwinism and Social Darwinism," *Antioch Review*, 19:33–46, 1959.

———— and **J. Milton Yinger:** *Racial and Cultural Minorities: An Analysis of Prejudice and Discrimination*, Harper & Row, Publishers, Incorporated, New York, 1965.

Singh, J. A. L., and **Robert M. Zingg:** *Wolf-Children and Feral Men*, Harper & Row, Publishers, Incorporated, New York, 1942.

Skinner, B. F.: *Walden II*, The Macmillan Company, New York, 1948.

Smelser, Neil J.: *Theory of Collective Behavior*, The Free Press, New York, 1963.

Smith, Delbert D.: "The Legitimacy of Civil Disobedience as a Legal Concept," *Fordham Law Review*, 336:707–730, May 1968.

Smith, Helena Huntington: *Cattle Barons and Range Wars: The War on Powder River*, University of Nebraska Press, Lincoln, 1967.

Smith, Lynn T.: "Some Major Current Rural Social Trends in the United States," *International Social Science Journal*, 21:272–285, no. 2, 1969.

Smith, Richard Austin: "The Fifty-Million-Dollar Man," *Fortune*, November 1957, pp. 176ff.

Smolinski, Leon: "Planning Reforms in Poland," *Kyklos*, 21:498–513, 1968.

Smutz, Robert W.: *Women and Work in America*, Columbia University Press, New York, 1959.

"Sociologists Invade the Plant," *Business Week*, Mar. 21, 1959, pp. 95ff.

Sorokin, Pitirim A., and **Carle C. Zimmerman:** *Principles of Rural-Urban Sociology*, Holt, Rinehart and Winston, Inc., New York, 1929.

————: *Contemporary Sociological Theories*, Harper & Row, Publishers, Incorporated, New York, 1928.

————: *Social and Cultural Dynamics*, American Book Company, New York, 1941.

Spengler, Oswald: *The Decline of the West.* Translated by Charles Francis Atkinson, Alfred A. Knopf, Inc., New York, 1926–1928.

Spiro, Melford E.: "Culture and Personality:

The Natural History of a False Dichotomy," *Psychiatry*, 14:19–46, 1951.

——: *Children of the Kibbutz*, Harvard University Press, Cambridge, Mass., 1958.

Spitz, Rene: "Hospitalism," in *The Psychoanalytic Study of the Child*, vol. 1, International Universities Press, Inc., New York, 1945, pp. 53–74.

Spock, Benjamin: *The Pocket Book of Child Care*, Pocket Books, Inc., New York, 1945, 1957.

Sprey, Jetse: "On the Institutionalization of Sexuality," *Journal of Marriage and the Family*, 31:432–440, August 1969.

Srole, Leo: "Social Integration and Certain Corollaries: An Exploratory Study," *American Sociological Review*, 21:709–716, 1956.

——, **Thomas S. Langner, Stanley T. Michael, Marvin K. Opler,** and **Thomas A. C. Rennie:** *Mental Health in the Metropolis: The Midtown Manhattan Study*, McGraw-Hill Book Company, New York, 1962.

Stannard, Una: "Clothing and Sexuality," *Psychology Today*, May 1971, pp. 24ff.

Starkey, Marion L.: *The Devil in Massachusetts*, Alfred A. Knopf, Inc., New York, 1949.

Stein, Maurice, and **Arthur Vidich:** *Sociology on Trial*, Prentice-Hall, Inc., Englewood Cliffs, N.J., 1964.

Steinbeck, John: *The Moon Is Down*, The Viking Press, Inc., New York, 1942.

Steiner, Stanley: *The New Indians*, Harper & Row, Publishers, Incorporated, New York, 1968.

Sterling, Claire: "The Aswan Disaster," *National Parks and Conservation Magazine: The Environmental Journal* August, 1971, pp. 10–13.

Stern, Bernhard J.: "Resistance to the Adoption of Technological Inventions," in U.S. National Resources Committee, *Technological Trends and National Policy*, 1937, pp. 39–66.

Stewart, Charles T., Jr.: "The Rural-Urban Dichotomy: Concepts and Uses," *American Journal of Sociology*, 64:162–158, 1958.

Stiehm, Judith H.: "The Teacher's Millstone," *Progressive*, 25:23–25, July 1961.

Stockdale, Jerry D.: "Structural Preconditions for Collective Action," paper presented at *The Society for the Study of Social Problems*, Washington, D.C., 1970.

Stoetzel, Jean: Cited in Alva Myrdal and Viola Klein, *Women's Two Roles: Home and Work*, Routledge & Kegan Paul, Ltd., London, 1956.

Stoltz, Lois Keek: "Effects of Maternal Employment upon Children: Evidence from Research," *Child Development*, 31:749–782, 1960.

Stone, Carol: "Some Family Characteristics of Socially Active and Inactive Teenagers," *Family Life Coordinator*, 8:53–57, 1960.

Stonequist, Everett H.: *The Marginal Man*, Charles Scribner's Sons, New York, 1937.

Stouffer, Samuel A.: *Communism, Conformity and Civil Liberties*, Doubleday & Company, Inc., Garden City, N.Y., 1955.

—— et al.: *Studies in the Social Psychology of World War II*, vol. 2, *The American Soldier: Combat and Aftermath*, Princeton University Press, Princeton, N.J., 1949.

Straus, Murray A.: "Deferred Gratification, Social Class, and the Achievement Syndrome," *American Sociological Review*, 27:326–335, June 1962.

Strauss, Anselm L.: "The Literature on Panic," *Journal of Abnormal and Social Psychology*, 39:317–328, 1944.

Street, Peggy, and **Pierre Street:** "In Iran, a New Group Challenges Us," *New York Times Magazine*, July 23, 1961, pp. 11ff.

Strodtbeck, Fred L.: "Husband-Wife Interaction over Revealed Differences," *American Sociological Review*, 16:468–473, 1951.

—— and **A. Paul Hare:** "Bibliography of Small Group Research," *Sociometry*, 17:107–178, May 1954.

Strother, George B.: "Creativity in the Organization," *Journal of Cooperative Extension*, 7:7–16, Spring 1969.

Stuckert, Robert P.: "African Ancestry of the White American Population," *Ohio Journal of Science*, 58:155–160, 1958.

Summary of the Report on Conditions of Women and Children Wage Earners in the United States, Bureau of Labor Statistics Bulletin no. 175, Washington.

Sumner, William Graham: *Folkways*, Ginn & Co., Boston, 1940.

Surface, Bill: *The Hollow*, Coward-McCann, Inc., New York, 1970.

Suttles, Gerald D.: *The Social Order of the Slum*, The University of Chicago Press, Chicago, 1968.

Szasz, Thomas: "The Psychiatrist as Double Agent," *Trans-action*, 4:16-24, October 1967.

Talmon, Yonina: "Pursuit of the Millenium: The Relation between Religious and Social Change," *European Journal of Sociology*, 3: 125-148, 1962. Reprinted in Joseph R. Gusfield (ed.), *Protest, Reform, and Revolt*, John Wiley & Sons, Inc., New York, 1970, pp. 436-452; and in Barry McLaughlin (ed.), *Studies in Social Movements*, The Free Press, New York, 1969, pp. 400-427.

Taylor, Miller Lee, and A. R. Jones: *Rural Life in Urbanized Society*, Oxford University Press, Fair Lawn, N.J., 1964.

Taylor, Telford: *Nuremberg and Vietnam: An American Tragedy*, Quadrangle Books, Chicago, 1970.

TenHouten, Warren D.: "The Black Family: Myth and Reality," *Psychiatry*, 33:145-155, May, 1970.

Terman, Lewis, M.: *Gifted Group at Midlife: 35 Years' Follow-up of the Superior Child*, Stanford University Press, Stanford, Calif., 1959.

Thomas, W. I.: *The Unadjusted Girl*, Little, Brown and Company, Inc., Boston, 1923.

—— and Florian Znaniecki: *The Polish Peasant in Europe and America*, Alfred A. Knopf, Inc., New York, 1918, 1927.

Thompson, Victor A.: *Modern Organizations*, Alfred A. Knopf, Inc., New York, 1961.

Thompson, Warren S.: *Danger Spots in World Population*, Alfred A. Knopf, Inc., New York, 1929.

Thompson, Wayne E., and John E. Horton: "Political Alienation as a Force in Political Action," *Social Forces*, 38:190-195, March 1960.

Thurlow, Lester C.: *Poverty and Discrimination*, The Brookings Institution, Washington D.C., 1969.

Tiger, Lionel: *Men in Groups*, Random House, Inc., New York, 1969.

Tinbergen, Nikolaas: *Study of Instinct*, Ox- ford University Press, Fair Lawn, N.J., 1969.

Toffler, Alvin: *Future Shock*, Random House, Inc., New York, 1970.

Tonnies, Ferdinand: *Community and Society*. Translated and edited by Charles A. Loomis, Michigan State University Press, East Lansing, 1957.

Toynbee, Arnold: *A Study of History*, Oxford University Press, London, 1935-1961.

Treiman, Donald J.: "Status Discrepancy and Prejudice," *American Journal of Sociology*, 71:651-664, May 1966.

Tripathi, B. D.: "On Minimizing Social Distance Between the Upper Castes and Harijans," *Interdiscipline*, 4:316-321, Winter, 1967.

Tuddenham, Read D.: "The Influence of a Distorted Group Norm upon Judgments of Adults and Children," *Journal of Psychology*, 52:231-239, 1961.

Tumin, Melvin M.: "Some Unapplauded Consequences of Social Mobility," *Social Forces*, 36:21-37, 1957.

Turner, Jay R., and Morton O. Wagenfeld: "Occupational Mobility and Schizophrenia: An Assessment of the Social Causation and Social Selection Hypothesis," *American Sociological Review*, 32:104-113, February 1967.

Turner, Ralph H.: "Role-taking, Role Standpoint, and Reference Group Behavior," *American Journal of Sociology*, 61:316-338, 1956.

—— and Samuel J. Surace: "Zoot-suiters and Mexicans: Symbols in Crowd Behavior," *American Journal of Sociology*, 62:14-20, 1956.

—— and Lewis M. Killian: *Collective Behavior*, Prentice-Hall, Inc., Englewood Cliffs, N.J., 1957.

——: "The Sense of Injustice in Social Movements," *Proceedings of the Southwestern Sociological Association*, 19:122-126, 1968.

Turner, Thomas B.: "The Liberal Arts in Medical Education," *Association of American Colleges Bulletin*, 44:71-77, 1958.

Tweeten, Luther, and Dean Schreiner: "Economic Impact of Public Policy and Technology in Marginal Farms and on the Nonfarm Population," in Iowa State University Center for Agricultural and Economic Development, *Benefits and Burdens of Rural Development*, Iowa State University Press, Ames, 1970, pp. 41–76.

Tylor, Edward: *Primitive Culture: Researches into the Development of Mythology, Philosophy, Religion, Language, Art and Custom,* vol. 1, John Murray (Publishers) Ltd., London, 1871.

Underhill, Ralph: *Youth in Poor Neighborhoods*, National Opinion Research Center, New York, 1967 (a).

———: *Youth in Poor Neighborhoods*, National Opinion Research Center, The University of Chicago, Chicago, 1967 (b).

United Nations: *The Future Growth of World Population*, New York, 1958.

U.S. Commission on Civil Rights: *Strangers in the Land*, Clearing House Publication no. 19, Washington, D.C., May, 1970.

United States Committee for Refugees: "The World's Refugees, 1970," *World Refugee Report*, U.S. Committee for Refugees, 206 West 40th Street, New York, 1971.

U.S. President's Commission on Campus Unrest: *The Report of the U.S. President's Commission on Campus Unrest*, Arno Press, New York, 1970.

Unni, K. P.: "Polyandry in Malabar," *Sociological Bulletin* (India), 7:62–79, 1958.

Urban America, Inc., *One Year Later*, Frederick A. Praeger, Inc., New York, 1969.

Useem, John: "South Sea Island Strike: Labor-Management Relations in the Carolina Islands, Micronesia," in Edward H. Spicer (ed.), *Human Problems in Technological Change*, Russell Sage Foundation, New York, 1952, pp. 149–164.

Van der Kroef, Justus M.: "Some Head-hunting Traditions of Southern New Guinea," *American Anthropologist*, 54:221–235, April 1952.

———: "The Changing Class Structure in Indonesia," *American Sociological Review*, 21:138–148, 1956.

VanderZanden, James W.: "Resistance and Social Movements," *Social Forces*, 37:312–315, 1959.

———: "The Klan Revival," *American Journal of Sociology*, 65:456–462, 1960.

———: *Sociology: A Systematic Approach*, The Ronald Press Company, New York, 1970.

Vaughn, James: "An Experimental Study of Competition," *Journal of Applied Psychology*, 20:1–15, 1956.

Vernon, Raymond: *Metropolis 1985: An Interpretation of the Findings of the New York Metropolitan Study*, Harvard University Press, Cambridge, Mass., 1960.

Vine, Margaret Wilson: *An Introduction to Sociological Theory*, David McKay Company, Inc., New York, 1959.

Vogel, Susan R., et al.: "Maternal Employment and Perception of Sex Roles among College Students," *Developmental Psychology*, 3:384–391, November 1970.

Von Hentig, Hans: "Redhead and Outlaws," *Journal of Criminal Law and Criminology*, 38:1–6, May–June 1947.

Wagstaff, Thomas: *Black Power: The Radical Response to White America*, The Free Press, New York, 1969.

Wakefield, Dan: "The Careful Conversion of the Nouveau Riche," *Esquire*, November 1961, pp. 105ff.

Wallace, A. F. C.: "The Modal Personality Structure of the Tuscarora Indians as Revealed by the Rorschach Test," *Bureau of American Ethnology*, Bulletin no. 150, 1952 (a).

———: "Individual Differences and Cultural Uniformities," *American Sociological Review*, 17:747–7750, 1952 (b).

Wallace, Samuel E.: *Skid Row as a Way of Life*, Harper & Row, Publishers, Inc., New York, 1965.

Wallerstein, James S., and **Clement J. Wyle:** "Our Law-abiding Law Breakers," *National Probation*, pp. 107–112, March–April 1947.

Walsh, Robert H.: "Intergenerational Transmission of Sexual Standards," paper read at American Sociological Association, Washington, D.C., 1970.

Warner, Lloyd W. and **J. O. Low:** "The Factory in the Community," in William Foote Whyte (ed.), *Industry and Society*, McGraw-Hill Book Company, New York, 1946, pp. 21–45.

Warner, Lucien: "A Survey of Psychological Opinion on E. S. P.," *Journal of Parapsychology*, 2:296–301, 1938.

Warner, W. Lloyd: "Murngin Warfare," *Oceania*, 1:457–494, 1931.

—— and James C. Abegglen: *Big Business Leaders in America*, Harper & Row, Publishers, Incorporated, New York, 1955.

—— and Paul S. Lunt: *The Social Life of a Modern Community*, Yale University Press, New Haven, Conn., 1941.

—— and ——: *The Status System of a Modern Community*, Yale University Press, New Haven, Conn., 1942.

Warriner, Charles K.: "The Nature and Functions of Official Morality," *American Journal of Sociology*, 54:165–168, 1958.

Wax, Murray L.: *Indian Americans: Unity and Diversity*, Prentice-Hall, Inc., Englewood Cliffs, N.J., 1971.

Weber, Max: *From Max Weber: Essays in Sociology*. Translated and edited by H. H. Gerth and C. Wright Mills, Oxford University Press, Fair Lawn, N.J., 1946.

Weller, Robert H., and David F. Sly: "Modernization and Demographic Change: A World View," *Rural Sociology*, 34:313–326, September 1969.

Wellman, Paul L.: *The Trampling Herd*, Carrick and Evans, New York, 1939.

Wells, Henry: *The Modernization of Puerto Rico*, Harvard University Press, Cambridge, Mass., 1969.

West, James: *Plainville, U.S.A.*, Columbia University Press, New York, 1945.

Westie, Frank R.: "Social Distance Scales: A Tool for the Study of Stratification," *Sociology and Social Research*, 43:251–258, 1959.

Whelpton, Pascal K., and Clyde V. Kiser: "Social and Psychological Factors Affecting Fertility," *Milbank Memorial Fund Quarterly*, 21:221–280, 1943.

Whittaker, David, and William A. Watts: "Personality Characteristics of a Nonconformist Youth Subculture: A Study of Berkeley Nonstudents," *Journal of Social Issues*, 25:65–88, Spring 1969.

Whittaker, James O.: "Cognitive Dissonance and the Effectiveness of Persuasive Communication," *Public Opinion Quarterly*, 28:547–555, Winter 1964.

Whyte, William F.: *Street Corner Society*, The University of Chicago Press, Chicago, 1955.

Whyte, William H., Jr.: "Urban Sprawl," in Editors of *Fortune*, *The Exploding Metropolis*, Doubleday & Company, Inc., Garden City, N.Y., 1958, pp. 115–139.

Wilder, Russell M.: "Experimental Induction of Psychoneuroses through Restriction of Intake of Thiamine," in Milbank Memorial Fund, *Biology of Mental Health and Disease*, Harper & Row, Publishers, Incorporated, New York, 1952, pp. 531–538.

Wilkes, Paul: "Mother Superior to Women's Lib," *New York Times Magazine*, Nov. 29, 1970, pp. 27ff.

Wilkins, Thurman: *Cherokee Tragedy: The Story of the Ridge Family and the Decimation of a People*, The Macmillan Co., New York, 1971.

Wilkinson, Doris Y.: "Collective Behavior Theory and Research: A Critique of Smelser's Approach." Paper read at American Sociological Association, Washington, D.C., 1970.

Williams, Roger J.: *Biochemical Individuality*, John Wiley & Sons, Inc., New York, 1956.

Wilson, Alan B.: "Residential Segregation of Social Classes and Aspirations of High School Boys," in Reinhard Bendix and S. M. Lipset (eds.), *Class, Status, and Power*, The Free Press, New York, 1966, pp. 335–342.

Winiata, M.: "Racial and Cultural Relations in New Zealand," *Phylon*, 19:286–296, 1958.

Winick, Charles: "The Beige Epoch: Depolarization of Sex Roles in America," *Annals of the American Academy of Political and Social Science*, 376:18–24, March 1968.

——: *The New People: Desexualization in American Life*, Pegasus Press, Indianapolis, 1969.

Winslow, Charles N.: "The Social Behavior of Cats," *Journal of Comparative Psychology*, 37:297–326, 1944.

Wirth, Louis: *The Ghetto*, The University of Chicago Press, Chicago, 1928.

Wissler, Clark: "Depression and Revolt," *Natural History*, 41:108–112, 1938.

Wittfogel, Karl A.: *Oriental Despotism*, Yale

University Press, New Haven, Conn., 1957.

Woelfel, Joseph, and **Archibald O. Haller:** "Significant Others: The Self-reflective Act and the Attitude Formation Process," *American Sociological Review*, 36:74–87, February 1971.

Wolf, Eleanor P.: "The Invasion-Succession Sequence as a Self-fulfilling Prophecy," *Journal of Social Issues*, 13:7–20, 1957.

Wolfers, D.: "The Demographic Effects of a Contraception Program," *Population Studies*, 23:111–140, March 1969.

Wolff, Robert J.: "Modern Medicine and Traditional Culture: Confrontation on the Malay Peninsula," *Human Organization*, 24:339–345, Winter 1965.

Womens' Bureau: *Wives—Their Contribution to Family Income*, Document WB 67-271, U.S. Department of Labor, Washington, D.C., 1967.

———: *Background Facts on Women Workers in the U.S.*, U.S. Dept. of Labor, Washington, D.C., 1970.

Woodward, Comer Vann: *The Strange Career of Jim Crow*, Oxford University Press, Fair Lawn, N.J., 1957.

Worsley, Peter: *The Trumpet Shall Sound: A Study of "Cargo" Cults in Melanesia*, MacGibbon & Kee, London, 1957.

Wright, Grace S.: *Subject Offerings and Enrollments in Public Secondary Schools*, Government Printing Office, Washington, D.C., 1965.

Yablonsky, Lewis: *The Hippie Trip*, Pegasus, New York, 1968.

Yalom, Irwin D., and **Lieberman, Morton A.:** "A Study of Encounter Group Casualties," *Archives of General Psychiatry*, 25:16–30, July 1971.

Yang, C. K.: *The Chinese Family in the Communist Revolution*, The M.I.P. Press Cambridge, Mass., 1959.

Yinger, J. Milton: *Toward a Field Theory of Behavior*, McGraw-Hill Book Company, New York, 1965.

Young, Leontine: *Out of Wedlock*, McGraw-Hill Book Company, New York, 1954.

Zahn, G. D.: *The Military Chaplaincy: A Study of Role Transition in the Royal Air Force*, University of Toronto Press, Toronto, 1969.

Zald, Mayer N., and **Roberta Ash:** "Social Movement Organizations," in Barry McLaughlin, *Studies in Social Movements*, The Free Press, New York, 1969, pp. 461–485.

Zilboorg, Gregory: *Mind, Medicine, and Man*, Harcourt, Brace & World, Inc., New York, 1943.

Zolla, Elémire: *The Eclipse of the Intellectual.* Translated by Raymond Rosenthal, Funk and Wagnalls, a division of Reader's Digest Books, Inc., New York, 1968.

Zorbaugh, Harvey: *The Gold Coast and the Slum*, The University of Chicago Press, Chicago, 1929.

Glossary

Accommodation Peaceful adjustment between hostile or competing groups; "antagonistic cooperation."

Acculturation Acquisition by a group or individual of the traits of another culture.

Achieved role or **status** A role or status attained through individual choice, effort, action, or accomplishment.

Adjudication Resolution of role conflict by decision of a third party.

Aggregation A gathering of people without conscious interaction.

Amalgamation Biological interbreeding of two or more peoples of distinct physical appearance until they become one stock.

Anomie A situation in which a large number of persons lack integration with stable institutions, to the extent that they are left rootless and normless.

Applied science Scientific methodology applied to the search for knowledge which will be useful in solving practical problems.

Ascribed role or **status** A role or status assigned according to hereditary traits without regard to individual preference, ability, or performance.

Assimilation Mutual cultural diffusion through which persons or groups come to share a common culture.

Association A group with its own administrative structure, organized to pursue some common interest of its members.

Attitude A tendency to feel and act in a certain way.

Audience A crowd with interest centered on stimuli outside themselves.

Authority An established right to order the actions of other people.

Bias A tendency, usually unconscious, to see facts in a certain way because of one's wishes, interests, or values.

Bureaucracy A pyramid of officials who conduct rationally the work of a large organization.

Caste system A stratified social system in which social position is entirely determined by parentage, with no provision for change of position.

Category A number of people who share some common characteristic.

Charismatic leadership Type of leadership in which the personality and image of the leader give him great authority and influence.

Clique A small group of intimates with intense in-group feelings based on common sentiments and interests.

Cognitive dissonance The degree of difference one perceives between his own beliefs or ideas and those of another person.

Collective behavior Behavior which originates spontaneously, is relatively unorganized, fairly unpredictable, and depends upon interstimulation among participants.

Collectivity A physical collection of people.

Commune Cooperative household shared by a number of persons, none of whom need be related by blood or marriage.

Community A local grouping within which people carry on a full round of life activities.

Compartmentalization Process of isolating parts of the personality from each other so that one is unaware of value conflicts; isolating roles from one another so that one is unaware of role conflicts.

Competition Process of seeking to obtain a reward by surpassing all rivals.

Concept An idea or mental image that embodies generalized or common elements found in a number of specific cases.

Conflict The effort to obtain rewards by eliminating or weakening the competitors.

Conjugal family Family with the married couple and their children as its core, with a fringe of other relatives.

Consanguine family Family with a group of married sisters and their children, or a group of married brothers and their children, as its core, with a fringe of spouses and other relatives.

Cooperation Joint activity in pursuit of common goals or shared rewards.

Counterculture A subculture not merely different from, but in opposition to, the conventional and approved culture of the society; e.g., the hippie subculture.

Craze A temporary obsessive interest shared by a number of people.

Crescive change Changes which occur without any choice, plan, or intention.

Cross-fertilization in social change Use in one field of discoveries and inventions from an entirely different field.

Crowd A temporary collection of people reacting together to stimuli.

Cultural base for invention The accumulation of knowledge and techniques available to the inventor.

Cultural change Changes in the culture of a people; often used interchangeably with social change.

Cultural drift A broad, sweeping, gradual change in values or behavior in a society.

Cultural integration The degree to which the traits, complexes, and institutions of a culture are harmoniously adjusted to one another.

Cultural lag The time lag between adoption of an innovation and accomplishment of the social and cultural adjustments which the innovation makes necessary.

Cultural pluralism Toleration of cultural differences within a common society; allowing different groups to retain their distinctive cultures.

Cultural relativism Concept that the function, meaning, and "desirability" of a trait depend upon its cultural setting.

Cultural trait Smallest unit of culture as perceived by a given observer.

Culture Everything that is socially learned and shared by the members of a society; social heritage which the individual receives from the group; a system of behavior shared by members of a society.

Culture complex A cluster of related culture traits.

Deferred gratification pattern Postponement of present satisfactions for future rewards.

Demography Statistical study of population composition, distribution, and trends.

Deviation Failure to conform to the norms of a group or society.

Deviation, primary The deviant behavior of a person who is conformist in the rest of his life organization.

Deviation, secondary Deviant behavior which follows from one's public identification as a deviant.

Diffusion The spread of culture traits from group to group.

Discovery A shared human perception of an aspect of reality which already exists.

Discrimination A practice that treats equal people unequally; limiting opportunity or reward according to race, religion, or ethnic group.

Ego According to Freud, the conscious and rational part of the self which oversees the restraint of the id by the superego.

Elite A small controlling clique within a group, association, or society.

Embourgeoisment Assumption of middle-class attitudes by people generally considered to be of working-class status.

Enacted change Change induced by deliberate decision or persons or groups.

Endogamy Requirement that mates be chosen within some specified group.

Ethical neutrality in science Seeking knowledge but avoiding value judgments or recommendations.

Ethnic group A number of people with a common cultural heritage which sets them apart from others in a variety of social relationships.

Ethnocentrism Tendency of each group to take for granted the superiority of its own culture.

Ethos Unifying spirit running through various aspects of a culture.

Exogamy Requirement that mates be selected outside some specified group.

Fact A descriptive statement of reality upon which all qualified observers are in agreement; a descriptive statement of reality which scientists, after careful examination and cross-checking, believe to be accurate.

Fad A trivial, short-lived, popular variation in speech, decoration, or behavior.

Family A kinship grouping which provides for the rearing of children and for certain other human needs.

Fashion A variation in speech, decoration, or behavior, of temporary duration but less trivial or brief than a fad.

Feral man Individual supposedly reared apart from human society and hence imperfectly socialized.

Folk society Small, isolated, often nonliterate, homogeneous society characterized by a high degree of group solidarity, traditionalism, and informal social control.

Folkways Customary, normal, habitual behavior characteristic of the members of the group.

Gemeinschaft A society in which most relationships are either personal or traditional.

Generalized other The totality of values and standards of one's community or one's social group, whose judgments one applies to his own behavior in forming his concept of self.

Geriatrics The study of the health problems of the aged.

Gerontology The study of the aged and their problems.

Gesellschaft A society based on contractual as contrasted with traditional relationships.

Ghetto Any part of a city in which the population is restricted to a particular ethnic group; historically applied to a Jewish district, but today often applied to Negro districts.

Group Any number of persons who share a consciousness of membership and of interaction; often used incorrectly to denote aggregation, collectivity, or category.

Group dynamics The scientific study of the interaction within small groups.

Human ecology The study of man in relation to his physical environment; a study of how people and institutions are located in space.

Hypothesis Tentative, unverified statement of the relationship of known facts; a reasonable proposition worthy of scientific testing.

Id According to Freud, the instinctive, antisocial, selfish desires and impulses of the individual.

Ideology A system of ideas which sanctions a set of norms.

In-group A group or category toward which one has a feeling of identity or belonging.

Influence The ability to affect the decision and actions of others without any formal authority to do so.

Innovation A new culture trait or complex, whether received through discovery, invention, or diffusion.

Instinct An inborn behavior pattern characteristic of all members of the species.

Institution An organized cluster of folkways and mores centered around a major human activity; organized system of social relationships which embodies certain common values and procedures and meets certain basic needs of society.

Invention A new combination or a new use of existing knowledge.

Labeling process The public identification of a person as a deviant (e.g., thief, rapist, homosexual).

Latent functions Unintended effects of a policy, program, or institution.

Law Regulations enforced by coercive power which is either organized or sanctioned by the society; sometimes referred to as "stateways."

Levirate Pattern in some societies whereby a widow automatically becomes wife to her deceased husband's brother.

Looking-glass self Perception of the self that one forms by interpreting the reactions of others to him.

Manifest functions Intended and realized effects of a program or institution.

Marginal man Individual torn between two or more cultures, partly assimilated into each and fully assimilated into neither; often an immigrant.

Marriage The approved social pattern whereby two or more persons establish a family.

Mass A relatively large number of people, spatially dispersed and anonymous, acting independently in response to the same stimuli.

Mass behavior The unorganized, unstructured, uncoordinated, individually selected behavior of masses in a mass society.

Mass hysteria An irrational, compulsive belief or behavior which spreads among a number of people.

Mass society A society in which primary-group, community-based, tradition-oriented relationships have been largely replaced by contractual, secondary-group, utilitarian relationships; characterized by anonymity, mobility, specialization, and individualism.

Mean Sum of all the items divided by the number of items; sometimes referred to as the "average."

Median The midpoint in a series of items arranged according to size.

Mob An emotionally aroused crowd taking violent action.

Modal personality A personality configuration which is typical of most members of a group or society.

Mode Value which appears most frequently in a series.

Monogamy Marriage form permitting only one mate (at a time).

Mores Strong ideas of right and wrong which require certain actions and forbid others.

Nativism Rejection of contemporary culture, with a desire to return to traditional patterns; rejection of "foreign" groups and influences.

Norm A standard of behavior. Statistical norm is a measure of actual conduct; cultural norm states the expected behavior of the culture.

Norms of evasion Customary, recognized ways of violating certain of the norms of a society.

Objectivity Observing and accepting facts as they are, not as one would wish them to be.

Oligarchy Rule of a group or organization by a small clique of self-perpetuating leaders.

Oppression psychosis Tendency for members of a group with a history of persecution to feel persecuted even in situations where they are not being mistreated.

Orgy The action of a revelrous crowd which transgresses the usual mores.

Out-group A group or category toward which one has no feeling of identity or of belonging.

Panic A collective flight based on a hysterical belief.

Personality The totality of behavior of an individual with a given tendency system interacting with a sequence of situations.

Polyandry A form of polygamy in which two or more husbands share one wife.

Polygamy A plurality of mates.

Polygyny A form of polygamy in which one husband has two or more wives.

Position The rank one holds in an hierarchical series.

Power The ability to control the actions of others, regardless of their wishes.

Primary group Small group in which people come to know one another intimately as individual personalities; distinct from the impersonal, formal, utilitarian secondary group.

Primitive Descriptive term for societies which are (or were) culturally homogeneous and relatively isolated, with fairly simple technological and economic organization, and usually preliterate.

Progress Social or cultural change of a kind defined as desirable according to some set of values.

Proletariat A working class which is conscious of its underprivileged and property-less status.

Propaganda All efforts to persuade others to an acceptance of a point of view.

Public A number of people who share an interest in a particular topic or activity, or are concerned about and divided upon an issue.

Public opinion An opinion held by a significant number of people; the dominant opinion among a population.

Pure science Search for knowledge for its own sake without primary regard to its practical usefulness or consequences.

Race A group of people somewhat different from other people in a combination of inherited physical characteristics, but the meaning of the term is also substantially determined by popular social definition.

Reference group Any group accepted as model or guide for our judgments and actions.

Relative deprivation Feelings of deprivation which tend to be proportionate to the gap between what one has and what he feels he should have, or between what he has and what others have.

Revolution A relatively sudden, usually violent, and relatively complete change in a social system.

Rite of passage Any ritual which marks movement from one status to another, such as the ceremonies attending birth, death, puberty, or marriage.

Role Expected behavior of one who holds a certain status.

Role playing Acting out the behavior of a role which one actually holds, as when a couple marry and set up a household.

Role taking Assuming or acting out the behavior of a role which one does not actually hold, as when children "play house."

Rumor A rapidly spreading report unsubstantiated by authenticated fact.

Sacred society A society with a homogeneous set of folkways and unified moral values which are revered as sacred and eternal.

Science A body of organized, verified knowledge which has been secured through scientific investigation; a method of study whereby a body of verified knowledge is discovered.

Scientific methods Methods of study which produce organized, verified knowledge.

Secondary group Group in which contacts are impersonal, segmental, and utilitarian, as distinct from the small, intimate, highly personal primary group.

Secular society Society with a diversity of folkways and mores; society in which religious influence is minimized.

Secularization Movement from a sacred to a rationalistic, utilitarian, experimental viewpoint.

Segregation Separation of two or more groups based on a desire to avoid equal-status social contact.

Self An individual's awareness of, and attitudes toward, his own person.

Self-fulfilling prophesy A prediction which starts a chain of events which make the prediction come true.

Semite People of Middle-Eastern origin, perhaps represented in most nearly pure form by the Bedouins of Northern Arabia; often used as a synonym for Jewish, but equally applicable to most Arabs.

Significant others Those individuals whose approval one desires and whose judgments will affect one's attitudes and behavior.

Slum A deteriorated area of the city inhabited by poor people.

Social change Change in the social structure and relationships of a society; often used interchangeably with *cultural change.*

Social class A stratum of persons of similar position in the social-status continuum.

Social contagion Process whereby members of a crowd stimulate and respond to one another and thereby increase their emotional intensity and responsiveness.

Social control All the means and processes whereby a group or a society secures its members' conformity to its expectations.

Social disorganization Disruption of existing culture by social change, as evidenced by failure of traditional social controls, role confusions, and conflicting moral codes.

Social distance Degree of closeness to, or acceptance of, members of other groups.

Social mobility Movement from one class level to another.

Social movement A collectivity acting with some continuity to promote or resist a change in the society of group of which it is a part.

Social order A system of people, relationships, and customs operating smoothly together to accomplish the work of a society.

Social processes Repetitive interaction patterns which are commonly found in social life.

Socialization Process by which one internalizes the norms of his groups so that a distinct self emerges unique to this individual.

Society A relatively independent, self-perpetuating human group which occupies a particular territory, shares a culture, and has most activities within this group.

Sociocultural change Changes in either the social structure and relations or in the culture of a society.

Sociology The scientific study of man's social life.

Sororate Pattern in some societies whereby a widowed husband automatically becomes husband to his deceased wife's sister.

Standardized birth- and death-rates Birth- and death-rates which are adjusted to what they would be if the population had the same age, sex, or other population characteristic as some "standard" population distribution which is used as a measure.

Status Position of an individual in a group, or of a group in relation to other groups.

Stereotype A group-shared image of another group or category of people.

Subculture A cluster of behavior patterns related to the general culture of a society and yet distinguishable from it; behavior patterns of a distinct group within the general society.

Superego According to Freud, the social ideals and values which one has internalized and which form the conscience.

Symbiosis (social) Mutual interdependence without conscious decision to cooperate.

Symbol That which stands for something beyond its own immediate meaning; especially a specific object representing a more diffused, generalized, or abstract concept. The flag, the cross, and Uncle Sam are examples.

Symbolic communication Exchanging meanings through words and other symbols which have no meaning in themselves, but to which agreed meanings have become attached; distinguished from exchange of meanings through instinctive barks and growls.

Utopia A perfect society.

Values Measures of goodness or desirability.

Variable Anything which differs from person to person, group to group, time to time, or place to place.